INDIAN SOCIAL PROBLEMS

VOLUME I : *Social Disorganization*

BY THE SAME AUTHOR

1. Indian Social Problems, Volume I, Social Disorganisation, (7th Revised Edition 2009), Allied Publishers, New Delhi.
2. Indian Social Problems, Volume II, Social Work, (6th Revised Edition 2009), Allied Publishers, New Delhi.
3. Social of Development–An Indian Perspective (2003), Allied Publishers, New Delhi.
4. Voluntary Social Organisations in India and Develop-ment—A Critical Appraisal (2008), Allied Publishers, New Delhi.
5. Introduction to Sociology (2008), 3rd Edition, Allied Publishers, New Delhi.
6. (a) Western Sociologiest on Indian Society, 1979, Routledge & Kegan Pual, London.
   (b) Western Sociologiest on Indian Society, 1979, Allied Publishers, New Delhi
   (a) Western Sociologiest on Indian Society, (Spanish Edition), 1984, Economia (Mexico, South America).
7. Western Thinkers on Indian Society (Revised Edition), 2000, Anamika Publishers, Darya Ganj, New Delhi.
8. Cooperative Movement in India, 1993, 2007, Mittal Publications, Darya Ganj, New Delhi.
9. India and The West (A Cultural Contrast 2004), Mittal Publications, Darya Ganj, New Delhi.
10. Buddhism and Its Various Manifestations (Ed.), Mittal Publications, Darya Ganj, New Delhi.
11. Indian Rural Problems (2002, 2009), Radha Publications, Darya Ganj, New Delhi.
12. Economic Thinking in India (1966, 1981, 2004), Radha Publications, Darya Ganj, New Delhi.
13. Casteism, Cooruption and Social Development in India (2004), Radha Publications, Darya Ganj, New Delhi.
14. World Civilizations and India (2007), Radha Publications, Darya Ganj, New Delhi.
15. Integral Sociology (4 Volumes)—An Anthology of the Writing of Prof. Radhakamal Mukerjee (2000) (Co-editor, V.P. Gupta), Radha Publications, Darya Ganj, New Delhi.
16. Radhakamal Mukerjee—An Eminent Scholar, Saint and Social Worker, 2008, (Ed.), Radha Publications, Darya Ganj, New Delhi.
17. The Bible of Hinduism 1985, 1988, Allied Publishers, New Delhi.
18. Village Development in India, 1983, (Co-Author, Dr. Tara Madan), Allied Publishers, New Delhi.
19. India's Social Transformation Volume I Problems of Economic Development 3rd Edition 1989, Allied Publishers, New Delhi.
20. India's Social Transformation Volume II Problems of Welfare and Planning 3rd Edition 1996, Allied Publishers, New Delhi.
21. India of Tomorrow—Problems of Social Reconstruction, (1998), Allied Publishers, New Delhi.
22. Society and Culture 1987 (In Honour of late Dr. Radhakamal Mukerjee), (Co-Editor Prof. R.M. Loomba), Allied Publishers, New Delhi.
23. Economic Problems of Modern Volume 1 (Ed. 1989), Allied Publishers, New Delhi.
24. Economic Problems of Modern Volume 2 (Ed. 1995), Allied Publishers, New Delhi.
25. Cooperative Movement in the Punjab (India), S. Chand & Company, (1958), New Delhi.
26. Changing Pattern of Indian Villages, (1959, 1964), S. Chand & Company, Ram Nagar, New Delhi.
27. Cooperative Farming and Service Cooperative in India 1961, S. Chand & Company, Ram Nagar, New Delhi.
28. The History and Development of Economic Thought (1964, 1978) Co-Author H.S. Dhooria.
29. Social Disorganization and Social Reconstruction in India, Karnatak University, Dharwar, (1973).
30. A Guide for Voluntary Social Workers in India (1984), The Indian Council of Social Welfare, Bombay.

GURUMUKH RAM MADAN

Indian Social Problems

SOCIAL DISORGANIZATION AND RECONSTRUCTION

VOLUME ONE

Social Disorganization

ALLIED PUBLISHERS PVT. LIMITED

NEW DELHI MUMBAI KOLKATA CHENNAI NAGPUR
AHMEDABAD BANGALORE HYDERABAD LUCKNOW

ALLIED PUBLISHERS PRIVATE LIMITED

1/13-14 Asaf Ali Road, **New Delhi**–110002
Ph.: 011-23239001 • E-mail: delhi.books@alliedpublishers.com

Khasra No. 168, Plot No. 12-A, opp. Wisdom Academy School, Kamta,
Surendra Nagar, **Lucknow**–227105
Ph.: 09335202549 • E-mail: lko.books@alliedpublishers.com

17 Chittaranjan Avenue, **Kolkata**–700072
Ph.: 033-22129618 • E-mail: cal.books@alliedpublishers.com

15 J.N. Heredia Marg, Ballard Estate, **Mumbai**–400001
Ph.: 022-42126969 • E-mail: mumbai.books@alliedpublishers.com

60 Shiv Sunder Apartments (Ground Floor), Central Bazar Road,
Bajaj Nagar, **Nagpur**–440010
Ph.: 0712-2234210 • E-mail: ngp.books@alliedpublishers.com

F-1 Sun House (First Floor), C.G. Road, Navrangpura,
Ellisbridge P.O., **Ahmedabad**–380006
Ph.: 079-26465916 • E-mail: ahmbd.books@alliedpublishers.com

751 Anna Salai, **Chennai**–600002
Ph.: 044-28523938 • E-mail: chennai.books@alliedpublishers.com

5th Main Road, Gandhinagar, **Bangalore**–560009
Ph.: 080-22262081 • E-mail: bngl.books@alliedpublishers.com

3-2-844/6 & 7 Kachiguda Station Road, **Hyderabad**–500027
Ph.: 040-24619079 • E-mail: hyd.books@alliedpublishers.com

Website: www.alliedpublishers.com

First Published, 1996

Seventh and Enlarged Edition, 2009

Edition, 2018

ISBN : 978-81-8424-453-3 (PB)

ISBN : 978-81-8424-456-6 (HB)

Published by Sunil Sachdev and printed by Ravi Sachdev at Allied Publishers Private Limited, Printing Division, A-104 Mayapuri Phase II, New Delhi - 110064

To

THE INTELLECTUALS

OF INDIA

FOREWORD

"SOCIAL RECONSTRUCTION" is both a gigantic as well as a delicate task. It is much more easily achieved in utopian imagination than through the slow process of directed or induced change.

Indian social research, especially in the domain of social institutions, interactions and relationships, has primarily been descriptive and exploratory so far. In view of the recent development of this science in India, this meagre achievement, consciously effected, is not to be decried but adequately eulogised. It has by now made available reliable materials, in keeping with the tenets of empiricism, on which the policy-maker, the planner and the implementor may safely rely in their endeavours rather than lean on mere surmises and conjectures.

After appraising the nature, type, extent and etiology of a social problem or a social situation, through the above method, all concerned are placed in a comfortable position to bring about social reconstruction on a scientific basis.

Dr. G.R. Madan, in Volume I of this series of two volumes, has discussed in a comprehensive manner some of the pressing social problems with which India is confronted since Independence. In this volume the author focuses on the concept and history of social work, welfare services in some of the major fields of social work, social security, social administration and social legislation and international welfare agencies which he considers crucial in a programme of social reconstruction. The materials marshalled in this volume represent those vastly scattered on the subject. Dr. Madan has woven them into a pattern which will not merely be handy but very useful both to the undergraduate and post-graduate students. I wish this publication a great success.

SUSHIL CHANDRA

Professor of Sociology
Lucknow University
September 5, 1966

PREFACE TO THE SEVENTH (REVISED) EDITION, 2009

THE SECOND revised edition of this book vol I was brought out in 1969. Since then the changes in this volume have been made at the end under the head Post-scripts in three chapters. The volume 2 of this book was published under the head Social Reconstruction in 1967. The second thoroughly revised edition of volume 2 was brought out under the title "Indian Social Problems" Vol. II under the head Social Work as the scope of Social Reconstruction was found to be wider then contemplated earlier.

The first edition of the book was brought out in 1967 under the title 'Indian Social Problems, Volume II Social Reconstruction'. The second thoroughly revised and enlarged edition was published in 1973 under the title 'Indian Social Problems, Volume II Social Work as the scope of Social Reconstruction was found to be wider than contemplated earlier. To deal with the topic of 'Social Reconstruction' two more additional books were brought out under the titles 'Social Change and Problems of Development in India' and 'Welfare State and Problems of Democratic Planning' in 1971 and 1972 respectively. However some of the problems were still not covered and another book 'India of Tomorrow Problems of Social Reconstruction' was brought out in 1975 to complete this series.

When the two books 'Social Change and Problems of Development' and 'Welfare State and Democratic Planning' were revised and enlarged in 1979 and 1984 respectively, their titles were changed as 'India's Social Transformation, Vol. I Problems of Economic Development' and 'India's Social Transformation, Vol. II Problems of Welfare and Planning' to show their interconnection in a more clear way. The book 'India of Tomorrow' was revised and its second revised edition was brought out in 1985. Thus the revised series was completed in 1985.

In the Third, Fourth, Fifth and Sixth revised editions of the book Indian Social Problems, Volume I and Third, Fourth and Fifth of Volume 2, no changes were made in the text and only two or three additional chapters were added at the end under the head Post Scripts. In the Sixth Revised Edition of Vol. I and Fifth Revised Edition of Vol. II published in (2002), I obtained the assistance from Miss Roli Kulshreshtha who had M.S.W. Degree from Lucknow University in 1996. She cleared her UGC-NET for lectureship examination in 1998, as I was busy in my Voluntary Social Work.

The three additional books to deal with Social Reconstruction which were earlier published under three different heads have now been published in one Volume pt blished under the title "Sociology of Development" (An Indian Perspective) in 2003. In the Seventh Revised Edition of Indian Social Problems Volume I and Sixth of Volume II changes have again been made in the last three chapters under the head Post-script.

The Hindi edition of these three books Indian Social Problems Volume I and Volume II and Sociology of Development (2003) have been published by Vivek Prakashan, 74 A, Jawahar Nagar, Delhi-110017.

Two books have recently been published under the head Introduction to Sociology (IIIed.) (2008) and Voluntary Social Organizations of India and Development (A Critical Appraisal) by Allied Publishers, New Delhi.

The Hindi Edition of the book "Introduction to Sociology" has been published under the head Samaj Shastra ke Siddhant (2008) by Radha Publications, Ansari Road, Darya Ganj, New Delhi.

I am grateful to the teachers, students and Voluntary Social Workers who have popularized these books inspite of many short comings. I will be happy to receive comments of the readers in the deficiencies of these books.

Interest has been shown by some teachers of Sociology to bring about some of these books in Regional languages. However the progress in this respect have been very slow.

The other books published or edited by me in various fields are given under the head "Books Published by the same Author" in this book.

Due to old age I will not be able to revise these books in future. Any Teacher interested in the subject can approach me in this respect.

July, 2009
45 EA, SFS Flats
Maya Enclave
New Delhi-110064

G.R. Madan
Visiting Professor of Sociology
Maharaja Surajmal Institute
New Delhi

Preface to the First Edition

This Work is mostly the outcome of lectures delivered to the undergraduate as well as post-graduate students in the Department of Sociology and Social Work, Lucknow University for seven years since 1956. The book is divided into two volumes. Volume I: "Social Disorganization" deals with problems of social defence including delinquency, crime, beggary, etc. along with problems of family and community disorganization. Volume II: "Social Re construction" deals with fields of social work in the broader sense including community development, labour welfare, housing, etc. It is for this reason that we have used in the title the term "Social Re construction" instead of "Social Work."

Social Work is not a new activity but has been undertaken since time immemorial. However, the concept of Social Work has rapidly changed since the beginning of the nineteenth contury when emphasis was first laid on preventive rather than palliative activities. According to Professor Robson two types of services emerged in England therefrom. One of them consisted of the social services which the state initiated during the nineteenth century to deal with public health, education, factory regulation and similar matters. The other involved the action taken in the twentieth century to relieve or prevent destitution. This action sprang from a changed attitude towards poverty. The scope of social work has increased so much that it has now become a profession available to all, although in India it has not yet achieved this status.

The expanding scope of social services is synonymous with the increasing functions of the modem state, which has gradually changed from police state to welfare state. Professor Myrdal in his book, *Beyond the Welfare State,* states that in the last half century the state in all the rich countries in the western world has become a democratic

"Welfare State" with fairly explicit commitments to the broader goals of economic development, full employment, equality of opportunity for the young, social security and protected minimum standards as regards not only income, but nutrition, housing, health and education for peoples of all regions and groups, After Independence India also adopted the objectives of a welfare state when the new constitution came into force. Some of the protective services which have been provided by the State directly or indirectly in the various spheres have been discussed in this volume, while rehabilitative services for maladjusted persons have been discussed in Volume I. However, it has not been possible to discuss all the services and functions which a "Welfare State" ought to perform.

I owe a debt of gratitude to my guru, Dr. Radha Kamal Mukerjee, whose life has always inspired me. My sincere thanks are due to Professor Sushil Chandra, M.A., D.LITT., Professor of Sociology, Lucknow University, who has spared some of his valuable time to write a foreword to this book. I am thankful to my pupil Sri Tej Narain, M.S.W., who prepared the index and Sri R.D. Saxena, who typed the manuscript.

Tagore Library G.R. Madan
Lucknow University
September 5, 1966

CONTENTS

FOREWORD *vii*

PREFACE TO THE SEVENTH (REVISED) EDITION, 2009 *ix*

PREFACE TO THE FIRST EDITION *xi*

Part One : Introductory

I SOCIAL PROBLEMS AND SOCIAL DISORGANIZATION 3

Study of Indian Social Problems—Nature of Social Problems in India—Social Problems: A Field of Applied Sociology—Scope of Applied Sociology—Applied Sociology and Social Work—Social Problems and Social Disorganization—Social Problems and Individual Disorganization—Social Organization Defined—Social Organization and Social Change—Social Change in Industrialized and Pre-industrialized Societies—Causes of Social Change—Rapid Changes in Material than in Non-material Culture—Social Control and Social Organization— Social Organization and Modern Society—Social Organization : its Equilibrium and Disequilibrium—Concept of Social Disorganization—Social Change and Social Disorganization—Causes of Social Disorganization—Causes Giving Rise to Social Problems—Social Disorganization in India—Scheme of the Book

II INDIVIDUAL DISORGANIZATION 32

Relation Between Individual and Social Disorganization—Individual and Society—Individual's Life Organization—Proper Life Organization and Disorganization—Causes of Individual Disorganization—Stages in Personal Disorganization—Types of Individual Disorganization—The Disintegration of Personality—Mentally Deranged—Causes of Mental Illness— Mental Illness in India—Services for the Mentally Ill—Suicide—Theories of Suicide—Causes of Suicide—Suicides in India

Part Two : Crime and Delinquency

III CRIME AND ITS CAUSES 55

Conception of Crime—Causes Leading to Delinquency and Crime—General Factors—Specific Factors—Biological Factors— Environmental Factors—Causes of White-Collar Criminality

IV JUVENILE DELINQUENCY 86

Juvenile Delinquency Defined—Extent of Juvenile Delinquency in India—Causes of Juvenile Delinquency—Truancy—Juvenile Vagrancy—Methods of Controlling Vagrancy—Prevention of Juvenile Delinquency—Preventive Measures—Method of Re-habilitation—Programmes Before Independence—Children Acts in other States—New Policy After Independence

V ADULT OFFENDERS 114

Classification of Criminals—Extent of Crime in India—Causes of Crime—Prevention of Crime—Treatment of Adult Offenders—Correctional Programme in India: Prison Administration and Reformation—Brief History of Prison Administration—Working of Prisons—The Prisons Act 1894—Probation—Working of Probation in India—Working of Probation Acts—Parole—Other Alternatives to Punishment—After-care of Prisoners—Developments during Five-Year Plans—Prevention of Crime and U.N.O.— Future Programme

Part Three : Social Vices

VI ALCOHOLISM AND DRUG ADDICTION 153

Alcoholism—Causes of Drinking—Casual to Habitual Drinker—History of Drinking in India—Progress After Independence—Programme During the Second and Third Five-Year Plans—Study Team on Prohibition (1964)—Drug Addiction—Opium—Charas, Ganja and Bhang—Central Organizations

VII GAMBLING AND SMOKING 180

Gambling and Speculation—Gaming, Wagering and Betting—Gambling Activities—Occasional and Habitual Gambler—Causes of Gambling—Disadvantages of Gambling—Gambling and Demoralization: Control of Gambling—Treatment of Gamblers—Smoking: Advantages and Disadvantages of Smoking—Bad Effects of Smoking—Economic and Social Effects—Causes of Smoking—Extent of Smoking in India—Control of Smoking

VIII PROSTITUTION 200

Causes of Prostitution—Causes of Prostitution for Males—Causes of Prostitution for Females—Two Types of Prostitutes—Procurers, Pimps and Brothel-Keepers—Prostitution and Personal Disorganization—Prostitution and Family Disorganization—Vice and Community Disorganization—History of Prostitution in India—Legislation on Prostitution—Extent of Prostitution in India—Programme After Independence: Recommendations of the Advisory Committee on Social and Moral Hygiene—Suppression of Immoral Traffic Act, 1956—Developments After 1956—Future Programme—Venereal Diseases and Prostitution: Social and Economic Effects—Extent of Venereal Diseases in India—Social Control of Venereal Diseases—Prostitution and Welfare Organizations—Association for Moral and Social Hygiene in India—League of Nations Advisory Committee on Social Questions

IX BEGGARY 226

Begging in Ancient Period—Beggary in Modern Society—Causes of Beggary—Types of Beggars—Techniques Employed in Begging—Extent of Beggary in India—Measures Taken in Ancient India—Present Methods of Rehabilitation—Action Taken During the British Period—Action Taken During the Five-Year Plans—Future Programme

Part Four : Maladjustment in Institutions

X POVERTY AND UNEMPLOYMENT 251

Poverty : Absolute and Relative—Measurement of Poverty—National Income of India—Causes of Poverty—Unemployment—Types of Unemployment—Causes of Unemployment—Evil Effects of Unemployment—Extent of Unemployment in India—Alleviating the Problem: Removal of Personal Disabilities— Economic Development to Remove Poverty and Unemployment—Unemployment Among the Educated—Removal of Seasonal Unemployment—Unemployment Owing to Difficulties in the Migration of Labour and Change in Technology

XI POPULATION AND HEALTH PROBLEMS 280

Theories of Population—Optimum Theory of Population—Growth of India's Population—Is India Overpopulated?—Birth Rate and Death Rate—Health: Medical Care and Public Health—Water Supply and Environmental Sanitation—Health Education—Nutrition—Other Health Problems—

Control of Population—Migration of Population— Increase in Production—Family Planning

XII EDUCATIONAL AND RELIGIOUS INSTITUTIONS 298

Educational Institutions—Social and Adult Education—Adult Literacy—Adult Education—Indiscipline Among Students—Education on Social, Moral and Spiritual Values—Religious Institutions: Hinduism and Social Progress—Reinterpretation of Religious Literature—Reorganization of Religious Institutions

XIII LEISURE AND RECREATION 318

Leisure and Recreation—Leisure and Recreation Defined—Recreation in Modern Society—Income and Leisure—Forms of Recreation—Recreational Activities Among Adults—Commercial Recreation—Meaning of Commercial Recreation—Causes of Commercial Recreation—Commercial Recreation and Disorganization—Cinema and Disorganization—Misuse of Leisure Time and Disorganization

XIV POLITICAL INSTITUTIONS AND CORRUPTION 338

Corruption in Ancient Period—Corruption Defined—Causes of Corruption—Forms of Corruption—White-Collar Criminals—Organized Crime and Community Disorganization—Extent of Corruption in India—Measures for Controlling Corruption

XV FAMILY DISORGANIZATION 356

Family and Society—Functions of the Modern Family—The Nature of Family Organization—Concept of Family Disorganization—Rapid Changes in the Role and Status of Partners—Factors Bringing Change in Functions of the Family—Causes of Family Disorganization—Personal and Impersonal Factors in Tension—Effects of Family Tension—Extent of Desertion and Divorce in India—Social Consequences of Desertion and Divorce—Divorce and Economic Position—Children of Divorced Persons—Desirability and Undesirability of Divorce—Avoidance of Family Tensions and Divorce—Future of Family Organization

Part Five : Community Conflicts

XVI COMMUNITY AND NATIONAL DISORGANIZATION 391

Nature of Community—Nature of Community Disorganization—Disorganized, Under-organized and Unorganized Community—Individual's Participation in

Community Organization—Process of Community Disorganization—Community Disorganization and Social Change—Community Conflicts and Inactivity—India and Social Change—Changes During the British Period—Changes After Independence—Migration and Community Disorganization—Migration of Displaced Persons—Conflict and Inactivity in Rural and Urban Communities—Casteism and Community Disorganization—Remedies and Reforms—Class Tension and Community Disorganization—Communal Tensions and Community Disorganization—Lingual and Regional Conflicts—Conflicts and Groupism in Larger Organizations: Universities, Municipal Corporations and Legislative Assemblies

XVII CRITICAL APPRAISAL 417

Suggestions—Balanced Advance on All Fronts—Reform in Religion and Education to Minimize Crime—Diagnostic Services for Prevention of Juvenile Delinquency—Vigilance Committees for Prevention of Adult Crime—Complete Prohibition as recommended by Study Team—Private Gambling to be Prohibited—The Problem of Smoking to be Examined by an Expert Committee—Amendment in the Act to Control Prostitution—All-India Legislation to Check Beggary—Educated Youngmen to Resort to Business and Manual Labour to Remove Unemployment—Adult Education for Acceptance to Family Planning Programme—Moral Education to Minimize Students' Indiscipline—Proper Use of Leisure Through Civic Clubs and Social Service Organizations—Honesty Among Politicians and High Officials to Check Corruption—Opening of Family Counselling Agencies to Avoid Family Conflicts—Constructive Work by Political Parties to Build the Community—Intellectuals to Take Part in Social Service Activities

Part Six : Postscript

XVIII SOCIAL DEFENCE PROGRAMMES 4

Scope of Social Defence Programmes—Individual Disorganization and the Mentally Ill—Suicide—Crime and its Causes—Juvenile Delinquency—Prevention and Control of Delinquency—Protection and Treatment of Juvenile Delinquents—An Integrated Programme for Juvenile Justice—Juvenile Justice Act 2000 and After—Treatment of Adolescent Offenders—Treatment of Adult Offenders—Probation— Treatment through Community Services—After

Care of Prisoners—Alcoholism and Drug Addiction—New strategy for Drug Abuse Prevention—Gambling and Smoking—Prostitution—Beggary-Uneven Progress in Different States—Voluntary Action in Social Defence Programmes

XIX PROBLEMS OF MAJOR INSTITUTIONS AND COMMUNITIES 475

Major Groups and Institutions in Society—Poverty and Unemployment-Removal of Poverty and Unemployment in Rural Areas-Poverty Alleviation in Rural India-Ninth Plan Strategy—The Sampoorna Grameen Rozgar Yojana—Programmes for the Educated Unemployed Swarnjayanti Gram Swarozgar Yojana—Swarn Jayanti Shahri Rozgar Yojana—Programmes for Urban Areas—Programmes for Employment During Tenth Plan and After—Programme for Female Employment—Population and Health Problems-Health Services—Some Programmes in the field of Population Control and Health—AIDS: A Major Health Hazard—Nutrition Programme—Educational and Moral Problems—Elementary Education-Imparting of Moral Education—Adult Education Proramme—Indiscipline among Students—Education Policy during 10th Five Year Plan and After—Problem of High Education in Eleventh Five Year Plan—Religious Institutions and Democratic Society—Leisure and Recreation—Political Institutions and Corruption—Family Disorganisation—Community Conflicts and National Integration—Problems of National Integration —Committee on Emotional Integration (1961)—Colloquium on National Integration (1966)—National Integration Council—National Integration Samities in Universities and Colleges—All India Scholars' Conference on National Integration—National Integration a Complex Problem.

XX SOCIAL WELFARE AND FIVE-YEAR PLANS 529

Concept of Welfare—Social Welfare and other Related Concepts— Scope of Social Welfare in India—Social Welfare Services and Welfare State—Welfare State and Planning—Economic Versus Social Planning—Social Planning and Social Policy—Planning of Social Welfare Services—Social Welfare and Five-Year Plans-—Fifth Five Year Plan to Eighth Plan—Changes made in Ninth Five Year Plan (1997-2002) and After—Main Emphasis in Tenth Five Year Plan (2002-2007)—Growth, Poverty and Employment, Social Development and Quality of life—Eleventh Plan (2007-2012)—Vision of the Eleventh Plan—The 27 National Targets—The 13 State Specific Targets.—State Social Welfare Department—Voluntary Social Welfare Agencies—Role of National Council of Social Welfare

INDEX 575

PART ONE

INTRODUCTORY

CHAPTER I

SOCIAL PROBLEMS AND SOCIAL DISORGANIZATION

A SOCIETY that strives to improve must be keenly aware of its social problems. "Social Problems are behaviour patterns or conditions that are considered objectionable or undesirable by many members of a society. These members recognize that the corrective policies, programmes and services are necessary to cope with and reduce the scope of these problems."[1] Thus, those adverse conditions that are not defined by the group as reprehensible or undesirable are not known as social problems. For example, if gambling is not regarded as objectionable by the community, it is not considered a social problem. These social problems may be distinguished from physical and biological problems such as soil erosion, floods, tempests, fires, etc. in the former case and heart diseases, cancer, tuberculosis and other organic ailments in the latter. Social problems seem deceptively easy to understand when compared to physical or biological problems. But when we try to change or control them they become resistant to change. For example, juvenile delinquency is a very pressing and persistent social problem. It has been studied intensively and considerable knowledge has been accumulated about it. However, the rates of juvenile delinquency are higher today than they were sixty years ago.[2] But in the case of malaria and other communicable diseases, with research in medicine, we have been able to control them to a great extent. Similarly, many other social problems in contemporary urban society such as adult crime, alcoholism, prostitution, gambling and casteism resist control.

Study of Indian Social Problems

The social problems in India in the past did not receive the attention they deserve. There are various reasons for it : (1) The teaching

[1] Richard C. Fuller and Richard Myers, "Some Aspects of a Theory of Social Problems", *American Sociology Review*, (February, 1941), pp. 24-32. Also see Weinberg S. Kirson, *Social Problems in Our Times* (1960), p. 4.

[2] Weinberg S. Kirson, *op. cit.*, p. 4.

of the science of sociology was neglected in this country. The post-graduate study in sociology was introduced only in 1919 at the University of Bombay. The first Graduate School of Social Work was started by the Tata Institute of Social Sciences in 1936. (2) Due to appalling poverty of the masses in the country the attention of the educationists and the statesmen was directed towards economic problems rather than towards social problems. Therefore, only those social problems, which were connected with economic problems received attention of the public, e.g. unemployment. (3) Some of the political leaders such as Mahatma Gandhi drew attention of the public towards certain social problems like drinking, casteism, conditions of women, but due to apathy of the British Government, much could not be done to improve the situation. (4) Some of the social problems, which cropped up as a result of rapid urbanization and industrialization in some of the Western countries were not so acute in this country due to its slow urbanization and industrialization. (5) The concept of "Welfare State" gained ground in some of the Western countries, which took interest in diagnosing and solving some of the social problems emerging there. But this concept was not accepted by the then British Government for this country and the old policy of *laissez faire* was followed in every sphere of life. (6) Even after Independence though the National Government accepted the "Welfare State" as its goal and was keen in tackling the various social problems confronting the country, yet much could not be done immediately in solving these problems because of certain other important problems confronting the nation which arose as a result of Independence, e.g. the problem of refugees, the problem of integration of princely states, the food problem, etc. It was in 1954 that the Central Social Welfare Board was set up by the Government of India and the first publication on social problems, viz. Social Welfare in India was brought out by the Planning Commission in 1955. But there is still much to be done.

On the other hand, the study of social problems to improve the society need hardly be emphasized. The needy, the neglected, the handicapped, the maladjusted and the unadjusted are to be helped and protected by the society. The "Welfare State" accepted as the goal in the Indian Constitution has further increased the responsibility of the state in providing welfare services to a growing number of citizens. The modern concept of a "Welfare State" presupposes a minimum economic standard wherewithal for maintaining man's physical well-being and a comprehensive network of protective and constructive services in the social field such as public health, medical care, labour welfare, social welfare and social education. The changing concept of social work from palliative to rehabilitative and protective activities has also increased the scope of welfare services. The emergence of social work as a profession has further emphasized the providing of these services on scientific lines.[3]

Nature of Social Problems in India

The nature of social problems in India is not very different from that in other civilized countries of the world, though there are certain problems peculiar to this country because of differences in culture, social set up and certain other historical and political reasons. For example, unemployment, gambling, crime, etc. are considered to be social problems in all the countries though the extent of the problem and the causes giving rise to them may differ due to differences in political, economic, social and cultural setting. But the problems of scheduled castes and scheduled tribes are peculiar to India because of the prevailing caste system. The problem of refugees arose after Independence as a result of the partition of the country. Similarly, the problem of negroes in the U. S. A. is quite peculiar to that country.

Social Problems—a Field of Applied Sociology

Both Sociology and Social Work study social problems. There is, however, some difference between the scope of Sociology and Social Work which we have discussed later in this chapter. In sociology, social problems are strictly within the field of applied sociology. There are certain sociologists who advocate that sociology being a science should study only the society as it is and should not pronounce any judgments or suggest any solution for solving those problems. The function of science is "is" and not "ought". But majority of the sociologists do not agree with this point of view. In their opinion all social sciences are light-bearing as well as fruit-bearing sciences and it is legitimate for them to suggest ways and means to solve social problems and improve society. The aim of social sciences is and ought to be human betterment and applied

[3] For Social Work as a Profession and change in the concept of Social Work see Chapter I, Vol. II.

sociology is concerned with human betterment. Professor Davis observes, "We want to build the society for the better. There are certain citizens who may be contented and do not want change, but we must be careful not to give them undue weight. So long as there are people who feel that they are not receiving justice or fair play to that extent society needs reconstruction. It is the function of applied sociology to reconstruct that society. The objective is that in free society (1) there should be a variety of thinking, (2) equality of opportunity by eliminating inequalities—economic and educational, (3) there is no exploitation of special privileges by a particular group, and (4) social order in which social intelligence, social efficiency and voluntary co-operation produce the maximum good."[4] Professor Ford points out, "The Practical or Applied Sociology may be designated as Applied Social Ethics or Social Policy and the study of the adaptation of social method to the achievement of moral purpose may be termed as applied social ethics."[5] Professors Gillin and Gillin remark, "Some of the earliest sociologists ignored the pathological aspects of human association. Some today think that these aspects are not a part of theoretical sociology. Possibly that attitude harks back to the fact that the study of social maladjustments was introduced by practical reformers. Increasingly, however, those who are interested in studying society as a dynamic rather than a purely static phenomenon, are convinced that social pathology is as much a part of sociology as medical pathology is a part of scientific medicine."[6]

The science of sociology is divided into two parts, theoretical sociology and practical sociology. Applied sociology is chiefly concerned with the getting of information, upon problems of social experience and finding methods for their amelioration and, if possible, their solution.[7]

Scope of Applied Sociology

The scope of applied sociology may differ from country to country, culture to culture, and from time to time. A social problem for one country may not be a social problem for another. Similarly, a

[4] Davis, Jerom , Sociology applied to Social Problems in *An Introduction to Sociology*, Davis, J., and Barnes, H. E. (Ed.) (1927), pp. 699 and 707.

[5] Ford, James (Ed.), *Social Problems and Social Policy* (1923), p. 1.

[6] Gillin, J. L., and Gillin, J. P., *Cultural Sociology* (1954), p. 739.

[7] Groves, E. R., and Moore, H. E., *Introduction to Sociology* (1947), p. 709.

problem considered to be social problem at one time may not be so at another time. However, there are certain social problems which are common to many countries.

In applied sociology, generally problems are divided into two categories, i.e. problems of social disorganisation or social rehabilitation and problems of social reconstruction. In the former category are included the problems of deviants, defective and dependents, e.g. criminals, delinquents, orphans, mentally defective, ill, blind, etc. In this case measures needed to cope with the evil are generally palliative, curative or rehabilitative in character. Something is done to help the poor, to educate the defective, to reform the criminals, to prevent poverty, defectiveness and crime. Thus, the method is curative rather than preventive. In the later category are included child welfare, women welfare, youth welfare, labour welfare, housing welfare, etc. Hence persons are normal but weak and need strength. In this case generally preventive and constructive methods are used. Education is given to the child so that he may be able to earn a normal living. His health is protected so that he may have normal health in adulthood. But generally in books on social problems and social welfare all the problems are dealt with together. In the applied sociology, Groves and Moore have included the problems of poverty, crime, immigration, race, the family, the social hygiene, mental defects, housing, public opinion, and the organisations and practices of modern philanthropy.[8]

Applied Sociology and Social Work

The terms Applied Sociology and Social Work are often used synonymously. The scope of both is almost the same, although in Social Work more emphasis is laid on rendering assistance through methods like social case-work, group work and community organization. Moreover applied sociology is a branch of sociology which is a science, whereas Social Work is now considered to be a profession.[9]

Social Problems and Social Disorganization

The terms "social problems" and "social disorganization" are closely related. When social problems (or a particular social problem) arise to the extent that the smooth functioning of the society

[8] Groves, E. R., and Moore, H. E., *op. cit.*, p. 710.

[9] For Relationship between Sociology & Social Work see Chapter I, Volume II.

is threatened, social disorganization is in existence. In other words, it is a number of social problems which bring social disorganization. Thus, when social problems are so many that the society cannot work smoothly or social progress is hindered, we call this a stage of social disorganization.

Social Problems and Individual Disorganization

As there is correlation between social disorganization and social problems, so is the relation between individual disorganization and the social problems. When an individual (or a group of individuals) is disorganized and is not functioning according to the norms laid down by the society the social problem is in existence. Generally speaking, a social problem can be seen as a significant discrepancy between social standards and social actuality.[10] "The individual who conforms to social norms is socially normal and, as a consequence, he considers himself normal. But the individual who is detected for violating the norms is a deviant. Whether a group member or alone, the deviant represents a social problem."[11] Generally it is a group of individually disorganized persons having the same problem which represents a social problem. Thus, when a number of persons are unemployed, the problem of unemployment is in existence.

Now let us trace the relation between individual disorganization, social problems and social disorganization. All these are interdependent and interrelated. It is often the case that one disorganized person affects others, thus giving rise to a social problem ; and one social problem leading to another, ultimately bringing social disorganization. But sometimes reverse is the process. First there emerges social disorganization all at once giving rise to social problems and then emerges individual disorganization. Thus, individual disorganization, social problems and social disorganization are interrelated and interdependent. It will, therefore, be proper to study social disorganization and individual disorganization first before we study various social problems. Again as social disorganization is always the resultant of some breakdown in the social organization, it will be necessary to understand "social organization" before we discuss social disorganization.

[10] Merton, R. K., "Social Problems and Sociological Theory" in *Contemporary Social Problems*, Merton, R. K., and Nisbet, R. A., (Ed.), (1961), p. 701.

[11] Weinberg, S. K., *op. cit.*, p. 8.

Social Organization Defined

"Since the term 'Social Organization' subsumes the whole function and structure of society it must include man, and all the ideas, knowledge, techniques, achievements, traditions, aspirations, fashions, folkways, mores and institutions which have interpenetrated within an existing social order. Social organization is then that totality of human personalities and conscious and unconscious attitudes, their crystallized and uncrystallized ideas and institutions, which in complex interrelationship make up the framework of human existence."[12]

The term "social organization" has been defined by very few sociologists because of its complexity. Professor Page in foreword to *Social Organization* points out that the fuzziness about the terminology "What is Social Organization?" is confirmed by examination of ten currently widely used textbooks, revealing that notwithstanding the fact that specific divisions of some of them carry the title "Social Organization" and contain extended discussion of the relation of social organization to change, to different types of groups, to disorganization, and to other sociological themes only two of the volumes define the concept and in only five does "Social Organization" appear in the indexes. The two definitions have a disarming simplicity, one stating that "organization refers to the way people relate themselves to one another", the other identifying social organization with ways in which "persons and groups making up a society are somehow held together". To these statements, which suggest a close affinity between organization and such concepts as integration, cohesion and equilibrium, may be added the explanation by Ely Chinoy that social organization and social structure are interchangeable concepts, both referring to "any interrelated system of roles and statuses[13]." However, it is to be pointed out that there are certain sociologists who consider "Social Organization" to be inclusive term which includes all human personalities, their culture and human relationships within its orbit, while "social structure" is concerned only with human relationships. Professor Nadel observes, "All the students of social structure are agreed that in studying 'structure' we study essentially the interrelation or arrangement of 'parts' in some total entity or 'whole'."

[12] Elliott, M. A., and Merrill, F. E., *Social Disorganization* (1941), *op. cit.*, p. 7.

[13] Greer, Scott A., *Social Organization* (1955), Foreword.

They are agreed, further, that the adjective "social" specifies the character of that "whole"—which is "society" or any of its subdivisions, and not "culture" and any of its sectors or provinces : which distinction is by now too well established to need further comments.[14]

In simple terms social organization is made of two words social and organization whereas social refers to human beings living together as a group in a situation requiring that they have dealings with one another.[15] Organization means a set of differentiated activities serving a common purpose and so correlated that the effectiveness of each is increased by its relation to the rest. Here "a set of differentiated activities" means the different groups and institutions which may contribute to the welfare or common purpose of the organization.[16] However, here we will like to distinguish this term from such other similar terms such as social structure, social system, etc. used in sociology. In this sense social organization is a broader term, as pointed out by Professor Nadel, and may include all the three systems, i.e. the social system, the personality system and the cultural system within its orbit. In other words, as pointed out earlier, social organization consists of three elements i.e. society, culture and personalities, and change in any of these elements is likely to effect social organization.

Again the term "social organization" has two meanings in sociology. First what "social organization" consists of and secondly, what is the stage when we say that there is social organization in the society as opposed to disorganization. This stage has to be defined in reference to some objectives laid down by any particular society. In this sense social organization may be conceived when human actions are not contrary to the ideals laid down by the society and the society is progressing towards particular goals set by it. These ideals may be with regard to residential stability, property ownership, business enterprise, religious discipline, etc.[17] "Social organization is a state of being, a condition in which the various institutions

[14] Nadel, S. F., *The Theory of Social Structure* (1957), p. 4.

[15] Webster's *New World Dictionary*.

[16] Hayes, E. C., *Introduction to the Study of Sociology* (1915), p. 409.

[17] Lemert, Edwin M., *Social Pathology* (1951), p. 3. There are some sociologists who think social organization and disorganization are not objective concepts as moral judgments enter into them. However, it needs pointing out that concepts referring to human behaviour have element of valuation and these concepts cannot be an exception.

in a society are functioning in accordance with their recognized or implied purposes."[18] In other words social organization implies a relative harmony between individual attitudes and social values.

However, it is to be pointed out that social organization is not something static but like a living organism where changes are taking place in the inner structure. If the changes are such that the society remains intact and is moving towards the goal set by the society, there is said to be social organization in society. As described by Mowrer, "Social organization is not something static, which once established will forever remain without change. In one sense, it is a hypothesis, an ideal-construct, emphasizing the relatively unchanging patterns of culture, as over against the changing aspects which are always present in every society."[19] Here culture includes four main elements—articrafts, techniques, beliefs and institutions, such as the church, the school, the family, and the government, etc. which represent the formalized patterns of co-operative activity organized for the performance of certain essential functions. The articraft are the physical objects of everyday life, while beliefs include society's moral and ethical notions, the principles of science, the philosophies, etc. by which man tries to understand his relationship with his fellows and the universe in which he lives. In this sense social organization is closely connected with social change.

Social Organization and Social Change

Life is dynamic and there is ceaseless change going on in the universe. The man though equipped with the experience of the past can never be certain of the future. The individual, the family, the local community, the nation and the world of nations are involved in varying degree in the process of social change, which renders the old truths uncertain and the new truths transitory. On the one hand, social change is a restless and dynamic process, on the other social controls tend to make it formalized and fixed. In this dynamic society, people are obliged to face new situations which necessitate new forms of response, new patterns of behaviour and new ways of thought. Sometimes they can meet the new situations with the experience and techniques acquired in the past. However, often problems arise for which previous experience offers no acceptable solution, and a certain degree of maladjustment is inevitable.

[18] Elliott, M. A., and Merrill, F. E., *op. cit.* (1950), p. 4.

[19] Mowrer, E. R., *Disorganization, Personal and Social* (1943), p. 3.

But if the maladjustment is not to the extent that society can still move towards social progress the social organization is still in tact and these disorganizing forces must be considered as a part of the normal dynamics of social life.

Social Change in Industrialized and Pre-industrialized Societies

The element of change has been present since the universe came into existence, but the change has been relatively slow in the past than at present. The life in pre-literate society was comparatively static and the society could adjust itself to the new situations with comparative ease. Problems of unemployment, housing, family disorganization, personal demoralization, etc. seemed comparatively simple, where there were no landlords, no sex taboos and no large scale migration. The social structure is built up through the introduction of new elements. When the process of social accumulation is slow, the social organization is stable. With rapid increase in the population and the introduction of new modes of life the relative stability of the social structure is threatened. The problems of the present society have become so complex that we are faced with an adjustment without precedent in human history. Change is taking place at rapid pace both in the material and non-material aspects and society is becoming an unstable equilibrium of conflicting forces.

Causes of Social Change

The causes of social change have been discussed by different writers in different ways. However, in general there are considered to be five main factors of social change, viz. biological, physical, psychological, technological, and cultural. In the biological factors may be included the hereditary changes and changes in population. (2) In the physical factors are included natural calamities such as earthquakes, floods, storms, exhaustion of soil, etc. (3) In the psychological factors are included changes through imitation and other social processes such as communication, conflict, competition, accommodation and assimilation. (4) The technological factors bring changes in the man-made conditions of living. (5) The cultural factors bring changes in the attitudes, beliefs, ideas, etc. of men.

Rapid Changes in Material than in Non-material Culture

Among these the technological factors are most potent as compared to other factors as they bring rapid changes in the material culture though at times other factors may bring about a vast social change. The changes brought in the material culture bring more rapid changes in human relations than changes in the non-material culture itself. There are various reasons for it. Firstly, the innovations brought about in the articrafts through new inventions and techniques are readily accepted by the people if they promise greater utility and do not disturb the larger social complex, whereas the new beliefs or philosophies are not readily accepted, if they would necessitate a radical reorganization of the culture complex. Secondly, it is often argued that the usefulness of one articraft against another can be readily tested and demonstrated. No one can question the superior utility of automobile over a horse or a cart or the superiority of electric light over gas light which can be easily demonstrated to the satisfaction of everyone. Thirdly, anyone may use either the automobile or the electric light without understanding how it operates and, generally, there is no necessary relationship between the understanding of the mechanism of many of the most widely used articrafts and their use by the great masses. Fourthly, changes in the manufacturing processes are readily adopted by the manufacturers as they promise greater profits.

On the other hand, to determine the utility of one belief as compared to another is a difficult task. It is also difficult to set up an objective criterion to test the utility of one belief as opposed to another. For instance, it is difficult to make out which belief leads to greater happiness, the belief in evolution or in divine creation. Similarly, the advantages of changes in governmental policy or in religious ideas or in relative position of women cannot be demonstrated.

Moreover, the beliefs in the sacred realm are enmeshed in the core of the personality of a person and to question them is to threaten the integrity of the personality itself. Thus, any suggestion of replacing the old beliefs with new ones is looked upon with misgivings or with outright hostility. Elliot and Merrill rightly observe. "Nothing changes so slowly as an idea. Once accepted notions are invested with sacred connotations. Men will shed their blood to protect their beliefs in what is right, whether such beliefs involve religious ideas, political philosophies or economic theories."[20]

[20] Elliott, M. A., and Merrill, F. E., *op. cit.*, p. 35.

This disparity in the rate of change between material and non-material culture is termed as "cultural lag". This we shall discuss again in detail later on.

Social Control and Social Organization

Social change, from whatever point of view it may be considered, is related to social organization and is always disbalancing it. On the other hand, the important forces keeping the social organisation in balance and bringing adjustment between the various elements of the society are social controls which consists of folkways, mores, laws, beliefs, attitudes, values and ideologies. These controls which the group imposes upon the members impart a certain consistency and stability to human activities. Unfortunately, as already pointed out, these elements of social control change slowly as compared to the modern techniques, which bring out rapid changes in the economic processes, and economic and social institutions, which affect the social relationships in a violent way. Sometimes social institutions, which in themselves constitute elaborate control devices, are rigid which render the task of social equilibrium difficult. The major institutions are family, the temple or mosque, the school, the state and the economic institutions. Religious ideas incorporated into the framework of the temple come to possess a definite rigidity. Educational ideas come to develop a vested interest in a particular form of training. The functions of the state are subject to rigidity where social situations demand changes. Similarly, joint family system may be adhered to, while changes are needed with the new situations

Not only the institutions are rigid in structure, but they tend to produce groups for the *status quo* on the ground of their validity. Those dominant groups generally enforce their values on the whole society which sometimes checks the maladjustments. The subordinate groups ignore their compulsives so long as their fundamental beliefs are not called into question, but a stage may come, when there may be serious maladjustment.

Social Organisation and Modern Society

Complete social harmony is manifestly impossible in a dynamic society. A society in which all persons unite in common definitions of all the important situations, has been reached only in the Utopias. Divergent ideologies and hostile class alignments are apparent in the surviving democracies. These elements are also present in the totalitarian states, even though they are concealed.

Complete social harmony implies a unanimity of opinion and a stability in techniques and behaviour patterns, which are inconceivable in a rapidly changing modern society. Stability was comparatively more in the ancient and medieval societies, than in the present ones, due to less transgression of mores. Majority of the persons accepted the duties and privileges assigned to them. In the modern period when social change is rapidly coming through new techniques and beliefs the equilibrium has become more unstable. Dr. Mowrer has mentioned three additional factors for the variant behaviour of individuals in the present society.[21] Firstly, there is the specialised functioning inherent in complex societies. The individuals in complex societies cannot learn all the culturally defined responses because of specialised vocations with the result that no individual can ever be exact counterpart of the social order. Secondly, the modern individual family functions as a culture-defining agency, interprets and distills the general culture complexes of the group in its own peculiar fashion under conditions of high emotionality with the result that there is some variation from the generally accepted notions. Thirdly, there is cultural participation by individuals outside the social order. The individuals in complex societies live a part of their lives either actively or imaginatively in other cultures either through actual travel or by distant communication bringing variant responses. The result of all these factors is the generation of a wide variety of variant response patterns out of which develops disorganization both individual and social. In the highly individualized life of modern urban society, where the individual is motivated by personal rather than communal ends, there is hardly any agreement between social and individual interests. Social harmony is often disturbed by the competition and conflict of hostile individuals, institutions, classes and nations. Social organization and social disorganization are in fact relative concepts dependent upon different degrees of disharmony of interests in a dynamic society. It may also be pointed out that complete harmony of interests and attitudes produces intellectual stagnation and uncritical acceptance of existing social values. As modern society becomes more and more complex and social change increases in rapidity, the pressure on social organization becomes more intense and the disorganiza-

[21] Mowrer, E. R., *op. cit.*, p. 26.

tion is the price which has to be paid for rapid social change and social progress.

Social Organization—its Equilibrium and Disequilibrium

Social evils are generally the results of existing social conditions. For example prostitution, crime and political corruption are the natural products of existing social conditions. The crimes against property grow out of the violation of mores which sanction private ownerships ; prostitution is the inevitable result of sex taboos between sexes and political corruption is the result of democratic process, where financial success is placed above political honesty. But at the same time it is necessary to note that society cannot exist without fixing certain rules. Without a general social agreement on basic issues society cannot be said to exist. As Louis Writh points out, "There is no society without an ethos, i.e. without shared values, objectives, preferences, and the well-founded anticipations of the members that all the others recognize the rules of the society and will abide by them."[22] However, it is difficult to say how far the rules imposed by the majority party or the dominant party over the whole society are beneficial to all. But to keep the social organization in a comparatively stable position it is necessary that all the members of the society must adhere to the rules which have once been laid down by the society. A society can exist only when a great number of men consider a great number of things from the same point of view ; when they hold the same opinions upon many subjects, and when the same occurrences suggest the same thoughts and impressions to their mind. When men begin to lose the fund of common understandings and expectations, social disorganization may be the result. When all the members of a given society are in virtual agreement on the definition of certain fundamental situations that society is harmonious and organized. When on the other side, there is general disagreement concerning the social implication of particular activities or creeds, the seeds of social disorganization have been sown.

Concept of Social Disorganization

So far we have discussed the concept of social organization and social change. Social disorganization is a relative phenomenon

[22] Writh, Louis, "Ideological Aspects of Social Disorganisation' *American Sociological Review* (August, 1940).

and the two, i.e. "social organization" and "social disorganization" are the dual aspects of the whole functioning of the social system. As there may be various degrees of social organization, so is the case with social disorganization. Social disorganization may thus be more or less, when the forces of social change create a threat to social stability and as a result of which there arise social problems. Social disorganization implies some breakdown in the social organization, which may be more or less according to the forces of social change operating at a particular time. In the words of Elliott and Merrill, "Social disorganization represents a breakdown in the equilibrium of forces, a decay in the social structure, so that old habits and forms of social control no longer function effectively."[23] Dr. Mowrer defines social disorganization as, "Whereas social organization consists of the co-ordination of individual responses as a consequence of the operation of conventionalized patterns of consensus and control, any change in the cultural context which impedes or destroys the functioning of the patterns of co-ordination which constitute the social order represents social disorganization."[24] Gillin and Gillin point out, "By social disorganization we mean such serious maladjustment between the various elements in the total cultural configuration as to endanger the survival of the group, or as seriously to interfere with the satisfaction of the fundamental desires of its members, with the result that social cohesion is destroyed."[25]

Social Change and Social Disorganization

As already pointed out there is a close relation between social change and social organization. Similarly there is a correlation between social change and social disorganization. When the present forces of social change are so violent that the existing social institutions and other means of social control are unable to control the new situation there arises social disorganization. As the ordinary forces of social change are constantly working in a dynamic society, some form of disorganization is always present. However, the society is not much alarmed as long as the form of social disorganization is such that it does not become a threat to the further progress of the society. According to Dr. Mowrer, "Social change and

[23] Elliott, M. A., and Merrill, F. E., *op. cit.*, p. 27.
[24] Mowrer, E. R., *op. cit.*, p. 26.
[25] Gillin, J. P., and Gillin, J. L., *Cultural Sociology* (1951), p 740.

social disorganization imply some break in the cultural context, some disturbance in the equilibrium among the various aspects of the culture pattern. But a society without social change and disorganization never exists, if for no other reasons than the appearance of hereditary variants and the failure of the imitative process to produce exact counterparts to the culturally defined responses."[26] Thus, social disorganization in true sense only takes place when there is a violent disturbance in the equilibrium of social organization. Prof. Giddings observes, "The dynamic nature of social interaction insures a constant rearrangement of the constituents of society. The resultant social change brings about the dissolution of certain institutional relationships and behaviour patterns which are imbedded in the social structure. This social upheaval which makes way for a new synthesis may bring in its wake a considerable amount of disorganization. Such confusion becomes particularly pronounced when the breakdown occurs more rapidly than the corresponding forces of reorganization."[27]

Causes of Social Disorganization

We have already mentioned the five main factors given by Maciver and Page which bring about social change. These factors are psychological, biological, physical, technological and cultural. When the changes brought about by these factors in the social structure are so disturbing that the present institution and other forces of social control are no longer able to control them by adjusting themselves to the new situations there arises social disorganization. Sociologists generally attribute one or two factors to be responsible for social disorganization at a particular moment. However, it is to be pointed out that the factors responsible for social disorganization at a particular period are so intermixed that it is difficult to locate as to which factor or factors are predominant. Elliott and Merrill observe, "In order to understand the full implications of a study of social disorganization, we must keep in mind the complex nature of all social phenomena. Out of man's fruitless search for unique causes has come a recognition of the multiple factors which account for such characteristics of modern society as the decline in the acceptance of revealed religion, the changing structure of the family, the increasing importance of the central

[26] Mowrer, E. R., *op. cit.*, p. 26.
[27] Giddings, F. H., *Studies in the Theory of Human Society* (1922), p. 231.

government, the 'lowering standards of morality' or other equal patent indices of a dynamic society. In the past these factors have all been regarded as singly responsible for social disruptions and social disorganization, and even today in the present world crisis, there are some persons who believe that all the disorganization of a dynamic society has its beginning in original sin. Other earnest souls ascribe the existence of such varied manifestations as crime, immorality, political corruption, unemployment and divorce to the decline of the traditional controls of orthodox Christianity. Others would rely on a reconstruction of the fundamental economic institutions to bring about the millennium. Still another group insists that the basis of all human woe lies in the biological field. If we would only eliminate the physically and mentally unfit, cry the eugenists, the social organism would automatically undergo a complete and rapid rejuvenation. Each of these partisans, however, ignores the selective nature of the interpretation, while on the other hand, any realistic social understanding must consider all the factors related to the particular manifestation of social disorganization, which is under investigation at the moment."[28]

Elliott and Merrill have ascribed the four main causes for the disorganization : (1) the social processes under the three main heads, i.e. cultural, political and economic, (2) cultural lag, (3) conflicting attitudes and values, and (4) social crisis. Dr. Mowrer has given five main approaches to the study of social disorganization, viz. social problems approach, bio-psychological approach, geographical approach, cultural approach and organic approach or microscopic—macroscopic relationship between the society and the individual. Prof. Sorokin has mentioned the change from the "idealistic" and "ideation" culture to "sensate culture" as the main cause of social disorganization. Prof. Karl Mannheim views that unplanned capitalism and policy of *laissez faire* are responsible for social disintegration in the present age, while Bertrand Russell observes that the lack of adjustment in institutions based on authority in the past is responsible for present social disorganization.[29] However, as pointed out above, it is not one but many factors which bring social disorganization. Let us discuss the views of these writers

[28] Elliott, M. A., and Merrill, F. E., *op. cit.*, pp. 27-28.

[29] See Park., R.E, and Burgess, E.W., *Introduction to the Science of Sociology* (1924), pp. 508-24.

along with that of others in brief which lead to social disorganization. These causes may he discussed under the following heads :

(1) *Psychological Factors of Social Disorganization.* Under the psychological factors may be included the social processes like immitation, conflict, competition, accommodation and assimilation. According to Park and Burgess there are five main processes including communication, conflict, competition, accommodation and assimilation which make up the dynamic organization of society.[30] When members of the society live in close proximity there is constant communication going on among them. This communication can function effectively only when there is common understanding or common consciousness. As complete unanimity of attitudes and values can hardly be reached in modern societies, communication is generally incomplete and fragmentary. Symbols used do not mean exactly the same thing to all men who use them. Words, phrases and ideas arouse different trains of thought in different persons and there is some disequilibrium in the society. Thus, communication may tend to bring about social harmony or may result in conflict or competition. Occasionally, conflict and competition may produce desirable social ends but in general they are destructive to the organization of the larger group. These processes operate in all the spheres such as cultural, economic, political, religious, etc.

In the cultural sphere the old social forms and patterns are imposed by the preceding generation upon the succeeding one. The cultural conflict between the older and young generation may result in disorganization of the adolescents, sex delinquency and sometimes resulting in family disorganization. The cultural conflict between groups in the same country may result in civil war or communal riots and between two nations in cold war, the serious consequences of which are readily apparent. In the political sphere may be included the phases of subordination and super-ordination in the sphere of state, business, or educational institutions. The disorganized phase of the political process may include such antisocial behaviour as delinquency, crime, disorder, revolt, etc. In the economic sphere the physically, mentally or economically weak persons are not able to compete with other persons because of lack of physical strength, mental incapacity or inadequate economic resources. This problem

[30] Russell, Bertrand, *Principles of Social Reconstruction* (1916), p. 26.

has become acute due to *laissez faire* and individualistic policy current at present.

(2) *Cultural Factors.* The cultural factors of social disorganization may be discussed under these heads : (1) The maladjustment in existing institutions, (2) cultural lag or disbalance in the material and non-material culture, and (3) cultural conflict. In the first case the maladjustment in the existing institutions may lead to social disorganization. For example poverty is considered to be the outgrowth of capitalistic system and the institution of private property which creates inequalities of wealth. According to Bertrand Russell in the modern world the principle of growth in most men and women is hampered by institutions inherited from a simpler age. By the progress of thought and knowledge, and by the increase in command over the forces of the phsyical world new possibilities of growth have come into existence, and have given rise to new claims which must be satisfied if those who make them are not to be thwarted. Institutions which give much greater opportunities to some classes than to others are supported by the former.

In the cultural lag approach, which was first developed by Ogburn, it has been pointed out that changes in the material and non-material culture are not uniform leading to social disorganization. We have already pointed out that changes in the material culture are readily adopted due to apparent utility of new articles, which bring immediate changes in human relations. On the other hand, the social institutions or mores which control social relationships generally remain rigid with the result that there may arise social disorganization. "Thus social maladjustment is the consequence of delay in the reciprocal changes in the dependent part of culture necessitated by discoveries and inventions in material culture."[31] This may also be called the technological factor of social disorganization. Rapid industrialization and urbanization bring so many problems of bad housing conditions, slums, industrial accidents, unbalanced ratio of sexes, etc. which ultimately lead to social disorganization.

In the cultural conflict may be included the conflicting attitudes or values of different groups or individuals, etc. The conflict between older and younger generation has already been discussed. The values are of two kinds, i.e. subjective and objective. Subjective values are those which are fixed by individuals or groups according to the situation or circumstances in which they are placed and which

[31] Ogburn, W. F., *Social Change* (1922), pp. 200-01.

are suited to their interests, whereas objective values represent the consciousness of the society and are formed on the basis of collective thinking and for the benefit of the whole society. These values often do not coincide, and out of their conflict may arise social disorganization. Class alignments have developed to secure benefits or privileges for particular groups regarding relief, taxation and regulation of business.

(3) *Physical or Geographical Factors.* The geographical factors include the nature of land, water resources, minerals, natural changes of seasons, storms, earthquakes, sea currents, rainfall, altitudes, etc. They may bring changes all of a sudden, e.g. floods or earthquake or they may be cumulative. The cumulative crisis may develop slowly out of a long line of sequential events. Frequent failure of rains for many years may bring famine.

(4) *The Biological Factor.* The cause of social disorganization here is considered to be the inter-mixture of races, marriage of deficient and unfit persons and population explosion leading to poverty and unemployment. Gobineau and his followers believe that the decay of all societies is the result of racial inter-mixture. This is due to the fact that races are not equal in capability. There are three races, the white, the yellow and the black. The white races are superior in capability and when interbred with other races, the quality deteriorates. However, this factor does not hold good in the present knowledge of biological science.

(5) *The Ecological Factor.* The ecological factor has been recently emphasized by many sociologists in the study of social disorganization. Here social disorganization is related to environment in terms of regions and neighbourhoods. Professor Shaw and his associates at the Institute of Juvenile Research in Chicago found that the delinquency was unevenly distributed in the city of Chicago.[32] While some areas showed no complaint of juvenile delinquency, from particular areas came large number of delinquents. Areas where delinquency was concentrated were found to be characterized by proximity to industry and commerce, physical deterioration, decreasing population in a period when the city as a whole was growing rapidly, dependency, absence of ownership of homes and absence of constructive agencies intended to promote well being and prevent maladjustment. Besides differences in crime due to

[32] Shaw, C. R. with the Collaboration of Mackay and others, *Delinquency Areas* (1929).

neighbourhood environments, Taft found two additional factors for such differences. He came to the conclusion that amount of social disorganization also varied in different regions due to difference in culture and density of population. According to his findings not only crime is concentrated in cities but with some exceptions, the larger the city the greater the per capita crime rate.[33]

(6) *Individual Disorganization leading to Social Disorganization.* This philosophically organic approach has been developed by Charles H. Cooley and his followers. Basic to this approach is the microscopic-macroscopic relationship between society and the individual.[34] In Professor Cooley's formulation, both are but different aspects of one and the same thing, i.e. social life, when one views social life from the point of view of the separate units of which it is made up, he sees the individual. When, on the other hand, his view is that of the collectivity he sees society. From this standpoint personal and social disorganization are inextricably bound up together and it is difficult to say which has grown out of which and both are cause and effect of each other and one cannot exist without the other.

Suppose at a particular stage there is social organization in the society. But due to psychological nature of man some new elements in norms are introduced by individuals. On the other hand, there is gradual relaxation of institutional control. Both these factors lead to personal disorganization. And if this personal disorganization is not checked it may develop into social disorganization.

(7) *Social Problems leading to Social Disorganization.* Social problems in the various fields such as economics, medicine, psychology, political science, sociology are considered to be the symptoms of social disorganization. For example, unemployment in the economic field, sickness in the medical field, mental illness in the psychological field, political corruption in the political field and divorces in the sociological field were considered to be problems threatening the smooth working of society. These social problems were considered to be the diseases of the society, which threatened the welfare of the society. The society could progress only when these diseases were removed or, in other words, these social problems were solved. This required some sort of collective action.

(8) *Degeneration of Values.* According to Professor Sorokin

[33] Taft, D. R., *Criminology* (1956), pp. 204-20.

[34] Mowrer, E. R., *op. cit.*, p. 23.

the cause of social disorganization in the present age is due to cultural degeneration in the sphere of values which has led to more wars, criminality, revolutions, suicides, mental disease, etc. In his opinion the present crisis is neither due to conflict of democracy versus dictatorship, capitalism versus communism, or nationalism versus internationalism or despotism versus liberty, nor that culture has reached its climax and must decline (Spengler holds that each culture is mortal and must decline), but it is degeneration of values in various spheres such as art, science, philosophy, religion, law, politics, economics, family, etc. More precisely, it consists in a disintegration of a fundamental form of western culture and society dominant for the last four centuries.[35] In his opinion there are three forms of culture (*i*) ideational, (*ii*) idealistic, and (*iii*) sensate. In the ideational culture there was a united system—a whole whose parts articulated the same supreme principle of true reality and value : an infinite, supersensory and super-rational God, omnipresent, omnipotent, omniscient, absolutely just, good and beautiful, creator of the world and of man. In the sensory culture the major principle is that the true reality and value is sensory. Only what we see, hear, smell, touch and otherwise perceive through our sense organs is real and has value. Beyond such a sensory reality, either there is nothing, or if there is something, we cannot sense it, therefore, it is equivalent to the non-real and the non-existent. As such it may be neglected.[36] In between these two cultures is the third one known as the idealistic. Its major premise was that the true reality is partly supersensory and partly sensory—that it embraces the supersensory and superrational aspect, plus the rational aspect, and finally, the sensory aspect, all blended into one unity, that of the infinite manifold, God.

The decline of ideational culture began at the end of the twelfth century. The idealistic culture was prevalent till the beginning of the sixteenth century when the sensate culture began to dominate. The modern sensate culture is—the sensory, empirical, secular and "this worldly" culture. In this culture the principal value that the true reality and value is sensory dominates, articulates in all its main compartments, in its arts and sciences, philosophy and pseudo-religion, ethics and laws, in its social, economic and political organizations, in its dominant ways of life and mentality. The

[35] Sorokin, P. A., *The Crisis of Our Age* (1941), p. 17.
[36] *Ibid.*, p. 20.

present crisis of our culture and society consist in the disintegration of the dominant sensate system of modern culture. But disintegration is not to the extent that it cannot be remedied.

Let us take one or two examples to explain how sensate culture has brought disintegration in the sphere of art and family. The morbid concentration of sensate art is on pathological types of persons and events. The heroes and other personages of the past were mainly God, deities, saints and the noblest of human heroes—the bearers of the basic positive values. Now it centres in the police morgue, the criminal's hide-out, and the sex organs, operating mainly on the level of the social sewers.[37] If we accept it as a faithful representation of human society, then man and his culture forfeit our respect and admiration. In so far as it is an art of man's debasement and vilification, it is paving the way for its own downfall as a cultural value. In the case of family which was a socially sanctioned union of husband and wife, of parents and children and of the circle of relatives shows signs of disintegration in many forms : the tie binding husband and wife into one entity, normally for life, has weakened and is, therefore, sundered more and more frequently by divorces and separations.[38] The bond uniting parents and children has likewise weakened, because of increasing percentage of marriages without children and the cleavage between the mores, beliefs, mentality, and social forms of conduct of parents and children has progressively widened. The conflict between fathers and sons has become sharper and deeper. As a union of relatives beyond the circle of husband and wife and parents and children, the family is virtually non-existent. As it has become more and more contractual, the family of the last few decades has grown even more unstable until it has reached the point of disintegration. The way out is that the sensate culture must shift to another basic form of culture—in our case from the agonizing sensate to the ideational or the idealist or integral.[39] "Our remedy, demands a complete change of the contemporary mentality, a fundamental transformation of our system of values, and the profoundest modification of our conduct towards other men, cultural values, and the world at large."[40]

[37] *Ibid.*, p. 67.
[38] *Ibid.*, p. 187.
[39] Sorokin, P. A., *op. cit.*, p. 316.
[40] *Ibid.*, p. 321.

Professor R. K. Mukerjee also holds a similar view. He points out that in the present age there is a decline of human character and the perversion of human sentiments and values. Science and technology while enormously enlarging man's practical skill to control the occurrence of values and use of objects, events and men for the realization of values do not enable him to apprehend the completeness of particular objects and situations in themselves, to realize them as intrinsic values and entities with their varied, potentialities of life experience.[41] According to him the recovery of chronically sick civilization is not possible without a new integrated framework of ideas and values that are of general validity for entire mankind, and that we may call Meta-civilization.[42] Meta-civilization integrates and coordinates ecology, ethology, psychology and social science with a philosophy of human values.

(9) *Lack of Proper Planning leading to Social Disorganization.* According to Karl Mannheim the uncontrolled capitalism and policy of *laissez faire* were responsible for personal and social disorganization in the present age. In his opinion the *laissez faire* policy in the old sense could no longer work and in the present stage of industrial society planning in some form or other was inevitable. He says that as a result of a process of fundamental democratization, the older type of restrictive democracy of propertied and educated elite has been increasingly displaced by a democracy of emotionalized masses. In a society in which the masses tend to dominate, irrationalities, which have not been integrated into the social structure may force their way into political life. This situation is dangerous because the selective apparatus of mass democracy opens the door to irrationalities in those places where rational direction is indispensable. Thus, democracy itself produces its own antithesis and even provides its own enemies with their weapons.[43]

Besides mass democracy, another cause of social disorganization is the development of new social techniques which have made minority rule possible replacing democracy by dictatorship. The large scale organizations, i.e. the factory, the army and the civil services lead to bureaucratic tendencies. They create over-disciplined factory worker or soldier who in consequence loses vitality

[41] Mukerjee, Radha Kamal, *Sickness of Civilization* (1964), p. vi.

[42] *Ibid.*, p. x. Also see his *Destiny of Civilization* (1964), p. vii.

[43] Mannheim, Karl, *Man and Society—In an Age of Reconstruction* (1940) p. 3.

whenever the plant closes down or when there is no one to give commands. There is a tendency to establish key positions from which central decisions are made. The very existence of key positions makes for minority rule. The end of *laissez faire* and the necessity for planning are unavoidable consequences of the present age.[44]

In his view religion has also ceased to be a creed and a social control inspiring patterns of behaviour and ideals of the good life. But it must take the task of an ultimate integration of all human activities.

(10) *Disintegration and Confusion of Roles.* According to Professor Faris one of the important causes of social disorganization is the transition from pre-industrial folk society to modern industrial civilization where the separate functions of members are not being performed successfully. In a rapidly changing society it is not entirely obvious what it is that constitutes the normal or non-pathological for standards are confused. In a stable society there is a team work and each member contributes his activity to the whole organization and draws his reward or benefit from the whole. When such a condition of high morale is obtained, the relatively individualistic satisfactions, the comforts and personal pleasures become of secondary importance. Of course, some defects of coordination are not as easy to perceive in the teamwork that constitute the whole social organization. The complexity is so great that the goals and the individual roles are not as clearly specified. Similarly, the aims of a society as a whole are not only not made explicit at any one time but they are not even understood to be the same by all the members. However, there are many functions which are clearly understood to be the responsibility of the whole society or separate institutions within it. For example, children are to be cared for and given an essential part of their cultural education in the family. Economic order is assumed to provide for the production and distribution of goods and wealth. The political order has many clear-cut responsibilities—the prevention of crime and disorder, the provision of many essential services to communities and to larger areas, and the defence of the nation. The religious institutions have the responsibility of preserving and transmitting their particular religious heritage. When any of these functions or others of the same order are being inadequately fulfilled, there is clearly a situation of

[44] Mannheim, Karl, *Freedom, Power and Democratic Planning* (1951), p. 8.

disorganization in the society.[45] In other words, "Social disorganization is disruption of the functional relations among persons to a degree that interferes with the performance of the accepted tasks of the group."[46]

(11) *Political Subservience.* In certain cases political subordination of one country to another has also led to social disorganization in the former one. The subordinate country is not allowed to develop its economy and institutions in its own ways and is made as a means to serve the dominant country. This happened in countries like India where there is mass illiteracy, poverty, etc. and effects of colonialism have been examined in detail in Chapter X.

Besides the causes described above there are some more which have been mentioned by sociologists as leading to social disorganization, e.g. war, business depression, formalism in the means of social control such as religion, law, etc. However, these have been discussed above under one head or the other indirectly and need no further examination.

Causes Giving Rise to Social Problems

We have already seen that social problem and social disorganization are closely related to each other. The social disorganization gives rise to social problems and vice versa. Thus, the causes giving rise to social problems are almost the same as that of social disorganization. Professor Timms observes, "The conditions giving rise to social problems have been described as states of social pathology, of social disorganization and of dissensus and deviation."[47] However, he also develops two general approaches to the study of social problems, viz. the process of deviation and the structural approach. In the first case he points out that some persons become deviants because of certain circumstances and then try to make a group of their own, thus creating social problems. This we shall discuss in detail in Chapter II. In the second case, i.e. structural approach he refers to the idea of anomie developed by Professor Merton. In a society like U. S. A. where the emphasis is on the cultural goal of success and the fact that many people in the society

[45] Faris, R. E. L., *Social Disorganization* (1948), p. 21.
[46] *Ibid.*, p. 21.
[47] Noel Timms, *A Sociological Approach to Social Problems* (1967), p. 20. Also see Dutt Gupta, Bela, *Contemporary Social Problems in India* (1964), Chapter I.

are deprived of access to the institutionalized means of reaching for their goals, high rates of criminal behaviour are the normal outcome.[48]

Professor Merton adds that the social problems can be usefully divided into two broad classes, the one described as "social disorganization", and the other, as "deviant behaviour", though there are some—for instance, family disorganization, criminal behaviour and community conflict—which are evidence of both social disorganization and deviant behaviour, though in differing compound.[49]

Social Disorganization in India

The causes which have led to social disorganization in India are almost the same as are operative in some other countries although there can be some variations due to some peculiar conditions prevailing in this country.

In general we can say that the problems of poverty and unemployment, rising population and low standard of living and illiteracy are the result of political subordination and *laissez faire* policy followed by the British Government in the past.

The problems of juvenile delinquency, drinking, gambling, prostitution, beggary, etc are mostly the product of rapid industrialization and urbanization on the one hand and dissolution of old institutions like joint family and village panchayat on the other. The problems of corruption, moral degeneration, etc. are mostly the result of more formalism in religion which has crept into it in the last few centuries. Community conflicts, lingualism, communalism, regionalism, etc. are mostly the product of new social structure which have emerged after Independence.

However, there is not one but many causes which have led to the emergence of a specific social problem. Again one social problem creates another one and they become enmeshed with each other. For example, poverty is the cause of low health, undernutrition, crime, etc.

India in a State of Disorganization. The next question is whether India is in a state of social disorganization. It is difficult to answer such a complex question. However, looking to the goals of society as laid down in the Indian Constitution on the one hand and symptoms of social disorganization on the other, we can say that our

[48] *Ibid.*, p. 26.
[49] Merton, R. K., *op. cit.*, p. 719.

country is in a state of disorganization. Of course, it is difficult to make any categorical statement on such a question, which is so complex and requires large amount of data to substantiate. However, looking to some of the symptoms such as rapidly growing population, poor standard of living, food deficit, malnutrition and undernutrition, large scale unemployment, beggary, illiteracy, prostitution, crime, corruption, too many political groups, strikes by students and labourers, we can say that the society is in a state of social disorganization. No doubt some processes of social reconstruction such as expansion of education for the children, programmes for agricultural and industrial development, etc. are also going on for the development of society. But taking the position as a whole the balance is on the negative side. The Education Commission (1964) observes, "Indian society is hierarchical, stratified and deficient in vertical mobility. The social distance between different classes and particularly between the rich and the poor, the educated and the uneducated is large and is tending to widen. . . . . As education is not rooted in the traditions of the people, the educated persons tend to the alienated from their own culture. The growth of local, regional, linguistic and state loyalties tend to make the people forget 'India'. The old values, which held society together, have been disappearing and as there is no effective programme to replace them by a new sense of social responsibility, innumerable signs of social disorganization are evident everywhere and are continually on the increase. These include strikes, increasing lawlessness, and a disregard for public property, corruption in public life and communal tensions and troubles. Students' unrest, of which so much is written, is only one, and probably a minor one of these symptoms."[50] According to Professor Faris in periods of general disorganization there arises among the people a sense of awareness that something is wrong, even though there is no clear analysis of the trouble. Affairs are not going as smoothly as formerly, and dissatisfaction spreads.[51] Applying this test, such conditions do exist in India, though to pronounce such a judgment without substantial data may not be justified.

Scheme of the Book

In the foregoing pages we have described the various factors

[50] *Report of the Education Commission* 1964-66, (1966), p. 2.

[51] *Ibid.*, p. 38.

leading to social disorganization. On the basis of that we may discuss the various forms of social disorganization under the following main heads :

(1) Individual difficulties such as physical, social or mental handicaps which may or may not lead to social disorganization.

(2) Certain handicaps as a result of which the individual becomes habituated to some social vice. This ultimately affects his life organization as well as others in the community bringing social disorganization in the society.

(3) Biological and physical factors which without proper control through modern technology create problems of mass disorganization such as population explosion and non-development of economic resources leading to poverty.

(4) Decay in the existing institutions whether educational, religious, recreational, family, etc. which ultimately affect the community.

(5) Change in values and conflict in roles due to the rapid spread of technology, industrialization, urbanization and mass communication creating problems of community and national disorganization.

Although these factors cannot be divided into watertight compartments and affect each other, yet on the basis of this division we shall discuss the problems of individual disorganization, crime, social vices, poverty and unemployment, population explosion, decay in institutions like educational and religious, family disorganization and problems of conflicting roles, community conflicts, and prejudices in the succeeding pages.

CHAPTER II

INDIVIDUAL DISORGANIZATION

WE HAVE pointed out in Chapter I that there is a very close relation between individual disorganization and social disorganization. Similarly, there is a close relation between individual disorganization and social problems. When a number of individuals suffer from a similar type of disorganization, a social problem is in existence. In other words, individual disorganization, social problems and social disorganization are closely interrelated to each other. Therefore, it will be appropriate to discuss how individual disorganization arises. In other words, what are the causes which lead to individual disorganization. However, before we do that it will be appropriate to discuss the relation between social and individual disorganization in detail so that we may be able to understand the causes of individual disorganization in a more clear way.

Relation Between Individual and Social Disorganization

We have already pointed out that individual and social disorganization are closely related to each other and are dual aspects of the same process. It could not be said whether personal disorganization grew out of the same dynamic processes which occasioned the breakdown of group consensus and produced social disorganization as well as individual disorganization. To Professor Cooley personal disorganization without its corresponding social disorganization was a contradiction in terms.[1] If social disorganization was cause and effect of individual disorganization, the same could be said for individual disorganization. Thus, both operated in a vicious circle.

However, let us find out a clear sequence how one grew out of the other. We shall first trace the emergence of individual disorganization from social disorganization and then take up the other case. The social disorganization may appear all of a sudden due to the operation of one or more factors discussed in Chapter I,

[1] See Mowrer, E. R., *op. cit.*, p. 24.

emergence of some social problems, or biological, psychological, geographical, cultural or technological reasons which may lead to the breakdown of institutional control and group consensus in the society. This breakdown in institutional control and group consensus will allow man's elemental nature to function unrestrained, and thus bring individual disorganization on a large scale. The second position can be that social disorganization may be of a milder nature and the formalism in institutional control still remains which functions outwardly, but internally the individual is left without guidance. The personal disorganization in this case may appear gradually assuming a larger form later on. Thus, personal disorganization may grow gradually or all of a sudden, out of social disorganization, and this individual disorganization may further intensify social disorganization.

Now let us take the other case and see how social disorganization emerges from individual disorganization. Here we may assume that some social disorganization is already present in the society but it is so mild that we can easily ignore it, and this we may call as social organization of a dynamic society. Here individual disorganization may arise because of various factors such as biological, environmental, loss of security or crisis in life, which we shall discuss in detail in succeeding pages. There can be two possibilities : (*i*) Individual disorganization may grow independent of social disorganization. For instance, if a person has ill health or is unable to meet his social demands it may lead to his physical or nervous breakdown and upset his personal plans and life schemes. He may seclude himself from the society. Here the relation between social and individual disorganization may thus seem remote. (*ii*) Suppose an individual is a leader or occupies a strategic position in society, which is often the case, then any disorganization in him leads to social disorganization if not checked. Each such disorganized individual affects other individuals and in so doing produces social disorganization.

Here the social disorganization can be of different degree depending upon the nature of individual disorganization. The disorganized person who wants to introduce new innovations into the society, will naturally have to face social disapproval. Dr. Mowrer points out that here the individual is faced with three alternatives : (1) revamping of the discordant elements to the degree that their variance is no longer apparent, (2) the seeking out of others who themselves have incipient trends in the same direction, or (3) to retreat in a subjective world.[2]

In simpler societies the first alternative is most commonly chosen. Social change is not eliminated, but it takes place by such minute increments that there is no realization that anything is happening. On the other hand, if the innovator finds his "heresy" encouraged by a sympathetic audience he resists the constraining influence of the larger group and tends to accentuate the variant response. The nature of this sympathetic audience group depends upon the nature of the resistance which a particular society sets up. The varying degree of social disorganization in this case depends upon the character of the sympathetic audience group which promotes the development of cultural innovation. The innovations which meet with organized resistance tend to result in marked social disorganization. If, on the other hand, these innovations are supported by spontaneous organized groups they do not lead to violent disturbances in the social order and become incorporated in the social order.

If the innovator, in the face of social disapproval, retreats into a subjective inner world his innovations lose their social character and become enmeshed in the development of his mechanisms, which further tend to insulate him from the normal influences of group life. In other words, he goes insane and because of the danger that he may harm others, he may be locked up in an institution. Some, however, may not go to that extreme, and are looked upon simply as disorganized personalities. This type of personal disorganization does not have much of its counterpart in social disorganization though such person may form a small group. This small group generally consists of innovators or inventors, or reformists or revolutionists who are extraordinarily intelligent. But if such a group consists of criminals, prostitutes, alcoholics, etc. who even when small in number affect others and ultimately the society.

Dr. Mowrer also points out that the tendency to variation in behaviour is more in complex societies than in simple societies due to (1) specialized functioning inherent in complex societies, (2) the family instead of group which works as a culture defining agency, and (3) cultural participation outside the particular social order.[3] Further that innovations of milder character receive ready accep-

[2] *Ibid.*, p. 29.

[3] *Ibid.*, p. 26.

tance, especially those in the material than in the non-material culture, because in the former case they do not form an integral part of the institutional pattern. Comparing the two, i.e. social and individual disorganization, he points out that whereas any change in the cultural context which impedes or destroys the functioning of the patterns of coordination which constitute the social order represents social disorganization, any form of variant behaviour which disturbs the integration of the attitude systems within the personality represents personal disorganization.[4] Having discussed the relation between individual and social disorganization, we pass on to concepts of individual organization and disorganization.

Individual and Society

The individual and society are closely related. Although individual is endowed with certain biological and mental capacities and potentialities at birth, he soon becomes a social animal. He is indebted to social influences for all that he is or hopes to be. No matter how much intelligent a man may be, he cannot advance without social influences. Since man has almost without exception, lived in some sort of social world, he has always been socialized in the course of growing up and come to possess individual self-consciousness. The group relations of the person furnish a major clue to his behaviour, whether that behaviour be defined as normal or delinquent. Thus, while studying a person, we have to study not only his various mental, physical and temperamental characteristics, which often offer a significant clue to the behaviour of the person and the understanding of his role in the various groups of which he is a member, but as Professor Burgess points out, "An adequate study of the person must include the nature and extent of his participation in the manifold groups of which he is a member, his personal behaviour pattern, his 'social type (i.e. Philistine, Bohemian, Creative)', and finally his philosophy of life, his life organization."[5] Professor Mead in his book, *Mind, Self and Society*, while studying the genesis of the self, makes clear the individual's basic dependence upon the dynamic forces of his social milieu. He says that the individual's very self, his personality, his human nature, are

[4] *Ibid*., p. 26.

[5] Burgess, E. W., "The Study of the Delinquent as a Person", *American Journal of Sociology*, May, 1923.

all social products, derived from his complex interaction with the social groups which make up his expanding environment. In the continuous interplay between the individual and his associates, the biological "individual" becomes a "person". In so doing, he takes a variety of roles in the various groups of which he is a member. His personality is a complex mosaic of these roles. Human nature is painfully acquired and is made possible only by contact with other persons. Without these contacts, man would remain less than a human being.[6]

Individual's Life Organization

Man is a purposive creature and he must have some purpose motivating his life. Each individual has evolved some scheme or some organization of his life incorporating a particular set of attitudes and values. Attitudes as we may define them are the tendencies to act in a specific way and social values are the meanings we attach to the objects the behaviour involves. The term "life organization" has been defined by Thomas and Znaniecki "as that structure of attitudes and values which have grown out of the social experience of each person and through which, consciously or unconsciously, he hopes to realize his basic purposes. An individual's life organization is thus his set of rules for guidance in the sphere of morality, law, social relationships, religion, business or recreation. These rules are the embodiment of the individual's values, by which he attempts to define each particular situation."[7] These rules constitute his code of behaviour, the things that he will and will not do, whether he be a gambler, politician, clergyman or stockbroker. With the infinite range of individual variations, each person sets up a life organization, based on what he is and what he wants to be.

The society tries to impose the socially sanctioned variety of life organization upon the next generation and, therefore, the individual's attitudes and values are in large part the product of such group norms and expectations. If the group values were sufficiently rigid or well-defined there would seem to be no reason for the individual's failing to conform to them. However, the group

[6] Mead, George H., *Mind, Self and Society* (1934). Also see *Social Disorganization* by Elliott, M. A., and Merrill, F. E. (1940), pp. 66-67.

[7] Thomas, W.I., and Znaniecki, F., *The Polish Peasant in Europe and America* (1927), pp. 1843, 1851.

definitions are not so rigid as they seem ; and disorganization of the individual is often the result.

Proper Life Organization and Disorganization

A proper life organization is one which is based upon a set of attitudes, habits and values which are in harmonious concord with the organization and purposes of the group. "The balance which applies in the life organization of an adjusted individual must come from maintaining perspective—from seeing life steadily and seeing it in the whole or in the acceptance of the Aristotelian 'golden mean'. A well-organized, creative person is one whose various social activities are in substantial reciprocal balance. The balanced person diversifies his talents and energies so as to include all of the essential phases of a well-rounded life. Calmly and sensibly he alternates work and play, waking and sleeping, activity and rest. He recognizes the relationship between means and ends and does not exhaust himself over the means if the ends themselves are unworthy. In short, his various life processes are integrated into a harmonious and smoothly functioning social whole."[8]

The unadjusted person, on the other hand, is essentially uncoordinated. For one reason or another he becomes one-sided, devoting too much time and energy to one group of activities and ignoring others which are equally important in his life scheme. Even if he does not become so maladjusted as to be adjudged undesirable, dangerous or immoral, he is regarded as an unbalanced person. When he deviates so much from the normal conception of balance as to be treated in an exceptional manner, he is then considered to be truly disorganized. He is one who fails to come up to social definitions. Personal disorganization is measured by the degree and severity of individual departure from the socially accepted norms. Our concept of imperfect and perfect disorganization or balanced and unbalanced personality is obviously one of degree. "We are all out of balance in certain respects. No one follows perfectly the via media, the middle way."[9]

As pointed out above an individual in his social contact is exposed to the norms of the social group. His own attitudes and values are in large part the product of such group norms and expectation. If these group values are sufficiently rigid and clear, the individual

[8] Elliott, M.A., and Merrill, F. E., *op. cit.*, p. 75.

[9] *Ibid.*, p. 76.

will have no difficulty in following them. But often it has been observed that group values are neither rigid nor precise. Disparity in opinion exists within the various political, religious, educational, economic and ecological groups within the same social structure. Thus the individual is often confused, the result of which may be maladjustment. Even where there is a relatively high agreement in social definition there is no necessary harmony between the individual and society. Therefore, it is not necessary that an individual will conform to those definitions though an average individual, because of examples and group pressures, may accept them outwardly, at least the social dictates, whether or not they coincide fortuitously with his own desire. Thus, the life organization of the individual, which is based upon his own peculiar set of attitudes, habits and values, is not necessarily in harmony with the organization and purposes of the group. Each individual has to learn, sooner or later, that he has to conform to the group, but it is not necessary that all may understand this so soon. In fact the growing realization of disparity between the individual and group purposes is the essential basis of maturity. There are many people who are unable to adjust their individual desires to the social purposes. They resist the orders vainly which are more powerful than themselves. These unhappy individuals curse the fates, the injustices of society which are hindrances in achieving their own egoistic ends. A serious derangement of their life organization may result. While rejecting the group definitions, they try to formulate definitions of their own. But only the strong and creative person can maintain his own equilibrium in doing so. The weak cannot operate effectively against socially accepted values. "The man who is too creative, who rejects too many social schemes, disrupts the established order and is generally adjudged dangerous to the continued safety of the group."[10] A person who does not wholeheartedly accept, or at least pretend to accept, all the schemes of the group for life organization, is branded a non-conformist a heretic and a menace to the common good. Sooner or later, either the group or the individual must yield as a defining and normative unit and it is usually the individual who must bow to the inevitable.

In simple or primitive societies it is easier to impose group schemes and patterns of life organization on the individual than in the modern societies due to the increased complexity of the modern culture.

[10] Thomas, W. I., and Znaniecki, F., *op. cit.*, p. 1899.

Despite the ability of superior individuals to erect a satisfactory life organization in the midst of the confusion in social thinking, a larger number of individuals are utterly unable to do so. Those who fail to construct a new life organization out of the remnants of the old, become the victims of disorganization. They become vagabonds, thieves, prostitutes, and lose their contact with the society, particularly with the primary group such as family, neighbours and friends whose sanction of his conduct impart validity to his life organization which he has adopted.

Causes of Individual Disorganization

Anything which upsets the harmonious functioning of an individual's daily living may disrupt his life organization and "disorganize" him. Elliott and Merrill have mentioned four kinds of factors or situations which often disturb the individual's pattern of living, viz. biological factors, environmental factors, loss of security and crisis in life, though some writers have discussed them under the former two. The biological factors include personal difficulties arising out of organic or functional disorder, i.e. physical illness, injury, mental deficiencies or personal inadequacies which may occasion a reorganization in an individual's life. The individual so handicapped may become maladjusted as he is unable to overcome his obvious disadvantages. The inadequacies in the social order or in other words environmental factors include such situations as economic distress, confusion, contradiction and conflict in social relations in the family, in the economic world, in religious institutions or in recreational activities, which may bring disorganization in his life. Thirdly, the child or the adult alike make a search for security. Much of the child's sense of security is based upon the fact that he is his parent's child and belongs to his parents in a very real sense.[11] As a child the individual's desire for security may be threatened by the sense of inadequacy which he experiences in comparison with the members of his family or his playmates. As an adult he may dread a comparison with his fellow workmen or other associates. The psychological need of the individual to feel himself an essential part of the universe is a recognized fact. Without the sustaining strength which many persons previously derived from religious faith, the modern materialist may conclude that his individual conduct and destiny are of no importance to the cosmos

[11] James S. Plant, *Personality and the Cultural Pattern* (1937), p. 96.

or to his fellows. He may decide to "live merrily for tomorrow we may die", or he may develop the profound conviction that "life is a poor joke" and not worth the candle. Upon neither philosophy can a satisfying life organization be built. Crisis in life, means sudden shocks in the life of an individual whether due to the death of his near relation or loss of service, which may disturb his life organization. We shall discuss these factors in detail in the next chapter.

Stages in Personal Disorganization

Queen and Mann have pointed out three stages in individual disorganization.[12] Everyone faces the necessity of a possible reorganization of his life, if he would remain a stable personality. Following a disruption in his plan of living, which is either due to death of his some near relation or due to some other difficulty, such as failure of business or loss of service, the individuals vary greatly to meet the new situation. The largest number of individuals are at first perplexed in their attempts to find a way out or to build a constructive plan of action. This marks a period of un-adjustment or the first stage of disorganization. If the individual works out an adequate solution, he soon becomes adjusted and life goes on more smoothly. However, occasionally it so happens that multiplicity of untoward factors seem to allow no possibility of adjustment. If the individual loses his stability, he may have a nervous breakdown. If there is no satisfactory solution, he may enter upon a further stage of disorganization called maladjustment in which he is more or less permanently unadjusted. The criminals or the prostitutes who have lost all sense of social values come in this category. This personal disorganization may also lead to insanity or suicide, which is the last stage of disorganization. Some persons may reach this last stage without passing through the second one.

Types of Individual Disorganization

We have already pointed out that individual disorganization arises because of various factors within the individuals such as organic handicaps or extraordinary ability, or (2) social situations which are generally beyond the control of the individual. But many a time both operate side by side and reinforce each other.

[12] Queen, S. A., and Mann, D. M., *Social Pathology* (1925), p. 17.

According to Elliott and Merrill all types of personal maladjustment represent in one way or another, the inability of the individual to achieve a satisfactory life organization from the point of view of the social definition of his social patterns.[13] Dr. Mowrer mentions the following characteristics of disorganized persons. (1) The behaviour of the disorganized person deviates from the culturally approved norms. (2) His behaviour arouses social disapproval which may vary from mild to marked (and even violent) one. (3) The disorganized person may respond to social disapproval in two ways, i.e. positively or negatively. The positive respond leads to the seeking out of others who also manifest trend in the same direction, while negative response results in the building up of a world of phantasy, or finds expression in regressive behaviour. (4) The objective in the positive response may be defined in two ways, i.e. in terms of the welfare of the society or on hedonistic lines. He further points out that in the complex societies the most apparent form of personal disorganization is that in which there is mild social disapproval and to which the individual responds positively. This is the realm of the innovator, whether he works with material objects or with techniques and beliefs. All inventions are met with some skepticism. However, as this type of personal disorganization is confined to relatively small segment of the person's response pattern, the social disapproval is very mild. In case of marked or violent social disapproval the innovation tends to result in the organization of cults or sects. In the process of cult and sect organization the objective may be defined in either of the two ways, i.e. in terms of welfare of the larger group or on hedonistic line for the restricted advantages of the cult or sect. In the latter case such groups may consist of criminals or those cases in which elemental appetite and urges exclusively dominate their personalities such as prostitutes. In case where the individual's response to social disapproval is negative or subjective, the person retreats into an individually defined inner world. This type of personal disorganization finds its extreme development in the psychoses and sometimes in suicide.

On the basis of above criteria Dr. Mowrer divided various types of disorganized persons into three main categories depending upon the degree of social disapproval their behaviour arouses and the response of the person concerned.

[13] *Ibid.*, p. 80.

(*a*) *Non-conformists.* Among the non-conformists are included inventors and innovators who are not satisfied with the present position and bring changes in their own environments and later on in the whole society. It is true that in the field of technology it rather looks awkward to say that the inventor is personally disorganized as his inventions are readily accepted. On the other hand, in such cases many attain considerable social prominence. However, it cannot be denied that they have personal disorganization to a certain extent, as they are too much absorbed in one activity and are not satisfied with the present position. In the field of ideas and beliefs the degree of personal disorganization is more marked, although here again sympathetic audiences sometimes become so large that their tendency to give ready approval with a minimum of demonstration of usefulness overshadows general social disapproval. Such people are generally included among the rebels.

(*b*) *The Rebels and Revolutionists.* In contrast to the inventor and the innovator, the rebel and revolutionist arouse marked social disapproval. The rebel may define his rebellion, however, in two widely contrasted ways, i.e. along social welfare lines or on hedonistic lines. If the definition is a hedonistic one, this type of rebellion includes the forms of behaviour ordinarily referred to as criminal. If rebellion is defined in terms of social welfare this takes a variety of forms all the way from the nebulous revolt of youth to the more complex and integrated forms expressed in radicalism and Bohemianism.[14] Among the mild type of rebels he includes : (1) the adolescents who demand changes in the non-material culture, that is, in beliefs, conventions, or economic, social or religious ideas, although their idealism is for a shorter period. (2) Some of the migrants who move to the cities because of superior or inferior abilities and are unable to adjust to the local social requirements. (3) The marginal man, who has been brought up in two different cultures, he being a racial or cultural harhid. (4) The casual labourer or hobo who is like a migrant, but unlike the pioneer, unable to find a relatively permanent place in any cultural area. The wanderlust for him has become a vice, and his rebellion against the social order finds no clear-cut patterning and remains transitory. (5) Among those whose behaviour arouses marked social disapproval are included the reformers and the revolutionists. Whereas the adolescents and others have no programme against the older generations and have only nega-

[14] *Ibid.*, p. 54.

tivistic protests against the *status quo*, the reformers and revolutionists have an organized and consistent programme of revolt. The reformer is partly a reclaimer and partly a radical because he seeks to reconstruct social conditions in conformity with the mores. On the other hand, the radical is concerned with reconstructing the social order along the lines differing from those which prevail at a particular time. Further, the reformer, partly radical, differs from the radical in that he advocates reconstruction of only a specific segment of the social order, rather than the whole. The programme of the reformer is to bring the behaviour of individuals and groups into harmony with the traditional standard which society accepts in theory but fails to live up to it in practice. The reformer enjoys a respectibility denied to the radical and revolutionist and is able to carry out the campaign for group support into the open. However, both have one fundamental feature in common that they have a desire for social approval and the formulation of a basis for protest in such terms as to win sympathetic approval upon the part of some group. As contrasted to a revolutionist a Bohemian is a person who vacillates from one revolutionary programme to another. Inconsistency is the essential characteristic of a Bohemian's behaviour and he shows a high degree of adaptability to new influences.

(3) *Maladjusted or Disintegrated Persons*. Among those disorganized personalities who are unable to adjust themselves to the circumstances he includes the mentally disordered, insane or who commit suicide. He says that when the individual abandons the campaign for achieving social approval and retreats into a subjective world he has become maladjusted, or insane.[15] But again there is a wide gradation in the degree of abandonment of the campaign for social approval. Thus, in the neuroses the individual has abandoned the struggle only in part, whereas in the psychoses there has been complete abandonment. It may be mentioned here that among the unadjusted personalities he includes those having conflicting roles, dual roles, the pseudo ill, phantasy roles, the alcoholics, the suicide, the sexual variant, the neutotic and the psychotic. Among these unadjusted persons majority of them have disorganized personality but not a disintegrated one. In his view those who are not able to accommodate the conflicting situations in a socially approved way, but have not given up the attempt to adjust are disorganized or unadjusted but not disintegrated or maladjusted.

[15] *Ibid.*, p. 247.

Although the above description given by Dr. Mowrer covers a variety of disorganized persons, yet there are many more who are not normal from the societal point of view. They are not pathological in the sociological sense because they are well adjusted to the situation in which they live, yet need protection of the society to develop properly and perform their obligations in a proper manner. Among these may be included the children, the poor, the women, the physically and mentally deficient, the old, the unemployed, the labourers, etc.[16] For example, a poor person who is normal may be adjusted to the situation, yet he is not able to keep normal health due to under-nutrition and fulfil other obligations in the family and the society because of insufficient income. Thus, he needs the assistance of the state to provide him free medical facilities, education to his children, etc. Such persons may be called the weaker sections of the community. The problems of all these weak and unadjusted persons have been discussed in these two volumes.[17] However, in this chapter we shall deal in brief with the maladjusted or disintegrated personalities.

The Disintegration of Personality

Personality disorganisation, as has already been pointed out, is the consequence of conflict among the several aspects of personality. In the drive towards unity, patterns of accommodation among these aspects are achieved which impede, rather than facilitate, the individual's adjustment to his social environment. The consequence is the development of a core of covert and inner responses which defy group demands for social approval, dislocating the individual in the social order. Where this dislocation becomes so great as to interfere markedly with the person's ability to support himself or to take care of his bodily needs, so that another has to care for him as he would be a person who is ill or he becomes likely to injure or shock the sensibilities of other persons he is regarded as having a mental disease. Again personal disorganization covers a wide range of patterns as from those who because of mental conflict had lives of mild frustration and social inefficiency to those who eliminate themselves from society or become such liabilities that they have to be cared for either privately or publicly. It is in the

[16] For details see Volume II, Chapter I.

[17] Volume I deals with unadjusted persons, while Volume II with weaker sections. However, this bifurcation is not strictly possible.

extreme form that personal disorganization finds expression in suicide or psychopathic behaviour.

Mentally Deranged

The insane or mentally deranged were long regarded with supertitious fear and were treated with a combination of cruel flogging and social avoidance. It was in the nineteenth century that human intelligence and sympathy were touched by the unnecessary sufferings of the insane. Instead of providing purely custodial, medical attention was directed towards the etiology of the disease and treatment of the patient, and the diseases were studied and classified on the basis of origin, characteristics, and possibility of recovery. The early history of the patient, the incipient stages of the disease were analysed and for the first time a truly scientific approach was made.

The mentally ill are generally divided into three categories. They are (1) brain syndromes (symptoms of brain disease or injury) with mental reactions, (2) psychotic disorders (which are essentially mental disorders with specific mental reactions), or (3) those of the psychoneurotic or neurotic type.[18] These again are subdivided into various categories.

According to Professor Munn such abnormal persons may be classified in two ways. One classification is in terms of whether the abnormality is structural or functional and the other in terms of whether it is a psychoneurosis or a psychosis.[19] The structural or organic personality disorders are those which have a known organic basis like syphilis of the nervous system or hardening of the arteries of the brain. Functional disorders, on the other hand, have no known organic basis, except acquired modifications of the nervous system which underlie the individual's peculiar attitudes towards himself and others.

Psychoneuroses (or neuroses) are relatively mild mental disorders. They include such symptoms as excessive fatigue and bodily complaints (neurasthenia), loss of memory or of sensory or motor functions (hysteria), and abnormal anxiety (anxiety neurosis). Although such disorders may cause great distress to the person afflicted with them, and be a nuisance to those who have to associate with him,

[18] Elliott, M. A., and Merrill, F. E., *op. cit.* (1961), p. 287.

[19] Munn, N. L., ***Psychology, The Fundamentals of Human Adjustment*** (1958), p. 182.

they are usually neither incapacitating nor dangerous. Institutionalization is rarely necessary. All personality disorders which fall within the psychoneurotic classification are generally assumed to be functional in origin, although thought by the patient to be organic.

Psychoses are much more serious than psychoneuroses. There is usually a marked psychological deterioration. The individual may have hallucination and delusions. He may, for example, see visions and hear voices. A psychoneurotic may call himself "neurotic" and even laugh at himself. But the psychotic is usually sure that he is all right and the world all wrong. Psychotics are often dangerous to themselves and to those around them, hence one must usually place them in hospitals where they can be treated and looked after. The psychotics may be divided into two categories as already seen. Those with known organic basis, like syphilis and alcoholism may be termed as organic or structural psychosis. Those without any associated organic pathology are known as functional psychosis. In the later case the maladjustments arise out of peculiar attitudes which the individual has developed toward his world, including his relation with other people.

Causes of Mental Illness

A little worry about the best solution to a given difficulty will not hurt anyone. Any crisis—whether a death in the family, an unexpected illness, an injury from an accident, being called into military service, the loss of job or disappointment in friend—calls for intelligence and external resources. Fortunately most people can make adjustment to the situation. However, some people have difficulty in shaking their anxieties and tensions while some create crises by their own emotional responses to situations. Such people become fearful and suspicious toward those with whom they are associated and thus become mentally disturbed. Further crisis in their life may upset the balance more and ultimately it may result in insanity and suicide. We have already discussed the stages of personal disorganization given by Queen and Mann in this connection. Thus, the causes of mental illness are both biological and situational. A major share of mental disorganization is the result of inability to adjust to the strains of modern life. The struggle for material possessions, the frustration of the job, aggression endangered by competition, the migration which involves marked cultural adjustment, the pervasive attempt to rise in the social scale, unhappy family relations—these and many other factors combine to increase the difficulty of living in the modern age.

Mental Illness in India

In this country the number of those who are mentally ill is not known due to the lack of facilities for such persons. No accurate statistics has been collected so far. It has been estimated that in U. S. A. the number of people who suffer from some sort of nervous or mental disorder is about 6 per cent of the total population.

Services for the Mentally Ill

The services for the mentally ill are also inadequate as compared to some of the advanced countries of the world. For example, in India there are only 20 hospitals as compared to about 1,000 mental hospitals in U. S. A. Similarly, there are only 10 child guidance clinics in India as compared to 650 in the U. S. A.

The total number of beds available in the mental hospitals at present is about 15,000. However, even if we take the ratio of mental patients at two per thousand of the population, as contrasted with 5 to 8 per 1,000 in the U. S. A. and 3.9 per cent in England, the number of patients who require hospital accommodation would be a million.[20] Similar is the position in case of child guidance clinics and other facilities for the mentally ill.[21]

Suicide

According to Durkheim suicide is the term applied to all cases of death resulting directly or indirectly from a positive or negative act of the victim himself which he knows will produce this result.[22] Suicide represents an extreme form of personal disorganization in an ordinary situation. However, in certain situations where the individual may kill himself because the group expects him to do so, it represents an index of social organization and group cohesion.

[20] Gobindaswamy, M. V., *Socio-Psychological and Mental Hygiene Problems in Social Welfare in India* (1956), p. 199.

[21] For more details see Volume II, Chapter XV, Mental Hygiene and Services for Mentally Handicapped.

[22] Durkheim, Emile, *Suicide* (Translated by J. A. Spaulding and George Simpson), (1951), p. 44.

Theories of Suicide

Suicide is a social phenomenon, with special reference to the relationships between the person and the group. However, it is also an individual phenomenon, in terms of the processes occurring with the psyche. Thus, theories of suicide can be divided into two groups the psychological and the sociological. The psychological theories stemmed from the writings of Freud. He postulates two contradictory wishes to which all behaviour may be traced, the will to live and the will to die. This death wish, however, can be turned upon one's self only by identification with someone else whom the individual has experienced a desire to kill. But not all suicide represents the fulfilment of the death wish alone. The ego wish, particularly as it is in part made of the sex wish may also become a part of the suicide pattern, especially with reference to the means of suicide. Thus, to poison one's self is to become pregnant, to drown is to bear a child, and to jump from a height is to deliver a child.[23]

Menninger expands upon the analysis suggested by Freud by breaking down the death wish as it operates in suicide into three distinct elements : (1) the wish to kill, (2) the wish to be killed, and (3) the wish to die. Accordingly in the absence of a wish to die or of a wish to kill in which the hated person has become incorporated into one's self, the suicidal impulse takes the form of extreme submission in which the individual obtains masochistic satisfaction.[24]

Under the sociological theory Durkheim mentioned three types of suicides which occur in different social situations. These types are the altruistic, the egoistic and the anomic. The altruistic suicide occurs when the integration of the individual with the group is very close. This type is found among many primitive peoples, where social integration is very strong. It is also found in more advanced societies such as India and Japan, when the sense of social responsibility is highly developed. Under the pressure of moral codes, persons who are old and enfeebled, women whose husbands are dead, and servants whose masters are deceased are expected to commit suicide.

Egoistic suicide occurs when the integration of the individual with the group is too loose and ill defined. Much of the suicide in

[23] William Healy *et al.*, *The Structure and Meaning of Psychoanalysis*, pp. 396-97.

[24] Karl, A. Menninger, *Man Against Himself* (1938), Part II. Also see Mowrer, E. R., *op. cit.*, p. 315.

modern society reflects this lack of integration. Consensus has broken down, leaving the individual isolated from many of the normal contacts of society. When the group is disorganized in this way, egoistic suicide becomes the predominant form of self-destruction. In this sense suicide is both a result of and an index of the relative degree of social disorganization in society.[25]

Anomic suicide results from a large scale lack of social regulation of individual behaviour. This type is closely related to egoistic suicide, but the emphasis in anomic suicide is upon the dissolution of norms that bind society together. It may arise from a severe break in the social equilibrium such as a business depression, an inflation, or a boom. The "will to live" among such persons is threatened by sudden changes in their way of life, whether an elevation or a decline in the social scale. For other persons, the mere existence in dynamic society makes adjustment difficult.

Causes of Suicide

The causes of suicide are complex as are the causes of any other social phenomenon. Many factors combine to cause one particular individual (and not another) to divert his aggressions upon himself in the form of suicide. However, in general the rates of suicide are higher in urban than in rural life. The social disorganization is, in general, greater in the city than in the country. Many primary relations break down in the city, social mobility is greater, social interaction is subject to more violent disturbances and crisis situations are more common. However, wide differences in suicide rate occur with respect to sex, religion, marital status, age, place of residence, economic conditions and other factors. Insecurity, frustration and self-aggression differently affect different groups and individuals.

Suicides in India

The statistics available for the year 1964 show that more males than females commit suicide. Similarly, the age group 18-30 is more vulnerable than the age groups 30 and above, and 18 and below. There is also variation in different regions. Madras has the highest number and next in order were Andhra, Mysore and Bengal whereas Bihar, Punjab and Assam had the lowest figures. It indicates that those states which are somewhat advanced in wealth and industry have a higher rate. Looking to the motives of suicide it will be seen

[25] Elliott, M. A., and Merrill, F. E., *op. cit.*, p. 317.

that the highest were from the dreadful diseases. Among the means of committing suicide the highest were from drowning ; next comes hanging and poisoning in order. All this is clear from tables 1, 2 and 3.

TABLE 1

SUICIDES IN INDIA IN DIFFERENT STATES IN 1964[26]

State	No.	State	No.	State	No.
1. Andhra	4022	7. Madhya Pradesh	1994	13. Punjab	897
2. Assam	870	8. Madras	4342	14. Rajasthan	N.A.
3. Bihar	319	9. Maharastra	3398	15. Uttar Pradesh	2589
4. Gujarat	1713	10. Mysore	3933	16. West Bengal	3426
5. J & K	N.A.	11. Nagaland	13	17. Other territories	561
6. Kerala	N.A.	12. Orissa	1647		
				Grand total ...	29,724

TABLE 2

SEX AND AGE COMPOSITION OF PERSONS COMMITTING SUICIDE IN 1964

Sex	Males	Females	Total	
Number	16,835	12,889	29,724	
Percentage	56.7	43.3	100.00	
Age group	Below 18 years	18-30 years	30 years & above	TOTAL
Number	6100	12724	10900	29734
Percentage	20.5	42.8	36.6	99.9

[26] Figures have been taken from *Accidental Deaths and Suicides in India 1964*, Central Bureau of Investigation, Government of India (1966).

TABLE 3

MOTIVES OF SUICIDE AND MEANS OF COMMITTING SUICIDE IN INDIA (1964)

Causes of suicide	M=Male F=Female	*Means of committing suicide*											
		Drowning	*Fire*	*Firearms*	*Hanging*	*Jumping*	*Machine*	*Poisons*	*Railways*	*Road*	*Other weapons*	*Other means*	*Total*
1. Dreadful disease	M.	1014	87	10	1256	104	2	496	342	18	13	267	3609
	F.	1281	135	4	667	91	4	355	55	14	2	127	2735
2. Quarrel with parents or in-laws	M.	198	33	13	484	20	2	263	131	5	11	73	1233
	F.	488	142	4	342	43	2	216	58	4	4	18	1321
3. Quarrel with married partners	M.	153	25	6	247	19	1	158	19	2	12	21	663
	F.	384	98	4	340	22	1	247	38	5	0	20	1159
4. Failure in examination	M.	154	29	11	114	18	4	112	61	46	6	107	662
	F.	76	22	2	41	23	2	34	9	6	1	34	250
5. Love affairs	M.	74	3	4	117	3	—	105	20	3	6	25	360
	F.	87	14	3	123	4	—	107	16	3	0	14	371
6. Religious sacrifices	M.	12	2	—	2	—	—	—	2	—	2	8	28
	F.	9	3	—	2	—	—	—	—	—	0	2	16
7. Political	M.	17	1	1	2	1	2	5	1	1	—	6	37
	F.	15	7	0	1	0	3	3	0	1	—	3	33
8. Poverty	M.	170	23	2	218	35	1	164	36	10	6	85	800
	F.	143	16	1	83	4	0	65	28	3	5	24	363
9. Disputes over property	M.	35	5	4	56	6	2	29	11	4	22	7	181
	F.	34	13	0	25	2	0	10	3	1	3	4	95
10. Insanity	M.	181	26	1	233	22	—	33	41	18	5	37	597
	F.	181	43	1	111	18	—	40	28	20	0	16	458
11. Any other cause	M.	2071	394	66	1479	439	145	921	602	251	42	2255	8665
	F.	2075	510	29	811	403	19	536	146	106	6	1447	6088
Male		4079	628	118	4208	667	159	2386	1316	358	125	2891	16835
Female		4764	1003	48	2546	610	31	1613	381	163	21	1709	12889
Grand Total		8843	1631	166	6754	1277	190	3999	1697	521	146	4600	29724

The trends of suicide cannot be known in India as it is for the first time that the statistics were collected on all-India basis in 1964. However, it cannot be denied that suicide must be on the increase in India as in some of the Western countries. The World Health Organization recently published a report setting forth the ten leading causes of death in highly industrialized developing countries. Nearly 70 per cent of all deaths were due to diseases affecting heart and blood vessels, cancer and accidents. It was reported that T. B. has fallen from its earlier important place among death causes "but suicide was listed with increasing frequency". This increase in suicide is attributed to social disintegration, fast diminishing family ties and the immense tension of modern living.[27]

[27] Varma, Paripurnanand "Suicides in India", *Social Welfare*, December, 1967, p. 8.

CHAPTER III

CRIME AND ITS CAUSES

WE HAVE pointed out in Chapter II the various types of disorganized persons, whose life organization is not in conformity with the norms and values set by the society. In other words, the conduct of these persons is in variance with the one approved by the society. Among these are included the non-conformists such as innovators and inventors ; the rebels including the criminals, sex offenders, adolescent rebels, the reformers and revolutionists, etc. and the mentally deranged. Against all these persons society has got some degree of social disapproval, depending upon the effect their behaviour has on the society. Among these the most important are the criminals who violate the law and against whom society has got marked social disapproval. The chief reason for this marked social disapproval is that the criminals are not only dangerous to the well-being of society, but to the individual liberty and property as well. As Dr. Gillin points out, "More important is the feeling of danger to ourselves and our property than the criminal induces."[1] Their study is, therefore, the most important in the field of individual disorganization. However, before we take up their study, it will be proper to discuss the conception of crime, which has gone under a revolutionary change in the past few centuries.

Conception of Crime

The most prevalent definition of crime in these days is the legalistic one, though it is not so comprehensive and has got many deficiencies. According to this definition, crime is an act in violation of the law and the criminal is a person who does an act in violation of the law. There are four other conceptions of crime given by different criminologists. Thus, in all there are five concepts of crime (1) demonological, (2) legal, (3) sociological, (4) socio-legal, (5) psycho-socio-legal.

(1) The earliest conception of crime was a demonological one. Long before formal governments came into existence, there were

[1] Gillin, J. L., *Criminology and Penology* (1945), p. 2.

well-recognized offences which were considered to be harmful to the group. Among these the most serious one was considered to be an open insult to the Gods, as the latter were considered to be the protectors and benefactors of the group, and any insult to them was a serious menace to the prosperity of the community. Not only that, but among the causes of crime, which are now considered to be biological or environmental ones, the old theory explained criminal conduct to devilish possession and instigation. "Since evil spirits infested the persons and must be driven out, the conventional notion of primitive punishment was either to drive away the evil spirits or to banish or execute the one possessed. In part, this doctrine was based upon the concept of protecting the community group against further outrages by the offending individuals, but far more important was the belief of the necessity and the desirability of pleasing the Gods."[2] Although the actual belief in witches and demons has gradually waned, it still persists to some extent in small culture pockets and even in civilized societies some people still think that wilful persons are thinking on the devil's side and must be chastened.

(2) The next most important and largely prevalent conception of crime is the legalistic one. According to Michael and Adler, "Crime is that behaviour which is prohibited by the criminal code."[3] Mr. Miller observes, "Crime is the commission or omission of an act, which the law forbids or commands under pain of punishment to be imposed by the state . . . and no act is a crime however wrong it may seem to the individual conscience, unless it is prohibited by law."[4] But in backward or the so-called primitive or preliterate societies, which do not possess a written or legislative body of criminal law, crime is considered to be a violation of the precious customs—the mores. Unfortunately this legal conception of crime discussed above is not an adequate one as already stated. Because : (*i*) Only those acts are considered as crime which are in violation of law, and not others, however bad the society may consider them to be. (*ii*) No difference is drawn between a misdemeanour, i.e. misbehaviour or ordinary crime and a felony—a grave crime. A petty infraction (violation) of the statutes or a homicide are equated

[2] Barnes, H.E., and Teeters, N.K., *New Horizons in Criminology*, New York (1944), p. 122.

[3] Michael, J., and Adler, M.J., *Crime, Law and Social Science* (1933), pp. 2, 3.

[4] Miller, Justine, *Hand Book of Criminal Law* (1934), pp. 16, 19.

at the same level. (*iii*) It does not explain the changing conception of crime, which changes from time to time, country to country, region to region or zone to zone in the same region.

(3) According to sociological conception, crime is an act which is socially harmful. The crime here is fundamentally a violation of conduct norms. It is a harmful act, deemed criminal by the public opinion and not an act which is necessarily in violation of the written code. Professor Reckless observes, "Criminal behaviour is a violation of the rules of the social order. Crime, sociologically speaking, is fundamentally a violation of conduct norms which contain sanctions, no matter whether found in the criminal law of a modern state or merely in the working rules of special social groups."[5]

This concept, too, is inadequate as all acts which are socially harmful are not considered as crimes in the civilized societies unless they are in violation of the criminal code.

(4) The socio-legal conception is an amalgamation of two conceptions, i.e. legal and social and attempts to overcome their deficiencies and inadequacies. According to this definition there are two elements in a proper definition of crime. Firstly, crime is an act which is believed to be socially harmful. But this is the belief of the dominant group within the society, which has the power to enforce its beliefs, through the enactment and promulgation of statutes upon that country and any person who acts contrary to this is subject to positive penalty. This current conception of crime is also not wholly adequate, as it does not take into consideration the total setting of the individual committing the crime.

(5) The fifth and the last is the psycho-socio-legal conception, which is a modern one. This takes into account the intention, constitutional and acquired characteristics as well as early established reactive tendencies of the criminal who is affected both by biological and environmental factors. However, this conception is not practicable because in this case (*i*) different punishments will be needed for different criminals for the same crime, and thus, uniformity of punishments cannot be maintained in the code, (*ii*) and the capitalists who make the law, would not allow it, otherwise to steal for bread would not be a crime.

The modern criminal codes, however, keep all these considerations in view as far as practicable. Mr. Justin Miller contends

[5] Reckless, W. C., *Criminal Behaviour* (1940), pp. 9-10.

that crime is the commission or omission of act which the law forbids or commands under pain of punishment to be imposed by the state. But he hastens to add that in most cases the law requires that there must be unlawful intent.[6] The criminal law in a modern society essentially contains the conduct norms of the political group, but it should be recognised that kinship groups, religious groups, fraternal orders, labour organizations, clubs and special associations in a socially differentiated society have conduct norms that impose sanctions in order to preserve certain recognized values.[7] Similarly, the biological and environmental factors of the criminals are now taken into consideration, while dealing with these in the courts, and correctional and rehabilitative measures are suggested instead of repriative punishment.

However, it will have to be admitted that the criminal codes of the modern society still contain the conduct norms of the dominant political group and it is the poor and not the rich who are mostly convicted. As Sellin observes, "The conduct which the state denotes as criminal is, of course, that deemed injurious to society, or in the last analysis, to those who wield the political power within the society."[8]

Causes Leading to Delinquency and Crime

It is to be pointed out at the outset that causes leading to crime or delinquency are almost the same. The difference in the nomenclature so far as the causes are concerned is only because of the age of the offenders committing the crime. However, there are other differences too so far as the intent of offenders and their treatment is concerned. These we have discussed in the next chapter. "Thus almost all causes and circumstances which lead to delinquency are also responsible for crime. As a matter of fact, delinquency is the prelude to crime. The only difference between crime and delinquency is that of age. The term 'crime' refers to offences committed at a matured age, whereas the term delinquency refers to offences committed at the pre-matured age."[9]

[6] Miller, Justine, *op. cit.*, p. 16.

[7] Reckless, W. C., *op. cit.*, p. 10.

[8] Sellin, Thorsten, *Research Memorandum on Crime in the Depression*, Social Science Research Council, New York (1937), p. 3.

[9] Srivastava, M. P., *Social Analysis of Adult Offenders* (A study of 50 cases kept in District Jail, Rae Bareli), an unpublished M. A. thesis submitted in the Department of Sociology and Social Work, Lucknow University (1961), p. i.

We have pointed out in Chapter II that the causes which lead to individual disorganization are four : viz. biological, environmental, loss of security and crisis in life. In the case of criminals these causes have been investigated by many a physician, anthropologists, psychologists, psychiatrists, criminologists, sociologists and economists, who have propounded different theories for the causation of crime. So far there is no unanimity among them, because of the uncertainty of these factors working in a particular individual. Professor Reckless observes, "It is impossible in the existing state of criminological knowledge to say just what are the causes of crime. Anyone who attempts to do this is far transcending the bounds of definite knowledge. A presentation of a list of causes, no matter how logical, could not indicate the degree of acceptance or the importance and the weight of any given causative factor, since no general agreement on such matters has taken place between scholars and researchers in the field of criminology. . . . However, we possess at present a body of theory, points of view, and more or less controversial conclusions from research."[10]

Up to the first decade of the twentieth century most of the criminologists have tried to explain crime in general, rather than the criminal behaviour of specific individual. It was between 1909 and 1914 that Mr. William Healy, a psychiatrist, made an epochal contribution to the study of the causes of crime. This was the result of his research work at the Juvenile Psychopathic Institute of Chicago. His method of study was the individual case method rather than the crime in general. This had not been widely used so far for the analysis of causative factors in crime. He studied 823 repeated juvenile offenders and came to the conclusion that in every case there were one major and, on an average, two and a half minor or a total of three and a half causative factors responsible for the causation of crime. The theories, expounded by the earlier criminologists which have now become classical, some now totally discard, partially accepted or modified, run in scale from physical, to topographical (study of limited area), and climatic factors through the biological, constitutional and psychological factors in the social environments, whereas modern researches have shown that not one but many factors may be responsible for the causation of crime. We may discuss these factors under two heads: (*a*) general

[10] *Ibid.*, p. 167.

factors, and (*b*) specific factors. In general factors may be included (1) the physical or geographic factors, (2) the sociological factors, (3) areal and regional differences, and (4) the factors of class, age, sex and race. Among the specific factors may be included the biological, and the environmental factors. The former are called general factors because they affect the community as a whole and not a particular individual.

General Factors

1. *Physical Factors.* Historians and sociologists have noted the influence of physical nature upon the development of society. Mr. Huntington, a proponent of the geographical school, has asserted that large proportions of persons born in winter will have low I. Q.'s, will become criminals, or suffer from insanity or tuberculosis.[11] "A number of Italian, and some French and German Criminologists have endeavoured to indicate correspondences between different geological features and crime rate. It must be confessed, however, that these attempts have not been very successful. Lombroso, for example, studied the influence of the geological differences upon political crimes and crimes against the person in different parts of France. These differences were so slight as to be negligible."[12] Lombroso has also tried to correlate geography, climate, seasons and weather to criminality in his book, *Crime, Its Causes and Remedies* (1918). But this relation is indirect rather than direct as Dr. Gillin points out, "While it is quite possible that climate, season and geological conditions have some effect directly upon the human organism, and thus determine to some extent whether the conduct shall be socially good or bad, the influence of the physical environment for the most part is indirect."[13] Buckle, Spencer, Semple, Giddings, and others have seen that the problem is not so simple but that the physical environment usually acts indirectly upon the density of population, economic development and cultural institutions."[14]

2. *Sociological Factors.* It has been observed that frequency of crime was less in undisturbed, isolated, homogeneous, unchanging primary group societies such as primitive tribes, folk communities,

[11] Gillin, J. L., *op. cit.* (1945), p. 70.
[12] *Ibid.*, p. 71.
[13] Gillin, J. L., *op. cit.*, p. 74.
[14] *Ibid.*, p. 70.

agricultural villages and religious sects than in people disturbed by change, impact, dislocation, migration, heterogeneity of population and cultural clash of conduct norm. In other words, the frequency of offence is affected by social integration or social disintegration in a society. But it must be pointed out that the relative amount of stability or instability is not offered as a cause of criminal behaviour, but is merely a background condition associated with the frequency of violation of important rules of society, because, many individuals even in an unstable situation do not become offenders, while some individuals even in a very stable society become violators. However, the chances of an individual's becoming a transgressor are greater in an unstable than in a stable social order.

3. *Areal and Regional Differences in Crime.* It has been observed by sociologists that crime varies in volume and form by areas and regions. One reason advanced for this is that it is due to variations in the social framework of crime and the factors attributed are varying social and legal definitions of offences, prevailing sentiments of people towards illegal or offending behaviour, prevailing facilities for law enforcement and the persistence of traditions or practices which conflict with the legal order of society, amount of change, mobility and disorganization, and of special types of persons or groups attracted to certain areas. Such areas and regions which have been compared are frontiers, political borders, intra-urban areas, metropolitan regions, cultural regions and rural versus urban communities. In a frontier area where there has been recent intrusion of an advanced community, a form of lawlessness develops because it has not yet developed a settled or stable socio-political order. Crimes of contraband appear at political borders as a normal reaction to restrictive measures of governmental control and as a pursuit which can take advantage of the difficulties of adequately policing both sides of a border.

The areas of high crime and delinquency rates in cities provide an unstable social setting in which individuals can become unadjusted to the ways of living required by the dominant moral group. In metropolitan regions, it has been suspected that crime decreases in per capita volume throughout the hinterland of a large urban community with the distance in miles from the centre of the dominant city. Sutherland reported special data for the Chicago region to show that the volume of crime decreases as the distance from the large city increases.[15] Regarding cultural regions Shaw found that basic socio-economic characteristics of areas in the city of Chicago affected the delinquency and crime rates. He found that areas of higher delinquency in Chicago were in and around the areas of industrial concentration, with certain special characteristic such as physical deterioration, economic dependency, declining population, etc.[16] However, it is to be pointed out that such differentials can only be significant to the comparative study of crime, but not causes of crime in and of themselves. They may receive potency and reinforcement from such factor, but they cannot be a cause in themselves.

4. *Effect of Class, Sex, Age, Race, etc.* It has been asserted that crime varies in amount by population categories such as social class, sex, age, race and nativity. The individuals in the lower class level of a society are suspected of displaying greater risks and liabilities owing to their sociological positions, for getting involved in crime and for being acted upon officially. Similarly, males are disproportionately more criminals than females because of the differential working of social institutions on the two sexes and because of physical disabilities of females as compared with males. The age factor in crime is revealed by a graph, which shoots precipitously up through the adolescent years, reaches its peak in the young adult age, and tapers off with advâncing age thereafter. Race, nativity or nationality factor in crime appears to be of importance mainly in a heterogeneous society, in which people differing in race, nationality and maturity occupy various levels of a minority status. Because of varying positions, minority peoples, as compared with the members of the dominant group, have differential opportunities to be violators, differential liability to be arrested and convicted for violations and they face differential problems of social adjustment.

The categoric risks for criminal violation expressing themselves through class, age, sex, race and nationality differentials are highly significant to the comparative study of criminal behaviour though not causes of crime in and of themselves.

Specific Factors

Under this head are included two main factors, viz. biological

[15] Sutherland, E. H., *Principles of Criminology* (1934), p. 122.

[16] Shaw, C. and McKay, H.D., *Social Factors in Juvenile Delinquency* (1931), pp. 60-108.

and environmental. There has long existed a feeling that one must resort to either of these dichotomous extremes to explain human conduct. Much of this zeal emanates from academicians and professional men who, it seems, felt emotionally bound to their respective disciplines and professions. While bulk of the accepted investigators in Europe were trained in the biological sciences, those in the United States have in the main been keen social scientists. Mr. Kinberg, perhaps, rightly points out, "One might venture the assertion that the tendency of European criminology is rather towards the individual, endogenous theory of criminality, while Northern American criminologists are more inclined to see its chief causes in social factors."[17] However, it is to be pointed out that all behaviour is bio-social. By this we mean simply that the biological equipment of the individual, e.g. his biological heritage, and the environment to which he has been exposed, i.e. his social heritage are operative in all of the social situations in which he participates. It is in fact through the interaction of these two heritages that one's personality is developed. Many sociologists, therefore, prefer to speak in terms of the interactive factors that are operative in determining behaviour. Similarly, we are yet unable to ascertain whether the relationship of any factor in a situation is one of influence or is merely one of association. Keeping these propositions in mind we have studied the views of ardent champions of the particularistic theories. These biological and environmental factors have again been divided into various sub-heads. We shall first take up biological factors.

Biological Factors

Biological factors may be studied under two main heads : (*a*) physiological, and (*b*) mental factors though sometimes it is difficult to separate the two.

(*a*) *Physiological Factors*

In physiological factors are included : (*i*) constitutional factor, (*ii*) hereditary factor, and (*iii*) glandular activity, though the hereditary factor can better be put directly under biological.

(*i*) *Constitutional Factor*. Lombroso was the first to draw attention to this biological fact. He contended that there was, among

[17] Kinberg, Olof, *Basic Problems of Criminology* (1935), p. 167. Also see Gillin's book, *op. cit.*, p. 65.

various kinds of criminals, a born criminal type which was characterised by irregularities of body and mind. Born criminals were supposed to possess a greater measure of anomalies than ordinary criminals, occasional criminals, and criminals of passion. These anomalies were also supposed to be much more frequent in the criminal than in the non-criminal population. "Some of the many anatomical and mental anomalies of the born criminals were : asymmetry of skull ; low retreating forehead ; strongly arched brows ; large outstanding ears ; sparse beard ; tatooing ; left-handedness ; relative insensibility to pain ; acuteness of vision ; obtuseness of the sense of smell or of taste, touch, and hearing ; lack of moral sense ; violent temper ; extreme vanity ; improvidence ; and so forth."[18] This was known as Lombroso's Theory. This theory was later on contradicted by Goring and Boas. Goring who carried research on English convicts in 1912 disapproved the physical anomalies among prisoners while Boas refuted his mental anomalies. Goring arrived at the proposition that crime must be explained by the heredity of weakness as well as by the inheritance of a predisposition to crime. However, the theory of Lombroso is still widely upheld by many important criminologists in Europe, who cling tenaciously to the notion that real criminals especially the recidivists possess a physical and mental make up that lowers their ability to live a law-abiding existence. However, their contention is slightly different from Lombroso. They contend that the inferiorities of the constitution are derived in large part from heredity and do not insist that there is a specific criminal constitution always possessing a definite set of physical and mental traits in combination. Greatly varying combinations of physical and mental characteristics and inferiorities are used to define and diagnose the constitutional criminals. One of the leading criminologists among them is Dr. Louis Vervaeck from Belgium.[19]

Another theory almost similar to this is given by Kretschmer, who carried out his investigations on 260 insane persons in Swabia. His theory is that the criminals possessed a certain type of physique and character. He was impressed with the fact that they displayed definite types of body build as well as characteristic and associated psychic disposition. The basic types of body build in his scheme are the asthenic, athletic, pyknic and certain mixed and unclassified

[18] Lombroso, Cesare, *Crime, Its Causes and Remedies* (1918), pp. 371-72.

[19] His book is *Syllabus du Cours d'anthropologie* (1926).

types. Regarding psychic disposition he found two mental types. Circular and schizophrene having cyclothyme and schizothyme temperaments. Kinberg who applied his findings to criminals came to the conclusion that the pyknics with their prevailing cyclothymic temperament commit principally the higher offences, while the athletics and asthenics with their prevailing schizothymic temperament are more prominent in the dangerous and serious crimes.[20] However, Mohr and Gundlach discovered that the convicts in Illinois showed a progression of physical and mental traits rather than clear-cut types according to Kretschmer's schematization.[21]

(*ii*) *Hereditary Factor*. After coming into prominence of that branch of biology dealing with the laws of heredity, and the widespread development of the applied science of eugenics the factor of heredity in human behaviour and social problems was given great emphasis. As pointed above, born criminal type was one way of relating heredity to criminal behaviour indirectly, while inheritance of criminal instincts, of specific patterns, of criminal tendency or predisposition were the other contentions made by criminologists. Goring's findings in this respect that crime must be explained by the heredity of weak-mindedness as well as by the inheritance of a predisposition have already been mentioned.

Several other studies have attempted to substantiate the hereditary factor in criminality by investigating the descendants of notorious degenerate families as to their physical, mental and social status. The first of these studies was made by Dugdale on the jukes family, an American white family of the early eighteenth century backwoods settlement. Pauperism, illegitimacy, intemperance and criminality were found to be rampant among the descendants of this family. Dugdale's general conclusions were : (1) heredity was the preponderating factor in careers of people where the constitution is modified or organically weak and that physical and mental capacity is limited by heredity ; (2) that where conduct depends on knowledge, environment has more influence than heredity has and that the use to which capacity is put depends on environment and training ; and (3) that heredity tends to produce an environment which perpetuates it (the licentious parent makes an example for the child to follow).[22]

[20] Kinberg, Olof, *Basic Problems of Criminology* (1935), p. 315.

[21] Reckless, W. C., *op. cit.*, p. 196.

[22] Dugdale, R. L., *The Jukes : A Study in Crime, Pauperism, Disease and Heredity* (1884), p. 65.

A generation later, eugenics saw the possibilities of exploring family descendants with a view to proving that dysgenic traits such as feeble-mindedness, alcoholism, prostitution, criminality, insanity, and pauperism were transmitted biologically in family strains.

More recently attempts have been made to demonstrate the biological inheritance of criminality by studying cases of criminal twins. Among these the most notable investigation is that of Mr. Lange in Bavaria. In the case of monozygotic twins which were supposed to be identical and to have divided from the same ovum, it was found that out of 13 sets, ten sets were found to be both criminal. In the case of dizygotic twins, which were supposed to be non-identical and to have developed from separately germinated ova, out of 17 pairs, only two of them had prison record. Thus, it was concluded that inherited tendencies do play a part in the causation of crime.[23]

Information from the case histories of intensively studied offenders has also been used to detect the working of the hereditary factor in criminality. Dr. Healy, in his pioneer study of 823 cases, found that no direct evidence of inheritance of criminalistic traits was found in those cases. Only evidence of indirect inheritance, meaning that heredity in determining physical and mental traits in the offsprings and in determining in part the conditions of rearing children were indirectly operating to produce delinquency. Burt, who studied English juvenile delinquents confirmed Healy's general conclusions. He found no evidence that led him to suspect that criminality was directly inherited. He too, discovered that heredity worked through physical and mental traits, which in turn might be related to delinquent behaviour.[24]

On the other hand, Dr. Adolph Lenz of the so-called school of criminal biology considers that hereditary predisposition is one of the outstanding factors in the causation of crime. The presence of mental disease and ailments, hysteria, epilepsy, neurotic traits, alcoholism and suicide in the familial and ancestral background is an indication that the individuals of the present generation will have difficulty in making adjustment. Such a background leads to mental disorder, crime, prostitution, vagabondage, quarrelsomeness, wilfulness, unsociability, homosexuality, perversities and drug addiction. He claims that instead of criminal inclination being

[23] Lange, Johannes, *Crime and Destiny* (1930), p. 46.

[24] Burt, Cyril, *The Young Delinquent* (1925).

inherited, it is predisposition to maladjustment that is inherited. The predisposition induces crime only where the pressure of the life struggle on the individual is in evidence.[25]

(*iii*) *Glandular Factor*. With the rise to prominence of endocrinology, the importance of glandular determination of physical and mental growth was revealed. Not only that but the functioning of the glands was made a basic determiner of temperament, intelligence, character and personality as well as of physical and mental pathology. Regular and irregular physical growth, certain mental deficiencies, temperamental types, body build, mental alienations and alterations, emotional stability and instability, and many other anatomical, physiological, neurological, and psychological problems became explainable partially or wholly in terms of abnormal or inadequate functioning of the ductless glands. It also bridged the gap between the body and mind and in part validated Kretschmer's contention that the type of temperament, character or mental set is grafted on to the type of physique. The functioning of the glands was the connecting link between the two. At the same time, glandular disturbances could account for many disharmonic, defective, unstable and inadequate qualities found in the suspected constitutional inferiority of criminals. Thus, the constitutional factor along with Kretschmer's types of physical traits and mental set up came into prominence as a cause of crime. The most sweeping claims for the glandular explanation of crime have been made by Schlapp and Smith in their book, entitled *The New Criminology* (1928), where the authors claim that mental deficiency which is paramount in the causation of crime, the intelligent higher type criminals and defective and deficient constitution of criminals are all explained by abnormal or deficient functioning of the glands.

However, it is difficult to conclude that these factors such as physiologic, hereditary, and endocrine do play a part in the causation of crime though it is equally difficult to contradict them. (1) For sometimes when begging, pauperism, prostitution, alcoholism and thieving are traced to heredity they may be transmitted more by social heritage than by germ plasm. (2) It is difficult to carry out tests on criminals and non-criminals because people possessing the same type of criminal constitution may not be criminals having different social environments. (3) The test applied for measuring

[25] Lenz, Adolph, *Die Sedeutung der Kriminalbiologie* (1931), pp. 222-24. Also see Reckless, W. C., *Criminal Behaviour*, p. 190.

constitution, or mental weakness may not be scientific. According to one investigation a person may be weak-minded while according to another the same may be normal. Similarly, in case of endoctrine determination exact consequences of normal or abnormal functioning of ductless glands are not known and comparison of glandular disorder between criminals and non-criminals has not been made, and the relation of glandular disturbances to conduct in the behaviour situation has been assumed and not investigated in detail. Thus, the etiology of crime has not been lifted from the realm of unwarranted claims and speculations into the realm of verified conclusion.

(b) *Mental and Psychological Factors*

The mental factors are in many respects related to the biological factors discussed above, but mental factors as such which include mental deficiency, mental disorders, mental mechanisms and motivation to criminal behaviour are treated as separate factors in themselves for the causation of crime.

(*i*) *Mental Deficiency*. While mental deficiency is one of the many earmarks of the so-called constitutional criminal, subnormality and feeble-mindedness have been considered important causes of crime in their own right, separate and apart from the larger frame of reference. Goring had concluded that weak-mindedness was an outstanding factor in the production of crime. Goddard relying on the results of psychometric testings of juvenile reformatory inmates, claimed that low-grade mentality was the greatest single cause of crime. He concluded that "at least 50 per cent of all criminals are mentally defective".[26] But the fact that an inmate in a penal institution is found to be feeble-minded is no reason to assume that mental condition operated as a causative factor of misconduct. At the same time we find that very often mentally defective persons do not get into difficulty with the law.

(*ii*) *Mental Disorders*. There is no clear indication at present that mental disorders play a very important part in the etiology of crime. Dr. East who studied about 234,000 persons admitted to prisons in England from March 1923 to March 1926 found that only about 2,000 i.e. 1.5 per cent were dealt with under the Lunacy and Mental Deficiency Act [27] and similar were the results shown by

[26] Goddard, H. H., *Feeble-mindedness: Its Causes and Consequences* (1926), p. 9.
[27] Quoted by Reckless, W. C., in *Criminal Behaviour*, p. 205.

the surveys made by the National Committee for Mental Hygiene (1931). Dunham who worked in the research division of the mental hospitals in Illinois, also came to the conclusion that the criminal insane comprised a very insignificant part of the total institutionalized insane.

(*iii*) *Mental Mechanisms*. Psychoanalysts have made certain unique interpretations of behaviour, whether criminal or neurotic, in terms of unconscious motivating forces, fixations, conflicts, frustrations, neuroses, inferiority, regression, guilt feelings, and psychic trauma. Dr. Lenz contends that the roots of our tendencies are to be found in the inborn drives that seldom crop out in conscious form. Only those drives cross the threshold of consciousness which are harmonious with the conception of self while the bad tendencies of the offender belong to his unconscious life. The same tendencies that lead to failures at home, at school, at work-in social life generally repeat themselves in criminal behaviour.[28] There are many others like Adler and Alexander who have made contributions in this direction. In so far as psychoanalysts in their interpretations of crime have called attention to motivations, mental conflicts and mental mechanisms that are reasonably apparent in cases, they have made a contribution. But when they proceed to fabricate the complexities of motivations, conflicts and mechanisms, they become fanciful beyond the realm of visible proof and validation.

(*iv*) *Motivation to Behaviour*. Besides psychoanalysts who have brought to the fore the importance of dynamics of motivation in the study of behaviour problems, psychiatrists, psychologists and sociologists have also brought forth, importance of motivating forces in human behaviour. Among these two important interpretations developed by Thomas, a sociologist, and Dr. Healy, a criminologist are as follows : W. I. Thomas says human motives could be reduced to four basic types of wishes. New experience, response, recognition and security. This system of motivation is based on organic needs arising from the body and the external social situations. Individuals either turn directly to delinquency in order to get their wishes satisfied or resort to delinquency as a result of blockages in the satisfaction of wishes in the normal channels. Whereas Healy contends that delinquent behaviour is "a response to

[28] Quoted by Reckless, W. C., in his book *Criminal Behaviour*, p. 212.

inner and outer pressures", i.e. a form of self-expression. Interreferences with the ordinary satisfaction of wishes by thwartings and deprivation lead to substitute satisfactions as a means of offsetting dissatisfaction. Although it can be said that unsatisfactory fulfilment of wishes and associated emotional distress is expected to constitute an important cause of crime yet it is difficult to differentiate delinquents from non-delinquents and also one cannot tell what role the course of motivation plays along with or to the exclusion of other causative factors.

Conclusion. Reviewing the physiological and mental factors in crime, we may say that (1) there is no concrete reason to believe that heredity plays a discriminating role in the production of crime even if we agree with Dr. Lenz that a potent inadequacy or reduced ability for making social adjustment could be biologically transmitted. (2) There is no justification to believe that a combined mental and physical constitution makes persons prone to become criminal, although various physical and mental difficulties might place a severe handicap on persons in ordinary social situation. The contentions of the endocrinologists cannot be put to objective observations, although glandular disorder might in some cases be an important factor in crime.

Feeble-mindedness and insanity are not considered to be important factors in crime, while failure to obtain adequate satisfaction of wishes, accompanied by severe emotional stress may be an important motivating force in crime, but it cannot be said to be the exclusive cause of crime.

Environmental Factors

While criminological research has called attention to the operation of biological factors in the causation of crime, efforts have also been made to indicate how situational factors are conducive to such a tendency. Situational factors have also been referred to as environmental factors. Of the great variety of research and study on the relation of crime to situational conditions, the most important are : (*a*) family conditions, (*b*) companionship factor, (*c*) community conditions, (*d*) economic conditions, and (*e*) religious and other factors. We shall discuss these factors one by one.

(*a*) *Family Conditions* There are various family conditions which have been considered responsible for the causation of delinquency such as break in the family unit, the size of the family, sibling position, unsatisfactory parent-child relations, demoralised home conditions, lack of discipline and control over children and economic inadequacy. Among these the most important are the broken home factor and unsatisfactory child-parent relations, as we shall see from the present researches made in these directions.

(*i*) *Broken-home Factor.* Where there is break in the family either due to death of the mother or the father or both or due to their divorce or separation it has been recognized to be one of the important factors in causing delinquency and, therefore, much attention has been given in recent researches to know its effect on crime. Breckinridge and Abbot, covering the family data in the records of over 14,000 children in the Juvenile Court of Chicago from 1899 to 1909 found that 34 per cent of the cases came from broken homes, (31 per cent of the boys, 47 per cent of the girls).[29] In the American juvenile court statistics collected by the Children's Bureau, 33 per cent of the boys and 52 per cent of the girls came from broken homes in 1927, while 29 and 48 were the respective percentages in 1928.

Cyril Burt in studying English juvenile delinquents found that the average number of defective home conditions in the family of delinquent children was 131 per 100 cases ; and 35 per 100 cases in the families of non-delinquents.[30] On the other hand, Shaw and McKay, found that juvenile offenders came from broken homes only slightly more than did school children in Chicago. However, they found that broken homes were more obviously a condition associated with delinquent boys than with school boys in the younger ages and in the socially disabled national and social groups. They came to the conclusion that it is not so much the break in family membership as the cumulative effect on internal tension and discord that operates as a causative factor in delinquency.[31] From above it may be suspected that broken homes play a greater part in the lives of younger than of older delinquents.

(*ii*) *Size of Family.* Various evidences pointing to the relation of delinquency to the size of family have been inconclusive. Theoretically, the larger the family, the more difficult it is to support and

[29] Breckinridge, P., and Abbot, E., *The Delinquent Child and the Home* (1912), p. 91.

[30] Burt, Cyril, *The Young Delinquent* (1925), p. 62.

[31] Shaw, C., and McKay H. D., *Social Factors in Juvenile Delinquency* (1931), p. 285.

to supervise ; consequently, children are neglected and get into trouble. However, no valid differential between the size of delinquents' families and non-delinquents' families has been established and no clear direct causation has been worked out between the size of family and delinquent behaviour. But it cannot be ignored that in lower class urban families which have a large birth-rate, neglect of children may lead them to trouble.

(*iii*) *Sibling Position.* Sibling position of the child in the family has been a case of much investigation. The New York Crime Commission (1930) discovered that the second child in the family committed the most severe crime, the next to youngest child was least likely to be delinquent, the youngest child was less likely to be truant than his older brothers, but more likely to commit offences than the next to youngest.[32] In view of the small number of cases and the prevalence of immigrant families in the sample the results of this investigation cannot be taken as reliable. In another study, Sletto found that there was no marked difference between the number of only children in the total delinquent group and in the matched non-delinquent group Delinquent boys who were only children were found not to differ from other delinquent boys in types of offence. However, in another study he points out that there are differences in delinquency ratio due to sibling position, which is due to the different roles that children develop in intra-family interaction. He states, "Delinquency involves non-conformity to cultural standards, such non-conformity may be more frequent among children who play certain roles in intra-sibship interaction than among children who play other roles."[33]

(*iv*) *Unsatisfactory Parent-Child Relationships.* Unsatisfactory parent-child relationships have been considered an important factor in behaviour problems of children. Bushong claimed that the ratio of delinquents produced by abnormal homes was three times as great as that produced by normal homes due to estrangement influences. From a detailed study of 153 juvenile offenders, in which family situations with reference to behaviour was one of the paramount interests, Healy and Bronner found that in only 20 per cent of the cases could the family relationships be considered

[32] The Crime Commission of New York State, *Crime and the Community*, (1930), p. 23.

[33] Sletto, Raymond F., "Sibling Position and Juvenile Delinquency", *American Journal of Sociology* (1934), pp. 665-67.

reasonably satisfactory.[34] However, how extensive is this factor which is related to the intra-family interaction between parents and children is not known. Similarly, to what extent parent-child discord is more characteristic of delinquent than of non-delinquent children is, likewise unknown.

(*v*) *Demoralised Homes.* The presence of demoralising conditions in the home such as alcoholism, immorality, and criminality has been cited as having an important bearing on child behaviour. Healy in his case study of 823 subjects found that out of 823 subjects, there were 157 or 18 per cent in which alcoholism, immorality and criminality among family members could be considered as related to delinquency of children and 28 cases or 3.4 per cent in which an immoral home environment was related to the misconduct of the children.[35] In another investigation Healy and Bronner found that alcoholism, immorality and criminality were present in 21 per cent of the subjects studied.[36] However, many criminologists have viewed that there may not be any direct bearing of these things on the etiology of delinquency. Many students of the relation of social situation to behaviour have for some time recognized the point that it is not so much what surrounds the child, but what he responds to in his surroundings that affects his behaviour most directly. Healy and Bronner also collaborate this view. "The evil influence of any (family) item can only be established in terms of its meaningfulness for the individual child."[37]

(*vi*) *Lack of Supervision or Control over Children.* Lack of supervision or control over children by parents has also been an important cause in juvenile delinquency. This lack of parental supervision may be in the form of actual neglect, ignorance of parents, temperament or personality of parents, absence of parents from home due to their employment, etc. Mr. Burt found that "his sample of English delinquents showed defective home discipline about 4.5 times more than in non-delinquents".[38] However, other case studies show that many children in spite of difficult home situations do not become

[34] Healy, W., and Bronner, A. F., *New Light on Delinquency and its Treatment* (1936), pp. 47-49.

[35] Healy, William, *The Individual Delinquent* (1915), p. 134.

[36] Healy, W., and Bronner, A. F., *Criminals, Their Making and Unmaking* (1926), p. 126.

[37] Healy, W., and Bronner, A. F., *New Light on Delinquency and its Treatment* (1936), p. 33.

[38] Burt, Cyril, *op. cit.*, p. 63.

delinquents. This was revealed by Healy and Bronner in their case study of 105 delinquent children and their non-delinquent siblings.[39]

To conclude we may say that the family influences and situations are very important factors in the production of delinquency and other forms of behaviour. However, the researches so far made cannot make any positive pronouncements. Obviously one cannot seize upon the mere presence of inadequate, disrupted, or discordant family situations to account for delinquent behaviour. It is necessary to have data in each case to indicate just how the child was affected and how he responded to the total family situations. The family is not the same family for any two children living within it, and it is necessary to find out just what the family world of the delinquent child really was or is.

The researches so far made regarding effect of family conditions have been mostly concerned with juvenile delinquency rather than with adult crime. The presumption, however, is that family conditions are as important in adult crime as in delinquency.

(*b*) *The Companionship Factor*. This has been studied from three angles. Firstly, there are many specific offences which are committed by a company of two or more than two persons. Secondly, the persons are likely to fall in the company of bad elements who are committing crime, and thirdly, a person may learn certain tricks from older offenders when in custody.

(*i*) It has been a matter of common observation that much delinquent and criminal activity is an affair of association of two or more individuals. For many specific offences, particularly the property offences, are committed by a group of two or more persons. Shaw and McKay in their study found that only 18 per cent of the boys taken to the Chicago Juvenile Courts in 1928 were lone-wolf offenders, the overwhelming majority being involved with one or more companions. Two-somes were the most prevalent, while three-somes almost as frequent.[40] Mr. Walsh describing the phenomenon of Crime in India observes, "In England a large proportion of crime is committed single-handed and the average number of offenders per crime must be under two. The average number per crime in the United Provinces must be nearer ten than two on account of the large proportion of agricultural fights and riots, village

[39] Healy and Bronner, *New Light on Delinquency and its Treatment* (1936), pp. 87-88.

[40] Shaw and McKay, *Social Factors in Juvenile Delinquency* (1931), pp. 195-97.

vendettas, communal riots, and dacoities, in most of which the number of offenders, runs into double figures, and in many of which it is quite large."[41]

(*ii*) It has been observed that sometimes boys, specially those roaming the streets of city slums, start something as a game, which often ends in delinquency. Similarly, the patterns and traditions of gang life may bring anti-social behaviour and ultimately may merge into a form of organized crime for older boys. It is not generally the whole gang which is delinquent, but often members pair off in two-somes or three-somes in delinquent activity.

Case studies and life histories of juvenile offenders frequently reveal bad companionship as a causative factor in delinquency, but how far it has immediate connection with delinquent acts has not been known. Healy in his pioneer analysis of 823 cases, found the companionship factor only in 44 cases as a primary cause, a secondary cause in 279 cases, which presented 34 per cent of the total.[42] Atwood and Shideler studied the participation in various social groups of 100 delinquent boys from the Indian reformatory and of 100 non-delinquent boys matched for age, colour and nativity. The results indicated that delinquent boys have a greater degree of group participation than do non-delinquent boys. "Apart from the mere gang participation, the study suggests that delinquent boys, by having more social contacts than non-delinquent boys have, are in the position of being greater risks for getting into trouble and getting caught."[43]

Companionship has been considered not so influential for girls as for boys—a fact often used to explain the much higher rate of delinquency among boys than among girls. It is also believed that if the companionship factor does not help in the causation of crime at the first instance, it does assist the maturation of a delinquent career, in its formative stages, and that up to a certain point it is important in the continuation in crime, in developing the techniques, attitudes and motivations to continue and progress in crime. Thus, its role as perpetrator of continued criminal activity may be more important than its role as cause of first or early offences. Also as the

[41] Walsh, Cecil, *Indian Village Crimes* (1929), p. 10.

[42] Healy, William, *The Individual Delinquent* (1915), p. 130.

[43] Atwood, B. S., and Shideler, E. H., "Social Participation and Juvenile Delinquency", *Journal of Sociology and Social Research* (1933-34), pp. 436-41.

offenders become more mature, they become lone-wolf offenders to survive in crime, while those in teaming are often caught.

(*iii*) The contacts in custody are considered to be important factors in the causation of crime. Lombroso contended that "the pick-pocket and cut-throat learn in prison, at the expense of the state, to make fake keys, to make counterfeit money, to engrave bank-notes and to commit burglaries".[44] Healy was very much impressed with the pernicious and contaminating effects of custodial experience. He remarked, "When offenders are thrown together, the worst knowledge has spread and a powerful stimulus has been disseminated towards antisocial conduct. Many a girl has testified to us that she learned more in the first twenty-four hours under custody than she knew in all her life before."[45]

While custodial contacts and friendship formed in penal institutions are important factors in the maturation of criminal careers, and in recidivism and help to explain continuation in crime, they cannot explain initial offences.

(*c*) *Community Conditions*. Among community conditions community disorganization, density and overcrowding, agencies of moral risk, and particularly the cinema are considered to be the factors responsible for the causation of crime.

(*i*) *Community Disorganization*. The sociologists have attempted to explain the existence and aggravation of social problem with the help of community or social disorganization due to the weakening of institutional and primary group influence over the lives and conduct of individuals. Social disorganization is the decrease of the influence of existing social rules of behaviour upon individual members of the group, whereas community disorganization is a phase of the former and includes decay of social opinion and decay of communal social solidarity. The main drawbacks of the application of this factor to the explanation of behaviour problems is that (1) all exposed persons are not disorganized, and (2) those who are disorganized are not affected in a uniform way.

(*ii*) *Density and Overcrowding*. Density of population in urban neighbourhoods has been considered a factor in the production of delinquency and crime, the thought being that the incidence is greater in the thickly populated areas than in the sparsely populated areas. Secondly, that children get into difficulty while roving into

[44] Lombroso, Cesare, *Crime : Its Causes and Remedies* (1918), p. 114.

[45] Healy, W., *The Individual Delinquent*, (1915), pp. 312-14.

the streets because of the inability of parents and neighbours to watch over their conduct. Elmer, who conducted research with regard to the first factor, however, came to the conclusion that ' it is not the density of population which is of great significance in juvenile delinquency but rather the transitional zone area (slum sections), where the details of the individual's life do not definitely fit into the established group organisations and activities" [46] Thus, according to him, it is the amount of disorganization rather than density of population which bears a close relation to juvenile delinquency.

As overcrowding per unit of area, so overcrowded housing has likewise a suspected relation to delinquency on the assumption that it makes family discipline and morality difficult to maintain and it drives children into unsupervised street play. Mr. Burt, in his study of delinquency in London, found that 21 per cent of his delinquency cases, as compared to 16 per cent of non-delinquents, came from overcrowded homes. The proportion for the whole country was 11 per cent.[47] But how far overcrowded housing is a factor in delinquency is difficult to say, as overcrowding in many peasant homes does not produce any delinquent behaviour. On the other hand, many sociologists are inclined to think that it is not the overcrowding, but the scheme of family life, particularly the family conflicts and inadequacies, which are likely to have direct bearing on behaviour problems. It is particularly so among the lower economic levels of urban dwellers who are suspected to have disorganized family life along with overcrowding.

(*iii*) *Agencies of Moral Risk*. Agencies or institutions of moral risk are frequently mentioned as an important factor in the causation of crime. Amusements of low moral tone, cheap dance halls, gambling parlours and dens of vice are considered to be responsible for the demoralization of young children. Many a times the criminals visit these places and pick up their companions from there or teach such practices to others.[48] Sociologists admit of the demoralising effect of these agencies in case of certain individuals, but how far they demoralise and what sorts of persons they demoralise are questions not readily answerable in the present state of knowledge.

[46] Elmer, M. C., *Maladjustment of Youth in Relation to Density of Population*. Proceedings of the American Sociological Society, (1926), p. 140.

[47] Burt, Cyril, *The Young Delinquent* (1925), p. 84.

[48] Kerawalla, P. C., *A Study in Indian Crime* (1959), p. 180.

(*iv*) *Cinema.* One of the most important agencies of commercialised recreation—the cinema—has been considered to be contributing to the demoralisation and delinquency of children and adolescents. But usually, exaggerated claims have been made by laymen, while moderate claims have been made by research. Healy, in his pioneer study of 823 cases, found only 9 cases in which excessive interest in moving pictures was considered as a minor factor in causation.[49] He contended that the moving pictures stimulate sex instincts and also mentioned the possibilities for the occurrence of bad sex habits under cover of darkness in the theatres. In some cases children steal to satisfy their appetite for pictures. But considering all sides of the question, the amount of delinquency produced by them corresponds but slightly to the immense number of pictures which are constantly shown. Burt has also come to the same conclusion when he remarks, "In comparison with the incalculable number of films that are manufactured and released, the offences resulting are infinitesimally few."[50] Blumer and Hauser, on the other hand, in their study of young offenders in Illinois found much heavier role of cinema in the production of delinquency than did Healy and Burt.[51] Perhaps the one reason for this was that the former specifically and exclusively paid attention to the effect of movies on conduct whereas the latter took note of it only when it happened to make itself visible in case studies.

(*d*) *Economic Conditions.* The effect of economic conditions in the causation of crime has been studied from three angles. Firstly, effect of class differential or economic status ; secondly, effect of different economic levels in areas, regions and countries, and thirdly effect of different business activity.

(*i*) Effects of the economic status of the criminal population as compared with the economic status of the general or non-criminal population have been studied. In this connection Bonger's theory has great importance. The Dutch criminologist, Mr. Bonger, has emphasized the environmental determination of crime as compared to the individual factors. He thinks that the basic cause of crime is the economic pressure of a capitalistic system. Under the capita-

[49] Healy, W., *The Individual Delinquent*, p. 136.

[50] Burt, Cyril, *The Young Delinquent*, p. 143.

[51] Blumer, H., and Hauser, P. M., *Movies, Delinquency and Crime* (1933).

listic system man has become egoistic and more capable of commiting crime. The capitalistic order has, therefore, had a prejudicial influence upon character especially upon the life and behaviour of the proletariat. He presents statistics to indicate that child labour, a by-product of capitalism, has been responsible for the increase in juvenile delinquency in countries that have become industrialized, and that a greater population of juvenile delinquents than of non-delinquents follow a trade (i.e. do work). Similarly, the lack of care of the children among the proletariat is another important factor.[52] He contends that long hours of work have a deleterious effect on behaviour, and bad housing conditions likewise have a bad effect upon conduct. Most of the criminals tend to come from bad housing quarters. Unemployment and economic insecurity, which are by-products of industrialism, are considered important factors in crime. Likewise illiteracy and lack of education are considered important factors in crime. For this he quotes statistics and claims that the illiterates supply, in general, a greater proportion of the criminals, a proportion much greater than that of illiterates in the general population.[53] He also offers statistics to prove that majority of criminals come from the poorer classes—from the non-possessors of the means of production.

Bonger appears to be strongly influenced by the socialistic theories of Marx and Engels, in placing the underlying blame for crime on the economic pressures created by the capitalistic system. Child labour, bad housing, illiteracy, insecurity, and poverty are all considered to be the offshoots of the capitalistic system.

No doubt, most of the factors to which Bonger draws our attention would receive considerable support from many persons, but it is to be pointed out that he is attempting to find out the primary cause of crime from which the secondary causes spring. But in the study of crime, as researchers, we are more concerned with direct causes rather than underlying causes. Suppose a wife deserter falls into the hands of the bad companions and commits a crime. Here the companionship factor is very close to the violating behaviour, whereas family discord is the important factor behind the desertion. The economic handicaps of the breadwinner are at the back of the discord, while the insecurity of the capitalistic system may be partly responsible for man's economic handicaps. Thus, the more

[52] Bonger, W. A., *Criminality and Economic Conditions* (1916), p. 409.
[53] *Ibid.*, p. 433.

remote and indirect the influence of factors are on behaviour the more difficult it is to ascertain their effect and thus lesser the importance. The class risks are just like other categoric risks for crime such as area variation, sex, age and race. There is no more reason to say that illiteracy or bad housing is a cause of crime than to say that the male, sex, the race, young adulthood or urbanism are causes of crime. Such items set the categorical risk for crime in general, but do not immediately call out antisocial behaviour in individuals.

Healy in his study of 823 cases found poverty as causative factor only in 63 cases, combining both major and minor factors. Similarly, Burt found that only 19 per cent delinquent children came from families classified as poor. From these studies we may conclude that poverty as direct cause of crime was in a very few cases. Poverty, however, may have a closer bearing on delinquent and criminal behaviour in countries where poor actually get involved in crime from sheer hunger and want. But the question also remains why some people from poor families involve in crime, while others do not. Even where poverty can be shown to be directly linked with delinquent behaviour, it may not be the sole or outstanding factor.

Regarding crime among different social classes, it is very difficult to point out which class is more liable to commit crime than the other. Even if it were possible to point out that a particular class was liable to commit crime, it could not be considered as a causative factor in criminal behaviour, since it merely indicates a risk rather than the factors that bear directly on behaviour.

(*ii*) The comparison by countries or areas was not possible due to differences in legal processes, police activities, crime reporting as well as social conditions which have great bearing on the volume of crime. However, Morrison in his study of volume of crime in different countries, having varying economic conditions concluded that there was no necessary connection between impoverishment and crime. He found that 1 out of 42 in England and 1 out of 195 in India were proceeded against criminally in 1888 and claimed that India should be by far the more lawless, if poverty was a cause of crime.[54] In his studies of moral conditions by districts, Quetelet found that the Creuse was the lowest in crime rate, the poorest and yet the most moral in France.[55] Likewise Luxembourg (Holland) the poorest and very moral, was low in crime. Thus, one is led to

[54] Morrison, Douglas, *Crime and its Causes* (1908), pp. 130-37.

[55] Quetelet, L. A. J., *Physique Sociale* (1869), pp. 198-99.

suspect that the change, disorganization and demoralization that attend industrial and commercial development are more likely than wealth or misery to be connected with volume of crime. Economic distress will more probably have an influence on crime in an actively developing urban area, than in a stabilized rural area.

(*iii*) Efforts have been made to shed light on the determination of crime by relating the volume of crime to the economic prosperity and depression. The method employed in such studies is to relate the volume of crime to an index of economic conditions such as the prices of grains or an index of business activity. The study made by Von Mayr for nine Bavarian provinces for the years 1835-36 to 1860-61 showed that the yearly fluctuations in the amount of total crime, and crime against property follow directly and fairly closely the fluctuations in the price of grain.[56] During these pre-industrialized times, high price of grain was supposed to mean hard times and low prices, good times, for the masses. Similarly, Winslow related prosecutions and admissions to penal institutions in the state of Massachusetts to an index of employment in the state for the period 1885 to 1929 and he came to the conclusion that about three-fourths of the years with a low employment index showed a tendency towards an increase in crime.[57] However, the question why certain classes or groups of people, exposed to these conditions, did not become criminal and others did, still remains.

(*e*) *The Religious and other Factors*. The studies of crime in India show that besides the factors discussed in the foregoing pages there are some other important factors too which lead to crime in this country. Among these may be mentioned (*i*) the superstition among illiterate persons, (*ii*) feuds and factions in villages, and (*iii*) exploitation of poor children by elders.

(*i*) *Superstition*. A strong belief in spells and sacrifice to obtain material wealth is a frequent cause of crime.[58] Many a times murders are committed in the belief that human sacrifice would reveal hidden treasure. Thus, superstition continues to exist in considerable measure among the illiterate and ignorant masses and among sche-

[56] Von Mayr, George, *Statistik der Gerichtlichen* (1867), pp. 189-205. Also quoted by Reckless, W. C., in *Criminal Behaviour*, p. 250.

[57] Winslow, E. A., *Report on Causes of Crime*, National Commission on Law Observance and Enforcement (1931), Vol. I, pp. 310-11.

[58] Rao, S. Venugopala, *Facets of Crime in India* (1962), p. 17.

dule tribes and aborigines and even among more advanced communities in varying degree.

(*ii*) *Factions and Feuds*. Factions and feuds in villages are a common feature in this country. The unfortunate legacy of the caste system which tended to create narrow channels of thought and a tendency to think and act in terms of little groups is the main factor in the creation of tensions. There are also a number of instances where blood feuds have been carried on between two branches of a single family. In villages so affected, unending criminal and civil litigation is the heritage of their residents. It is really intriguing to see with what fervour and determination they are pursued as matters touching the honour of the leaders and their forefathers. Sometimes innocent persons are included in these cases who were never a party to the crime. These innocent persons when involved in a criminal case without any reason later retaliate and adopt criminal career to take revenge of their grievances. The case of the famous dacoit, Man Singh, is a point in instance.[59]

The recent developments consequent on the introduction of democratic forms of government, periodic elections and introduction of local self-government through village panchayats have, in some cases, sharpened the old animosities wherever they exist, or given them a new twist.[60]

(*iii*) *Exploitation of Children by Adults*. Exploitation of children for the purpose of stealing by bad elements of society engaged in antisocial activities is very common in big cities like Bombay. Miss Hansa Sheth in her investigations found that there was a fair good number of children who were exploited by gangs headed by adult criminals for stealing telephone wires and electric equipment from trains.[61] Similarly, the smugglers make use of juveniles and females for transporting the illicit liquors and foodgrains as in case of their detection, punishment is corrective and light. The employers sometimes also exploit the children who then take to stealing with a feeling of revenge. Miss Sheth found that in some cases the employers did not make adequate or any payment to their servants. The servants in order to recover their wages stole some articles of their employers and were later caught by the police.[62]

[59] Rao, S. Venugopala, *op. cit.*, p. 51.

[60] Rao, S. Venugopala, *op. cit.*, p. 57.

[61] Sheth, Hansa, *Juvenile Delinquency in an Indian Setting* (1961), p. 108.

[62] *Ibid.*, p. 108.

Conclusion. To conclude we may say that among biological and environmental factors, environmental factors have been subjected to more rigorous, objective, critical and statistical tests of validation than have been the biological ones. Looking back over the numerous efforts to throw light on the causes of crime, it appears that more progress has been made in discounting than in arriving at validated and scientifically acceptable findings. Thus, the progress in the etiology of crime has been more negative than positive. More is known as to what is not acceptable than what is acceptable.

However, it needs pointing out that in spite of so many efforts to invalidate the findings of particular theorists, there are still three schools which are currently battling for supremacy in the explanation of criminal and delinquent behaviour ; the constitutional school (led by Lambroso and others), the psychogenic school (led by neo-freudians and some psychiatrists in America who believe that repetitive and serious criminality is often related to personality disorders such as inadequate personality, emotionally unstable personality, passive aggressive personality, sexual deviation, etc. that are the result of developmental conditions which reach back into early childhood) and the sociological school (mostly Americans believing in social factors of crime).[63] The positive verified knowledge about the etiology of crime does not appear to be possible in the near future because of many uncontrollable factors which operate to produce antisocial behaviour. Thus, we can only find differential risks a liability for crime such as can be found for age, race, sex, class, region or area. As Professor Reckless rightly observes, "Crime is a phenomenon whose appearances can be studied and charted but whose existence cannot easily be explained. If such an approach to the study of crime finally emerges, it would mean that criminological study by statistical and observational methods would conform to something akin to the astronomical approach to the study of heavenly bodies, whose behaviour in time and space can be accurately plotted and predicted, but whose reason for existence can only be guessed at."[64] In fact, it is the study of individual criminal which will lead us to the right way, if we were to understand the factors which made him criminal. It was the professional psychiatrist, Dr. William Healy, author of the *Individual*

[63] For details see Reckless, W. C., *The Crime Problem* (1961), pp. 233-44.

[64] Reckless, W. C., *Criminal Behaviour*, p. 256.

Delinquent, who first used the individual-case method for the scientific study of the delinquent.

Causes of White-Collar Criminality

So far we have analysed the various factors, general and specific which induce criminal behaviour in ordinary citizens and for which they are considered to be criminals by the dominant political group in a country. But there is another type of criminal behaviour, which is not totally disapproved by the upper class and the dominant political group, even though it is harmful to the well-being of the society as a whole. This is the behaviour of white-collar criminals of which very little comes to light. Dr. Barnes points out that need and greed explain most crimes.[65] And it is the latter which is the most potent factor in these cases. This white-collar crime may be defined approximately as a crime committed by a person of respectability and high social status in the course of his occupation.[66]

In the modern age material success forms an important part of prestige, therefore, both white-collar and lower class criminals generally have a distinct desire to gratify their economic wants. To the poverty-stricken youngster, who lives in a delinquency area, the gang to which he belongs provides the educational process by which he becomes familiar with the techniques of crime. For the college graduate who becomes the white-collar criminal, business and professional associates are the mentors. The rewards for unethical behaviour afford many temptations. Such men build homes in the best neighbourhood, acquire a comfortable fortune through shoddy merchandise, illegal operations and legal assistance to criminals. So chances of detection are not great.

This is because there is confusion in values. Certain offences are condemned irrespective of the individual who commits them. If a banker murders his wife, he will suffer the same penalty as a poor man does. But the gradations between respectability and condemnation are ill defined and often distort social conceptions of crime. All offenders come to accept the values of the group with which they are associated and look upon their behaviour as a necessary means to a desired end. Generally, crime becomes the only possible way of getting what they want and they learn the criminal behaviour from their associates. The young graduate who first

[65] Barnes, H. E., *Society in Transition* (1939), p. 677.

[66] Sutherland, E. H., *White Collar Crime* (1965), p. 9.

enters a business or a profession may have ethical scruples against evasions of the law or dubious practices. But eventually his desire for financial gain and social prestige influences him to accept the philosophy of his associates. Business is business. A doctor practices medicine to make a living. If patients want treatment he may prescribe them whether they are needed or not. The average is actively interested in promoting social welfare only when there is extreme pressure to do so, or when he has had some consistent education in social values.

The illegal economic activities of the upper social classes are not apt to be severely condemned by the society as a whole or by law enforcing bodies. As Dr. Sutherland observes, "There is significant share of crime in America which is largely ignored .... They are criminals in the legal sense ; they have broken laws which, *ipso facto* indicate them to be serious offenders. They have even manipulated the laws to their own advantage and subverted the purpose of the government through corrupt practices. But their behaviour has not resulted in prison sentences or even in social rejection."[67] The upper class social groups have prestige. They are articulately, the leaders and the creators of public opinion. It is not, therefore, surprising that the somewhat more brutal methods of the underworld are patterned to a marked degree, after those of their social superiors. The main reason why they succeed so often is because of the collusion between business, politics and crime.[68] The social disorganization in the upper class partially becomes responsible for the social disorganization among the lower classes.

[67] Sutherland, E. H., "White Collar Criminality", *American Sociological Review*, February, 1940.

[68] For further details see Chapter XIV.

CHAPTER IV

JUVENILE DELINQUENCY

AMONG the various social problems which the modern society has to face, juvenile delinquency as one occupies an important place. Along with many other social problems juvenile delinquency has emerged as a result of rapid urbanization and industrialization in the recent period. Social conditions obtained in the process of urbanization have affected the family pattern of the country to a great extent resulting in an air congenial to the growth of this type of disorganization. A large number of children moving from rural areas or living in slums and groping for adjustment in urban areas have proved vulnerable to this process and as a result the number of socially maladjusted children has recorded a gradual rise. Mr. G. C. Dutt observes, "Juvenile delinquency is rapidly becoming a serious menace in India and with the progressive industrialization of many parts of the country, which were essentially, rural areas uptill a few years ago, this problem will soon assume the same proportions as in many of the western countries."[1]

It is, however, not to be supposed that the delinquency among children was altogether non-existent in the country before. It might have been there but in a far less proportion. The joint family system, the compact and self-sufficient pattern of the traditional Indian village, the vigorous social control of the local community and such other factors offered a kind of automatic check on the growth of delinquency in the past. For this reason, the instances of children found to have indulged in delinquent behaviour were rare. However, the actual position of the delinquents to some extent came to be known only after the advent of legislative efforts to deal with the problem. A recent study of juvenile delinquency in a rural and semi-urban area shows that the problem of delinquency was also serious in rural areas. The survey showed that 11 per cent of the juvenile population in the age group 7 to 21 years com-

[1] Intelligence Eureau, Government of India, *Seminar on Social Defence*, March 1964 (1965), p. 30.

mitted delinquent acts, as compared to 17 per cent in the town.[2]

Juvenile Delinquency Defined.

Delinquency, as defined by Friedlander, is a juvenile misconduct that might be dealt with under the law.[3] Cyril Burt defines delinquency as occurring in a child "when his anti-social tendencies appear so grave that he becomes or ought to become the subject of official action", whereas William H. Sheldon regards delinquency "as behaviour disappointing beyond reasonable expectations". It is clear that different social scientists have defined juvenile delinquency according to their own light and experience. Some have made the concept too wide to incorporate all problems of juvenile misbehaviour while others have focussed only on that behaviour which amounts to a criminal offence.[4] The Second United Nations Congress on the Prevention of Crime and Treatment of Offenders (1960) points out that if the term "juvenile delinquency" is restricted to those juveniles in each country who have committed criminal offences, it would seem that no universal definition is needed. Allowance could be made for the wide variations found in the legal systems of the many countries of the world, but the inclusion under the "juvenile delinquent" of acts which are not serious and which can be classified as behaviour problems could be ruled out. If a clear and restricted definition of juvenile delinquency is established would it not be possible to focus more attention on the kinds of behaviour which need to be prevented ?[5] Thus, it is now generally agreed that juvenile delinquency should be demarcated from other problems of juvenile misbehaviour. "By juvenile delinquency should be understood the commission of an act which, if committed by an adult, would be considered a crime."[6] Although the term juvenile delinquency may be confined to problems of serious misbehaviour, in many countries children having problems of misconduct, truancy, vagrancy, destitution, etc. are also dealt by the state.

[2] Dr. Kishore, B. R., "Incidence and Causes of Juvenile Delinquency". (A Survey of Rural and Semi-Urban Area), *Social Defence*, January, 1966.

[3] Friedlander, W. A., *Introduction to Social Welfare* (1957), p. 44.

[4] Chandra, Dr. Sushil, *Sociology of Deviation in India* (1967), p. 42.

[5] *Report of the Second United Nations Congress on the Prevention of Crin and Treatment of Offenders* (1960), p. 52.

[6] *Ibid.*, p. 52.

Extent of Juvenile Delinquency in India

It is difficult to know the extent of this problem in any country because of certain reasons. (1) There is no satisfactory definition of crime, and the only workable definition is a legalistic one. According to this definition only those persons are considered criminals who violate the existing laws. However, there may be persons who violate mores but they cannot be convicted as criminals as these mores are not mentioned in the statute books. Thus, the data cannot be obtained regarding such criminals. (2) All crimes are not known to the police and one has to be caught and convicted to be a criminal because many crimes may not be reported legally for one reason or the other such as inefficiency of the administration or apathy of the public. (3) A delinquent is only caught when he has repeated his act many a time. Because it is only when the behaviour pattern is of an aggressive and antisocial nature and harmful to the public weal that the child concerned will come under the purview of law, and this is the stage when the existence of problem is already known. (4) There may be large number of children who may have behaviour problems and still be included under the delinquents. (5) Majority of the cases coming to the courts generally represent the under privileged groups whose parents lack cultural or economic resources.

With these limitations only a part of the violation of law can become the subject of analysis from the standpoint of study of crime. Besides these difficulties we in our country do not have accurate statistics of even those who are brought into courts. It is in few states only that we have complete statistical data about those who are brought to courts. Up to the year 1950 in Bombay alone there was a separate department for the administration of the Children Act. The annual administration reports furnished information regarding juvenile delinquency and vagrants, but not about truants. The reports indicated the number of cases admitted and disposed off during the year by the juvenile courts and also furnished figures about the cases pending at the close of the year. The cases are classified according to sex, community, native place, and mental and physical defects. The young offenders are also classified according to the type of offences, namely, theft, house-breaking, and similar offences against property, gambling, travelling without ticket, other offences under the Railway Act, assault and indecent assault, violating Defence of India Rules, attempted suicide, murder, rape, breach of prohibition order, escape from custody and miscellaneous offences. Data was also available in some other states in respect of age, sex, caste, and types of crimes committed by different categories of delinquents. But they were not adequate. The data collected by the Ministry of Education in 1950 showed that juvenile courts were functioning only in four states in that year, namely, Bombay, Madras, West Bengal and Delhi, and they were working only in some towns of those states. During 1950, cases against 15,196 children—12,915 boys and 2,281 girls—were brought before these courts, about two-thirds of which were reported in Bombay alone.[7] (The number of juvenile courts was larger in the State of Bombay than in any other state.) During 1950, the total number of cases of child delinquency put up for trial in all states except Uttar Pradesh, for which figures were not available, was 40,119, including 37,040 against boys and 3,079 girls. The distribution of these cases, according to the nature of offences was as follows :

TABLE 4(*a*)

Nature of Crime	*Number*	*Percentage*
Against Property	13,568	33.8
Against State	5,853	14.6
Against Person	3,016	7.5
Against Morality	1,098	2.7
Vagrancy	4,984	12.5
Other Offences	11,600	28.9
Total	40,119	100.0

However, the report points out that in view of non-uniformity in the legislative measures on the subject in force in different states, the disparity in the upper age of protection and the probable variation in the efficiency of the agencies administering such laws, these figures cannot be taken as an accurate index of the respective incidence of children delinquency in these states.[8]

Since then some progress has been made in this direction. The Bureau of Delinquency Statistics and Research of the Children Aid Society, Bombay, collected some statistics from seventeen states in 1956 for six years (1948 to 1954) regarding juvenile arrests

[7] Report of Delinquent Children and Juvenile Offenders in India, Ministry of Education, Government of India (1950), p. 3.

[8] *Ibid.*, p. 5.

affected by the police during that period. These states included Andhra, Bombay, Madhya Pradesh, Madras, Orissa, East Punjab, West Bengal, Hyderabad, Madhya Bharat, Mysore, Pepsu, Rajasthan, Saurashtra, Travancore Cochin, Ajmer, Delhi and Vindhya Pradesh.[9] According to this report the number of such juvenile offenders was 12,268 in 1949 and rose to 16,757 in 1954. Since 1958 these statistics are being collected on regular basis by the Intelligence Bureau, Ministry of Home Affairs, Government of India. These figures may be seen from the following table.[10] However, these figures are to be read with caution as (1) some of the states have not enforced the Children Acts properly, (2) these figures sometimes include cases of homeless, neglected and destitute children, and (3) there is a variation in the upper age limit of children to be dealt under the Children Acts.

TABLE 4(*b*)

Year	*Total number of cases*	*Males*	*Females*
1950	40,119	N.A.	N.A.
1958	41,920	N.A.	N.A.
1959	47,925	45,782	2,143
1960	49,276	46,893	2,383
1962	53,803	51,227	2,576
1964	66,158	63,468	2,690

It will be seen that the juvenile delinquency is on the increase.

Causes of Juvenile Delinquency

The causes of juvenile delinquency are many and these we have discussed in detail in the last chapter. A man's behaviour is a highly complex resultant of interrelated factors, and elaborate investigation of delinquency has given us conclusive evidence that there is no single predisposing factor leading inevitably to delinquent behaviour. "The delinquent child is generally a child handicapped not by one or two but by usually seven or eight counts. A child can overcome one or two handicaps, such as the death of one parent or poverty and poor health. But if the child has a drunken unemployed father and an immoral mother, is mentally deficient, is taken out of school at an early age, and put to work in a factory, and lives in a crowded

[9] A Report on Juvenile Delinquency in India, Children Aid Society, Bombay, pp. 122-25.

[10] See *Crime in India*, 1958 to 1964.

home in a bad neighbourhood, nearly every factor in his environment may seem to mitigate against him. Such children constitute the largest share of those who get into serious trouble and are brought into court."[11] Besides these direct causes which lead to crime, there are general risks such as age, sex, class, caste, areal and regional variations in crime, which throw some light on the problem of delinquency. Similarly, the types of crimes—murder, theft, burglary, sex offences—also throw some light in understanding the problem of delinquency.

To prevent delinquency and to rehabilitate those who have become delinquents certain measures will have to be taken. But before we describe those measures it might be appropriate to discuss the problems of truancy and vagrancy which often lead to delinquency. In many cases truants and vagrants are also treated on the same lines as the delinquents and the Children Acts also cover these persons.

Truancy

With mass education, not adopted to the aptitude of each child and neglect of children by parent due to economic distress and certain other reasons, truancy has an important part to play in juvenile delinquency. Along with other environmental factors, the school bears its own share of responsibility for delinquent conduct. It supervises a large share of younger children's waking day than do the parents. As Elliott and Merrill point out, "One of the most frequent predisposing factors to other forms of delinquency is truancy, which has been called the kindergarten of crime."[12] Frequently the school fails to provide ample stimulation in the subjects presented, and from this standpoint it well deserves its indictment.

Shri Raj Nath Khanna, who made a detailed study of 54 cases between the age of 11 to 15 years in a middle school in the city of Lucknow in 1951 came to the conclusion that the truancy was the result of so many cumulative influences, i.e. (*i*) unsystematic system of school education, (*ii*) unsuitable conditions at home, (*iii*) companionship factor and the attempts of these truants to imbibe the behaviour of their senior companions, (*iv*) predominance of play in the mind of a student, (*v*) attempt to escape from school punishment, (*vi*) inability to cope with home task, and (*vii*) age of

[11] Elliott, M. A. and Merrill, F. E., *op. cit.*, p. 111.
[12] Elliott, M. A. and Merrill, F. E., *op. cit.*, p. 138.

the truant more than the usual.[13] These truants exhibited many other behaviour patterns such as gambling and wandering which were not conducive to their welfare and proper development. Out of these 54 delinquents, 44 were found ordinary truants, 7 delinquents and the rest 3 as misbehaved. Out of these 44 ordinary truants, 15 also had slight delinquent traits, and they stole money ranging from one anna to Rs. 10 from their homes. Out of these 7 delinquents, one stole a box, 3 spent away their school fees which they got from their parents and 3 sold away their books and stationery. These were found habitual pilferers and stole money, books or stationery of other students. Thus, it is clear that truants develop the delinquent traits gradually if not checked at the proper time.

These truants were classified in another manner also if they were casual or partial truants who absented themselves from the class due to strictness of certain teachers, or they were habitual offenders. Among these habitual offenders there were some who were found incorrigible and were termed as recidivists. These recidivists were regular absentees who instigated others to leave the class and threatened them if they happen to complain against them. They had generally disorganized homes. The number of these casual, habitual and recidivists was 17, 16 and 11 respectively.

To gauge the extent of truancy in India it might be significant to note that these 54 students were picked up from a total number of 225 students in a middle class school after consulting their roll call register. In other words, the percentage of such truants to the total number was 24 per cent. Thus, we find a fairly high percentage of truants in our schools.

Among these truants we have also delinquents which is an aftermath of truancy. Generally, a truant goes out of the school in search of pleasant experience. He finds companions and forms a group. Their play takes the form of gambling with stakes and if there is loss the truant resorts to borrowing and ultimately to stealing, which is clearly a delinquent trait. Even if he gains, he uses this gain for bad purposes such as smoking, drinking and cinema show, which ultimately lead him to delinquent career. The Crime Commission of New York State (1928) observed, "Where truancy habits are well established, other delinquent habits often exist. Wandering

[13] Khanna, Raj Nath, "Juvenile Truancy and School". Thesis submitted in J. K. Institute of Sociology and Human Relations, Lucknow University, for Diploma in Social Sciences (1951).

about the streets, picking up with other truants, concealing his whereabouts from his parents, the child is almost certain to become a petty thief and commit other increasingly serious offences."[14]

The Joint Committee on Methods of Preventing Delinquency, New York, observes, "Where these is some provision for more adequate enforcement of school laws and greater insight in dealing with backward children, fewer cases of delinquency occur. The trained visiting teachers have done much both to minimise problems of school attendance and to iron out behaviour problems."[15] According to Mr. Khanna all those factors which lead to truancy need to be mitigated if the truancy is to be effectively checked.[16] The problems of child should be investigated by the social worker and his parents and teachers should beappraised of those problems. The child should be given due love, affection and security at home, the system of education should be modified and there should be recreation for them at school and home. Thus, good family environments, better education system and recreational facilities at school and home play an important part in mitigating this evil.

As already pointed out, truants are treated like delinquents in most of the civilized countries, where truancy is considered to be one form of delinquency. In England juvenile courts deal with their cases like delinquents. In one state of U. S. A. the delinquent has been defined "as a child who violates any law of the state, or is incorrigible, or knowingly associates with thieves or immoral person, is truant, or visits policy shop or gambling den or saloon, or dram shop, or wanders about aimlessly, etc." and thus truants are included in delinquents.

Juvenile Vagrancy

Vagrancy like truancy is another state in the formation of delinquent career. Children are generally studied when they are caught by police and have become delinquents. But they develop these traits gradually. Dr. William Healy observes, "The first known delinquency occurred at 8 years or earlier in 24 cases and after

[14] Crime Commission of New York State, *From Truancy to Crime—A Study of 250 Adolescents* (1928). Also see Elliott and Merrill's book, *op. cit.*, p. 139.

[15] Joint Committee on Methods of Preventing Delinquency, New York, *The Problem Child in School* (1925), pp. 253-80.

[16] Khanna, R. N., *op. cit.*, p. 11.

12 years in only 22 per cent. The delinquent had been a delinquent for more than a year before his first court appearance in 87 per cent of the cases."[17] These are generally the neglected, ill-cared and wandering children known as waifs. Professor C.C. Carstens defines neglected children as "those whose interests are not properly protected by responsible persons, organisation or governmental bodies."[18]

These children generally come out of poor or disorganized families or broken homes which could not provide them basic needs, i.e. nutrition, clothes, companionship, education, recreation and affection which are essential for the child's personality. The child who is unable to get these needs generally exhibits some abnormalities which may even be antisocial. In quest for satisfaction of these needs he may become a waif and may end in delinquency. In fact the causes leading to vagrancy are similar to those of delinquency already discussed.

In a study of 50 waifs in the city of Lucknow between the age of 7 to 14 years, Mr. S. S. Srivastava found that out of these 50 waifs, 36 were casual gamblers, 10 were habitual and 4 were non-gamblers.[19] Thus, the first symptom for the waif to move towards delinquency was to start gambling and slowly and gradually to become a habitual gambler, a trait of delinquency. He also found that out of these 50 waifs, 20 were resorting to begging. Out of these 20, 11 were habitual and the rest 9 were casual beggars. Those who were neither habitual beggars nor gamblers, showed other signs of vagrancy like wandering, roaming, uttering most filthy language or indulging in other antisocial activities pertaining to sex, and even resorting to stealing. Out of the 50, 19 showed certain patterns of delinquency and were senior in age. Some of them resorted to drinking and indulged in other antisocial activities like stealing and quarrelling. Some of these had been caught while doing antisocial activities, but somehow they escaped from the grips of law. All these fifty waifs were smokers.

During the shop hours in the evening when there was much

[17] Quoted in *Report of the U. P. Jail Enquiry Committee* (1946), p. 50.

[18] Carstens, C. C., *Neglected Children in Encyclopaedia of Social Sciences*, p. 37.

[19] Srivastava, S. S., "Juvenile Vagrancy". Thesis submitted for Diploma in Social Services at J. K. Institute of Sociology and Human Relations, Lucknow University, (1950).

rush in the market they went to central business places in small groups. During day time they visited open places near the river, or zoo or other playgrounds in the city, where they kept themselves busy in kite flying, gambling, and gillimarble. It is at these places that they get new associates and take part in gang activities.

Among these 50, only 4 were literate and the rest were illiterate. Some of these were sent to school by their parents, but they became truants, and ultimately left the school. Majority of these had illiterate parents—mostly low-paid workers—and did not care for their education. They wished them to join as labourers after 14 years of age and before that they could while away their time by wandering. These juvenile vagrants who develop wanderlust may, in course of time, become delinquents or if they get a proper vocation they may become normal citizens.

Methods of Controlling Vagrancy

To check vagrancy and begging which lead to delinquency, Vagrancy and Begging Acts have been passed in various states—Bengal, Madras, Bombay, Bihar, while in some other states there are no special laws for dealing with these persons; but beggary is prohibited in the municipal areas. Unfortunately, these acts have not been put into practice and also there is not sufficient number of institutions for maintaining these beggars and vagrants. Under the Bengal Vagrancy Act II of 1943 a vagrant means a person asking for alms in any public place or remaining in any public place or wandering about in such a condition or manner as makes it likely that he exists by asking alms. Under these various acts the beggar or vagrant is supposed to have committed an offence and he is apprehended by the police, produced before a magistrate, and committed to a workhouse or a special home. But it also requires the setting up of special institutions—workhouses for the able-bodied beggars and special homes for the infirm and the disabled before these provisions can be enforced. There are certain other difficulties such as non-uniformity of laws in the various states which do not allow to take comprehensive measures to tackle this problem on rational basis. We have discussed these problems in detail in the chapter on Beggary.

Prevention of Juvenile Delinquency

In order to prevent juvenile delinquency we have to deal not only with maladjusted children and youths whose difficulties bring them before the law, but also with those who, while not violating laws, prove to be hard to educate in the family or who are disturbing others in school and in the street. Thus, truants, problem children, vagrants and neglected children are also to be protected along with delinquents in the broader sense of the term.

In preventing delinquency there are two types of methods to be used, preventive and rehabilitative (or curative).[20] In the former case, factors leading to delinquency are to be mitigated as far as possible while in the later one it is to be seen that those who have committed delinquent acts do not repeat them and become normal citizens.

Preventive Measures

We have already discussed the causes of delinquency which are many. Friedlander has summed up these factors as follows : "Among these various factors may be hereditary and biological elements, such as poor health, physical handicaps, abnormalities, glandular disturbances, various degrees of mental deficiency or even psychosis, emotional instability, insecurity, uncontrolled sex drives or neurotic behaviour. Other factors may be contributed by environment, neglect or rejection by parents, siblings and friends, detrimental influences by a broken home, criminal attitudes of the family, neighbours, or predatory gangs in a slum area. There may also be poverty in the family, gambling, bad companions, irregular or poor education, lack of healthy recreation, excitement through the radio, television, the newspapers, crime stories, comic books and movies."[21] In order to offset the effects of these factors the following measures may be suggested.

1. *A Team Work of Private and Public Agencies Devoted to Preventive Work.* To counter the dangers which lead youth to crime, a whole-hearted team work of public and private agencies devoted to the task of crime prevention is necessary. "These include schools, churches, parent-teacher associations, youth organizations, group work agencies (such as YMCA, YWCA, YMHA, boy scouts, girl scouts, and boys' clubs), probation officers of the juvenile courts, social workers and police-women and officers of juvenile bureaus

[20] Sometimes three terms, i.e. control, prevention and treatment are used in prevention programme, and one method may be useful both for treatment and prevention, e.g. probation.

[21] Friendlander, W. A., *op. cit.*, p. 442.

of police department. If all the members of these groups assist parents and guardians in locating difficult children in danger of maladjustment, in recognizing early symptoms of unhappiness, conflict, and insecurity, help can be found."[22] The Seminar on Social Defence, 1964, laid special emphasis on the formation of boys' clubs and boys' aid societies, etc. by police officers trained in the field of juvenile delinquency to control and prevent delinquency in India.[23]

2. *Training of Members and Staff of all Organizations* Careful training of members and staff of all organizations concerned with delinquency control is essential in order to enable them to recognize the danger and bring parents and youths in contact with the agency which has the facility to help them.

3. *Establishment of Child Guidance Clinics*. Child guidance clinics and mental hygiene clinics are important for the treatment of seriously disturbed and maladjusted children. There may also be diagnostic facilities in the schools.

4. *Education of the Family*. The family is to be strengthened by conscientious casework of public and private social agencies, education for family living and social hygiene and counselling.

5. *Establishment of Wholesome Recreational Agencies*. Prevention of delinquency requires the establishment of wholesome recreational agencies (sports, playgrounds, community centres, concerts, drama, puppet shows) and developing social group work and youth groups.

In rural areas to provide healthy recreation, neighbourhoods, schools and churches should open their meeting halls and playgrounds for sports, recreation and cultural activities and youth organizations and citizens' groups should assume the responsibility for carrying on these programmes.

6. *Assistance to Under-privileged Children*. Schools, churches and other character-building agencies should be encouraged to serve under-privileged children for poor areas and to assist law-enforcement agencies, including juvenile police bureaus.

7. *Propaganda*. The newspapers, magazines, radio, television and and motion pictures should interpret juvenile delinquency in terms of honest reports about causes and protection of youth, rather than

[22] Teeters, N. K. and Reinemann, J. O., *The Challenge of Delinquency : Causation, Treatment, and Prevention of Delinquency*, New York, 1950, pp. 580-621.

[23] *Seminar on Social Defence* (1965), *op. cit.*, p. 33.

stressing the sensational aspects, scandals and a false heroism in delinquent behaviour.

In California (U. S. A.) in 1941 the Youth Correction Authority Act was passed under which a Youth Correction Authority was set up which co-ordinates all facilities in educational, medical and rehabilitation work, for juvenile delinquents carried on in social agencies, children's institutions, training schools, clinics and hospitals. Besides the rehabilitation programme, the Youth Correction Authority assists in the development of facilities for sports, recreation and leisure time activities for children and young persons on the community level as a preventive measure. Professor Jagannadham mentions three steps for the prevention of delinquency in India. (*a*) Improving the environment which include improved housing, increased recreational facilities, better schooling, reducing economic insecurity, raising income level of poor families, etc. and these do not directly concern children. (*b*) Spotting potential delinquents by predictive tests. Children may be identified by school teachers or specialized agencies in contact with home. (*c*) Reducing recidivism and seriousness of delinquency through treatment.[24]

However, so far as preventive programmes in India are concerned, not much has been done so far. The United Nations report on Juvenile Delinquency observes, "Perhaps the weakest link in the entire chain of the early diagnosis, prevention, treatment and control of juvenile delinquency in this region is the preventive aspect . . . . As seen in the present survey it is not so much the juvenile who is a potential delinquent as his social environment which creates a predisposition toward delinquency. Hence most of the protective and preventive legislation is directed not towards the prevention of potential or predelinquency in the juvenile himself, but towards the prevention of cruelty to juveniles or of crime against juveniles by adults, and towards the punishment of adults who victimise juveniles. There is hardly any diagnostic or prognostic services which might lead to the early detection of the problem personality."[25] In fact, there are few child guidance clinics, recreational centres and other social welfare agencies, as mentioned above, in this country.

[24] United Nations, Department of Social Welfare, *Comparative Survey of Juvenile Delinquency* (Part IV Asia and the Far East), (1953), p. 101.

[25] Jagannadham, Dr. V., "Prevention of Juvenile Delinquency": *Social Defence*, October, 1965.

Method of Rehabilitation

The fact that children, offered proper guidance, training and help towards rehabilitation, would develop into socially normal individuals came to be recognized in the last century in almost all the civilized countries of the world and India had also followed suit. The principle of differential treatment of children is now a valid fact. Prior to that time children were tried and convicted of violations of the law in the same way as adults except that a child below seven years was not regarded as responsible and, therefore, could not commit crime. It was during the first quarter of the twentieth century that separate courts for the hearing of juvenile offenders were widely established, the age span ranging all the way from ten to a maximum of sixteen, seventeen, eighteen or even twenty-one years. The juvenile courts have the jurisdiction in connection with violations of the law by the juveniles along with their jurisdiction over questions of dependency, neglect and incorrigibility. The question of the possibility of non-responsibility became the basic task of juvenile courts. Whereas an adult was presumed to be responsible for his acts, the juvenile was thought much less likely to be, particularly if he approached the lower limit. As time went on, the point of view that he was not in a strict sense accountable for his delinquent behaviour was well established, and the assumption that treatment called for was some sort of remedial programme rather than punishment. The action so far taken for the prevention and treatment of juvenile delinquency may now be discussed under two broad heads, viz. (*a*) programmes before independence, and (*b*) after independence.

Programmes Before Independence

(1) *Apprentices Act*, 1850. The earliest step taken in this direction in India was the Apprentices Act of 1850 which provides for the binding of children, both boys and girls, between the ages of 10 to 18 as apprentices.[26] The act was intended for the benefit of children especially orphans and poor children brought up by a public charity to train them for trades, crafts and employment by which they may gain a livelihood when they come to full age. The father or guardian may bind a child above 10 and under 18 up to 21 years of age for a period not exceeding 7 years. A female child may be so bound until her marriage. The act contains several safeguards for the

[26] For details see *Social Legislation—Its Role in Social Welfare*, p. 145.

protection of children so bound. The act also dealt with children who committed petty offences. It authorized magistrates to commit such children as apprentices to employers and provided for controlling the relations between the two. Evidently, the underlying motivation of the Act was to divert the misdirected energies of juveniles towards the learning of some trade and craft to have honest living.

(2) *Reformatory Schools Act.* The next important legislation in connection with the treatment of juvenile delinquents was the Reformatory Schools Act of 1897, which can be considered a landmark in the history of treatment of delinquency. Under this act courts were empowered to send youthful offenders (boys only) sentenced to transportation or imprisonment for detention in a Reformatory School for a period not less than three and not more than seven years if they considered him to be a proper person to be an inmate thereof and be at the time of conviction under the age of 15. No person may be detained in a Reformatory after he attains the eighteenth year. The State Governments may establish and maintain Reformatory Schools or may recognize any other school conducted in conformity with the Act. Every school must provide: (*i*) sufficient means of separating the inmates at night ; (*ii*) proper sanitary arrangements, water supply, food, clothing and bedding for the inmates ; (*iii*) industrial training ; and (*iv*) an infirmary to receive them when ill. Under this Act some Reformatory Schools were established at places like Lucknow (U. P.), Hissar (Punjab), Hazaribagh (Bihar), Secunderabad (Andhra Pradesh) and Jubbulpore (Madhya Pradesh), and they are reported to have done useful work.[27]

(3) *Provision in Criminal Procedure Code.* Besides this Act there is a general provision in the Criminal Procedure Code (1898) under Section 399, which states that when anyone under 15 is sentenced to imprisonment for any offence, the court may direct that such person, instead of being imprisoned in a criminal jail should be confined in a Reformatory established by the State Government. But this section shall not apply to any place in which the Reformatory Schools Act 1897 is in force. Section 562 of the C. P. C. also permitted discharge of certain convicted offenders on probation of good conduct and release with admonition. Under Section 82 of the Indian Penal Code children under seven are not to be held responsible for

[27] See *Social Legislation—Its Role in Social Welfare* (1956), pp. 152-55.

their criminal acts. Section 83 of the same Code relaxes this age up to twelve in case of children who at the time of committing a breach of law did not attain sufficient maturity of understanding to judge for themselves the nature and consequences of their conduct.

However, all these measures did not have the desired effect and separate Children Acts had to be passed to deal effectively with problem children. The Indian Jail Reform Committee, 1920 observed that "a child offender was the product of an unhealthy environment and what was needed was not punishment but a fresh chance of living in community in better surrounding". The Committee recommended a specialized treatment based on a social investigation into the environment of the child. These remarks had their effect in the early enactment of Children Acts and development of Borstal schools.

(4) *Children Acts and Establishment of Certified Schools and Juvenile Courts.* The interests evinced by the League of Nations and with the advancement of public opinion, the care of delinquent children received a fresh impetus. In the twenties of the present century comprehensive laws in respect of children were passed by various provinces in India.

The various legislative attempts dealing with the problem of juvenile delinquency can be broadly classified into two categories. The first category of Acts includes the series of Children Acts, beginning with the Madras Children Act of 1920 followed by the Bengal and the Bombay Children Acts passed in 1922 and 1924 respectively.[28]

The other series of Acts deal with the specific pattern of anti-social behaviour among children or with children affected by certain wider social problems. Under this come the Juvenile Smoking Acts and the Suppression of Immoral Traffic Acts passed in various provinces from time to time since 1911.

The Children Acts not only deal with the problem of juvenile delinquents who are convicted, but also with the problem of needy children in general and cover the pre-delinquent, or the near delinquent, the delinquents, the destitute and the neglected children and also provide for care and protection of children in moral danger as well as uncontrollable children.

When the Madras State first passed such an act (Madras Children

[28] Kulkarni, D. V., *Juvenile Delinquency in Social Welfare in India* '(1955) p. 344.

Act, 1920) it was found that prior to this enactment there was lack of any power to protect a young child with potential criminality until he had committed a crime and was convicted, and there was nothing that could be done for a girl at all. The waifs and strays of the streets and those who were keeping bad company could not be saved from a life of crime. Even the Reformatory Schools Act did not apply to boys incurring imprisonment or failure to furnish security. "Sec. 31 of the Reformatory Schools Act and Sec. 562 of the Criminal Procedure Code permitted discharge of convicts after admonition, but those powers were rarely used. The law did not operate until after conviction and afforded no means of rescuing the young who had not actually become criminals. Also, it did not enforce the responsibility of parents for the good conduct of their children which is one of the most important principles of English Law."[29]

It was to remedy these defects and to provide for the custody, trial and punishment of youthful children and young persons that this act was passed, repealing the Reformatory Schools Act. The main provisions of this act were :

(*i*) No child under 14 years of age can be imprisoned under any circumstances and no young person between 14 to 16 years of age can be imprisoned unless he is certified to be of an unruly or depraved character. The person under 14 years was termed as child and between 14 to 16 as a young person.

(*ii*) Any person arrested on a charge and is under 16 is required to be released or bailed except in very grave offences. The detention in no case be in a jail with other prisoners and they must be detained in a separate building preferably in charge of a person other than a police officer.

(*iii*) The child or youthful offender cannot be sentenced to death or imprisonment except when he is unruly or depraved and is unfit to be sent to a Certified School. Person below 12 were to be sent to junior certified schools and 12 to 16 to senior certified schools.

(*iv*) Committal to a school is not compulsory. The court has alternative methods of dealing with the youthful offender. It may discharge him after due admonition, it may hand him over to his parents or guardians or any adult relative if the latter undertakes, on a bond, to be responsible for his good behaviour for 12 months.

[29] *Social Legislation--Its Role in Social Welfare*, p. 156.

(*v*) The court may couple the sentence mentioned against item (*iv*) with an order of supervision under a Probation Officer, or some other person. It is the duty of the Probation Officer to visit, advise and befriend the youthful offender and obtain suitable employment for him.

(*vi*) The court can also pass order for whipping and fine in certain cases.

(*vii*) For the protection of other children, the court may direct the detention of certain children under 14 years of age (or 15 in exceptional circumstances) in Junior Certified Schools or commit them to suitable custody where they remain until they attain their sixteenth year. The grounds on which children may be so taken in for protection are referred in detail, e.g., any child without a home or abode or means of subsistence ; any child wandering or without a parent or guardian ; a child whose parent or guardian is unfit to take proper care due to drinking habits, or is criminal or undergoing imprisonment, etc. The parent or guardian of a child unable to control it may also bring it before the court for detention.

(*viii*) The State Government may establish Juvenile Courts to hear charges against children or young persons Where there is no separate court, the court shall sit either in a building or room different from its ordinary sittings or on different dates or at different times from those fixed for its ordinary sittings except where the child or young person is tried jointly with an adult. No child or young person shall be handcuffed. Police officers conducting them shall be in plain clothes.

(*ix*) For the purpose of giving effect to the act, the State Government may establish junior and senior Certified Schools and Auxiliary Homes. A junior certified school is for the training of children and a senior certified school is for the training of youthful offenders. Auxiliary Homes are attached to certified schools for the reception of inmates of certified schools. The State Government may also recognize any school or home and such recognized schools or homes are called Private Certified Schools or Private Auxiliary Homes. All such schools are liable to be inspected by the Chief Inspector.

(*x*) No body should be detained in a senior certified school after he has attained 16 years of age. Three months before the due date for release, the school must notify the Probation Officer, or the District Magistrate in order that he may arrange for his after-care. Every discharged inmate is given a letter addressed to the Probation Officer or the District Magistrate who is expected to hlpe the pupil towards a fair start in life and protect him against temptations to relapse into crime. The Headmaster is expected to keep track of a discharged inmate for three years after release and to keep himself informed by obtaining half-yearly reports, from the District Magistrate or the Probation Officer.

Children Acts in other States

The Acts passed in other states are almost on the lines of Madras State except Bombay, which differs somewhat in certain respects from the Madras Act.[30] Here any boy or girl who has not attained 16 years of age is treated as a child instead of 14. Juvenile courts are to be established under the act. The State Government is authorised to establish and maintain industrial schools for the reception of children and youthful offenders. Any private industrial school or educational institution may be certified by the State Government. The State Government may declare any place as a Remand Home. The Government may similarly notify "Fit Persons Institutions" having their object the reception or protection of children or the prevention of cruelty to children, which undertake to bring up or provide facilities for bringing up children entrusted to its care in conformity with their religion of birth. "Places of Safety" are places or institutions for the temporary reception of children. There are many other provisions which are slightly different from the Madras Act.

These acts have worked with varying success in different states, the more progressive being Bombay and Madras. In certain states like Madhya Pradesh, East Punjab and Uttar Pradesh, these acts have not been properly enforced. If some progress is to be made in this direction, all these acts will have to be brought under one uniform procedure and enforced in right earnest.

(5) *Juvenile Smoking Acts.* As already stated other acts deal with the specific pattern of antisocial behaviour among children or with children affected by certain wider social problems. Of these the juvenile smoking acts are in force in majority of the states —Punjab, Bengal, Assam, Madhya Pradesh, Rajasthan and Uttar

[30] Some of the other states which passed Children Acts are Madhya Pradesh (1928), Delhi (1941), Mysore (1943), Punjab (1949) and Uttar Pradesh (1951).

Pradesh. The Punjab Act of 1918, the earliest, forbids the sale of tobacco in any form in which it can be smoked, to any person under 16. Penalty for violation of the prohibition is a fine of Rs. 10, 20 or 50 for the first, second or subsequent offence.

Any tobacco found with a person appearing to be under 16 or found smoking in any public place may be seized and destroyed by certain persons named in the Act ; for example heads of villages, teachers, members of municipalities and district boards, legal and medical practitioners and magistrates. Similar provisions are provided in the acts of other states. But unfortunately these acts were rarely enforced.

(6) *Suppression of Immoral Traffic Acts to Protect Young Girls.* The Suppression of Immoral Traffic Acts are in force in various states, which though do not declare prostitution by itself a crime, they deal with particular activities connected with its practice such as soliciting in a public street or place, living on the earnings of the prostitution of another, procuring, importing, unlawful-detention for prostitution, permitting use of premises for a brothel, which are rendered as punishable. Some acts also contain provisions for rescuing minor girls from brothels or from moral danger. In some states these provisions are contained in the respective Children Acts while in certain states—U.P., Bombay and Madras—there are acts for the protection of minor girls. There are also provisions in the Indian Penal Code for the prevention of immoral traffic.[31]

(7) *Probation of Offenders Acts.* After the passage of Children Acts, certain states enacted the Probation of Offenders Acts which contemplated authorized supervision by Probation Officers. But the scope of the Probation Acts is not confined to children only. Moreover, in certain states provision existed even in Children Acts, under which the courts could place children under the supervision of certain persons. However, under the Probation Acts the Juvenile Courts can place the youthful offenders under the supervision of Probation Officers even for grave charges, provided he has no previous conviction. The first was the Madras Probation of Offenders Act, 1936. Such Acts were later passed in Madhya Pradesh, Uttar Pradesh and Bombay.

(8) *Borstal Schools Acts for Adolescents.* These Borstal Schools

[31] For further details see Chapter on Prostitution.

Acts were passed to accord a special treatment for adolescent offenders, that is offenders between 15 and 21 years of age (between 16 and 21 years of age where children acts are in force).[32] These Acts were in force in the States of Madras, Andhra, Punjab, Bengal, Madhya Pradesh, Uttar Pradesh, Bombay and Mysore. The earliest act was the Madras Borstal Schools Act, 1926.

A Borstal School is a corrective institution wherein adolescent offenders are given industrial training and other instructions and are subject to such disciplinary and moral influences as will conduce to their reformation and prevention of crime. The period of adolescence is the most critical in an individual's life and it is necessary to prevent habits of immorality and crime from being formed. It was considered undesirable to familiarize adolescents with ordinary jail life and bring them into contact with adult prisoners. So these acts authorized the states to establish Borstal schools for the detention and training of adolescent offenders. The main features of these schools are : (*i*) the special and individual training of the inmates, and (*ii*) the conditional release of those who appear to deserve the privilege, to enable them to make a living. The acts apply only to male members. The period of detention is between 2 to 3 years but the Inspector-General, on the recommendations of the Visiting Committee consisting of official and non-official members, may permit the discharge of any inmate, who has completed six months of detention and if his conduct has been good and there is a reasonable probability that the inmate will abstain from crime and lead a useful and industrious life. Released persons are placed under the supervision of Probation Officers who attend to the after-care of inmates. In Uttar Pradesh there is the Borstal School Act of 1938, but it is not operative. In its place there is the Juvenile Jail in Bareilly which is run on the lines of a Borstal School. All juvenile offenders under 19 years of age and not more than 21 years of age at the date of conviction sentenced to imprisonment for not less than a year are detained in this jail. It is a correctional institution.

Above are some of the steps which were taken before Independence in connection with control of juvenile delinquency in India.

[32] It may be pointed out that Reformatory Schools Acts were for persons below 15 years and persons in Reformatory Schools could be detained up to 18 years of age.

It might be appropriate to give a brief account of the institutions connected with juvenile delinquency before we discuss the programme after Independence.

1. *Juvenile Courts*

The separation of the treatment of juvenile delinquent from that of adults has given rise to the institution of Juvenile Courts. In India in accordance with Children Acts they generally deal with children below 16. Whereas in certain other countries they sometimes deal with cases up to 21. They have slightly different procedure from the ordinary course, where pleaders are not allowed to plead, the public is excluded from hearing the case and the police officers come in plain clothes. The policy is to have specialization of the magistracy and they are given training to deal with problem children and in child psychology.

In the states, where Children Acts have been in operation it is laid down that problem children may be dealt with by juvenile courts. As the act gives option, the number of juvenile courts in this country is small. According to the report compiled and published by the Union Ministry of Education in 1950, there were only 39 juvenile courts in India, 30 in Bombay, 4 in Madras and the rest in other states.

2. *Remand Homes*

When a child is apprehended under the Act, he is brought before the magistrate within 24 hours and until the special investigations in respect of the child are complete he is kept in the remand home. The child is kept in the remand home until the final disposal of the case. In addition to being a place of safety it has become a place where the important function of observation and classification is performed before the investigation starts. When the child has been proved guilty and as some measure for his welfare is to be taken, the boy at that time is ordered to remand. The hearing is adjourned to a week or fortnight. The child is observed by an expert staff, i.e. Probation Officer or a social worker on whose recommendation the final disposal is made. Sometimes persons convicted are remanded for a few days and released.

These homes are mostly run by private welfare agencies and are supported both by the government and the public. The exact number of such remand homes in this country is not known except in Bombay

State, where their number was 30 in 1956, corresponding to 30 juvenile courts.

3. *Certified Schools*

In the states where Children Acts have been made applicable certified schools are established for the treatment of children. Here the children, except mentally sub-normal, are sent for long-term treatment. They are managed by voluntary bodies or by local authorities and are financed by public funds. There are generally two types of schools, i.e. junior and senior, junior for boys under 12 and senior for boys under 16. In junior schools generally general as well as technical education is imparted.[33] In Bombay in 1951 there were 9 government-managed and 19 privately-managed schools, whereas in Madras there were one senior and 2 junior certified schools for boys and one combined junior and senior managed by the government and 8 privately managed schools. The figures about other states were not available. The children are generally confined there up to a certain age limit and for about 2 to 3 years but the school authorities can make an early discharge. After their release they are put under the charge of a welfare or probation officer, who watches their activities.

4. *Auxiliary Homes*

Just like remand homes there are auxiliary homes attached to certified schools for the reception of inmates of certified schools. Here the delinquents who have been convicted are kept for sometime and studied by a social worker and then they are sent to the certified school according to the nature and aptitude of a young offender.

5. *Foster Homes*

They are specially for delinquent children, under 10, who cannot be sent to approved or certified schools unless the court is satisfied that they cannot be dealt with otherwise. These are generally run by voluntary agencies and the governments give grants to them.

6. *Fit Persons Institutions*

Under the Bombay Children Act 1938, the Government is autho-

[33] In certain countries there are three types of schools, junior for children under 13 years, intermediate for those between 13 and 15 and senior for those between 15 and 17 years. In junior primary education, in intermediate primary and technical education, and in senior only industrial training is given.

rized to notify "fit person" institutions, which have for their object the reception and protection of children or the prevention of cruelty to children and undertake to bring up or provide facilities for bringing up children entrusted to their care in conformity with their religion of birth. These non-government institutions are utilized for the reception and training of children dealt with under the Children Act. There are specific institutions for specific type of children. There were about 100 such institutions in the Bombay State in 1956.

7. *Uncared Children Institutions*

The children in the pre-delinquent or near delinquent stage, who are mostly found in a state of destitution or neglect are cared for in the various orphanages and children's institutions situated all over the country managed by private philanthropists. However, it is to be stated that many of these institutions do not maintain proper standards and need inspection. An Act known as the women's and children's Institutions (Licensing) Act of 1956 has been passed to control such institutions.

8. *Reformatory Schools*

In states where there are no Children Acts or they are not in force delinquent children are sent to Reformatory under the Reformatory Schools Act, 1897. These reformatory schools are meant for the education and vocational training of delinquent children with much regard to the type of crime committed. The delinquents are removed from bad environments and placed in the reformatory school for some time after which they can adopt some vocation learnt in the school. Young offenders, under 15, convicted of any offence punishable with transportation or imprisonment are detained for 3 to 7 years.

There were 5 reformatories in India in 1951, at Hissar, Jubbulpore, Hazaribagh, Lucknow and Secunderabad and were working satisfactorily.

9. *Borstal Institutions*

Borstal system is a system of detaining juvenile-adult delinquents, named from the first correctional purpose reformatory of the kind at Borstal. Under Borstal system special treatment is provided for adolescent offenders between the age of 15 to 21 years (between

16 and 21 years of age where Children Acts are in force). Thus, these are corrective institutions for the adolescent offenders not served by certified schools. There are two types of Borstal institutions, viz. close and open. Open institution is a camp or building in the open country with no surrounding wall. Closed institution is a converted prison building, where maximum security can be afforded when necessary, though the main gates generally remain open and a large part of the activities is carried on outside the walls. The training is industrial and other instructions, and varies according to the age, record and character of the inmate. The work is intentionally arduous, along with physical exercise and education so as to deter them from committing crime again. The training is different for boys and girls, such as in mixed farming, building and engineering for the former and laundry, cooking and housework for the latter.

The term of Borstal is 2 to 3 years but the date of release is decided by the Borstal authorities according to conduct and progress of the inmate. For after-care the person is attached to Borstal associate or Probation Officer, whose duties are to see that he is fitted in the trade for which he has been trained.

There are Borstal schools in Madras, Bengal, Bombay and Mysore states at present. There is no Borstal institution in U.P. in spite of the presence of Borstal Act. There is a juvenile jail in Bareilly which is run very much on the lines of a Borstal school where juvenile offenders under the age of 21 are sent for correctional purposes.

10. *Probation*

As method of Probation is applicable both to children and adult offenders, we shall deal with it in detail in the following chapter. It is used as a preventive of delinquency, where certain persons in danger of becoming offenders, are placed on probation. In the first instance of offence it is tried to bind the offender over for good behaviour, preferably under supervision. It is subject to a recognizance of a sum of money which his parents are required to pledge as security, that the conditions imposed will be complied with. There may also be specific conditions, e.g. to go to school, to live at a place, etc. It is generally for three years and may be for persons already convicted. There is provision for the use of this method under the various Children Acts. Children can be put under the supervision of Probation Officers or other guardians under the Madras Children Act.

New Policy After Independence

We have seen above that from 1920 onwards when the Children Acts were passed in the states of Madras and Bombay and which were adopted with some modification by other states there have been no visible efforts to deal more effectively with juvenile children. On the other hand, public consciousness regarding the problems of children has been gradually growing. But it did not gather the momentum it deserved. It was only after Independence that the work in the field of child welfare in general including that in respect of delinquent children gained further importance.

It was found that all the states had not yet passed Acts for the protection of children and even in those which passed the Acts these have not been implemented in a proper manner. The deficiencies of these acts were :

(*i*) In some acts a distinction is made between children and young persons. Those below 14 years of age are called children and between 14 to 16 are called young persons. The protective sections are applied to children only.

(*ii*) The acts have left a loop-hole in making the provision of necessary machinery optional. The children are still produced for trial before ordinary courts. Even where juvenile courts are established the jurisdiction to try children has not been exclusively conferred on them and it is open to the prosecution to bring children up before the ordinary courts.

(*iii*) Where Probation Officers have been appointed and are attached to the court, the magistrates continue to regard them as superfluous. This could be remedied by making the consideration of a Probation Officer's report compulsory.

(*iv*) The application of the protective sections of the Children Acts is left to the Magistrates, who, in the public mind, are invariably associated with crime and punishment.

(*v*) The Acts set a limit to the period of detention or to the age up to which children may be detained in institutional care. Thereafter the acts are silent. But follow-up and after-care is necessary if the child is to be rehabilitated in the real sense. All releases should continue to be under supervision for a time. Certain percentage of apprenticeships and employments must be kept at the disposal of Institutions for children to complete the programme of rehabilitation.

Such steps were necessary if the juvenile delinquents were to be rehabilitated in the real sense, problem children were to be corrected and neglected children to be protected.

It was with a view to tackle the problem of juvenile delinquents in an earnest way that in 1949 the Conference of Education Ministers called by the Government of India discussed the problem of juvenile delinquency at length and appointed a small committee of experts to go into it and frame a model Children Act.[34] The Government of India formulated a Children Bill on the recommendation of this expert committee and circulated it to the states for illiciting their opinion.

The Indian Parliament passed the Children Act in December 1960. The Act is, however, applicable to Union territories only. The Act applies to boys up to 16 and girls up to 18 years of age, but they can be committed and kept in the institutions under state care up to the age of 21.[35] The Act has two different bodies to deal with children. One the Children's Court and the other the Child Welfare Board, both consisting of "Bench of Magistrates". The latter deals with the larger number of children who are considered socially handicapped such as neglected, abandoned, deserted and destitutes. The Act also provides for separate institutions for neglected children and juvenile delinquents, known as Children's Homes and special schools. However, such watertight compartmentalization for the two types of children does not seem desirable as it is likely to attach stigma to the special schools and consequently to the inmates.

Some of the after-care institutions have also been opened in the country as was recommended by the Bureau of Delinquency Statistics and Research, Bombay in its Report. The Report pointed out that a Bal Audyogic Kendra should have shelter, food and proper employment and supervision for at least 100 juveniles and should have trades like carpentry, cane-work, powerloom, weaving, tailoring, etc. The Central Social Welfare Board has played an important role in encouraging voluntary agencies to take such type of programme. However, this type of programme still needs to be developed further.

[34] *Report on Delinquent Children and Juvenile Offenders in India,* Ministry of Education, Government of India, 1950, p. 6.

[35] *Seminar on Social Defence* (1965), p. 38.

In April 1965, the Planning Commission appointed a Study Group under the Chairmanship of Smt. M. Chandrasekhar to examine the problem of begging, vagrancy and juvenile delinquency and formulating schemes for its control for the Fourth Plan.

Regarding juvenile delinquency the Group noted that Children Acts were in force in all the states excepting Assam, Bihar, Orissa and Rajasthan. However, the Acts were not uniform and properly enforced. The Group recommended that all the above four states which do not have Children Acts should enact them on the lines of the Central Children Act, 1960 within the Fourth Plan period and the other states should enforce them properly and throughout their territory.[36] We hope that proper action will be taken by all the states as recommended by the Group to control delinquency.

Conclusion. "Many of the states today, although have passed Children Acts, have not been able to enforce them. In the matter of provision of machinery contemplated by the Act, progress in this direction has been very low. Some of the Acts themselves have left a loop-hole in making the provision of necessary machinery optional. It would even seem that a failure to provide such machinery was foreseen, for certain courts of a prescribed status are authorized to apply the provisions in the absence of a juvenile court. In some states children are still produced for trial before the ordinary courts. In some others even where juvenile courts are established, they do not have appropriate atmosphere and function in the same locale as the adult court. In some cases the jurisdiction to try children has not been exclusively conferred on the established juvenile courts and it is open to the prosecution to bring children before the ordinary criminal court. This could not have been the original intention of the Children Acts and the defects in the drafting has to be remedied."[37] Some states have not been able to implement the Act lly because of lack of appropriate probation system and institutions. In some cases children are still kept in mixed institutions. Only 5 to 6 states have regular juvenile courts with appropriate machinery to implement the Children Acts.

[36] *Social Defence*, January, 1966.

[37] Basu, Smt. Sita, "Juvenile Delinquency, After-Care and Correctional Practices" in *Seminar on Social Defence* (1965), p. 39.

CHAPTER V

ADULT OFFENDERS

THE ADULT offender differs from the juvenile delinquent in that he is older and his rebellious pattern of personality is more firmly established. His acts of rebellion cover a wider range and tend to include violations of social norms seldom found among juveniles. The wider range of offences makes it difficult to compare adult with juvenile delinquents, since the more heterogeneous categories tend to show the greatest expansion at the expense of the more homogeneous. The adult offenders are the recidivists who have committed crime time and again. As Elliott and Merrill observe, "Not only are adult male prisoners those with a long history of petty juvenile delinquencies, but approximately half have had a reformatory, prison or jail record as adults. According to the statistics for 1937, almost half that is 49.2 per cent of the total prisoners for whom there was information, had been formerly sentenced and committed to juvenile institutions or to jails or prisons. It is possible that there were others equally guilty whose earlier offences had escaped either sentence or commitment but who were actually, if not legally recidivists."[1]

Classification of Criminals

Criminals have been classified by different sociologists and criminologists on different basis. This classification has been done on the basis of (1) causation of crime, (2) personality of the criminal, (3) type and gravity of offences committed, (4) on class basis, etc. on the basis of causes of crime which we have discussed in detail in Chapter III. Lombroso classified criminals into four main categories, i.e. (1) born criminals, (2) criminals by passion, (3) insane criminals, and (4) occasional criminals. These were again subdivided into various categories.[2] Elliott and Merrill divide these criminals into three groups, i.e. born criminals, the criminaloids

[1] Elliott, M. A. and Merrill, F. E., *op. cit.*, p. 165.

[2] For details see Sethna, M. J., *Society and the Criminal* (1964), pp. 90-97.

or occasional criminals, and criminals due to some mental defects. The occasional criminal is not a born criminal but because of circumstances there have developed criminal habits. However, there is no validity in such a classification as we have already seen that each criminal is a unique person with unique roles in his group contacts. The other basis on which we can logically classify criminals is the type of offences they have committed or the seriousness of the offences. On the basis of severity of offences criminals are classified as felons or misdemeanants. The severity of offence depends upon the social values attached to any act. Some social values are almost universally accepted. Out of human experience certain of these values, and rules and regulations pertaining to them have come to be regarded as more important than others. For example, murder, rape, burglary, counterfeiting are all rather generally regarded as serious offences. Other offences vary with culture. Social change, changes in social opinion and the conception of right and wrong, political ideologies, and all such things affect crime and the criminal code. Thus, on the basis of severity of offences we call an offender a felon or misdemeanant. In general a misdemeanant is one who has committed a petty offence, which is punishable by fine or imprisonment in a local jail. The term felon is applied to serious offences punishable by death or by imprisonment. But there can be no unanimity as to the definition of felonious conduct, because an act which may be considered felonious in one country may be considered misdemeanour in the other. The other classification can be according to specific offences such as crime against property, sex crime, crime against life, crime against traffic laws, liquor laws, etc. or the particular type of crime committed. Thus, we call a person a murderer, a thief, a burglar or a pick-pocket according to the type of crime committed by him. But such a classification does not give any explanation as to why a man commits a particular type of crime and for this we have to analyse the causes of crime. Sutherland has given yet another important classification on the basis of class to which the offender belongs. White-collar class of criminals who belong to upper class and generally escape punishment, and ordinary criminals or the lower class criminals who come chiefly from under-privileged economic and social classes and whose behaviour is condemned and punished by law.

There is yet another classification, whether the criminal is a casual, habitual or serious offender.

EXTENT OF CRIME IN INDIA

We have already pointed out in the last chapter the various limitations inherent in knowing the exact volume of crime in any country. Even otherwise the crime statistics available from different states of India were not uniform. It was only in 1953 when the Annual Conference of the Deputy Inspector General of C. I. D. decided for the first time that the Government of India should standardize the crime statistics in the country and these should be published annually by the Director, Intelligence Bureau, Ministry of Home Affairs. The number of cognizable offences reported under the Indian Penal Code from 1948 to 1963 may be seen from the following table.

TABLE 5(*a*)

NUMBER OF COGNIZABLE CRIMES REPORTED IN INDIA FROM 1948 TO 1963

(*in thousands*)

S. No.	*Year*	*No.*	*S. No.*	*Year*	*No.*	*S. No.*	*Year*	*No.*
1.	1948	626	7.	1954	556	13.	1960	606
2.	1949	654	8.	1955	535	14.	1961	625
3.	1950	635	9.	1956	585	15.	1962	674
4.	1951	649	10.	1957	581	16.	1963	659
5.	1952	612	11.	1958	591			
6.	1953	601	12.	1959	582			

From the above table it will be seen that there has been wide variation in the volume of crime from year to year and that it particularly decreased in the years between 1953 to 1955. No scientific explanation for this variation can be given unless the various causes leading to crime in each year are thoroughly examined. However, a number of states in 1956 attributed increases in crime due to better reporting facilities made possible by opening new police stations and improvement in communication.[3]

Besides these serious crimes which are now classified by the Government of India under the following main heads recognized by the United Nations Social Welfare Board and the International Police Organization to have a uniform procedure (see table 2) there are many other minor crimes committed by the people.

[3] Intelligence Bureau, Government of India, *Crime in India*, 1956 (1958), p. 1.

TABLE 5(*b*)

COGNIZABLE CRIMES IN INDIA (1958-1963)

Total cognizable crimes	1958	1963
1. Murder	10,661	10,754
2. Kidnapping and abduction	6,043	6,924
3. Dacoity	4,658	4,997
4. Robbery	7,120	7,694
5. House-breaking	1,24,695	1,37,025
6. Theft (cattle	23,832	23,557
ordinary)	2,12,271	2,18,930
7. Riots	24,942	28,114
8. Criminal Breach of Trust	16,017	18,438
9. Cheating	9,503	8,854
10. Counterfeiting	555	289
11. Miscellaneous	1,50,690	2,40,629
(*a*) Against persons	1,05,893	N.A.
(*b*) Against property	41,638	N.A.
(*c*) Others	3,159	N.A.
Total	5,90,987	6,58,830

For example in 1958 the total number of criminal cases reported in India was 31,39,115 which included besides cognizable offences mentioned above, road violations, gambling, prohibition crime, prostitution, vagrancy, public nuisances, etc.[4] Even if we ignore the bulk of petty prosecutions, the number of crimes committed is very large.

Again there is a variation in the incidence of crime per lakh of population in different states. For example in 1959 the highest incidence of crime per lakh of population was 275 in Madhya Pradesh and the lowest was 102 in Uttar Pradesh.

However, it is interesting to note that rate of crime in India was much lower than in some of the industrially advanced countries. This is evident from the figures compiled by the International Police Commission for the year 1952 [see table 5(*c*)].

Causes of Crime

We have already discussed the causes which lead to criminal behaviour in detail in Chapter III under biological, mental, social

[4] Central Statistical Organization, Government of India, *Statistical Abstract of the Indian Union*, 1965, p. 681.

and economic factors and need no repetition. The causes leading to white-collar criminality and the possible methods of controlling them have been discussed in Chapter XIV.

TABLE 5(c)

VOLUME OF CRIME REPORTED PER HUNDRED THOUSANDS OF POPULATION FOR THE YEAR 1952[5]

Country	*Murder*	*Serious theft including robbery and burglary*	*Simple*	*Total number of offences*
1. U. K.	0.8	258.6	910.7	1342.2
2. U. S. A.	4.7	325.2	985.5	1322.4
3. France	4.8	64.8	365.9	1484.3
4. Japan	3.3	6.9	135.7	1605.5
5. India	2.9	46.0	69.2	165.1

Prevention of Crime

The crime prevention programme may be discussed under two heads, viz. prevention programme and treatment or correctional programme. The former is used to avoid the occurrence of crime and to mitigate its causes and the latter to restore the individual to a normal condition of living after he has committed the crime. In the preventive programme the best method to control crime is to check its occurrence in the childhood period and for that we have suggested various methods in the last chapter. Besides those measures, the other programmes suggested by Aschaffenburg are : "to curb the sale, distribution, and use of alcohol ; to relieve the wretchedness of the lower classes by eliminating overcrowded housing and by educating the masses to appreciate the values of family life and intellectual pleasures ; to care for the sick and incurable ; to regulate aid to the poor ; to establish unemployment offices ; to increase the use of social insurance against sickness, accidents, and unemployment, to foster compulsory saving accounts; to curb illegitimate births, in order to prevent the demoralization of children ; to care for released prisoners especially in obtaining work for them ; to develop adequate policing and energetic prosecuting along with a strengthening of public feeling for strict

[5] Rao, S. Venugopala. *op. cit.*, p. 9.

observance of law and the abandonment of publicity of crimes and trials in the press." Mr. Rao points out that although measures like development of predelinquent contacts through child guidance clinics and visiting teachers system may be useful to spot out criminal tendencies at an early stage, yet their use in this country can be limited. He lays stress on trained and adequate police force and the revival of old village organizations known as vigilance committees to obtain public cooperation in the prevention of crime. These organizations should consist of select village elders who would be expected to keep an eye on local bad hats and check the movement of suspicious strangers. Similar organizations will also be needed in towns and cities.[6] But in spite of these performances it may not be possible to check crime completely because of complex factors leading to crime, and treatment programme will be necessary for those who have once committed a crime.

Treatment of Adult Offenders

From Punishment to Reformation. It was pointed out in Chapter III that the conception of crime has gone under a revolutionary change with the discovery of new factors leading to crime particularly the environmental factors. This has brought change in the treatment of criminals particularly the juvenile, though there has been some change in the treatment of adult offenders as well. In the case of juvenile delinquents attempt is made towards reforming and re-educating them instead of punishing them. In the case of adult offenders also the same attitude is now developing, though not much is done in practical life. Despite the reformatory motive which prompted the founders of present day reformatories there has not been any thorough instance upon adjusting the behaviour problems of the adult criminals. So far efforts have been made to provide reformatories only for youthful and first offenders. But there is no reason why methods suitable for dealing with juvenile delinquents should not be applied to adult offenders.

It is generally held that the juvenile is too young to be held accountable for his misconduct, as he is the victim of circumstances over which he has had no control, and everything possible should be done to secure his adjustment. But even the adults are very often the victims of circumstances and become a greater problem only

[6] *Ibid.*, p. 177.

after their institutionalization. In order to understand why this movement of reformation has been a slow one we will have to study some of the methods adopted from time to time in dealing with the offenders. These may broadly be discussed under four heads : (*i*) Justifications of Punishment, (*ii*) Forms of Punishment, (*iii*) Trends in Punishment, and (*iv*) Types of Prisons.

(*i*) *Justifications of Punishment*. We are not concerned here with the history of different concepts and modes of punishment in different societies which have gone under many changes with the progress of society and the readers are advised to see some basic books on penalogy.[7] In the modern age the concepts and modes of punishment are an accumulation through the ages. New ideas and patterns of punishment have come into circulation while others have lost currency. The reasons why society punishes are bound up with several conceptions, attitudes and values as well as with more recent justifications and motives. As given by Professor Reckless "some of the still existing justifications of punishment, some of them antique and some of them more recent in origin, may be listed as follows : (1) retribution, (2) atonement, (3) deterrence, (4) protection, and (5) reformation. These stereotyped rationalizations justifying the use of punishment, are current in the modern society today."[8] The common man usually justifies the use of punishment mainly in terms of retribution and atonement, which are undoubtedly the oldest justifications. The more sophisticated persons usually justify punishment in terms of deterrence and protection, while the reformers express a faith in the use of punishment as a means of reformation.

Retribution is probably the oldest and the most ancient justification for punishment, according to which a wrong is righted by an offender's receiving his "just deserts". It involves a "get even" spirit —an eye for an eye and a tooth for a tooth and is based on instinctive human reactions ; which may be called wrath, anger, resentment or revenge. Atonement or expiation is likewise an ancient justification for punishment. The offender is made to atone or pay reparation for his crime through suffering. The demand for expiation is generally as frequent as is the demand for retribution and both

[7] Kindly see Reckless, W.C., *Criminal Behaviour*, Chapters XIV to XVIII, and Barnes, H.E. and Teeters, N.K., *New Horizons in Criminology*, Chapters XVII to XXI.

[8] Reckless, W. C., *Criminal Behaviour* (1940), p. 270.

motives are usually found re-enforcing one another. The trend in modern society to do away with physical torture and to withdraw the application of punishment from the public eye has lessened to some extent the force of expiation though the community is still able to take satisfaction in the fact that justice has been done although hidden from view. Deterrence has the assumption that if society failed to bring culprits to justice and to punish them for their misdeeds, it would thereby encourage crime and consequently the crime will increase. Punishment is, therefore, supposed to hold crime in check to have a deterrent effect on criminal behaviour. In modern societies, deterrence is probably the most apparent and plausible of the still existing justification for punishment. Beccaria, one of the foremost leaders of penal reforms, observes, "The intent of punishment should not be to torture the criminal or to undo the crime (expiation) but the purpose should be to prevent others from committing a like offence."[9] Protection is linked with notion that punishment is necessary, to protect society from criminal acts of plunderings, and has been growing in importance especially since the increasing utilization of imprisonment as a form of sentence. While imprisonment is supported by all the conceptions justifying punishment in general, it is also thought of as a safety device. Confined behind prison walls, the offender is considered unable to harm society.

Reformation which is the modern concept of punishment developed in the era of widespread use of prison sentences. Later on reformatories were established with a programme of work, education, recreation and religious services, in order to assist in rehabilitating the offender and preparing him for his entrance back into law-abiding society. The indeterminate sentence, with a mark-off of so much time from the full length of the sentence for good behaviour in prison, and the accompanying use of parole as a form of conditional release before full expiration of the sentence were also additions to the modern prison system, calculated to foster quick reformation of the offender.

(*ii*) *Forms of Punishment*. The forms of punishment and the ways in which they were executed have also undergone a considerable change in the course of time. The most common forms of punishment in times past have been death, physical torture, mutilation,

[9] Beccaria, C. B., *An Essay on Crimes and Punishments* (1728), p. 51.

branding, public humiliation, fines, forfeiture of property, banishment, transportation and imprisonment.[10] But this list is not exhaustive. Also every form of punishment has had several variations and applications. For example, the death penalty has included hanging, execution, electrocution, crucifixion, burning on the stake and so on. Imprisonment has included incarceration in dungeons, guard-houses, galleys, jails, workhouses, houses of correction and penitentiaries.

Some of the above-listed forms of punishment are more characteristic of advanced than of unadvanced societies. Imprisonment, for example, rarely occurs in primitive societies. The idea of imprisonment for punishment of offenders appears to have developed from the practice of providing detention for prisoners of war, although there is no certainty about such a contention. In advanced societies, that developed tribunals of justice, some sort of detention places or jails were needed to confine offenders until they were called for trial. In spite of this, imprisonment as a penal sentence did not become prevalent in Europe until the nineteenth century. It grew as a substitute for the death penalty, transportation, exile and public degradation—particularly the death penalty. As something has to be done instead of death penalty and other sentences, workhouses, houses of correction and penitentiaries arose to take care of the unexecuted and unpardoned criminals. Lengthy penal sentences required a convict prison or a penitentiary—a prison that was not a place of detention while awaiting trial and not a place of short sentences, but a place for a lengthy stay. In other words, modern prisons had to await the development of a concept of imprisonment as a punitive measure, to fill a need not provided for by any other punitive measure and to take up the slack in the declining usage of the older forms of punishment. But important, too, is the fact that the concept of imprisonment and of the convict prison is related to reform agitations that arose at the end of eighteenth century and aimed at humanizing the penal system and the evils of indiscriminate mass congregation of prisoners in the jails and the writings of Montesquieu, Beccaria, John Howard, Jeremy Bentham and many other philosophers and agitators for social and political reforms were in large part responsible for the motivating power behind the reformation of the penal system.

[10] Reckless, W. C., *op. cit.*, p. 265.

Dr. Sutherland has made another classification for modes of punishment into four fundamental types : financial loss, physical torture, social degradation and removal from the group.[11] Under financial loss would come fines, forfeitures, compensation, and such like. Under physical torture would come flogging, mutilation, burning, and all methods of inducing physical pain. Under social degradation would be included such methods as branding, the use of pillories and stocks, etc. and under removal from the group would come execution, imprisonment, banishment and transportation. However, one would find that all these forms are overlapping one another as, for example, imprisonment is often accompanied by considerable physical torture and removal from the group involves serious loss of status.

This classification of the forms of punishment may serve a useful purpose in indicating the range of application, but we are more concerned with specific patterns of punishment. For example, it is not enough to be aware that a society uses imprisonment, but, it is vital to understand that it sentences offenders on such and such terms to such and such penal institutions for such and such penal offences. Thus, the incarceration of an offender in a dungeon is a far different thing from sending an individual to a juvenile reformatory. Both are forms of imprisonment, or forms of removal from the group, but these two specific usages are markedly different in pattern.

(iii) Trends in Punishment. Unless a society completely overhauls most of its basic institutions in a comparative short space of time as has been done in Russia or China the system of punishment is likely to change slowly. Replacements and modifications in the system are sped up considerably by reform agitation, but such agitations are very rare as penal reforms have never been a mass movement. In consequence the changes in the penal system have been slow. However, the most important trends in the field of punishment have been (1) the mitigation of punishment, (2) the decline in the severity of punishment, (3) the individualization of punishment, and (4) the substitution for punishment.[12] For example, allowing some reduction in time of sentence as a reward for good behaviour, indeterminate sentence empowering the prison authorities to increase or decrease sentence within a minimum and maximum

[11] Sutherland, E. H., *Criminology* (1924), p. 317.
[12] Reckless, W. C., *Criminal Behaviour*, p. 279.

limit given by the court, parole system (a conditional release for imprisonment), probation (suspended sentence) and such other methods are instances in point. Similarly, crime was first regarded as an abstract juridical entity, dissociated from the circumstances attending its commission and the personality of the offender, and the law had to determine the penalty for each offence. A system of punishment graduated in proportion to the gravity of the crime was next adopted. However, gradually insanity, nonage, drunkenness and coercion had to be admitted as legitimate defences in determining culpability. From these it has been a short step to adjust punishment to the offender taking into account the offender's nature, background, impulses, handicaps and extenuations in determining his punishment. This has taken long to establish itself and though now it is theoretically considered sound its practical application is still in check.

(*iv*) *Individualization of Treatment.* Individualization of treatment was used at three stages, i.e. prior to commitment, during commitment, and after release. The greater use in the first direction means greater use of probation and rehabilitation of the individual offender before the categoric execution of penalties. In the second case, it means progressive use of the individualized treatment programme in institutions to offset the limitations of mass handling. In the last case, it meant a more extended use of elastic release procedure with supervision for individual cases to ensure greater post-institutional adjustment to society. It is also to be pointed out that if this trend towards the individualization of punishment is able to proceed further, it will succeed in dissolving or displacing retributive punitive measures and in substituting treatment for what was once called punishment. The substitute practices for traditional punitive measures will be individual treatment and if by such a method the control of crime can be achieved progressively, crime will be looked upon much like a physical disease, not in terms of legal responsibility, but in terms of a restoration of the individual to a healthy state. As Gandhiji observes, "Jails must be converted into hospitals for their treatment and cure. The jail staff should be transformed into physicians. The prisoner should be made to feel that they are his friends."[13] In fact, commission of crime is a sign of disease

[13] Planning Commission, Government of India, *Social Legislation—Its Role in Social Welfare* (1956), p. 389.

and the causes of particular diseases should be investigated and removed.

It is in the light of these developments that we have to view the programmes being taken for the treatment of adult offenders in this country. However, before we deal with that programme let us mention in brief the two types of prisons which came in vogue in the beginning.

(*v*) *Types of Prisons.* In the beginning there were two types of prisons. One was the Pennsylvania system and the other Auburn system. In the former case the idea was to have solitary confinement to aid penitence and reform. There was separation of the hardened from the petty offenders and of men from women. Here labour was provided in separate cells while work in common during the day and separation in cells at night were the principal tenets of the latter system. These systems were gradually replaced by the Irish system or the progressive stage system, which converted the prisons into an adult reformatory the purpose of which was to train the prisoners to resist temptation and lead a law-abiding life after discharge.

CORRECTIONAL PROGRAMME IN INDIA

The programme for the treatment of adult offenders being undertaken in this country may be discussed under the following heads : (*i*) Prison Administration and Reformation, (*ii*) Probation, (*iii*) Parole, (*iv*) Other alternatives to Punishment, and (*v*) After-care of Prisoners.

(*i*) *Prison Administration and Reformation*

Brief History of Prison Administration

Prison has been defined as "a place properly arranged and equipped for the reception of persons who by legal process are committed to it for safe custody while awaiting trial or for punishment".[14] As places of detention, prisons are old institutions ; as places of punishment they are, however, comparatively modern. Imprisonment at that time was not the common form of punishment and the usual punishments were beheading, mutilation, branding, fines, confiscation of property and banishment. The use of prisons as places of detention has continued since old times, but their use as

[14] *The Oxford Dictionary,* Vol. VIII, p. 1385.

a form of punishment for certain type of offenders initiated towards the middle of the sixteenth century.

In India, too, the early prisons were only places of detention and offenders were detained until trial and judgement. With the advent of British rule the administrative structure in the country began to assume a new form. At first little alteration was made in the existing legal system. The Regulating Act was passed in 1773 which established the Supreme Court at Calcutta to exercise "all civil, criminal, admiralty and ecclesiastical jurisdiction, and indicated the intention of the British Government to introduce English rules of laws and English superintendence of law and justice".[15] The English criminal law which was first applied to Englishmen came to be applied to Indians. The Indian Penal Code and the Criminal Procedure Code which had long been in preparation were enacted in 1859 and 1860 respectively. The Indian Penal Code defined each and every offence and prescribed punishment for it, while the Criminal Procedure Code laid the procedure for prosecuting the criminals. The imprisonment as a form of punishment (or the modern prison system) which was first applied in India in 1773, came to be applied on uniform basis throughout India in 1860.

The Criminal Procedure Code of India requires that a Court convicting any offender must pass sentence on him according to the Indian Penal Code unless it proposes to proceed under section 562 which provides for the release of certain convicted offenders on probation of good conduct. The punishments that may be inflicted on offenders convicted under the Indian Penal Code may be death, transportation (it has been replaced by imprisonment since 1st January, 1956), imprisonment rigorous or simple, forfeiture of property or fine. In addition, a sentence of whipping[16] can also be passed. The appropriate government may remit the whole or any part of the punishment without conditions or upon conditions accepted by the prisoners. Similarly, any order of the criminal court restricting the liberty or imposing any liability upon any person or property may be suspended, remitted or commuted by the appropriate government.

[15] Bhushan, Vidya, "Prison Administration in U. P.", Unpublished Thesis (1953), p. 12.

[16] Under the Whipping Act 1909, Whipping was provided as an additional mode of punishment but it was subsequently abolished in 1955 under Whipping Act of 1955. See *Social Legislation—Its Role in Social Welfare* (1956), p. 294.

The Institution of Jails, as is understood these days, is of British origin and was introduced in India as part of British administration. Before the institution of jail, the system of punishment did not require any financial burden on the part of the government. The Directors of East India Company were reluctant to spend money on jails and although jails were modelled on British lines, there was not enough accommodation and there was inadequate food, clothing and medical attention for the prisoners. Thus, the conditions in jails were extremely bad.

In 1835 Lord Macaulay drew attention of the Government of India to the terrible conditions of Indian jails. On his recommendations a Committee was appointed to look into the conditions of Indian jails and the Committee submitted its report in 1838. The main recommendations of this Committee were : (1) that central jails should be built to accommodate prisoners of over one year's sentence and that they should not accommodate more than 1,000 prisoners each, (2) that Inspector-Generals of Prisons should be appointed in all Provinces, and (3) that sufficient buildings should be provided in all jails to accommodate prisoners comfortably. In pursuance of the recommendations of this committee many central prisons were constructed in various Provinces and some other reforms were also carried out.

The Second All-India Committee was appointed in 1864. This Committee also made many useful recommendations some of which are : (1) It fixed minimum space for each prisoner in Jail, viz. 54 superficial feet and 640 cubic feet per prisoner. (2) It recommended for improvements in diet, clothing and bedding and insisted upon regular inspection of prisoners. (3) Employment of Medical Officers to be in charge of central prisons and district jails. (The average death rate in 1864 amongst jail prisoners was 40 per thousand and the Committee attributed this high mortality mainly to the absence of medical supervision resulting in many unfit prisoners being employed on hard labour.) (4) Every central jail should have cellular accommodation for 15 per cent of its population. (5) The juveniles should be kept separate from other prisoners and that they should be given education.

The Third Jail Committee was appointed in 1877 and reviewed jail administration in general. It framed certain rules for keeping accounts in jail, method of obtaining supplies, etc.

The Fourth All-India Committee was appointed in 1889, which

laid down elaborate rules for prison administration. The committee also recommended the separation of undertrial prisoners and the classification of prisoners into casual and habitual. It also recommended building of a hospital in each jail.

The next All-India Committee was the Prison Conference of 1892. It resurveyed the whole jail administration and laid down further detailed rules. The Prison Act of 1894 was mainly the outcome of the efforts of this conference. Thus, the Prison Act of 1894 came into being which governs all the prisons in the country. The act restricted and regulated the use of whipping, cellular confinement and penal diet. It provided for the classification of different types of offenders and tried to secure uniformity of treatment of all offenders in jail. The detailed provisions of this act have been discussed later on. However, it is to be pointed out that in spite of all this "it was the idea of deterrence which influenced prison policy until the appointment of the Indian Jails Committee in 1919. The prisoners were engaged in unproductive, irksome and hard labour and were subjected to a prison discipline enforced with vigour, on pain of severe corporal punishment, penal diet, etc."[17]

The sixth and the last Jail Committee was appointed in 1919 and submitted its report in 1920. This is a very valuable report and touches upon all aspects of jail administration such as prison staff, separation and classification of prisoners, prison labour and manufactures, discipline and punishment, reformatory influences in prison, prison hygiene, medical administration, aid to prisoners on release, probation and Borstal treatment. With regard to the ultimate object of prison treatment the Committee observed, "That prisoners while in prison should be brought under such influences as will not only deter them from committing further crimes but will also have a reforming influence on their character is the next principle, which should, we conceive, be accepted. This proposition, has now been established by the general concert of penologists throughout the world, and is today questioned by hardly anyone. The general tendency of modern ideas is towards the view that severity alone has little effect in reclaiming the criminal, and that what is required is rather humanizing and improving the influences which will lead to the prisoners realizing the essentially evil results

[17] Planning Commission, Government of India, *Social Legislation* (1956), p. 390.

of crime on himself and others, and will result in a real reformation of character and purpose. The place which the various reformatory agencies, religion, education, rewards for good conduct, the hope of release, the encouragement of industry, and the like should occupy in any scheme is a matter of detail."[18]

Soon thereafter, on the introduction of the Montagu-Chelmsford Reforms, jails and other like services became state subjects. The Provincial Governments showed great enthusiasm for jail reform and under the influence of the recommendations of the above committee greater attention was paid to the provision of better food, living conditions, sanitation and health measures. Education, recreation and religious and moral instructions became a feature of jail life, supplying the reformative influence. Amenities like letters, interviews and remissions were made more liberal. Separate jails were established for habitual offenders. Revising Boards were appointed to recommend the reduction of long-term sentences of individual convicts. The philosophy of prison labour underwent a change, providing for the reformation and rehabilitation of the offenders. Several states appointed a series of Jail Reform Committees with a view to improving the prisoners' lot in the jails under their jurisdiction. The Committees appointed in different states were Punjab Jail Reform Committees (1919 and 1948), Uttar Pradesh Jail Committees (1929, 1938 and 1946), Bombay (1939 and 1946), Mysore (1941). Bihar (1948), Madras (1950) and Travancore Cochin (now Kerala) (1953)[19]. Apart from these committees, Conferences of Inspector-Generals of Prisons have been held from time to time. The suggestions made by them relate to administration of jails, classification of prisoners, introduction of remission system and concessions to prisoners, abolition of short-term imprisonment, better treatment to prisoners, etc.[20] However, only some of the recommendations could be implemented due to paucity of funds as we shall presently see.

As a result of the recommendation of the above committees and conferences, in most of the states prisoners are now getting soap and oil every week. Schemes for the eradication of illiteracy among prisoners have been introduced. The number of male nurses to

18 Report of the Indian Jails Committee (1919).

19 Planning Commission, *Plans and Prospects of Social Welfare in India 1951-1961* (1963), p. 143.

20 *Ibid.*, p. 144.

look after sick prisoners has been increased. Jails have been electrified with a view to enabling prisoners to read and write and play games before light-out time. In some states in certain more important jails welfare officers have been appointed to organize and promote welfare activities for the prisoners.

Open air jails have been set up in Kerala, Uttar Pradesh, Maharashtra and Rajasthan wherein prisoners are allowed to work in free conditions of life.[21] Wage earning schemes have been introduced in the jails in Assam, Bihar, Kerala, Madhya Pradesh, Maharashtra, Madras, Mysore, Rajasthan, Uttar Pradesh, West Bengal and Delhi, whereby prisoners can earn while working in the jails. They are allowed to send part of their earnings to their families and dependents. The theory of "hard labour, hard fare and hard bed" as a part of treatment in jails was no longer good. This was the position before the First Five-Year Plan. At this place it would be appropriate to discuss the working of the prisons in some of the important states to have a more clear idea about the actual position.

Working of Prisons

The Working of prisons in various states is governed by the Prison Act of 1894. Therefore, it would be appropriate to discuss in brief the main features of this Act before dealing with the working of prisons.

The Prisons Act of 1894

In order to provide for the convicts who are under imprisonment, the first Prisons Act was passed in 1894. The main provisions in this Act are :

Prison and its Officers. Under this act, a prison is defined as a jail or a place prescribed by the State Government for the temporary or permanent detention of prisoners, but places for the detention of persons while in police custody and subsidiary jails are excluded from the definition. Under this act it is the duty of the State Government to provide accommodation for the prisoners in prisons constructed and regulated in accordance with the provision of this act. There shall be an Inspector-General of Prisons for each state. For each prison there shall be a Superintendent, a Medical Officer, a Medical Subordinate, a Jailor—and such other officers as may be necessary.

[21] *Ibid*., p. 144.

Separation of Prisoners. There must be separation between male and female prisoners. Male prisoners under the age of 21 shall be separated altogether from other prisoners ; those that have arrived at the age of puberty shall be separated from those who have not ; unconvicted criminal prisoners shall be kept apart from the convicted and civil prisoners from criminal ones.

Convicted Prisoners. Convicted criminal prisoners may be confined together or individually in cells. No cell shall be used unless furnished with the means of enabling the prisoners to communicate at any time with the Officer. Every prisoner so confined shall be visited at least once a day by the Medical Officer or medical subordinate.

Employment of Prisoners. No criminal prisoner shall be kept on work for more than nine hours a day. The Medical Officer shall examine them while employed from time to time and their weight shall be recorded on the history ticket once a fortnight. A prisoner shall not be employed on labour if in the opinion of the Medical Officer his health will suffer on that account. He may be given such other labour as the Medical Officer considers suitable. Criminal prisoners sentenced to simple imprisonment shall be provided with employment, if they desire, but they shall not be punished for neglect of work except by such alteration in the scale of diet as may be permitted by the rules in the case of neglect of work.

Health. Sick prisoners and prisoners desiring to see the medical subordinate shall be reported to him without delay and all directions of the Medical Officer regarding alteration of discipline or treatment shall be given effect to and all such particulars shall be entered on the history ticket. Every prison must have a place for the reception of such prisoners.

Prison Offences. Various acts committed by a prisoner are declared as prison offences under this act, such as wilful disobedience of prison regulations ; any assault or use of criminal force ; use of insulting or threatening language ; immoral, indecent or disorderly behaviour ; continuously refusing to work ; filing, cutting, altering or removing handcuffs, fetters or bars without due authority ; wilful damage to prison property, etc. For these offences the Superintendent of the prison may determine and award any of the punishments mentioned in the act, such as formal warning ; changing of labour to a more irksome or severe form ; loss of privileges under the remission system, substitution of gunny or other coarse fabric for clothing ; imposition of handcuffs or fetters ; separate confinement ; penal diet ; whipping, etc.

The Prisons Act of 1894 governs the administration of all jails other than subsidiary jails, where short-term prisoners are confined.[22] It leaves all details of internal administration to be determined by rules made by the State Governments. There are, thus, wide disparities in standards and methods between one state and another.

Bombay. "In a pamphlet on jail reforms issued in February 1954, by the Director of Publicity, Government of Bombay, it is stated, that the State jail policy accepts and acts on the view that the basic purpose of jail administration is not retribution or revenge, but reformation and rehabilitation of men and women who find themselves in jail for various reasons. The jail reforms are meant to give human treatment to prisoners without in any way affecting the institutional discipline."[23] The Jail Administration Report for 1953 reports that out of an average daily population of 20,000 only 338 people were given bar-fetters in 1953. Cellular confinement and whipping were never used in recent years ; penal diet, hard labour and sack cloth are abolished by rule. Several amenities like radio, canteen, games, etc. are provided. All Central and District jails provide educational facilities. In some jails wages are paid at one-fifth of the rates for similar work outside. During the year under review 865 prisoners remitted a total sum of Rs. 12,000 to their families.

West Bengal. It is reported that there has been a considerable liberalization in the treatment of prisoners in the jails. Sack cloth, penal diet, whipping and bar-fetters are given up in practice. Cellular confinement is very rare ; hard labour is given up altogether by rule. Adult education is introduced. Radios are provided, documentary films are shown, magazines and newspapers are made available in all central jails. In the central jails, prisoners themselves look after the preparation and distribution of food, maintain discipline, look after sanitation amenities and sports under a panchayat system. They also recommend punishment in case of minor indiscipline

[22] The law relating to all prisoners confined by order of Court including those confined in subsidiary jails was passed in 1900, known as the Prisoners Act of 1900.

[23] Planning Commission, Government of India. *Social Legislation* (1956), p. 295.

and their recommendations are generally accepted. In three Calcutta jails, wages are paid for all work done.[24]

Uttar Pradesh. Uttar Pradesh is one of the pioneer states in introducing some revolutionary reforms in the prison system after Independence. The first step in the direction of providing facilities and training for self-reliance to prisoners was taken in 1949, when the Central Prison, Lucknow, was converted into a model prison. The Prison has a reception centre where a detail personal study of the new entrant, being a casual prisoner, is made through enquiries regarding personal case history, family relationship, social and economic background, psychological and mental defects, police reports, judgement and other material. He is processed through a detailed programme of educational, physical and vocational training for 6 months, during which period his honesty, industry and aptitude for co-operation are judged. When he passes through the tests successfully and is found fit, he is given the choice to join the model prison, where he has to work on his own and pay to the state his cost of maintenance. In the prison there are cottage industries, vegetables and agricultural farming, etc. to give them work similar to and on similar terms as outside the prison in order to develop self-reliance. Out of the sale proceeds of the produce they are required to pay for the raw materials used, the rent of land and their own maintenance cost. The balance is at their disposal which they can remit to their dependents or may use for purchases from the jail canteen which is run by the inmates themselves on co-operative basis. Every effort is made to promote friendly feeling between the staff and the prisoners, who manage their own affairs through a panchayat. They are thereby entrusted with responsibility. From the security point of view the Model Prison is a mixed institution, where prisoners can be kept under maximum, moderate and minimum security depending on the individual's progress. They are gradually admitted to higher privileges and at one stage they are allowed to work outside the jail both day and night without watch and ward. The best-behaved are also allowed to pay short visits to the city or other places of attraction. Dramatic performances, cinema-shows, lectures, debates, musical entertainments, religious celebrations and games are available to the inmates. Thus, they are prepared to take their place in society after release.

[24] Planning Commission, Government of India, *Social Legislation* (1956), p. 256.

The Open Prisoners' Camp. Another bold and new experiment in the treatment of prisoners was conceived in 1952 by Dr. Sampurnanand, the then Home Minister. It strikes a departure from the age-old practice of confining prisoners within well-guarded buildings and putting them to hard fruitless labour. No doubt, in recent years prisoners have been engaged in remunerative production whether in prisons or convict settlements, but even this does not take the prisoners' mind off the situations and conditions in which they were forced to commit crime, nor does it enable them to adjust themselves without stress to outside conditions when released.

In this scheme about 2,000 prisoners were employed in the construction of a dam over the River Chandraprabha, 12 miles from Chakia, in Benares District—a dam which will irrigate a vast area and obviate floods. The prisoners are housed in tents or hutments in the open, untrammelled by guards and are working on the construction of that dam. The camp has been named as Sampurnanand Camp after the name of its originator.

There is a variety of work and prisoners are carefully chosen from all the jails in the state and put to such work as is suitable to them. There is no police escort and the jail warders act only as guides. Complete freedom of movement and association is provided. They have a wide campus where they can move and play. There are good feeding arrangements, a well-equipped hospital and recreation in the shape of music and cinema shows, etc. The staff also lives on the premises and this promotes better understanding, between them and prisoners, because they live a corporate life. There are no walls around this camp and there is no police surveillance. Prisoners work with ordinary labourers. The Education Officer attached to the Camp is in-charge of a literacy scheme for the prisoners. The teachers and welfare officers at the camp assist the work of reformation and rehabilitation.

The prisoners are paid wages. A part is paid to them and the balance is kept as savings to be handed over at the time of release. The prisoner pays for his meals and he is free to buy anything he likes at the canteen. Remission for good conduct and efficiency is allowed. The dignity of labour and man is instilled in the hearts of the prisoners and each is made to feel he is on his honour.

The inmates of this camp by their excellent work and discipline fully justified the confidence reposed in them. The success achieved encouraged the opening of another camp with 3,000 inmates in

Naugarh in the same district. In the time of two years they have displayed a high sense of discipline which is proved by the number of escapes which were only 20, and is negligible as compared to the corresponding figures for the closed jails. These results raise high expectations which it is hoped will be realized. At present there are two permanent camps—one at the Government Churak Cement Factory (District Mirzapur) which was established in 1956 and another at the Agricultural-cum-Industrial Camp in Sitarganj (District Nainital) established in 1960. The number of prisoners in these camps in 1962 was about 1,400 and 800 respectively.

As is clear from the above account a good deal of change has been brought about in the treatment and approach to prisoners, yet much more still remains to be done.

(ii) Probation

Probation as a means of treating offenders came long after the system of imprisonment was developed. The failure of imprisonment to cope with crime called for other methods. Probation was urged for first offenders and for others who might be effectively treated outside a penal institution. It was first applied on a large scale to juvenile delinquents when the creation of the juvenile court system (about 1,900) gave an impetus to the practice of sparing the convicted person a prison experience. In the words of Barnes and Teeters, "Probation, as applied to modern courts, seeks to accomplish the rehabilitation of persons convicted of crime by returning them to society during a period of supervision, rather sending them into the unnatural and too often socially unhealthy atmosphere of prisons and reformatories .... Successful probation entails an adequate investigation into the facts of the defendant's environment, character and previous record ; a wise selection by the court of the offenders capable of benefitting by the treatment, and a zealous but sympathetic prosecution of his duties by the supervisory staff."[25]

Probation is not a pardon but only a conditional suspension of punishment. Throughout the period of probation the original offence remains punishable in the case of violation of any condition of probation or in case the offender commits another offence. The suspension is only in order to promote the offender's rehabilitation.

[25] Barnes, H. E. and Teeters, N. K., *New Horizons in Criminology* (1944), p. 373.

"It is increasingly recognised that probation treatment is a highly skilled service requiring specific technical training. It is the application of modern scientific case-work methods to individuals outside the Institutions. It is a sort of community treatment which permits normal social experience not available in the Institutions. Its advantages are that it does not disrupt the offender's relationship with his family, with his friends, with the opposite sex and with his occupation. It saves a good deal to the State and the community, but that is, not, however, the best reason for its application."[26]

It is in the wake of successful experiments made in other advanced countries that the system of probation was introduced in India also. Such provision was first made in the Criminal Procedure Code and later on separate Probation Acts were passed by the various states.

Working of Probation in India

Under sections 562 to 564 of the Criminal Procedure Code the court has the power to release certain convicted offenders on probation of good conduct or to release them after admonition. Section 562(1) of the C. P. C. reads as follows : "When any person not under twenty-one years of age is convicted of an offence punishable with imprisonment for not more than seven years, or when any person under twenty-one years of age or any woman is convicted of an offence not punishable with death or imprisonment for life and no previous conviction is proved against the offender, if it appears to the Court before which he is convicted, regard being had to the age, character, or antecedents of the offender, and to the circumstances, in which the offence was committed, that it is expedient that the offender should be released on probation of good conduct, the Court may, instead of sentencing him at once to any punishment, direct that he be released on his entering into a bond, with or without sureties to appear and receive sentence when called upon during such period (not exceeding three years) as the Court may direct, and in the meantime to keep the peace and be of good behaviour."

Section 562(1-A) makes provision for release with admonition and reads as follows : "In any case in which a person is convicted

[26] Planning Commission, Government of India, *Social Legislation* (1956), p. 506.

of theft, theft in a building, dishonest misappropriation, cheating or any offence under the Indian Penal Code punishable with not more than two years' imprisonment and no previous conviction is proved against him, the Court before whom he is so convicted may, if it thinks fit, having regard to the age, character, antecedents or physical or mental condition of the offender and to the trivial nature of the offence or any extenuating circumstances under which the offence was commited, instead of sentencing him to any punishment, release him after due admonition." (Nothing in this section shall affect the provisions of section 31 of the Reformatory Schools Act, 1897).

Under section 564 it is further stated that "The Court before directing the release of an offender under section 562 sub-section (1) shall be satisfied that the offender or his surety (if any) has a fixed place of abode or regular occupation in the place for which the Court acts or in which the offender is likely to live during the period named for the observance of the conditions.

Later on special probation acts were passed in the various states such as the Madras Probation of Offenders Act (1937), the United Provinces First Offenders Act (1938), Bombay Probation of Offenders Act (1938) and so on. Under these various acts provision is made for the appointment of Probation Officers by the states. The duties of the Probation Officers are to pay or receive visits from the offender at intervals fixed in the order and have to see that the conditions of the bond are observed. He has to report to the Court upon his behaviour. He has to assist and befriend the offender and endeavour to find suitable employment for him. He may advise the court to alter or relax the conditions of bond or to discharge the bond.

Working of Probation Acts

The Madras Probation of Offenders Act is the first of its kind in India. Before the passing of this act various annual conferences of Inspector-Generals of Prisons since 1925 recommended for the passing of an All-India Probation Act, but the Government of India did not favour All-India legislation and recommended to the states for such legislation on Provincial basis. Madras State was thus first to enact such a legislation.

To begin with, the act was first applied to the city of Madras and six other districts and was later extended to other districts.

The Madras Presidency Discharged Prisoners Aid Society was constituted for administering the Act and the work was subsidized by the Government. But after some years of its working the Government realized that no satisfactory probation system could be built on an honorary basis. Accordingly in 1946 the service was provincialized and was placed under the Inspector-General of Prisons. There is a Chief Probation Officer to supervise the work of the District Probation Officers. There were 43 Probation Officers in the State in 1955 and out of these 5 were women.

A Committee of the Discharged Prisoners Aid Society functions as a Probationary Advisory Committee and its functions are to popularize the probation system and to help probationers with money and in other ways in their rehabilitation.

"The probation department as worked in Madras is now converted into a multi-purpose service assisting the Courts and correctional institutions in several ways. They are in charge of the after-care of children released under the Madras Children Act ; the adolescents discharged on licence or on release from Borstal Schools ; the after-care of prisoners prematurely released under the Advisory Board Scheme ; the women discharged from the Stri Sadhana and Vigilance Home ; they enquire into disputes between spouses in maintenance claims before magistrates either to effect a rapprochement or to report to the Court on the means of the husband."[27] In the year 1952 alone 5,250 persons were placed on probation and the total expenditure was about Rs. 3 lakhs. If all these were placed in Institutions the expenditure would have been nearly Rs. 16 lakhs and thus saving to the state and society is considerable.

However, all is not well with this system. As it has been observed, "Apart from the popular misgivings about the system, the courts are still far from regarding the Probation Officers as their 'eyes, ears and conscience' and there is still a feeling that, however estimaable, it is a dispensable adjunct to the administrative machinery."[28]

In Bombay the probation work is entrusted to the Bombay State Probation and After-Care Association, Poona, which provides a constructive method of dealing with adult offenders in lieu of committing them to jail. There are District Associations with trained Probation Officers who make proper enquiries regarding home circumstances, antecedents and character of the accused in order

[27] *Social Legislation, op. cit.*, p. 313.
[28] *Social Legislation, op. cit.*, p. 313.

to advise the courts on the suitable disposal of the cases. Later on when the offender is put on probation the officers are required to make reports every month to the courts concerned regarding the progress and conduct of probationers placed under them and copies of their reports are sent to the above Association in Poona, where they are scrutinized and instructions to the concerned Probation Officers are issued where necessary. In Bombay, this work is carried out by one of the Chief Officers of the Bombay State Probation and After-care Association and his staff. The total number of Probation Officers in the State in 1954 was 173, out of which 153 were voluntary officers and 20 recruited directly. In addition to the work done under the Probation Act, they also do the work under the Bombay Borstal Schools Act and the Bombay Children Act.

In Uttar Pradesh although the Probation Act was passed in 1938, it was in force only in 16 out of 51 districts of the state in 1956. There were 25 Probation Officers. All first offenders under the age of 24 years not convicted of offences punishable with death or transportation for life may be placed on probation. As the Probation Officers are not available in all the districts of the state, full benefits of this legislation cannot be availed of. In 1953, 1,700 cases were handed over to the Probation Officers. Women convicts are denied the benefits of probation for want of women Probation Officers.

No such special acts were passed in other states till 1956 nor were there any probation officers. Thus, only restricted use of provisions contained in the Criminal Procedure Code has been made so far. The subject of Probation is an important one and considerable attention has been paid to it in recent years. Professor Reckless has recommended for its application on a liberal scale as we shall see at the end of this chapter.

(*iii*) *Parole*

It is another method of individualized treatment. "Parole is a conditional release granted to a prisoner who has served a part of his sentence in a penal Institution. While that is also a community treatment conditionally applied and the methods of supervision closely resemble those employed in probation (perhaps the same Probation Officer is in charge both of probation and parole), there is still a distinction between the two. In the case of the parole there has been a period of institutional treatment. Parole is an adjunct to institutional treatment whereas probation is an alternative to it Another significant point is that the future conduct of the parolee is judged by an administrative authority, whereas in the case of probation it is the Court that orders further disposition."[29] In the words of Barnes and Teeters, "It is a form of release, but it always presupposes some sort of supervision, for it is not freedom. There can be no parole without a previous sentence following a conviction by a court or jury, or without an institutional experience. The parolee must have been released from some sort of institution under some sort of supervision. Hence it must never be confused with probation nor with pardon."[30] Thus, the granting of parole is merely permission to a prisoner to serve a portion of his sentence outside the walls of the prison. As against probation he continues to be in the custody of the authorities, both legally and actually, and is still under restraint. Parole, wisely and efficiently administered, guarantees to the community that the released prisoner is a potential asset because of his institutional training, and it is one of the bulwarks of a progressive penology.

Closely correlated in function and usage to parole is the system of indeterminate sentence, though it is not in vogue in this country.

It is in the light of this parole system or indeterminate sentence introduced in some other advanced countries that Release of Prisoners for Good Conduct Acts were passed in some of the states in this country. The Punjab State gave a lead in this direction when the Punjab Prisoners' Probational Release for Good Conduct Act was passed in 1926. Subsequently, such acts were passed in Assam (1938), Uttar Pradesh (1938), and the Central Provinces and Berar Prisoners' Act in 1939. Under these acts a Provincial Government may release a prisoner on licence subject to conditions, if from his antecedents or conducts in prison he is likely to abstain from crime and lead a useful and industrious life. He will be placed under the supervision of a servant of the state or a secular institution or a person willing to take charge of him. A licence is revocable. On revocation the prisoner shall be recommitted and shall serve the unexpired term of the original sentence. He also forfeits any remission earned before his release.

[29] *Ibid.*, p. 310.

[30] Barnes, H. E., and Teeters, N. K. *New Horizons in Criminology* (1944), p. 814.

The Uttar Pradesh Prisoners' Release on Probation Act 1938, also provides for the conditional release from prison of prisoners before the completion of their term of imprisonment. The Provincial Government may by licence permit the release of any prisoner, if satisfied from his antecedents and his conduct in the prison that he is likely to abstain from crime and lead a peaceable life. It shall place him under the supervision of a Government Officer or any person or secular institution professing the same religion as the prisoner and willing to take charge of him. Any person escaping from supervision or failing to return to prison upon revocation of any licence would be liable to imprisonment for a further term of 2 years or fine up to Rs. 2,000 or both in addition to the liability to serve the unexpired portion of the original sentence.

The Uttar Pradesh Government also made Ticket of Release Rules under section 401 of the Code of Criminal Procedure in 1950. Under these rules any prisoner may apply to the State Government for release except in case of certain offences such as against the state, or relating to Indian Armed Forces, etc. Any prisoner who has served three years of his sentence may be released on a personal bond with sureties for a period not exceeding a month. The application is to be sent to the Inspector-General of Prisons through the District Magistrate and the case is finally considered by a Board of Release. If the Board gives its consent, the State Government then issues a ticket in triplicate and a guardian is appointed who may be a Government servant or other person or secular institution or society or a Probation Officer. The Guardian takes charge of the prisoner from the Superintendent of the Jail. It is the guardian's duty to look after the conduct of the prisoner and to see that the conditions of the ticket are fulfilled.

If there is any breach, he may report to the District Magistrate. When the District Magistrate receives information of any breach of conditions of ticket he should summon the prisoner and after hearing him if he appears, he shall recommend to the Government whether the ticket should be revoked. If the ticket is to be revoked he may order his arrest and detention in prison pending the orders of the State Government. Such a temporary release is also available under the Central Provinces and Berar Prisoners' Act of 1939, under which any prisoner serving a sentence of not less than 3 years may be released for a period not exceeding 10 days in a year, under certain conditions.

(*iv*) *Other Alternatives to Punishment*

They include such measures as recognizance, binding over, pardon, commutation and reduction of sentences for good behaviour. Recognizance is the practice of obliging persons, about whom there is probability of future misbehaviour, to assure the public that such offence as is apprehended shall not occur. It is a caution against a repetition by the offender of the same offence. The use of binding over in respect of actual offender is due to the realization of the fact that short-term imprisonment has a demoralizing and contaminating influence. It also serves as a rehabilitative measure.

The two important forms of mitigation of punishment are pardon and commutation of sentences. The pardoning power is, however, to be used very cautiously, because of the abuse of power by the authority concerned. Commutation is a lesser degree of the pardoning power. It is not a pardon but a change from a higher to a lower penalty in the scale of punishment. A death penalty may be commuted to life imprisonment or a sentence of imprisonment reduced in length by commutation. The reduction of the length of sentence for good behaviour in prison is another measure for the commutation of sentence.

(*v*) *After-care of Prisoners*

"The concept of after-care of prisoners is derived from the penological thought that regards reformation and rehabilitation as the ultimate aim of penal administration."[31] This after-care aspect of prisoners on release from the prison after completion of sentence or on premature release for the proper rehabilitation of prisoners has received much attention in these days. Generally, a convict loses some of his civil rights, he is stigmatized by the society and finds difficult to get a government or private job and readjust himself in the society. As Barnes and Teeters point out an ex-prisoner is ill prepared for life after prison because of various handicaps from which he suffers such as loss of civil rights, stigma of conviction, follow-up by the police, etc. They observe, "The Prisoner returning to society is seriously handicapped under the most favourable conditions. This is specially true in so far as obtaining work

[31] *Report of the Advisory Committee on After-care Programmes*, Central Social Welfare Board (1954), p. 214.

is concerned."[32] No doubt some welfare agencies in some advanced countries provide after-care services for ex-prisoners and help them in providing jobs, but very little attention has been paid to this aspect in our country. Some Discharged Prisoners' Aid Societies were organized as early as the end of the nineteenth century—U. P. Discharged Prisoners' Aid Society (1894), Bengal (1907) and Bombay (1914). But for want of official support and public sympathy these agencies could not flourish. The Indian Jails Committee (1918-1919) emphasized for help to the released prisoners. It was on the recommendation of this Committee that fresh stimulus was given to this work.

In response to this need Madras Prisoners' Aid Society was formed in 1921. This was followed by similar societies in Central Provinces (1925), Punjab (1927), Bengal (1928), Bombay (1933), Delhi (1935) and United Provinces (1937). Some of these societies also formed District Committees for the implementation of their aims and objects. The aim of these societies was to render aid to discharged prisoners and also establish after-care hostels for these released prisoners who had difficulty in returning home. However, it is to be pointed out that some good work was done only in Bengal, Uttar Pradesh, Madras and Bombay.[33]

In order to provide such services on a large scale, and on scientific lines, the Central Social Welfare Board appointed an Advisory Committee on After-Care Programmes in 1954 to look into the conditions of present services and suggest certain measures for their improvement. The Committee after reviewing the work of present societies has suggested a comprehensive plan for the after-care services, including after-care services for orphan children, physically handicapped, the delinquent children, the widows and beggars. The Committee has discussed two aspects of the after-care programme, i.e. vocational rehabilitation and social rehabilitation which are mutually interdependent. No doubt some after-care homes have been set up for various types of persons in some of the states, but few of them relate to services for ex-prisoners and the work has not been entrusted to voluntary agencies. The Study Team on Social Welfare rightly remarks, "It is a matter of regret

[32] *Op. cit.*, p. 805.

[33] See *Report of the Advisory Committee on After-care Programmes* (1954), pp. 214, 231.

that voluntary efforts of these agencies have not been effectively utilised in the execution of the programme."[34]

Developments During Five-Year Plans

The above is an account of the work done for the treatment of adult offenders in this country. Although some new and bold experiments have been made at some places to create self-reliance among prisoners, so that they may settle as normal citizens after their release from the prison, yet the progress is still far from satisfactory. Many of the prisoners commit crime again to take abode in the prison, as they are not able to adjust themselves in the society. As Barnes and Teeters observe, "Any one who has worked with prisoners or ex-convicts realizes that the majority of them have lost the self-esteem upon which they must rely to make good in a highly competitive world. Self-esteem bolsters up confidence; when they lack it they are completely demoralized. . . . He comes out of even the most progressive prison today with the brand 'ex-convict' indelibly seared on his soul to betray him wherever he goes."[35] Professor Reckless observes, "Available statistics on previous convictions of offenders show that the recidivism rate is high."[36] If this is the state of affairs in a country where individualized treatment has made much headway, the conditions cannot be better in this country. Thus, though something has been done in this country yet much more still remains to be done.

After Independence the Government of India has given enough thought to this problem. In order to chalk out some uniform programme for the reformation and rehabilitation of the adult offenders they invited Dr. Walter C. Reckless, a United Nations' Expert and a well renowned criminologist, to study and report on jail administration in India in 1952. He made a study of the jail administration in India and submitted a report "The United Nations Report on Jail Administration in India". Progressive measures of jail administration and liberal use of the probation system as an alternative to institutionalization are among the important recommendations of Dr. Reckless. To these we shall refer in detail in the following pages.

[34] *Report of the Study Team on Social Welfare and Welfare of Backward Classes* (1959), p. 94.

[35] *Ibid.*, p. 801.

[36] Reckless, W. C., *Criminal Behaviour*, p. 357.

In March 1957, the Government of India appointed a Committee of Inspector-Generals of Prisons to evolve a common jail manual for all the jails in the country, to examine the Prison Acts and other central legislation on the subject and to recommend prison reform to be applied uniformly throughout the country. The committee submitted its report in 1959.

The Committee recommended that the prevention and control of crime, treatment of offenders and after-care of prisoners should be treated as a unified programme of social defence. The Department of Prisons and Correctional Services should exercise jurisdiction over prisons, juvenile delinquency, probation and after-care services.[37] The report made detailed recommendations with regard to care, welfare, discipline, training and scientific treatment of adolescent and adult offenders. The Prisons Acts of 1894 and Prisoners Act of 1900 were to be revised. It also recommended the amendment of certain sections of the Indian Penal Code and the Criminal Procedure Code. The recommendations of the Committee were still under consideration of the Government.

During the Second Five-Year Plan social defence schemes were included among centrally sponsored schemes. Central assistance, in so far as it relates to welfare services in prisons including assistance for the appointment of welfare officers, diversification and modernization of jail industries and other welfare services, especially those for women prisoners and their children was extended.[38] It was proposed to have one welfare officer for each of the 66 more important jails in the country. These programmes were continued to get central assistance in the Third Plan. Here it will be appropriate to mention some of the developments which have taken place at the international level.

Prevention of Crime and U. N. O.

The General Assembly of the United Nations in their resolution in December 1950 provided for the convening every five years of an International Congress on the prevention of crime and treatment of offenders. The first congress was held in Geneva in 1955, the second in 1960 in London and the third in 1946 in Felkets Hus (Stockholm). The third congress discussed two programmes : (*a*) prevention

[37] Report of the All-India Jail Manual Committee, 1957-59. Also see Sushil Chandra's *Sociology of Deviation in India* (1967), p. 219.

[38] *Plans and Prospects of Social Welfare in India* 1951-1961 (1963), p. 146.

10

in the predelinquent stage through family education, protective programmes, police services, etc. and (*b*) prevention of recidivism. This last required four measures : (*i*) control of criminogenic factors conducive to recidivism such as detention pending trial, inequality in the administration of justice, etc. ; (2) adult probation and other non-institutional measures ; (3) special prevention and treatment measures for young offenders ; (4) prevention of criminality by abnormal offenders and their treatment.[39]

Future Programme

In spite of some active efforts made by the Central and State Governments in the prevention of crime and reformation of prisoners in the last few years, many more steps are still needed to reach desirable standards. The following few suggestions may be helpful in this connection.

1. *From Punishment to Treatment*. The use of imprisonment as a corrective is a recent trend and it has slowly led to the concept of the re-education of the criminal. The penal and correctional administration must operate on the principle that majority of adult offenders are improvable and can be returned to society in a better condition. The officers in the various units of correctional administration need to recognize the distinction between amenities and treatment. Amenities help to improve the lot and the conditions of offenders while serving sentence, treatment aims at the change of attitudes, habits and approach to life of the individual offender. Though in India, food, shelter, clothing and medical attention have been improved and have reached satisfactory standards, there has not been much change in the attitude of the staff. Therefore "social rehabilitation and re-education of the prisoner for good citizenship as the aims of prison policy must be placed in the forefront".[40] To make a better person out of the prisoner, the prison staff must be engaged with him directly through admission interviews, orientation, interpretation of rules or action taken, classification for special treatment, encouragement, counselling, guidance, discussion sessions, talks with visiting family members, re-adjustment in programmes, and preparation for release. Much will depend upon

[39] Central Bureau of Correctional Services, Ministry of Home Affairs, *Social Defence*, January 1966, p. 1.

[40] *Social Legislation, op. cit.*, p. 394.

the personal relationships established between the prison staff and the prisoners and on the impact of various constructive programmes within the jail. The jail personnel must be a specialized one having proper qualifications and training.

2. *To Reduce the Number of Undertrials.* It is urgently necessary to reduce the number of undertrials languishing in jails by speeding up Police investigations and Court trials. They must be provided with work when undertrial and paid wages for the work done. To leave him in idleness is to contribute to his moral and physical disintegration.

3. *Short Sentences to be Discouraged.* Short sentences of imprisonment should be discouraged as far as possible. Fine, judicial reprieve, recognizance, warning, dismissal and filing can be used as alternatives. Probation yet untapped has great potentialities. We must grow out of the superstition that the jail system is the only instrument of social control. The other methods are more economical and they are to be preferred because they do not create fresh problems for the prisoners and his dependents.

4. *Fines and Default Imprisonment to be Reduced.* Imprisonment in default of payment should be reduced to the minimum. While at present the fines are related to the gravity of the offences, they should in future be related to the means of the offender.

5. *Premature Releases.* There is a limit beyond which imprisonment becomes merely punitive detention. For the ordinary prisoner what cannot be done in two or three years in an institution is not likely to be done even in five or ten years. It is far better to develop a system of premature release under supervision. Full-time Revising Boards are necessary if they are to work effectively. The merely advisory function of the existing Boards whereupon the State Government is to order the release at its discretion involves a process which checks its extensive use.

6. *More After-Care Services.* There should be full-time after-care service for prisoners released before due date or after completion of their sentence. Without it the prisoner who has no place to go will be forced to seek his old haunts and his old friends and all the efforts made over him will have been wasted. A programme of after-care must address itself to the problem of the prisoner's social and vocational rehabilitation and set him on his own feet to an honest and independent living. Considering the prevailing prejudices against an ex-prisoner the state should give the lead in

facilitating his rehabilitation by a preparedness to re-employ him if he has earned a good chit from the probation and after-care agency. Unless this is done jails will continue to be places which foster at public expense future criminals who, embittered by the society's refusal to give them a chance to live as honest citizens even after they have paid their dues in the hard coinage of punishment, will be driven to further antisocial behaviour.

7. *Increased Use of Probation.* Professor Reckless points out that authorities and officials from many countries of the world have agreed that probation is perhaps the most economical and satisfactory way of handling the average juvenile and adult offender. Therefore, its use should be made on an extensive scale. All courts may be authorized to apply its provisions and it need not be confined to first offenders only. It is also not necessary to exclude its application to certain offences considered serious. The factors to be considered and the conditions which may be imposed on any particular offender must be left to the discretion of the Court. Courts should be required to state their reasons for not applying the probation method before passing a sentence of imprisonment.

There must be full-time Probation Officers and all releases must be required to be under their supervision. Successful termination of probation should completely exonerate the offender from any blame or stigma. It will facilitate the work of probation officers if there are hostels for probationers where they can stay and where the officers may visit them. This will also enable the courts to dispense with the requirements of sureties which is another factor limiting its use. The Government of India introduced the All-India Probation Bill in Parliament which became an Act in 1958, known as the Probation of Offenders Act. It is hoped that this Act will be enforced by all states on uniform basis.

8. *Improvement in Their Living.* Although there has been much improvement in the amenities such as food, shelter, clothing, medical facilities, etc. provided to the prisoners, yet there is a need for further improvement. The diet provided to the prisoners should be more varied according to the work done by the individual prisoner.[41] Literate persons should be allowed books on Sundays and in their spare time. The prison libraries should be improved.

9. *Individualization of Prisoners.* There should be psychological clinics attached to jail hospitals as is done in U. S. A. The field

[41] Sethna, M. J., *Society and the Criminal* (1964), p. 314.

workers attached to these clinics should collect data from their homes and about the past history of prisoners so that individual treatment can be rendered. Those who are insane, feeble-minded or defective should be put in separate institutions.

10. *Proper Labour and Payment of Wages.* Sometimes prisoners are given work which they do not like. Each prisoner should be assigned work which suits his background and can be useful after release. Those who have been working as farmers should be put on farms and those with industrial background in factories.

Prisoners should be paid for the work done and they should be required to pay for their meals and other conveniences in the prison. This system has already been introduced in many states and need to be adopted in others. Wages should be paid according to the quantity and quality of the work done. This will give incentive to the industrious workers. In the case of disobedient or lethargic prisoner who refuses or fails to do the work assigned to him or who is guilty of breach of prison discipline or of insubordination instead of resorting to fettering or flogging, he should be deprived of wages. Thus, he should be brought to understand the value of and necessity of work.[42]

It is hoped that if the suggestions made above are put into practice they will go a long way in the reduction of crime.

[42] Sethna, M. J., *op. cit.*, p. 312.

PART THREE

SOCIAL VICES

CHAPTER VI

ALCOHOLISM AND DRUG ADDICTION

ALCOHOLISM and drug addiction are harmful not only for the individual but also for his family and the society at large. The World Health Organization Expert Committee defines, "drug addiction as a state of periodic or chronic intoxication, detrimental to the individual and to society, produced by repeated consumption of a drug either natural or synthetic. Its characteristics include : (*a*) an overpowering desire or need (compulsion) to continue taking the drug and to obtain it by any means ; (*b*) a tendency to increase the dose ; and (*c*) a psychic (psychological) and sometimes a physical dependence on the effects of the drug."[1] This definition covers both alcoholic drinks—a synthetic form of drug, and other drugs which have a narcotic (sleeping) effect and are used for self-indulgence. Although the disorganising effects of these alcoholic drinks and other narcotic drugs are almost similar and are only a matter of degree, the use of the former is more rampant. We shall first take up alcoholism and then drug addiction.

Alcoholism

There would not have been the problem of alcoholism, as we see it today, had it been possible to restrict its use to moderation. On the other hand it would have been a boon to the society because its moderate use has certain beneficial effects too. It is generally asserted that if alcohol is used in a moderate quantity, (1) it makes life in our highly tensioned world more tolerable ; (2) it is a valuable social lubricant ; (3) it unlocks the door to a more vivid inner life ; (4) as a drug, a narcotic which by relaxing the control of the higher brain centres dulls painful feeling or promotes pleasureable ones ; and (5) as a drug it is used in the treatment of the sick. But it is its excessive use which has caused it to be impeached through the ages as a serious social evil, and as such has been a subject of agitation.

[1] Quoted in article "Drug Addiction in India" by K. Mitra, in *Social Welfare in India* (1960), p. 149.

The difficulty is that once a man starts drinking he becomes addicted to it and goes on increasing its dose, which has a very harmful effect both on the individual as well as the society. The percentage of those who can stick to its moderate use is very very small. There is a well-known proverb "Once a drinker always a drinker." "The truth is that all hard drinkers start with moderate drinking and gradually increase the quantity to become addicts."[2] As Mr. Mitra points out, "the characteristic of such drugs is that the attraction of their effect, irrespective of whether they are produced by stimulation or by narcotism is of such a degree that people once accustomed will resort to them in utter disregard of the adverse effects produced on themselves either mentally, morally or physically."[3]

Problem Drinkers. Thus, there are two types of drinkers: (1) those who can stand their liquor and may be called as moderate drinkers and (2) those who cannot and are known as problem drinkers. A problem drinker is one whose drinking becomes a personal and social problem to him. According to Dr. Durfee a problem drinker is one, "if as a result of drinking (*i*) his health is endangered, his peace of mind is affected, his home life made unhappy, his business jeopardized and his reputation clouded, and (*ii*) drinking has become his routine."[4]

Causes of Drinking

Different reasons have been given by various writers such as Caltin, Starling, Bonger and Janet, which may be summarised as below.[5] Men generally start drinking because of its beneficial effects but later on become addicted to it, which has a detrimental effect.

1. *Misery Drinking.* Men drink, because they are miserable, because life holds no joy for them or any other prospect other than

[2] *Report of the Prohibition Enquiry Committee, Planning Commission*, Government of India (1955), p. 7.

[3] Mitra, K., *op. cit.*, p. 149.

[4] Durfee, Charles, *To Drink or not to Drink* (1937), p. 11.

[5] Caltin, George E.C., has mentioned serial numbers 1, 2, 7 and 9 as the major factors of drinking in his article "Alcoholism in the Encyclopaedia of Social Sciences" (1930). E. H. Starling has stated serial numbers 2, 4, 5 and 8 in his book *The Action of Alcohol on Man* (1923). W. A. Bonger has mentioned the first four factors in his book *Criminality & Economic Conditions* (1916) and Pierre Janet, the last, i.e. Social Inadequacy in his book *Psychological Healing* (1925).

a dreary and unending round of toil. In such a life scheme drink is a blessed palliative medicine.

2. *Occupational Factor*. Men drink because their occupation has completely exhausted them. They look forward eagerly to the respite which intoxication affords after the heat of the blast furnace or the stench of the stockyards.

3. *Bad Housing and Lack of Recreational Facilities*. Men drink, because their houses are so cold, dark, dismal and sordid, that they cannot stay there for a long time. The failure of community to satisfy the emotions in a sane and healthy manner also leads to such craving.

4. *Ignorance*. Men who do heavy manual work have long been deluded by the belief that alcohol furnishes added strength and vigour with which they can pursue their labour. This illusory feeling of physical vitality after the consumption of alcohol is the cause of drunkenness.

5. *Inherent Nervous Defects*. These are the born drunkards whose neurological heritage is such that they are unable to face reality. In their desperate effort to flee the world these unhappy persons become hopeless alcoholics.

6. *God's Curse or Gift*. Some persons believe that men drink because they are steeped in original sin. Others maintain with equal conviction that men drink because the Lord intended that they should have occasional movements of pleasant oblivion from this vale of tears—and placed the grapes on earth for that particular purpose.

7. *For Companionship and Fun*. Men drink for companionship, for fun, for conviviality for what the Germans call *Gemutlichkeit*, a compound of all three.

8. *Fashion*. Drinking to excess is a "perversion of the hard instinct", brought about by the pathetic attempt of one individual to enter into rapport with his fellows.

9. *For Business Reasons*. Men drink for business reasons in the capacity of either potential customers or sellers. The great game of "entertaining the visiting buyer" falls into this category.

10. *Sudden Success in Business*. Many cases of drinking arise after apparent success in business or professional life.

11. *Urbanization*. The urbanization and mechanization of life along with material mindedness which modern civilization has brought, has also been responsible for the increase in drinking.

12. *Social Inadequacy.* There are certain persons who are unable to face the hard realities of life and start drinking to overcome their social inadequacy temporarily which later on takes the form of habitual drinking.

Among these various causes Dr. Caltin has mentioned companionship as the chief cause of drinking, while Mr. Bonger gives Misery Drinking and Dr. Janet the social inadequacy. The last two causes may be discussed in detail.

Misery Drinking. The Dutch criminologist, W.A. Bonger, has given considerable insight to the problem of misery drinking among the proletariat and has clubbed together some of the factors given above under the head Misery Drinking. He points out a number of ways in which alcoholism is fostered among the workers by the miserable condition of their socio-economic environments, such as nature of occupation, long hours of work, bad and insufficient food, bad housing conditions, economic uncertainty and ignorance. (1) He points out that certain occupations expose the worker to excessive heat or excessive cold. In order to blunt the resulting feeling of discomfort, the worker often resorts to alcohol. (2) Workers often use alcohol in a vain effort to increase their resistance to fatigue from long hours of labour. (3) Many workers are chronically undernourished, others are unable to buy a variety of food sufficient to provide an adequately varied diet. They use alcohol as a supplement to a diet to counteract the monotony of food. (4) Many workers live under miserable housing conditions. Their homes are so cold, dark, dismal and sordid that they take refuge in the brightly lighted dram shop. Here they find warmth, companionship and the opportunity to escape temporarily from the dismal routine of their lives. (5) The uncertainty of employment, the constant threat of unemployment and the prospect of a dependent old age are among the grim spectres which take them to drink, so as to serve as a consolation for their troubles. (6) Ignorance of the true effects of alcohol is another factor of drink among them.

Social Inadequacy. According to Dr. Janet the chief cause of starting drinking is the social inadequacy. The impulse to imbibe is often precipitated by a severe crisis in the life of the individual. Men and women may have had no difficulty in avoiding the dram shop prior to a severe shock or readjustment in their life schemes. These interruptions are varied. Overwork, a sudden change in environment with resulting nostalgia, or a sudden rise or decline in the social scale may produce a feeling of inadequacy without artificial stimulation. "Quarrels between friends and lovers, breaches of conjugal faith, disappointment in love may all reduce the individual to extreme melancholy. In great many cases Janet observed this fundamental feeling of incompleteness in his patients both before they became alcoholic and after they were confirmed addicts."[6]

The victim of these crises may take his first drink as an experimental method of dispelling the gloom which envelops him. He is usually rewarded by a given feeling of warmth and well-being in the early stages of intoxication and depression follows after some time. In order to perpetuate this pleasant relaxation the novice tries to experiment again and again and gradually becomes an alcoholic.

Casual to Habitual Drinker

Professors Elliott and Merrill have given five stages through which a person has to pass till he becomes a complete drunkard and his personality is completely disorganized.[7] By easy and imperceptible stages, alcohol becomes increasingly important as a value in the life organization of the individual. They are (*i*) morning drink, (*ii*) escape drinking, (*iii*) increasing consumption, (*iv*) drinking and social functions, and (*v*) extreme behaviour.

The first danger signal for the frequent drinker occurs when he begins to drink in the morning and alcohol has lost its convivial function. Alcohol has become a drug by which the drinker whips his jaded and depressed nervous system to such a pitch that he can get through the day. The second stage starts when a person begins to feel that he cannot face a difficult business problem or a period of emotional stress without recourse to considerable quantities of alcohol. Such drinking is a fruitless attempt to escape from reality. Among business and professional classes it corresponds to the phenomenon which we call "misery drinking" among the proletariat. The motive of escape is similar, although the way of life of the two classes is widely different. Many of the cases of alcoholism among businessmen result from this attempt to flee from the social and economic complexities of daily life. The third stage is evident.

[6] Elliott, M. A., and Merrill, F. E., *op. cit.*, p. 282.

[7] *Ibid.*, p. 282.

when the person discovers that he is drinking more and more in the course of every month or every year. This phenomenon of increase in consumption is a symptom of personal disorganization and gradually the values of the drinker are changing. A stage may come when the potential alcoholic may feel that he has become so dependent upon alcohol for stimulation and enjoyment that he cannot face an evening without it. Alcohol has become an absolute necessity for dispelling the boredom enveloping a friendly social gathering. Thus, it is no more a pleasant adjunct to a party and a complete transvaluation of all values has taken place. The fifth stage reaches when such persons drink in excess and commit indiscretions. When such extreme behaviour becomes chronic, the drinker has reached a dangerous stage of incipient alcoholism. Those persons who habitually become involved in fights without provocation, who continuously insult innocent by-standers, and persist in playing absurd and dangerous pranks on their friends have almost completely lost their sense of values. They have broken with the normal world and have come close to the pathological.

It will not be out of place to discuss stages of intoxication here, ranging from first drink to complete forgetfulness which Mr. Emil Bogen has described in his book *The Human Toxicology of Alcohol.* They are sub-clinical stage, stimulation, confusion, stupor and coma. The first stage is brought about by the moderate doses of alcohol and the effects are apparent in the higher centres of the brain and the faculties of judgement, reflection, observation and attention are blunted. In the second stage when the dose is increased the drinker is stimulated and begins to lose his self-consciousness and his self-control. He is often unable to retain the control of his emotions and his moods. Such person may brood while his fellows laugh. In the third stage the drinker experiences a definite reduction in the previous symptoms of stimulation. There is an increasing difficulty in physical coordination. The hearing is dulled, the speech is incoherent and the muscular coordination necessary for walking becomes increasingly difficult. At this stage the drinker cannot stand erect, nor can he walk straight. At this stage he reacts very little to the external environments and becomes increasingly unable to coordinate. He cannot stand up easily nor can he sit down. He is continually on the verge of unconsciousness. In the last stage he becomes completely unconscious and he is now dead drunk. He breathes slowly and with difficulty. In this condition he is often close to death. However, the actual amount of alcohol which will bring out such fatal results differs from person to person. The important fact, however, is that alcohol taken in large quantity is poisonous which may cause the death of the drinker.

Besides social effects discussed, excessive drinking has physical effects too. The effects of alcohol upon the human organism are many and varied. Taken in moderation in the form of wine or beer, it has no harmful effect and rather has a healthy effect. As Mr. Raymond Pearl suggests, on the basis of exhaustive researches upon animals, that a certain amount of alcohol actually favours the physical growth of the organism.[8] Nor even a periodic dose is permanently injurious to the physical mechanism. It is only acute drinking, as any other form of poisoning, which carries a train of ill effects. Chronic gastritis, cirrhosis of the liver, multiple or peripheral neutritis, gout, and delirium tremens are the pathological effects of acute alcoholism. Besides these specific diseases, the resistance to all diseases is appreciably lowered by heavy and periodic consumption. He is also more subject to violent death from accident and other causes than is the non-drinker.

Those who favour the use of alcohol generally advocate that (1) moderate use of alcohol with meals does not interfere with health or length of life, (2) its medicinal effect, and (3) used in moderation does not cause intoxication. While its opponents point out that (1) morbidity rate of drinkers is high than that of non-drinkers, (2) its medicinal effect is not so important, while it is a habit-forming drug which is both depressant and narcotic in its effects upon the human organism, and (3) even its moderate use causes intoxication. Some truth appears to be on both the sides.

Drinking and Individual Disorganization. A healthy life organization can only be erected upon the basis of normal and healthy social relationships. When used to excess alcohol modifies these relationships, changes the reality of former social values and brings about highly individuated attitudes. The excessive drinker may forsake his home, his family and his business. When under the influence of alcohol he may be talkative or gloomily silent. His conversation may seem vulgar to the sober observer. When flown with wine he may be a liar, a scoundrel and may even commit

[8] Pearl, Raymond, "Alcohol, Biological Aspects", *Encyclopaedia of the Social Sciences*, Vol. I., pp. 621-22.

murder. Though it will not be appropriate to say that any adult who occasionally takes a drink is a candidate for personal disorganization yet even the intelligent and good looking people under prolonged indulgence may disintegrate and ultimately end in complete individual disorganization.

Drink and Family Disorganization. The problem of drink and family disorganization are closely allied to that of personal disorganization. In U. S. A. many divorces are granted on the grounds of drunkenness. Drink is also a motivating factor in many family tensions. When husband and wife in an alcoholically stimulated entertainment pay attention to someone else, it creates tension between the two later on. Sometimes savage quarrels result, which are enhanced by friends who hasten to impart any additional information concerning the temporary breach of moral standards of the erring spouse. Such quasi-promiscuity is not conducive to the highest type of family relationships. It is generally said that liquor has been a traditional enemy of love and marriage because of this unfair competition. Many habitual drinkers feel uneasy in the presence of women. They infinitely prefer the relaxation of masculine preferably slightly intoxicated. Chronic alcoholics often become completely disinterested in the opposite sex.

Tensions, by over-indulgence were previously brought out by man. But today this friction has been greatly increased by increase in drinking among women and family disorganization has increased due to latter's drink. A strong prejudice against drink on the part of a husband or wife of one who drinks is a constant source of friction in the family and leads to divorce later on. Mothers when they find that children are subjected to the vagaries of an alcoholic father, to save their children from such bad effects often resort to divorce. In lower class families where people have neither the knowledge of law nor the resources for divorce, drunkenness often causes untold misery. The family legally retain its solidarity but the normal cohesion is completely shaken.

Drink and Community Disorganization. The public hall or hotels where drinking along with other allied activities such as dance, prostitution, gambling goes on brings community disorganization. The elements of privacy, of clandestine drinking in an atmosphere conducive to over-indulgence, encouragement to excessive drinking by keeping girls as entertainers, permission of gambling and such other entertainments is often a menace to public decency. The increased presence of women both as patrons and entertainers is the most disorganizing element in such taverns.

Prostitutes openly solicit in many such places, which are often conducted in close association with establishments of commercialized vice. Young girls are engaged to act as "hostesses" in order to stimulate the consumption of liquor. Such a combination of alcoholic indulgence and sexual license have a disorganizing effect both upon the hostess and the patron. Thus, drink in taverns or hotels brings community disorganization in many ways.

History of Drinking in India

The use of intoxicating drinks in India dates back to ancient times. There is sufficient evidence to show that their consumption was looked upon with disapproval by Hindu scriptures and society. Generally, the people were sober and the use of liquor was confined to the lowest strata or residium of society. Increased habit of drinking in medieval times may be attributed in part to the example set by kings and their courtiers. But it is encouraging to note that "throughout the course of Hindu and Muslim periods, the masses generally remained free from the evil of drink and drugs—this is corroborated by foreign travellers including Fa Hien, Vasco Da Gama, Bernier and Tavernier who visited India at different times".[9] Various method of controlling the drink traffic were tried at different times with varying degrees of success. Such attempts were, however, few and far between and at least there was no attempt to derive any material revenue from the traffic because their consumption was insignificant.

The British Government did not follow the Indian tradition and tried to enforce the pattern in vogue in England with regard to drinks and other drugs. The year 1790 saw the enactment of excise laws and framing of excise rules in British India in consonance with the policy of maximum revenue with the minimum of consumption, a policy that was followed in the United Kingdom. But this policy had no salutary effect. On the other hand, the consumption of liquor increased much with the coming of British rule. The consumption of liquor was extended among the people by the personal example set by the average Englishman. The restraint fostered by tradition, religion and social customs over a long period

[9] *Report of the Prohibition Enquiry Committee* (1954), p. 4.

gave way to new forces set free by the British rule. The trade in liquor also went into a new and expanding phase. A system of controlled monopolies came into existence for the manufacture and sale of liquor. The demand created by the drink habit on the one hand and supported by trade interests on the other resulted in increased consumption. Drinking was given a social acceptance and more and better opportunities were provided for drinking than before. It became possible to have a drink under almost every circumstances, in restaurants, cinemas, messes, clubs, railway refreshment rooms and even in railway dining cars. Certain other external factors such as industrialization and urbanization indirectly contributed to the spread of drinking in larger cities. The worker living under the complex conditions of industrial areas away from the influence of family life felt the need for some kind of stimulant. The Indian Excise Committee was appointed in 1905 with a view "to examine the excise administration of each province, to consider how far it is calculated to give the fullest practical effect to the general policy which has been laid down and to suggest such alteration as may seem desirable".[10] The policy of the Government of India is described below.

The Indian Excise Committee (1905-06) observed that "the consumption of all classes of foreign liquor has largely increased .... The consumption of 'tari', unless properly controlled, is liable to lead to much drunkenness .... The consumption of country beers is causing much drunkenness in certain areas and the beers made are sometimes very deleterious .... The imported liquor which were mostly of cheap varieties were in demand by middle classes of the native population whose consumption by them tends to show a rapid increase."[11] Regarding the industrial workers they observed, "About a dozen large cities consumed a quarter of all the spirits recorded as drunk in India."[12]

The Government of India in their excise policy enunciated in 1905 pointed out: "the Government of India have no desire to interfere with the habits of those who use alcohol in moderation and it is necessary in their opinion to make due provision for the needs of such persons. Their settled policy, however, is to minimise temptation to those who do not drink and discourage excess among

[10] *Report of the Indian Excise Committee* (1905-06).

[11] *Ibid.*, pp. 141-42.

[12] *Ibid.*, p. 27.

those who do, and to a furtherance of this policy, all considerations of revenue must be absolutely subordinated. The most effective method of furthering this policy is to make the tax on liquor as high as it is possible to raise it without stimulating illicit consumption to a degree, which would increase instead of decreasing the total consumption and without driving people to substitute deleterious drugs for alcohol, or a more or less harmful form of liquor."[13]

The above policy with minor changes was in operation in all the Provinces for thirty-two years till 1938 when it was replaced in several Provinces by prohibition applied to selected areas, while in the rest of the areas the old excise policy still remained in force. During this intervening period a number of organizations—social, religious or political, impressed upon the Government of India that the excise policy followed by them was not effective in reducing the consumption of liquor and drugs but the Government evinced little interest in the work of such organizations. It was only after 1920 that abolition of liquor and drug shops became the popular demand when the Indian National Congress passed a resolution to this effect. Mahatma Gandhi, the great advocate of prohibition, placed it as one of the eleven demands before the Viceroy in 1930 for the settlement of Indian problems. After the introduction of Montford Reforms in 1921, several Provincial Governments enacted local option laws, which recognized the principle of self-determination on the part of local bodies in the matter of restricting the sale of intoxicating liquor within their respective jurisdiction. But this local option principle did not prove very effective because the abatement of drinking in a particular local area led to increased drinking in the neighbouring areas. Illicit distillation and smuggling also contributed to its failure. The movement towards prohibition slowly gained momentum after the introduction of Montford Reforms and resolutions to the effect that prohibition should be declared as the ultimate goal of excise policy was passed by Legislative Councils in several Provinces. However, it was only in 1937, when with the inauguration of Provincial Autonomy, Congress Ministries assumed office in certain provinces that real efforts were made to implement the policies of prohibition in selected areas.

[13] *Report of the Prohibition Enquiry Committee* (1954-55), p. 6. Also see *Report of the Indian Excise Committee* (1905-06), p. 26.

Between 1937 to 1939 five Provinces—Madras, C. P., Bihar, Orissa and N. W. F. P. (West Pakistan) — passed comprehensive legislation enacting prohibition. Madras was the first among them to make a beginning in this direction, where Salem District was declared dry in October 1937 and other Provinces followed suit. For example in Bombay and U. P. the prohibition programme was introduced in 1938. These experiments, however, remained in operation for a short time when war broke out in 1939 and the Congress Ministries resigned.

Progress After Independence

The policy regarding the use of alcohol after independence may be discussed under three heads : (*i*) Prohibition Programme from 1946 to 1956, (*ii*) Programme during Second and Third Plan, and (*iii*) 1966 and after.

(*a*) *Progress from* 1946 *to* 1956. The above programme was revived in 1946 when popular Ministries took up office in various states. The prohibition programme made good progress in some Provinces and by 1955 there was complete prohibition in the state of Madras, Andhra and Bombay while in states such as Assam, Kerala, Madhya Pradesh, Orissa, Punjab, Uttar Pradesh, Mysore and Himachal Pradesh there was partial prohibition and in the rest there was no prohibition at all. In the states where partial prohibition was in operation the dry areas ranged from one district in the whole of the state, as in Punjab, to 70 per cent of the total areas as in Mysore. In some states comprehensive prohibition legislation has been passed, while in others partial prohibition has been enforced by special notification on the basis of restrictive powers vested with Governments under the Excise Acts. The position with regard to various states was as follows :

In Bombay in 1946 the popular Government decided to introduce total prohibition in the state in stages over a period of four years. In pursuance of this policy the supplies of country liquor and drugs (and the number of toddy trees to be tapped) and quotas of sales of foreign liquor were curtailed progressively by 25 per cent each year from April, 1947 onward, culminating in total prohibition from April, 1950. The period of four years was allowed in order to give an opportunity to the drinkers to change their habits of using intoxicants, for the dealers and others engaged in the trade to switch over to other avocations and to enable the State Government to make the necessary administrative and other arrangements to meet the situation arising from the enforcement of complete prohibition. The foreigners were, however, allowed to drink and were granted foreign liquor licences. In consequence the illicit consumption of country spirit decreased from 10 lakh gallons in 1947 to 5 lakh gallons only in 1953, fermented liquor from 10 lakh gallons to 1.5 lakhs and wine from 36 thousand gallons to 7 thousand gallons in 1953. There was also progressive decrease in the consumption of toddy.

In the composite state of Madras the prohibition was introduced area-wise in three stages. Eight districts were made dry in 1946, eight more in 1947 and the remaining in 1948. There was provision for exemption in case it was needed for medical, scientific or such other purposes and foreign tourists and members of the armed forces. In consequence the illicit consumption of country spirit has come to nil while that of foreign liquor has substantially decreased.

The position in partial prohibition states was as follows. In Uttar Pradesh there was prohibition in 11 out of a total of 51 districts besides three pilgrim centres, representing about one-sixth of the total area of the state. The State Government was committed to the total prohibition as the ultimate goal. Substantial progress was also reported to have been made in the states of Orissa, Madhya Pradesh and Kerala where partial prohibition was in force.

Prohibition Enquiry Committee (1954-55). The above was the position, in a nutshell, when the Prohibition Enquiry Committee was appointed by the Planning Commission, Government of India in 1954 with Shriman Narayan as Chairman "to examine the experience gained regarding measures adopted by State Governments to promote prohibition with a view to assessing the extent to which these have been successful and analysing the practical difficulties—administrative, economic, social and others—which have come in the way of implementation of the programme of prohibition and to make recommendation for a programme for prohibition on a national basis".[14] The Planning Commission, while appointing the Committee, pointed out, "Article 47 of the Constitution lays down as a Directive Principle of State Policy that the state shall endeavour to bring about prohibition of the consumption, except

[14] *Report, op. cit.*, p. 2.

for medical purposes of intoxicating drinks and of drugs which are injurious to health. Experience gained in a number of states in implementing the programme of prohibition has suggested the need for further study of the problems connected with administration, co-operation and support from the community, financial aspects, co-operation between neighbouring areas, etc. With the object of developing a national programme for the fulfilment, with wide public support, of the Directive Principle of the Constitution, it is desirable at this stage to review the experience gained and to find solution for the problems and difficulties encountered in recent years."

The Committee after discussing the specific benefits accrued from prohibition and the difficulties encountered, came to certain conclusion and made its recommendations. The findings of the Committee may thus conveniently be discussed under four heads, i.e. (1) Specific benefits accrued, (2) the difficulties encountered, (3) conclusions, and (4) recommendations.

(1) *Specific Benefits Accrued.* Among the specific benefits which accrued in states like Madras, Bombay, Andhra and Madhya Pradesh where appreciable steps were taken they mentioned reduction in consumption, economic benefits and social gains.

(*a*) *Reduction in Consumption.* In Madras most of the old addicts had given up drinking excepting for a hard core which still remained to be dealt with. Estimating their number it was pointed out that out of 20 to 23 lakhs people who used to consume arrack toddy only twenty-five per cent remained to be reclaimed. More or less similar was the number in Bombay State and about thirty per cent of the previous addicts were still consuming liquor and drugs. In Andhra no statistics were available, but it was noted that the decrease in the number of addicts was more marked in the case of arrack toddy and ganja than in the case of opium and foreign liquor.

(*b*) *Economic Benefits.* The money, which now remained unspent on account of the non-availability of intoxicating liquor and drugs, found its use in fruitful directions. Debts incurred before were now being repaid, houses were being repaired or rebuilt, earthen utensils were being replaced by copper and brass ones. They were now able to afford better food and clothing and make even ornaments for their wives, give toys to their infants and education to their children. Most of the ex-addicts were able to improve their farm lands, purchase farm equipment and even live-stock. Thus, prohibition brought about a marked change in the standard of living of the poor working classes. It was observed that the industrial labour on account of prohibition was able to retain twenty to thirty per cent of the wage bill previously spent on drink. Some economic surveys to this effect conducted in Bombay (Ahmedabad) and Madras (Salem) have reaffirmed the same conclusions.

(*c*) *Social Gains*. Improvement in the condition of addicts had been a great asset to the society at large. The ex-addicts had now regained the lost social prestige and were looked upon as active and useful members of the society. Addicts have become conscious of their rights and duties as citizens. They actively participate in social and political activities. Family quarrels and street brawls have been eliminated. Regarding health the condition of ex-addicts has considerably improved. The improvement in the standard of living has improved the social and physical health of the family as a whole.

(2) *Difficulty Encountered*. The difficulties which the State Governments had to face for complete prohibition were as follows :

(*a*) *Administrative*. The administrative difficulties arose due to (*i*) lack of proper enforcement staff and want of adequate facilities for transport ; (*ii*) facilities afforded for smuggling by the peculiar geographical situation of some states and border problems created by adjacent wet states ; (*iii*) absence of protection to witnesses and the lenient attitude of magistrates in general, in prohibition cases ; and (*iv*) the comparatively simple process of manufacture of illicit liquor and the easy availability of base material for such purposes.

(*b*) *Legal*. Under the legal difficulties were mentioned: (*i*) the inadequacy of punishment for grave offences and procedural difficulties ; (*ii*) the absence of control over inter-state trade in spirituous and medicinal preparations and ineffective control over manufacture and sale of these preparations within the limits of states.

(*c*) *Social*. Under social difficulties were mentioned : (*i*) the absence of active support towards enforcement of prohibition and consequent indifference towards prohibition offences ; (*ii*) lack of adequate facilities for counter-attraction and propaganda ; and (*iii*) lack of specialized institutions dealing with addicts.

(*d*) *Economic*. In economic difficulties are included: (*i*) the lucrative nature of smuggling and distillation which lure the unemployed to engage in such illegal activities ; and (*ii*) unemployment created by the introduction of prohibition among toddy-tappers.

Similar difficulties were experienced in the partial prohibition states, with further implications due to the area-wise introduction of prohibition which gave stimulus to smuggling and illicit traffic.

(3) *Conclusions*. The Committee after assessing the benefits and the difficulties encountered in these states where prohibition was enforced came to the conclusion that the measure of success achieved in these states was by no means small. Consumption of liquor was considerably reduced and the quantity of illicit liquor now consumed by addicts who have not given up drinking was much smaller in comparison with the quantity of illicit liquor consumed in prohibition days. A distinct gain was that the prohibition of toddy had been successful. In case of other liquors prohibition has succeeded in weaning away a large number of casual drinkers who were generally averse to breaking the law. The younger generation was saved from acquiring the habit of drinking. No doubt there had been increase in offences on account of illicit practices in prohibition states, but the extent of such malpractices was often exaggerated. In the partial prohibition states, the success of prohibition has been limited on account of the existence of wet and dry areas side by side, but the consumption of alcoholic drinks and intoxicants has been reduced to a considerable extent in dry areas. Despite all difficulties experienced in the working of prohibition, they were of the opinion that prohibition was not only a sound policy but also a practical proposition and thus they recommended for nationwide prohibition programme. They also pointed out that in non-prohibition states the excise policy of minimum consumption and maximum revenue had, in reality, failed to achieve the objective of reducing consumption. While maximum revenue was being raised from a helpless people exposed to continuing temptation no tangible results had been secured in minimizing consumption. The supply of liquor near at hand made for sympathetic drinking.

Not only that but drink habit has been gradually spreading among classes hitherto not accustomed to it. "In larger urban areas, almost every witness affirmed that the drink habit was steadily on the increase. For instance, the Excise Commissioner of West Bengal was positive that the evil of drink has spread alarmingly amongst the younger generation and even among some of the women-folk of the upper classes in Calcutta. The Delhi State Government reports that students coming from well-to-do families have picked up the habit of visiting hotels where liquor is served. Some women belonging to advanced families have also been noticed to have taken up the drinking habit though their number is quite small. . . . We were informed that in the main industrial areas, such as coal mines, jute mills and the like, and amongst concentrations of labour in the Assam tea gardens and the large irrigation and other projects, liquor has entrenched itself into the economic life of the workers. The liquor traffic is enlarging."[15] Thus, year after year the drink was gathering new recruits. Liquor was habit forming and with the habit once formed it was hard to obliterate the craving.

With the above observation the Committee strongly recommended that prohibition should be regarded as an integral part of the Second Five-Year Plan and a uniform national policy alone will meet the requirements of the situation.[16] The target date for complete prohibition was fixed as 1st April, 1958. They also recommended for the appointment of a Central Committee to review the position from year to year. They recommended various steps to be taken in three categories of the states, viz., (*i*) states which have not yet enforced prohibition, (*ii*) states where partial prohibition is in force, and (*iii*) states where complete prohibition is in operation.

(4) *Recommendations.* With regard to states where no beginning towards prohibition was still made, from 1st April, 1956 : (*i*) there should be stoppage of drinking in hotels, bars, restaurants, messes, clubs, cinemas and in parties and functions except in hotels serving tourists and visitors which should provide separate room for serving liquors, and (*ii*) all advertisements relating to drinks should be stopped. Besides these two steps, (*iii*) the number of liquor shops in both rural and urban areas should be progressively reduced, (*iv*) liquor shops should be closed for an increasing number of days in a week, (*v*) a proportionate reduction should be effected in the quantity of supplies to the shop, (*vi*) the strength of distilled liquor produced by distilleries in India, should be progressively reduced, (*vii*) the closure of shops in and near specified industrial and other developmental project areas should be given high priority, and (*viii*) removal of shops to places away from living quarters in villages and towns.

[15] *Report, op. cit.*, p. 40.
[16] *Report, op. cit.*, p. 46.

Such steps were also to be taken in states where there was partial prohibition and complete prohibition was to be enforced at once. They also recommended for complete prohibition in the armed forces and appealed to foreign embassies not to serve liquor at public receptions where Indian citizens were invited. The public servants should observe total abstinence as it was found to be one of the chief factors in the failure of prohibition policy in U. S. A. and some other countries. Prohibition laws cannot be worked by those who lack faith in the policy and, therefore, abstinence should be made a rule of conduct for government servants.

In the states where there was complete prohibition in force (*i*) no permits should be issued on health grounds as they are misnomers ; (*ii*) tourists and visitors from abroad may be allowed to have liquor privately in their homes on the basis of special permits, but they should not be allowed to indulge in drinking in public after the target date ; and (*iii*) as in the prohibition states there was a tendency on the part of addicts to consume denatured spirits after these were rendered potable as a substitute for liquor and the abuse of industrial alcohol was one of the contributory causes for the repeal of prohibition in the U. S. A., satisfactory formulae may be devised to render industrial alcohol non-potable with a view to prevent its diversion, dilution and adulteration for drinking.

They also recommended various steps with regard to the manner and method of enforcement of prohibition laws taking in view the difficulties experienced by states where prohibition was already in force. The enforcement of prohibition had two aspects, viz. (*i*) legal and administrative, and (*ii*) the creation of public opinion. While law and, proper administration were essential, prohibition also demanded public cooperation. For this the measures suggested were as follows :

1. *Appointment of Administrator*. To achieve coordination between the two wings of the enforcement machinery, i.e. (*a*) legal and administrative, and (*b*) educative and preventive, an Administrator of Prohibition should be appointed in each state. The administrator will have control over the two wings of enforcement, but he will have no powers to interfere with the normal administration of the Police Department. The educative wing will be directly under him.

2. *Prohibition Boards*. There should be a Prohibition Board in each state consisting of representatives of both the wings of the

enforcement machinery as well as some representatives of public opinion, which will consider the details of policy and review the progress of prohibition programme from time to time. Similarly, there should be Prohibition Committees in each district and even up to the village and mohalla level.

3. *Legal and Administrative Aspects.* There should be a Prohibition Act in every state on the model of Bombay and Madras Acts. Prohibition offences should be treated on par with other offences and the police should be made responsible for legal enforcement of prohibition. Within the police department, there should be a special enforcement branch for prohibition work consisting of trained personnel. Mobile squads of police be organized especially for attacking sources of illicit supplies of liquor and drugs. The material used for illicit distillation should be destroyed by them.

4. *Education and Propaganda.* A regular, organized campaign should take the place of sporadic propaganda. The educative wing should educate public through all existing social organizations which have experience of this kind of work. Among them may be included temperance associations, local leaders, women's associations, trade unions, religious organization, etc. The Education Departments have a special function to perform in the matter of educating students and the young in regard to alcohol and habit-forming drugs. The press should be fully utilized to rally public opinion around prohibition.

5. *Preventive Measures.* Counter attraction centres in the form of recreation centres should be established on a large scale both by the states and non-official organizations. Special efforts should be made to persuade ex-toddy tappers to take up suitable cottage industries. Liquor contractors and vendors should be weaned off from their present occupations and encouraged to take up more productive lines of work.

6. *Persuasion of Habitual Drunkards.* It is of utmost importance to keep in touch with the families of habitual drunkards. Though drunkards offer hard resistance to persuasion, the force of persuasion even after many disappointments, will begin to make itself felt. Both the Government and non-official social agencies can co-ordinate their activities in this direction.

7. *Financial Aspect.* The loss from excise duties should be made good by steepening of estate duties, rationalization of rate structures and tightening up of tax collection. On the other hand, prohibition,

if effectively enforced, will contribute to the general economic prosperity of the country by raising the purchasing power of the people, by stimulating and increasing savings and by improving their general standard of living.

Programme During the Second and Third Five-Year Plans

The above Report was considered by the Planning Commission in consultation with State Governments and Central Ministries and was generally approved, though the target date suggested by the Prohibition Enquiry Committee as April 1958 was not accepted. The Planning Commission in the Second Five-Year Plan recommended that each State Government should approach the problem in terms of phased programmes setting out specific targets to be achieved over the whole field of social and administrative action within a reasonable time on the lines recommended by the Prohibition Enquiry Committee. In the states which have already introduced prohibition further steps should be taken for effective enforcement and increased public cooperation. Where partial prohibition was introduced, states were to consolidate and strengthen prohibition throughout their territories.[17] As a first step, as recommended by the Committee, in states where prohibition was still not introduced it was suggested that advertisements and public inducements relating to drink should be discontinued and drinking in public premises (hotels, hostels, restaurants, clubs, etc.), and at public receptions should be stopped. A series of other steps to be taken subsequently were also suggested, e.g. progressive reduction in the number of liquor shops, increasing number of dry days each week, reduction of supplies and of proof strengths of liquor and encouragement to inexpensive and soft drinks.[18]

The Planning Commission in the Third Five-Year Plan observed that although action had been taken in a number of states on the suggestions made by the Prohibition Enquiry Committee, yet for the country as a whole, progress had been slow.[19] They further pointed out, "It is not envisaged that States should fix target dates for introducing complete prohibition, for such target dates are in practice difficult to work out or to adhere to. However, a country-wide approach would make it easier for all states to ensure imple-

[17] *Second Five-Year Plan* (1956), pp. 607-09.
[18] For details see Committee's recommendations already mentioned.
[19] *Third Five-Year Plan* (1961), p. 722.

mentation and to check inter-state and inter-district smuggling. The various measures recommended in the Second Plan constitute a limited but practical programme which should be implemented in the course of next two or three years. It should be possible also for states which have introduced prohibition in some districts to extend it steadily to other areas, care being taken to provide for appropriate dry belts between districts which have prohibition and those in which prohibition has not yet been introduced. Periodical review and evaluation of progress would suggest further steps. In pursuing the programme for prohibition two important considerations should of course be kept in view. Firstly, the customs and traditions of the tribal people must be fully respected. Secondly, due attention must be given to the convenience and requirements of foreign visitors and tourists and of foreign missions."[20] The Commission also laid stress on the creation of a growing public opinion in favour of prohibition and financial assistance to voluntary organizations for educational activities as mere enforcement through police and excise staff will not serve the purpose.

This was the position in the beginning of the Third Five-Year Plan when China attacked India in November 1962. Some of the states, including Uttar Pradesh, reversed their policy of prohibition.[21] This was mostly done on the pretext of financial losses, though political corruption by vested interests may be another reason behind it.

Study Team on Prohibition (1964)

In January 1963 the Chief Ministers of States, after an informal discussion on the various aspects of prohibition came to the conclusion that there should be no relaxation in the existing system. As a consequence the Planning Commission appointed a Study Team on Prohibition in April 1963 with Sir Justice Tek Chand as Chairman to study the working of the prohibition programme for the country as a whole. The Team was especially entrusted to assess the magnitude of illicit distillation, examine the existing legislation on prohibition, suggest methods for securing maximum cooperation

[20] *Ibid.*, p. 724.

[21] Uttar Pradesh introduced partial prohibition throughout the state—in place of the earlier complete prohibition in 11 districts. Under partial prohibition important national days and 57 other days have been declared as dry days throughout the states. But this was an unfortunate position.

of voluntary organizations for prohibition onforcement and study the financial aspects of the prohibition programme. The position of prohibition programme when the Team was appointed was as follows :

TABLE 6

POSITION OF PROHIBITION PROGRAMME IN INDIA IN 1963

States having complete prohibition	*Partial prohibition*	*Mostly wet*
1. Gujarat	1. Andhra Pradesh (58% area)	1. Bihar
2. Madras	2. Assam (3 districts)	2. Rajasthan
3 Maharashtra	3. Kerala (59%)	3. Uttar Pradesh
	4. Madhya Pradesh (17%)	4. West Bengal
	5. Mysore (81%)	5. Delhi
	6. Orissa (41%)	
	7. Punjab (One district)	

The Study Team was much pained to see the increasing consumption of Alcohol in Wet States. It observed, "The picture which we now have of the wet states, is of increasing consumption. In order to realize this revenue the states have to encourage, if not, instigate the citizens to drink—the more frequent and excessive the libations, the better for the states treasury. . . . But certain basic facts regarding revenue from liquor need being borne in mind. When states are entering on the credit side of their ledger the liquor revenue, they are apt to omit from the debit side numerous expenditures involved in items like the cost of maintenance of convicted inebriates in jails, of alcohol caused crimes, cost of investigation and the conduct of cases in courts in which intoxicating beverages have played a part ; the damage done to person and property ; of hospitalization because of alcohol caused diseases, of absenteeism in factories and loss in hours which are a dead loss to production as also to the wage-earner ; damage done to machines and shorter life span because of drinking."[22]

The Study Team after studying the various aspects of the program-

[22] *Report of the Study Team on Prohibition* (1964), p. 214.

me in detail endorsed the implementation of steps recommended by the Planning Commission in the Third Five-Year Plan and also suggested a four-phased programme for the wet areas to have complete prohibition by 1975-76 after the third phase is over. The Team observed, "It would have been excellent if a uniform policy of prohibition could be followed all over the country. But under the circumstances, realistically speaking immediate and complete prohibition in wet areas is not feasible. This would lead to a tremendous upsurge of illicit activity and weaken the social fibre through lawlessness, corruption and allied evils. . . . We, therefore, recommend for wet areas a phased programme of movement towards total prohibition. Along with this programme we suggest supporting measures such as tax and price changes and changes in the system of supply so that the profit of illicit activity and the accompanying evils of lawlessness, corruptions, etc. may be kept at the minimum."[23]

In the first phase the proof strength of liquors be reduced. In the second phase there should be further reduction in the proof strength and public consumption of alcohol may be stopped by cancelling all on-licences and the licences for clubs, hotels and other public places. The addicts and habitual drinkers of an age above 40 to be given permits for hard liquor. In the third phase there was to be further reduction in the proof strength and it should generally be reduced to 5 per cent or less. These three phases were to be completed by 1975-76. In the fourth phase they will come in line with the dry areas and only addicts and habitual drinkers of an age above 40 years may be put on permit system. The toddy may be allowed to be served subject to a ceiling of 5 per cent alcohol within a prescribed limit and its production and sale should be under government control.

The Team also recommended many social, legal and penal measures to curb illicit distillation and sale and corruption The Team endorsed the recommendation of the Planning Commission made in the Third Five-Year Plan regarding educational work on Prohibition through voluntary organizations which were to be provided adequate financial assistance. It also recommended that the scheme of Nashabandi Lok Karya Kshettra (Centres for educational work on Prohibition) sponsored by the Planning Commission and run so far on a pilot basis should be extended so as to provide

[23] *Report, op. cit.*, p. 506.

for at least one Kshettra in each district and important industrial projects and urban areas.

Drug Addiction

Among other drugs may be included opium, charas, ganja, bhang, cocaine, etc. Among these charas, ganja, bhang and cocaine are obtained generally from hemp plant (plant of mulberry family yielding a coarse fibre, narcotic drug, etc). These are obtained from the leaves and flowers of local plants and do not have adverse effects on the physiology and well-being of the consumer as alcohol and opium. Opium drug is a class in itself and was perhaps introduced into India by the Muslim traders in the ninth century A.D. and its cultivation was soon extended to India. Opium and other drugs, i.e. charas, ganja, bhang and cocaine are consumed mostly by the poor and labouring classes. We shall discuss opium and the other four drugs separately.

Opium

Opium is either eaten in the form of a pill or drunk in solution with water. As a medicine it affords relief in digestive disturbances, cough and pain and produces sleep. The infants are often doped with opium in poor houses to keep quiet and allow their mothers to carry on their work. But the difficulty is that many people become addicted to it. Opium is also used in smoking. In 1907 an agreement was reached with the Chinese Government for gradual reduction of export of opium to China and the exports were completely stopped in 1913-14. As regards internal consumption of opium the policy followed before Independence has been one of regulating the use of opium for other purposes mainly through the device of stepping up the rate of duty. As regards smoking it is encouraging to note that under the Opium Smoking Act, passed in various Provinces, from 1948 onwards smoking was totally prohibited in all the states by the end of 1953 except to those who were registered. The policy in respect of registered smokers was to issue an annual quota and to stop it after their death. The excise policy of restricting consumption by stepping up the rates of taxation proved ineffective. In 1948 Excise Ministers' Conference was organized by the Government of India at New Delhi, wherein it was decided to abandon the present excise policy in favour of physical control on the supply of opium with the object of prohibiting oral consumption of the drug by March 1959. In pursuance of this policy a progressive cut of 10 per cent every year was to be made in the quota of opium allowed to the state excise departments. An annual reduction of 10 per cent from 1949 onwards has been put into force, so that the supply could be reduced to nil in 1959. It is to be noted that the production and distribution of opium is completely under the control of the Government of India and it was not difficult to prohibit it completely. The Prohibition Enquiry Committee rightly observed, "Opium is marching to its doom slowly but surely."[24] Thus, prohibition of opium is now in force in all the states of India.

Charas, Ganja and Bhang

Charas, ganja and bhang are the products of hemp plant. They are the narcotics most extensively indulged in by the poor classes. Charas is the resinous exudate obtained from the Cannabis plant grown in Central Asia. Experiments conducted in India have proved that this resinous matter did not materialize on hemp plants grown in India. Charas was imported by the Punjab Government from Yarkand to Leh in Kashmir State and warehoused in Punjab from where it was distributed in most of the Provinces. The supplies of charas were cut off in 1940-41 owing to the stoppage of production and export of the drug by the Sinkiang Government, and when the existing stock was exhausted its use automatically stopped. It is reported that many of the charas addicts who are mostly confined to United Provinces, Punjab and Delhi have now taken to smoking ganja as a substitute.

Ganja and Bhang. Ganja consists of the flowering tops of the hemp plant, while bhang consists of the dried leaves. Ganja, like charas, is generally smoked, while bhang is usually drunk. Bhang is also occasionally smoked. The narcotic effect of bhang is much less compared to that of either ganja or charas. The cultivation of these plants is restricted to small areas, and is licensed and carried under supervision of local excise officer.

The traditional policy of deriving maximum revenue with minimum consumption did not yield any satisfactory results. In respect of ganja, the Delhi Conference of 1949 referred to above, suggested its gradual prohibition. The State Governments agreed to follow this policy and took steps with a view to stop the use of

[24] *Report, op. cit.*, p. 53.

this drug over a period of years. The cultivation of the hemp plant has been discontinued in the prohibition states. In Madras under the Madras Prohibition Act of 1947 the possession of hemp drugs was entirely prohibited except by licences for the purposes of manufacturing medicinal preparations. In Bombay under the Bombay Prohibition Act of 1949 limited quantities of these drugs were made available from Government depots to registered addicts only ; gradual cuts are made in the quotas to wean them away from the use of hemp drugs. Similar steps have been taken in other states too. The issue price as well as the retail prices of ganja and bhang have been greatly increased in most states. For instance, in Bengal the rate of duty on ganja was gradually increased from Rs. 40 per seer in 1932 to Rs. 236 in 1951, and that of bhang from Rs. 3.50 per seer to Rs. 60 per seer in 1949. The Prohibition Enquiry Committee recommended their complete prohibition by April 1958 and for a progressive reduction in the number of shops and the quantities issued for consumption in the interim period. The sale of ganja and bhang are now prohibited in most of the states.[25]

Cocaine. This is obtained from cocoa leaves and is used as a drug. This drug was introduced in India sometime between 1890 and 1900. The use of this drug was at one time most prevalent in Northern India. The Government of India on account of its increased consumption imposed a ban on its import and prohibited the cultivation of cocoa plant inside the country. Though the vice has gradually died down in the country there are still a few cases of smuggling. Their number was 17 in 1953 and the total weight of the drug involved was 17 tolas only.

Central Organizations

A central organization—Narcotic Intelligence Bureau—was set up by the Government of India in 1936 under Articles 11 and 12 of the Geneva Convention of 1936 which coordinates the preventive activities of the Central and State Governments in respect of drug addiction. During the past few years, this has brought out history sheet records of 398 persons as traffickers in narcotics. These history sheets which contain all available information on the identity and criminal record of the traffickers are supplemented by periodical

[25] For details see *India—A Reference Annual*, 1965. Publications Division, Government of India, pp. 109-11.

investigations, the results of which are circulated to state excise and police authorities. These efforts have resulted in several big seizures and in smashing up some of the powerful rings of drug traffickers in India.

There is also a Central Committee to review the progress of prohibition programmes, to coordinate activities in different states and to keep in touch with their practical problems. This Committee was constituted on the recommendations of the Prohibition Enquiry Committee by the Ministry of Home Affairs which met for the first time towards the end of 1960.[26]

[26] *Third Five-Year Plan* (1961), p. 723.

CHAPTER VII

GAMBLING AND SMOKING

It is difficult to define the term "gambling" because many a time gambling activity cannot be separated from business transactions. The *Oxford Dictionary* explains the word "gamble" as : "Gamble means to play games of chance for money especially for unduly high stakes. The word gamble would not ordinarily be applied to the action of playing for stakes of triffling amount except by those who condemn playing for money altogether."[1] Mr. Stocking says, "The term gambling designates the deliberate waging or staking of important or valuable considerations upon events, which, so far as parties to the wager can know, lie in the realm of pure chance, or luck."[2] However, it is to be pointed out that many a time it is very difficult to draw distinction between a gambling act and an ordinary business transaction as referred above.

As Mr. Stocking himself points out, "The line between gambling and other activities is often hard to draw. Even in the most static circumstances chance plays an important part in the distribution of gains and losses ; and wherever the factor of pure chance can be segregated, activities that are essentially gambling may develop. Ordinary commercial transactions involve calculations based on rational data to the future course of the market ; but the data are never exhaustive, and in default of certainty action may be dominated by a spirit of 'plunging' virtually identical with gambling. It is particularly difficult to distinguish the gambling element from others in the specialized transactions known as speculation."[3]

Gambling and Speculation. In its simplest form speculation is the act of buying and selling commodities, securities or rights in order to benefit from changes in the prices. In so far as the speculator is governed by rational calculations based on factual data, however inadequate, the transaction is essentially commercial. When he

[1] *Oxford Dictionary*, Vol. IV, p. 35.

[2] Stocking, Collis, *Gambling in Encyclopaedia of Social Sciences* (1934), Vol. VI, p. 555.

[3] *Ibid.*, p. 556.

buys or sells simply in the blind hope that the market will turn his way he is gambling. Professor Reckless remarks, "It is difficult to make a sharp distinction between gambling and speculation or even the ordinary risks of business or other every-day activities."[4] Mr. Hardy points out two types of speculation. (1) Investment of resources in the effort to create wealth under conditions which involve more than ordinary uncertainty as to the results. (2) Speculation is the buying and selling of commodities, securities or land in the hope of realizing a profit from fluctuations in prices. However, he points out in the end that in spite of the distinction between speculation and gambling the two activities are closely related, particularly regarding the end, in view of the effects upon the individual. In both the objective is the same, to gain a relative advantage at the expense of the rest of the community either by superior knowledge or by superior luck. Speculation and gambling tend to undermine the appreciation of the value of money and of the value of work. They involve the same unpleasing willingness to profit by the misfortune of others and the same temptation to risk more than one can afford to lose.[5]

In the words of Dr. Bergler the difference between investment and speculation is : speculation means trying to make a great deal of money out of a small amount of money ; investment means trying to prevent a great deal of money from becoming a small amount of money. This definition pinpoints the difference between the harmless investor and the shrewd speculator. But the former may have to take chances, since risk is inherent in stock trading even when choice is deliberately limited to "solid" stocks. The latter does not concern himself with the solidity of a stock or the firm foundations of a business but instead speculates on "outsiders" among stocks, or risky propositions that "have to" make a killing. In not-too-exaggerated cases, the investor is not a gambler. The speculator, on the other hand, is always a pathological gambler.[6]

He also mentions three kinds of speculators. (1) The non-gambling, one-time speculator who succeeds in making a killing, takes his money, and retires to Florida. But such a speculator is a rare exception. (2) The small speculator—small in the sense of

[4] Reckless, Walter C., *The Crime Problem* (1955), p. 382.

[5] Hardy, Charles O., *Speculation Encyclopaedia of the Social Sciences* (1934), Vol. XIV, p. 290.

[6] Bergler, Edmund, *The Psychology of Gambling* (1958), p. 68.

money involved. He is the little man who spends every free minute in the brokerage office, or phones "his" broker twenty times daily. He trades in the stock market, loses and is always in *hock.* (3) The big speculator-gambler, who claims that he is not the sucker he considers the small speculator to be. What distinguishes him, he claims, is the "large concept", some knowledge of business, and "intuition". But he also points out that when scrutinized with the analytic microscope, there is no difference between the latter two types. Messrs. Sen and Das define speculation as, "Speculation comprises those activities which are based in the intelligent anticipation of coming events. It means the buying or selling of a commodity with a view to profit from the future changes in prices."[7] Speculation is different from gambling. Gamblers are persons who try to make a profit by assuming unnecessary risks. Often they themselves deliberately create the risks which they bear. For example, it is, of course, unnecessary whether England or Australia will win the test. There is uncertainty but none need bear it. A speculator, on the other hand, assumes necessary and natural risks. For example, the price of jute may rise or fall six months hence. There is a risk which must be assumed by somebody if the production is to run smooth.

Although speculation aids production and is beneficial from the economic point of view, yet this requires expert knowledge and honest dealing. While there are manipulative speculators who dupe the public and make them suffer unnecessary losses. They create a false opinion as to the general conditions of demand and supply and thus make the common man suffer. They may control the whole or most part of the supply of commodity and can then dictate market prices. Instances of successful corners are thus rare. It may be argued that what is lost by one is gained by the other and, therefore, there is no economic loss. But this is wrong. The marginal utility of sum lost by a person is more than the same gained by another person and particularly the rich one.

Gaming, Wagering and Betting. A wagering contract has been described as one by which two persons, professing to hold opposite views touching the issue of a future uncertain event, mutually agree that, dependent upon the determination of such event, one shall win from the other, and that the other shall pay or hand over to him,

[7] **Sen, S. N. and Das, S. K., *An Introduction to Economic Theory* (1947), p. 157.**

a sum of money or other stake ; neither of the contracting parties having any other interest in that contract than the sum of stake which he will so win or lose there being no other real consideration for the making of such contract by either of the parties.[8] Whereas a bet may not be regarding the future uncertain event and may be upon a past event, e.g. whether a particular horse won a race in a certain year or not.

Gaming in the ordinary sense means there must be a game of contest and participation by the bettors as players and not as on-lookers. The element of chance or uncertainty of result is common to gaming as well as to wagering or betting.

A lottery is a scheme for distributing prizes by lot or chance.

"Gaming" and "gambling" are synonymous terms except that the latter is suggestive of a practice more reprehensible from frequent indulgence. To game or gamble means to use cards, dices or other instruments according to certain rules with a view to win money or other things waged upon the issue of the contest.

Gambling Activities. Of purely gambling activities the simplest are those for which the circumstances of chance may be re-established easily and frequently at the will of the participants and in which the elements of skill and foreknowledge of the outcome are reduced to a minimum. The simple games of cards, in which the results are more dependent on fortuitous distribution than on the skill of play, have enjoyed wide popularity among gamblers. In simple dice and card games the duration of suspense and uncertainty between the casting of the dice or the dealing of the cards and the examination of the results is relatively short and allows frequent repetition. There are gambling activities such as sedentary games and athletic contests, which require fortitude and skill and in which some of the participant may participate directly in the play. In these may be included horse-racing and animal combats where the participants simply sponsor one side.

Professor Reckless has mentioned the following media most widely utilized for gambling : (*i*) card games, among which the most popular are bridge and rummy, (*ii*) dice, (*iii*) lottery and number games, (*iv*) horse-racing, (*v*) sports and athletic contests, and (*vi*) automatic gambling machines. But he has not included business speculation in gambling activity which Dr. Bergler does. Dr. Bergler remarks,

[8] Raju, V. B., *Gambling Acts of India* (1949), p. 7.

"Gambling is not only something done with cards and dice, it concerns more than betting on horses, roulette or the number racket. Gambling takes many forms and among them is business speculation"[9] He divides gambling activities into three categories and includes among them business transactions as well. These three categories are : (*i*) Games of pure chance : roulette, dice, screeno, etc. (*ii*) Games in which chance is combined with skill, reasoning, "secret information", and the ability to bluff : the stock market, poker, bridge, pinochle, horse-racing, etc., and (*iii*) games of pure reasoning : chess.[10]

He further points out that the devotees of games of pure or semi-pure "reasoning" are highly contemptuous of the adherents to games of pure chance. And both types behave as if they were world apart. Nevertheless, he concludes in the end, all three groups are alike genetically and psychologically, only the covering cloak is different. This conception is covered even by his definition of the gambler, when he says, "The popular concept of a gambler is that he is a person who wants to make as much money as he can with the least expenditure of time and effort."[11]

Occasional and Habitual Gambler. There are two types of gamblers, habitual and casual, as is the case with a drunkard or an alcoholic. For the habitual gambler Dr. Bergler has given six characteristics. "(*i*) Gambling is a typical, chronic, and repetitive experience in his life. (*ii*) Gambling absorbs all his other interests like a sponge. (*iii*) The gambler is pathologically optimistic about winning and never 'learns his lesson' when he loses. (*iv*) The gambler cannot stop when he is winning. (*v*) No matter how great his initial caution, the true gambler eventually risks more than he can afford. (*vi*) The gambler seeks and enjoys an enigmatic thrill which cannot be logically explained, since it is compounded of as much pain as pleasure .... Thus the title of gambler is reserved for a specific group of neurotics .... The person who indulges only occasionally in games of chance is not a pathologic gambler. Nor every 'Sunday gambler' is meant."[12] Regarding the gambler's conscious motivations, he adds, "In the myth of the eternally lucky gambler only the success is remembered ; the failure is forgotten .... For this he

[9] Bergler, Edmund, *op. cit.*, p. 66.
[10] *Ibid.*, p. 56.
[11] *Ibid.*, p. VII.
[12] *Ibid.*, p. 7.

calls upon three additional arguments—all of them irrational but to him completely convincing: (*i*) he is subjectively certain that he will win and he is a fanatic in his belief in ultimate success, (*ii*) he has unbounded faith in his own cleverness, and (*iii*) he claims that life itself is nothing but a gamble. He believes that luck alone has made many millionaires."[13] But luck alone is not enough, only the combination of luck-plus-personal initiative spells success. Greenson has mentioned three classes of gamblers: (*i*) Normal person (who) gambles for diversion or distraction and can stop gambling when he wants, (*ii*) Professional gambler (who) selects gambling as his means of earning a livelihood, and (*iii*) Neurotic gambler (who) gambles because he is driven by unconscious needs and who is unable to stop gambling.[14]

Causes of Gambling. It has been pointed out by Dr. Bergler that tendency to gamble is found in every person. In some personalities this latent tendency can be awakened, and the person becomes actual gambler. Thus, in his opinion the cause of gambling is hereditary, and neurotic person, when brought in such environments, his nerves become crammed. He affirms, "The confirmed gambler is neither gullible nor greedy, but markedly neurotic, according to the modern school of thought. It is held that the hectic gambler knows perfectly well that the odds are against him—that he notoriously refuses to stop when winning—and that, therefore he wants to suffer the excruciating thrill of losing. This craving for disaster is, of course, pathological — a condition that may require psychological attention."[15] However, Prof. Reckless points out that although neuroticism may be a causative factor in some gamblers, one must be cautious in inferring neuroticism merely from the fact that the person is a chronic gambler and then using neuroticism as an etiological explanation.[16]

Disadvantages of Gambling. As the definition of a gambler itself points out, that he is an idle person depending upon chance and hates work, a parasite living on the earnings of others. Professor Stocking points out, "The earliest opposition to gambling seems to have manifested itself when it began to interfere with activities,

[13] *Ibid.*, p. 9.

[14] Greenson, R. R., "On Gambling", *American Image*, Vol. 4, No. 2 (1947), p. 63.

[15] **Bergler, Edmund,** *op. cit.*, p. 241.

[16] *Ibid.*, p. 388.

which in the opinion of the ruling authorities should have first claim upon the time and energy of the masses. In ancient communities laws were passed to discourage the masses from gambling, and at later dates antigambling laws were aimed specially at the activity as practised by the working classes. Gambling also sets at defiance the bourgeois philosophy which holds that private property is something which the individual has earned and which in the nature of the case tends to be commensurate with the service rendered. Rewards which are determined by chance have no place in a system based upon such a premise."[17] Another difficulty is the malpractices of professionals associated with gambling. At all times an important factor in arousing antagonism to gambling has been the association, almost inevitable with sharp practice. For example, loaded dice, marked cards, sleight of hand, manipulations in play, machines rigged to the advantage of the house, race horses "doped" or "sponged", prize fighters bribed by insiders to "throw" the bout, false tips in the bucket shops, such devices are innumerable. It is for all these reasons that in established societies more or less serious attempts were made either to prohibit or to regulate gambling in its more notorious forms. But such regulations are among the most difficult to enforce adequately even by an honest and intelligent police administration because of the ease with which gambling operations can be carried on under cover and because of the extremely spasmodic interest of the public in the suppression of gambling.

Gambling and Demoralization

(*a*) *Gambling and Personal Disorganization*. We have pointed out above the disadvantages of gambling. It tends to promote idleness, dishonesty and other vices ; and thus has a pernicious influence on the character of those habituated to it. The inveterate gambler regards it as the easiest way of making a good fortune and heedless of the fallacy underlying his notion, he gives himself up to it with the infrequent result of bringing about his financial ruin. Ordinary pursuits of life possess little attraction for him, and moral degradation, a frequent concomitant of poverty soon overtakes him. Sometimes he resorts to crime such as theft, extortion and even murder in order to find money for gambling. It drags the person into extreme moral degradation and ultimately into extreme

[17] Stocking, Collis, *op. cit.*, p. 557.

poverty, which leaves him no alternative, but a recourse to evil means. Sometimes utter disappointment compels him to commit suicide.

As in the case of drug addiction and alcoholism, gambling begins to dominate a person's life and reduces him to derelict status. The chronic gambler may use ingenious means for securing money for gambling. This may lead to further demoralization of the individual as he becomes more deeply involved in gambling and resulting financial losses.

(*b*) *Gambling and Family Disorganization.* His evil habit is not confined to him alone. Every one coming in touch with him runs the risk of contracting the vice with all its consequences. Poverty at home may bring conflict between husband and wife, ultimately leading to divorce and family disorganization.

(*c*) *Gambling and Social Disorganization.* Gambling as a crime may be merely personal vice comparable to alcoholism or a criminal career. But it is often suspected that other offences such as forgery, passing bad cheques and petty crimes against property may be committed in order to pay gambling debts. Besides, gambling often occurs in combination with excessive drinking and bad associates, which lead to further disorganization.

Extent of Gambling in India. To know the magnitude of gambling is a great problem. No separate statistics about the offences in connection with gambling are available for the country. In Bombay State where investigations were carried by Miss Kerawalla into the structural pattern of criminal behaviour in 1956, it was found that gambling offences were on the increase, which is evident from the following table :

TABLE 7

GAMBLING OFFENCES IN BOMBAY CITY[18]

	1928	1938	1945	1952	1955
1. Number of bucket shops raided	14	31	110	10	2
2. Number of gaming houses other than bucket shops raided	109	977	525	1200	1525
3. Number of cases regarding house race betting	129	40	99	42	48
4. Other cases of gaming in public places	676	1056	1838	7280	8516
5. Number of persons arrested in connection with gambling offences	2101	5662	7274	21290	23348

[18] Kerawalla, P. C., *A Study in Indian Crime* (1959), p. 135.

Control of Gambling

As in other countries, efforts have been made in this country to control gambling since long. Manu advocated its total prohibition. He prohibits all games with dice, as also betting on animal races or fights. He classes gambling with theft and condemns it even though it be resorted to for mere recreation. According to him, gambling constitutes a source of danger to the state ; and those who practise it, whether in public or private, are offenders liable to any punishment the rulers might deem fit to impose. Manusmriti says, "The king should diligently keep gambling and betting away from the State. For these two vices destroy the State and sovereigns themselves." (221). "He who does these himself or causes them to be done by others, secretly or openly, may be punished by the ruler with punishment upto the death, at the ruler's discretion, like cheats and impersonators, pretending to follow vocations other than their rightful ones." (224-228). Under the Mohammadan Law, too, gambling was punishable as an offence.

In the British Rule the first Gambling Act was passed in 1867 with a view to put an end to the practice of keeping common gaming houses and of public gambling and fighting of animals prevalent in the provinces of Agra and Oudh, the Punjab, Delhi and the Central Provinces. In the same year a separate act was passed for Bengal as the previous Act was applicable in these provinces only. A common gaming-house under the Act, was defined as "a house, the owner or occupier of which levies a toll (generally a percentage on the winning) for its use for gambling on games of chance".[19] The existence of such houses was believed to be mainly responsible for the crime attributed to gaming in general and thus a source of danger to society. Prior to this keeping of a common gaming house was no offence. Public gambling was prohibited even before the passing of this Act.

However, it is to be pointed out that the Act did not completely prohibit gaming. Games of skill were not forbidden ; nor games of chance provided they were played in a "private house" and not a "common gaming house". A "private house" means any house whose owner or occupier gratuitously permits its use for gaming purposes, whereas a "common gaming house" means any house in which instruments of gaming are kept or used for the profit or gain

[19] Raizaday, B. N., *The Public Gambling Act* (1927), Introduction, p. xi.

of its owner or occupier, whether by way of a charge for the use of the instruments of gaming or of the house, or otherwise howsoever. Gaming as such was not defined under this Act. Gaming as defined by the Bombay Prevention of Gambling Act, 1887 means "any transaction by which a person in any capacity whatever employs another in any capacity whatever or engages for another in any capacity whatever to wager or bet."[20] In this Act gaming includes wagering or betting. The objective of the Act of 1867 was to discourage gaming only in so far as it was believed that it led to the injury and demoralization of poor persons. The penalty was more for the keepers of common gaming houses than for the actual gamblers. Money found in a common gaming house in course of a search was forfeitable under the act. However, the act made provision only against the keepers of common gaming-houses and the frequenters of such houses and did not inflict severe penalty on gamblers if they played in a house, where no tax was charged. Thus, the Act did not approach the private gambler directly. Such gaming goes on, on an extensive scale in clubs and other private places.

Because of the loop-holes in this Act, a new game or form of betting known as *satta* came up and became very popular with the poor classes. In order to remove some of the defects in the Act of 1867 and check *satta*, various amendments were made by the three states—United Provinces, Central Provinces and Punjab, while separate acts were passed by other States to control gambling, e.g. the Bombay Prevention of Gambling Act, 1887, the Madras Gaming Act, 1930, Rajasthan (1949), Orissa (1955), Delhi (1955), etc.[21]

In spite of all these acts in various states gambling is still resorted to by a large majority of the people and some forms of gambling are even exempted from the law such as horse-racing and gaming in private houses, which have demoralizing effect.

Horse-racing is allowed under two conditions, when such wagering or betting takes place (*a*) on the day on which such race is to be run, and (*b*) in an enclosure which the licensee of the race course, on which such race is to be run, has set apart for the purpose under the terms of the licence issued under the Race Course Licensing Act.[22]

[20] Sami, S. M. A., and Iyer, K. J., *Gambling in India* (1947), p. 82.

[21] For details see Mathur, L. P., Commentaries on Gambling Acts in India (1962).

[22] *The Bombay Prevention of Gambling Act*, 1887, Section 3.

But horse-racing is also an evil, and is one of the forms of gambling. An excerpt from a letter written to Gandhiji by an English lady will make it more clear, "You will earn the gratitude and thanks of thousands of wives, both European and Indian, if you can succeed in putting a stop to betting at the races. My husband was an ideal husband—until he took to betting at the races. We are now in debt, and, although he draws a good salary and does not drink alcohol, we are hard up, and I am sure this is the experience of very many wives. I have often implored him on my bended knees not to go to the races, but to no purpose. And does it not seem very hard that wives and children should suffer because their husbands cannot refrain from going to the races and losing money? It is true that alcohol is ruining thousands but betting at races is certainly ruining tens of thousands.... By practically robbing the public, the W.I.T. Club can afford to pay its European Employees handsome salaries. If you were only in the know I am sure you would agree with me that hanky-panky tricks are carried on by the Turf Club and thus the public are cheated and robbed of a lot of money. Do, for God's sake, try and right matters. Things were certainly better when the book-makers were allowed to take bets on the race course."[23]

Gambling on race course was introduced from abroad. Gandhiji advocated that the protection of law that gambling enjoys on the race course even to a limited extent must be withdrawn. Sometimes it is argued that horse-racing is necessary for breeding good horses. But it can be possible to have horse-racing without gambling. Similarly, gambling cannot be an aid to good breeding of horses. He strongly advocated to the popular governments in 1946 to put an end to this evil. In Harijan he wrote, "I do not know all the intricacies of horse racing. All I can say is that if it is within the competence of a popular government to put an end to the evil it should certainly do so."[24] He further pointed out that law alone will not be able to stop gambling, unless it is backed by public opinion. He said it was much more difficult to root out this evil than drinking which was socially disliked. "Betting at races is a part of the gambling mania. If only the people will non-cooperate, the evil will die a natural death. Thousands who attend the race course, do so merely for fun. They attend either to see horses run breathlessly,

[23] Gandhi, M. K., *Drink, Drugs and Gambling* (1952), p. 159.
[24] Gandhi, M. K., *op. cit.*, p. 165. Also see *Harijan* (18-8-1946).

or because it is the fashion, but they, nevertheless, aid and abet the ruin of many a gambler.

But betting is, I apprehend, more difficult to deal with than drinking. When vice becomes a fashion and even a virtue, it is a long process to deal with. Betting is not only fashionable, but is hardly regarded as a vice. Not so drinking. Fortunately, it is still the fashion to consider drinking a weakness, if not positively a vice. Every religion has denounced it with a more or less vehemence. But betting has escaped such special attention. Let us hope, however, that the vigilant public will find a more innocent recreation than attending the race course and thus show its disapproval of gambling at the race course.

The law must be against this gambling. But it is of no avail if public opinion is not behind it. It is, therefore, necessary for workers to bestir themselves. They must not be satisfied till the evil is rooted out. The war against gambling is an uphill task, but it must be tackled."[25] Dr. Bergler points out, "Gambling is a rather static phenomenon. I believe this is because it is a uniquely convenient way of expressing childish megalomania. Society ridicules the man who makes an out-and-out claim to omnipotence, and brands him a psychotic. The gambler, however, entertains the same unreal fantasy under conditions that can be mis-understood by the outsider as having a 'rational' aim — that of winning money. This pseudo-rational social approval perpetuates gambling."[26]

Treatment of Gamblers

Nothing has been done so far in the way of rehabilitation and psychotherapeutic treatment of gamblers. Greenson and Dr. Bergler, to whom we have already referred, point out that only adequate therapy is psychoanalysis. Dr. Bergler points out, "Gambling is a complicated neurosis, but it is generally not recognised as such. In the outer world, the unfortunate gambler—who often ends in suicide—simply bears the stigma of immorality. The only chance of changing him lies in psychoanalytic treatment, where the prognosis is favourable."[27] But this method can be useful for treating neurotic gamblers only, and cannot be applied in case of demoralized or professional gamblers. Even in case of neurotic gamblers

[25] Gandhi, M. K., *op., cit.* pp. 160, 163.
[26] Bergler, Edmund, *op. cit.*, p. 240.
[27] *Ibid.*, p. 239.

the treatment is only temporary as the neurotic gambler relapses because "feelings aroused by winning and losing are interwoven with guilt feeling that full satisfaction is impossible and frustrated wishes return again and again, seeking gratification".

The gambler can only be helped through deterrent punishment, friendly advice, or religious teachings.

Smoking

The custom of tobacco smoking is so ancient that it is impossible to state where and when it originated.[28] However, so far India is concerned tobacco was imported into this country from America by Portuguese in the beginning of the seventeenth century.[29] Dr. Koskowski remarks, "In India, tobacco has been known since 1605 and in 1610 it was already being cultivated in Ceylon ; by about 1619 it was being exported to the ports of the Red Sea. Tobacco smoking became common soon after the introduction of the plant. The Portuguese also introduced snuff taking into India. The Brahmans confined themselves to taking snuff and never smoked tobacco, because a cigar once soiled with saliva cannot be replaced in the mouth."[30] While tobacco smoking came to India from America as did the plant itself, all the utensils used for smoking are of local origin. The smoking of water-pipes also originated and developed locally and the water-pipe was known as *hooka*. There are several types of water-pipes but all are based on the idea of passing the hot smoke through water in order to cool it and purify it of toxic substance.

The forms in which tobacco is used at present are : cigars, cigarettes, bidis, pipes, tobacco chewing, tobacco eating and licking and snuff-taking.

Advantages and Disadvantages of Smoking

Many advantages and disadvantages of tobacco have been claimed by its supporters and opponents. Its devotees believed that it has a mysterious influence on the activity of the mind, is responsible for the poet's inspiration, the formation of political talents, and the creation of new ideas, achievement of discoveries and great enter-

[28] Koskowski, W., *The Habits of Tobacco Smoking* (1955), p. 39.

[29] Gupta, Dauji, *Tobacco Industry in India*, unpublished Ph.D. Thesis, Lucknow University (1964), p. 2.

[30] Koskowski, W., *op. cit.*, p. 48.

prises. It was also considered a panacea for many ailments. However, with the passing of time antagonism has gradually developed against this false panacea both in medicine and in other intellectual activities. The controversy became alive during the middle of the nineteenth century and still continues, though the opponents are now stronger. In view of the enormous spread of the smoking habit the tobacco problem is today a question of the greatest moment.

Bad Effects of Smoking

The evil effects ot smoking may be discussed under two heads, viz. (*i*) Biological, and (*ii*) Economic and Social.

Biological Effects. As a result of a large number of researches it has now been established that excessive cigarette smoking is the chief factor responsible for lung cancer besides many other diseases caused by the use of tobacco. Among other diseases Dr. Ochsner has mentioned heart disease, circulatory ailment, cerebral haemorrhage, blindness (from nicotine amblyopia), loss of sense of taste and smell, nervousness and irritability, indigestion, respiratory diseases such as smoker's cough, smokers' throat, smoker's larynx, impotency (in man) and sterility (in women).[31] He further says, that unless one dies earlier from something else, the risk of death from lung cancer about the age of fifty-five is heavy. The risk of getting lung cancer will depend upon the amount a person has smoked and the number of years he has maintained that habit. Incessant smokers, for the most part, can choose the site of their cancers. The cigarette smoker may prefer to risk cancer of the lung ; pipe smoker cancer of the lip ; cigar smoker cancer of the tongue. If started in young age, it can disguise existing nutritional defects, e.g. of vitamins and interfere with normal development of the body as it emerges from childhood to puberty. At puberty a deficiency of vitamins or of an essential foodstuff may be compensated from psychological standpoint only by the use of tobacco which would tend to hide the undesirabie effects of the lack of function of the thyrcid gland, suprarenals and other glands of internal secretion and of the autonomic nervous system.[32]

Economic and Social Effects

Economically, smoking entails enormous loss to the individual,

[31] Ochsner, Alton, *Smoking and Cancer* (1954), p. 2.
[32] Koskowski, W., *op. cit.*, p. 272.

his family and the nation. There is economic loss to the individual and the family because of the expenses incurred on tobacco or cigarettes which can be utilized for other purposes. Many a time fires are caused by the negligence of tobacco smokers. There is also a loss of work and effort caused by this habit. "Such losses can reach 15 to 25 per cent due to invalidism caused by affections of the circulatory system and other organs, abbreviation of life and the reduction in the efficiency of human work."[33] There is also a loss of time too. It has been estimated that every man who takes snuff does so at least every ten minutes. Every inhalation with sneezing and the consequent cleaning of the nose takes $1\frac{1}{2}$ minutes, hence 2 hours and 24 minutes are lost in every 24 hours by snuff taking. This is equivalent to $36\frac{1}{2}$ days per year.[34] In India lot of money is spent on the import of foreign made cigarettes and tobacco which creates difficulty in foreign exchange.

The use of tobacco in modern times is an expensive luxury. It has a bad effect specially on the youth and is often associated with other bad habits such as gambling, drinking and undesirable social contacts in badly ventilated premises. Dr. Benjamin Rush observed that smoking and chewing provoked drunkenness. Similarly, Dr. Osler observes, "Many alcoholic patients in whom the attacks seem to be without existing cause, if questioned closely, are found to be great tobacco smokers, and the cause of that outbreak is really a recurrent poisoning by tobacco. Usually the history is that they smoke, especially the cigarette smokers, incessantly and to excess. This finally makes them nervous. Then they smoke more to quiet their nervousness until finally they seek another narcotic to quiet them. Then they naturally turn to alcohol."[35]

Classification of Smokers. Smokers may be divided into various categories, namely, non-smokers, light smokers, moderately heavy smokers, heavy smokers and chain smokers. According to Dr. Ochsner a non-smoker is one who has not regularly smoked one cigarette per day for twenty years. A light smoker is one who has consumed from one to nine cigarettes a day for the same period. Smoking from ten to fifteen cigarettes daily makes one a moderately heavy smoker, and if one has smoked from sixteen to twenty a day for twenty years, he is a heavy smoker. An excessive smoker con-

[33] Koskowski, W., *op. cit.*, p. 93.
[34] *Ibid.*, p. 93.
[35] Ochsner, Alton, *op. cit.*, p. 80.

sumes from twenty-one to twenty-four cigarettes a day. More than that makes him a chain smoker.[36] Here he is using this span of twenty years, because he is relating the susceptibility of these various types of smokers to cancer. For he says, "A man of fifty who has smoked a pack of cigarettes a day for twenty years has fifty times more chance of contracting lung cancer than a non-smoker."[37] Such classification can also be made for persons who use pipe or cigar or some other form of tobacco.

Causes of Smoking

There are various reasons which force people to start smoking. One may start smoking for sake of company, to minimize certain pains, to cure certain diseases, as a fashion or because his parents are smokers. A person who once becomes addicted to it, it becomes difficult for him to leave this habit. So far as college students are concerned, Dr. McHugh, Professor of Psychology at Duke University, found that his college students started smoking because they wanted to appear more grown up, to relieve a sense of inadequacy, to attain proper status in a group, to become what they regarded as men and women of the world.[38]

In France a snuff box was an essential part of a gentleman's costume from the seventeenth to the nineteenth century.[39] "In England, grandmothers smoked pipes in theatres, and when the fashion of snuff-taking was introduced, aristocratic ladies fed their noses with snuff mundungus. In fact snuff became more indispensable to the toilet of ladies of high society than soap. In the late nineteenth century the 'new woman' often smoked in order to demonstrate her emancipation and to emphasize her equality with men."[40]

It has been called a communicable disease—in a sense that desire to smoke originates from the advocacy of smoking by smokers, much of it unconscious. Saturation with nicotine turns habit into addiction. Like the opiates, nicotine causes definite physiological changes. The body becomes dependent upon a daily dose of nicotine and tends to want larger and larger doses. Dr. Lennox Johnston—

[36] *Ibid.*, p. 3.
[37] *Ibid.*, p. 3.
[38] Ochsner, Alton, *op. cit.*, p. 59.
[39] Koskowski, W., *op. cit.*, p. 38.
[40] Koskowski, W., *op. cit.*, p. 87.

a British investigator, has come to the conclusion, that addiction to tobacco, like addiction to opium, is a specific disease—an intermittent intoxication.[41] Mahatma Gandhi says, "Smoking, I consider, to be a vice. It deadens one's conscience and is often worse than drink in that it acts imperceptibly. It is a habit which is difficult to get rid of when once it seizes hold of a person. It is an expensive vice."[42]

Extent of Smoking in India

Some statistics are available about the manufacture and import of tobacco and cigarettes and also about the number of people using it. In 1928 Mahatma Gandhi estimated that India paid for unmanufactured tobacco and cigarettes 213 lakhs of rupees per year. The import of unmanufactured tobacco which was 1.25 million lbs. in 1923 rose to 5 million in 1927. There was a corresponding increase in the import of cigarettes. This excluded the amount of tobacco grown in our own country.[43] The position had deteriorated after Independence. Not only the consumption of tobacco products has increased after Independence but there has been considerable shift in the smoking habits of the people. The consumption of tobacco which was 538 gms. per capita in 1943-44 rose to 578 gms. in 1951 and 590 gm. in 1956, as may be seen from table 8.

TABLE 8

PER CAPITA CONSUMPTION OF TOBACCO PRODUCTS IN INDIA[44] (IN GRAMS)

	1943-44	47-48	50-51	55-56	60-61	62-63
1. Cigarettes (F. C. V.) of Flue Cured Virginia Tobacco	34	36	35	38	53	52
2. Other cigarettes	16	15	26	36	43	49
3. Bidis	73	100	132	175	166	189
4. Snuff	4	6	7	11	12	13
5. Cigar	38	63	65	53	46	41
6. Hookah	251	123	151	140	90	89
7. Chewing	122	153	162	137	140	141
Total	538	496	578	590	558	575

[41] Ochsner, Alton, *op. cit.*, p. 58.
[42] Gandhi, M. K., *Drinks, Drugs and Gambling* (1952), p. 155.
[43] *Ibid.*, p. 156.
[44] *Tobacco Export*. Also see Dauji Gupta, *op. cit.*, p. 265.

It will be noted from the table that the consumption of snuff, bidis and cigarettes has increased much more than of other products.[45] Both cigarettes and bidis are more harmful than hookah, whose consumption has decreased. The snuff besides health hazard also wastes a lot of time. The increasing use of cigarettes and bidis is likely to be more pronounced with further improvement in the living standard and rapid urbanization. The rapid increase in the production of cigarettes may be seen from table 9.

TABLE 9

NUMBER OF CIGARETTES MANUFACTURED IN INDIA[46]

Year	*Number of cigarettes manufactured in millions*
1951	21,448
1956	26,304
1961	46,470
1964	46,206

Due to the increasing use of cigarettes we have also to import some tobacco from outside, which adds to our foreign exchange problem. The figures for import and export of tobacco may be seen from table 10. The total number of factories and labour employed in tobacco products may also be examined from table 11.

TABLE 10

IMPORT AND EXPORT OF RAW TOBACCO[47]

(Figures in 000)

	1961-62		1962-63		1963-64	
	Quantity	*Value*	*Quantity*	*Value*	*Quantity*	*Value*
	Kg.	*Rs.*	*Kg.*	*Rs.*	*Kg.*	*Rs.*
Imports	1083	10720	1177	11323	951	8284
Exports	44421	140363	60240	179487	63874	210912

[45] The Bidi consumption which was 197 bidis per capita in 1939 rose to 700 in 1967. "Bidi Industry" in *Enterprise Journal* of Vidarbha Industries Association, Nagpur, October, 1967, p. 23.

[46] *Statistical Abstract of the Indian Union* 1965 (1966), p. 136.

[47] *The Times of India, Directory and Year Book* 1965-66, p. 44.

TABLE 11

FACTORIES AND LABOUR EMPLOYED IN TOBACCO PRODUCTS[48]

	1956		1962	
	Factories	*Labour*	*Factories*	*Labour*
1. Bidi	1580	71,328	1467	72,090
2. Cigar	64	2,941	24	948
3. Cigarettes	30	9,514	14	1,159
4. Snuff	13	468	28	809
5. Jerda products	168	4,904	235	9,203
6. Others	466	58.463	400	77,106
Total	2321	1,47,616	2,171	1,71,665

Control of Smoking

Because of the various bad effects of smoking—biological, economic and social, the total prohibition will bestow many benefits, as the general health of the individual will improve with the resulting benefits to the health and moral well-being of the community as a whole. But there are some people who argue that it is extremely difficult to eradicate smoking completely, since it has become a psychological infection. Therefore, attempts should be made to remove (*i*) nicotine and carcinogens from tobacco smoke or from tobacco itself, and (*ii*) to restrict its use. Mahatma Gandhi says, "Smoking has attained alarming respectability. When a vice reaches that state it becomes difficult to eradicate."[49] To minimize its harmful effects and to restrict its use the following steps may be suggested.

(1) *Removal of Nicotine*. The extraction of nicotine from tobacco leaves can be done with water or similar solvents. To remove the toxic substances from tobacco smoke, without diminishing the characteristic aroma of tobacco, two types of filters have been suggested, one for the basic water-soluble nicotine, and the other for ether-soluble carcinogens.[50]

(2) *Restriction on Excessive use*. To help anyone to stop smoking is not easy. It is really a psychological problem. As already pointed out the psychological urge is reinforced by a pharmacological

[48] *Statistical Abstract of the Indian Union* 1956-57, p. 565 and 1965, p. 454.

[49] Gandhi, M. K., *op. cit.*, p. 156.

[50] Koskowski, W., *op. cit.*, p. 271.

craving—a real hunger for tobacco, which is more difficult to stop. Physicians have a great responsibility on setting a good example to their patients by their controlled approach to the use of tobacco even if complete abstinence is not feasible. It has been seen that some heavy smokers have successfully reduced their consumption of tobacco and then either stabilized their smoking on a moderate level or stopped entirely. Another way of minimizing health risks, particularly lung cancer, is to switch over from cigarettes to pipe and cigar. But one should not draw too heavily on pipe as it may develop mouth cancer.

In the case of chain smokers, it has been found that it is advisable to stop smoking completely once for all. Certain drugs have been found to cause complete distaste for tobàcco in all its forms. One type of chewing gum may be replaced by another gum according to the taste.

Dr. Ochsner has given some suggestions to stop smoking : (*i*) The smoker should stop smoking abruptly, completely, and permanently. (*ii*) He should try to know the reason why he started smoking. He should ask himself whether it really gives any benefit, e.g. relief from fatigue. (*iii*) He must build up his resolution, i.e. his determination must be strong. He should try to know its bad effects and consequences, e.g. cancer, etc. and then try to resolve. (*iv*) He should throw away all smoking paraphernalia ; cigarettes, cigars, cigarette holders, pipes, even ash trays and cigarette containers. He should tell his friends that he has stopped smoking on the advice of his physician so that they may stop offering him cigarettes. (*v*) He should eschew the company of heavy smokers. (*vi*) The first day and a half after one has stopped smoking is the crucial period. Therefore, one should resolve not to smoke during this period, after which the intensity will decrease. (*vii*) He should adopt substitute habits to minimize the craving for tobacco. For example, one should take a drink of water, an apple or some other fruit when one feels an impulse to smoke. One may go for a good walk or have an agreeable companionship. (*viii*) One should also keep note of the benefits and call them to the attention of his friends. For example, how much money and time you have saved, regained your health and have been freed from so many diseases.

CHAPTER VIII

PROSTITUTION

PROSTITUTION has been generally defined as promiscuous (i.e. indiscriminate) intercourse for hire whether in money or in kind. In the words of Mr. Geoffrey, "Prostitution may be defined as the practice of habitual or intermittent sexual union, more or less promiscuous, for mercenary inducement."[1] Professors Elliott and Merrill remark that prostitution has been frequently defined, but all definitions are in essential agreement, namely, that the practice involves illicit sex union on a promiscuous and mercenary basis with accompanying emotional indifference. Prostitution is not to be confused with the illicit sex union of lovers, for there is no affection in prostitution. Nor is the mistress who receives monetary blandishments, a prostitute, for usually she is not promiscuous and her sex favours are granted on an affectional basis.[2] Thus, there are three important constituents of prostitution, viz. (*i*) illicit and promiscuous sexual intercourse, (*ii*) mercenary basis whether in cash or in kind, and (*iii*) lack of affection or personal interest. The Advisory Committee on Social and Moral Hygiene observes, "Adopting Flexner's definition three elements namely, barter, promiscuity, emotional indifference should be present."[3]

Prostitution as a commercialized vice has existed in the world from time immemorial, though its institution has never been recognized by the society as such. As the world's oldest profession prostitution has undoubtedly existed in some form as long as society has attempted to regulate and control sex relationships through the institutions of marriage and the family. Society has not recognized it because it brings in its train not only the personal disorganization of the persons concerned, but also affects the life organization of the family and the community at large.

[1] Geoffrey, May, "Prostitution" in *Encyclopaedia of the Social Sciences*, Vol. XII, (1935), p. 553.

[2] Elliott, M. A. and Merrill, F. E., *Social Disorganization* (1941), p. 242.

[3] *Report of the Advisory Committee on Social and Moral Hygiene* (1954), p. 30.

Causes of Prostitution

The causes of prostitution fali under two main heads, viz. biological and socio-economic. The first one is a natural phenomenon, while the second one is the creation of society. The biological course operates through sex urge in human beings. It is only by applied efforts that a man can control his sex desires, but it is not possible to do so in all cases. It is also the reason that man like the anthropoid apes can prostitute his sex by introducing sexual stimuli into intrinsically non-sexual situations, which is not possible in other lower species. Among the socio-economic factors have been included many, the most important being the poverty of the female who in the absence of any other means of support for herself or for her children resorts to prostitution. Davis Kingsley has explained prostitution on the basis of dominance and subordination.[4] In most of the societies the male is the dominant factor in sex equation. This dominance is based upon both superior physical strength and certain traditional social forms. The female attempts to equalize this situation by attracting and holding the attention of the male by the use of the only power at her command—sexual stimulation and satisfaction. Among other socio-economic factors may be included modern industrialization and rapid urbanization which have affected the sex ratio in the cities, lack of family and social control, lack of moral teachings, more contacts between men and women during employment, overcrowding, commercialized recreation including cinemas and dancing hall, drinking and late marriages to keep higher standard of living..

From the causes discussed above the most predominant cause which operates among males is the sexual urge, the chief cause which affects females is their economic dependency.

Causes of Prostitution for Males. It has been observed that different causes work in three different groups of males when they are classified on the basis of their marital status. These three groups are (*i*) the unmarried persons, (*ii*) the married persons, and (*iii*) the widowers.

(*i*) The cause of prostitution for unmarried persons lies in unfulfilment of their sexual urges and the social barriers to their satisfaction. The double standards of morality which are different for males and females further encourage it. While women are stig-

[4] Kingsley, Davis, "The Sociology of Prostitution" in *American Sociological Review* (October, 1937), pp. 745-56.

matized for illicit intercourse, no such strong social disapproval is shown against men. The postponement of marriage because of economic necessity further contributes to the increase of prostitution among bachelors. Among other causes may be included sex stimulating literature, indecent shows, lustful conversation, use of alcohol, lack of moral teaching and curiosity for sex experience. Another belief is that sex relationships are necessarily periodical for reasons of health, although modern medicine rejects this theory and insists that psychological motives rather than those primarily physical are present in the satisfaction of sex desire.

(*ii*) A fair percentage of married persons resort to prostitution. The reasons given are (*a*) unsatisfactory marital relationship, because of the indifference or distaste which their wives have for the sex relationship, (*b*) to escape from the emotional tensions in their marriage which exists because of temperamental or cultural differences between the couple, and (*c*) there are certain happily married persons who seek to escape the monotony of the marriage relationship. The wish for new experience in the form of new sexual conquests motivates them to seek out prostitutes.

(*iii*) The divorced man is often lonely and establishes a relationship with a prostitute for companionship, and many times the sex drive itself causes men, who have become accustomed to regular sex relationship in marriage, to resort to prostitution when their relationships have ended.

Causes of Prostitution for Females

Dr. Punekar and Miss Rao who conducted a study of prostitutes in Bombay have mentioned 26 causes which led those women to prostitution. They have grouped these causes under six major heads. In the first group are included death of parents or husbands, etc. In the second group are included economic causes such as poverty and destitution ; in the third are included domestic causes such as ill treatment or neglect by parents, husband or relatives, etc. In the fourth group are included kidnapping, deception, bad influence, etc. In the fifth group are included causes of physiological significance such as sexual urge, illegitimate pregnancy, etc. and in the six causes relating to mental disposition or attitude such as ignorance, desire for easy life and low moral values.[5] They further

[5] **Punekar, S. D. and Rao, Kamla,** ***A Study of Prostitutes in Bombay*** **(1962), pp. 90-95.**

point out that any of these causes may occur as contributory causes, predisposing or direct causes depending upon each case. In other words, there are always more than one cause which lead one to prostitution. For example, the death of parents of a girl may render her vulnerable to prostitution, but the direct cause may be the exploitation of her by a procurer. However, we have discussed these causes under the following heads :

(*i*) *Economic Factors.* The chief cause for women or young girls accepting this profession is their poverty. Having no other visible means of support or in order to eke out a scanty wage, they often resort to this profession. Mr. Bonger has discussed in detail these economic factors which are responsible for underprivileged girls entering prostitution, such as immoral environments, early employment and poverty. Most of the prostitutes come from the underprivileged economic groups. Their parents are unable to provide the proper physical or moral care for their adolescent daughters. The morality of their children is endangered owing to inadequate housing conditions where they are forced to sleep in the same room with older persons. Early employment brings them into contact with immoral influences at an age when they are not equipped to make their own definitions and decisions. In many cases they are forced to work with men and women who give them a vicious initiation into the techniques and practices of promiscuous sex relationships. Both absolute and relative poverty affects sex behaviour. Because of absolute poverty many girls resort to prostitution in order to live. Relative poverty refers to the lack of many of the small luxuries, to attain which they resort to prostitution.[6] The League of Nations Advisory Committee on Social Questions also observes, poverty, overcrowding and low wages are clearly contributory causes of prostitution.[7]

(*ii*) *Social Values Against Unchastity.* A girl who had illicit sex experience because of some reasons is often made to feel that she had nothing left to lose because she has already lost all. Social values with respect to chastity tend to make it difficult for such a girl to regain her social status and conform to the accepted standards. The girl who has made a "mis-step" but is inherently decent is often made to feel that she has sinned unpardonably and irrevocably.

[6] Bonger, W.A., *Criminality and Economic Conditions* (1916), pp. 321-56).

[7] League of Nations, Advisory Committee on Social Questions, Enquiry into Measures of Rehabilitation of Prostitutes (1938), p. 7.

(*iii*) *Mental Deficiency or Certain Temperamental Traits.* Mental deficiency is also sometimes considered to be the cause of prostitution. A large share of both the young sex offenders and the common prostitutes are rated low in mentality.[8] The League of Nations' Advisory Committee on Social Questions found that a third of the women described in the cases submitted to the Committee were either mentally abnormal or subnormal.[9] In temperamental make-up are included such traits as are likely to cause unhappiness and failure, viz. excessive restlessness, lack of self-confidence, lack of affection, defiance of authority and irascibility.

(*iv*) *Ignorance.* Vice rings operating in large urban areas frequently exploit girls from surrounding rural communities. Often they are lured by offers of employment. They accept positions as maids, unaware that they may be more or less forced into prostitution.

(*v*) *Unhappy Marital Relations.* Unhappy marital relationship with the husband causes many women to resort to prostitution. Loose habits of the husband may also lead to such an action.

(*vi*) *Inordinate Sex Desire.* Certain girls have inordinate sex desire and crave for sex stimulation for its own sake.

(*vii*) *Desire for New Experience etc.* There are many other factors which may lead women to prostitution. Of these desire for new experience, either for sex experience itself or for the promiscuous social contacts leads to such experience. Desire for finery may also enter in or she may have been stimulated by a type of literature which places a premium on thrilling sex adventure. It is also possible that when a girl is under the influence of alcohol she may undergo her first sex relationship. Her continued use of immoderate alcohol may further affect her sexual promiscuity. Childhood assaults also initiate many into prostitution.

(*viii*) *Vested Interests.* Highly profitable nature of the business makes many girls to resort to prostitution. For the most part, the profit motive is important to the persons who operate the houses of prostitution. High profits in this enterprise attract large capital in this business. In order to attract fresh recruits in the form of young girls, an elaborate organization is maintained. The specific function of this organization is to interest young girls in prostitu-

[8] Elliott, M.A. and Merrill, F. E., *Social Disorganization* (1941), pp. 64-67.

[9] Mowrer, E. R., *op. cit.*, p. 318.

tion and to keep them in the business when they have once entered. In a survey of prostitutes in the Bombay city, it was found that one third of the non-hereditary prostitutes left their homes and entered the brothels under conditions which may be broadly termed as "involuntary", that is, due to deception, kidnapping or being forced into the profession with no choice whatsoever.[10]

(*ix*) *Restrictions on Widow Remarriage.* In India there are two additional social factors which increase prostitution. They are difficulties in widow remarriage and some other social customs such as *Devadasi* system which force many women to prostitution.

Widows who are unable to remarry because of social customs prevailing in society often resort to prostitution to eke out existence for themselves and their children.

(*x*) *Devadasi System.* The *Devadasi* system is prevalent in some of the South Indian states such as Madras, Bombay, Mysore, etc. Under this system the women who are dedicated as *devadasis* to Hindu deities and idols are considered unfit to marry later on and this leads them to a life of prostitution.

Some social customs among the Naiks in Uttar Pradesh (it is a particular caste), the Numbudri of Malabar, the Kulina system of Bengal also produce this evil under which girls are destined to prostitution irrespective of their own wishes.

The Association for Moral and Social Hygiene in India which conducted its investigations into the causes of prostitution points out, "that investigations have shown that though illiteracy, poverty and ignorance are the three big factors which increase commercialized vice in India as in other countries, yet these factors are by no means the only causes. The real cause is the 'demand' for the supply. This demand is sometimes enhanced by tribal customs and semi-religious customs, by inherited family traditions, by such systems as non-marriage of child widows, the existence of tolerated districts in cities and towns, 'red-light' tents in melas and the dowry system."[11] The Advisory Committee on Social and Moral Hygiene (1955) has put prostitution due to *Devadasi* system under the religious and traditional group and the prostitutes from the Naik and other such communities under the hereditary group.

[10] Punekar, S. D. and Rao, Kamla, *op. cit.*, p. 193.

[11] Kabir, Smt. Shanti "A Programme of Moral and Social Hygiene in India" in *Social Welfare in India* (1955), p. 422.

Two Types of Prostitutes

Prostitutes may be divided into two groups, i.e. (*a*) the overt, and (*b*) the clandestine group. The overt group includes professional registered as well as unregistered prostitutes, who generally live in brothel houses. But there are many prostitutes who are nominally employed at other type of work, notably in personal service or as entertainers. Such girls are accustomed to practice prostitution as a more or less regular supplement to their legitimate earnings.

The clandestine prostitutes include a wide variety of women who enter into sex relationships for mercenary considerations. Firstly, there is the occasional prostitute who alternates periods of reforms with period of active prostitution. Secondly, there is the incidental prostitute, who augments a scanty legitimate income by the sale of sex favour. Girl clerks employed in department stores often supplement their wages by recourse to such illicit sources. Cast-off mistresses often enter prostitution as a last resort after all other resources have failed. Thirdly, married women on occasion resort to such mercenary and adulterous practices usually serving a restricted clientale. Fourthly, the coincubinage system under which the mistress or her guardians (if she is a young girl) enters into agreement with a male member for a minimum stipulated period. Unlike common prostitution which is generally characterized by indiscriminate sexual indulgence, here the relationship is between two parties. In India the mistresses mostly belong to the class of professional singing girls or temple girls who sang and danced at the temple ceremonies in the olden days.[12]

Procurers, Pimps and Brothel-Keepers

The male component of the prostitute is known as a procurer or a pimp. He is the person who makes business contacts for the prostitutes and generally acts as her "guide, friend and philosopher". In return he lives upon the earning of the prostitute or prostitutes. They are found in almost all the countries where prostitution exists. The Advisory Committee on Social and Moral Hygiene (1955) has drawn the difference between the two. "Procurer is a person whose business it is to find a steady supply of girls, study the demand in the area they are serving, seek their victims in distressed areas

[12] Punekar, S. D. and Rao, Kamla, *op. cit.*, pp. 160-68.

of towns and villages, reject those who have lost their charm and freshness and have perhaps become diseased and replace them with new victims.... whereas the pimp is one who brings to each brothel the appropriate client — he or she would know where to suit the special preferences of the customer, advertise the charms of the inmates of the special houses, and tempt the footsteps of those who need entertainment to certain specific houses. The procurers are often the old prostitutes who have given up the profession due to ill health or age, while the pimps may be taxi drivers, rickshaw coolies, tongawallas or special agents operating in the areas."[13] Another term, "brothel-keeper", has also been mentioned by the committee. She is one who provides accommodation for the new-comers, to help them purchase all the requirements of the trade by advancing loans, finds doctors and cares for them in times of illness, and solves a hundred problems they may have to face. She usually takes 50 per cent of their earnings.[14]

Prostitution and Personal Disorganization

Social values in the realm of sex are at present confused and paradoxical. Chastity and faithfulness have been held up as the primary virtues for women, while men have been overlooked in the sexual disorder. Prostitution is a necessary counterpart to the socially sanctioned licence for men. So long as this double standard remains this evil is bound to remain.

The personal disorganization resulting from prostitution is due to the fact that the person concerned receives condemnation at the hands of men and women and is excluded from the society. Women, as pointed out above, usually suffer great personal deterioration than men due to the existing double standard. However, the participation in vicious conduct may not always result in complete collapse of personal organization at once and may come in stages. Professor Reckless has given two stages of maladjustment as an aftermath of unsocial sex activities: (*i*) the dual person, and (*ii*) the demoralized person.[15] In the first instance those individuals who lead a double life may not suffer a complete moral collapse. The most that can be said is that their personal efficiency is generally

[13] Report of the Advisory Committee, pp. 14-15.

[14] *Ibid.*, p. 15.

[15] Reckless, Walter C., "Vice and Personal Disorganization", *Journal of Applied Sociology*, December (1926), pp. 134-38.

impaired by the mental conflict and physical strain on their marginal existence. In the second instance vice often results in complete personal demoralization. Repeated violations of the code are almost certain to bring about irremediable loss of status. Eventually the individual man or woman may lose all contact with the respectable elements of the community and may resign himself or herself to a life on the fringe of society. Thus, the prostitutes and pimps, for example, may have but slight opportunity or incentive to retrieve the stability of their life organization. When this complete change in basic attitudes towards society and social values has taken place, complete demoralization results. He also points out that sometimes the person may not pass through these two stages and a single offence against the mores of the groups may irrevocably doom the transgressor to a life beyond the pale. This may be the case when pregnancy occurs or the act becomes known to the public at the time of commission or is of a violent nature, or he or she gets a disease which shows its effect afterwards.

Another type of behaviour connected with vicious conduct is subsumed under the concept of the unorganized person as opposed to the disorganized person. As Mr. Thomas points out a certain type of girl "cannot be said to fall, because she has never risen. She is not immoral, because immorality implies a loss of morality, but amoral—one who has never had a moral code."[16] The values of the amoral group are quite different from those of the society. The individual does not consciously offend the moral code. Such a person has been brought up in such environments that his or her social definition of promiscuous sex conduct is quite different from that of society at large. Such attitudes are extremely difficult to eradicate. We have some castes in India, e.g. Naik and Numbudris where such attitudes develop from the early environments.

Prostitution and Family Disorganization

Prostitution not only affects the personal organization of the man or woman concerned, but also affects his or her family as well. The married person may get some venereal disease from the prostitute, which may affect his wife and children. Similarly, a married woman who resorts to clandestine prostitution may get the disease from her other client. "Prostitution does not exact its full price

[16] Thomas, W. I., *The Unadjusted Girl* (1923), p. 98.

in social ostracism, shame and stigma. Fully half of those suffering with venereal disease have acquired it through promiscuous sex relationships. The other half are innocent victims—the wives and children of men who acquired the disease in premarital or extra-marital contacts."[17] Children of parents suffering from venereal diseases are likely to be maimed for life and many a time are born blind. Illegitimate sex relations of the wife or husband may also be the cause of friction in the family and divorce may be the ultimate result.

Vice and Community Disorganization

Prostitution not only breaks down the life organization of the person who is so involved, but it also brings widespread disorganization of the community in which it operates. It has two aspects. One is its commercial aspect and the other the health aspect. Prostitution when allowed to operate tends itself to commercial exploitation and becomes institutionalized. In its institutional form, it becomes deeply rooted in the deteriorated local community of the larger city. This means that due to its relatively permanent position in the city it becomes still more accessible to the public and as a result still more profitable. This situation in turn strengthens the hands of the persons engaged in this business.

The institutionalized prostitution may take two forms : (1) There are the vice resorts in their obvious form, which vary in size, in number of inmates, in number of patrons, and in general degree of elaborateness. In this group may be included brothels, the call flats, disorderly hotels and tenements which are devoted exclusively to prostitution. Alcohol may be sold or indecent shows added as an additional attraction, but solely for the purpose of increasing customers for the primary business. (2) There are places which cater to vice under cover of some more or less legitimate business. Under this come many disorderly hotels and restaurants. Such hotels and restaurants supplement their income by profit from illicit resources. Frequently the profits from prostitution become the primary revenue. At the hotels and drink shops the entertainers frequently solicit, and men who have come to while away an idle hour may yield to the blandishment of their enchanters.

Prostitution through the spread of venereal diseases also brings

[17] Elliott, M. A. and Merrill, F. E., *op., cit.* p. 264.

in train many other social problems. As Elliott and Merrill observe, "The venereal diseases—syphilis, chancroid and gonorrhoea—are of vital social concern not only because they are epidemic and devastating diseases but also because they are factors in so many other social problems. Venereal disease produces a large share of insanity. Its victims are particularly likely to commit violent crimes. Children of syphilitic parents are apt to be maimed for life. Many are born blind. The result of syphilitic and gonorrhoeal infections are so appalling that they rank as the major public health problems in the western world."[18]

History of Prostitution in India

The profession of prostitution in India is as old as in some of the other countries of the world. "The origin of this institution is shrouded in mystery, yet some of the authorities on the problems associate it with religious practices, which in the beginning were of a customary nature. The cause of shame prevented it for a time from degenerating into licence, but the strong tide of circumstances forced it into a mercenary affair."[19] Various efforts were made in the past to arrest its growth by the state through legislation or by public opinion with little effect. There was segregation of prostitutes in a town and a list of them kept by the state. Kautilya laid down the rules for keeping the public women (prostitutes) under control.[20] The reference to prostitutes also comes in Mahabharata and Jataka stories, and all Hindu Shastrakaras such as Manu, Gautam, and Brihaspati recommended for suppression of prostitution. During Mohammadan period also prostitution was much in vogue and many Mohammadan kings had their Harem. However, the rapid urbanization and industrialization during the British period increased this evil, and certain legislative measures were taken to stop it.

Legislation on Prostitution

The East India Company made certain regulations dealing with sexual offences. Later on provisions were made in the Indian Penal

[18] *Ibid.*, p. 265.

[19] Jayakar, R. B. K., "Prostitution and Immoral Traffic in India" in *Social Welfare in India* (1955), p. 353.

[20] *Kautilya's Arthashastra*, Book II, Chapter 28. Ganikas were segregated in the southern portion of a town. A superintendent should be appointed to keep information about the health and pecuniary conditions of the Ganikas.

Code to deal with sexual offences, whose object was to protect the modesty and to protect women against forced illicit sexual intercourse. The Code provided an imprisonment up to one year or fine or both for insulting the modesty of any woman by any word, sound, gesture, or exhibition of any object, or intruding on her privacy. Similarly, a penalty of two years' imprisonment or fine or both was provided for the offence of assault or use of criminal force upon a woman with intent to outrage her modesty (S—354). Kidnapping or abducting a woman, in order that she may be compelled to marry any person against her will, or in order that she may be forced or seduced to illicit intercourse with any person, inducing a woman to go from any place, in order that she may be seduced to illicit intercourse by criminal intimidation or by abuse of authority or under any other compulsion inducing a girl under 18 years of age, by any means whatsoever, to go from any place or to do any act, in order that she may be forced or seduced to illicit intercourse, kidnapping or abducting any person in order that she may be subjected to the unnatural lust of any person, each of these was a grave offence punishable with imprisonment of either description for 10 years or fine or both (S—366).

Selling, letting for hire or otherwise disposing of, or buying, hiring or otherwise obtaining possession of any girl under 18 years of age for any unlawful or immoral purpose was made an offence (S—372).

Sexual intercourse with a woman under 16 years of age was rape notwithstanding that she may have consented to it and punishment for rape was up to 10 years (S-375). Sexual intercourse by a person with the wife of another man without the consent or connivance of that man constituted the offence of adultery (unless it amounted to rape) punishable with imprisonment up to 5 years or fine or both (S-497). The woman herself was declared free from any liability as an abettor. Enticing a married woman, in order that she may have illicit intercourse with any person or concealing or detaining her with such intent was an offence punishable with imprisonment for 2 years or fine or both (S-498).

It will be seen from above that the provisions made in the Indian Penal Code did not make prostitution illegal, nor did it make procuring a criminal offence under all conditions. As far as adult females were concerned the provision was that it must be accompanied by kidnapping, abducting or criminal intimidation. It was an offence in case of minor girls under 18 years of age for their buying and selling for immoral purposes and importing into India girls under 21 years of age for immoral purposes. Brothel-keeping was not illegal. Thus, the efforts on the part of the Government of India to check prostitution were salutary.

The credit of having some effective checks on prostitution goes to Bombay State when the Bombay Prevention of Prostitution Act was passed in 1923. Under this act living on the earnings of the prostitution of another ; soliciting in a public street or place ; procuring ; keeping, managing or assisting in keeping or managing a brothel ; permitting use of premises for a brothel, and prostitution in prohibited areas were offences. The brothel was defined as any house or place with the occupier or the person in charge thereof, habitually allowed it to be used by more than one person for the purpose of prostitution. Later on such acts were passed in some of the other states such as Madras (1930), Bengal (1933), Uttar Pradesh (1933), Punjab (1935), Bihar (1948), Madhya Pradesh (1953) with certain variations. In some acts there was provision for the discontinuance of the use of premises either as brothels or for common prostitution and for the removal of prostitutes from specific areas. Some separate acts were also passed to protect certain girls who were made prostitutes under certain social customs. These acts were the U. P. Naik Girls Protection Act (1929), the Bombay Devadasi Protection Act (1934), and the Madras Devadasi (Prevention of Dedication) Act (1947). Under the U. P. Naik Girls Protection Act District Magistrates were empowered to call for particulars from persons having the guardianship or control of Naik girls under 18 years of age and to restrict or regulate their movements to protect them from being trained to the profession of prostitution and to remove them from immoral surroundings. Under the Devadasi Acts any ceremony or act intended to dedicate a woman as a *devadasi* with or without her consent was made illegal act because previously such *devadasis* were later on exposed to prostitution as they could not marry.

Under the Cantonment Act of 1924 Officers Commanding a station were given certain powers for the discontinuance of brothels in cantonment areas. Under the Municipalities Acts certain states such as U. P., C. P., Bihar, etc. authorized the Municipalities to put certain restrictions on prostitution, such as loitering for prostitution or the discontinuance of the use of brothel in the vicinity of a place of worship or an educational institution, etc. Similarly, Children Acts contain provisions to protect children. A child frequenting the company of a prostitute or living in a house used for immoral purposes or exposed to the risk of seduction or prostitution may be taken under protection or placed under supervision.

In spite of all these acts the problem of prostitution could not be tackled. Firstly, because prostitution by itself was no crime and the acts dealt only with particular activities connected with its practice. Secondly, the law defines its policy towards the problem and provides the tools to the officials entrusted with its enforcement. But the mere existence of law is no guarantee that the problem itself is being tackled effectively. It was difficult to get at the pimps, the procurers and the property owners who let their premises for this purpose. Thirdly, many a time the police officials were apathetic or corrupt and there was no special police force or special courts for this purpose. Fourthly, the enactment passed for the suppression of immoral traffic also varied from state to state and sometimes there were many deficiencies in the law. For example, there was no restriction on brothels away from educational institutions, religious place or any other public place. In some states there were no such special acts, and the action could be taken only under the provisions of the Indian Penal Code which were not sufficient for suppression of Immoral Traffic. Even in special acts no alternative or proper protection could be provided to those who fell into the snares of traffickers. The Advisory Committee on Social and Moral Hygiene observed, "The question of exploitation of women and girls generally is so closely linked up with prostitution that it is impossible to suggest measures to wipe out the one without taking into consideration the other."[21] Fifthly, sometimes it is also asserted that prostitution is an ancient profession as old as the world itself and it is impossible to stop it. As it is pointed out that, "there is an undercurrent of feeling that not only it is inevitable as an institution, it is even desirable. It is a safety valve, absorbing as it does, the violent passions of the dissolute and saves society from ugly overtures."[22]

On the other hand, greatest stigma is attached to the prostitute. Prostitution recks personality and affects marriage relationships. Prostitution affects family life, communicates diseases and thus

[21] Committee Report, *op. cit.*, p. 17.

[22] *Social Legislation, Its Role in Social Welfare* (1956), p. 384.

brings social disorganization. Often women are forced into this profession and are unwilling agents. Prostitution operates under a network of brothels, pimps and procurers. Helpless women and girls are led through force or persuasion into prostitution and these agents subsequently live on their earnings. In the larger cities particularly this ranks among big business with high returns. Under cover of concubinage and the pursuit of the arts of dancing and singing prostitution goes on. Wayward girls, girls who may have conceived, unwanted widows, deserted wives, and destitute women—all drift to its "protection".

Extent of Prostitution in India

In countries which nominally control the practice of prostitution through the licensing of brothels and police inspection some estimates have been made, while in some other countries exhaustive survey has been conducted by the governments or other social institutions to know their number. However, it is very difficult to know the clandestine prostitution which goes on a large scale. In India no such effort was made either by any government, research student or welfare agency before Independence. The Association of Moral and Social Hygiene in India collected some statistics from some of the states during the year 1949-50, which are as follows. No complete information was available from other states.

TABLE 12

NUMBER OF BROTHELS IN SOME STATES IN INDIA (in 1950)

	State	*Total number of brothels*	*Total number of prostitutes*
1.	Bombay	269	12,058
2.	West Bengal	5,065	N.A.
3.	Delhi	482	N.A.
4.	Orissa	213	N.A.

The Government of India in their report to the League of Nations in 1933 described their general policy towards prostitution as one of abolition. They said, "There were no licensed houses or prostitutes and no compulsory medical supervision of prostitutes in the country. On the whole there were neither registration of brothels nor of prostitutes, though under a voluntary informal system the names of the inmates of European brothels in Calcutta and Karachi were furnished to the police."[23] They have also stated that their policy towards the import of foreign women for immoral purposes was to discourage it and to render it difficult. In this connection they had amended the Indian Penal Code in 1923 to give effect to the International Convention for the Suppression of Immoral Traffic, 1922 and the importing into India of any girl under the age of 21 years to be used for immoral purpose was made an offence.

Though the policy declared by the then Government of India was one of abolition, no effective steps were taken to implement it. Under the various acts passed by some states brothel-keeping was not altogether illegal and most of the efforts were only to check soliciting in public places and to regulate the location of brothels.

The Association for Moral and Social Hygiene in England had been carrying out active campaign for the programme of moral and social hygiene and started its work in India in 1875. It was owing to the efforts of this association that procuring of Indian and Japanese women for British troops stationed in India was stopped. Similarly, it was the result of its efforts that Suppression of Immoral Traffic Acts were passed in some of the states.

Programme After Independence

It was looking to the evil of prostitution which brings in its train personal, family and community disorganization as well as the exploitation of helpless girls and women that after Independence, the Association for Moral and Social Hygiene intensified its campaign for checking of this evil. It has been regularly holding all-India Conferences since 1951. In these conferences it was urged that the existing laws in various states for the suppression of immoral traffic were not enough and needed drastic changes. It would be better if uniform legislation on all-India basis is passed. In the third all-India Conference (1953), they recommended that both individual as well as commercial prostitution should be abolished. The Resolution said, "This Conference is of the considered opinion that individual and commercial prostitution are linked with and aid and abet each other and, therefore, individual prostitution along with commercial prostitution should be condemned and abolished in the best interest of society."[24]

[23] *Ibid.*, p. 255.
[24] Kabir, Smt. Shanti, *op. cit.*, p. 431.

The Central Social Welfare Board in pursuance of the International Convention signed at Geneva in May, 1950 for the suppression of immoral traffic in women and girls and on the recommendation made at the various all-India Conferences of Moral and Social Hygiene, appointed an Advisory Committee on Social and Moral Hygiene in December, 1954 with Smt. Dhanwanthi Rama Rao as Chairman to investigate the problem in all its aspects throughout India.

Recommendations of the Advisory Committee on Social and Moral Hygiene

The Committee besides mentioning the following measures for the suppression of immoral traffic, also recommended for comprehensive legislation on all-India basis to check prostitution. It pointed out that it would be impossible to introduce other measures in the absence of such legislation.

It recommended that for the proper enforcement of laws: (*i*) There should be an Inter-State Police Organization in order to link up activities all over the country. (2) No institution should be allowed to come forward to care for and protect such women and girls unless both its *bonafides* and ability are tested. (3) There should be a special police squad for the enforcement of this act of which women should form a fair percentage. (4) Women produced before courts should be remanded to approved places or remand homes, where they can be contacted by social workers and probation officers. (5) Special courts should be constituted, consisting a few trained women to look after the social and human aspects of the problem and not solely from the point of view of guilt determination and, (6) Whoever resorts to any brothel or other public place for the purpose of prostitution should be punished.

For the reclamation, rehabilitation and after-care of the women rescued from the brothels and those who are in moral danger these should first be brought to District Vigilance Shelters and from there they should be removed to proper institutions. For this there should be two types of institutions : (1) Regional Women Institutes for the women in moral danger, and (2) Remand Homes for those under arrest and waiting trial. The Regional Women Institutes should be established by the Central Social Welfare Board, while Remand Homes should be established by the State Governments. They should be imparted proper training in these institutions.

Suppression of Immoral Traffic Act, 1956

On the lines recommended by the above Committee the Parliament passed the Suppression of Immoral Traffic in Women and Girls Act in 1956. This very comprehensive act, without making individual prostitution illegal, gives wider power to the states to deal with this in a systematic way. The main provisions of this act are :

Under section 3 of the Act any person who keeps or manages, or acts or assists in the keeping or management of a brothel is to be vigorously dealt with (i.e. a rigorous imprisonment between one to three years and fine up to Rs. 2,000). Similarly, under sections 4 and 5 any person over eighteen who knowingly lives, wholly or in part, on the earnings through prostitution, or procures or attempts to procure a woman or a girl for the purpose of prostitution is to be severely dealt with (imprisonment of one year or more). Under section 7 any woman or girl who carries on prostitution, and the person with whom such prostitution is carried on, in any premises which are within a distance of two hundred yards of any public place are to be punished. Under section 8 soliciting in a public place is prohibited. Under section 13 special police officers are to be appointed for dealing with offences under this act. There is also provision for the detention of girls in protective homes which are to be established by the states or by private social welfare agencies. Under section 19 prostitutes have been given right to seek protection in a protective home and under section 20 magistrates have been authorized to remove any girl or woman carrying on prostitution at any place from there to any other place which they consider proper.

Under this act not only the keeping of brothels, and procuring and living on the earnings of prostitutes is illegal, but both the prostitute and the person with whom such prostitution is carried on within a distance of two hundred yards from any public place are punishable. The magistrates are also empowered to remove prostitutes from any place, which they consider harmful to the public.

Another important piece of legislation, the Women's and Children's Institutions (Licensing) Act was passed in the same year.

Developments After 1956

Along with the appointment of Advisory Committee on Social and Moral Hygiene another Advisory Committee on After-care Programmes was appointed by the Central Social Welfare Board in

1954. The Reports of both these Advisory Committees were considered by a committee consisting of the representatives of the Central Social Welfare Board, the Planning Commission and the Union Ministries of Home, Finance, Commerce and Industry, Health and Labour. The outlines of schemes were drawn up for implementation and were included in the second plan among centrally sponsored programmes under the head : Social and Moral Hygiene and After-care Programmes.[25] Under the scheme it was proposed to establish in all 80 state homes and 324 district shelter or reception centres in various parts of the country. The homes where women involved under the Suppression of Immoral Traffic Act were to be kept were to be known as Protective Homes. It was also decided that pending the set up of protective homes such women could also be put up in rescue homes set up under the After-care Programme provided proper arrangements for segregation were made. The table below shows the number of rescue homes, reception centres and protective homes to be set up during Second and Third Plan periods in various states.

TABLE 13

RESCUE HOMES, RECEPTION HOMES AND RECEPTION CENTRES IN INDIA (1956-1966)

States	*Rescue homes*	*Reception centres*	*Protective homes*
1. Andhra	1	7	—
2. Assam	2	8	2
3. Bihar	2	—	2
4. Gujarat	1	6	—
5. Kerala	1	6	—
6. Madhya Pradesh	3	14	—
7. Madras	2	5	—
8. Maharashtra	1	13	1
9. Mysore	3	5	—
10. Punjab	1	3	2
11. Rajasthan	2	5	2
12. Uttar Pradesh	1	14	5
13. West Bengal	2	3	2

The Act actually came into force with effect from May 1, 1958. With the enforcement of this act some tangible results have been

[25] *Plans and Prospects of Social Welfare in India* 1951-1961 (1963), p. 135.

achieved. But a good deal still remains to be done. The voluntary social welfare agencies should actively associate themselves with the state programme. In this connection the work done by some of the voluntary organizations like the Delhi Branch of the Association for Moral and Social Hygiene in India and some other institutions in Madras and Bombay is praiseworthy.

The League of Nations Advisory Committee on Social Questions observes "that special rehabilitation services can only be built successively on a foundation of wider social measures. It will be useless to train prostitutes in institutions if social custom, bad labour conditions and the absence of insurance against unemployment and ill-health will throw them back into prostitution."[26] This work will have to be done at the village level by employing them in cottage or village industries as vast majority of the prostitutes in the city are women from rural areas. Their education and vocational training are also essential to make them fit for employment and avoid their exploitation.

Future Programme

No doubt, if in the light of present legislation strenuous efforts are made it may be possible to close these brothels which encourage prostitution. Temptation for men may also be reduced as they now must make more strenuous efforts to locate the women. But still other measures (mentioned below) will be necessary to root out the evil.

(*i*) *Sex Education.* Men and women should be educated as to the dangers of venereal diseases from such a source, and its effects on marriage relation in case of married persons. There is need for educating the public mind on the gravity of the consequences of the evils of prostitution both to the individual and to society as a whole. The proper teaching of the value of self-control should begin early at home and then at schools. There should be sex education and some training for family life to young people in schools and colleges. Some suitable literature for the education of the young should be distributed by some social welfare agencies It is encouraging to note that some work on these lines is being done by the Association for Moral and Social Hygiene in India.

[26] League of Nations, Advisory Committee on Social Questions, *Enquiry into Measures of Rehabilitation of Prostitutes* (1938), p. 28.

(*ii*) *Employment Opportunities for Women.* There should be more employment opportunities for the girls who are forced to this profession under economic stress.

(*iii*) *Removal of Certain Social Customs.* The widow remarriage should be encouraged and the system of dowry which debarred many girls from marriage may be discouraged.

(*iv*) *Double Standards to be Discouraged.* The notion of double standards now prevalent should be discouraged. As Smt. Ranganayaki observes, "It is in reality impossible to have a double-standard morality in matters of sex for without male chastity, female chastity is impossible. As a result of a double standard of morality which demands of woman to be chaste, and expects man to be irregular there developed *tolerated* vice."[27]

(*v*) *Publicity and Propaganda.* The public should be enlightened about the law and to report any such nuisance in their surrounding areas. The films stimulating sex interest and other such literature should be discouraged. The branches of the Association for Moral and Social Hygiene should intensify their vigilance programme. There should be social workers employed by such agencies to look after this work and make a report to the police.

Venereal Diseases and Prostitution

Venereal diseases are so designated because they are ordinarily acquired through sexual contact. Physicians estimate that 95 per cent of syphilis, for example, is so acquired, although kissing and careless contact with contaminated towel and clothing account for a small percentage. Among these diseases the two most serious widespread are (*a*) syphilis and (*b*) gonorrhoea, A third one is chancroid which is generally regarded as less serious.

Syphilis is the most dangerous and "invades the tissues, nervous system, and bones and gives rise to ailments which imitate practically every disease to which flesh is heir.[28] It has been estimated that 15 per cent of all blindness in U.S.A. is due to syphilis. As a physical scourge, syphilis exacts severe tolls from men than women.[29] Gonorrhoea, on the other hand, affects women more seriously than it does men. Because of their bodily structure, the

[27] Ranganayaki, "Can We Prevent Prostitution?" in *Social Welfare*, April 1958, p. 22.

[28] Thomas, Parran, *Shadow on the Land, Syphilis* (1937), p. 298.

[29] Elliott, M. A. and Merrill, F. E., *op. cit.*, p. 265.

disease easily invades the female genital organ. Chancroid produces a local ulcer and is generally regarded as less serious.

Syphilis, a contagious and epidemic disease, is caused by a micro-organism called the spirochaeta pallida. The mucous membranes of the eye-lids, mouth, or genital tracts are most susceptible to its penetration. Once within the bodily tissues the germ multiplies rapidly, invading the blood stream and lymph. Within two days the organism may infect all parts of the body. In the early stages appears a hard chancre or sore at the point of initial contact and invasion, followed by a rash or skin eruption, ultimately invading the bones, liver, lungs, eyes and nervous system and ultimately causing death. Pregnancies among syphilic women result in serious consequences. Many infected children are born blind, many have defective hearing, others have loathsome physical stigma or paralysis of various types.

Gonorrhoea is even more widespread than syphilis. It is caused by the bacteria called gonococcus. Both men and women suffer from inflammatory diseases, acute endocarditis, septicemia, and arthritis resulting from gonorrhoea, although women seem to suffer in greater number from these afflictions. Both sexes are rendered sterile by the disease. Many women become partially or totally invalid. Babies of both sexes suffer from gonococcal ophthalmia. It has been estimated that in U.S.A. 25 per cent of all blindness is transmitted by infected mothers to the unborn foetus.

Social and Economic Effects

Venereal diseases are of vital concerns not only because they are epidemic and devasting diseases but also because they are factors in so many other social problems. They create insanity among the sufferers and its victims are also likely to commit crime. Children of syphilitic parents are apt to be maimed for life and many are born blind.

There is a tremendous economic waste from syphilis in the loss of working hours alone. In addition there is an enormous annual cost of care for syphilis in private and public institutions and this is particularly so in mental and nervous institutions. Because of the inability of the lower income groups to secure treatment, these diseases set in motion a vicious economic circle. Because of the disease they are unable to work, which affects their families. They are also exposed to other infections because of bad housing conditions and low vitality.

Extent of Venereal Diseases in India

"Venereal diseases appear to have entered this land with the arrival of Vasco De Gama's ship at Calicut in 1498. Within a few months of his soldiers' landing there, it spread like wild fire all over India. It is still known as Farangi Rogan."[30]

No statistical data about the extent of venereal diseases in this country is available. The scanty information which could be collected by the Association for Moral and Social Hygiene in India from some of the states is as follows :

TABLE 14

EXTENT OF VENEREAL DISEASES IN INDIA

State	*Total no. of new cases treated*		
	1948[31]		1951[32]
Bombay	34,928		6,675
West Bengal	35,381	(Males 25,836) (Females 9,545)	N.A.
Bihar	26,282		87,334
Madras	92,852		1,50,286
Punjab	945		N.A.
U. P.	3,679		93,446
Orissa	N.A.		95,244

Even these figures are rough estimates because no separate statistics are collected by the states annually either from the public hospitals or from the private practitioners. In Madras where some sincere efforts have been made to check this social evil and the public has been informed about the consequences of these diseases some correct data is available. Some venereal disease clinics have also been opened in Madras City and in several other places for the treatment. These figures indicate a rough estimate about the extent of this problem in this country.

Social Control of Venereal Diseases

If the country is to be saved from the ravages of these diseases some measures will have to be taken to check these diseases. Some of these are as follows :

(*i*) *Social Rejection of the Profession.* A part of the treatment

[30] Jayakar, R. B. K., *op. cit.*, p. 363.

[31] Figures given by Smt. Shanti Kabir, *op. cit.*, pp. 423-26.

[32] Jayakar, R. B. K., *op. cit.*, p. 370.

must be accounted for in the social rejection of prostitution. The demand should also be eliminated by acquainting young people with the dangers of these diseases.

(*ii*) *Spread of Information.* Information about venereal diseases should be issued in bulletins and pamphlets to make the public aware of their consequences and advise them to report themselves in public hospitals for treatment. The work should be taken on more intensive basis by the A.M.S.H.I., which is actively engaged in this task.

(*iii*) *Establishment of Venereal Disease Clinics.* Special venereal disease clinics should be opened as has been done by the Madras and Bombay Governments. There should also be special departments for the treatment of these diseases in all public hospitals. In these clinics there should be free confidential and effective treatment of these diseases. There should be free blood test examinations and treatment of all antenatal cases to ensure the birth of normal healthy children free from all congenital blemishes. There should be provision for special training in venereal diseases in medical colleges.

(*iv*) *Segregation of Diseased Patients.* Diseased prostitutes must be handled the same way as any other person suffering from contagious or communicable disease.

Prostitution and Welfare Organizations

There are many social and religious organizations which take part in the suppression of immoral traffic directly or indirectly. Among these the most important are (1) the all-India organization, namely, the Association for Moral and Social Hygiene in India, and (2) the international agency, i.e. the League of Nations Advisory Committee on Social Questions.

Association for Moral and Social Hygiene in India

This association is an off-shoot of the Association for Moral and Social Hygiene in England which started its programme of moral and social hygiene in India in 1875 and established its branch in Calcutta. It became an independent organization in 1928 and was named as Association for Moral and Social Hygiene in India. Later on it had branches at the various Provincial headquarters. After Independence there was a complete change in the organizational structure of this organization, and from high British officials as members, it became completely Indianized having non-official character. Shrimati Rameshwari Nehru who was also a member of the General Committee during the British regime became its first President. Since 1951 this Association is holding Annual Conferences to invite attention of the public to this social evil.

Since its very inception, as we have already pointed out, the Association has been taking active part in the suppression of immoral traffic and was responsible for getting such acts passed in the various states. After Independence the Association took active part in the rehabilitation of the destitute and widows who had no means of support, along with other welfare organizations. Since 1950 the Association has resumed its most specific duties which can be divided into five categories : (*a*) Investigation and research, (*b*) legislation, (*c*) education and propaganda, (*d*) medical and public health work, and (*e*) rescue and rehabilitation. Some of these have already been mentioned in the foregoing pages. The future role of this organization lies in the complete suppression of immoral traffic in this country. Its branches in various states can take up this work for the rehabilitation of rescued women with the assistance of Central Social Welfare Board and State Social Welfare Departments.

League of Nations Advisory Committee on Social Questions

The First World War emphasized anew the dangers of uncontrolled venereal diseases. Accordingly in 1919 the League of Nations (Covenant, art. 230) was entrusted with general supervision over the execution of agreements with regard to the traffic in women and children.[33] The League of Nations formed an Advisory Committee on the Traffic in Women and Children in 1922, which have investigated on various problems relating to traffic in women and children on an international level. The problems on which investigations have been carried and reports submitted are : traffic in women at national and international levels (1927), law and penalties in various countries relating to pimps and souteneurs, the problem of licensed houses of prostitution, the traffic in obscene publications, enquiry into measures of rehabilitation of prostitutes (1934) and other kindred subjects relating to the varied aspects of prostitution. The Advisory Committee on Social Questions replaced the Traffic in Women and Child Welfare Committee in 1937.

[33] May, Geoffrey, "Prostitution" in *Encyclopaedia of the Social Sciences*, Vol. XII, p. 557.

Since the formation of the United Nations Organization this work is now being looked after by the Economic and Social Council. We have already mentioned about the International Convention held on its behalf in New York in 1950.

It also published a report in 1959 *The Suppression of the Trafficking in Persons and of the Exploitation of the Prostitution of Others* which is based on research carried out in various countries of the world.

CHAPTER IX

BEGGARY

BEGGARY is as great a social problem in India as are juvenile delinquency and crime. Beggary is a symptom of individual as well as social disorganization. It is a form of personal disorganization as it indicates the failure of the individual to adjust himself with his social milieu. It is a symptom of social disorganization as the beggar in the street at once reminds us of the ill-organized society which is not able to adjust him properly.

Beggars are a phenomenon of the civilized society and closely associated with the emergence of private property. So long as men lived blood bound in small groups, hazards of life were shared by all. In Europe a beggar is mostly a product of industrial revolution, where the spirit of individualism shattered the sentiment of community feeling and an individual became isolated and helpless when he fell into distress. In India also though begging is an old profession, it has changed its form in the modern period and the problem has become a colossal one.

Begging in Ancient Period

In India the institution of beggary is often traced to the ancient educational system which provided for training in the *Ashram* and where pupils used to support themselves and their guru by asking alms just enough for the day. But the spirit behind such type of begging for alms was not that of parasites but of seekers for truth and the householders thought it their duty to support them. There was no idea of caring for a certain group of people who were unfortunate or distressed.

Manu also approves the maintenance of some people by others. He says in verse LXXXVI, "in the *Krata Cycle* Austerity is the highest, in the *Trta* knowledge is described as such, in the *Dvapar* they call the sacrifice the highest, charity alone in the *Kali cycle*." He also adds, "What the *Brahman* eats is his own. His own what he wears and his own also what he gives, it is due to the good will of the *Brahman* that other people enjoy things. When he obtains clothing either by begging or otherwise it does not mean that he has acquired from others ; what it means is that he is employing what is his own in the covering of his body." In view of the facts given above it appears that Manu sanctioned at least two classes of people, so far as giving of gifts or charities was concerned, one the giver and the other the receiver of gifts. But then a beggar was not a nuisance to others but discipline to one-self. Mendicancy was not an occupation, but it was only a form of austerity. Living by alms is only permitted during certain stages and conditions of life. Besides, begging was conceived as an ideal and all learned people were to beg as a discipline which made it a virtue without degenerating it into parasitism or loathsome mendicancy that it is today.

Beggary in Modern Society

The beggar problem of today is somewhat of different nature than it was in the past. There are many causes—the economic system and the social changes, when the joint family system, the village community and the *varna* system are not able to support the disabled, the mentally ill and the poor—which throw thousands into beggary. With the development of a more complex economic system and the resulting disintegration of the family, the afflicted member has to fall back upon his own resources. Charity which has been a part of our social heritage is coloured and directed by a sense of guilt and personal interests. This encourages healthy people to beg. But beggars have also become unscrupulous persons and sometimes adopt cruel practices to win sympathy of the people. Some racketeers have also made it a business who combine to produce cripples and decrepits out of the poor. They maim young children and produce monsters by artificial means who are thrown on the streets to crawl and beg. These conditions create sympathy, cause fear and bewilderment and charity flows indiscriminately towards them. Thus, it is a complex, socio-economic problem. It is a social problem because the beggars are a burden upon society and are a great menace to public health. The beggar becomes a nuisance when he lays before somebody and attracts his sympathy by constant pressure in an inhuman way. It is an economic problem so far as larger the number of beggars the greater the strain on income. Dangerous and harmful is the condition of those who ... able-bodied and invite other idlers and vagrants to join them, while degrading is the position of those who beg because they do not get the support from the society for their proper rehabilitation, whether they are sick, blind, deaf, dumb, lame, leper, mentally defective, poor or unemployed. Thus, it is a complex problem and should be treated and studied in all its phases. It is only by a scientific approach that we can understand its implication and offer remedies.

Definition. It is very difficult to give any definition of a beggar. In simple words, "A beggar is one who asks for alms or charity or performs such actions which derive sympathy from others and who give something in return." In England the beggar is described as, "consisting of every person wandering abroad, or placing himself or herself in any public place, street, highway, court or passage, to beg or gather alms, or causing or procuring any child or children (under 16) to do so. It also comprises every person wandering abroad and endeavouring, by the exposure of wounds or deformities, to obtain or gather alms or endeavouring to procure charitable contributions of any nature or kind, under false or fraudulent pretence."[1] The Bombay Beggars Act of 1945 has defined, "Begging as soliciting or receiving alms in a public place whether or not under any pretence such as singing, dancing, fortune-telling, performing tricks and selling articles, exposing or exhibiting any sore, wound, injury, deformity or disease whether of human being or of animals, for the purpose of obtaining or exhorting alms."[2] A person without means of subsistence and wandering about or found in public places or allowing himself to be used as an exhibit for the purpose of begging is also covered by the definition.

Causes of Beggary

It is difficult to give particular cause or set of causes to the institution of beggary as is the case with a criminal. A set of causes such as physical inability, mental derangement, personal or social maladjustment, poverty, custom of alms giving, unemployment, disruption of joint family, whether singly or in combination may produce a situation which may result in beggary. Thus, there cannot be one single cause of beggary but it is a result of multiple factors and instead of generalized causes we may better say of such situations which favour the institution of beggary. For the sake of clarity

[1] Quoted by Cama H. Katayun in "Types of Beggars" in *Our Beggar Problem* (Ed.), M. Kumarappa (1945), p. 4.

[2] Planning Commission, Government of India, *Social Legislation, Its Role in Social Welfare* (1956), p. [illegible].

we may discuss these situations under the heads—economic, social, biological, religious and others, but many a time these situations overlap. For example, old age may be a biological as well as an economic cause. Though the underlying cause in each case is the poverty of the family or lack of employment when the family is not in a position to support, the handicapped, but at the same time absence of security measures from the society forces them to beg.

(*a*) *Economic Causes*. The three main economic causes are poverty, loss of employment or under-employment and lucrative business.

(*i*) *Poverty*. One of the main factors which forces people to take to beggary is destitution. Having no sufficient means to support themselves or their families many persons resort to begging. Lack of employment opportunities in villages either because of tiny holdings or non-availability of other work forces thousands to resort to begging when they cannot find employment in the cities. Dr. R. K. Mukerjee rightly observes, "Obviously the most common cause of beggary in India is the loss of agricultural employment in the villages. For several decades the number of landless workers deprived of subsistence from the land has been steadily rising. All landless individuals cannot be absorbed in industrial employment."[3]

(*ii*) *Loss of employment and Under-employment*. But poverty alone cannot be held responsible because all those who live on poverty line do not take to beggary. A man begs not only when he is poor but also when he is unemployed or under-employed.

In a survey conducted in Lucknow City of 200 beggars in 1947, it was seen that many labourers beg to supplement their incomes. "They migrate to Lucknow to find jobs which they can hardly get. Therefore they have no option except to support themselves and their families by begging. Not only that one can find at the Charbagh Station that poor children and adults alike not only earn their livelihood as coolies but also they subsist and increase their earnings by collecting alms, because their earnings do not suffice even for keeping their body and soul together. It shows that they are not only unemployed but also they are under-employed."[4]

(*iii*) *Lucrative Business*. Owing to easy gains and sufficient income

[3] Mukerjee, R. K., "Causes of Beggary" in *Our Beggar Problem* (1945), p. 20.

[4] Srivastava, S. K., *Some Problems of Beggary in Lucknow*, a Thesis submitted for M.A. Class in the Department of Economics and Sociology, Lucknow University (1947), p. 47.

from begging many people make it a profession instead of doing honest labour. Not only that, many make it a business and exploit others by investing some amount in this business. There are groups operating in big cities which force many children to this profession. As Dr. R. K. Mukerjee observes, "The gang trains persons how and where to beg, acts as a foster parent to children that are deliberately maimed in order to evoke sympathy of the passers-by in the street and generally speaking look after their welfare. India had, for centuries this shadowy organization which has its Sirdars or capitalists and a large number of intermediaries, the ramifications of whose business extend to distant villages and hamlets. They arrange for beggars' accommodation in some slum or tenement and advance them food, cash or dirty clothes from day to day, their wage-earners bringing home every evening the hard day's collection or alms from the different mohallas of the cities so that all have a share in the gains of this organized beggary."[5] Sri S. Bahadur observes, "A study made by the sub-committee disclosed a most disturbing state of affairs. It appeared that gangs of professional kidnappers existed practically in all states of India. They kidnap or entice away children from the possession of their parents and then commit inhuman cruelties on them to make them into objects of pity so that they could be exploited for the purpose of beggary in public places. Many specific cases were mentioned by the sub-committee in its report and a typical case was a kidnapper, Karamat Ali, who with his associates lifted a three-year old girl from Katihar Railway Station in Bihar, broke both her legs and arms and blinded her by poking fingers into eyes, thus converting her into an object of pity so that they could exploit the people's sentiments and collect charities."[6]

(*b*) *Social Causes.* Among the social causes are family disorganization, lack of parental control, community disorganization, break up of joint family system and social custom.

(*i*) *Family Disorganization* Family is an integral part of our social relationship which influences our patterns of behaviour and activities. Any disturbance in our home condition especially in the case of a poor one leads to a breakdown of family, which in return gives rise to beggary. It may be death of parents, death of the hus-

[5] *Ibid.*, p. 20.

[6] Bahadur, S., "Kidnapping of Children for the Purpose of Begging" in *Seminar on Social Defence* (1965), p. 53.

band, death of the breadwinner, step-parental treatment, maltreatment, disruption in the family or desertion by the husband. Majority of the children who beg have nobody to support them.

(*ii*) *Lack of Parental Control.* In the industrial centres parents do not have the required control over their children, where often the mothers also go to factories for work. The result is that children's energies may turn to any direction. If they fall into bad company they may develop wanderlust which may lead to beggary. They loaf about from one city to another and beg for food or money.

(*iii*) *Community Disorganization.* Disorganization in rural community may also be responsible for increase in beggary. In the Hindu period, when village councils were functioning properly, it was considered to be their duty to look after the poor, the disabled and the infirm.

(*iv*) *Break-up of Joint Family System.* In the past the Hindu joint family supported the handicapped, orphans, blind, etc. But owing to break-up of the joint family system in the present age such persons are often thrown in the streets.

(*v*) *Social Custom.* Some of the castes and tribes ask for alms only because begging is their hereditary profession. They are often migratory in character. Castes like Sain, Bhatt, and tribes like Nats and Beriyas beg from door to door.

(*c*) *Biological Causes.* Among the biological causes may be mentioned sickness, physical or mental defects and old age.

(*i*) *Sickness or Disease.* The diseases may be curable and preventive in the beginning, but in the long run may become chronic and incurable. Diseases like syphilis, T. B., skin diseases and leprosy turn most people into beggary. Dr. R. K. Mukerjee remarks, "Leprosy with its accompanying disablement, disfigurement and social oppression is one of the principal causes of beggary in India and is at the same time most difficult to handle."[7] On the other hand, there are not sufficient welfare institutions which can look after them.

(*ii*) *Physically Disabled or Infirm.* The physical defects like blindness, deafness acquired in the beginning or got later on force many people to beg as the economic condition of their family is not such as to afford the maintenance of these disabled persons. The number of such persons is very large in this country. According to census of 1931 there were 6.01 lakhs blind, 2.3 lakhs deaf, and

[7] Mukerjee, R. K., *op. cit.*, p. 20.

1.47 lakhs lepers. No such figures were collected in 1941, 1951 or 1961 census.

(*iii*) *Mentally Deficient*. There are persons who are mentally deficient or insane and cannot earn any living and they are forced to begging.

(*iv*) *Old Age*. Persons who become physically weak in old age and cannot do any work and at the same time have nobody to support become beggars to get some money and sustain themselves. The number of such persons is also large in this country.

(*d*) *Religious Causes*. Among religious causes may be included religious mendicancy and indiscriminate alms giving.

(*i*) *Religious Mendicancy*. Religious mendicancy facilitates a man to beg under the garb of a *Sadhu* or *Fakir*. Such people take the form of religious mendicants only as means to an end. But religious mendicancy may be the result rather than a cause of beggary as it may result from the family breakdown or poverty.

Sometimes one is forced to beg by way of atonement for his or her sin, e.g. killing of the cow. This is done for religious purification.

(*ii*) *Indiscriminate Alms-giving*. Indiscriminate alms-giving by the public because of their religious sentiments encourages beggary. Most of the beggars are encouraged to remain in this profession because of good prospects of income which they cannot earn by honest means. There are many social customs which force us to give something or other to the beggars, orphans and religious mendicants. Among the Hindus during *Shradh* observance, birth and marriage ceremonies and at certain other religious days and among Muslims in the month of Ramzan it is obligatory to offer alms.

Charities are also given by various temples, mosques, *dharamshalas*, gurdwaras, shrines and by many public philanthropists. This charity, religious or otherwise, encourages beggary to a great extent.

(*e*) *Other Reasons*. Among other reasons may be mentioned those who are forced to beg.

There are persons upon whom beggary is enforced. There are orphans, and waifs and strays who are sometimes deliberately maimed or disfigured in order that their guardians or some other persons may earn their living. Many normal parents also trade on their children's infirmities using these as sources of supplementary income.

A survey carried out by a Committee of the Deputy Inspector-Generals of Police, C.I.D. in 1956 showed that most of the "Ashrams" which kept young boys were bogus and had been established with the sole object of exploiting them for begging and most of these children in these "Ashrams" were procured by kidnapping them from their lawful guardians.[8]

Types of Beggars

We have discussed various causes which may force or induce a person to become a beggar. On the basis of these causes we may classify beggars into various types so as to analyse the problem in a scientific way and suggest measures for the rehabilitation of each type.

(1) *Able-bodied Adult Beggars.* Among these may be included those adult beggars who beg either because they are unemployed or under-employed and have no other sources to fall back upon or they do not work and prefer begging to work. This latter class of beggars shirk all the responsibilities of an honest citizen and are a burden upon the society. They encourage honest workers to take to beggary. They also include wandering women with babies in their arms who invoke the sympathy of gentle ladies in the name of "poor fatherless children". Although they are able to work they wilfully refuse or neglect to do so.

(2) *Able-bodied Child Beggars.* These may include: (*a*) Those child beggars whose parents are not able to support them and deliberately encourage them to beg. (*b*) Due to some type of disorganization in the family or because of the death of parents, or loss of mother or father, maltreatment by the parents, neglect by parents, the child leaves home and resorts to begging. (*c*) He has been exploited by some beggar-organization, which gives him a hand to mouth living and exploits for its own ends. (*d*) Inmates of social institutions which have insufficient funds and ask the inmates to beg.

(3) *Hereditary Beggars.* Because of social customs in certain communities they consider begging as their hereditary profession. Among these may be included : *Nats*, *Bajigars*, *Sains*, *Jugglers*, *Bhats* and *Kanjars*. They do not attach any social stigma to this profession and take to it from their very childhood. To some of them their children are an asset who can excite more pity in human heart and can earn more and support their parents.

[8] Bahadur, S., *op. cit.*, p. 53.

(4) *Sick or Diseased Beggars.* These beggars suffer from chronic and incurable diseases such as leprosy, venereal diseases, tuberculosis, skin diseases, etc. They spread such diseases not only among themselves, but are a great danger to the society at large and infect the innocent passers-by by their contact.

(5) *Physically Disabled.* Among these may be included blind, deaf, dumb and crippled. They may be males or females and young or old.

(6) *Mentally Deficient.* They may be mentally deficient or mentally defective, i.e. insane.

(7) *Infirm or Old.* They are physically weak owing to old age and are not in a position to work.

(8) *Religious Mendicants.* There are religious sanctions for the foundings of mendicant orders. Among these may be included *Bairagis*, *Faqir*, *Darvesh*, *Kabir Panthi*, *Nanak-shahi*, etc. with their paraphernalia of saffron robe, wood-bead necklace, bowl in hand or purple coloured decorated with ashes, etc. These religious mendicants may be divided into three categories :

(*a*) *Sadhus* and *Faqirs* who are in charge of petty or large shrines, the guardianship of cemetries, mosque, temple or similar other religious offices.

(*b*) *Faqirs* and *Sadhus* of various sects such as *Sanyasis*, *Kabir Panthis*, *Faqirs* roaming from place to place in the garb of regular order, and living on alms.

(*c*) Bogus religious mendicants who hardly know the names of orders to which their external signs show them to belong. Their dress places them in better position in comparison to their rivals in this profession.

Techniques Employed in Begging

It will be interesting to note that the beggars employ various types of techniques to exploit the religious sentiments, spiritual beliefs and human nature of their patrons. These techniques may be discussed under five heads, viz. ordinary techniques, (2) techniques employed by religious mendicants, (3) use of coercive methods, (4) use of tricks, and (5) deforming of body.

(1) *Ordinary Techniques.* The beggar employs his techniques in such a manner so as to appeal to human sentiment and arouse sympathy on the one hand and adjust himself to the varying situations and circumstances on the other. The desire to make oneself

comfortable in this life and the life beyond characterizes most of the human beings. The blessings that the beggar showers on the giver of alms has a direct reference to the fulfilment of this desire. Women are more easily lured by such stimulated pleadings, such as predicting good health and longevity of their husbands and children, while old men and women are fit subject for the glorification of their future life and the means necessary for securing it.

When he is unable to elicit any response in this way he starts relating tales of misery and ill luck that have befallen him. If he is diseased or if he is harbouring some sore or untreated wound he exposes it to attract their sympathy. In addition to display of handicaps imposed upon him by nature, he employs various other means such as evidence of his incompetency in printed letters and giving some false pathetic stories. Sometimes they give melodious songs or show certain tricks to attract the attention of the passers-by.

Dr. Sen Gupta points out that the beggar in his begging appeals banks upon the sentiments inherent in human nature and attempts to touch the personality at all its vulnerable points. "He appeals to your religious sentiments, to your sense of dependence on Divine grace when he shouts, 'May God give you happiness' (*Tumko Parmatma sukhi rakhkhey, baba*) ; he appeals to you as a parent when he blesses your children (*Tumhara bal bachcha sukhi rahey*) ; he appeals to your sense of greed when untold wealth and even a kingdom is promised to you in exchange for a price, and seeks your protection for himself and his starving family ; and finally he tells you of his illness, hard luck, bereavement and utter destitution."[9]

Dr. Sen Gupta has also mentioned about the psycho-physical techniques which the beggar employs in order to make his appeal effective. In order that his appeal may be effective it must have three ingredients. It should (*a*) attract attention, (*b*) appeal to emotion, and (*c*) impress the need of the beggar upon the mind of his patron. These three types of techniques are as follows :

(*a*) *Variable Techniques to Attract Attention.* The meaning conveyed by begging appeal are rendered more effective with the aid of certain subsidiary factors. The same hard luck brings more coppers when it is associated with occasional sobs and sighs than

[9] Sen Gupta, N. N., "Mental Traits of Beggars" in *Our Beggar Problems* (1945), p. 28.

when it is a continuous whine. The successful beggar must be a good actor, he must vary his speech and demeanour with the normal procession of changes that characterize mental life. Thus, intonation, facial expressions and general bodily postures must undergo alteration as they do for people in grief and agony.

(*b*) *Use of Stereotypes to Appeal to Emotions.* The old tales heard in childhood, the precepts transmitted from the early days of society, the myths of fairies, gods and demons that assume queer human shapes—all stir in our breast when we listen to them and yield to the beggar's plaintive wails.

There is always a temptation for the beggar to take to stereotypes. Lodged in the wayside the beggar sees the stream of humanity pass by in a never-ending succession. He does not wish them to return ; each face passes on even as the wavelets in the stream pass on never to return. It is not necessary for the beggar, therefore, to try to variegate his voice and gesture ; they fall on new ears, new eyes and new minds. To render the begging appeal into stereotypes is to economize energy.

(*c*) *Impresses Upon the Mind of his Patrons According to Situation.* The beggar is not slow to seize upon special occasions and particular situations. A successful beggar is never loth to sing to the praise of the presiding deity. The same beggar who seems to be a devout *Vaishnava* in front of one temple is transformed into a *Shakta* before another. They pose victims of starvation and disease just in front of sweet-meat shops and small hotels. Those who feel the gnawing hunger are bound to relent to others from sheer fellow-feeling.

Thus, he concludes that skill in the use of the psycho-physical techniques of intonation and pitch variation, emotional expressions, facial contortions, bodily postures, the ability to watch the flow of words with situations and finally, quickness in perception of the possibilities of an environment enter into calculation in making a success of begging.

(2) *Techniques Employed by Religious Mendicants. Sadhus* and *Faqirs* generally employ one of the following techniques for collecting alms both in kind or cash, i.e. (*a*) organizing some religious feast, *bhandara* or the like, (*b*) removing any natural calamity or disease, e.g. epidemics, small pox, cholera or to bring rains, (*c*) making pilgrims to all the religious centres, (*d*) giving blessings to people and an assurance of a happy life beyond, or (*e*) constructing

a temple or a mosque. They are aware of the fact that they cannot get alms in abundance, if they appeal to the public directly.

(3) *Use of Coercive Methods.* Some of us might believe that modes of begging mean the employment of humble ways of collecting alms, and that a beggar always appeals apologetically to the public sentiments, but there are other ways by which a beggar makes his way through and forces the people to give something or the other.

A beggar may force a man by turning himself as a nuisance to him by holding or touching the feet, by coming nearer the people, by showing such wounds or actions of abnormality physical or mental so that one may like to avoid his or her sight. One can avoid such person only by giving some money to him. Some particular types of beggar, known as Murchias would bleed before one who does not pay. Similarly, some *Sadhus*, e.g. *Nagas*, would threaten a hunger strike if they are not properly provided for.

(4) *Use of Tricks.* Apart from the various techniques used by the beggars, they employ various tricks and trickeries in order to make their appeal more effective. Some beggars excite the people by exhibiting some strange natural phenomena—a cow with four tongues or birth of a queer boy. Indian jugglers and snake charmers may show new feats. Some become palmists and show strange charts to attract the passers-by.

(5) *Deforming of Body.* The most sinister of the tricks is that when the child if deformed at the time of birth or in early childhood to be used as instrument for beggary. The crippled children are used as means to an end. Many beggars are given training in their noses, lips and ears closed by various devices. They have got a strange and indirect organized method of begging and are governed by elaborate codes of behaviour, discipline and ceremonial drinking parties.

A beggar leader may have under his control several beggar children and others whom he provides with the necessary food, clothes and shelter. All the earnings by these beggars go to his pocket. The greater the contribution of an individual beggar the greater the amenities provided by the gang leader.

In Madras city where a survey of beggars was carried out in November 1953 it was found that the method used for begging, were ordinary, exhibiting wounds, exhibiting new-born babies, singing religious songs, exhibiting pregnancy or exhibiting dead bodies.[10]

In conclusion we may say that the most successful beggar is he

[10] See *Social Legislation, Its Role in Social Welfare* (1955), p. 247.

who can extract the largest amount of money out of his victims by the method he uses and in order to achieve this end he must be a successful actor. His appeal, expression, words and gesture must differ with different situations to attract human sympathy. The lesser the mental plasticity and variability of behaviour, the lower the income from begging and lower the status and position of the beggar in his beggar society for these depend upon his income which itself is dependent upon his mode of begging.

Extent of Beggary in India

The Planning Commission points out that although accurate statistical data regarding the number of beggars are not available, it is now roughly estimated that there are about 2 million beggars of all categories in the country, largely concentrated in big cities and towns. Of these, about 71 per cent are males and 29 per cent females.[11] After Independence many surveys of beggary have been carried out in various cities of Uttar Pradesh and cities like Bombay, Nagpur, Madras, Delhi and Calcutta some details of which have been given later on in this chapter.

Measures Taken in Ancient India

In ancient times the problem of beggary was different from today and so were the different methods of their rehabilitation. Dr. Moorthy points out that in all earlier societies it was incumbent upon the family, the clan or the tribe to support their own helpless members and this applied to *Vedic* societies as well.[12] Preventive relief measures in India in the past took the form of institutional design and ethical regulations. The *Varna*, *Ashrama* and the joint family system were the two most efficient and co-operative institutional endeavours to restrain shifty and adventurous living, to limit and reduce to a minimum the social burden of vagrancy and mendicancy. According to the *Varna* scheme of life *Kshatriyas* and *Vaisyas* were to provide for the other two *varnas*, i.e. *Brahmin* and *Sudras*, *Brahmins* were to engage *Sudras* in their service and support them and their families according to their work and needs

[11] Planning Commission, *Plans and Prospects of Social Welfare in India* (1963), p. 146.

[12] Moorthy, M. V., *An Historical Survey of Beggar Relief in India in our Beggar Problem* (1945), p. 71.

and if the *Brahmins* were not able to maintain and support them it devolved upon the *Kshatriyas* and the *Vaisyas* to engage and support the *Sudras*. These two *varnas* were also to engage *Brahmins* as their family priests and maintain them handsomely. Of course, begging was allowed to the students and the *Sanyasis;* its scope was strictly limited with rules and regulations and the persons of *Grahastha Ashrama* were obliged to help them. Living by alms was only permitted during certain conditions and stages of life. The *Varna* institution defined the scope and methods of mendicancy, distributed the social burden of poor relief and prevented haphazard and promiscuous begging. The institution of joint family system was an important factor in the prevention of needless beggary. If there was a lame or blind member in the joint family or a widowed girl or a parentless child, they had rights of life-long protection and maintenance along with other members. These benefits and regard to family members were strictly enforced by the state. Kautilya says, "When a capable person other than an apostate (who has left his religion) or mother neglects to maintain his or her child, wife, mother, father, minor brother, sisters or widowed girls, he or she shall be punished with a fine of twelve panas."[13] It was also laid down that "when without making provision for the maintenance of his wife and sons, any person embraces asceticism, he shall be punished."[14]

But both these institutions have some limitations in the present set up. The *Varna* system though made some provision for the employment of those in distress it did not provide for the fluidity of employment and created class and caste distinctions which are repugnant to modern ideas and ideals of social justice, solidarity and integrity. The joint family organization is an efficient medium of relief only when there are large resources at its command and when there are willing workers who replenish and rehabilitate the resources as they get constantly exhausted. With limited resources and expanding members a joint family will soon collapse. In spite of these two preventive methods, there must have been many helpless ones and numerous hungry and unemployed who needed assistance. And this relief was given either by the individuals, the institutions, the village community or the state. Our religion

[13] Kautilya's *Arthasastra*, Book II, Chapter I, Translated by R. Shama Sastry (1923).

[14] *Ibid.*, Book II, Chapter I.

sanctions charity by individuals and institutions like *Dharamshalas* which provide for boarding and lodging of the poor. Manu says, "the king should always give gifts and do other kinds of charities to a learned *Brahmin*, to one who is affected by disease or affliction, to one who is young (an orphan), to him who is very old and also to him who is born in a noble family."[15] Kautilya also mentions the same thing when he says, "the king shall provide the orphans, the aged, the infirm, the afflicted and the helpless with maintenance. He shall also provide subsistence to helpless women when they are carrying and also to the children they give birth to."[16] He also mentions about "workhouses" for the unemployed.

From the foregoing account it is clear that beggar relief in India was not neglected. The methods of relief expressed themselves in highly institutionalized devices and ways of living such as *varna* and joint family system and prevented the problem of begging from growing to unmanageable proportions. Owing to difficulties in communications the problem of mendicancy was localized and each region was called upon to solve its own beggar problem and the citizens knew the beggars intimately. The state took care of the poor and the helpless. However, it must be said that though the economic help was given to them by answering to their physical needs, yet except in rare cases, it did not conduce towards the unfolding of their personality as the modern conception of social work could not be thought of then.

Present Methods of Rehabilitation

The problems of beggars of today are of somewhat different nature from what they were in the past. Not only the conception of giving relief has changed, but also the situation and, therefore. new methods of rehabilitation are to be found according to the new situation. Firstly, beggars are persons and relief that is to be given is not only to remove temporarily the hindrances in the way of living but we have to create permanent advantages and channels for good living. Secondly, the new civilization has destroyed old institutions, which are in a staggering stage. The *varna* and *ashrama* obligation has become anchoretic, the joint family is disorganized, the old charitable institutions like *dharamshalas* have become effete and

[15] Manu, *Manusmriti*, Chapter VIII, Sloka 395.

[16] Kautilya's *Arthasastra*, Book II, Chapter 1, Translated by R. Shama Sastry (1923).

functionless. The individuals are motivated not by higher ideals of charity but by a sense of guilt and personal interests and have started institutions to grind their own axes.

The competitive industrial economy of our times has *destroyed* the old cooperative rural economy from its place and engages man in a ruthless struggle for existence. Mobility has made the problem grow out of dimensions and the state has thrown up its hands and disclaims its responsibility for the growth of beggars.

Thus, the competitive economy is to be changed, new social obligations are to be instituted, mobility of beggary is to be controlled, old institutions are to be rehabilitated on new lines and the state has to assume full responsibility. In future the duty is not to be upon the individual as such as it was in the past but more upon society and the government.

Action Taken During the British Period

Some sporadic measures were taken during the British regime by some of the states in this country to check beggary by state legislation, as had been done in some of the western countries such as England, Belgium, Switzerland and Germany. Even in ancient India Kautilya made begging a penal act. Men or women suspected of joining any of the holy orders were apprehended by the police and stringent measures were taken against them.

In this direction the lead was given by the state of Bengal during the Second World War. The problem of beggary became acute as a menace to public health and sanitation when beggars affected with leprosy and other infectious diseases occupied the Air-Raid Shelters. The Calcutta Rotary Club, the Salvation Army and the European Association and some social workers agitated for concerted efforts to tackle the problem of the city's vagrants by suitable legislation. The Bengal Vagrancy Ordinance was passed in May 1942 and this was later on replaced by the Bengal Vagrancy Act of 1943. The Act though applicable to the whole state was in force only in Calcutta city and certain other parts of the state. Under the act all police officers, above the rank of head constables, in these areas were authorized to apprehend apparent vagrants and produce them before special magistrates.[17] One Receiving Centre and two Vagrant Homes were opened in the beginning and their number was 5 in

[17] *Social Legislation, Its Role in Social Welfare*, p. 243.

1951 with a total capacity of about two thousand inmates. There were separate homes one each (1) for adult males over 14 years of age, (2) for adult females over 14 years, (3) for children between 5 to 14 years of age. (4) for leprosy patients, and (5) for the old and infirm.

In the first three categories of homes there is segregation between mentally deficient, insane, suffering from communicable diseases, and so on. There is a Vagrancy Advisory Board consisting of both official and non-official members which meet every month to advise the Government on matters relating to the administration of the Act.

There is no fixed period of detention under the Act but they are generally kept for 2 to 3 years. Primary schools are run in the first three category of homes and various types of training are provided in these homes. Facilities for medical treatment are provided. There is a leprosy specialist in the Leprosy Vagrant Home, while venereal disease cases are treated in the Medical College.

There are various methods of discharge : (1) repatriation to their home states is one method, (2) inmates who find employment, (3) those whose well-wishers offer to take them on an undertaking not to permit them to resort to vagrancy again, (4) those who have earned Rs. 75 in wages on outside work or Rs. 50 from wages in the home, and (5) in case of women inmates who are married, such inmates are discharged on these grounds.

Even before the passing of this Act the Bengal Rural Poor and Unemployed Relief Act was passed in 1939, under which Union Boards were to be constituted for the administration of poor fund which was to consist of voluntary contributions, contributions from State Government, District Board and Union Board. The aid was to be given to those who were unemployed for more than a month or without means of subsistence.

Similar Acts were also passed in the states of Madras (1945), Bombay (1945), Mysore (1944) and Kerala (1945) before Independence and in Bihar (1952) after Independence. Besides, this special legislation passed for the prevention of beggary some of the states like Punjab (1916), Central Provinces (1922) and Uttar Pradesh (1916) had made certain provisions in the Municipal Acts for the checking of beggary. Section 248 of the Uttar Pradesh Municipalities Act 1916 prohibits begging importunately for alms or the exposure of any sore or wound, etc. in any street or public place and prescribes imprisonment for one month or fine of Rs. 50 or both for the offender. In other states some action could be taken under section 109 of the Code of Criminal Procedure (1898) whereby a magistrate of the first class on receiving information that there is within such limits a person who has no ostensible means of subsistence, or who cannot give a satisfactory account of himself, may require such persons to show cause, why they should not be ordered to execute a bond, with sureties, for their good behaviour for such period, not exceeding one year as the magistrate thinks fit to fix. However, except in few states like Bombay and Madras no effective steps were taken to apprehend beggars and rehabilitate them.

In 1951 the Act was in force only in Greater Bombay. There were separate institutions for the able-bodied male and female beggars, for the old and crippled, for the male blind and the leper and the lunatic. There were five government institutions, four mental hospitals and nine private institutions—in all 18 certified institutions with accommodation for about 2,000.[18] In Madras the Corporation of Madras had a Poor House for the old and destitute. There were also special homes in some other towns too. In Delhi State the provisions of the Punjab Municipal Act 1916 were in force and there was one poor house for the destitutes with a capacity for 500, but there was no provision for beggars suffering from leprosy or other infectious diseases. In Madhya Pradesh, Kerala and Mysore there were two to three small beggar homes. In Uttar Pradesh in Lucknow City a Poor House was started by a Social Service League in 1941. But the capacity of this Poor House was limited and also there were no special institutions for different types of beggars. After their release from the house on the expiry of conviction period they again resort to begging, because no measures were taken for their after-care.

Action Taken During the Five-Year Plans

In 1953, the Research Programme Committee of the Planning Commission sponsored two survey projects dealing with beggary, one in Delhi and the other in Madras. The Delhi survey conducted by the Delhi School of Social Work showed that there were about 3,000 beggars of all categories in the state, and their annual earnings total about Rs. 10 lakhs. The Madras survey showed that there

[18] *Ibid.*, p. 248.

were about 7,443 beggars in Madras out of which 4,396 were able-bodied, 1,153 diseased, 1,435 disabled and 459 insane persons. Similar surveys have been carried out in Nagpur, Bombay, Calcutta and some other cities of Uttar Pradesh.[19]

Most of these surveys revealed that the majority of beggars were able-bodied and had resorted to begging as an easy way of earning livelihood. For the Second Plan period the Ministry of Home Affairs proposed that each state should have at least one home for 100 old, infirm, diseased or disabled beggars at a suitable place within the state.[20] These homes could be set up under the Central Assistance Scheme. It was proposed to have 26 beggar homes in different states. Such assistance was also continued during the Third Plan to set up 33 more beggar homes. To check the exploitation of children for begging in 1959 the Indian Penal Code was amended on the recommendations of the Committee of the Deputy Inspector-Generals of Police set up in 1956. By this amendment if any person who, not being the lawful guardian of the minor, employs or uses such minor for the purpose of begging was to be severely punished.[21] Begging here has been defined as soliciting or receiving alms in a public place, whether under the pretence of singing, dancing, fortune-telling, performing tricks or selling articles or otherwise and it also includes exposing or exhibiting with the object of obtaining or exorting alms, any sore, wound, injury, deformity or disease, whether of himself or of any other person. In 1964 the Ministry of Home Affairs in consultation with the Planning Commission sanctioned a project for controlling and for eradication of juvenile beggary and vagrancy. This project includes institutional services in the shape of establishment of homes for the care of children 7-14 years of age, in all cities and towns having a population of 1 lakh and above and in important places where the incidence of begging is very high.

However, in spite of all these efforts the problem of beggary still continues.

Future Programme

In some states there is no adequate legislation to check beggary.

[19] For details see Chandra, Sushil, *Sociology of Deviation in India* (1967), pp. 137-42.

[20] *Plans and Prospects of Social Welfare* (1963), p. 148.

[21] *Seminar on Social Defence* (1965), p. 55.

In some states there is some legislation but it is not adequate. For example, in Punjab the acts prohibit begging in municipal towns. But there is no provision to establish beggar homes. In other states there is adequate legislation. But there is absence of workhouses or other institutions for the rehabilitation of beggars when they are caught. On the other hand, in the public mind all begging is associated with poverty. There has been a resistance on the part of Magistrates to consign a beggar to jail. Neither fine nor a sort of imprisonment can solve the problem. The man is back again on the streets. Thus, the problem is to be tackled rationally and scientifically.

Firstly, public opinion is to be created that all begging cannot be equated with poverty. While poverty is to be removed by appropriate social security measures, begging must be considered as an antisocial act and should be treated as such. The problem is to be treated in a humanistic way. They are not to be treated by the society as social pests and outcastes but with all sympathy and tolerance they need as an integral part of the society, only grown abnormal through force of circumstances and deserving of all care and help. A large proportion of able-bodied beggars call for a stern application of the law to drive such persons out of the profession. Thus, on the basis of these suggestions the following steps will be necessary.

(1) *Uniform Law in all States.* There should be comprehensive and uniform law on all-India basis to tackle the problem on a rational basis. As pointed out above at present in some states there are no special laws to tackle the problem in a systematic way and in some states where there are such laws, the laws are defective. All those persons who beg or exploit through beggary are not considered as beggars but only those who actually beg. It is optional for the states to set up special institutions such as workhouses for the able-bodied beggars and special home for the infirm and the disabled. Thus, there should be comprehensive legislation on all-India basis to deal with all types of beggars.

(2) *Provision of Workhouses.* There should be workhouses for able-bodied persons who should be imparted training in different types of industries and then steps should be taken to secure employment for them to rehabilitate them permanently, otherwise they may resort to begging again. Where it is possible to provide employment before training it may be done so. There should be separate houses

for men and women. There should be special homes for disabled and infirm persons. These homes should be different for disabled, diseased, deaf, dumb, lame persons, etc. They may be provided work according to their capacity and the diseased should receive proper treatment.

(3) *Child Care Institution.* There should be separate homes or institutions for children where they should be provided training along with general education.

(4) *Reception Homes.* Some Reception Homes will have to be set up in each state, where all beggars are sent at the first instance for classification and medical examination. After their careful study for a few days they are to be sent to the institution for which they are considered to be fit.

(5) *Rehabilitation on State Basis.* Owing to easy means of communication and no strict checking on railways, beggars move from place to place and many a time there is a large concentration of beggars in a particular state. If the problem is to be solved in a more rational way the beggars will have to be rehabilitated in their home states. It is not only a question of expenditure but differences in language and food habits and the feeling that they do not belong to the states in which they were apprehended retard their rehabilitation. If the legislation is passed on all-India basis there will be no difficulty in rehabilitating the beggars in their own states because there will be proper provisions for their rehabilitation in each state.

(6) *Comprehensive Social Security Measures.* As at present, administered relief is forced on the persons concerned for the period they are confined, provisions will have to be made for their dependents through comprehensive social security measures.

(7) *Grant of Outdoor Relief.* Grant of outdoor relief in a suitable form to all those who do not require institutional custody should be permitted. Conditions of eligibility for relief may be defined. Grant of relief may be left to local committees without requiring a magisterial order or commitment in each case.

(8) *Licensing of Religious Mendicants.* It is very difficult to distinguish between real and imaginary religious mendicants. However, some type of licensing will be necessary in their case, if this problem is to be tackled comprehensively. Some of these *sadhus* as we have pointed out earlier do not beg openly in streets or from the general public.

(9) *Creation of Public Opinion and Collection of Funds by New Methods.* Public opinion will have to be aroused against indiscri-

minate charity and how it is against the modern conception of social work. Not only it discourages honest persons to work, but it also wrecks the personality of the person who accept alms.

(10) *Development of Country's Economic Resources.* Besides these measures healthy conditions are to be created in society through various types of development schemes, so that none who is able-bodied and equipped with normal intellect should be unable to support himself and his family. For this both development in the industrial and agricultural field is necessary.

(11) *Family Welfare Services.* It was pointed out in the beginning that many children and women beg owing to some types of family disorganization in the family such as maltreatment by parents or husbands. In such a case family social services rendered by trained social workers will be of much importance in reducing such tensions.

In April 1965, the Planning Commission appointed a Study Group to examine the problem of begging, vagrancy and juvenile delinquency and formulating schemes for its control for the Fourth Plan. The Group after examining the problem in detail has suggested that for the Fourth Plan period, certain areas be selected in each state for instituting certain intensive programmes for eradication and control wherein all aspects of the problem of begging might be tackled on a comprehensive basis. Pilot projects of this nature might provide the necessary experience for solving the problem on a wider scale in successive plan periods. Under this scheme a double track system has been proposed for tackling the problem, namely, one of Social Assistance, wherein people will be assisted on the basis of needs recognized for the purpose, and the other in which, those begging wilfully and professionally would be punished like adult offenders. Different institutions are to be created to cater to the needs of beggars in different circumstances.[22]

If training and work are provided for the able-bodied and institutional care or outdoor relief is given to handicapped persons the problem can be solved satisfactorily. But the solution of the problem is not so easy as we may think. Poverty, unemployment and diseases are the general problems of the under-developed countries and will require long time to achieve satisfactory standards of living for each. These problems have been discussed in detail in the subsequent chapters.

[22] *Social Defence*, October 1965.

PART FOUR

MALADJUSTMENT IN INSTITUTIONS

CHAPTER X

POVERTY AND UNEMPLOYMENT

POVERTY and unemployment are the two major social problems causing sickness, personal, family and community disorganization. They have been in existence since the dawn of civilization and one method or the other was devised to help the poverty stricken, the dependent and the unemployed. But since the technological advancement, industrial revolution and new concept of democracy unemployment has assumed a new shape. While workers and employees organized separately with diverse functions, poverty and dependency of many stand in better contrast with the enormous riches of the few. The causes of poverty and unemployment may be slightly different, but the effects of both are almost the same. Similarly, the remedies of both may be different but they are often similar. Sometimes under-employment and poverty are equated with each other. Therefore, we shall deal with them separately at places and at others in a combined way.

Another term used parallel to poverty is dependency, although the word "dependent" has a different meaning in a general sense. For example, a young child is dependent upon his parents or a wife upon her husband, but relationships here are not pathological. But a child placed in an orphanage or a wife without means of support whose husband has died is dependent in the pathological sense. Thus, dependency is that condition of life in which one depends for his subsistence either in whole or in part upon some other agencies than his natural supporters.

Poverty—Absolute and Relative

Poverty and richness are relative terms. The poverty line in any given society is determined by the customs and mode of living. The poverty line in India is not at the same point as in the U. S. A. or in the U. K. As defined by Gillin and Gillin "Poverty is that condition in which a person, either because of inadequate income or unwise expenditures, does not maintain a scale of living high enough to provide for his physical and mental efficiency and to enable him and his natural dependents to function usefully according to the standards of the society of which he is a member."[1]

Poverty is relative to the scale of living in a given group or a country. For example, a whole group may be better off relatively than a whole group in another culture and yet feel poor in comparison with others in the same community. Thus, poverty is relative to the conditions of others in the same culture group. Status is determined by relative position. Further, the scale of living may be different in different social groups in the same culture, and each group tends to formulate a standard of living, what is considered necessary for a decent living. The actual scale of living compared with the standard of living measures the extent of poverty.

Another term used is absolute poverty and relative poverty. A person may be relatively poor among the persons of his own group who are relatively rich, whereas absolute poverty means that he is not able to maintain a minimum decent standard of living to maintain himself and his family.

Measurement of Poverty

One way of measuring the richness or poverty of a country is the availability of goods and services for consumption in a particular year. This we call the national income or dividend of a country. However, to measure national dividend of a country is an elaborate task and requires the services of expert economists. Sometimes it is difficult to decide which items should or should not be included in the national income and there is difference of opinion among the economists over this. For example, the services rendered by domestic servants or housewives should be included in national income or not, though one of them is a paid worker and the other unpaid. Similarly, the goods consumed by the cultivator at home without bringing it to the market cannot be estimated easily.[2] According to the United Nations publication on National Income Statistics the net national product is the aggregate of the net values added in all branches of economic activity during a specified period together with the net income from abroad.[3]

[1] Gillin, J. L. and Gillin, J. P., *An Introduction to Sociology* (1942), p. 721.

[2] For details see Wadia, P. A. and Merchant, K. T., *Our Economic Problem* (1952), pp. 678-80.

[3] United Nations, *National Income Statistics of Various Countries* 1938-47 (1'

Economic welfare may be said to be measured by the amount of national income accrued in a particular period. Other things being equal, economic welfare is greater if national income is greater. However, while looking at the national income figure as an approximate index of economic welfare, we should take into consideration all the relevant factors involved e.g. the extent to which the economy of the country is non-monetary, the distribution of income (for inequality of income distort value), age composition of the population, the price index, etc. Thus, while making comparisons from country to country we have to be careful not only regarding the extent to which the respective economies are monetary and non-monetary, but also regarding the differences in prices, standard of living, habits, etc. For example, the same income per head would have an entirely different significance in two countries so wide apart from each other as India and England, because the scale of values is different, not only owing to difference in taste, but also because external conditions impose different standards of requirement. Broadly speaking owing to the warmer climate of India, an appreciably smaller expenditure is required on food, clothing, fuel and housing than in England. However, in spite of these limitations, the national income has some utility in measuring the standard of living of any country.

National Income of India

Various estimates about the national income of India have been made from time to time by different economists beginning by Dadabhoy Naoroji in 1868. Dadabhoy estimated the income per capita in 1868 as Rs. 20, Digby as Rs. 18 in 1899, Dr. Rao as Rs. 65

TABLE 15

NATIONAL INCOME OF SOME SELECTED COUNTRIES[4]

Country	*Per capita national income in rupees*	*Country*	*Per capita national income in rupees*
India (1948-49)	255	Pakistan	240
Australia	3070	Sweden	3520
Canada	4210	U. K.	2700
France	2280	U. S. A.	6970
Japan	480	U. S. S. R.	1500

[4] Wadia, P. A. and Merchant, K. T., *op. cit.*, p. 695.

in 1931 and Government of India as Rs. 204 in 1945-46. However, due to differences in price levels and different methods used in arriving at these figures these estimates were not comparable. The most reliable estimate of the national income has been made only after Independence when a National Income Committee was appointed by the Government of India in 1948. It estimated the national income per capita as Rs. 255. As compared to other countries the income in our country was very low as may be seen from Table 15.

The estimates made by the Statistical Department of the United Nations for British India excluding the Princely States from 1931-32 to 1948-49 show that our national income was lower in 1948-49 than in 1931-32 and so was the case with per capita income.

TABLE 16

NATIONAL AND PER CAPITA INCOME OF INDIA EXCLUDING PRINCELY STATES (IN CONSTANT PRICES)

Year	*National Income (in million Rs.)*	*Population (in millions)*	*Per Capita Income (Rs.)*
1931-32	17,120	206	83
1945-46	18,530	242	77
1946-47	18,295	244	75
1948-49	16,958	246	70

It will be seen that there has been no improvement in National Income in the decade and a half before Independence. The improvement made after Independence has been discussed later on.

Causes of Poverty

The causes of poverty have been discussed by different sociologists in different ways. Gillin and Gillin have mentioned the causes of poverty and dependency under five heads : (1) incapacity of the individual, (2) adverse physical environments, (3) economic factors, (4) defects in social organization, and (5) war. In the incapacity of the individual they include the hereditary weakness of the individual such as weak and sickly body, depressing aptitudes and attitudes towards work as a result of early conditioning and physical handicaps because of accident or disease such as blind, deaf, dumb, mentally deficient or disordered. In the adverse physical environments are mentioned the poor natural resources, adverse climate and weather, insects, pests and the like and natural disaster. Among economic factors are included shortage of capital and technical know-how, uneven distribution of wealth, business depression and technological changes which may replace labour. The defects in social organization arise due to rapid technological changes, when it is difficult to make economic and social arrangement to cope with new situations. These defects include educational shortcomings, inadequate health machinery for the protection of new occupational diseases, bad housing and employment of husband and wife outside home leaving little time for socialization of children and difficulties of youth to find employment because of inexperience. In the war most active and strong are skilled, some are disabled, many women become widows and inflation affect standard of living.

So far as India is concerned some of the above factors also apply in this country, but some are peculiar due to its different political and social set up. We may discuss these factors under personal, political, economic, biological, technological and social.

(1) *Personal Factors*. Among the personal factors may be included the physical weakness, defects or diseases which may be hereditary or accidental. All these factors effect the efficiency of the worker to compete in the world and have adequate earnings.

(2) *Political and Economic Factors*. Due to political subordination of the country the British Government exploited the situation in their own interest. While the industrial revolution in the eighteenth century brought many changes in agriculture, industry, transport and economic thinking in the West, leading to a higher standard of living there, "India was made subservient to the industries of Great Britain and was encouraged to produce raw material only in order to supply material for the looms and manufactories of Great Britain."[5] Dr. Mukerjee observes, "The seventeenth century saw India as Agricultural Mother of Asia and Industrial Workshop of the World. The end of the eighteenth century witnessed the rapid decline of Indian industries, the complete ruin of Indian shipping and loss of her political sovereignty."[6] There was a rapid decline in urban handicrafts due to (1) the disappearance of the indigenous court, (2) new taste of the ruling classes for foreign machine-made goods, (3) deliberate policy of the government to import raw

[5] Dutt, R. C., *Economic History of India* (1919), p. 67.

[6] Mukerjee, R. K., *Economic History of India* 1600-1800 (1946), p. 29.

material from India and to put tariffs on Indian-made goods imported in England as against duty free goods imported from England to this country, (4) competition from cheap machine-made goods manufactured on large scale, (5) less cost of transportation for foreign-made goods due to revolution in transport system and especially after the opening of Suez Canal in 1869, (6) too rapid construction of railways which did not allow the artisan to adopt to new circumstances, and (7) laissez faire policy of the government which did not lend any helping hand to the struggling handicrafts or new large-scale industries.[7]

There was no improvement in agriculture too. The Zamindari System introduced by the British Government led to the exploitation of tenants by the zamindars. They tried to charge the maximum possible rent from the tenants making them poorer and poorer. The further division of land with increasing population and growing ruralization because of the exodus of artisans to rural areas increased the number of small cultivators and uneconomic units of farms.

The Government did not render any assistance to the cultivators to use new techniques of agriculture. There was also no expansion of education facilities. The Government followed the laissez faire policy even in such matters. The result of all this was the further lowering of the standard of living of the masses.

(3) *Biological Factors.* We have already pointed out that the population rose rapidly in this period. There were two reasons for this. Firstly, due to improvement in transport the occurrences of famines decreased. Secondly, the science of medicine brought reduction in the death rate, while birth rate continued to be the same due to the absence of family planning programme. We have discussed this in detail in another chapter.

(4) *Technological and Environmental Factors.* Due to non-protection of industries these could not develop much and as a consequence there was no development of technical know-how. Sometime some basic raw material is also not available, e.g. kerosene oil and certain metals. Uncertainty of rains may be another factor.

(5) *Social Factors.* Among social factors may be included the joint family system, the caste system and the religious beliefs which have been an impediment in the development of industrial

[7] For further details see my book, *Changing Pattern of Indian Villages* (1964).

growth. The joint family system discourages young persons to go out and strive for new ventures. Due to minimum security provided by the family, people become lethargic and develop the stay-home habit.

The caste system was a hindrance to the development of new industries and it discouraged some persons to leave their traditional occupation lest they may be outcasted.

Some of the religious beliefs such as the Karma theory and the concept of Maya also discouraged certain Hindus to work hard although these beliefs were mostly confined to ignorant and illiterate people. Some believed that as we could not change our fate, there was no use of much effort and the results were preordained. Similarly the concept of Maya led some of the persons to belief that this world was illusionary and there was no use in acquiring much wealth.

Poverty and Disorganization. The poor have such a low income that it is very difficult for them to manage affairs of the family—food for children, their clothing, medical care, education and other opportunities. Such people become discouraged and cannot perform their functions properly. Under these conditions we cannot have healthy individuals, educated children, socialized men and women interested in the progressive development of our social organization. The children are forced to work at an early age to supplement the family income. Sometimes women are compelled to work, even when there is nobody to look after the children at home. When family members are not given proper food, there may be illness, mental breakdown and conflict, because of lack of minimum necessities.

Unemployment

The problem of unemployment is common to all the countries, whether industrially advanced as well as backward, although the causes and extent of such unemployment may differ from country to country. The term unemployment is a complex one and somewhat difficult to explain. As Professor Pigou rightly observes, "Unemployment is one of those many terms in common use the general significance of which is understood by all, but which is nevertheless somewhat difficult to define with accuracy. Are we, for example, to include among the unemployed those who are idle because they do not want to work. Are we to include sick persons, or workmen out on strike or the various classes of individuals who are for one reason or another unemployable. Any decision upon these points is more or less arbitrary."[8]

In simple terms then we may say that unemployment is said to exist in a country where the able-bodied persons of working age who are willing to work are not able to find work at the current wage levels. Under this definition people who are unfit for work due to physical or mental disability or are not willing to work, are excluded from the category of the unemployed. In the former category may be included children, the sick, the aged and the disabled and may be called the unemployable, while in the latter category may be included sadhus, beggars and non-working property holders and they may be called parasites. Professor Pigou adds, "Unemployment means unemployment among the wage-earning classes and in respect of wage work only. Thus, it does not include all the idleness of wage-earners but only that part of it which is, from their point of view and in their existing condition at the time, involuntary. There is, therefore, excluded the idleness of those who are definitely incapacitated from wage-earning work by extreme old age, infirmity or temporary sickness. There is also excluded the idleness of those who are idle, not from necessity but from choice."[9]

However, there are writers who count all those persons unemployed, who are willing to work, including the incapacitated because of illness, or certain other handicaps, which can easily be corrected. It is due to this difference of opinion over the term unemployment that the types of unemployment or causes of unemployment have been described differently by sociologists and economists.

Types of Unemployment

Various types of unemployment as distinguished according to different causes are : (*a*) casual and seasonal unemployment, (*b*) frictional and technological unemployment, (*c*) temporary unemployment, (*d*) voluntary unemployment, (*e*) cyclic unemployment, (*f*) unemployment arising from shortage of capital, equipment or other complementary resources, and (*g*) involuntary unemployment and underemployment which is mainly found in underdeveloped countries.

(*a*) *Seasonal or Casual Unemployment.* In many industries there

[8] Pigou, A. C., *Unemployment* (1913), p. 17.

[9] *Ibid.*, pp. 14-15.

are sudden fluctuations of activities in a particular period of the year. At one time activity is very brisk and the employer requires a large labour force to deal with the rush of work. At other times work is comparatively slack, when a part of the labour force becomes unemployed. This is the case with dock workers, building constructions, etc. There is thus a floating surplus of the unemployed called the "Reserve of Labour".

In some industries the workers get jobs only for a certain period of the year or in a particular season. Such is the case with woollen industry, sugar industry, etc. Work is carried in sugar industry in our country from November to April or May and the workers remain idle during the intervening period. This is also the case with agricultural labourers.

This seasonal or casual employment makes the labourers of migratory character. The hardships and privations of uncertain existence on the road demand a hardy constitution and only the strongest can survive in such conditions.

(*b*) *Frictional and Technological Unemployment*. Frictional unemployment is caused by changes in the industrial structure which are constantly occurring. Modern businesses are essentially dynamic, throwing some workers out of employment for the time being. Demand is constantly shifting from one product to another leaving behind a trail of unemployment. There may be loss of time between different jobs.

Technological advancement creates unemployment in another way as well. The increase in technology means a displacement of human labour. With the advance in technology some manufacturing processes have become so perfect as to be virtually automatic. Some of this displaced labour may be absorbed in the production of new commodities, but it is a fact that advance in technology reduces the demand for labour.

(*c*) *Temporary Unemployment*. When young men have completed their education and training they remain unemployed for a few years, because of overcrowding in the labour market of inexperienced persons for jobs. Older persons who have had a few years experience have some advantage in the competitive market.

(*d*) *Voluntary Unemployment*. Voluntary unemployment is that which is caused by the refusal of labour to accept a cut in the rate of real wages. But such unemployment cannot exist under full equilibrium conditions, when there is free competition.

(e) *Cyclic Unemployment.* The unemployment may be caused due to cyclic functions of the industry. The course of business shows a wave-like movement, consisting of alternating periods of booms and depressions. These trade cycles exercise great influence on the volume of unemployment which decreases when trade is good and increases when it is bad.

There are many explanations and theories of the business cycle. Lord Keynes maintains that a boom is generated when investment exceeds savings. A slump or depression similarly results when savings exceed investment. This is probably over-simplification, but it is basically true. Various theories regarding the origin of trade cycle have been advocated, such as climatic theories (Jevons, Moore and Beveridge), theories of over-saving or under consumption (Hobson, Major Douglas), monetary theory (Hawtrey) and psychological theory (Pigou).[10] But we may add, the trade cycle is the result not of one single factor, but a multiplicity of factors, among which sometimes one and sometimes another becomes dominant.

(f) *Unemployment Arising from Shortage of Capital, Equipment or Other Complementary Resources.* This type of unemployment is found mainly in underdeveloped countries. In India, in common with other underdeveloped countries, production is carried on with insufficient amount of real capital per head of the population. In almost all processes of production the techniques are relatively backward leading to various forms of unemployment, seasonal unemployment in agriculture, and disguised unemployment in certain other industries. It may perhaps appear strange that in underdeveloped economy, in which there is shortage of goods and services should at the same time have insufficient employment opportunities resulting in a surplus labour force.

(g) *Involuntary Unemployment or Underemployment.* Lord Keynes gives the concept of involuntary unemployment for underemployment. He defines the concept of involuntary unemployment as that when a person is willing to work at a lower real wage than the current real wage, whether or not he is willing to accept a lower money wage. In simple words mere engagement in some productive occupation does not necessarily mean absence of unemployment. People who are partially employed or are doing inferior jobs while they could do better jobs are not adequately employed. It is called

[10] For details see my book, *History and Development of Economic Thought*, Chapter XVIII.

a state of underemployment, which is equally bad for the prosperity of a country.

Underemployment is present both in rural as well as urban sectors. As most of the occupations are overstaffed, the wages consequently paid are extremely low.

Causes of Unemployment

We have discussed above the various types of unemployment, and the causes giving rise to such types of unemployment. However, let us discuss those causes in brief in a more clear way. The causes may be divided into two broader categories, viz. subjective and objective, or internal and external, or (*i*) personal, and (*ii*) technological and economic.

(*i*) *Personal Factors.* Personal factors include defects in character, physical disability, etc. which in other words means physical, mental and moral deficiency of the labourers. Many a time a person in spite of his desire is not able to work owing to his deformity, weak mentality, accidents, defective education and training, etc. However, it is to be noted that to call these causes as entirely personal may be sometimes throwing the responsibility on the wrong shoulders. Many physical deformities are doubtless due, directly or indirectly, to the factory system, obligation in which case falls on the employer. Elliott and Merrill have mentioned the following under the personal factors.

(*a*) *Age Factor.* They point out that both young and old persons have disadvantage in getting employment. This is because young men who have completed their education and training at this age find difficulty in getting jobs because of their inexperience. Similarly, persons above forty years and particularly those past fifty and sixty have the highest proportionate incidence of unemployment. With so many younger persons glutting the labour market, older men have often been unable to get good jobs. This scrapping has been justified on the ground that older people produce less, are more prone to accidents, and are less adaptable. However, the real reason for discriminating against them is that they will be candidates for pensions and their retirement age will add to the cost of insurance. The Planning Commission observes, "The older persons are precluded from public employment because of age bar, while private employers prefer young persons to older people."[11]

[11] *First Five-Year Plan*, Government of India (1952), p. 658.

(*b*) *Vocational Unfitness.* Too many young people have no understanding of their own abilities or interests and no particular task in mind when they get training. Willingness to do anything may seem to indicate a worthy desire on the part of the person seeking work. Employers, on the other hand, may seek qualified and competent trained workers. Similarly, there may be more men trained in a particular profession than required. The demand is less than the supply and hence unemployment.

(*c*) *Illness and/or Physical Disabilities.* Many workmen are temporarily or permanently unemployed because of illness or other physical disabilities. Illness induced by industrial conditions or the hazards of the particular industry account for a larger number. Industrial accidents are often fatal and sometimes make the workers permanently disabled. Other specific dangers of industry are the occupational diseases. In addition to those who are physically disabled because of illness or accident we have the blind and the crippled who not only constitute a problem unto themselves but augment the number of both the unemployed and the unemployable.

(*ii*) *Technological and Economic Factors.* Among these factors are included mostly those causes which we have already discussed under the head "Types of Unemployment". The major factor in the unemployment complex may be ascribed to dislocations in industries and to disorganization of economic structure. Because of advances in technical skill and highly specialized division of labour, able-bodied and capable men are unable to secure jobs. "Unemployment which is not due to personal disabilities may be classified as (*a*) cyclical, (*b*) technological, (*c*) seasonal, and (*d*) that due to problems in labour turn-over because of lack of mobility in the labour supply. Labour problems are also closely related to other phases of our economic order, such as disturbed market conditions, low buying power, high tariffs and the like. In final analysis, however, our present problem of unemployment seems to be the result of both technological changes and the cyclical aspects of business conditions which are deeply rooted in problems of production and distribution."[12] In addition to these causes we have already pointed that in underdeveloped countries insufficient amount of real capital per head of population also leads to various forms of unemployment disguised or manifested.

[12] Elliott, M. A and Merrill, F. E., *Social Disorganization* (1941), p. 441.

Evil Effects of Unemployment

Unemployment whether of a permanent or temporary nature has many bad consequences not only for the worker himself but for the worker's family and the community at large. He suffers from personal disorganization, his health is affected, his family and the community is also affected. We may discuss these evils under four heads : (*a*) personal disorganization, (*b*) effect on health, (*c*) family disorganization, and (*d*) community disorganization.

(*a*) *Unemployment and Personal Disorganization.* Unemployment whether of a seasonal or permanent nature undermines the life organization of a worker. The unemployed person faces a discouraging outlook. In his book, *Labour Market*, Mr. Lescohier observes, "Unsteady employment undermines the worker's physique, deadens his mind, weakens his ambition, destroys his capacity for continuous sustained endeavour, induces a liking for idleness and self-indulgence, saps self-respect and the sense of responsibility, impairs technical skill, weakens nerve and will power, creates a tendency to blame others for failures, saps his courage, prevents thrift and hope of family advancement, destroys a workman's feeling that he is taking good care of his family, sends him to work worried, underfed, plunges him in debt."[13] Unemployment affects the personal organization of different persons in different ways say : (1) new entrants, (2) experienced persons, (3) old persons, (4) casual workers, and (5) underemployed.

The new entrants, i.e. the young persons who have just finished their education and training and have entered in the labour market are full of enthusiasm and vigour. When they cannot get employment they become disillusioned and cynics. Having no outlet for creative energy they become delinquents and commit robberies or bank hold-ups. The anti-social activities offer the only chance to the undisciplined and recalcitrant youth. Many college students feel that they have been educated which might be much useful to secure a job but become disappointed when they find no market for their services.

The plight of the experienced unemployed person, who has lost his job is equally unfortunate. The disorganizing effect is not upon the worker only but upon his family as well. The ex-wage-earner discouraged and depressed may become cynical, irritable and disagreeable in his home. The unemployed often become unable to

[13] Lescohier, Don. D.. *The Labour Market* (1919), p. 107.

do steady work, unreliable, inefficient and "good for nothing" Moral values of the group are distorted or lose their significance. With savings exhausted and credit denied he may become a rebel. He may steal because his children need bread. Because of their inability to face economic insecurity and loss of status for themselves and their family, some may end in suicide.

No experience is perhaps so full of bitterness and so conducive to loss of self-respect as economic insecurity during old age. Struggling against the inevitable such dependence in itself produces a sense of defeatism. The frustrated desire for security, the loss of status, the isolation from former contacts may bring out serious emotional maladjustment, if not actual disorganization. For some, the maladjustments of dependent old age eventuate in suicide.

The effect on casual workers is almost similar as in the case of the unemployed. Of all the seasonal labourers the migratory casual workers represent the most maladjusted of men who toil. Being mobile they have no permanent community interest nor family ties to act as a stabilizing force. Subjected to little restraint so long as they perform the tasks set before them and frequently living under inhuman conditions, there is a large personal disorganization among them.

The unemployed are not the only persons who suffer disorganization. Equally serious is underemployment for the worker which frustrates hopes and brings loss of status. Many capable men are available for the same job, hence all tend to be underpaid. Old standards of living must give way. Children must not be well educated. The loss of status and sense of defeat may be quite as disorganizing as dependency on charitable relief for others.

(*b*) *Unemployment and Low Health.* Those who are unemployed have insufficient resources to maintain their own and family members' health. The limited diet, the low consumption of essential food elements, the inability to pay for ordinary medical care, all these enter into the picture. Worry and anxiety about inability to provide for dependents further affects their health. The problem of low health is most serious in the low-income group.

The stress and strain of worry, the restlessness and lack of usual activity, the new obligations for wife and children may all affect his health.

(*c*) *Unemployment and Family Disorganization.* In addition to the physical and mental deprivation, and the havoc unemployment wrecks on the personality of the breadwinner, it affects his family as well. When the regular income fails, the families fall back upon their own savings, however, low they may be. After the meagre savings are exhausted the inevitable borrowing either in cash or in goods starts. Valuable articles are sold and ornaments are mortgaged. Families suffer starvation by resorting to unbelievable economics in food. Bodies sapped through such undernourishment become prey for ill health. Thus, there is an almost universal failure among the unemployed and underpaid labourers to take adequate care of their family members' health.

In desperation the children may be induced to industry earlier, their education may be stopped, and the wife may seek employment knowing fully well that her husband can secure nothing. She, thus, assumes a double load. The father can seldom cook or care intelligently for the children. The working mother may do her job as well as her housework. Her energy is soon exhausted and she becomes irritable with a nervous breakdown in the offing. If she is not working, her anxiety concerning the husband's unemployment may affect her mind, the children may likewise become irritable and the whole family organization may be threatened. The family may often be broken up to secure help from relatives or friends.

(*d*) *Unemployment and Community Disorganization.* Owing to unemployment in a country its resources are not utilized to the full extent and production is less than the maximum. This affects the standard of living of the people. Owing to illness, crime and mental illness many social problems arise leading to social disorganization. Those unemployed are not only a problem to themselves but are a charge on the society. Hospitalization, emergency relief, increase in police strength and scenes of family disputes are examples of costs that are borne by the public.

Extent of Unemployment in India

The problem of unemployment and underemployment seems to have been there for a long time, but no exact estimate about the magnitude of the problem in quantitative terms was available till 1951. The Planning Commission in the *First Five-Year Plan* rightly points out, "There has been no attempt so far for collecting statistical material on employment and unemployment, the only published figures at present available are the registration and placement of employment exchanges. These figures cannot, however, give an idea of the total volume of unemployment. Firstly, employment exchanges are confined to industrial towns and the figures of registration and placements which they compile are restricted mostly to the industrial and commercial sector. Secondly, even in the industrial sector, there is neither compulsion for the unemployed to register with the exchanges, nor is there any obligation on the part of the employer to recruit labour only through these exchanges. Even the information regarding unemployment among the industrial workers is thus inadequate. Thirdly, in the nature of the case, employment exchange statistics cannot indicate the amount of disguised unemployment which is otherwise believed to exist. This means that the extent to which qualified persons have to accept work which does not give them the income which persons with similar qualifications get elsewhere cannot be assessed from these data. There is also to some extent registration of persons who are already in employment and who desire to seek better jobs. This tendency is reported to exist in the more qualified section of registrants, but to the extent a region maintains these persons on the register of employment seekers, there is an over-estimate of the number unemployed."[14]

However, it was noted by the Planning Commission that the problem has been aggravated in the last hundred years or so because of (*i*) rapid growth of population, (*ii*) the disappearance of the old rural industries which provided part-time employment to a large number of persons in the rural areas, (*iii*) inadequate development of the non-agricultural sector from the point of view of employment, and (*iv*) a large displacement of population as a result of partition.

Urban Unemployment. In 1954 a preliminary survey of urban employment was undertaken at the suggestion of the Planning Commission by the National Sample Survey. This survey placed the magnitude of urban unemployment at 2.24 millions. It also sought to establish a rough relationship between the number unemployed and those who remain on the live registers of the exchanges. According to this survey it was estimated that about 25 per cent of the unemployed register themselves with the exchanges. The number on the live register which was 3.37 lakhs in March 1951 rose to 7.05 lakhs in March 1956. On the basis of this it was estimated that the magnitude of urban unemployment at the end of First Plan, i.e. in March 1956 may be of the order of 2.8 millions. Allowing for frictional unemployment, the Planning Commission

[14] *First Five-Year Plan*, p. 651.

put the number of urban unemployed as 2.5 millions. To this may be added the number of new entrants to the urban labour force. It was estimated that in the next five years about 4.2 millions persons would be added on this account.

Rural Unemployment. As pointed out above no estimate of the magnitude of unemployment in the rural areas was available in the beginning of First Five-Year Plan. During the First Plan period some surveys of unemployment in rural areas were made by some states. But because of differences in the concepts used, a comparative statement for different regions could not be compiled. The only systematic enquiry undertaken was Agricultural Labour Enquiry (1954) according to which in 1951 the level of rural unemployment was 2.8 millions. The National Sample Survey has also begun to attempt periodical appraisals of unemployment in urban and rural areas, but the data with regard to rural areas were not available by the end of First Plan period. The Planning Commission estimated that the number of new entrants to the rural labour force in 1956-61 may be 7.5 millions. The following table shows the number of job opportunities which should have been created if unemployment was to be eradicated.

TABLE 17

UNEMPLOYMENT SITUATION IN INDIA

	First Plan		*Second Plan*			*Third Plan*		
	3/1951 Number of unemployed	*3/1956 Back log. of unemployed*	*New entrants during Second Plan*	*Employed during Second Plan*	*3/1961 Back log. of unemployed*	*New entrants during Third Plan*	*Employed during Third Plan*	*3/1966 Back log. of unemployed*
	1	2	3	4	5	6	7	8
(1) Urban (in millions)	1.4	2.5	4.2	6.5	N.A.	14.0	10.5	N.A.
(2) Rural (in millions)	N.A.	2.8	7.5	1.5	N.A.	3.0	3.5	N.A.
Total	N.A.	5.3	11.7	8.0	9.0	17.0	14.0	12.0

Besides the problem of unemployment the problem of underemployment was also quite acute in India which was to be solved.

It is also to be pointed out that the above estimates exclude unemployment due to personal factors, such as illness, physical handicap, old age, etc.

Alleviating the Problem

In order to meet the problem of unemployment and under-employment various measures were to be taken. These could be discussed under five heads: (*a*) removal of personal disabilities, (*b*) unemployment among the masses, (*c*) educated unemployed, (*d*) seasonal unemployment, and (*e*) unemployment due to immobility of labour and technological changes.

(*a*) *Removal of Personal Disabilities*

The personal disabilities of a person include illness, physical handicaps, old age, inexperience, etc. and for this the methods suggested are socialized health services, adequate wage provisions to maintain health, vocational rehabilitation, vocational education and educational planning, workmen's compensation and other social security schemes, and new vocational opportunities.

(*i*) *Provisions of Health Services.* In order to put the worker back to work in the shortest possible time so that he and his family may not suffer from lack of income it is necessary to provide him medical facilities free of cost or at a nominal cost. Thanks to the passing of Employees' State Insurance Act, 1948 under which many of the factory workers are provided medical facilities and cash benefits under the sickness insurance scheme. But this is not enough as it covers only a very small percentage of the urban population, which is working in factories covered by the Indian Factories Act. Adequate medical facilities will have to be provided to all the population both in the rural as well as urban areas at a nominal cost as is done in U. K. if this loss of employment is to be saved.

(*ii*) *Adequate Wages.* Along with adeqúate medical care, adequate wages are a first line of defence for the health of workers. A large percentage of population in this country is under-fed owing to poor income, and is susceptible to many diseases. This is a very big problem and we can only raise wages through increase in productivity and proper economic development, which is a long-term question. This we shall discuss in the subsequent pages. In the agricultural sector where the wages are too low, Minimum Wages Act was passed in 1951. But it has not yet been enforced.

(*iii*) *Vocational Education and Educational Planning.* Educators generally think they are preparing young people for life and not for making a living. Various faculties of man should be developed because man cannot live by bread alone. On the other hand, there is no life without a good living and educators must recognize the importance of preparation for a life work as part of the educational process. There is a glut of educated people in the market for clerical jobs, while there is a shortage of technicians. To correct this tendency to some extent many technical institutes for the training of young men have been opened during the First and Second Five-Year Plans but this lag is still to be removed. The Planning Commission has observed, "It seems necessary that the plans for education, especially in the post-primary stage will have to be so framed that our future requirements will not suffer for want of structural adjustments."[15] The problem of educated unemployed has also been discussed separately.

(*iv*) *Rehabilitation of the Physically Handicapped.* For those who cannot work because of physical injuries and handicaps, some steps will have to be taken by the welfare agencies providing services for particular type of handicapped persons. The number of such persons who are blind, deaf, dumb, without some limb, or are suffering from diseases which make them handicapped to do some job is very large in the country, and different steps will have to be taken to rehabilitate them.

The government or private social agencies should provide them work through production centres. Some special training will have to be given to these persons, before they can be employed.

The government should give grant to social agencies which provide services or maintain physically disabled persons who cannot work, e.g. persons suffering from chronic diseases or certain other disabilities.

There should be free treatment by the state of those who suffer from certain disability before they can be put to work again. For example, if a person loses a limb in an accident, the state should provide him an artificial limb and also assist him in securing employment. Similar provision can be made for mentally defective persons.[16]

(*v*) *Workmen Compensation.* To those workers who suffer injury

[15] *Ibid.*, p. 657.

[16] For further details regarding the programmes for the rehabilitation of physically and mentally disabled persons see Chapters XIV and XV of Volume II.

during the course of work in the factory and become disabled or suffer death some provision for them and their families is necessary. Under the Workmen's Compensation Act 1923 provision for such temporary or permanent disablement does exist. But it applies only to those establishments which come under the Indian Factories Act.

(*vi*) *Discovering Occupational Opportunities for Young Men.* Securing a first job is the major hurdle for young persons seeking job. Guidance to such young men can be provided through employment exchanges who can provide them with jobs or can advise them to prepare for the available work. The Planning Commission observes, "The University Commission has observed that the utility to employers of graduates with certain qualifications, e.g., commerce, can be increased if the present purely theoretical knowledge imparted in colleges is supplemented by practical training. Its recommendations to impart such practical training either during college terms or during the periods of vacation deserve consideration."[17] Similarly, employers are usually reluctant to engage persons without experience. This difficulty can be solved only with the help of employers by providing apprenticeship training to such persons. This, however, also implies sufficient employment opportunities for these young persons and is a question linked with economic development.

(*vii*) *Employment for the Older Workers.* If we would secure work for older people, several things have to be kept in view : (1) more liberal policy is to be followed by the employers, and (2) the necessity of the middle-aged possessing qualifications for higher jobs. This sometimes means further training which may be provided by employers. The Planning Commission remarks, "it is only by reservation of certain number of posts in public service and by persuading private employers to engage such persons, especially those with family responsibility that the unemployment of such persons can be tackled."[18]

(*viii*) *Comprehensive Social Security Measures.* Social provisions for financial aid to those who face economic disabilities alleviates the suffering which unemployed entails. The relief can be given by passing comprehensive social securities acts as has been done in some of the industrially advanced countries such as United Kingdom and U. S. A. Such measures include non-contributory pensions,

[17] *First Five-Year Plan*, p. 657.
[18] *Ibid.*, p. 658.

pensions for the invalid, widow pensions, unemployment assistance, medical assistance and rehabilitation of the disabled on the one hand, and sickness insurance, pension insurance, unemployment insurance and workmen's compensation on the other. A beginning in this direction has already been made by passing some of the acts such as the Employees' State Insurance Act 1948, Employees Provident Fund Act 1952, etc. But much still remains to be done.

The problem of unemployment assistance is a huge one in India owing to a large number of unemployed persons and limited financial resources of the state. The real solution lies in providing employment to those who seek employment.

(*b*) *Economic Development to Remove Poverty and Unemployment*

To create new employment opportunities in an underdeveloped country where there is large scale unemployment and underemployment, development of all the economic sectors of agriculture, industrial as well as others through proper planning is essential. In the First Five-Y • r Plan the Planning Commission pointed out that to tackle the problem of unemployment, foremost consideration was to be given to the rural sector for two reasons : firstly, on account of the magnitude and seriousness of the problem and secondly, because the offer of better employment opportunities in the rural sector will have a salutary effect on the unemployment situation in the urban sector. But the urban sector was not to be ignored altogether, because the increasing pressure on land has forced a large number of able-bodied persons to go to town and cities in search of employment. In order to reduce the incidence of rural unemployment the measures suggested were the starting of major and minor irrigation works ; land reclamation schemes ; the revival and development of rural industries and old handicrafts ; the extension of mixed farming ; and undertaking of public work programmes in slack agricultural seasons.

In the urban sector the main steps contemplated were (*i*) expansion of large scale industries and the starting of new ones, and (*ii*) to save the existing small scale industries and to encourage the starting of similar new industries. The development of agriculture, industries, roads, major and minor irrigation works and building and construction activities will indirectly lead to development of tertiary sector.

It means that there will be more demand for transport, storage, banking and other services.

In the Second Five-Year Plan the Planning Commission pointed out that in the context of economy with relative abundance of labour a general bias in favour of comparatively intensive labour techniques is both natural and desirable, but specific investment decisions involving a choice between alternative techniques have to be made in the light of a number of considerations. However, in order to have a proper industrial base in future it was intended that the additional employment should be largely in the non-agricultural sector. But that does not mean that the agricultural sector was to be altogether ignored. Moreover, the quantum of additional work, for persons working on land was not to be measured in terms of jobs but in the forms of additional income accruing to them. It was estimated that provision for more irrigation facilities would provide opportunities of work on full-time basis, while reclamation of land and expansion and development schemes of plantations, pepper and horticulture would provide employment to about 1.5 million new entrants to the labour force in rural areas.

Considered in these contexts the employment opportunities were likely to be significant, but the problem of unemployment could not be solved. The Planning Commission itself pointed out, "Considering the magnitude of existing unemployment and additions to labour force (see Table 17) it would be incorrect to hold out the hope that full employment could be secured by the end of the second plan. The goal has to be achieved by a series of planned efforts lasting over a period beyond the second plan."[19] It was estimated that the total employment generated in the First Plan period in the public and private sectors excluding the fields of commerce and trade was of the order of 4.5 millions, and with double the size of the employment efforts, the additional targets of employment cannot be more than 10 millions, i.e. 8 millions in the urban sector and about 2 millions in the rural sector. However, actually employment opportunities were created for 8 millions instead of 10 millions. During the Third Plan it was estimated that 17 millions will be added to the labour force, while additional employment will be provided to about 14 millions (10.5 millions in the non-agricultural sector and 3.5 in the agricultural sector). Thus, there were to be 12 millions unemployed by the end of Third

[19] *Second Five-Year Plan*, p. 112.

Plan. The steps suggested by the Planning Commission to increase employed opportunities during the five-year plans may be summarized as follows :

(1) *Development of Agriculture.* The employment opportunities in the agriculture sector may be increased through the construction of major and minor irrigation projects, land reclamation, expansion and development of plantation, intensive cultivation, and horticulture.

(2) *Development of Fisheries and Forest.* The development of forest and fisheries is also to go ahead along with development of agriculture.

(3) *Development of Industries.* Development of industries may include (*a*) large-scale industries, (*b*) small industries, and (*c*) village and cottage industries including handicrafts. The development of large-scale industries should cover industries, minerals, transport and communication and power. The small-scale industries are to be developed by giving them proper protection and integrating them with large-scale industries. The entrepreneurs are to be given proper guidance and also provided with finance. The village industries are to be developed through provision of finance, marketing facilities and avoiding competition between large-scale and cottage industries through levy of cess. Similarly, handicrafts are to be developed through such methods.

(4) *Building Construction Activities.* The construction activity may be increased in all industries including construction of houses for labourers and middle class people.

(5) *Development of Tertiary Sector.* The employment opportunities in the fields of education, health, social services and offices are to be created by the expansion of these services. The trade and commerce will automatically expand with increase in the level of income of the people.

TABLE 18

NATIONAL INCOME AND PER CAPITA INCOME IN INDIA

Year	*National income*	*Per cent increase*	*Per capita*	*Per cent increase*
1948-49	8650	—	249.6	—
1950-51	8850	—	247.5	—
1955-56	10480	+18.4	267.8	+ 8.2
1960-61	12730	+21.5	293.3	+ 9.5
1965	14660	+15.2	299.4	+ 2.1

As a result of all these measures for the economic development of the country the national income of the country has increased from Rs. 88,500 millions in 1951 to 146,600 millions in 1966 as may be seen from Table 18.

However, due to large-scale increase in population and defective planning the per capita income is still very low. The increase was much less during the third plan than in the first two plans due to war with China, when large amount of resources had to be diverted to defence purposes. Also the income is unevenly distributed.

The estimates for distribution of income made by Ojha and Bhutt for the years 1953-54 to 1956-57 show that the upper 10 per cent households have an income of 28 per cent, while the lowest 20 per cent have an income of 8 per cent of the whole.[20] The inequalities are more in urban areas than in rural areas (see Table 19).

Looking to the range of incomes we find that about 95 per cent of the families had less than Rs. 3,000 as their annual income.[21] (see Table 20).

TABLE 19

INCOME DISTRIBUTION IN INDIA AMONG VARIOUS GROUPS

(1953-54 to 1956-57)

	Rural Sector	*Urban Sector*	*Both*
Top 5% having an income of	17	26	20
Top 10% ,, ,, ,, ,,	25	37	28
Top 20% ,, ,, ,, ,,	39	49	42
Bottom 60% ,, ,, ,, ,,	39	33	36
Bottom 20% ,, ,, ,, ,,	9	7	8

TABLE 20

INCOME DISTRIBUTION 1953-54 to 1956-1957

(Average at Current Prices)

S. No.	*Income group*	*Households* (000)	*Total income in rupees (crores)*	*Income per household*
1.	Rs. 0- 3000	77,074 (95.3)	8294 (80.4)	1076
2.	Rs. 3001-25000	3,777 (4.5)	1520 (14.7)	4314
3.	Rs. 25001 and over	165 (0.2)	504 (4.9)	30535

[20] Ojha, P. D. and Bhatt, V. V., "Pattern of Income Distribution in an Underdeveloped Economy: A Case Study of India", *The American Economic Review*, September, 1964, p. 714.

[21] Ojha, P.D. and Bhatt, V. V., "Distribution of Income in the Indian Economy" in *Reserve Bank of India Bulletin*, September, 1962, p. 1367.

(c) *Unemployment Among the Educated*

Although we have pointed out earlier under personal factors that to remove unemployment among the educated, educational planning and emphasis on vocational training is necessary, yet because of acute unemployment among the educated in our country certain special steps have been suggested in the Five-Year Plans to remove chronic unemployment among them. The Study Group on Educated Unemployed (1955) appointed by the Planning Commission included among educated persons with and above matriculation and equivalent education standards.[22] They include both technical and non-technical personnels.

The problem of unemployment among the educated is not a new one. Between the two wars unemployment among the educated assumed serious proportions. The war, to some extent, helped in relieving this situation by providing opportunities in the armed forces and industries dependent upon war. After the end of the war owing to demobilization of armed personnels and large-scale retrenchment in industries producing material for armed forces the problem again came to the forefront. The number of educated unemployed registered at employment exchanges increased from 86 thousand in 1947 to 126 thousand in 1951, out of which 41 thousand were technical and 85 thousand non-technical. As against this the employment opportunities were found to be 6 thousand (12 per cent) for technical personnels and 3 thousand (4 per cent) for clerical personnels. The Study Group estimated their number to be 5.5 lakhs in 1955. This shows that unemployment in this class is on the increase and suitable measures appear to be necessary. The Study Group also observed that 14.5 lakhs of educated persons will be added to the labour force during the Second Plan. Thus, the problem to be tackled during the Second Plan, if unemployment among the educated was to be eradicated, was the creation of about 2 million jobs for this group.

TABLE 21

EDUCATED UNEMPLOYED IN INDIA

Number of unemployed	1947	1951	1956	1961	1966
Technical (in lakh)	0.42	0.41	—	—	—
Clerical ,,	0.44	0.85	—	—	—
Total ,,	0.86	1.26	5.50	10.00	N.A.

[22] *Second Five-Year Plan*, p. 121.

The main reasons given for unemployment among the educated were : (*i*) rightly or wrongly there is an impression among the public that investment in education by an individual should yield for him a return in terms of a remunerative job, (*ii*) an educated person naturally looks for a job suited to his particular type of education he has received with the result that there has been an abundance of supply in regard to certain occupations and professions and shortage in others, depending upon the development of education in the country, (*iii*) Then, again, there are regional preferences shown by the educated which complicate the problem ; and (*iv*) there is a general disinclination among the educated to look for employment other than office jobs.

In the First Five-Year Plan the Planning Commission suggested that Government should help educated persons (*a*) by advancing loans for establishing small scale industries requiring capital from Rs. 500 to Rs. 5,000, providing vocational training facilities, and also assist in procuring raw material and the disposal of the finished goods, and (*b*) start Industrial Estates which provide factory sites with such facilities as transport and supply of electricity, water and gas laid on to small amateur manufacturers on a rental basis, and (*c*) should take those measures discussed under educational planning and measures like apprenticeship training by employers.

During the Second Five-Year Plan the Study Group estimated that Central and State Government projects included in the Second Five-Year Plan were likely to yield a million jobs. About 2.4 lakhs will replace the retired educated persons, while private sector will absorb about 2 lakh people leaving the size of the problem substantially unchanged during the period of the plan.

Against this background the Study Group suggested certain fields as capable of providing employment opportunities for the educated. The main criterion laid down for the selection of schemes was that these were urgently needed for the envisaged institutional reorientation of production relations and for that they deserved higher priority in connection with economic development. (*a*) In the former category of schemes the Group included strengthening of co-operative organizations in the sphere of production and distribution. (*b*) In the latter group were included a large group of small industries which were divided into three categories : (*i*) manufacturing industries, namely, hand-tools and small tools, sports goods, furniture, etc. (*ii*) feeder industries like foundries, forge shops, tool and gauge making shops, automobile shops, machinery parts, electroplating and galvanizing shops and so on, and (*iii*) servicing industries like repair shops for automobiles, bicycles and other machinery. (*c*) The Group further recommended for the setting up of orientation camps which would help remove the disinclination on the part of the educated to undertake manual work. Such camps would assist in discovering the vocational aptitude of the youth and if a liaison was established with a prospective buyer it would be possible for the latter to pick up educated people from the camp for suitable employment. (*d*) Another recommendation made for removing the hardships felt by the educated youth was the establishment of university employment bureaux.[23]

The Planning Commission accepted the recommendations of the Study Group. However, it pointed out that the problem of educated unemployed called for long-term measures. *Ad hoc* measures designed to alleviate unemployment in the short run can hardly produce lasting results. The expansion of education and training facilities should be closely linked to the future requirements of the economy. There should be systematic examination of openings for educated and trained persons in different categories and the necessary information should be widely disseminated through programmes of educational and vocational counselling, university employment bureaux, etc. Development of the co-operative sector in the rural economy and of small-scale and medium industries will offer growing opportunities for absorbing educated persons in gainful and productive work. Changes in the system of education should keep in view these and other lines of development envisaged in the Second Five-Year Plan.[24]

In the Third Plan it was estimated that the number of those educated who were unemployed was nearly one million on March, 1961 and 3 millions more will be added during the Third Plan period. Expansion in agriculture, industries and transport will provide a large and increasing demand for persons with skill and vocational or technical training. Reorganization of the system of education and provision of facilities for technical and vocational education are, therefore, of paramount importance. In the immediate future, it is in rural areas that through rural programmes large employment opportunities for the educated unemployed are likely to become

[23] *Ibid.*, p. 123.
[24] *Ibid.*, p. 124.

available. It is proposed that as a preparatory step a few educated persons should be selected and put through short period of training for specific jobs. The scope for regular and continuous employment within the rural economy will greatly increase with the development of co-operatives for credit, marketing and farming, growth of processing industries, development of scientific agriculture and establishment of democratic institutions at the district, block and village level. It should also be possible to assist fairly large number of educated young persons to set up small industries at rural centres at which power may be made available. These industries should be organized on co-operative basis as far as possible to provide financial, technical and marketing facilities easily. The development on such lines will keep the educated leadership in the rural areas.

(*d*) *Removal of Seasonal Unemployment*

We have already pointed out that in some industries there is seasonal unemployment because these industries employ workers only for a particular period in the year, such as sugar industry and agriculture. To eliminate this seasonal unemployment in factories the manufacturers can take up the production of some other commodities in the slack season. "In U. S. A. certain manufacturers, as for example, sled and winter sports goods factories have added lines of porch furniture. Toy manufacturers have added electric goods to their products."[25] In the agricultural sector a large number of labour is employed. The Planning Commission have introduced a special rural works programme during the third plan under which special schemes for irrigation, afforestation, soil conservation, drainage, land reclamation and improvement of communication have been taken to remove unemployment during slack seasons in the rural areas.

(*e*) *Unemployment Owing to Difficulties in the Migration of Labour and Change in Technology*

As pointed out in the foregoing pages there is sometimes chronic unemployment and underemployment in a particular area or region of the country because of its backwardness, and the labourers feel difficulty in moving to far off places to secure employment. In such cases rapid economic development of that particular area is essential. Such areas are found not only in our country but in other countries

[25] Elliott, M.A., and Merrill, F. E., *Social Disorganization*, p. 461.

as well. The Planning Commission has suggested certain measures for the development of such backward areas. Government can increase employment opportunities in such areas by (*i*) giving priority to them in the matter of location of projects in the public sector unless other considerations justify the location of such projects elsewhere, (*ii*) providing loans to local businessmen and industrialists at relatively favourable terms, (*iii*) reserving a certain percentage of contracts in the public sector for persons belonging to these areas, and (*iv*) adoption of other fiscal measures to induce inflow of private capital.

For those persons who become unemployed owing to change in technology or change in demand, some measures are necessary. Such persons are generally older ones. In this case a survey of the "middle-ages jobless problem" in New York State emphasized the importance of a more liberal hiring policy on the part of employyers, and the necessity of the middle-aged possessing qualifications for new jobs. Sometimes this means further training. For some it means training in particular crafts and skills. We have already discussed about these measures under the head "employment for older workers".

CHAPTER XI

POPULATION AND HEALTH PROBLEMS

THE wealth of a country depends ultimately on two factors, viz. (1) the gifts of nature including the soil, the climate, the mineral resources, etc. and (2) the human factor that is the quantity and quality of manpower or working population. As man advances in civilization, the influence of the physical environments plays a diminishing role as compared to the human factor. Even with the best natural resources a country will make a poor show in the production of wealth if the people are lacking in the ability and strength to make the best use of the resources at their disposal.

Theories of Population

Modern theories of population start with Malthus who wrote his "Essay on Population" in 1798. Studies of animal life had already drawn attention to the tendency for animals to increase beyond the means of subsistence provided by Nature. Moreover, in Malthus' time the mechanical methods of agriculture which have given rise to the phenomenal increase in production of food stuffs were not yet known. Further, the enormous increase in production of wealth which the Industrial Revolution made possible in the second half of the nineteenth century was still in the making. These were the conditions under which Malthus enunciated his theory that there is a tendency for population in every country to increase faster than the means of subsistence. Such a tendency is attended by the operation of positive checks like increase in the death rate by war, famine, plague and diseases in general. If such consequences are to be averted, moral restraint and the operation of prudential considerations should be brought into play by the spread of education. However, the hundred years that followed the enunciation of the Law of Population by Malthus witnessed a phenomenal increase in population in Europe, accompanied by a constantly improved standard of living. In the years that followed the first world war observers of social phenomena called attention to the unprecedentedly precipitate decline in birth rates in Western Europe and the U. S. A. Unless, they said, there was an increase in net fertility within a few decades there would be a stationary population. Not only that, but now the bogey of overpopulation is replaced by that of depopulation, as there is a tendency towards a declining population. However, this is in contrast with the rapidly increasing population in the Asiatic countries.

Optimum Theory of Population

The optimum theory of population which has been formulated more recently tells us that at any given time or under any given particular conditions, other things being equal, there is what may be called a point of maximum returns attained when the population is so exactly fitted to the circumstances, that returns would be less if it were either less or more that it is. This population has been called the optimum population. The optimum varies from time to time as conditions determining production vary. So far as India is concerned looking to the resources available and the population, India is overpopulated at present.

Growth of India's Population

The population increase in India was slow prior to 1871, when the first official estimate was made by the Government of India, though the estimates made prior to that date may not be very accurate. The estimates made before 1871 by various authorities as mentioned by Professor Davis are as follows :

TABLE 22
ESTIMATES OF POPULATION IN INDIA FROM 300 B. C. TO A. D. 1871[1]

Date	*Millions*	*Average annual percentage growth*	*Date*	*Millions*	*Average annual percentage growth*
300 B. C.	100-140	—	1845	130	—
A. D. 1600	100	—	1855	175	2.97
1800	120	0.09	1867	194	0.86
1834	130	0.24	1871	255	6.84

This stability in the population may have been the result of positive checks like war, plague and famines regularly pruning off the surplus population, but late marriages and the higher educa-

[1] Davis, Kingsley, *The Population of India and Pakistan* (1951), p. 25.

tion among the three *varnas* in ancient time and the custom of infanticide in middle ages for this slow growth of population also could not be ruled out.

The establishment of British rule which lessened warfare and banditry on the one hand and the extension of communication and advancement in medicine during the period, which checked diseases and famines, may have accelerated the rate of population growth. The following table indicates the growth of population from 1881 to 1961 :

TABLE 23

GROWTH OF POPULATION IN INDIA FROM 1881 TO 1961

Before partition			*After partition*		
Date	*In millions*	*Rate of annual increase*	*Date*	*In millions*	*Rate of annual increase*
1881	250	—	1941	315	—
1891	279	1.16	1951	357	1.26
1901	284	0.16	1961	437	1.89
1911	303	0.65			
1921	305	0.09			
1931	338	1.02			
1941	349	1.41			

There was less increase in population from 1891 to 1911 due to certain serious famines and diseases like plague and influenza during this period but after that the rate of growth has been quite steady. The annual rate of increase of little more than one per cent may not be very high but its gravity can be realized as soon as it is translated in absolute figures of additional mouths to be fed, with the limited resources.

Is India Overpopulated?

There is a growing pressure of population on the means of subsistence. Attempts have been made to estimate population pressure by reference to the cultivated area ; 2.5 acres per capita are said to represent the minimum size of cultivated land necessary for keeping the individual in health and efficiency.[2] Keeping in mind the fact that in many parts of India two crops are raised during the year, and the food requirements may be less in the East than in the colder countries of the West, we may safely assume that 1 acre per capita

[2] Wadia, P.A. and Merchant, K. T., *Our Economic Problem* (1954), p. 104.

i.e. 5 acres per family may be the minimum size of the agricultural holding necessary for the subsistence of a family of five souls. However, the cropped land per capita in India was 0.97 acre in 1951.[3] This must have gone down with further increase in population. However, it may be mentioned that food supply alone cannot give us an adequate coefficient of overpopulation, the industrial production can also effect upon the number of people a country can afford. In other words the number of people that can be supported in any country per square mile will depend upon the stage of economic development which the country has reached and on its natural resources. Thus, a highly industrialized country can support a far larger number of people than a country like India with a population mainly dependent upon agriculture carried on by methods handed down from early days. As compared with the density of countries of similar size, India has a very high density as is clear from Table 24.

TABLE 24

AVERAGE DENSITY OF SELECTED COUNTRIES[4]

	Date	*Area sq. mile in thousands*	*Population in thousands*	*Density*
(*a*) *Larger Countries*				
1. Indian Union	1941	1,220.5	318,863	261
2. Prepartitioned India	1941	1,581.0	338,998	246
3. Greater China	1939	4,287.0	450,000	105
4. United Kingdom & Colonies	1939-43	1967.0	106,413	54
5. U. S. A. & Territories	1939-40	3685.0	150,147	41
6. U. S. S. R.	1939	8351.0	192,667	23
7. Brazil	1940	3286.0	41,565	13
8. Canada	1941	3466.0	11,507	3
9. Australia & Possessions	1943	3065.0	7,332	2
(*b*) *Intermediate Countries*				
10. Japan	1940	147.5	73,114	496
11. Germany	1939	226.3	79,530	352
12. Pakistan	1941	361.0	70,135	194
(*c*) *Smaller Countries*				
13. England & Wales	1940	58.3	41,862	718
14. Holland	1943	12.7	9,130	717
15. Switzerland	1941	15.8	4,226	269

[3] *Census of India*, Volume I, Part 1B. Appendices to the *Census Report*, 1951, p. 72. Also see Wattal, P. K., *Population Problems in India* (1958), p. 132.

[4] Davis, Kingsley, *op. cit.*, p. 18.

Professors Wadia and Merchant remark, "No one who has carefully followed the history of population problem in India in its different phases can dispute the statement that there are more people in India than the soil and its present productive capacity can support. By far the major part of Indian manpower is underfed, diseased, illiterate and unskilled. Even with 'plain living and high thinking' which has been the ideal of Hindu civilization, one is inevitably driven to the conclusion that there exist in India today, under the present state of her industrial efficiency double the size of the population which could live with a moderate degree of opportunity for moral and national development."[5]

Birth Rate and Death Rate

India's population problem arises primarily out of an extremely high fertility accompanied by high mortality which is only slowly declining.[6] The increase of population in any country is a function of two variables, the death and the birth rate. The survival rate gives us the net increase of population, that is, the difference between births and deaths. In India the birth rate and death rate are both very high as compared to some of the advanced countries. A high birth rate and a high death rate in themselves are evidence of an enormous wastage of life. The causes of high birth rate are generally attributed to three factors, viz. (1) environmental or climatic and physical, (2) economic, and (3) socio-religious outlook of the people. It has been pointed out that births in any year fluctuate according to months. Also in tropical countries where puberty is early, marriages may take place in the early age. Among the economic factors, it has been pointed out that people of little means, tend to have larger families than the well-to-do. Where there is no stake in life, the arrival of an additional child is a source of additional income, as the child may be put to work at an early age to supplement the meagre resources of the family. Poverty is usually also associated with lack of education, the absence of prudential considerations and a consequent attitude of irresponsibility in relation to marriage and procreation. The socio-religious outlook of a class or country also influences birth rate in many ways. In India the marriage is universal. Marriage in India is sacramental and is considered to be obligatory for ail. To have a large family is an indication of the blessings of

[5] Wadia, P. A. and Merchant, K. T., *Our Economic Problem* (1954), p. 155.

[6] Chandrashekhar, S., *Hungry People and Empty Lands* (1952), p. 151.

the Gods. On the other hand, the barrenness is regarded as a terrible punishment for crimes committed in previous life. Not only marriage is obligatory, but also early marriage is preferred. A father would regard it a disgrace if he did not settle his daughter's marriage, before the age of 15. The custom and institution of child marriage has also been responsible for high birth rate. Although the Child Marriage Restraint Act has been passed in 1929, many marriages are contracted in contravention of the law. The joint family system also encourages early marriage and more children, as much of the responsibility is borne by the family.

Discussing the factors that contribute to high mortality in underdeveloped areas, the U. N. Report points out, "High mortality is associated with low per capita income, high rates of illiteracy, a large population of males engaged in agriculture, and a large number of persons per physician.... Although statistics are rarely available for other factors such as housing conditions, nutrition, public sanitation, etc. it is probable that similar relationships between these factors and different levels of mortality would obtain."[7] In India the high rate of infant mortality may be attributed to ignorance and the inability and unwillingness of the people to avail themselves of maternity services. It is also, however, true that in India there is a shortage of maternity and child welfare centres as well as other medical facilities as we shall see in the following pages. It is also true that where people are so deeply sunk in poverty it is impossible to take adequate care of the children in the shape of feeding, nursing and medical assistance, even if they were educated and familiar with the laws of hygiene and sanitation. The bad housing conditions and insanitary environments also contribute to increase in death rate. We shall examine this aspect again under the "State of Health".

There are other aspects of population too, such as their distribution between city and country, the sex ratio, the age composition, occupational distribution, the handicapped groups such as deaf-mute, dumb, blind, insane, persons suffering from various diseases such as leprosy, education, etc. which effect the wealth and prosperity of a country. However, due to limitation of space we have not discussed these factors here.

[7] United Nations Population Division, *The Determinants and Consequences of Population Trends* (1953), p. 49.

Healtn

We have pointed out in the beginning that both the quality and the quantity of population play an important part in the production of wealth. We have already discussed about the quantity of population. In this section we shall deal with the qualitative aspect.

Health is fundamental to national progress in any sphere. It is the measure of energy and productive capacity in any country. Loss of health effects productivity as well as efficiency in the national production. Health does not mean merely the absence of disease but complete adjustment of individual to external environments physical and social. Thus, it is a positive state of well-being of the individual having harmonious development of physical and mental capacities. Therefore, health involves not only medical factors, but social, economic and educational factors as well. The Health Survey and Development Committee rightly observes, "The term health implies more than absence of sickness in the individual and indicates a state of harmonious functioning of the body and mind in relations to his physical and social environment so as to enable him to enjoy life to the fullest possible extent and to reach his maximum level of productive capacity."[8]

It is difficult to obtain statistics of positive health, but the statistics of mortality and average expected life point out something from the negative side. The comparative data of three countries with regard to annual death rate, infantile mortality and expectation of life will throw some light over this point.

TABLE 25

DEATH RATE, INFANTILE MORTALITY & EXPECTATION OF LIFE (1951)

Country	*Death rate (per 1000)*	*Infantile mortality*	*Expectation of life*	
			Male	*Female*
U. S. A.	9.6	29	65	70
U. K.	11.6	30	66	71
India	16.5	127	32	32

The special vulnerable groups in any community are children, women during reproductive stage and old people. Nearly 40 per cent of the total deaths are among children under 10 years of age and half of them take place within the first year of life. Maternal mortality was estimated to be 20 per thousand in 1951. Epidemic diseases

[8] *Report of the Health Survey and Development Committee* (1946), p. 7.

such as cholera, small pox and plague and certain other diseases like fevers, dysentery, diarrhoea, tuberculosis, etc. also take away a large toll.

Causes of Low Health. The Health Survey and Development Committee (1946) which surveyed the causes of low state of health in this country pointed out the following important ones :

(1) Lack of proper medical care—curative and preventive.
(2) Lack of hygienic environment conducive to healthful living, i.e. lack of safe water supply and sanitation, and absence of proper removal of human waste.
(3) Low resistance due to lack of adequate diet and poor nutrition.
(4) Lack of general and health education.
(5) Lack of proper housing.

Besides there is also the problem of school health, mental health and food adulteration. We shall deal with all these problems in brief here except the problem of housing which has been discussed in detail in Volume II.

Medical Care and Public Health

There was serious shortage of medical personnel and medical facilities before Independence and this shortage was especially so in the rural areas. In 1951 it was estimated that there was one hospital for 50 thousand population in rural areas as compared to 24 thousand population in urban areas. Similarly, 75 per cent of the doctors lived in urban areas as compared to 25 per cent in rural areas. In order to remove this disparity and to provide more medical facilities both in rural and urban areas certain efforts were made under the Five-Year Plans. The programme in the rural areas envisaged the integration of hospital services with the public health programme and the hospitals were to become health centres in the full sense of the term. The pattern of development for rural areas was to have primary health units at the block level and secondary units at the tehsil and district level. The functions of the primary health units are to provide personal health services, particularly for mother and children, school health, control of communicable diseases, water supply, sanitary improvements, family planning and health education to the public. Mobile dispensaries were to be associated with the primary health units.

There were to be special provisions for the control of malaria, tuberculosis, venereal diseases, filariasis, leprosy, small pox, cholera, etc.

There has been substantial progress in various health programmes during the three Five-Year Plans. The measures adopted for the control of malaria and communicable diseases like filaria, tuberculosis, leprosy and venereal diseases have been successful to a great extent. The number of hospitals and dispensaries has also increased substantially.

We have already pointed out that the maternal mortality rate as well as infant mortality rate is very high in India as compared to some advanced countries of the world. In the rural areas the programme is to provide maternity and child health centres as part of primary and secondary health unit centres. At the secondary level there is to be a woman doctor having specialised training in this branch and two health visitors whose main function would be training of dais, supervision of midwives and dais and care of maternity cases needing hospitalization. Maternity and child welfare services provided by the primary health centres are supplemented by services provided by welfare extension projects and by voluntary organizations. The ultimate aim was to have one unit of maternity centre for a population of 10,000 to 12,000.

The progress made in some of these facilities during the Five-Year Plans may be seen from the following table :

TABLE 26

PROGRESS OF MEDICAL FACILITIES DURING FIVE-YEAR PLANS

Categories or units	1951	1956	1961	1966
(I) Hospitals and Dispensaries including primary health units	8600	10000	12600	14600
(II) Primary Health Units	—	725	2800	5000
(III) Medical Colleges	30	42	57	75
(IV) Annual Admission	2500	3500	5800	8000
(V) Control of Communicable Diseases				
(*i*) Malaria (units)	—	133	390	390
(*ii*) Filaria (units)	—	11	48	48
(*iii*) B. C. G. (Teams)	15	119	167	167
(*iv*) T. B. Clinics	110	160	220	420
(*v*) Leprosy Subsidiary Centres	—	33	135	235
(*vi*) V. D. Clinics	—	—	83	189

(VI) Maternity & Child Health Centres	1951	1856	4500	10000
Amount Spent (Rs. Crores)	1941-51	1951-56	1956-61	1961-66
	N.A.	140	225	341
Birth rate (per 1000)	39.9	41.7	40.7	N.A.
Death rate (per 1000)	27.4	25.9	21.6	17.2
Infant mortality-Males	190	161	142	N.A.
Infant mortality-Females	175	147	128	N.A.
Expectation of life	32	38	42	50

Water Supply and Environmental Sanitation

The provision of an environment conducive to healthful living is an essential requirement for the maintenance of public health. In countries where water supplies and waste disposal have been attended to cholera, typhoid fever and dysentery have almost disappeared. The Environmental Hygiene Committee (1946) suggested a five-year plan to tackle this problem of safe and adequate water supply. While it has not been possible to make provisions according to that plan, steps are being taken in urban as well as rural areas on the lines suggested by the above committee. The expenditure incurred in the three Five-Year Plans for water supply and sanitation was Rs. 49, 76 and 105 crores respectively.

In rural areas, states aim at providing simple type of safe water supply for all villages within a certain period. The Governments are to give grants which are to be supplemented by contribution by the people by way of voluntary labour or money. In respect of sanitation simple types of latrines which require no special servicing are to be provided. The State Governments are to offer technical service and some inducement like supply of water seal squatting slabs on a subsidized basis.

Health Education

In its widest sense health education is the very foundation of a successful public health programme. Much of the illness is the result of ignorance of simple hygienic laws and indifference to their application in practice. To implement the programme of health education, the Central Health Bureau was established in 1956 in the Directorate General of Health Services and several states have also set up such bureaux. "Among the most important aspects of health education are personal hygiene, environmental sanitation, prevention of communicable diseases, nutrition, physical exercise, marriage guidance, pre-natal and post-natal care, maternity and child health, etc."[9] The different sections of the community are to be addressed in a manner suitable to each. The medical personnel at maternity and child health centres are to carry this message to women. Instructions about health education in children are to be given in schools. Adults are to be instructed during their recreation, adult education and by publicity through literature, cinema, radio, audio-visual aids and health exhibitions in melas.

Nutrition

It is perhaps the most important single factor in the maintenance of health and resistance to disease. There is a direct relation between the nutrition and the productive capacity of an individual. Though cereal and pulses form the major portion of human diet and supply carbohydrates and proteins, etc. a satisfactory diet should contain in addition to foodgrains, adequate quantity of other foods such as milk, vegetables, fruits, meat, fish and eggs. There is both undernutrition and malnutrition in this country. It was estimated that in 1950 the availability of cereals and grains and pulses including imports of these two was 13.7 oz. and 2.1 oz. per adult as against the requirements of 14.0 oz. and 3.0 oz. per adult per day respectively. Similarly, there is a great deficiency of protective foods in the country. Thus, the diet of the population as a whole is defective.

A Joint Committee of the Indian Council of Medical and Agricultural Research has suggested the daily requirements of food per adult per day, cereal 14 oz., pulses 3 oz., green leafy vegetables 4 oz., root vegetable 3 oz., vegetable oil and ghee 2 oz., fish and meat 3 oz. and egg one. However, "generally, in most parts of India, the diet is composed of cereals and is lacking in protective and body building foods such as milk, meat, eggs, vegetables and fruits. Diet surveys undertaken at the instance of the Indian Council of Medical Research over two periods, 1935-38 and 1955-58, show that while there has been no appreciable change in the consumption of cereals and pulses, there may well have been a small reduction in the consumption per capita of some of the non-cereal foods. Food deficiencies bear most harshy on growing children among the poorer sections of the population."[10] Other important elements in the problem are the loss of nutritive elements in food, due to the adoption of wrong methods of cooking, as in rice and vegetables and of processing as

[9] *Third Five-Year Plan* (1961), p. 665.

[10] *Ibid.*, p. 673.

in rice milling, waste of fruit and fish, on account of lack of transport and refrigeration facilities and diversion to low priority uses as in the case of milk used in the preparation of sweets.

At the present stage when there is shortage of cereals and food-grains and other protective foods particularly milk, the problem of improving nutrition falls broadly under two heads namely (1) education of the public and of various groups of workers in nutrition, and (2) measures to meet the nutritional requirements of vulnerable groups within the country. Information and guidance about the nutrition, about conserving the nutritive elements in food and avoiding wrong use and wastage, should be made widely available through demonstration and the work of voluntary organizations and mahila mandals in the villages as part of the community development programme. At the same time, groups such as doctors, nurses, health visitors, school teachers and others should receive special short-term training in nutrition. Among the vulnerable groups those requiring the greatest attention are expectant and nursing mothers, infants, pre-school children and school children, specially in the lower age group. School children are best cared for through the mid-day meal programme. For expectant and nursing mothers and infants there is some provision at the maternity and child welfare centres for the free distribution of protective foods like milk, vitamins, etc. However, so far education in nutrition is concerned, there has not been much effort so far, nor it seems possible unless adult education programme succeeds.

Other Health Problems

Among other health problems we have discussed (1) the school health, (2) mental health, and (3) food adulteration.

School Health. With the expansion of educational facilities the number of children going to schools has increased from 44 millions in 1961 to 64 millions in 1966, out of which 50 millions are of the age group 6-11 years. Care of the health of such a large number of children is vital for the community. The School Health Committee pointed out that the incidence of sickness and disease among school children due to malnutrition and other preventive causes was extremely high. It recommended that the states should ensure during the Third Plan certain minimum services for the care of health in the schools. These were (1) clean drinking water and sanitary facilities in school, (2) arrangement for medical inspection,

(3) follow up service in association with the primary health unit in the development block, and (4) instruction of teachers in health education.[11]

Mental Health. The Central Government recently constituted an Advisory Committee on Mental Health. The Committee has emphasized the importance of mental health services in programmes for the development of public health and medical facilities. Rapid industrialization and the movement of population from rural to urban areas brings in train certain tensions and problems of maladjustment. In order to meet such situations there is need of making curative services available in mental hospitals and preventive mental hygiene services in general hospitals.[12]

Food Adulteration. Adulteration in articles of common consumption such as ghee, milk, oils and fats, spices, flour, pulses, etc. occurs all too frequently in towns and villages. "Problems of food adulteration have been recently considered by the Central Council of Health at a special seminar and a series of suggestions have been put forward. These include proposals for deterrent punishment under the Prevention of Food Adulteration Act, 1954, strengthening of the machinery for inspection of foodstuffs and of the available laboratory facilities, and improvement and speeding up of administrative and other procedures connected with food offences."[13] However, such measures are not likely to bear much fruit unless the morale of public and officials is raised who combine to use these malpractices.

Control of Population

The recent increase in the population and pressure exercised on the limited resources of the country has brought to the forefront the urgency of the problem of family planning and population control. The size and quality of the country's population are of utmost importance to national welfare and planning. As seen before while death rate has been lowered by the application of medical science, the birth rate continues to be fairly constant.

In order to solve the population problem in the country three methods have been suggested by the demographers, economists and other social scientists. These include (1) the family planning

[11] *Ibid.*, p. 665.

[12] For further details see Chapter on Mental Hygiene, Volume II.

[13] *Third Five-Year Plan* (1961), p. 669.

method, (2) migration outside the country or redistribution of population with the country by shifting people from densely populated areas to less populated areas, and (3) by increasing our industrial and food production on such a large scale so as to double the national income within the next few years. However, the last two have their limitation in the context of our country as we shall presently see and the only method available at present is family planning. We shall discuss the last two first and then the first, i.e. family planning.

Migration of Population

Dr. R. K. Mukerjee makes a strong plea for a policy of mass migration of Indians in large numbers to settle the empty spaces in the world.[14] Curiously enough this plea has been taken as an indication of growing Hindu Imperialism by western demographers. Dr. Vogt observes, "A heavily industrialized India backed by such population pressures, would be a danger to the entire world".[15] So long as racial prejudices and white immigration policies remain dominant, in a world which is euphemistically characterized as "one world" there can be no hope for emigration to solve our population problem. Thus, when western economists and demographers talk of emigration as a remedy for overpopulation, they have in mind only the white people. The Asiatic people never exist in their calculations, though Chinese and Indians are the only people who really need the help of emigration to solve their problems.

With regard to the redistribution of population inside our own country, whatever possibilities of redistribution exist, they do not justify any hope that it can materially help in solving our problem. There are also the new forces of inter-state jealousies caused by lingualism and provincialism.

Increase in Production

To increase our production in the agricultural and industrial field so as to rapidly raise our national income is again beset with numerous difficulties to which we have referred in detail in another book.[16] Even in the case of food, as already said, it is difficult to increase its production substantially in the near future. The Research Group of the Political and Economic Planning Organization, London

[14] Mukerjee, Radha Kamal, *Races, Land and Food* (1946).

[15] Vogt, William, *Road to Survival* (1948), p. 228.

[16] For details see Welfare State and Planning in India.

perhaps rightly observes, "In over-populated areas conservatism may become a lethal factor once population starts to increase sunstantially. Change to the new in custom, cultivation, and crop, and in much else besides, may be brought about by the triple agency of education, leadership and demonstration, or in contrast, by the spur and whip of control. Change by persuasion is slow ; changes under compulsion and control may be swift though often unstable. There lies the crux of whole dilemma."[17]

Family Planning

The main appeal for family planning is based on consideration of health of mother and better care and upbringing of children, thus contributing to the health and welfare of the family. The first problem is to create motivation in favour of family planning in the minds of the people and next is to provide advice and services based on acceptable, efficient, harmless and economic methods.

In the First Five-Year Plan the Planning Commission pointed out, "It is apparent that population control can be achieved only by the reduction of birth-rate to the extent necessary to establish the population at a level consistent with the requirements of national economy. This can be secured only by the realisation of the need for family limitation on a wider scale by the people. . . Measures directed to this end should, therefore form part of the public health programme.[18] As a result of this policy family planning advice and service were made integral part of the services in hospitals and health centres. However, it may be pointed out here that the programme in the beginning was very slow. During the First Five-Year Plan only 147 family planning clinics were set up, while the progress during the successive plans has been rapid as is clear from Table 27.

In addition to these clinics family planning services are also provided at 1,864 rural and 330 urban medical and health centres.[19] A number of sterilization centres have also been set up. The programme is guided by the Central and State Family Planning Boards. All States have set up special units for family planning work. The family planning education has been interwoven with other construc-

[17] Political and Economic Planning Organization, London, *World, Population and Resources* (1955), p. 36.

[18] *First Five-Year Plan* (1952), p. 522.

[19] *Third Five-Year Plan* (1961), p. 675.

ive activities, especially the work of the primary health centres, community development blocks and voluntary organizations. For certain sections of the population the provision of supplies free of cost or at subsidized rates has been made.

TABLE 27

FAMILY PLANNING CLINICS IN INDIA

	To the end of		
	First Plan	*Second Plan*	*Third Plan*
Urban	126	549	2100
Rural	21	1100	6100
Total	147	1649	8200
Amount spent in rupees (crores)	0.65	5.00	50.00

Besides the propagation of family planning methods emphasis is to be laid on moral and psychological elements, on restraint and on such elements as education of women, opening up of new employment opportunities for them and raising the age of marraige. Mahatma Gandhi was opposed to artificial family planning methods and laid emphasis on moral restraint. He said, "It is one thing when married people regulate the number of their progeny by moral restraint and totally another when they do so in spite of sexual indulgence and by means adopted to obviate the result of such indulgence. In one case people gain in every respect, in the other there is nothing but harm."[20] However, the method of moral restraint does not seem to be feasible.

The recent researches carried out at various places reveal that roughly 40 per cent of the currently married females are willing to take family planning advice, but in spite of this favourable attitude the use of contraceptives is very low.[21] At present, however, not more than 2 per cent among the currently married females of the reproductive age groups in the rural areas use family planning methods. Of these a majority use rhythm method, and that also the wrong one.[22] Thus, the need is to encourage the family planning methods in large number.

[20] Gandhi, M. K., *Self-Restraint versus Self-Indulgence* (1947), p. 8.

[21] Agarwala, S. N., *Some Problems of India's Population* (1966), p. 147.

[22] *Ibid.*, pp. 145-46.

Regarding the methods of family planning there are many. Among these may be included (1) coitus interruptus, i.e. withdrawal, (2) moral restraint and safe period, (3) intra-uterine contraceptive devices, i.e. loop or plastic coil, diaphragm, jelly, applicator, condom, foam tablets, (4) oral tablets, and (5) sterilization including vasectomy and ligation. Some of these methods can be used in combination. A recent survey about the use of various methods in Lucknow city shows that besides sterilization among these the most popular is loop as is clear from Table 28. The survey further indicates that out of 1.28 lakh couples in the city in 1965 only 11,729, i.e. 9 per cent of the acceptors used any method.[23]

TABLE 28

COUPLES USING VARIOUS TYPES OF CONTRACEPTIVES IN LUCKNOW CITY

Sl. No.	*Method of contraception*	*No. of persons accepted*	*Per cent*
1.	Intra-uterine contraceptive devices (Loop)	3,341	28.48
2.	Diaphragm and jelly	240	2.05
3.	Jelly and Applicator	276	2.35
4.	Condom	2,950	25.15
5.	Condom and Jelly	2,809	23.25
6.	Condom and foam tablets	1,854	15.81
7.	Foam tablets	259	2.21
	Total	11,729	100.00

The table also shows that so far emphasis has been laid on the artificial methods and not the natural ones, i.e. rhythm and coitus interruptus which are quite simple and less expensive and are widely used in other countries.[24] For example in the U. K. of the couples married in the year 1940-49, 46 per cent were practising withdrawal and of those married in 1960, 28 per cent were practising it. Similarly, 36 per cent couples married between 1940-50 were using safe period, and of the couples married in 1950-60, 16 per cent were depending upon it.

[23] Sethi, Miss Nirmal and Agarwal, Dr. S. K., "Family Planning Programme (A Review)" in *Aspects of Women Welfare in India* (Ed.), G. R. Madan (1967), p. 52.

[24] Agarwala, S. N., *op. cit.*, pp. 147-48.

The Planning Commission also list some of the difficulties in making this programme a success. They add that (1) to equip thousands of primary health centres and in due course their sub-centres, with personnels and supplies, (2) to utilize the services of diverse agencies as private medical practitioners, indigenous doctors and village dais along with the family planning clinics and the primary health centres, and (3) production of contraceptives on the scale needed are major tasks to be tackled.[25]

However, it is also to be pointed out that the control of population is not a matter for legislation or for executive action, but a matter that entirely lies within the choice of individual parents who are to be educated into a sense of their social responsibilities. This means population problem is related to broader social policy, i.e. economic development. Thus, we will have to fight on all fronts, i.e. social, religious, economic and political and to control social phenomena is an uphill task.

[25] *Third Five-Year Plan* (1961), p. 678.

CHAPTER XII

EDUCATIONAL AND RELIGIOUS INSTITUTIONS

THE educational and religious institutions have an important role to play in the social progress of any country. The importance of education hardly needs emphasis in the modern age of science and technology. "Education has always been important but perhaps never more so in man's history than today.... In a world based on science and technology, it is education that determines the level of prosperity, welfare and security of the people."[1] The religion has also an important role to play in a democratic society where there is freedom to hoard and use the material goods for selfish purposes ignoring the claim of others, the community and the nation. Modernization, if it is to be a living force, must derive its strength from the strength of the spirit. Modernization aims, among other things, at creating an economy of plenty which will offer to every individual a larger way of life and a wider variety of choices. While the freedom to choose has its own advantages, it also means that the future of society increasingly depends upon the type of choices each individual makes.

In the modern society where the control of tradition and family is less and freedom more, the individual has much more discretion than in a traditional society. The individual may make the choice either with reference entirely to his own personal satisfaction or in a spirit of service to the community and to further the common good. The religion plays an important role in controlling the animistic and selfish tendencies of a person and channelling them in the service of humanity. Thus, the inculcation of moral and spiritual values is as much important for modernization as are the advancement of science, technology and economic resources.

Having realized the importance of these two institutions in the modern age let us discuss their position in India.

[1] *Report of the Education Commission* 1964-66, (1966), p. 2.

Educational Institutions

"Education is not foreign to India. There is no country where the love of learning had so early an origin or has exercised so lasting and powerful an influence, writes a distinguished indologist Dr. Thomas. In ancient India religion was the main spring of one's activities and it saturated educational ideals too. The educational system aimed at the building of character, the development of personality and the preservation of the ancient culture of the mother land."[2] As the Upanayan Sanskar was compulsory for all the three varnas, education was compulsory for all the boys. "But by about the end of the seventh century B.C. the vedic rituals and learning had become more and more complex. Education was mostly confined to the Brahmans and the Upanayan was being gradually discouraged among the non-Brahmans."[3]

The growth of the modern system of education in India, in suppression of the traditional indigenous system of education which has developed in this country throughout centuries past may be traced back to the establishment of the British rule in India in the beginning of the nineteenth century.[4] Since then various Commissions and Committees were appointed from time to time during the British rule to find out the deficiencies of the existing system and suggest improvements. Among these some important ones were the Indian Education Commission (1882), the Universities Commission (1902), the Calcutta University Commission (1917) and Abott Wood Committee (1937). But the steps taken to improve the system have been sporadic.

After Independence some systematic attempts have been made to reorientate the educational system to suit our current needs. In order to study the problems of education in the changing context various commissions, committees and study groups have been appointed from time to time. Among these the most important are the University Education Commission (1948), the Secondary Education Commission (1953) and the Education Commission (1962-1964). According to these reports some of the defects of the present system of education are :

(1) There is not sufficient literacy among children as well as

[2] Mukerjee, S. N., *Education in India Today and Tomorrow* (1964), p. 2. Also see Mookerjee, R. K., *Ancient Indian Education* (1947).

[3] Mukerjee, S. N., *op. cit.*, p. 2.

[4] Nurullah, S., and Naik, J. P., *A History of Education in India* (1951), p. 1.

adults and this is particularly so in the rural areas. For example, in 1951 the percentage of literate persons in the country was 17 per cent and even if we were to exclude children below 10 years of age, the percentage was only 20. Further the percentage of literacy among persons above the age of 10 years from urban and rural areas were 35 and 15 respectively.

(2) Illiteracy was more among women than among men. While women constituted about half of the population, the percentage of female children of age group 6-11 years studying in primary schools in 1951 was 25 per cent of the total as compared to 42 per cent of both males and females.

(3) Majority of the children leave their studies before reaching the IVth class. In 1949-50 the percentage of such children leaving the school before that class was 60 per cent leading to enormous wastage of national resources.

(4) Many children take more than one year in one class due to poor quality of teaching and faulty method of education.

(5) There is more emphasis on academic and theoretical education which is not related to every day practical aspects of the world.

(6) There is absence of adequate facilities for technical and vocational education which forces large number of students to go in for general education than is justified by the requirements of the society.

(7) There is a lack of agricultural institutes and universities to impart education for agriculture and carry on research work.

(8) There is a dearth of trained teachers and in 1949-50 the percentage of untrained teachers was 41 in primary and 46 in secondary schools. More so there is a dearth of women teachers. The scale of pay and conditions of service of teachers are generally very unsatisfactory which is a major cause of low standard of teaching.

(9) The high cost of education especially at the university level prevents many intelligent students from proceeding to higher studies.

(10) The period of schooling at various stages such as primary, middle, high, intermediate or university level is not suited to the various objectives to be achieved at every stage.

(11) There is a lack of civic and moral education at various levels.

(12) There is often indiscipline among the students.

The above Commissions and Committees have suggested various measures to remove these deficiencies and defects. Some of these have been implemented during the successive five-year plans. These include the expansion of education at all levels, particularly at the elementary level for children of the age group 5-14 years to implement the provisions of the Indian Constitution, (2) larger emphasis on basic education, (3) diversification and comprehensiveness of education at the secondary stage through multipurpose schools, (4) more provision of training for untrained teachers and training of teachers in basic education and especially for women, (5) improvement in the standards of college and university education, (6) more facilities for technical and vocational education, (7) establishment of rural institutes and agricultural universities, (8) scholarships to poor students, (9) improvement in the service conditions and emoluments of teachers, (10) some programmes for adult education, etc.[5] However, in spite of some progress in various directions there are many deficiencies which need further attention These deficiencies can be discussed under (*i*) Basic and elementary education, (*ii*) Secondary education, (*iii*) University education, (*iv*) Scientific and technical education, (*v*) Rural education, (*vi*) Social and adult education (*vii*) Moral and spiritual education, and (*viii*) Student indiscipline. However, due to limitation of space it is not possible to deal with all of these here and these have been discussed in detail in another volume.[6] Here we want to confine our study to only three problems, viz. (1) The Adult and Social Education, (2) Moral and Religious Education, and (3) Students' Indiscipline as they are directly related to social disorganization.

Social and Adult Education

We have already pointed out that the percentage of literate to the total population was 17 in 1951 and this rose to 24 per cent in 1961 and 29 in 1966. But unfortunately India was more illiterate in 1961 and 1966 than in 1951 with an addition of 36 million illiterate in 1961 and 56 million in 1966.[7] This happened despite unprecedented expansion of primary education because of faster growth of population and failure of adult literacy programme. So far as social education is concerned the concept of adult education or adult literacy was found to be too narrow by the National Planning Commission to be able to meet the various needs of the adults. It was, therefore, widened "to include in addition to literacy, the health,

[5] For details see my *Changing Pattern of Indian Villages*, Chapter XIV.
[6] For details see my *Welfare State and Planning in India.*
[7] *Report of the Education Commission* (1964-66), 1966, p. 423.

recreation and home life of the adults, their economic life and citizenship training".[8] Thus, the problem can be divided into two categories, i.e. literacy programme and programme of social education (or adult education).

Adult Literacy

The importance of social education and particularly adult literacy which is the first step towards adult education has not been fully realized by the National Planning Commission. Even in the Third Plan it pointed out "As sufficient progress has not been achieved so far in this direction, the problem is now being studied afresh with a view to working out means for the rapid expansion of adult literacy."[9] Since then nothing concrete has come out. Even in social education programme the adult literacy is the last item to be taken instead of the first.

However, it need be emphasized that the programme of adult literacy is of fundamental importance for the all round development of the country. Unless this succeeds many of our other programmes such as cooperative movement including cooperative farming, the whole programme of community development including family planning and even the scheme of universal elementary education for children cannot make much headway. Professor Humayun Kabir says, "No programme of compulsory universal education for children can possibly succeed without the active support of adults. A state may pass a law making education compulsory, but unless the people support such laws no state can enforce them by military or police measures. It has also to be remembered that countries educationally backward will be economically backward.... Oral education must also increasingly give place to education through the written word. Memory which is the vehicle of oral education can no longer cope with the multiplicity and complexity of facts. Education which enabled primitive man to overcome the opposition of natural forces must today help him to overcome the problems created by the clash between different social forces and ideas. It must also increase human resilience to enable man to accept innovations from abroad, so long as they contribute to human welfare."[10] No doubt there are certain harmful effects of literacy too.

[8] Government of India, *First Five-Year Plan* (1952), p. 542.

[9] *Third Five-Year Plan* (1961), p. 599.

[10] Kabir, Humayun, *Education in New India* (1959), pp. 77-78.

For example, it has been observed that "the most rapid advances in the liquidation of illiteracy have been made in recent years under forms of government which are far from democratic, in order to control the spirit and soul of the individual by means of the printed word. And the nation that has committed the greatest crime against humanity has the highest percentage of literacy in the world."[11] Similarly, the advertisements, cheap newspapers, novels, etc. affect the mind of persons. But at the same time the advantages of literacy are so many that they overweigh the disadvantages. For example, it is impossible to make rapid progress in this technological age without universal literacy. Literacy provides knowledge in some of the basic tools of communication. In the words of Paul A. Witty and Golda Van Bushirk, "Reading and writing are tools by which a man may help himself. Without them he is handicapped in partially every undertaking".[12] Illiteracy is definitely correlated to working efficiency. A literate person, with the exception of the very simplest work involving only the exercise of physical strength, is essential to the efficient performance of production job. Literacy is also essential for the successful working of democracy. Firstly, because the enlightened and informed electorate will give us a wider choice for leadership. (2) Equal opportunity will be provided to all. (3) The literate voter can exercise his will in electing the popular representative. The UNESCO observes that although experience has shown that the impact of an idea is usually far greater when it is presented through several media, e.g. discussion, demonstration, poster, films, radio, newspapers, bulletins, books, yet "sooner or later reading is essential to the promotion of human welfare. This view is supported by the results of detailed studies of the merits of reading matter, radio, television and the cinema. As pointed out by Dale, there is no substitute for reading in achieving many types of personal development and social progress. Printed matter now contains a greater range of information, deals with more problems, and is a source of more pleasure and satisfaction than any other available media. It can also be read and re-read at the reader's convenience and at its own rate. He is thus able to reflect at will on the issues discussed and the suggested courses of action,

[11] Narain, Raj, *Education for Literacy—Its Nature, Function and Dynamics* (1950), p. 26.

[12] Witty, Paul A., and Golda, Van Buskirk, "Beam in the Eye" in *Childhood Education*, October, 1944. Also see Narain, Raj, *op. cit.*, p. 32.

and to reach more considered conclusions."[13] Some of the other advantages we have already mentioned.[14] In fact literacy is the basis of the modern way of living.

Having realized the importance of literacy it is essential that we must spread literacy in our country if we have to modernize it. The progress so far has been very slow. Experiments in adult literacy have been made in many countries and we can benefit from those experiences to avoid pitfalls. A plan should be drawn up for the country as a whole to eradicate illiteracy within a particular period. No doubt there is a provision in the budget of the C. D. Block for social education both in stage I and stage II Blocks for Rs. 70 thousands and Rs. 50 thousands for five years respectively. Generally a teacher of the local school or some voluntary worker is employed for this purpose. But these teachers are generally untrained in adult education methods. On the other hand, the attendance is also very thin at these schools with the result that energy and money is wasted without any result. The supervision of this programme is entrusted to A. D. O. Social Education, but his time is mostly taken in other miscellaneous jobs. Therefore, if the programme is to succeed it must be taken up earnestly and systematically. Another problem is provision of suitable literature. Mr. Luhach rightly observes, "Indeed, providing good literature for new literates is three-fourth of the problem. It is a permanent problem. The masses will become literate in a few years, but they will continue all their lives to need easy literature adapted to the level of the masses."[15]

Adult Education

Besides literacy which is the first step in adult education the programme of educating the adults in recent knowledge needs due attention. So far it has received scanty attention. The International Conference on Adult Education points out, "In the light of the social, technological and economic forces operating in modern society, adult today faces problems of a magnitude unknown to earlier

[13] UNESCO, Monographs on Fundamental Education — X, *The Teaching of Reading and Writing — An International Survey* by William S. Gray, (1956), pp. 18-19.

[14] For further details see Narain, Raj, *op. cit.*, pp. 32-51. Also see UNESCO Monographs on Fundamental Education — X, *op. cit.*, p. 19.

[15] Luhach, Frank C., "A Mass Literacy Campaign for India" in *Adult Education in India and Abroad* (Ed.), Sidhanta, N. K., and Others, (1949), p. 43.

generations. There is, therefore, a more urgent need for educational provision to help the adult population recognize the nature of problems, the possibilities, and the difficulties inherent in rapid social and technological change, the choices available, and the extent to which adults can, through education and knowledge, make wise choices and decisions. This educational assistance is only possible through adult education.... Recognizing these facts the conference recommends that adult education should be recognized by governments at all levels, by educational organizations and by the teaching profession as an essential and important branch of the total national educational system."[16] In this programme the universities have a special role to play. They should have special department of adult education. These departments should have provision of high level adult education workers and conduct research into problems related to adult education.

Recently the Education Commission 1962-64 has recommended for a bold programme in Adult Education. The Commission recommended that every possible effort should be made to eradicate illiteracy from the country as early as possible and that in no part of the country, however backward should it take more than 20 years to do so.[17] They have also recommended for various follow up programmes so that they may not relapse into illiteracy again. To draw up a comprehensive plan there should be set up a National Board on Adult Education as recommended by the Committee on Plan Project in their Report on Social Education.[18]

Indiscipline Among Students

In the past few years it is alleged that there has been increase in student indiscipline. It has manifested in the form of strikes and demonstration often leading to violence, walk-out from classrooms and examination halls, ticketless travels, clashes with the police, burning of buses and cinema houses and, sometimes, even mishandling of teachers and University officers. There are variety of causes which have brought about these ugly expressions of uncivilized behaviour. "These include the uncertain future facing the educated young man which breeds frustration and irresponsibility, the mecha-

[16] *Report of the International Conference on Adult Education*, New Delhi, India, July 28-30, 1961, (Eds.) Keuffer, Helen and Dutta, S. C., p. 4.

[17] *Report, op. cit.*, p. 425.

[18] *Ibid.*, p. 425.

nical and unsatisfactory nature of many curricular programmes ; the inadequate facilities for teaching and learning in the large bulk of institutions ; the poor student-teacher contact, the inefficiency and lack of scholarship on the part of teachers ; the absence of imagination and tact combined with firmness on the part of heads of institutions ; the teachers' politics in some colleges and universities ; interference of political parties in the work of students' unions ; the falling standards of discipline among the general citizens and their weakening civic consciousness and integrity which affect the students as well.[19]

Besides these the two other important causes are the defective constitution of some of the students' unions and lowering of moral standards. About the functioning of the unions Dr. Z. N. Dastur rightly points out, "Few student union leaders are 'better students' and few student unions are truly representing the student bodies. Most unions in fact, act only as anti-administrative bodies."[20] He also mentions about the clash among adolescents and their parents, who are unable to adopt to the rapid changes through which these adolescents are passing.

Due to complexity of causes, it is not easy to remedy the situation and efforts will have to be made by the agencies concerned, the students, the parents, the teachers, the political parties and the government to solve this problem. The following are some of the measures suggested in this connection.

(1) The educational deficiencies that contribute to indiscipline should be removed. These include the improvement in teacher-pupil ratio, changes in curriculum, change in the examination system and more and regular work from the students, youth counselling services and employment exchanges in the universities.

(2) To avoid clash between the authorities and the students there should be joint committees of students, teachers and the heads of the institutions and consultation among these should be very often.

(3) The election of students unions should be on indirect basis so that the so-called student leaders do not indulge in antisocial activities to gain popularity and win election on that basis. Similarly, there should be some qualifications for office-bearers. For instance,

[19] *Report of the Education Commission* (1966), p. 296.

[20] Dastur, Z. N., "Why Are Our Young People Indisciplined" in *Social Welfare*, April, 1966, p. 24.

those who have failed in the examination more than once or have been in the university for more than four years should not be allowed to become office-bearers. The programmes of the union should be interesting and constructive.

(4) The political parties and teacher politicians should refrain from taking part in the students unions. The teachers' prestige should be above question. They often do not perform their duties properly and this affects the students as well.

(5) There is need of civic, moral and spiritual education among the young so that they may have respect for teachers, elders and the laws of the country.

Education on Social, Moral and Spiritual Values

We have already emphasized that knowledge without a lack of essential values may be dangerous and, therefore, inculcation of right type of values among younger generations is of utmost importance. "The University Education Commission (1948) considered both its philosophical and practical aspects and made certain valuable proposals for reforms. However, except in a small number of institutions, they were not implemented."[21] In 1959 the Central Advisory Board of Education appointed a special Committee on Religious and Moral Instructions. The Committee recommended that one or two periods a week should be set aside in the school time-table for instructions in moral and spiritual values. At the primary stage such instruction will generally be imported through interesting stories, including stories drawn from the great religions of the world. At the secondary stage, there may be frequent discussions between the teacher and the pupils on the values sought to be inculcated. However, not much progress was made in this direction. The Education Commission (1955) felt much concern over this problem and said that the education system should emphasize at all stages the development of fundamental social, moral and spiritual values. For this they recommended that (1) The Central and State Governments should adopt measures to introduce education in moral, social and spiritual values in all institutions under their control (or local authority) on the lines recommended by the University Education Commission and the Committee on Religious and Moral Instructions. A general study of the different religions of the world

[21] *Report of the Education Commission* (1966), p. 19.

should be a part of the first degree courses and a graded syllabus of three years should be prepared for this purpose In the first year it can deal with the lives of great religious leaders, in the second, selections from the scriptures of the world with a universal appeal and in the third year with the central problems of the philosophy of religions concerned. Students may also be encouraged to meet in groups for silent meditation. (2) The privately-managed institutions should also be expected to follow suit. (3) The University Departments in Comparative Religion should be specially concerned with the ways in which these values can be taught wisely and effectively and should undertake preparation of special literature for use by students and teachers.

The Education Commission (1966) also emphasized that "education about religions" should be provided in the schools and colleges. They point out that in a multi-religious society like ours, it is necessary to define the attitude of the state to religion, religious education and the concept of secularism. The adoption of a secularist policy means that in political, economic and social matters, all citizens, irrespective of their religious faith, will enjoy equality of rights, that no religious community will be favoured or discriminated against, and the instructions in religious dogmas will not be provided in state schools. But it is not an irreligious or antireligious policy ; it does not belittle the importance of religion as such.... In such a society, however, one has to make a distinction between "religious education" and "education about religions". The former is largely concerned with the teaching of the tenets and the practices of a particular religion, generally in the form in which the religious group envisages them, whereas the latter is a study of religions and religious thoughts from a point of view—the eternal quest of the spirit.[22] They further observe that it would not be practicable for a secular state with many religions to provide education in any one religion. It is, however, necessary for a multi-religious democratic state to promote a tolerant study of all religions so that its citizens can understand each other better and live amicably together. It must be remembered that, owing to the ban placed on religious instructions in schools and the weakening of the home influences which, in the past, often provided such instruction children are now growing up without any clear idea of their religion and no chance of learning about others. In fact the general ignorance and misunderstanding

[22] *Ibid.*, p. 20.

in these matters are so widespread in the younger generations as to be fraught with great danger for the development of a democracy in which tolerance is related as a high value. They suggested that "a syllabus giving well chosen information about each of the major religions should be included as a part of the courses in citizenship or as part of a general education to be introduced in schools and colleges up to the first degree. It should highlight the fundamental similarities in the great religions of the world and the emphasis they place on the cultivation of certain broadly comparable and moral and spiritual values. It would be a great advantage to have a common course on this subject in all parts of the country and common text books which should be prepared at the national level by the competent and suitable experts in each religion."[23]

How far it will be possible to provide such education in the schools is yet to be decided. However, we have another aspect to discuss in this connection that is the religious education in religious institutions.

Religious Institutions

We have already pointed out in the beginning of this chapter that religion has an important role to play in the economic development and modernization of a democratic country. In fact unless the importance of religion is not properly recognized it might be difficult to have a balanced development in a democratic country. Professor Smith perhaps rightly observes, "I do not know what the economists or the other technical experts may say, but certainly the historians may confidently affirm that a highly relevant question in the evolution of a society towards any given goal, such as prosperity or health, is the question of how far; in every situation that arises from day to day, in ordinary life or in public procedures, in making choices men choose the alternative that is most conducive to national welfare. Nothing is more important in human life, one must perhaps always be emphasizing, than human freedom. Nothing is more consequential in social development than how men exercise their freedom : what in fact they choose, and how resolutely they strive for whatever it is that they opt to go after. To consider economic advance without pondering morale and motivation seems to me naive, if not disastrous.

"What one chooses, among various alternatives is a moral question.

[23] *Ibid.*, p. 605.

The question of drive has traditionally been, in part, at least, a religious one. Accordingly, it is not difficult to argue that the transformation of a society is a question with moral and religious implications. Development depends not only on men's notions of what is possible, but also on their notions of what is good, the force of their motivations and the quality of their acting. Modernization is a total process. Or at least, the less total it is, the less rapid. To think that one part of a man's or a country's life can be modernized without the other parts, is to discover that at best such modernization proves fragile, or slow, if not altogether deceptive."[24]

The religious education is not only necessary for modernization and economic development of the country, but it is an end in itself, for the development of an individual personality. As Hertzler points out "More institutions, or better institutions, or more socialized groups, or any other form of social machinery or environmental conditions cannot be ends, but merely efficient and necessary means to the real end. And one must finally conclude that this real and final end is the production of human beings, personalities, souls. The fact that society is essential to man does not make society greater than he, for society grows out of the individual, his needs and attributes.... Progress is mainly concerned with the fulfilment of self, the maximum realization of the various individual potentialities in a socially acceptable way, the harmonious exercise of human faculties and powers.... Thus progress consists in exercising the powers of living in their highest form in an attempt to achieve and enjoy relative fullness of life."[25] He also cautions that this realization of self and fullness of life does not mean a rampant and unrestrained individualism. Unrestrained individualism implies laissez faire, and laissez faire means struggle for all and thwarting of life for most men ; instead of spiritualizing men it brutalizes them. Achievement of self must be canalized by the highest ethical and social requirements. It is not in the acquiring for self, but in investing self in the doing of the world's work that the fullness of life is realized. Most human beings are most fully themselves, when they most fully give themselves to noble public causes.

We have to impart religious education to all age groups and to

[24] Smith, Wilfred Cantwell, *Modernization of a Traditional Society* (1965), pp. 46-47.

[25] Hertzler, J. O., *Social Progress — A Theoretical Survey and Analysis* (1928), pp. 89-90.

all classes. In order to do that we will have to change the ways and means of imparting that education. Not only that but the contents of education have also to be changed to suit the democratic ideals.

There is a lot of truth in Max Weber's contention that there is a close connection between religion and economics. He points out that the rise of mature capitalism in Europe was affected by the emergence of Protestant, especially Calvinist, ethics. In a preliminary way he established that in contemporary Germany areas predominantly Protestants were wealthier than primarily Catholic sections of the nation. He asserts on the basis of painstaking historical study that modern or mature capitalism, emerged not simply by inner economic necessity, but as if it were pushed by another rising force, the religious ethics of Protestantism, again especially Calvinism. Mature capitalism is not based on simply the acquisitive urge. It is a rational activity, emphasizing order, discipline, and heirarchy in organization.[26] It regards the performance of acquisitive behaviour as a kind of calling. It lays stress on success as such, not on the joys which economic success can purchase.

In India not much emphasis has been laid on this aspect in our economic development and planning. Perhaps this is the most neglected aspect of our democratic planning. Some books in Economics deal with the contents of Hinduism and how it is related to economic development, but lot of research is needed as to how to transmit religious values among the masses which can be helpful in our economic progress. There are some people (particularly humanists) who think that we can transmit moral values such as honesty, truthfulness, etc. without the help of religion. But some philosophers think that it is not possible to do so. It is for this reason that we want to emphasize that there should be reorganization of our religious beliefs so as to inculcate virtues like honesty, temperance, justice, truth, concern for others, etc. among masses. Professor Lillie observes, "The question is whether morality requires the support of religion or whether morality as we know it, can exist permanently without religion. History shows that it certainly can do so with no great appearance of harm to itself for limited periods, and it is possible that something in the way of morality may exist

[26] Timasheff, N. S., *Sociological Theory — Its Nature and Growth* (1961), pp. 170-71. For details see Weber, Max, *The Protestant Ethic and the Spirit of Capitalism*, translated by Parsons, Talcott (1930).

permanently without a supporting religion. There are, however, several reasons for thinking that morality without religion would be very different from what it has been in the past and that some of its very highest forms would disappear altogether. These reasons, by a different turn of expression, are those which make the existence of God a postulate of the useful, if not of the necessary kind in ethics.... Immortality promised to believers by many religions gives a new significance to morality, by making the moral struggle worthwhile and by making it reasonable to attribute great intrinsic value to each human personality. Morality is at the same time other-worldly in a different way. The good man has his affections set not on the things of this visible world and on the satisfaction that can be obtained from material things, but in a realm that is in some sense more spiritual."[27] Having discussed the importance of religion in teaching ethical values it would be appropriate to discuss if Hinduism or Islam can help in achieving this objective.

Hinduism and Social Progress

It is difficult to define Hindu Religion, because the religion of Hindus is amorphous and complex and lacks a "church" and a clearly defined body of dogmas.[28] Hindus worship countless deities for a variety of reasons. Even those who do not believe in God ; but believe that Vedas are the direct revelation of God, are considered to be Hindus. According to Dr. S. Radhakrishnan Hinduism is more a way of life than a form of thought.[29] Therefore, it will be appropriate if we describe some of its salient features. The main principles of Hinduism are the belief in the theory of karma, birth and rebirth (or transmigration of soul), the four main objects of life i.e. Dharma, Artha, Kama and Moksha, Ashram system, Varna system or caste system and the ultimate aim as Moksha. Besides it also includes two more tenets, i.e. the doctrine of Maya and that the world is "divine". Without going into the details of these tenets which have been discussed elsewhere in detail,[30] the question to be seen is whether Hinduism in the present form is a hindrance in social progress. The answer to this question cannot be given

[27] William, Lillie, *An Introduction to Ethics*, London (1959), pp. 340-42.

[28] Srinivas, M. N., *Caste in Modern India and Other Essays* (1962), p. 149.

[29] Radhakrishnan, S., *Hindu View of Life* (1920), p. 77.

[30] For details see Madan, G. R., *Changing Pattern of Indian Villages* (1964), pp. 330-35.

categorically in positive or negative form. If we look into the real meanings of these tenets the answer is that Hinduism is not a blockade in social progress but aids in material progress. But if we look into the fact as to how it is practised by the large masses at present it is a hindrance in our progress. It is because of this practice that some of the Western people think that Hinduism is a great hindrance in the material progress of India. It is alleged by those thinkers that the Hindu religion bids a man turn his back upon all material advantages as (1) this world is an illusion (Maya), (2) the sense of infinite (God does everything), and (3) the attainment of Moksha is the only aim of life. As a result of all this the Hindu religion and spirituality foster a pessimistic attitude and a universal indifference to the material side of life. But if we look to the past history of India, this contention appears to be untrue. If the Indian mind would have been exclusively taken up by thoughts of the other world, as has been frequently assessed the Indian people would not have made achievements in the sphere of positive sciences. It is well known that the ancient Indians laid the foundations of mathematics and mechanical knowledge. However, it cannot be denied altogether that at present majority of the illiterate masses are confused over these doctrines and their thinking is a hindrance in the material progress.

Another assertion is that in spite of the fact that majority of the Hindus believe in God and many of them visit temples yet there is a lot of corruption in public life, generally people are dishonest, speak lies and think in terms of personal gain ignoring the claims of community and the nation. There is a lot of truth in this statement, because there has entered more formalism in religion and people do not do what they believe.

Thus, if we wish to make religion a vehicle of progress in our present development many reforms will be needed in its interpretation and ways of imparting instructions.

Reinterpretation of Religious Literature

(1) Firstly the right interpretation of the doctrines of Hinduism to the masses through proper books in their own language is very essential. This can be possible through proper translation of religious books by learned persons or body of persons as has been done in the case of the Bible. The Gita is one such book which needs authentic translation. Only that translation should be published and

not others which contain irrelevant things. The other sacred books should also be translated with the approval of that body.

(2) There are innumerable religious sects in India and they have their own literature. It would be necessary to get that literature scrutinized through regional bodies formed for this purpose. It will be interesting to note that in Uttar Pradesh alone there are 66 sects and subsects of religious mendicants.[31] This excludes the reformed organizations like Arya Samaj, Brahmo Samaj, etc. which do not have such mendicants.

(3) It is not only a question of proper translation of religious books but proper interpretation through properly educated persons. Many of the Sadhus, preachers and priests have little education and interpret the texts in wrong ways. Thus, training and education of such persons is highly desirable.

Reorganization of Religious Institutions

We have numerous temples and deities in our villages and towns which are worshipped by the people. However, many of these temples remain uncared for a long time. As Professor Srinivas observes, "In some temples worship is offered everyday, in others once a week, while still others come to life only annually or once every few years, when the festival of the deity is being celebrated."[32] However, even in those temples which open regularly or weekly there are not adequate rooms for meditation and sermons to a group of people. In few temples where there are rooms, there are not regular sermons which can have a lasting effect on those who attend the temples. Thus, there has entered too much formalism in our religious institutions. The people go to the temple to do some image worship and then come back without imbibing any religious qualities. In the last hundred years there have been some reformist movements like the Brahmo Samaj, Arya Samaj, and the Ramakrishna Mission as a reaction to Christianity. They have attacked on some of the forms of image worship and laid stress upon the inner purification and good life of man. These organizations have halls where people meet collectively at regular intervals and there are sermons by educated

[31] Tripathi, B. D., *The Religious Mendicants of Uttar Pradesh*, Ph. D. Thesis, Lucknow University (1966), p. 1.

[32] Srinivas, M. N., *Religion and Society Among the Coorgs of South India* (1952), p. 181.

priests or laity. However, the impact of these movements has been confined only to few urban educated people.

On the other hand, one of the most significant things which impressed me in the Western countries and American society was their organized religion which is the base of their morality, social service and successful democracy. Most of the people attend the churches at least once in a week and there are regular classes and sermons for all groups of people, children, youth and old. All adults in Protestant denominations are asked to participate in religious discussion, and are not mere listeners of what is said by priests. Thus, what is needed is consolidation and reorganization of our religious institutions on a wider scale. In this connection the following suggestions may be worthwhile to pursue.

(*i*) All the temples should be registered and they must prescribe to certain minimum standards with regard to building, equipment, etc. All registered institutions should be governed by democratic set up. There should be proper arrangements for meditation and sermons in all these temples. No temple should be the private property of an individual and proper accounts should be maintained for it. There is legislation in certain states such as Mysore, Bombay, Bihar and Orissa though not so far-reaching as in Madras for controlling the administration of Hindu religious endowments.[33] However, this legislation is not applicable to all institutions. The rest of the states had no such legislation even. The Ramaswami Aiyer Commission (1960) recommended that those states where there are no enactments governing Hindu religious endowments should speedily undertake suitable legislation in this behalf. It further suggested to the Central Government the desirability of bringing into operation a uniform pattern of legislation dealing with the administration and management of religious endowments of all the communities of India.[34]

(*ii*) The preachers appointed in such institutions should be well qualified. And there should be regular training programme for such preachers as is done by Christian denominations. Even the Commission has recommended that each state should set up one or more religious institutions for systematic instructions to temple priests in Sanskrit, Hindu scriptures and rituals.[35] It also recommend-

[33] Srinivas, M. N., *Social Change in Modern India* (1966), p. 144.
[34] *Report of the Hindu Religious Endowments Commission* (1962), p. 172.
[35] *Ibid.*, p. 57.

ed for the creation of four central institutions in different parts of the country in which religion would be studied along with humanities as in colleges of divinity in the West.[36]

(*iii*) Some welfare activities should be taken up by certain religious institutions, where there is enough income. This work has been taken by some institutions, e.g. Rama Krishna Mission, Shivanand Divine Life Society, etc. However, there are many other institutions which have large incomes but the income is not properly utilized.

(*iv*) The All-India Bharat Sadhu Samaj was formed by Sri Gulzari Lal Nanda, the then Home Minister, Government of India in 1956.[37] His chief aim was to store up the scattered moralizing force lying in the unorganized community of religious mendicants and utilizing the same for the moral regeneration of the masses. His belief was that the samaj would be a reliable weapon for fighting out corruption in the country.

On an experimental basis the Bharat Sadhu Samaj mobilized 200 sadhus for launching an effective drive against corruption and for the promotion of Sadachar (good conduct) Movement in September, 1965, which lasted for 3 months. In this undertaking the Samaj was assisted by Samyukta Sadachar Samiti and Bharat Sewak Samaj.[38] The specific aim of this campaign was to purify the administration and public life from corruption, nepotism and adulteration. In January 1966, it also decided to impart spiritual and moral education in 1,000 schools and colleges in different parts of the country during that year. However, the Samaj has not achieved much success in its aims. Because (1) many of the religious mendicants have not co-operated with it. (2) State interference in the community of religious mendicants is not liked by many. (3) The *ad hoc* nature of these lectures could not have a lasting effect.

Therefore, what we need is a committee of mendicants and non-mendicants belonging to different religious organizations who should ponder over these problems and chalk out a scheme on the lines suggested above. The government's function should only be to watch the interest of public. The procedure should be uniform for mendicant and non-mendicant organizations.

[36] *Ibid.*, pp. 73-74.

[37] Smith, D. E., *India as a Secular State* (1963), p. 260.

[38] Tripathi, B. D., *op. cit.*, p. 325.

Some such steps are also needed in the case of Muslim religious institutions.[39] However, being not much conversant with them, it is not possible to give any suggestions.

[39] Professor Smith expresses such views in his book, *Modernization of a Traditional Society*. I also experienced the same type of corruption in Muslim countries which I visited in the Middle East.

CHAPTER XIII

LEISURE AND RECREATION

LEISURE is as important as work. Man feels tired after work and wants to recoup strength so as to gain efficiency. People have always had some free time, but in recent years much free time has come with such suddenness that very few are aware of its far-reaching significance. Never before there has been a period in the history of the world during which leisure has been so widespread as it is now. Society may find its greatest asset in the constructively used leisure of its citizens, but too much free time without adequate preparation for its use may become a serious problem.

People must work to make a living. While work is necessary for subsistence and progress and no country has ever been able to exist without it, but culture depends chiefly for its existence on leisure. "Labour and leisure go together, but the tone of society is conditioned largely by the extent and the uses of the time remaining after the practical necessities of life have been attended to. If people engage in creative and constructive activities, civilization is advanced ; if they indulge in useless and destructive activities, the social order deteriorates and social progress is retarded."[1]

In early days majority of the people devoted most of their time to work. The intense struggle for existence required this, which left little time for creative work. Also in the agricultural economy people used to live in primary, face to face and familiar relations with each other. Leisure was thus no problem where the whole family worked together and had recreation together. As soon as humanity experienced more leisure, even though for a long time it was confined to a small group, progress was accelerated. The machine has brought an unprecedented amount of leisure time for the common man, which was previously the sole prerogative of the upper classes. This large amount of leisure has been welcomed by some of the recipients, because it has been used for productive and constructive purposes. But at the same time many of the social scientists have been perturbed over it because of its grave implications upon the mores,

[1] Neumeyer , M. H. and Neumeyer, E. S., *Leisure and Recreation* (1958), p. 4.

attitudes and values of the groups. How does the new leisure affect the structure and functions of modern society. How is it affecting individuals. What are people doing with their new-found spare time? These and other questions are raised to call attention to the social significance of the new leisure.

Leisure and Recreation

No uniformity exists in the way people spend their leisure. Any activity may be a recreation to one person and boresome work to another. Also the same activity may be either labour or relaxation to the same person at different times. In a heterogeneous population various cultural groups have different interests. Although recreation is now considered a right not only of children but for all age groups, yet it is not necessary that all classes of people will make proper use of it. Some supposed that workers would use the longed for leisure wisely, devoting much time to self-improvement and social betterment, than spending it in idleness, mischief and even in carrying on criminal activities. That many have used it properly is evidenced by the progress of community recreation, club programmes, adult education, cultural activities and welfare programmes yet many have misused it leading to litigation in villages and filling the cinemas and drinking shops in the urban areas. Thus, people use their leisure activities in a variety of ways and there is no uniformity of either their choices or of the forces that influence them. Few people are well-equipped to select their leisure activities wisely. Hence, many are inclined to over-indulge in certain favoured pursuits to the exclusion of other available undertakings.

Leisure and Recreation Defined

Definitions of leisure vary a great deal but the chief emphasis is on the element of time. According to *Dictionary of Sociology*, "Leisure is the free time after the practical necessities of life have been attended to. The adjective leisure means being unoccupied by the practical necessities, as, leisure hours ; the adverb leisure applies to slow, deliberate, unhurried undertakings."[2] While it is true that leisure is the free time after all duties, obligations, and other practical necessities have been attended to, the line of demarcation between necessities and spare time is not rigid. Work is usually considered as the anti-thesis of leisure. A paid job imposes certain obvious and

[2] *Dictionary of Sociology*, (Ed.), Fairchild, H. P. (1944), p. 175.

formal duties. Yet, for some, work may be so enjoyable that it is equivalent to leisure. Similarly, sleep is usually considered as a necessity, but sleep beyond necessity may be a leisure time activity. Eating is equally classified as a necessity, yet Lundberg regards it as one of the major leisure activities. The routine eating of meals may not be regarded as leisure, but when members of the family eat their meal together or entertain friends at dinner, the activity assumes a different meaning.[3] What has been said about work, sleep and eating may apply also to other necessities, yet for practical purposes, leisure may be thought of as time that is relatively free from obligatory pursuits.

Leisure is not to be confused with idleness. Whereas leisure is freedom or opportunity to do something specific or implied, idleness is generally forced and the person is not capable of doing something he wants to do. Thus, leisure is an opportunity to engage in some kind of activity, which is not required by daily necessity. "Recreation has been defined as a form of leisure time experience in which physical, mental, or spiritual satisfaction comes to the individual from participation in certain forms of activity."[4] It is presumably something people really want to do and do not have to do, in contrast to those things they must do to earn a living.

Recreation includes any activity pursued during leisure, either individual or collective, that is *free* and *pleasurable* having its own immediate appeal, not impelled by a delayed reward beyond itself or by any immediate necessity.[5] According to Bela Dutta Gupta the various objectives of recreation include pleasure and enjoyment, satisfaction of the self, balanced growth of organism, restoration of creative skill, spirit of healthy competition, socialization, the general tenets of good citizenship, development of character and therapeutic measures and health.[6] He further adds, "Recreation is any activity engaged in during leisure or free time, and primarily motivated by the personal satisfaction derived from it. Since interests of different individuals are different activities engaged in during leisure or free time may also be unlike and take any of the four forms, cultural recreation, social recreation, educational recreation

[3] Lundberg, G. A. *et al.*, *Leisure : A Sub-Urban Study* (1934), pp. 99-100.

[4] Braucher, Howard, "Recreation", in *Social Work Year Book* (1949), p. 424. Also see Elliott, M.A., and Merill, F. E., *Social Disorganization* (1950), p. 586.

[5] *Dictionary of Sociology*, *op. cit.*, p. 251-52.

[6] Dutta Gupta, Bela, *op. cit.*, p. 300.

and physical recreation. But these different categories do, by no means mean that a water-tight division exists in them. On the contrary, there is too much of 'spill over' from one to the other. As for example pleasure derived during leisure time from art, music, drama and literature may be taken as cultural, social, educational and physical recreation all combined."[7]

This makes recreation almost synonymous with leisure. However, the emphasis in leisure is on the time element, whereas recreation refers to the way leisure is spent. One can conceive of spending leisure in other ways than the pursuit of some form of recreation, although in a broader sense most forms of recreation are free time activities and many leisure pursuits have some recreational values. Recreation offers a unique insight into the culture of people. Cultural values are expressed in the activities which are performed in the leisure time. A large portion of the major forms of recreation is carried on in groups or informal association with other people, though it is true that leisure is spent in individual activities with no immediate social contact with others. It may also be pointed out that the term recreation is generally applied to activities of young people and adults to differentiate those activities from the play life of children which is usually more spontaneous and unorganized than certain forms of adult amusements.

Recreation in Modern Society

The place of recreation in modern society cannot be fully understood without a consideration of the significance and development of leisure, because the increase of free time is chiefly responsible for the demand for recreation. At the same time the recreation activities are affected by geographic and ecological factors, the population situation, political and economic organization, science and technology, education and culture, and community life. The modern machinery has affected leisure in that it has produced an abundance of goods and more free time. Recreation has its physical, mental, emotional, moral, social and civic benefits. It is usually important for the development of well-balanced personalities and social welfare. Unfortunately the average man has not been educated to use his free time to the best of his advantage. The society has not sufficiently planned and organized the leisure resources in order to provide adequate facilities for the masses. On the other

[7] *Ibid.*, p. 303.

hand, the mass forms of recreation have become popular and have assumed a large place in modern life. In other words the problem of leisure has not, as yet, received serious consideration in the social sciences. Moral philosophy, from which the social sciences are only beginning to free themselves treated leisure for the most part as an evil, and correspondingly exalted hard work as a virtue. The reason for this glorification of work is not for us to seek. We have emerged only recently from ages during which the production of material necessities was the overwhelming predominant concern of man. But today, machines and power supplies have removed the necessity for our age-long fear of being unable to wring from the earth the means of subsistence. "The topics of leisure and recreation have, consequently, for the most part been regarded as sentimental subjects for intellectual dilettantes, and not subjects for serious philosophical thought or scientific investigation."[8]

Income and Leisure

Another problem is the rising income of the people in the modern age. "In terms of cash returns or incomes many sections of workers have had an improved standard of living in the past fifty years. Real wages have arisen in many trades. But quite apart from actual rates of payment, or earnings, the fall in the birth rate in European and American countries has been great enough to cause an increase in the average family income. The expenditure on leisure, therefore, of those with smaller incomes has increased."[9] On the other hand, many forms of recreation have become commercialized. Endless devices are offered to the idle person, each to be enjoyed only on condition that he has money to pay. Without money he is condemned, unable to share in the pleasure and pastimes which press on him on all sides. Such commercial amusements are usually regarded as relatively passive form of entertainment for spectators, as contrasted with more active recreation provided by community recreation centres. The business of providing entertainment for the people has become very profitable. While some persons in the field of commercial recreation are interested in providing wholesome entertainment, the profit motive is uppermost. All the programmes are evaluated in terms of financial returns. We shall discuss these in detail later on.

[8] Lundberg, G. A., *et al.*, *op. cit.*, p. 9.

[9] Burns, C. D., *Leisure in the Modern World* (1932), p. 19.

Forms of Recreation

The recreational activities are of various types. They may include play, games, sports, athletics, certain amusements, art forms, hobbies, social clubs, welfare activities, etc. The activities which can be recreational ones differ from person to person depending upon one's age, sex, class, attitudes, habits, etc. According to Neumeyer and Neumeyer recreation from the standpoint of organization and support may be broadly classified into three categories, viz., (1) the spontaneous free play kinds, which are not promoted specifically by organizations and institutions, (2) commercial amusements and various forms of mass entertainments, and (3) the communally fostered and conducted, whether public or semi-public or private. However, they also point out that this three form classification of activities is somewhat arbitrary, for recreation activities are so varied that they cannot easily be classified even from the point of view of organization and sponsorship. We have discussed in detail the different forms of play and recreational activities which can be useful for children and youth in Volume II and which are being developed for these groups in villages, towns and cities.[10] Here we want to discuss the recreational activities for adults whether ordinary or commercialized.

Recreational Activities Among Adults

Not much data is available about the recreational activities in which adults of this country spend most of their leisure time. To assess the use of leisure in two segments of society two postgraduate students in the Department of Sociology and Social Work, Lucknow University, carried out investigations in the city of Lucknow. One dealt with "Leisure in Upper Class"[11] and the other "Leisure in Middle Class Women."[12] The surveys were not very exhaustive. However, some of the results are as follows.

The first survey pertains to 50 upper class male adults whose income was Rs. 500 and above per month. In the sample were included lawyers, professors, doctors, government officials and businessmen in equal proportion. The activities in which they were presumed to be interested included cinema, radio, restaurants,

[10] For details see Chapters IV and V, Vol. II.
[11] Rai, Pramod Kumar, "Leisur in Upper Class", M. S. W. Thesis (1960).
[12] Jain, Asha Rani, "Leisure in Middle Class Women", M.A. Thesis (1963).

clubs, intoxicants, prostitution, painting, music, dancing, reading, chatting, sleeping and religious activities. Some of the results are shown in Table 29.

TABLE 29

USE OF LEISURE IN URBAN AREAS (LUCKNOW CITY)

S. No.	*Kind of Recreational Activity*	*Among upper class men*		*Among middle class women*	
		Interested	*Not interested*	*Interested*	*Not interested*
1.	Cinema	78	22	76	24
2.	Radio	74	26	82	18
3.	Restaurant	64	36	72	28
4.	Club goers	52	48	28	72
5.	Drinking	42	58	N.A.	N.A.
6.	Smoking	60	40	N.A.	N.A.
7.	Painting	6	94	10	90
8.	Music	8	92	84	16
9.	Dance	4	96	78	22
10.	Games	46	54	32	68
11.	Reading	94	6	92	8
12.	Chatting	88	12	100	—
13.	Sleeping	66	34	N.A.	N.A.
14.	Religious Activities	38	62	96	4

The second survey was confined to 50 middle class educated women in the income range of Rs. 250 and above, half of which were working women and the other half non-working. Besides their household duties which included management of kitchen, cleanliness and decoration of house, nurturing and upbringing of children, nursing the sick, tailoring, knitting, embroidery and handicraft which are their traditional duties these women were interested in certain recreational activities noted in the above table. Let us analyse some of these activities in detail to arrive at some conclusion.

Among these activities the cinema and radio are very popular forms of recreation these days in urban areas both among men and women. The visiting of restaurants among women has become very common in urban areas although in the past generally the women were confined to their homes.

Participation in club is another recreational activity in which urban class people are interested. However, clubs are of various types and it would be advisable to discuss these types in brief before we study the participation of these groups in club activities. "Clubs are an association of persons usually formed and run by its members for the common object of satisfying their urge for different types of amusements, recreation and hobbies, for spending their leisure time and for developing social relations among its members. Though a club is, broadly speaking, supposed to be a venture of its constituents, it is not unusual for clubs to be a purely business enterprise, e.g., night clubs, dance clubs, clubs offering facilities for particular sports, like Billiard Saloons."[13]

These clubs may be divided into various categories. Firstly, those which have their own premises and have facilities for various games and sports, outdoor and indoor and for different types of recreational activities. The membership of these clubs is mostly confined to men only. Most of them have bars attached to them and are usually open daily during fixed hours. Among these clubs were mentioned the Mohammad Bagh Club, Lucknow Club, Catholic Club, Avadh Gymkhana and Refah-i-Am Club. Secondly, those clubs which are more in the nature of a social and moral organization. They do not have their own premises and carry on their activities through weekly or similar periodical meetings. They also usually have the wives of the male members as members of the clubs. Among these clubs were mentioned the Rotary Club and the Lions Club. They are mostly the local units of international organizations. Thirdly, there are clubs which confine their membership to a particular department, institution or a creed, e.g. University Club. Fourthly, the clubs of business type, e.g. night clubs, dance clubs, etc. Fifthly, the professional organizations or social institutions.

In the first survey although no such distinction was made between these various clubs, the investigator had asked about their membership to the first or third category of clubs. In the second survey the participation of women was determined with respect to second category only. The first survey shows that majority of the upper class men attended recreational clubs though there was a fair percentage (48 per cent) who do not attend any club. The position may be much worse among the lower classes, who generally do not attend any such club. Thus, many of the adults do not participate in clubs, which are necessary for a democratic society to mould public opinion, and have good and healthy recreation as well. We have also seen that majority

[13] Jain, Asha Rani, *op. cit.*, p. 84.

of the clubs among the elite group are such where drinking and gambling goes on and may have pernicious effect on the personality of members taking part in such activities. The number of women attending clubs is very small as there are few such organizations for women. Chatting is very common among the women and they waste a lot of their time in this activity. It is also interesting to note that among the upper class people there are few (38) who are interested in religious activities. As pointed out in Chapter XII this is likely to have a very bad effect upon the morale of people. The data about the time spent in social welfare and political activities was not collected though it would have served very useful purpose.

In the villages people take part in various types of recreational activities such as folk songs, stories, poetry, dance, drama, village sports such as wrestling, kabaddi, etc.[14] But how much time they spend in these activities and what are their effects upon the development of their personalities and the society in general is yet to be found out. However, as one detailed survey in a village points out, "There are not many organized pastimes or forms of recreation in the village. The fact is that the villagers are so busy eking out their meagre subsistence that they hardly have any leisure and when they do have any free time they do not know how to utilise it to their advantage. Even the few rich villagers who do not have to work all day do not appear to turn to their leisure to much advantage, but waste it in idle gossip, gambling, etc. No plays, dramas or dances are arranged so that any talents which the villagers might possess are latent. There are no means by which the hidden potentialities in them may be drawn out and expressed for the benefit of themselves and society."[15]

Under the community development programmes some recreational activities like adult education programme ; community centres having libraries, radios, reading rooms ; games ; and cultural activities like Bhajan Mandalies were organized. But such activities have not taken root in the rural society. Thus, much more efforts will be needed to have healthy recreational activities for the rural areas.

[14] For details see Deva, Indra, "The Sociology of Bhojpuri Folk Literature", Ph. D. Thesis, Lucknow University (1958). Also see Singh, V. N., "A Sociological Study of Bundelkhand Folklore (Uttar Pradesh)", Ph. D. Thesis, Lucknow University (1966).

[15] Majumdar, D. N., *Caste and Communication in an Indian Village* (1958), p. 301.

Having mentioned the recreational activities in which people take part let us discuss the role of cinema and other commercialized agencies which affect the society in many ways.

Commercial Recreation

The problem of commercial recreation is a modern one and is comparatively greater in some of the highly industrialized countries. The machine has brought an unprecedented amount of leisure time for the common man which was previously the sole prerogative of the upper classes. The municipalities and city corporations which are responsible for providing healthy leisure time pursuits for the residents have not been able to cope with the problem. On the other hand, the responsibility for this vital community need has been assumed by persons whose only thought is commercial exploitation. The weakening of moral and religious teaching and lessening of family control have further widened their scope. The individual who has become materialistic and has enough money to spend, spends more and more on commercialized recreation to forget the complexities of modern urban life, while exploiters try to attract him by appealing to his sensual pleasures. All this has a disorganizing effect. Dr. Jain points out, "Today there is an increase in leisure, which is now considered to be the right of all and not the privilege of a few. It is an outcome of industrialization and of changing economic and social pattern which has resulted in the reduction of the working hours, increase in wages, development in communications and primary education. The economic motives have further commercialized this leisure." He further adds, "In early times public had no proper means of passing their leisure. Even in England in the latter half of the last century, leisure time was passed at a public house or a street corner. The position was similar more or less in other countries also. As time passed, public found some outlet or the other to pass their leisure hours, and horse-races and matches became popular. News of Wellington's Campaign in Spain were not awaited with greater national eagerness than reports on the prospects of famous horse-races and prize-fights. Many might say that today the public is much more interested in test-matches, but the truth remains that no other source attracts such a large number of persons today than the cinema."[16]

[16] Jain, R. K., *The Economic Aspects of the Film Industry in India* (1960), p. 15.

Unfortunately the effects of this commercialized recreation in the urban areas, are of more disorganizing nature than of organizing ones. Recreation takes the form of decreation bringing disorganization in the individual as well as the society. As Elliott and Merrill rightly point out, "Althouth the etymology of the word, recreation, would suggest that any sociological analysis of this topic be made under the concept of personal, family and community organization and integration, its actual operation, particularly in the urban community, necessitates a statement of its role in the disorganization and disintegration of these basic units in the social structure."[17]

Meaning of Commercial Recreation

Commercial recreation has been defined by Todd as, "more or less highly organized amusement enterprises engaged primarily for profit making. The essential point is that the providing of such recreation is to be considered as a business organized and managed by private individuals or groups which capitalizes the leisure time of its patrons through their response to opportunities to enjoy amusements or recreation in return for the payment of admission fees."[18] Another aspect of this commercial recreation is that there is an increasing propensity of persons to pay generously for the privilege of being amused. Carpenter speaks of commercial recreation as spatially restricted, passive and vicarious, serving as an emotional catharsis, often governmentally regulated, and occasionally dispersed to the periphery of the city by certain ecological and social forces.[19] Among these may be included prize-fights, movies, baseball, games, taxi, dance halls, cabarets, pool halls, hotels, brothels, amusement parks, gambling dens and other such recreational institutions. However, out of these only few are found in our country due to its slow industrialization and urbanization.

Causes of Commercial Recreation

Among the causes of commercialized recreation are included (1) the profit motive, (2) the sensual effect, (3) more purchasing power, (4) lack of other recreational facilities, and (5) modern industrialization. As pointed out above commercial recreation brings much profit to the persons who operate them, and is considered to

17 Elliott, M. A., and Merrill, F. E., *op. cit.* (1941), p. 865.
18 Todd, Arthur J. (Ed.), *Chicago Recreation Survey*, Vol. II (1938), p. 1.
19 Carpenter, Niles, *The Sociology of City Life* (1931), p. 250.

be one of the most prospering industries. In U. S. A. it has been estimated that from one-seventh to one-fifth of the entire national income is annually spent upon commercial recreation and powerful vested interests are represented in the profitable business of entertaining the American public. As it gives momentary pleasure to the persons who patronize them, they are attracted by its sensual pleasure. Because of its sensual effect even though people have not enough means to afford other necessities, are attracted by it. More purchasing power in the hands of some persons also attracts them, who do not find other alternative to spend. They go to such institution for the sake of fun and company. Lack of other recreational activities is one of the important causes for patronizing them. In big cities owing to lack of space there are not enough playgrounds or other healthy recreational activities to amuse the city dwellers. The absence of other social institutions also encourages it. In the joint family system there was enough recreation in the home itself. When all the members of the family were at home they could spend some time in family gossips. Also there was control of elders over the younger ones. The break-up of joint family system has lessened this control. Many a time a male or female alone comes to city to seek employment. In the absence of family they generally visit such recreational agencies for passing their spare time. Similarly, lack of religious interests which used to take lot of spare time in the past, has led many to resort to such type of recreation. The modern industrialization also encourages this. No doubt the advance in technology has given us certain advantages and we have enough leisure time to make further scientific advancement and improve our civilization, but its bad effects also cannot be ignored. When a large majority of the common people have enough leisure time, it becomes a problem for them how to spend it. The leisure time pursuits many a time lead to individual disorganization. The monotony of machine life increases the need for change and recreation. When a person has to do the same thing daily, he feels dull and monotonous. To relieve himself of this monotony he may resort to unwholesome recreational activities.

Commercial Recreation and Disorganization

The commercial recreation is disruptive to personal and community organization, and unsound and demoralizing attitudes, values and life schemes are acquired. It is mostly the adolescent and adults who often participate in these activities, except cinemas which are also visited by young children. It is not because that the commercialized agencies for recreation are inherently of disorganizing effect, but because they are operated for the profit motive and the persons who operate these facilities for amusement do not conceive their task to be that of preserving the public morale. For example, if a young girl falls in with unscrupulous characters at a public dance hall, or if a young girl spends the night in a hotel with her ("boy friend"), it is of no immediate concern to the management and even less to the shareholders. Thus, the result is often disruptive to the life organization of many persons who patronize or serve these agencies. As Mr. Janes Addams points out, "Responsibility for this vital community need has been taken from the civic body and assumed by persons whose only thought is commercial exploitation. As a consequence, they do not hesitate to assist actively in the disorganization of adolescents and those adults whose life patterns are not solidly integrated."[20]

In U. S. A. such institutions include the cabaret, the night clubs, the hotel, the road houses, the dance hall, the taxi dance hall, the brothels, the highway dine-and-dance establishments, the gambling dens and motion pictures.

In India we do not have such comparable institutions except some dance halls, night clubs, or hotels in metropolis cities and motion pictures in other towns. Such dance halls or hotels are mostly attended by upper class people. In such places some type of entertainment is given. These people often dine, sip a glass of wine and listen to music. There are singers and entertainers who augment their scanty salaries by circulating freely among the patrons and soliciting for immoral purposes. Sometimes prostitutes may also visit such places. The entertainment provided is often of a sensual nature appealing in many cases to the passions of male patrons. The disorganization in such an arrangement is apparent. The excessive use of alcohol, gambling and sex delinquency bring personal and community disorganization.

Cinema and Disorganization

The Role of the Movies. The cinema is evidently the most effective in creating social attitudes and values in our country than all other agencies of commercial recreation put together. The popularity of the

[20] Addams, Janes, *The Spirit of Youth and the City Streets* (1909), p. 7.

cinema is due to the fact that in a big city the average man is either poor or belongs to middle class and for him the cinema provides the cheapest source of entertainment giving some relief from the daily anxieties of life by lifting him for sometime to make-believe or an imaginary world. Dr. Jain points out, "In India, the impact of the movies is all the more. Indians are not very much fond of social gatherings and club-life mainly because majority of the people cannot afford that. The musical gatherings, poetic symposium, etc. remain too costly for an average man and do not attract a large number of people. Cinema being cheap and within easy reach of every one thus commands a better patronage. Further, in middle ages, theatres and festivals formed an integral part of a high life. In those days audience was organic. But modern audiences are atomized in spite of their mass character."[21]

A glance at the following table will show the growing popularity of cinemas in India.

TABLE 30

GROWTH OF CINEMAS IN INDIA

Circuit	1928	1938	1948	1952	1955	1959
1. Bombay	77	297	600	669	623	767
2. Central	15	204	306	531	609	686
3. Northern	81	330	320	405	535	740
4. Bengal	45	251	404	529	629	744
5. South	57	575	1373	1399	1161	1348
Total	275	1657	3003	3533	3557	4285

These cinemas included permanent, temporary, touring and seasonal. Permanent cinemas are those which have *pucca* buildings and have licences subject to renewal every year in order to ensure that all the required formalities have been observed. Temporary cinemas are granted licences for a short period, and such licences are subject to a renewal after the expiry of the term. As the term of licences is generally for a short duration, the cinema gets the name of temporary cinema. Touring cinemas are generally housed in tents or in tinsheds. The investment in such cinemas is very small in comparison with those falling in other categories. The seasonal cinemas are permanent

[21] Jain, R. K., *op. cit.*, pp. 15-16.

cinemas, but they work only in some particular seasons and are generally found at hill stations.

Another table shows the number of films produced annually in the country.

TABLE 31

OUTPUT OF FEATURE FILMS IN INDIA[22]

Language	1921	1941	1947	1951	1956	1961
Hindi	23	79	186	100	123	98
Non-Hindi	5	88	95	119	173	205
Total	28	167	281	219	296	303

It is also to be stated that while majority of the other recreational agencies operate in the large urban areas the cinema is affecting both urban and rural population. Another aspect of the question is that a vast majority of the population visits them and they include children as well as adolescents.

Movies and Adolescents. The cinema serves a very real social mentor for the child or adolescent who is confronted for the first time with the bewildering chaos of the modern world, with its variety of choices of conduct and definitions of the situation. In the picture, these choices are already made for them by persons on the screen, whose conduct he takes as final. He regards them as the faithful reproduction of the real world. That atmosphere grips his interest and stirs his imagination.

The movies in this sense are educational institutions and serve as important agencies both for inculcating the cultural heritage of the past in the young generation and for introducing new cultural traits and standards of conduct. Thus, they serve as effective educational institutions, because they arouse emotions and stir the romantic fancy of the adolescents.

This is not all. Adolescents often receive confused and disconnected impressions from the picture, involving contradictory standards of conduct which he is unable to reconcile. For example, a murderer or a gangster may live a life of excitement and luxury for a greater part of the picture, only to fall victim to police in the end. "Crime

[22] Figures taken from *India — 1962*, Ministry of Information and Broadcasting, Government of India, p. 153.

does not pay" is the moral, or see the dead gangster. But many a time the gangster's glorious life and not his untimely end puts vivid impression upon the adolescent's mind. The movie also thus influence in another way.

The attitudes and values of young men may be social or unsocial depending upon (1) the content of the picture, the skill and sympathy with which the various characters are portrayed, and (2) the social environments in which he has been brought up. Thus, all movies are not disorganizing to all adolescents, nor are some movies to all adolescents. The process is a selective one, affecting different groups and individuals directly and indirectly in a wide variety of ways. There are diverse views as to the exact role of the movies in relation to disorganized conduct. On the one hand, there are those who see in every portrayal of criminal or vicious conduct a direct incitement to crime and vice among adolescents, while on the other hand, there are equally zealous persons who believe that they provide a thoroughly clean and wholesome type of recreation and deter the budding criminals by pointing out the unpleasant inevitability of punishment in one form or another for all major transgressions. The claims of these two groups have been examined and weighed by various researchers, under three heads :

(*i*) *Inculcation of Antisocial Attitudes.* The Payne Studies of Motion Pictures and Youth in U. S. A. have made an attempt to essay the role of the motion pictures in the lives of the modern young men.[23] The studies point out that the role of cinema in stimulating antisocial attitudes in adolescents is evidenced by the subject matter of the pictures which they see. The theme of 1,500 feature pictures in the years 1920, 1925 and 1930, i.e. 500 from each year were analysed. Three principal subjects were dominant : love, crime and sex. The pictures in which the dominant theme was love were built about such situations as : (1) love conquers all—against a back-drop of personal adventure, thrills and suspense, (2) the vagaries of courtship are carried on under extravagant conditions and difficulties, and (3) then we have marriage and its difficulties, involving the eternal triangle in a variety of serious or comic aspects. Crime pictures were found to deal with such situations as : blackmail in its various forms ; political corruption and the link between organized crime and corrupt politics ; racketeers of different types —

[23] These Studies were published in the year 1933

gangsters, professional gamblers, hold-up men and murderers. Sex pictures were related to those which depicted romantic love, the principal difference being the inordinate stress placed upon the manifestations of sex in its more obvious and sensational form. Such themes included extramarital relationships, dissolute living marked by extramarital sex relationships, prostitution and similar conduct, and sex situations, for their own sake, where the principal purpose of the picture was to portray the sexual attractions of leading characters against an exceedingly slender plot. The majority of such themes either clearly impart false values to such life situations as romantic love or inculcate definitely antisocial attitudes in the adolescent.

(*ii*) *Its Relationship to Delinquent Behaviour*. An even more concrete indication of the role of the movies in generating or encouraging antisocial behaviour in young people is shown by their relationship to delinquent behaviour. In this connection the study of Blumer and Hauser is worth citing.[24] The investigators were interested to know the role of the motion picture in the lives of delinquents and criminals of both sexes. The study was made on truants and behaviour problem of school boys and girls ; young criminals in a state reformatory ; ex-convicts, and girls and young women delinquents in a state training school. The interviewers were assured about the secrecy of information given by them. It was found that the influence of movies in bringing delinquency and crime may be direct or indirect. Thus, motivation may take the form either of directly inciting persons to delinquent or criminal behaviour or of inculcating certain antisocial attitudes which predispose them to such conduct.

The direct role of movies in bringing about delinquency and crime was seen in the fact that under the influence of the motion picture, the adolescents indulged in conduct ranging in degree of severity from minor delinquencies, petty thefts, and the like to such activities as robbery with a gun, and even murder. Forty per cent of 110 inmates of a penal institution stated that they received the idea of carrying a gun from the movies : 28 per cent indicated that they gained both the desire for and the specific idea of a hold-up from the movies ; 20 per cent claimed that they received active suggestions as to the various techniques of stealing from the movies ;

[24] Blumer, Herbert and Hauser, Philip M., *The Movies, Delinquency and Crime*

21 per cent stated that the movies taught them ways of stealing and ways of eluding the police.

Indirectly the movies are instrumental in forming general patterns of social attitudes which are receptive to criminal suggestions. Many traits that form the ultimate basis for criminal behaviour are partly conditioned by the motion picture. The patterns of conduct that operate as indirect influence in delinquency and crime include such divergent elements as the idea of "easy money" and luxury to be gained from a life of crime, the stimulation of daydreaming on the part of the adolescent which lays the foundation for future overt delinquent behaviour, and the depiction of specific methods of criminal techniques.

However, in both the cases it is to be pointed out that this effect cannot be completely explained in simple terms of unitary cause and effect. Delinquent and criminal conduct do not result wholly from a single cause, even from so powerful a single cause as the motion picture. This agency operates as one of the factors, which actively predispose a juvenile to commit a delinquency. Delinquency arises from a combination of factors of which the motion picture may be one of them.[25]

(iii) Its Relationship to Sex Delinquency. Another type of conduct in which movies exert a powerful influence is the conditioning of attitudes in adolescents which result in promiscuous sex behaviour. The study of Blumer and Hauser shows, that many young men and boys report that their sex emotions are often highly aroused by passionate love scenes in the cinema. In many instances, this excitement may be communicated to the girl, with the result that illicit sex relations may be entered into after the performance. Under the stimulus of such a motion picture, a relationship between a boy and a girl may progress from an innocent adolescent flirtation to an illicit sexual contact. In certain instances, the sexual stimulation of adolescent boys in the movies has resulted in criminal rape committed either by individuals or by groups.

We have seen above that the movies definitely have some disorganizing effect in spite of their educative and recreational value to some extent. But it is also to be pointed out that their influence upon a particular person or group is directly related to the previous set of attitudes and values of the larger group, i.e. their cultural

[25] For further details see Chapter III.

base. Children who live in disorganized neighbourhoods and communities are,on the whole, most susceptible to the adverse influence of the movies. Those who come from areas where primary controls operate effectively are less liable to be influenced by delinquent or criminalistic suggestions in the movies. In other words, an adolescent who has lived in the delinquent interstitial areas will have acquired a set of attitudes and values that will readily respond to suggestions of antisocial conduct in the movies. Mr. Burt rightly observes, "Delinquency is encouraged rather than specifically generated by the motion picture. Those who have already acquired an anti-social set of attitudes and values may be stimulated to commit delinquent acts. But unless the behaviour pattern is already firmly established, the movies will have little disorganizing effect."[26] Dr. Jain concludes by saying, "To sum up the entire position in regard to the influence of the cinema on the society as a whole in India, it can be held that the greater danger of cinema is that it creates confusion in our minds. Survey of criminals has proved in almost all the countries that the inculcation of artificial and false values of life in a child or in adult mind, if unfit to be reconciled in actual life creates a tendency towards crime. And the cinema strengthens it by creating an artificial world and confusion of values on the one hand, and by teaching them the techniques of committing crimes on the other. But it alone cannot be held responsible for exercising bad influence and the cinema alone does not create decisive influence unless the child or man himself/herself is already vulnerable."[27]

Misuse of Leisure Time and Disorganization

It is also to be pointed out that leisure time not only when spent in these commercial recreational institutions is of disorganizing character, but also if otherwise improperly utilized may bring individual and social disorganization. In Cleveland Recreation Survey conducted under Mr. Thurston in 1918 it was revealed that approximately 75 per cent of the juvenile delinquency in the city grew out of the misuse of leisure.[28] Thurston divided these delinquents into five groups according to specific relationship between their spare

[26] Burt, Cyril, *The Young Delinquent* (1925), p. 143.
[27] Jain, R. K., *op. cit.*, p. 30.
[28] Thurston, Henry, W. O., *Delinquency and Spare Time*, Cleveland Recreation Survey (1918).

time and the type of offences committed. (*i*) This group contained delinquencies that were so considered by the community rather than from the inherently antisocial character of the activity itself. Such activities as playing on and about freight trains, in railroad yards, and other forms of trespassing on private property result from the normal tendency of children to wander about the city. (*ii*) Lack of specific agencies for wholesome recreation and the convenience of unwholesome agencies caused the second general type of delinquency. (*iii*) Adolescents in this group were considered delinquent because they had stolen money or otherwise performed a delinquent act in order to get money for recreation of a commercialized variety. (*iv*) In the fourth category were listed those who committed a delinquent act in order to gain status in the group with which they were associated in their leisure time, i.e. girls who stole money or committed sex delinquencies in order to buy new clothes. (*v*) The last group is composed of those adolescents whose extreme distaste for the activity that occupied them during the greater part of the day (usually work or school) caused them to seize upon any available method of recreation, no matter how disorganizing it might prove to be. It was pointed out that though most of the delinquencies outlined above were relatively harmless in the beginning, they may result in serious offences. Thus, assault, robbery, gambling, immorality, prostitution and even murder may directly result from such activities, which seem at first perfectly innocent.

The chief cause of leisure time disorganization is lack of adequate recreational facilities as mentioned above. Its effects are more on the children than on adults, because child and play are two inseparable things. Children become entangled in recreational delinquencies because they have nothing better to do and adopt whatever means that come to hand. Such forms of recreations are not inherently vicious, but delinquency may result from such acts which are in themselves perfectly harmless as we have seen above. The child thus appropriates the street, the alleys, the railroad tracks, the vacant plots, and the docks as a playground often at the imminent risk of life, limb and social values. We have already mentioned the effect of truancy and vagrancy on juvenile delinquency in Chapter IV.

CHAPTER XIV

POLITICAL INSTITUTIONS AND CORRUPTION

In the earlier days the communities were small and people knew each other. But with the formation of larger units some kind of control and authority came to be exercised by the rulers and administrators. However, under such a system the privileges of certain groups and inequalities were recognized in various spheres. The feudal system in Europe and the caste system in India are instances in point. The people were bound by the rules of custom and religious ethics. Even where political democracy prevailed it was confined to a selected group of people and often to a limited area.

With the formation of absolutist nation states during the sixteenth and seventeenth centuries in Europe[1] and of the democratic state during the nineteenth century there has been rapid change in the functions of political institutions and public administration.[2] The absolute nation state arose as a protest against various restraints which limited efficiency : the restraint of the Empire ; of the Church and of the feudal system.[3] This later gave place to modern democratic state because of reformation and industrial revolution where the worth of the individual was recognized. The democratic state which in earlier stages implied political and civic equality, later sought for economic and social equality as well. With this new concept of democracy the democratic state took the form of democratic welfare state. This implies a tremendous change in the structure of the government and a large increase in its functions. Without going into the evolution and complexity of modern democratic welfare state, functions of public administration and the mass democracy which have been discussed elsewhere,[4] here we want to

[1] Lindsay, A. D., *The Modern Democratic State* (1943), p. 1.

[2] *Ibid.*, p. 1. Also see Laski, H. J., "Democracy" in *Encyclopaedia of the Social Sciences*, Vol. V (1937), pp. 76-84.

[3] Lindsay, A. D., *op. cit.*, p. 5.

[4] For details see my book, *Welfare State and Democratic Planning.*

confine our discussion to political institutions, public administration and their relation to corruption.

Corruption in Ancient Period

In the early days, the smaller areas of the states where people knew each other, and because of its limited activities the problem of corruption was not so acute. Even if the corruption was there its forms were different. "In primitive and medieval societies the scope of public authorities was minimum. Many of the matters that were looked after by the community have now become a function of the State. Often offices were hereditary and requisites which would today amount to bribery were congruous of the currently accepted standards of integrity. The smaller compass of state activities and the lack of fluid resources set limits to the opportunities and capacity to corrupt and be corrupted."[5]

In the close type of society where offices were limited to few people of the upper classes the corruption was limited. The new form of democratic government at various levels such as village, town, city, state and central and the expansion of government activities have led to the various forms of corruption. The impersonal nature of the government, where the loss is to the corporate body or the state and by corruption the interests of both parties are served it is very difficult to deduct it. Thus, the problem is a complex one involving social, economic, legal, political and other factors. However, before we deal with these factors it will be appropriate to discuss what is corruption.

Corruption Defined

As corruption is a very complex phenomenon and takes various forms it is rather difficult to define it. It involves all types of persons and groups such as politicians, officials, policemen, and other citizens including businessmen, industrialists, bankers, etc. whether as individuals or groups including white-collar criminals who break the laws and do not live by honest means. The Committee on Prevention of Corruption (1964) observes, "In its widest connotation, corruption includes improper or selfish exercise of power and influence attached to a public office or to a special position one occupies

[5] Government of India, Ministry of Home Affairs, *Report of the Committee on Prevention of Corruption* (1964), p. 6.

in public life."[6] It further adds while it is true that the securing of some kind of pecuniary or other material advantage directly or indirectly for oneself or family, relative or friends, constitutes the most common form of corruption, other forms of the evil are coming into existence in the ever-increasing complexities of modern society. Professor Muhar observes, "Corruption may assume several forms. It may merely mean the exertion of some undue influence, political or otherwise, on the public functionary or it may be consequence of some invisible family or caste bonds and it may be the result of some financial inducements. Whatever the shape it takes, the essential element is the attempt to influence, from the outside, the operations of the due process, it being of little consequence, whether the influence is towards correction, expedition or deprivation."[7] As defined by Robert C. Brooks, "Political Corruption is a wilful failure to perform a specified duty in order to receive some direct personal gain. Such corruption involves an unlawful act performed for some tangible or intangible quid pro quo."[8] The corrupt individual defines the situation as one of personal aggrandizement, instead of service and co-operation. Corruption is not confined to any particular person whether a politician or a business man, but is a product of the mores of an acquisitive society, where financial values are uppermost and the pragmatic sanction of conduct lies in its pecuniary sense.

Another term used in place of corruption is "graft". Graft is an illicit profit earned by corrupt means especially in public life. Graft is a comprehensive category and covers a variety of sins. The irregularities subsumed under the terms may range from the cigar accepted by a policeman who has overlooked a minor traffic violation to a swindle (cheat money out of person or fraudulent scheme) in a metropolitan area, which costs the community millions of dollars. "Graft is the abuse of control over the power and resources of the state for the purpose of personal or party profit which need not be pecuniary in nature . . . in fact graft is merely a particular phase of corruption."[9]

[6] *Ibid.*, p. 5.

[7] Muhar, P. S., "Corruption in the Public Services in Indta" in *Aspects of Administration*, (Eds.) Avasthi, A., and Verma, S. N. (1964), p. 145.

[8] Brooks, R. C., *Corruption in American Politics and Life* (1910). Also see Elliott, M. A., and Merrill, F. E., *Social Disorganization* (1950), p. 525.

[9] *Ibid.*, p. 536.

The graft involves two elements. Firstly, there is abuse of power which may be legal, customary or ethical, i.e. either it violates the law, or runs contrary to customary practice or it is contrary to the best ethical standards and secondly, it involves definite and ascertainable profit, which may be pecuniary or it may be in the nature of special favours gained to the dispenser of the graft. Each of the grafting agencies defines community situation in a selfish and highly individualistic manner.

Causes of Corruption

Corruption in one form or another has always existed. Kautilya in his Arthasastra refers to the various forms of corruption prevalent in his time. Nor is corruption peculiar to India. In his book on *Ethics of Government*, Paul H. Douglas, Senator from Illinois points out, "Corruption was rife in British public life till a hundred years ago and in U. S. A. till the beginning of this century. Nor can it be claimed that it has been altogether eliminated anywhere."[10] However, the scope of corruption was limited in primitive and medieval societies. As already stated there are many factors which give rise to corruption. However, there is a general belief that there has been a great rise in corruption in our country after Independence. The main factors of corruption are : (*i*) large areas of political bodies, (*ii*) close connection between politics, and big business, (*iii*) the spoil system of democratic government, (*iv*) expanding activities of the government and scarcity of commodities, (*v*) change in values, (*vi*) expansion of money economy, and (*vii*) lack of adequate machinery to deal with corruption.

(*i*) *Large Areas of Political Bodies*. Forms of Government for the local community were established in a period when the communities were small, homogeneous and the majority of the citizens were both interested in and informed about the central political problems. The collective will of the community could then find adequate expression through the mechanism of local government, whereas the machinery is now manipulated in the interests of the small and plundering group. Certain politicians, racketeers, high officials, big businessmen, bankers and legislators now profit by using the local governments (municipal corporations, state governments or central government) for their own ends, while the ordinary members of the community often receiving only a minimum of

[10] *Report of the Committee on Prevention of Corruption* (1964), p. 6.

government services. The political structure of the local community becomes disorganized and no longer performs adequately, the functions for which it was originally organized.

(*ii*) *Close Connection Between Big Business and Politics.* The close connection between big business and politics at many places encourages corruption. The great corporate interests have collaboration directly or indirectly with corrupt political interests. While tax reductions and privileges of all kinds are in the hands of government, in return the corporate interests give financial assistance and adopt corrupt practices and cooperate during election campaigns. Similarly, the gangsters employ some practical techniques to further the cause of their political ally at the time of election, because the success of such politicians at the polls is of vital concern to them, as their future freedom for molestation and as well as continued enjoyment of special privileges depend upon their success. He not only votes himself but persuades his friends and relatives to do the same. The good citizens unwillingly aid the gangster and his political allies by remaining apathetically away from the polls. The activities of such gangsters include (1) the falsification, transference and substitutions of ballots, (2) the kidnapping of workers of other parties and even their murder, and (3) proceedings subsequent to the announcement of election returns, such as investigation into illegal election practices or the quashing of indictments upon some technicality.

(*iii*) *The Spoil System of Democratic Government.* The spoil system of democratic government under which the political party in power removes important and responsible city, state and national officials for no other reason than a change in political control from one party to another. There is a group of functionaries called civil servants, but their prestige is inferior to that of politically appointed officers in various capacities. Certain inefficient and incompetent persons are brought into administration.

(*iv*) *Expanding Activities of the Government.* The more the government functions increase, the more the corruption, because of the impersonal nature of the state whose interest suffers at the cost of officials and non-officials who take undue advantage from community funds. Such persons include certain business groups, the corrupt politicians, the corrupt officials and policemen, the owners and operators of vices and the white-collar criminals. The assumption of new responsibilities by the government has resulted in the multiplication of the administrative processes. Administrative powers and discretions are vested at different levels of the executive, all the members of which are not endowed with the same level of understanding and strength of character. Where there is power and discreation, there is always the possibility of abuse, more so when the power and discretion have to be exercised in the context of scarcity and controls and pressures to spend money.

(*v*) *Change in Values.* The corruption is a product of the modern materialistic out-look of the society where financial values are uppermost and those who have pecuniary success are praised by society. They are not concerned with means, whether they are within the laws or not, but are concerned with getting things done.

(*vi*) *Expansion of Money Economy.* In the money economy it is easy to give and take currency notes. The corrupt people can conceal huge amount of money earned by unfair means. When paper money and banks were not in existence it was difficult to hoard money and keep it safe.

(*vii*) *Lack of Adequate Machinery to Deal with Corruption.* "In addition to the various circumstances mentioned above we are of the opinion that two of the major contributory factors for the growth of corruption are, firstly, the partially acknowledged unwillingness to deal drastically with corrupt and inefficient public servants and, secondly, the protection given to the services in India which is greater than that available in the more advanced countries."[11]

Forms of Corruption

Having discussed the general causes of corruption we may discuss the various forms of corruption, i.e. corruption by (*a*) politicians, (*b*) officials, (*c*) policemen, (*d*) businessmen, (*e*) individuals, or white-collar criminals.

(*a*) *Corruption Among Politicians.* The patronage principle is the one which is adopted by the political party to win the largest amount of political support (votes) in exchange of certain appointments (jobs). Such appointments are given to persons, who can produce results in elections without any other consideration of qualification for those assignments. If these appointments were made on the basis of merit, the community would not suffer, but lot of disorga-

[11] Committee Report, *op. cit.*, p. 10.

nization arises from this patronage system which sanctions inefficient workers whose sole qualification is their political zeal and activity.

Apparently the patronage system does not infringe upon the civil service positions. But actually this is not the case. Positions are often filled by, "temporary appointment" pending civil service examination. These appointments are then renewed and examinations are indefinitely postponed.

Similarly, corruption finds its way into legitimate business by roundabout ways. The party in control has the power to purchase material and services for public works and enterprises. When the purchasing agent of the service has complete autonomy, he may demand a percentage of the total cost of any project or enterprise which he awards. In case where law stipulates that contracts under a certain amount may not be allotted on open competitive biddings, large illegal contracts may be awarded by dividing the total contract into small pieces to those firms whom the authority favours. Where the competitive bidding cannot be avoided, specifications in the contract may be so worded that only the company to which they want to favour had the equipment to meet requirements. Patent articles may be demanded, under the full knowledge that the favoured company can possibly fulfil it.

(*b*) *Officials and Corruption.* The above corruption may be done with the connivance of officials. Corrupt officials may be lax in enforcing contracts that a favoured firm may use shoddy material and make an extraordinary gain. Sometimes dummy contractors are introduced to get undue gratifications. They are fraudulently awarded a contract by the authorities to supply certain articles or services, which they purchase from the manufacturers at the lowest possible cost and then resell them at a handsome profit without risking a penny.

In some cases the government officials do not dispose off the cases in proper time. The anxiety to avoid delay many a time forces the client to pay some money. This has been called as "speed money". "Speed money is reported to have become a fairly common type of corrupt practice particularly in matters relating to grant of licences, permits, etc. Generally, the bribe giver does not wish, in these cases, to get anything done unlawfully, but wants to speed up the process of the movement of files and communications relating to decisions."[12]

[12] Committee Report, *op. cit.*, p. 9.

(*c*) *Graft and the Police.* Laws are placed on the statute books against gambling, theft, liquor and prostitution. But they are seldom enforced with strict and implicit severity. Men have always been able to enjoy these forbidden pleasures, provided they are willing to pay for them. Bribery is the means by which payments are made and the laws are ignored. The vice interests and the corrupt politicians are combined against the better elements of the community. The former are able to marshall tremendous financial resources with which to bribe public officials to overlook violations of the moral legal codes.

Against the tremendous power of the vested interests of vice and corruption, the honest police officials have a difficult task in maintaining honesty in their force. The officers and other public servants are often more subservient to a politician than they are to their own bosses. In addition, the honest police or other public officials must be eternally on their own guard or they may be hoodwinked by the dishonest members of their own force who advance their own interests in thwarting their best efforts. An overzealous patrol man who reports a glaring violation of the law may find to his disappointment that this violation has been committed with the full knowledge and consent of superiors.

(*d*) *Businessmen and Corruption.* It has been seen above that corruption cannot be practised by persons in authority alone, unless the businessmen or other citizens collaborate with them. These persons want to get some privileges by paying to the officials or the politicians. Therefore, they encourage corruption to get something illegally or irregularly done by the persons in authority. The Committee observes, "Corruption can exist only if there is someone willing to corrupt and capable of corrupting. We regret to say that both this willingness and capacity to corrupt is found in a large measure in the industrial and commercial classes.... To them, corruption is not only an easy method to secure large unearned profits but also the necessary means to enable them to be in a position to pursue their vocation or retain their position among their own competitors. It is these persons who indulge in evasion and avoidance of taxes, accumulate large amounts of unaccounted money by various methods such as obtaining licences in the name of bogus firms and individuals, trafficking in licences, suppressing profits by manipulation of accounts to avoid taxes and other legitimate claims on profits, accepting money for transactions put through without accounting for it in bills and accounts (on money) and undervaluation of transactions in immovable property."[13]

(*e*) *Individuals and Corruption*. The citizens may break the laws without bribing the officials. For example, they may pay less taxes by showing less profits, etc. "The Income Tax Investigation Commission in the 1,058 cases investigated by it, detected concealed income of the order of Rs. 48 crores. Concealed income amounting to Rs. 30 crores was disclosed by the assessees themselves under the Voluntary Disclosure Scheme of 1951 in 20,912 cases and the amount disclosed thereby was six times the amount originally reported. An unofficial estimate of the Central Board of Revenue is that about Rs. 45 crores of tax is evaded annually by the assessees in the higher income group, the evaded income being about Rs. 230 crores. Much of this tax is evaded without any connivance with any government servant."[14]

The white-collar criminals can be included in this category. Here corruption may be equated with criminal act or behaviour. In fact criminal behaviour and corruption are correlated as we shall see just now. Elliott and Merrill rightly remark, "In fact, political corruption and organized crime are so closely related that one cannot be considered without the other."[15]

White-Collar Criminals. Dr. Sutherland holds that there are two types of criminals : (1) the lower class criminals derived chiefly from the underprivileged economic and social classes whose behaviour is condemned and punished by law, and (2) the "white-collar" criminals who have broken laws so extensively and of such a nature as to indicate they are serious offenders.[16] The latter have manipulated laws and subverted the purposes of Government to their own advantage, but their behaviour has seldom resulted in prison sentences or social rejection. In fact, they have often been elevated to high places and have dictated or influenced the policies of governments. These criminals may be called "white-collar criminals" because they are for the most part in the upper socio-economic class. White-collar crime he calls "a crime committed by a person of respectable and high social status in the course of

[13] Committee Report, *op. cit*., pp. 11-12.

[14] Committee Report, *op. cit*., p. 19.

[15] Elliot, M.A., and Merrill, F.E., *op. cit*., p. 548.

[16] Sutherland, E. H., "White-Collar Criminality" in *American Sociological Review*, February, 1940.

his occupation". Sutherland has made a detailed and extensive study of the problem as represented in the illegal activities of 70 of the largest manufacturing, mining and mercantile corporations in America, in his book, *White-Collar Crime* (1949). He checked the records of each corporation and tried to determine the number of violations of laws with reference to : (1) restraint of trade, (2) misrepresentation in advertising, (3) infringement of patents, trademarks and copyrights, (4) unfair labour practices, (5) financial fraud and violation of trust, (6) violations of war regulations, and (7) other offences. He found that 980 decisions were made by the courts and commissions against the corporations, in which they were held guilty of violating these various laws, and thus each corporation averaged 14 violations. Two corporations were guilty of 50 violations and in 18 of them the verdicts were rendered by criminal courts.

Thus, the recent research of Sutherland has destroyed the validity formerly attached to the belief that the upper middle class and upper economic and social groups are much more law-abiding than other groups. On the other hand, the upper middle and upper classes protect themselves against the full measure of the law and thus tend to retain the respect of the community. In fact, criminal conduct is commonplace among major industrial leaders.

Even when laws are enforced, there has been a differential implementation of them on a class basis. In spite of all this members of the upper middle class believe fundamentally in the validity of law and order, even when they break their own laws. They have not always recognized that only when all groups accept the responsibility entailed in good citizenship that we may expect greater acceptance of the validity of the laws, when applied to lower class offenders.

The inability of this class to appreciate in full this need results in the emergence and growth of white-collar and economic crimes, renders enforcements of the laws, themselves not sufficiently deterrent, more difficult. This type of crime is more dangerous not only because the financial stakes are higher but also because they cause irreparable damage to public morals. Tax evasion and avoidance, share-pushing, malpractices in the share market and administration of companies, monopolistic controls, usury, under-invoicing or over-invoicing, hoarding, profiteering, substandard performance of contracts of constructions and supply, evasion of economic laws, bribery and corruption, election offences and malpractices are some examples of white-collar crime.[17]

Organized Crime and Community Disorganization

Political corruption and notorious criminal behaviour go hand in hand. A city which is politically corrupt is a city where many types of illegal activities go on without any action. The murders go unsolved, gangsters and racketeers ply their activities unhindered. Corruption not only promotes crime, but it itself is a crime. Undermining the public welfare for the advantage of the few, taking the people's money for illicit purposes, and padding the public pay rolls—this is robbery, by whatever name . ' is disguised. It is the corrupt politicians and officials who make other crimes possible. Without the collusion between corrupt politicians and criminals, organized crime will be minimized. It is often the petty offender who is caught and punished by the legal system while the organized type of crime or crime committed by upper class people goes unpunished. It is the lawlessness promoted by the organized crime of the underworld and the organized illegal activities of many forms of business enterprise which have a disorganizing effect in community life. When corrupt officials are caught, they are criminally indicted, but they rarely receive the full penalty of the law as even the court room feels the strength of the politician's power.

Among the organized crime may be mentioned racketeering, gambling, bootlegging or smuggling (liquor), kidnapping, etc. Racketeering may be defined as criminal conspiracy for the purpose of exploiting various types of business and industry, legal and illegal, for profit. Racketeers carry on activities like illegal prostitution in hotels, supply of liquors in prohibited areas, counterfeiting and such other activities which bring large profit and at the same time have disorganizing effect on the community. Thus, racketeering has taken many forms, but has always been motivated by the object of "easy money".

Extent of Corruption in India

We have discussed the extent of crime in India in Chapter IV among the lower class people. But these are only the reported crimes and there are many thefts which are not reported. Not only there is loss of property and life in such crimes, but

[17] Committee Report, *op. cit.*, p. 11.

to this must be added the whole cost of administering justice. This includes local, state and national police; the cost of maintaining courts, jails, prisons, reformatories, and probation and parole services which involves a huge amount of public funds. The loss due to corruption and organized crime is even much larger to the community. It has not only disorganizing effect upon the community as a whole but there is a huge loss to the public funds by less collection of taxes on the one hand and paying more to businessmen and contractors on the other. It ultimately effects the poor man.

However, it is difficult to detect the cases of corruption, bribes and malpractices, because of their dubious nature. In the case of evasion of taxes it is much more difficult to detect because generally in such cases only one person or party is involved. Even where two parties are involved both get some benefit at the expense of state, which is impersonal. However, the Committee on Prevention of Corruption (1964) observed that corruption increased during the Second World War and more after Independence. The immense war efforts during 1939 to 1945 which involved an annual expenditure of hundred of crores of rupees over all kinds of war supplies and contracts created unprecedented opportunities for acquisition of wealth by undoubtful means. The extension of economic activities of the government with a large armoury of regulations, controls,

TABLE 32

COMPLAINTS ABOUT CORRUPTION, VIGILANCE CASES AND FIRMS INVOLVED IN VIOLATION OF IMPORT/EXPORT REGULATIONS[18]

Year	*Cases under Vigilance Division*		*Complaints received by special police establishment*	*Firms involved in violation*	
	Complaints	*Vigilance cases*		*No.*	*Rupees in lakhs*
1956-57	4676	616	N.A.	N.A.	N.A.
1957-58	8540	3694	2733	N.A.	N.A.
1.4.58 to 31.12.58	8313	3714	3310	90	77
1.1.59 to 31.12.59	10649	10035	3995	58	50
1.1.60 to 31.12.60	10721	13305	2755	74	37
1.1.61 to 31.12.61	10481	15116	3380	156	48
1.1.62 to 31.12.62	20461	19277	3847	73	26

[18] Committee Report, *op. cit.*, pp. 14-15.

licences and permits provided new opportunities. The quest for political power at different levels made successful achievement of the objective more important than the means adopted.

As there was no machinery to deal with corrupt politicians, and only public servants could be comprehended with the existing law, the extent of corruption could only be known among them. The figures in Table 32 give some idea about the extent of the problem.

However, this should not mean increase in cases of corruption. (1) Because increase in complaints and investigations may be due to more intensified efforts against corruption. (2) All the complaints and vigilance cases do not relate to charges of bribery and corruption. Some of them are in respect of other types of disciplinary offences. However, it cannot be denied that corruption is on the increase due to the various factors mentioned above.

Measures for Controlling Corruption

The problem of corruption and white-collar crime is very complex and there are many interlocking factors involved in it. The political system, the politicians, the businessmen, the officials, the ordinary citizens and our social values are wrapped in it.

The parliamentary system of government in which there are more than one political parties in the country, is considered to be an ideal one, yet in actual practice it suffers from so many drawbacks, such as political corruption, inefficiency of the government, etc. They often promote legislation which is favourable to particular groups who have big industrial concerns or run commercialized vices. As Mr. Sullivan points out, "Actually, organised crime could not exist if it were not fostered by corrupt politicians and corrupt police."[19] But at the same time it is to be pointed out that collusion between politics and crime could not exist if there were any genuine concern for social welfare on the part of the citizens as a whole. The civic interests of the majority of people are obscured by concern for their own advancement. The tragedy is that the average citizen is so busy in making his own livelihood or contriving to augment it that he seldom develops any true civic consciousness. The business enterprises in which he invests his time and money are often organized according to dubious ethical principles, although within the law. Virtually any business practice is condoned so long as the clients

[19] Sullivan, Edward D., *Rattling the Cup on Chicago Crime* (1929), Chapter 13.

do not suffer heavily and object to its ethics. In fact, "Corrupt business practice, corruption in politics and organized crime constitute a formidable interlocking directorate of community disorganization. All are interested in the same goal—reward without effort."[20] The reason for such conditions lies in the tragic dichotomy in social values. Every human being admires honesty, courage and decency. But concern over such fundamental abstractions is overbalanced by the more powerful desire to taste the forbidden fruits of wealth, social privilege and social favours. Freud points out that every individual is a battleground between conflicting inclinations, those arising out of a desire to conform to the dictates of his conscience and those tendencies to aggression which arise out of his own frustrations. Thus, the forces promoting the community well-being and those striving for selfish ends at the expense of community are often in conflict within the individual.

But this conflict has to be reconciled through proper education so that democracy may work successfully. Every individual ought to put community welfare above his own welfare, if those are in conflict. It mostly lies with the national leaders to reconcile the problem of social well-being with the tendencies of those in political control who act to their own advantage. Such responsibility is not only that of the political leaders but also of public servants such as police officials, administrators directly concerned with public funds such as Income Tax Officers, Sales Tax Officers, and other tax collectors concerned with public money to discharge their duties honestly, judges concerned with justice to perform their duties impartially, etc. Let us discuss the role of some of these in brief detail. Besides, sometimes there are administrative delays which compel certain persons to bribe to expedite their work.

Thus, the measures which can be suggested to check white-collar crime and corruption are (*i*) honesty among politicians, public servants and businessmen, (*ii*) change in social values, (*iii*) civic sense among the public, (*iv*) administrative measures to avoid delays, (*v*) restriction on government functions, (*vi*) adequate legislation, and (*vii*) proper machinery to enforce laws against corruption.

I. *Honesty Among Politicians, Officials and Businessmen.* As stated above corruption is a complex phenomenon and the politicians, officials and businessmen are all inter alia involved in it.

[20] Elliott, M. A., and Merrill, F. E., *op. cit.*, p. 555.

Thus, to lessen corruption, honesty among all these sections is necessary.

(*i*) *Honesty Among Politicians.* It has already been pointed out that parliamentary system is the best system of government so far discovered by human beings. But it too has certain deficiencies and weaknesses. The politicians misuse the power to serve their own ends which brings loss to the community. Therefore, honesty among politicians is most essential. The Committee observes, "There is a large consensus of opinion that a new tradition of integrity can be established only if the example is set by those who have the ultimate responsibility for the governance of India, namely, the Ministers of the Central and State Governments."[21]

(*ii*) *Honesty Among Public Servants.* These public servants may be divided into three categories (*a*) policemen, (*b*) other public servants, and (*c*) judges.

(*a*) *The Policemen.* The police officials are responsible for maintaining peace and avoiding and detecting crimes. Many policemen are honest, but some of them often accept bribe and let the culprit go. Or, sometimes they lack training and are unable to apprehend offenders, whether murderers, bank robbers or highway robbers. This gives a sense of insecurity to the public.

Police executives should be well-trained men conversant with the law, criminology and the social science. They should be well versed in the personnel of gangsters and vagabonds, should know the city and have full knowledge of what is happening in every section of the community. The subordinate police should also have good training and high morals. Further, the police force should also be sufficient to have proper vigilance. No doubt if all the members of the community are basically concerned with carrying out community responsibilities, police needs might be relatively less. But as things stand, where religious control is less, and material prosperity is honoured, the civic corruption is on the increase, which need increasing vigilance on the part of the police.

(*b*) *Officials.* Among the officials may be included tax collectors and officials directly concerned with the use of public funds such as officials of public works departments, ticket examiners, etc. Such officers must work honestly if the state is not to suffer undue loss.

(*c*) *The Courts.* Even where policemen are attempting to do an honest piece of work, interference through political controls may

Committee Report, *op. cit.*, p. [illegible]1.

result in dismissal of cases. Therefore, judges have to be impartial and have to work without any political pressures. The recent enquiries by the Committee reveal that corruption exists in the lower ranks of the judiciary all over India and in some places it has spread to the higher ranks also.[22]

II. *Change in Social Values.* Dr. Sutherland's researches on the white-collar criminality had made us realize that criminality is a common human trait rather than confined to particular persons. If social acceptance makes one type of criminal respected and another subject to the stern disapproval of the group, we will have to find the basis for reorganizing our approach to the treatment of crime. But we shall reconcile differences in social definitions of crime only by altering the basic requirement for achieving respect from that of possessing wealth to one of accepting the responsibility for abiding by legal restrictions in order to promote the common good. Thus, we will have to build up a more generally accepted code of behaviour among all ranks and conditions of men. Those who commit such acts should be discarded and given due publicity.

III. *Civic Sense Among General Public.* The civic sense is to be developed among the general public. People must observe honesty and follow laws. Public welfare must be put before private interests. The ideals of honesty and social welfare must be put into practice. The Committee observes, "It is a matter of serious concern that at present education is thought of merely as process of sharpening the human brain with a view to utilising it for materialistic ends.... Ways and means have to be found to ensure that idealism and patriotism have their proper place in the ambition of our youth. The lack of moral earnestness, which has been a conspicuous feature of recent years is perhaps the greatest single factor which hampers the growth of strong tradition of integrity and efficiency."[23]

IV. *Administrative Measures.* The Committee on the Prevention of Corruption (1964) observes that the main effort for checking corruption in each department and for creating an environment which will discourage any temptation to stray away from the path of integrity must come from within the department concerned. The procedure for the exercise of power, and levels at which power is to be exercised is to be thoroughly examined.[24] The administrative

[22] *Ibid.*, p. 109.
[23] *Ibid.*, p. 109.
[24] *Ibid.*, p. 42.

delays should be avoided as far as possible. This will be possible if public have easy access to officials and are supplied necessary information at the enquiry office.

V. *Restriction on Government Functions.* There is need of restriction on government functions. It is true that under the modern concept of welfare state the government cannot divest itself from all regulatory functions. But it would be of interest if government takes up only those functions which are necessary for it. It should not take up those functions which can safely be entrusted to the public. The main criteria in assigning these functions to various agencies should be the public good.[25]

VI. *Legislative Measures.* The substantive law relating to bribery, corruption and criminal misconduct is contained in the Indian Penal Code and the Prevention of Corruption Act, 1947. However, under the existing legislation only public servants are covered. It would be better if all the Ministers, Deputy Ministers, Parliamentary Secretaries and members of local bodies are also brought into the purview of this legislation as recommended by the Committee on Prevention of Corruption, 1964. The persons who offer bribes or try to influence public servants indirectly through parties, feasts, etc. should also be severely dealt with.

VII. *Proper Machinery for Enforcement of Laws Against Corruption.* During the Second World War the Government of India felt that the enormously expanded expenditure for the purpose of war has brought a situation in which unscrupulous and antisocial persons, both officials and non-officials, were enriching themselves at the cost of public. Therefore, an organization known as the Special Police Establishment was created in 1941 to deal with such persons. In March 1947 the Prevention of Corruption Act was passed to deal with corruption cases in a more effective manner. Some amendments were made in this Act on the recommendations of the Bakshi Tek Chand Committee set up in 1949 to review the working of this Act. To cope with expanding government activities an Administrative Vigilance Division in the Ministry of Home Affairs was set up in August 1955, along with vigilance units in various Ministries or Departments. The Vigilance Division was to provide the necessary drive, direction and co-ordination to various units in the Ministries or Departments. A Commission of Enquiry was appointed by the

[25] For functions of Welfare State see my book, *Welfare State and Democratic Planning*.

Government of India in December, 1956 to inquire into and report on the administration of nine Dalmia-Jain Companies. The Commission submitted its report in June, 1962. It suggested certain changes in the Indian Companies' Act of 1956 to avoid certain malpractices in the administration of Companies and also recommended for the re-integration of administrative departments dealing with different aspects of the corporate sector. However, the machinery was still inadequate and the Committee on Prevention of Corruption (1964) recommended that a Central Vigilance Commission should be set up with more extensive powers to deal with these cases effectively. This Commission has now been set up.

For dealing with cases of corruption against Ministers the Committee recommended that the Prime Minister or Chief Minister should refer the matter to the Committee, whose members should be drawn from a panel constituted by the President of India. The Committee may consist of three persons one of whom should be a man from judiciary. The Committee may take the assistance of Central Bureau of Investigation for investigations, if necessary. There should also be a code of conduct for the members of parliaments and assemblies and they should not use undue influence with ministers or officials to get permits, licences, etc. If there is any breach of the code it should be investigated by the Committee of Privileges.

For dealing with corruption among judiciary the Committee recommended for the setting up of vigilance organizations in all High Courts under the overall guidance of the Supreme Court.

However, in the end the Committee points out that it is a long-term problem which requires firm resolve and persistent endeavour for many years to come.

CHAPTER XV

FAMILY DISORGANIZATION

THE family is by far the most important primary group in society. "Though almost everybody is born in a family and seems to know and understand what family is from first hand experience, yet the many special studies which have been devoted in recent years to 'The family' bring out very prominently how very difficult it is to define precisely and briefly the institution of family."[1] In a recent study of the family Burgess and Locke have defined, "family as a group of persons united by ties of marriage, blood or adoption ; constituting a single household ; interacting and communicating with each other in respective social roles of husband and wife, mother and father, son and daughter, brother and sister ; and creating and maintaining a common culture".[2] They also point out that the two necessary elements in the definition of a phenomenon are that (*i*) it should be wide enough to include all cases to be covered, and (*ii*) it should be specific enough to exclude all marginal cases, like the household, kin, fraternity, etc., if we are concerned with defining the family. Maciver and Page have defined family as follows : "Family is a group defined by a sex relationship sufficiently precise and enduring to provide for the procreation and upbringing of children. It may include collateral and subsidiary relationships, but it is constituted by the living together of mates forming with their off-spring a distinctive unity."[3]

In spite of so many variations in the form of family from country to country we may point out that in a broader sense a family consists of husband and wife and their dependent children, though in India where joint family system prevails "a Hindu joint family consists of all the descendants in the male line from a common ancestor, their wives and unmarried daughters".[4] Even in joint families there is a lot of variation. "On the basis of number of generations living

[1] Parbhu, P. N., *Hindu Social Organization*, (1954), p. 204.
[2] Burgess, E. W., and Locke, H. J., *The Family*, (1954), p. 8.
[3] Maciver, R. M., and Page, C. H., *Society*, (1950), p. 238.
[4] Mulla, M. D., *Handbook of Hindu Law*, (1955), p. 128.

in one household, the presence or absence of married couples, and the number of dependent members, four distinct types have been differentiated by Ross and five by Desai."[5]

Among various forms of family there may be a family without children ; or with adopted children , or with a man having a different abode of his own from the women and children ; or with more than one wife or husband or both ; or in which there is the widowed mother with her children ; or in which there is the single mother with her adopted child, etc. However, it is the monogamous type of normal family consisting of mother, father and their children which is found in most of the civilized countries and the form which is likely to predominate in future. Here we are concerned with this type of family.

Family and Society

The family in its earliest origins began as a reproductive or biological association, but gradually it has developed into a primary social unit of the highest importance to the individual and the society both. As Maciver and Page observe, "of all the organizations, large or small, which society unfolds, none transcends the family in the intensity of its sociological significance. It influences the whole life of society in innumerable ways, and its changes, reverberate through the whole social structure. It is capable of endless variation and yet reveals a remarkable continuity and persistence through change."[6]

The family as an institution has many important functions to perform. It has emerged in order to satisfy certain very basic biological, psychological and social needs of man. And even though recent social and economic changes have deeply affected the form and character of the family, yet they have not changed the basic biological facts and the social needs which create the essential functions of family. Though some of the original functions such as the educational, the economic, the recreational and the religious have been gradually taken away by other social and state agencies, yet its basic functions which centre round the primary bio-psycho-social needs of man have not been affected. In the words of Maciver and Page, "The primary functions of the modern family include (*i*) the procreation and the care and nurture of the young, (*ii*) the

[5] Dutt Gupta, Bela, *Contemporary Social Problems in India*, (1962), p. 75.
[6] *Ibid.*, p. 240.

more stable satisfaction of the sex needs of the partners, and (*iii*) the sharing of a home, with its combination of material, cultural, and affectional satisfactions. Only in a successful family are these three functions so united that each of them reinforces and enriches the satisfaction of the others. Sex becomes not a detached phenomenon as it tends to be in extramarital relations and usually is in prostitution—but part of a larger experience of meeting common problems. And the nurture of the children takes place within the focus of the home which, as considerable evidence seems to indicate, is a more favourable environment for them than that of the state nursery or other public or private agencies. The modern family, increasingly denuded of its older socio-economic activities stands or falls on its ability to harmonise the needs and satisfactions involved in its three essential functions."[7]

According to Shri P. N. Prabhu, "Apart from economic security, the family in many societies affords a religious security to its members. This is particularly true of the Hindu family. The Hindu parents find a spiritual immortality through their sons."[8] "The members used to perform their daily sacred sandhya rites before the same fire, and the daily sacrifices and worship used to be performed at the common hearth."[9]

The interaction of each of the members with others in the family is of profound significance in determining the individual's mental attitudes and his behaviour in society. The psycho-social influence of the family environment on the child is so deep and so quick, that in the view of the psychologists the child acquires almost all its personality and character traits of later adulthood before five, and according to some, even earlier. The recreational needs of the family are often provided by the members themselves, though they have lessened in the urban areas. "The family, the home, is the place where one can look to for personal psychological peace and security. It is the retreat to which man retires after the day's work and his dealings with the outside world to relax, to recoup, and to regain his physical and psychic balance in order to be able to deal effectively with the outside environment again."[10] "All the altruistic attitudes of man could be traced to their roots in the family life.

[7] *Ibid.*, p. 264.
[8] Parbhu, P. N., *op. cit.*, p. 214.
[9] *Ibid.*, p. 222.
[10] Nimkoff, M. E., *The Family*, pp. 76-77,

Co-operation, self-sacrifice, services to humanity, universal brotherhood, love of living beings, have been traced back to their origins to co-operation in the family life."[11] The family also provides for the satisfaction of what Thomas regards as the four "fundamental wishes or desires, viz. the wish for new experience, for security, for recognition and for response."[12] The new experiences, the new stimuli, the new associations the child meets within the family environment aid in its mental and social development. The satisfaction of the need for security begins with the physical and emotional security, given to it from birth onwards by embracing, caressing, nursing and other kinds of personal attention. The need for recognition is satisfied through the roles the child plays in the family, the attention he secures, the statuses he occupies, the approvals he gets therein. The need for response is satisfied through the affection and the comradeship he receives in the family. Shri P. N. Prabhu remarks, "In some civilized societies and predominantly among the Hindus, the original biological functions and the satisfaction of the sex were positively made subservient to the higher values of life, to moral and spiritual life and to life after death."[13]

As the family performs such an important function necessary for a healthful existence, it has come to be characterized as a social and economic unit. All of the mores, folkways, and institutional controls developed in regulating courtship, the marriage ceremonies and the intimate and public relationships of husband and wife are part of the superstructure reared upon the family's vital needs and traditional functions. Thus, "the traditional family performed a variety of functions, which may be subsumed as economic, protective, educational, religious, recreational, biological, affectional, and status giving. . . . This multi-functional pattern no longer exists, except in an attenuated form. The changing society has shifted functions from one institution to another and has removed first one and then another of its traditional functions from the family, until today it is in many respects a mere shadow of its former self."[14]

Functions of the Modern Family

As already pointed out in the foregoing pages that although the

[11] Ellwood, C. A., *Sociology in Its Psychological Aspects*, (1919), p. 213.
[12] Burgess, E. W., and Locke, H. J., *op. cit.*, p. 302.
[13] Parbhu, P. N., *op. cit.*, p. 215.
[14] Elliott, M. A., and Merrill, F. E., *op. cit.*, p. 361.

urban family still performs all its old functions several of them are no longer important as they were before. The economic function on the production side has diminished in importance, though its consumption side still remains with the family. The function of education has been taken away by the State and the family now performs a less educational function. The modern church school in the West has taken up most of the religious training of the children and this combined with the declining role of religion in general has minimized the religious role of family. Similar other traditional functions have been taken up by other institutions. For example commercialized recreational agencies have taken up the recreational function of the family. The status giving function of the family is in a state of flux and the emphasis is more upon the individual and his abilities rather than upon the individual as a member of a particular family group.

The two continuing important functions of the family are its biological and affectional aspects and have assumed greater importance with the decline in importance of the other ones. The biological functions refers to the family's role in providing the socially accepted relationship within which children are born and reared. Marriage also provides the intimate and affectionate response which each individual craves. As social beings men and women require personal and sympathetic understanding which is best secured in the various subtle relationships of marriage. The affectional function may include sympathetic understanding, gratification of the ego, a feeling of emotional security, the sense of being loved and appreciated, and finally the many physical attentions husbands and wives may give to each other.

The Nature of Family Organization

As we have seen above family is the most intimate social group. The unity of any group is a function of the similarity of values and attitudes among the various members and the family is no exception. Thus, complete family organization depends upon the unity of interacting personalities which are held together by certain psychological factors in a normal family. When these factors are present, the family may be said to be an organized unity and when they are not, the family, becomes disorganized. The individual members in a family must knit up the loose webs of their life organization under new and different circumstances. This is particularly so in the case of husband and wife, who have been recently brought together. According to Elliott and Merrill the family organization is characterized by the following three factors, each of which is present to some degree in the normal and unified primary group.

(*i*) *Unity of Objectives*. The organized family possesses a unity of objectives. That is, its members possess similar attitudes on the most important aspects of their joint activities, such as the care and discipline of the children, their education, the allocation of various items in the family budget, the location of the home, the question of sex relations, and other matters of a deeply personal nature.

(*ii*) *Unity of Personal Ambitions*. Complete harmony of personal ambitions with the welfare of the family may be difficult in a democratic society because of different life organizations and different personalities, yet in a well-organized family the individual members must subordinate their interests to the welfare of the family as a whole. For instance, a father, who does not give up his expensive living in order to feed and clothe his family adequately, is failing in a basic function.

(*iii*) *Unity of Interest*. Unity of interests in almost all respects is mostly possible in an agricultural joint family, where in matters of religious practices, education, recreation and economic activities the various members participated as a unit. Such an indentification is difficult in modern urban life, where members of the family develop different interests by virtue of their roles in various secondary groups. However, a similarity of such interests, i.e. religious, recreational, educational, and economic is more favourable to organized family as reciprocal relationships of family life operate more smoothly in such circumstances.

All families are subject to infinite gradation in these criteria of family unity. Perfectly organized families are rare, as is the case with completely disorganized families. Majority of the families struggle through. Their relationships are often marred by bickerings or tensions but they still continue to function on a fairly acceptable plane. For some, however, the tensions become so great that the individuals cannot continue their relationship. These tensions may be gradual developments, growing out of cultural dissimilarities or disparities in age, religious differences, economic difficulties or differences over fundamental values. The cumulative and precipitate crisis which disorganize the individual may also bring about disoganization of the family group. This may take the form of persistent domestic discord which may render harmonious relationships difficult although there may never be an open break in the formal unity of the family, or the tensions may take the extreme form of desertion or divorce. This disorganization of the particular family is then complete both sociologically and legally. Dr. Mowrer calls the first stage as the disintegration of the family and the second as the disorganization of the family. We shall now discuss these factors which lead to disorganization of the family.

Concept of Family Disorganization

In the broadest sense, family disorganization may be thought to include any sort of non-harmonious functioning within the family. Thus, it may include not only the tensions between husband and wife, but those arising between children and parents as well. Tensions between parents and children often present serious problems of adjustment if they are not to result in permanent friction and such disagreements may also result in tensions between husband and wife. However, the children's conflict with parents does not threaten the family organization to so marked a degree as the conflict between husband and wife over fundamental social values, which makes the rifts more serious, leading to the family disruption. Therefore, our discussion of the family disorganization will be mostly confined to the disruptions of the marriage relationship occasioned by tensions between husband and wife. This conjugal relationship is the central bond uniting the family in any society. When this bond is broken, the family is then automatically broken. The existence of the family groups as a functioning unit depends upon the continuation of many personal relationships, which are reciprocal. When this relationship is broken there comes the breakdown in the family organization.

Family disorganization in the external manifestation may take the form of desertion, separation, divorce, physical violence or use of abusive language. But these manifestations are only the superficial symptoms of a breakdown in the intimate relationships within the family. The legal or social function of the normal family life may be maintained even when these personal relationships are at a minimum. Family may continue to live under the same roof because of religious beliefs or economic or social motives which may prompt the wife or the busband to live in the marriage bond, from which love and affection have since long fled. Similarly, the duty towards children or fear of disapproval of parents may keep them together. In some cases the outward family life may be maintained while affectionate interests are satisfied elsewhere.[15] At the same time we must recognize that every normal family experiences conflicts which it is expected to overcome. "Every man and women enter marriage from a separate background, with different ideas and attitudes born out of his or her own experience. Each possesses a scale of values developed out of a particular social group. Under the circumstances, it is not surprising that distinctive personality traits of the one may unconsciously or consciously irritate the other. Only by integrating the husband's and wife's individual desires and attitudes can a successful family life be achieved with a harmonious functioning of the interacting personality."[16] However, it is to be pointed out that tension in family life is growing in the modern age because of the rapid changes in the role and status of the partners. Therefore, before we discuss the causes of family disorganization in detail we may discuss these changes in brief to understand the causes of family conflict in the modern context.

Rapid Changes in the Role and Status of Partners

Many of the adjustments within the family are a matter of unconsciously conforming to traditional attitudes, of accepting roles which conform to the social values expressed in the mores. For example, most women are content to submerge their identity in adopting their husband's name, without raising a question as to the underlying significance of the practice. Similarly, most men assume the economic burden and support of the family quite aside from the obvious economic contribution which their wives might easily make. Many husbands generally have the final decision in establishing a residence, in matters of family finance, and in disciplining the children though in these days there is a notable increase in the number of wives who share in such authority. Similarly, many husbands have presumed that a woman should be *ipso facto* happy

[15] Kinsey has estimated that approximately one-half of all married men have sexual intercourse with one or more women other than their wives at some time during their marriage. Kinsey, A. C., *Sexual Behaviour in the Human Male*, (1948), p. 585.

[16] Elliott, M. A., and Merrill, F. E., *op. cit.*, p. 334.

as his house-keeper, cook and body servant and they find difficult to understand any rejection of these roles.

But when the socially sanctioned patterns of family life become too rigid or conflict too seriously with personal attitudes, the serenity of family life is disturbed. The family, like any other human institution, should be organized to meet the present needs of men. New inventions, new standards of living, and new external situations necessitate adjustments in life schemes and redefinition of social values. Old situations yield to the new and, therefore, the social values along with attitudes of persons must change with time if the family organization is to be preserved. If a woman is gainfully employed in the industrial world or achieves a professional success, she will look to her husband as a comrade rather than as a lord or master. Similarly, the wife may see no valid reason why marriage should confine her to the four walls of the home. This challenge of social values has contributed to the chaos in family standard. But part of this chaos is due to the undefined attitudes of the women to their future role. Women are not certain what they want. They have proved that they can master the arts and sciences if they apply their energy in that direction. But unfortunately professional achievement is no measure of individual happiness. In their distinctive role as wives and mothers they have to continue to perform their vital role, both in the family and in the world outside.

Status and role in marriage are also in a process of rapid change, as husband and wife are called upon to assume new social positions and play new parts in the society and family. The traditional pattern of family structure evolved with the time. But the situation has so altered by the rapid changes in the technology that many former patterns no longer apply, while in numerous cases these patterns are the only guide the individual has to his own behaviour or that of his spouse. The role patterns are thus disorganized and the family group partially breaks down. Confusion in role exists in such matters whether the wife shall be employed or who shall manage the household finances and train the children. Formerly, family rights and duties were clearly defined. Today the uncertainty and ambiguity of roles in the family mean that many persons are unable to adjust to their marital obligations. They are never quite sure what their roles actually are. The wife today faces the major confusion in status and role, not because of any temperamental weakness or genic incapacity, but because her behaviour has changed more drastically than that of man. Often she is gainfully employed, participates increasingly in higher education, and bears fewer children than before. In addition to these roles she is expected to be companion, counsellor, practical nurse, romantic love object, and mistress—statuses that are difficult to fulfil satisfactorily even if she was consensus as to their complicated nature.

Moreover, different groups stress her different roles. Business groups tend to emphasize the companion and partner roles. The college professor's wife may be expected to become a junior scholar. The lower economic groups stress the mother and earner roles, while in certain groups wife is expected to play all of these roles. Under the strain of such confusion and bewilderment the family relationships may be strained. Thus, actually new definitions of status and role for the wife involve a corresponding adjustment in the husband. There would be little conflict in the family organization if the husband did not feel that his position was threatened. In the present situation, however, when their roles and statuses are not clearly defined as husbands and wives, they have difficulties in adjustment. At present there is no one consistent pattern for the good wife to follow. Neither she nor society as a whole is sure which of these roles is best for her or for the family. In a sense, each person is forced to improvise his or her role, with no traditional pattern to guide him or her.

Many persons are advocating that family is not what it used to be. This may be true, because husbands and wives no longer play their traditional roles and maintain traditional statuses. But this trend, on the other hand, is deplored by many who consider the old family norms the only possible or desirable ones. They speak of the decline of the family and fail to realize that the family as such is not declining, that merely a particular type of family is in process of change. A new family structure is gradually emerging with different statuses and roles for its members. As Maciver and Page rightly observe, "Economic change has deeply affected the form and character of the family, but it does not affect the basic biological facts and social needs which create the essential functions of the family. We may, in fact, look upon these changes as an aspect of the greater evolutionary process of society, in which its organizations have become specialized to perform more limited and more exclusive functions."[17]

[17] *Ibid.*, p. 254.

Factors Bringing Change in Functions of the Family

Having discussed the changing functions of family and the roles of partners within it, it would be appropriate to discuss the factors which have brought these changes before discussing the causes of family disorganization in the modern family. These factors are economic, political, social and philosophical or religious.

(*a*) *Economic Factors*. The Industrial Revolution has brought series of social changes which have altered the economic basis of society. A striking change has resulted in family organization from this social and economic revolution. Before the advent of the factory system, most of the production processes necessary to life and happiness were carried on within the home. Within the domestic domain the wife and mother boiled and brewed, spun thread and wove it into cloth, which were later used in the house. The family was in a sense a virtually self-sufficient unit. The old order has given place to new, and this is particularly so in urban areas, where there is separation of home from the place of employment. The home is no longer the place where consumption goods are produced or raw products transformed. Instead it has become a distribution and consumption centre conveniently located for the purposes of the family. These changes in economic functions have altered nearly every phase of family relationships.

Likewise, the structure of the family has been markedly modified. More and more married women are joining the ranks of the industrially employed. Family life depends upon its economic base, and the ways a family earns its living goes far towards determining the nature of family organization. However, it needs pointing out that although home is no longer the place where goods are manufactured or processed, it is still the most important consumption centre. In this respect the role of the family has not changed significantly. Carefully planned buying, adequately balanced budgets and reserves for the rainy day must be taken into account if the family is to maintain its economic equilibrium.

Industrial expansion and the consequent increase in the standards of living have made luxuries to take the place of necessities. Many a time multiplication of wants has often exceeded the increase in income. This has affected the family life in a negative way. The young wife may be unhappy because she cannot dress as well as she would like. A recent study in U.S.A. indicated that "spending the family income" constitutes the second most difficult area of marital adjustment (the first being sexual adjustment).[18]

In the earlier periods, many women married as much for economic considerations as for reasons of affection and abiding love. But today many of them who are economically independent look for more than economic support in marriage and are chiefly concerned about sympathy and affection. They are also less willing to endure an unhappy marriage than formerly, since they are in a position to support themselves. On the other hand, many husbands are conservative in their attitudes towards the employment of married women and often resent having their wives work for income. This is a basic conflict which modern society has not resolved and provide the source for much family instability.

The children of the employed mothers are to be cared for in their homes by older members of the family or placed in foster homes, nursery schools, and kindergartens. If they are to be left to their own devices some of these range the streets and get into serious types of juvenile delinquency. Others suffer from emotional deprivations of their isolated status and their personalities experience serious strain. It is difficult to say that we have outlived the child's need for love and affection. Thus, the ambitious woman has to be made to realize that her duty to her child is more important than any economic function that she can render. We are still not in a position to understand as to how the interests of women as persons and their roles as mothers can be affectively reconciled.

(*b*) *Political Factors*. Among the most significant of the changing political aspects of the family is the (*i*) decrease in the family sovereignty, and (*ii*) the change in the legal status of both married and unmarried women.

In many countries the state has recognized the necessity for depriving unfit parents of their right to complete control and authority over their children and the doctrine of family sovereignty is in danger. The state requires the parents to take proper care of their children and deprives them if they are not providing suitably for them. The state as "the larger parent" has assumed the right and authority to protect children against neglectful, ignorant, and vicious parents through the establishment of juvenile courts. The state has assumed, such family prerogatives as the supervision of

[18] Landis, J. T., "Length of Time Required to Achieve Adjustment in Marriage" *American Sociologist Review*, December, 1946.

the child's education, health and conduct. Compulsory school attendance, health clinics, mental examinations, probation officers, laws affecting cruelty to children and to check juvenile delinquency are the extensions of state's assumption of sovereignty over parents and children. However, there is the danger that the state assuming so much responsibility the parents may disavow all responsibility for their children.

The emancipation of women and their successful entrance into politics, education and employment have given them new status. Though there are still certain discriminatory laws against women legally or socially, yet their status has changed a lot. Since child-bearing and child-care impose certain physiological incapacities and limitations upon women, some special protective legislation for them appears to be necessary. Such special provisions do exist in our Constitution.

(*c*) *Social Factors.* The economic and political factors stated above which have altered the structure of the family do possess a social aspect too. But besides those there are certain other distinctive factors which have effected the family relationship and can best be designated as social. Among these may be mentioned (*i*) the mobility of population, (*ii*) higher education of women, (*iii*) changes in sex morality, (*iv*) increasing urbanization, and (*v*) commercialized recreation.

With rapid movement from place to place, family solidarity becomes thin. Standards of conduct, codes, and conventions accepted by the new environments are often foreign to native patterns. The conserving influence of the close neighbourhood is often absent. Higher education among women makes family stability difficult. The girl who attains educational equality with the husband will be a different kind of wife from the one who has no such comparable status. She will probably insist upon a voice in family decisions. Higher education also makes difficult for many women college graduates to marry at all, since the available number of males with higher educational attainments than their own is comparatively small. Men also tend to marry women who have had less education than themselves to maintain the myth of male superiority. Highly educated women may also insist upon getting an employment, which may bring some conflict in the family. Higher education of the wife also bears some relation to the size of the family. Generally speaking, the higher her education the smaller the family will be. The changing sex morality in which many young persons engage in sexual intimacy is also endangering the stability of the family, as the entire family structure is based upon the acceptance of the conventional morality.

The urbanism has brought differentiation in economic interests which is an important factor in the comparative disunity of the urban family. The father earns his bread away from home and his wife often has no comprehension of the task which he performs. As a consequence, she fails to understand his fatigue or boredom when he returns from the office or factory, unless she is a working wife. Similarly, the husband may have little appreciation of the nervous exhaustion which his wife experiences after a day's work. When the work of the family centred about the farm or cottage vocation, there was a meeting of minds, an understanding among the members concerning the nature of their various tasks. The urbanization and industrialization have made this family consensus difficult.

The overcrowded conditions under which the urban family must live have made an additional contribution to its instability. The modern city apartment lacks privacy, so essential to an integrated personality. There is seldom a suitable place to "spread out" for each member of the family is continually under the close supervision of the others. Virginia Woolf in her book *A Room of One's Own* (1929) made a strong plea for individual privacy for creative living and thinking.

The crowded city home offers little opportunity for leisure-time activities. Seldom does the urban family actively partake of any recreational event as a unit, and the recreational functions have been assumed by other agencies particularly the commercialized recreational agencies whose effects are often disorganizing upon the young and adolescents. Recreation in the old-fashioned sense of creating one's own good times through games, music, and conversation is becoming virtually a lost art for many city families.

(*d*) *Philosophical or Religious Factors.* Philosophical factors include changing beliefs, ideals and social values of the group, which have affected family life. Among these may be included (*i*) decline of the religious theory of marriage, (*ii*) materialistic and individualistic philosophy, and (*iii*) proposed new philosophies.

(*i*) The decline of the religious theory of marriage and the consequent acceptance of the contractual basis have been important factors in altering the conception of the nature and permanence of family. Marriage is no longer regarded as a sacrament to be broken only by death, but has become a contract which may be broken by desertion, separation and divorce.

(*ii*) The growing secularism of the modern world has fostered this secular attitude towards marriage. The deterioration of religious controls in matters of family life has been accompanied by a widespread acceptance of a materialistic philosophy which has accelerated family disorganization. Hedonistic creed has created this tendency as to why a man should subject himself to a life which yields little pleasure. The emphasis on material comforts and the insistence upon high standard of living also affects family stability. Similarly, the emphasis upon the individual's right to happiness and insistence upon living one's own life wrecks family harmony. The successful marriage implies mutual sharing, giving and taking, with necessary sacrifices to personal whims.

(*iii*) Some new philosophies of marriage have been advocated by certain individuals which have been taken too liberally. For example, Ellen Key in her book, *Love and Marriage* (1911) advocated the philosophy of freedom to enter free unions if they were sufficiently mature and sufficiently in love, while Mrs. Dora Russel in her book, *The Right to be Happy* (1927) advocated the idea of sex freedom as a means of attaining individual happiness. But even the foremost protagonists of sex freedom apparently cannot tolerate all that such freedom entails. E. C. Parsons advocated for the trial marriage. Such marriage was to be entered into with the idea of permanence if it proved satisfactory, but there was to be the privilege of breaking off an unsatisfactory marriage without recourse to legal machinery. All of these proposals have received the due share of their criticism, but they reflect the changing environment in which the family exists.

Maciver and Page have emphasized on three main factors bringing change in the role of women and affecting family life. They are (*i*) decreased control of the marriage contract, (*ii*) changing economic role of women, and (*iii*) decline of religious control. The marriage contract today is entered into more autonomously by both men and women. People are less subject to parental control and other forms of social pressure concerning whom and when they shall marry. The principle of male dominance and female obedience has been affected by changing economic role of the women. Thus, an important factor in bringing about the new character of the marriage contract is the increasing degree of economic independence attained by women and this has resulted towards equality in status. Marriage has become today essentially a civil contract, though it is often attended by religious rites. This has affected the sexual asceticism and realities of sex and the new position of women and of family life has been realized. They further add, "Not only economic and religious changes but the whole process of modern civilization within which they fall has worked towards giving women a new position in society and especially in their relation to men. The reduction of the functions of the family, the lightening of the tasks of home, bringing more leisure to larger number of women, the shortening of the period of child bearing or the lengthening of the interval between the arrival of successive children, these and other conditions have transformed the family into a new kind of partnership and created new problems for the family of the present and of the future."[19]

Causes of Family Disorganization

There have always been men and women who found their marriage ties bitter, their life together unhappy. A changed economic and social order has only facilitated release from such bonds. Marriage has now taken on a more personal aspect so far as wishes, desires and attitudes of the contracting parties are concerned. Maciver and Page point out that, "the modern instability of the family is revealed by the frequency of divorce, separation, desertion and other evidences of disharmony or lack of cohesion which come to light particularly in the courts, in social work, and in marriage clinics".[20] This is mainly due to less social pressure and replacement of domination by co-operation and stability is more in autocracy of one than in mutual consent. Thus, the number and intensity of tensions affecting the stability of the family has increased. Family tension is any conflict situation which generates opposing attitudes between its members particularly between husband and wife. In a sense tension grows out of an original disparity in attitudes and values and as the tension increases greater antagonism in attitudes develops.

[19] *Ibid.*, p. 258.
[20] *Ibid.*, p. 268.

Personal and Impersonal Factors in Tension

These tensions are the result of vast impersonal forces and personal antagonisms. However, the latter plays a greater part in family breakdown, which means disparities in attitudes and values which make life together intolerable to one or both. Hornell and Hart observe, "Marriage is more than a sex relationship with prescriptions for caring for offspring. In fact it is a functional relationship between two personalities involving some varied items as habits, friendships, aversions, property, ideals, attitudes, purposes and potentialities. When husband and wife love each other, their two personalities function more effectively, because of the marriage relationship. When husband and wife thwart each other, or attempt to enslave each other, the marriage is a disaster."[21]

Some of these tensions arise out of personality structures of the mates and make them more or less incompatible at the outset. These personality characteristics may include temperament, philosophy of life (disparity of values), personal behaviour patterns and psychopathic personalities which in the beginning may be hidden in the romantic fallacy. The other tensions may arise out of economic and occupational situations, cultural differences (including education), differences in social status, matters of ill-health, parent-child relationships, and interference of in-laws. Thus, these factors are both personal and impersonal. However, it may be pointed out that family conflict and disintegration often result from a combination of factors rather than from one specific item. It is, however, true that one particular situation may set a long list of factors into operation, and play an important role in the development of family tension.

(a) Personal Factors

(*i*) *Romantic Fallacy.* We have pointed out above that romantic fallacy brings many lovers together these days because of less parental control in the choice of mates and founded on freedom of choice owing to rising democracy and other social forces such as emancipation of women in religion, in economic affairs, in politics and above all in the power of marital choice. In fact equality of sexes was an important factor in the romantic courtship, which gives the individuals more liberty.

[21] Hornell and Hart, Ella, "Unsuccessful Marriages", in the Journal, *The World Tomorrow*, June, 1927.

A marriage which is based exclusively upon the dreaming and extravagant vagaries of romantic idealism without consideration of money, social position, cultural dissimilarities and parental objections, faces a tremendous handicap. The wives and husbands who are convinced that romantic happiness is the sole criterion of marriage are likely to think that something has happened when the edge has worn off the first careless rapture. They may believe that the only way that they can recapture this romantic infatuation is with another spouse. On the other hand, marriage is a practical and serious relationship, not romantic interlude. The person later on concludes that he has made an unfortunate initial choice and the joy of true romance may be realized more completely with someone else.

To many persons romantic love is the essence of all affectional function of the family. These persons enter marriage with ideas derived from many romantic sources the movies, popular magazines, and the like. But the affectional function includes a variety of interpersonal relationship that are necessary if the individual is to develop into a social adjusted human being. Thus, besides the sex attraction, sympathy and conjugal affection are other necessary important elements of affection which young persons do not realize at that stage. As Mr. Thomas points out, "The wish for response is the basis of the affectional functions of the family. This sentiment is primarily related to the instinct of love and in the tendency to seek and give signs of appreciation in connection with the other individuals. The romantic love expects to seek and give signs of appreciation at all times and at all places. In fact, he confidently expects to devote his life to this enchanting activity, an expectation that is approximately realized during the few weeks and months of marital intimacy. But the continuation of such a relationship ultimately decreases in intensity and satisfaction, unless supplemented by the calm pleasures of conjugal affection. During this period of decreasing romantic ecstasy, many persons begin to question the validity of their marriage. They do not realize that romance is not all to the successful union."[22]

Thus, the romantic fallacy is the cause of many family tensions for newly-married young couples. In the beginning they could not understand fully the biological attraction which makes each think the other the most charming person in the world. In after years, no

[22] Thomas, W. I., *The Unadjusted Girl* (1923), p. 17.

amount of good breeding or social training can keep them from recognizing the disparities in temperament, attitudes, habits or emotional nature or other factors, such as social status, etc. which often make marriage seem unpleasant to let down after the expectations of courtship. For marriage is a way of life involving continuous effort if adjustments are to be made satisfactorily. Personal tensions are often disturbing for young married people, who cannot understand "how they ever could have loved each other", when they have quarrelled over some minor matter.

(*ii*) *Clashing Temperament*. In the initial acquaintanceship, when each is bent on making a good impression on the other, the real personality and temperament are not brought to light. Later, however, clashes in temperament may take on a violent aspect. The overcritical, pessimistic, nagging wife may make life wretched for the happy, carefree youth who prefers a gay party to spending the evening at home. Or, again one person may be quick-tempered, choleric, and the other quiet, slow to anger. Highly individualized temperaments take on a characteristic pattern of behaviour, which the other resents and dislikes despite a certain bond of affection.

(*iii*) *Philosophy of Life*. More important than temperament is the role of individual's philosophy of life in the marital relationship. If both husband and wife possess some identity of important values, as expressed in the social attitudes, their marriage problems will tend to be adjusted successfully. On the other hand, if they differ on fundamental values, the relations are likely to be strained easily. For example, conflict will always be imminent if the woman's highest aim is social ascendancy, the whirl of bridge parties, and tea parties whereas her husband prefers intellectually stimulated contacts, the new books on art and philosophy, and friendships of a scholarly sort.

(*iv*) *Personal-Behaviour Patterns*. The personal-behaviour patterns may include both habits and the more generalized manner of conduct. Irritating petty habits, insignificant though they may seem, may bring high marital friction. A woman may talk so loudly on the street that she embarrasses her husband. A husband may be accustomed to eating something in the street, whereas his wife was reared in a home where such conduct was an offence to "good manners". Both of these divergences present serious implications because they present a disregard for values which the other has accepted as important.

Even in the most successful marriages there are irritating little habits and mannerisms of which the other was not aware at the time of marriage. If these can be accepted without any serious adjustment of life values, in a spirit of tolerant give-and-take, they may cause no serious trouble. But if they are not able to develop the power of tolerance serious troubles may arise.

(*v*) *Psychopathic Personalities.* Psychopathic personality of one partner or the other may affect marital relationships. Such persons have mental instability and are often charged with cruel and inhuman treatment, mental cruelty, or physical violence (and have the symptoms of psychosis and neurosis).

(b) Social and Cultural Factors or Impersonal Factors

(*i*) *Economic Tensions.* The economic tensions cover a variety of sub-classification and may be due to (*a*) sheer poverty, (*b*) business reverses, or (*c*) economic independence of the wife.

(*a*) *Sheer Poverty.* Despite romantic ideal of love, long-continued worry over financial matters is not conducive to healthy marital relations. Poverty is "of course" a relative term. An income which a middle-class family defines insufficient may be enough for a lower-class family. A person whose income is not enough to meet the necessities of life in a particular position may affect his temper. His wife may be sympathetic, but she is equally worried. Irritated and distressed because the children want shoes or there is nothing to eat she may lose temper, or her husband may leave the house.

(*b*) *Business Reverses.* Business reverses may sometimes bring troubles, particularly when the wife comes from an upper class family and is of aristocrat nature and she is not able to readjust with the existing lower income.

(*c*) *Economic Independence of Wife.* The college girl who has had special training and tasted of success in her field frequently finds herself loath to give up her work when she marries, while the husband may resent her taking job. Where wife and husband are both in the same profession, but the wife's capacity is recognized as surpassing her husband, her spouse may resent playing the inferior role. The professional jealousy in such circumstances may affect marital relations. Similarly, the economic dependence of wife who has a professional career before marriage may become thorn in flesh. She may find it difficult to adjust her experience to fit the scale of her husband's purse. It is often impossible for her to achieve standards of consumption which she enjoyed previous to marriage. As a result she may become dissatisfied with the whole relationship.

(*ii*) *Occupational Tensions.* Closely related to economic tensions are those developing out of the peculiar nature of the day's work. The mobility necessary to a particular line of work is often a source of family tension. Sometimes, they become so accustomed to living apart that they get on each other's nerves when they are together for a long time. Similarly, unstable occupation from store clerk to the insurance business or from salesman to window dresser, the continual readjustment and lean income period inevitably entail family hazards. Burgess and Cottrell found that frequent change of position is correlated with low scores in marriage adjustment.[23]

Occupational misfits may be another cause of marital discord. No amount of income in a business to a young man of literary and academic taste can bring contentment. Disgusted with the business world, which he feels is prostituting his intelligence, he may not be in the proper psychological frame of mind to enjoy the social relationship which his family brings. There arises a conflict between his ideals and practices which may easily be a source of friction in the family.

(*iii*) *Differences in Cultural Background.* When husband and wife come from different cultural backgrounds, there may be no grave difficulty, if both have approximately the same education and are somewhat cosmopolitan in their taste. But persons having different cultural background in the absence of above similarities may find it difficult to adjust. Burgess and Cottrell found that the cultural background of both husband and wife to be one of the five groups of factors affecting family adjustment.[24]

(*iv*) *Disparity in Age.* Any wide disparity in age is likely to mean divergences in attitudes and interests. Regarding age at the time of marriage though there can be no absolute rule as to the ideal age for marriage, yet those marriages appeared to be more successful when both parties were fairly mature or in any case the bride was over twenty-one. Because she then had insight and emotional maturity for marital problems. The age is, however, only one element in this complex relationship.

[23] Burgess, E. W., and Cottrell, L. S., *Predicting Success or Failure in Marriage* (1939), pp. 264-66.

[24] Burgess, E. W., and Cottrell, L. S., *op. cit.*, "The Impress of Cultural Back-grounds", Chapter VI.

(*v*) *Ill-Health.* At the first instance, a sick wife or husband may conjure up a real emotion of sympathy. But long continued ill health, with its drain on the family budget, the irritability because of nervous tension may, however, become a source of many family difficulties. Lack of stimulating contacts, monotonous aspect of house work coupled with the husband's indifferent expression of affection may lead to her nervous breakdown. Good health must be an accepted premise of satisfactory marriage.

(*vi*) *Parent-Child Relationships.* Although childless marriages on the whole are admittedly less successful than those with children, the children themselves may be the centre of family tension and family conflict. There may be disagreement as to the policy of discipline, the type of training, the nature of the child's education, social activities and so on. The father may become jealous of the attention which the wife gives to her children, especially in case of a son, and feel that he is largely shut out from his wife's affections. Similarly, the mother may resent the favouritism which the father displays for his daughter.

(*vii*) *Interference of In-laws.* Parents are often imbued with ambitions and the desire for their children's happiness, and consequently they often insist upon imposing their decisions upon the reluctant children. They may insist that the daughter-in-law is too extravagant, or she is un-cooperative, or she is unsuited to her task as a mother. In countless ways their undue criticism may play havoc with youthful marriage.

In India due to the prevalence of joint family system the interference from the in-laws is too much. In one of the surveys conducted among 414 couples in Uttar Pradesh, who married under the Special Marriage Act, 1954 it was found that 92 out of 114 respondents reported had some irritants in their married life ; they were 54 husbands and 38 wives and the rest did not answer this question. The irritants reported by the marriage partners related to almost all aspects of married life—age, attitude and temper and behaviour of spouse, children, dress and food, habits of spouse, health, housekeeping, income and expenditure, in-laws, servants, sexual relations, manner of talking and language used. Among these the most frequently reported irritants in the married life of these respondents were those relating to attitudes and temper of spouse. These were the greatest source of annoyance for the husbands and the second greatest for the wives. In-laws became the next greatest source of irritation in the marital life of the couples, complaints in regard to them obtained the highest frequency in the wives' list and the third highest in the husbands' list. Their narrow-mindedness, uncertain temper, partial treatment and interference in the couples' affairs, this was the first complaint of both the husbands and the wives ; living with in-laws, for some wives, a nuisance. . . . In order of frequency the third group of irritants related to family income and expenditure. The fourth group of irritants pertained to the condition of health in the family while behaviour of spouse, habits, talk and language were the next three sources of friction in married life.[25]

We have also seen in Chapter II that many of the married couples committed suicide in India due to conflict with their in-laws. An analysis of 37 female mental patients (10% of the total institutional female population) revealed that most of them had unhappy relations with their spouses and in-laws, especially with mothers-in-law.[26]

It may also be pointed out that Indian women have to bear a lot of hardships to adjust themselves properly in the new family. "She does not choose her partner through 'courtship' and enters passively into the strange environment and unknown setting of her husband's family. She has to perform there several delicate roles as a wife, daughter-in-law, sister-in-law and above all the role of 'Grihlaxmi'. She has to discharge her duties with the dexterity of an infallible person. Doing twenty-four hour's service to every one in the joint family is her sacred duty ; but committing even insignificant human mistakes is not pardonable." "Every one demands too much from her but they have little to offer in return. This is the stereotype position of a wife in a typical Indian family. The impact of modern education, social legislation, urbanization and industrial development has sufficiently changed woman's place in our society. Nevertheless she has to encounter innumerable difficulties to adjust herself in the husband's family."[27]

[25] Khan, Nasir Ali, "The Emerging Pattern of Marriage (A Sociological Study of Civil Marriages)", Ph. D. Thesis, Lucknow University, (1963), pp. 242-43.

[26] Mohan, Brij, "Social Work and the Problem of Mental Disorders", Ph. D. Thesis, Lucknow University, (1963), p. 308.

[27] Mohan, Brij, "Dynamics of Marital Adjustment (With special reference to the Patterns of Adjustment in the Indian Family)", Lucknow University, *Journal of Social Work*, December, 1967, p. 52.

Effects of Family Tension

Even though relatively few people find the perfect happiness they assume that marriage had in store for them, many husbands and wives muddle through their domestic problems. They recognize that marriage has much to offer in companionship, sympathetic understanding and conjugal affection. If there are children, the parents find much of their happiness in providing a suitable environment for them and in accepting their role as parents. They eventually realize that the romantic raptures of motion pictures do not exist in everyday life and the calm and pleasant companionship, the dependence of husband and wife in the petty details of their daily life, and similarity of basic values—these are the factors which contribute to the happiness of family life. Majority of men and women thus make fairly satisfactory adjustments, whether from force of habit, social pressure, or for inescapable destiny.

For some couples, however, life does not go on smoothly owing to various reasons discussed above, which tend to interrupt the process of living together. They believe their marriage impossible to continue under such circumstances. Some disorganized families maintain their legal solidarity for reasons of religion, prestige or social pressure, while others severe such bond. Desertion and divorce are the final stages of family disorganization. Divorce is legal status, while desertion is an unofficial indication of the same thing when husband or wife has moved out of the house. Desertion is more among the lower classes than among the upper classes, because of illiteracy and legal and financial difficulties. Desertion may be temporary or permanent. Temporary desertion may be due to low family income and is considered as "poor man's vacation". He leaves his family in order to escape some financial responsibility or when a domestic difficulty has developed he may escape and when the scene has quietened down, he may return. Permanent desertion is a complete break with his family and this has been done after having made certain successive attempts at readjustment. It is a final termination of unsatisfactory relationships.

Extent of Desertion and Divorce in India

No statistics are available about the deserted families in India. Data are also not available about divorces given under the Special Marriage Act, 1954 and the Hindu Marriage Act, 1955.

Social Consequences of Desertion and Divorce

The consequences of both desertion and divorce are similar except that wife and children suffer much more emotionally in the former case because it entails a humiliating rejection of the spouse. It also carries with it lack of certainty. Will the husband return? He may have met death unnoticed. Such are the other problems which the wife and her children have to face.

Disorganization of the family does not end with divorce or desertion. This crisis is the final outcome of the long process of family disorganization. But it is final in the sense that it represents a formal break in a previously intimate relationship. Both husband and wife have to adjust to the new situations. If there are children, their lives must continue in new and strange circumstances. Thus, many consequences follow from divorce.

(*i*) *Personal Disorganization of Divorced Persons.* A certain degree of moral turpitude is often bestowed on the parties in divorce, on the ground that one or both must have committed an immoral or at least an undesirable act. Divorced persons, therefore, often have a sense of guilt, either conscious or unconscious, which complicates their reactions to other persons, whose attitudes in turn are coloured by moral condemnation. When the divorced person is viewed suspiciously by many righteous persons, his difficulties in readjustment are considerably increased.

Divorce also represents a fundamental change in role and status for all concerned. This change may bring crisis in their lives. Only those with a strong and well integrated life organization may survive it with comparative ease. But one has to adjust to the new situation. The preliminary attempt at readjustment is naturally along the line of former behaviour patterns, formal ways of defining the whole situation. But this reversion is never wholly successful largely because of its incomplete character. An entirely new life organization must be worked out, which takes into consideration all of the manifold factors in the new situation.

It is just possible that even before desertion or divorce many such persons may have developed symptoms of personality disorganization as a result of emotional crisis to which they have been subjected. These psychological manifestations include suppressions, regressions, ambivalent motivations, blockages, cleavage between lust and love, loss of self-confidence and ambition, doubts, indecision, nightmares, morbidly transferred attachments or aversions—all these and more. Such persons may face further crisis after the desertion or divorce.

The crisis which each divorce entails for the parties involved varies with the particular situation. However, it has been observed that divorces or desertions which have taken place in case of those whose marriages were arranged by their parents involve less crises than in case of those who married for love.

(*ii*) *Divorce and Sex Adjustment*. The explosive and imperious character of sex urges creates a great problem for satisfactory personal reorganization because of visceral tensions. Both habit and nature in man are united in the sex activity of married life. When these twin forces are suddenly interrupted the life organization is in serious danger or derangement. The disorganization may be either temporary or permanent and the result will be determined by the degree to which the person is drawn to some overexpression of sex behaviour and the success with which this urge is transferred, sublimated, repressed or allowed to run riot. Rigid repression may be practised. One may become deeply interested in some other love object, be in work, children, or various substitutes may be sought which offer physical release. Divorced males often seek satisfaction with casual companions and personal disorganization is the result.

Divorced woman is often faced with more difficult situation. She is often subjected to a variety of insulting proposals merely because of her ambiguous status. No matter how virtuous she may be, she is often considered fair game by all the amateurs. Some of them may become prostitutes.

(*iii*) *Divorce and Injured Ego*. There are very few instances in which both parties have come to an agreement about the dissolution of marriage and it is often one party which presses for such an action. Such a situation is extremely humiliating to the person who feels that he or she is lacking something to fill the life of the other. The rejected person with injured ego often feels difficult in adjusting his or her personality.

(*iv*) *Divorce and Habits*. A large number of contacts and relationship of marriage life are habitual in character. There is some element of habituation even in the periodicity with which a married couple may have sex relations. Many other activities of married life become even more completely routinized down to such petty details as frying the bacon and buttering the toast. When the marriage is broken such habits struggle to find their usual expression. Their inevitable failure to do so brings unrest, dissatisfaction and sadness to each party.

(v) *Divorce and Social Relationships.* A wide variety of complications are introduced into the social relationships of both the parties after desertion or divorce, which may consequently result in personal disorganization of some sort. Firstly, his or her relationships to other persons, both those who are aware of this changed status, and those who are not, become subtly altered. Gossip in all its poisonous and malicious forms is an irritating and often an object of terror to the divorced person. It is often believed that every divorced person is guilty until he or she has been proved innocent. The friends of divorced persons also often become suspicious of them. They are thus forced to cut off arbitrarily from many of the groups with which they were formerly connected. The maladjustment resulting from the lessening of these contacts is particularly bitter because of the high emotional tensions involved. Sometimes whole groups or even communities may be driven into two hostile camps over the divorce of a prominent couple. In such situations the divorced person is forced to redefine his situation at the same time that he is making new friends. Lacking this ability and cut off from the old values, personalities may become disorganized.

Divorce and Economic Position

Many masculine occupations and professions are dependent upon the goodwill and respect of other persons. This interested circle may range from the relatively small group of clients or medical practitioner or a grocer to the entire country when the divorce of a leading person is considered. This all-important goodwill may be severely affected by a divorce depending upon the reason for divorce. Many employers also take into consideration the marital status of their employee for permanency, promotion, etc.

Alimony represents another problem for the husband, when it is granted to the wife by the court. Such awards imply the ability of the husband to support two households, which middle or lower income groups do not have.

In case alimony is not granted or is insufficient wives are forced to take employment to support themselves or their children, unless help is coming from some other sources. The employment which she gets may not be of the type for which she is fitted by training or inclination and may affect her personality. The divorced women who have never worked before must often face severe economic handicaps. The divorced woman may contract illicit sexual relationships because she is unable to support herself. In the lower social level many prostitutes are recruited from this group who exploit their only resource, when they face the world alone.

Children of Divorced Persons

In the family children are accustomed to look to their parents for affection and security. The sudden interruption of this relationship in the primary group is a shock to the child's developing personality. He has been reared in an atmosphere of strong affection and when this tie is broken he is bewildered and does not know which way to turn. His position may take various forms, which are discussed below.

Children with Re-married Parents. One situation is that the divorced parents may remarry. This is very often the case in Western countries, but rarely so in our country. But the new home can seldom take the place of the old. The new step-father or mother will always be fundamentally a stranger, lacking the wisdom and affection found in the old. For the average child of divorce, the intangible aspects of family solidarity have gone out of his life. Few children, however, may make a satisfactory adjustment to their new status. When the parents remarry, the additional complexities of step-parents and half-brothers and sisters arise. A bewildering variety of roles is created for the child. Strange adults, brothers, and sisters are suddenly introduced into his life and he finds the adjustment very difficult. His parents are completely absorbed in the new families and the child of the first marriage may find himself without a real home. From such complex situations personal disorganization looms as an unpleasant possibility.

Children with Divorced Persons. Children in the broken home where father or mother is absent often fall prey to juvenile delinquency, adolescent crime, sex offences or become vagrants. A sense of guilt often attaches to the children of divorcee because their parents have somehow transgressed the mores and such a child must face a moral problem which a child whose parents have died never faces. If the divorced woman lacks economic resources, the child may go for employment at an earlier date before completing his education. The child's difficulty may be carried over to the play group. The child who lives with one of his divorced parents is often susceptible to the humiliation of his playmate, who have parents. Thus, his role in the group may undergo a subtle change and his status suffers for no fault of his. Emotional maladjustment may even continue many years after he has left the play group and he may be prone to various symptoms of personal disorganization such as missing classes, smoking, and loitering in the streets.

Children With Joint Family Members. In case where joint family system prevails divorce may not affect the children. In such cases children often remain with the mother's or father's family and do not experience drastic interruption. Uncles and aunts act as substitute to fathers and mothers and the continuity of the basic family relationship remains substantially unbroken.

Desirability and Undesirability of Divorce

Divorce is nearly always really a tragedy, for it generally means disorganization of the personalities concerned and of their children as we have seen above. Sometimes one party wants a divorce in order to marry another person. This leaves the other mate to feel that he or she has been judged and found wanting, that he or she failed to pass the test of a successful and co-operative spouse. This makes the divorce process an emotional upheaval for the rejected person. Or, the rejected person may feel humiliated because his pride is hurt.

Because marriages have proved unstable in the modern society, many critics of manners and morals believing in old social values blame divorce for the current problems of family disorganization. But this appears to be one-sided reasoning, because divorces occur after the family is disorganized and when one or both the parties have a strong desire to dissolve their relationship. They do not occur in happy, well-adjusted families. Divorce in fact gives only a legal status to the marriage already disrupted. On the other hand, there are many unsatisfactory and unhappy marriages which are not terminated because of religious belief, pressure from in-laws, small children who need care, inability of the wife to make her own living and fear of loss of prestige.

But it is also to be pointed out that widespread divorce is prejudicial to public interest, and often partial divorce or separation is allowed at the first instance so that the parties may reconcile during that period, and have a normal family life again. Wholesome family life is desirable in the first state, because (*i*) it is conducive to effective living and, therefore, to effective citizenship, and (*ii*) for responsible parenthood and adequate care and training for the children, which is nowhere well supplied outside the family system.

Avoidance of Family Tensions and Divorce

We have discussed the various factors which cause tensions between husband and wife in a family and ultimately lead to desertion or divorce. The effects of such tensions, desertion or divorce are not conducive to the welfare of the individual, the family and the society at large. Therefore, steps must be taken to mitigate such tensions in the early stages by various means such as proper education of the spouse before and after marriage through literature, family counselling agencies, courts and services after divorce.

(*i*) *Education About Proper Choice of Mates.* The uneducated young in the modern age of democracy, stimulated by movies and other literature, are more prone to romantic marriages which bring difficulties in marital relationships after some time either due to differences in their cultures, attitudes or fundamental values. They must be made aware of the consequences of such marriages and may be advised to leave such matters to their parents, who can better choose for their companion according to their own cultural setting, because conjugal affection, rather than romantic love, forms the basis of a truly successful marriage. Elliott and Merrill rightly point out, "Conjugal affection is not included in the romantic complex, based as the latter is upon unfamiliarity, excitement, personal attraction and similar considerations.... Conjugal affection, on the other hand, comprises an intangible but nevertheless fundamental group of expectations, attitudes and values that insure a successful marriage. It involves such considerations as complete communication between husband and wife ; their just participation in various activities ; the harmonious mutual adjustment of the many habitual relationships of marriage ; consensus derived from similar definitions of important situations ; and finally the simple fact of personal friendship."[28] In this connection the system of tallying *Patris* (horoscopes), which to some extent indicate the nature of the parties is worth pursuing. Also marriages within their own castes or at least within their class can be more successful owing to similarities in cultures.

[28] *Ibid.*, p. 381.

25

In spite of all such advices still many young persons are likely to marry mates of their own choice. In such cases they must be taught that romance is not the only sound basis of marriage and the marriage should not be dissolved when romance is on the wane. They should be informed that love which enables a marriage to endure is something finer, deeper, and more realistic than the romantic love of the movies and popular stories. Mr. Landis points out, "Many divorces arise because the romantic expectations with which young people often enter marriage are frustrated by the unromantic realities of the marital situation. If these expectations could be modified in the direction of greater realism, a large number of marriages might conceivably be saved."[29] Elliott and Merrill remark, "Men and women are demanding greater personal satisfaction from the estate of matrimony. But then one has to work harder at making marriage a success. Also greater emphasis upon personal happiness in marriage deserves analysis as to its essential validity. Life exacts difficulties as well as pleasures and is full of petty annoyances, disappointments and disillusionment, both in and out of marriage. Probably no married people were completely happy before marriage, nor they can expect to be completely happy after marriage. Many young men nourished in the romantic tradition may blame their marriage if they feel unhappy whereas the difficulty may lie either within themselves or in situations external to marriage."[30]

(*ii*) *Family Counselling Agencies.* Often there are tensions in the family owing to the reasons already stated such as differences in temperament, attitudes and social values ; economic difficulties, ill health, conflict on child's training, etc. There should be family counselling agencies with trained social workers in family matters. They should try to analyse the situation and suggest methods for removing that tension. Such family counselling agencies are found in some of the industrially advanced countries particularly U.S.A. But unfortunately such agencies have not found their due place in India. The first family welfare agency was started in Bombay in 1950, which is reported to be doing good work. Besides counselling service to the client it renders some practical assistance. Community

[29] Landis, Paul H., "Control of the Romantic Impulse Through Education", in the journal, *School and Society*, August , 1936.

[30] *Ibid.*, p. 450.

resources like schools, hospitals, trusts and charities are approached to render all the necessary help to the client and the family.

There are also courts of domestic relations in U.S.A. which are presided by persons of wide social experience and social understanding which help in preventing temporary discord through reconciliation of domestic relations, which otherwise often lead to permanent family disruption. All those welfare agencies which add to the welfare of the family, and ease tensions, e.g. maternity and child welfare centres, agencies rendering financial assistance to the economically backward families or family planning clinics should be assisted and encouraged by the state.

(*iii*) *Counselling Courts*. When the matter comes to the court for divorce they should try to gather the facts of the case through the social worker and analyse it before giving decision. Let us cite one example here. Once a husband went to a court for divorce on the ground that his wife often scolded him and called him vicious names. She talked wildly, wept, and went into tirades of rage whenever he remonstrated. The attorney was a man with unusual amount of insight into the human nature. He said, "Is not she rather frail? The rush of city life is probably too much for her nerves. You might take her to the country." The husband said, "You may be right. I think I will call on a doctor." He consulted a psychiatrist on the way home. Gradually her health improved and her emotional disturbance was over. The husband came to understand the source of her peculiar behaviour and became much more tolerant and sympathetic in his attitude.

(*iv*) *Help After Divorce*. In spite of these measures there may be certain cases where there is constant tension in the family which is not only affecting the life organization of the husband and the wife but also their children. In such cases some employment or financial assistance should be provided to her for her own and the maintenance of children. Because many such women resort to prostitution if they are not able to secure employment, and this leads to further social disorganization. No other environment has proved so favourable for the upbringing of children as the home which the parents create, if the home is relatively harmonious, but if it is utterly inharmonious or positively harmful, the state must seek to protect the children in some other way.[31]

[31] Maciver, R. M., and Page, C. H., *op. cit.*, p. 276.

Future of Family Organization

To be sure, the instability of the modern family as measured by divorce and separation and economic discord, will continue to increase for some time. Because these are the by-products of man's attempt to evolve a new pattern of human relationships. Formerly, social and economic pressures made it imperative for the family to hold together in spite of other difficulties. But today it must depend much more on its intrinsic strength.

Part Five

COMMUNITY CONFLICTS

CHAPTER XVI

COMMUNITY AND NATIONAL DISORGANIZATION

It might be appropriate to discuss at the outset the difference between the terms "social disorganization" and "community disorganization". While the term "social disorganization" is a general one indicating disorganization in any society, the term "community disorganization" is applied in a narrower sense indicating disorganization in any particular community or physical configuration. Professor Chinoy points out, "Society is the most inclusive group and when viewed as a group rather than as a network of relationships or a system of institutions we may call it a community. When societies are considered in relation to their geographical location the term community is frequently used".[1] Having distinguished the terms "society" and community let us explain the term community.

Nature of Community

The community has two relative aspects, viz. the geographical and the psychological. Geographically, it may be considered as a contiguous distribution of people with their social institutions. Psychologically we may think of community in terms of the elements that combine to make it a dynamic and living entity. Since both these elements are important, the community may be considered to be a complex social unity that has both a physical locus and a psychological consensus.[2] Some of these clusters such as neighbourhoods, villages, towns, cities, suburbs, show hardly enough organization, hardly enough "commonness" among their members to be called communities. But this is precisely part of our enquiry. The geographic clustering which constitutes a village or town or city ordinarily sets in motion certain processes which tend to make these localities into communities. But sometimes these natural

[1] Chinoy, Ely, *Sociological Prospective* (1954), p. 30.

[2] Elliott, M. A., and Merrill, F. E., *Social Disorganization* (1950), p. 473.

processes fail, or are blocked, and a community fails to develop or falls apart.[3]

Though we have expansion of communities from the dimensions of village and the city to that of the region and the nation and perhaps to world, yet the smaller communities have their own importance. As civilized beings we need both the smaller as well as the larger circles of community. The larger community brings us opportunity, stability, economy and the constant stimulus of a richer and more varied culture, while in smaller community we find the near and more intimate social satisfaction. Both these are essential to the full life process. Therefore, we may deal either with rural or urban communities or sometimes with both as a region, state or a nation. In our analysis of community disorganization we have to remember the infinite complexity of the community. We must thus consider the individuals, the families, informal social organizations and organized institutions that are related and interrelated in the social structure of the community. Community is more than individuals. It has an existence of its own.

Thus, within the community there are various groups and organizations whose some interests are common, while others clash. Again there are communities within the community, whose interests may be common or clash with each other. For example, a factory located by the Central Government in Gorakhpur city may benefit that area and may be good from the national point of view. But the interests of other regions in the same state, or other states as against Uttar Pradesh may suffer. Thus, we have to understand the complex structure of the community as a whole.

Nature of Community Disorganization

Community disorganization like social disorganization is always a relative phenomenon. Every community has some tensions and disruptions, some institutions that are not functioning adequately and some signs of incomplete consensus. But just as no community is completely organized, so no community is completely disorganized. "The vitality and effective functioning of the community are dependent upon harmonious co-operative efforts and consensus of social definition in agreement as to general ends and purposes. When this common definition is translated into co-operative activity

[3] Coleman, James S., "Community Disorganization" in *Contemporary Social Problems*, (Eds.) Merton, Robert K., and Nisbet, Robert A., (1961), p. 553.

towards some common end, we have community efficiency."[4] Thomas and Znaniecki hold, "Communal vitality is measured by the degree of harmony with which any action affecting the community as a whole is carried out. When the local citizens cease to be concerned about their community welfare, the social organization of the community is threatened. This is true where no great corruption exist and it may be manifest in the increasing tendency to stress the economic, religious, or hedonistic aspects of the human activity at the expense of the social."[5] When a sizeable portion of the community puts its own economic interests, its own religious sectarianism or its own pleasure above the welfare of the group, community disorganization is apparent. On the other hand, if the community is well organised there will be little difference between the definitions of individual and of social welfare. The citizens would perform their share of civic duties honestly and diligently.

There will be community disintegration and disorganization if different groups whether on the basis of caste, class, sect or rural urban prejudices fought to serve their own interests at the cost of community interests. Such types of groups could only be useful if they served the interest of the community at large as well. The criteria for social integration is measured by the gradual increase in the number of schools, libraries, recreational facilities and other such welfare activities in which the public takes active part, there is less disparity of income between various social classes, there is less corruption, more employment and the various groups in a community work in a harmonious manner to develop individual and group responsibilities, and at the same time serving for the welfare of the community.

Disorganized, Underorganized and Unorganized Community

Again a distinction has to be drawn between various terms such as organized, disorganized and unorganized community. According to Coleman a community is well organized if it can act collectively towards the problems that face it. If it cannot, then it is disorganized relative to these problems, though there may be a great amount of apparent organization.[6] Such inability to act can come about in

[4] Elliott, M. A., and Merrill, F. E., *op. cit.*, p. 476.

[5] Thomas, William I and Znaniecki, Florian, *The Polish Peasan Europe and America* (1927), Vol. II, p. 1171.

[6] *Ibid.*, p. 556

two ways : through an absence of any collective effort, or through the existence of conflicting collective efforts that cancel each other out. Thus, a disorganized community is one when there is any serious breakdown in the customary mode of control or it is unable to function properly due to factionalism or conflict between groups or classes within the community.[7] It is also supposed that a community can be disorganized only upon the presumption that a previous state of organization has existed.

"On the other hand an unorganized community is one which lacks organization. An adjustment of relationships may not have been achieved because of newness, as in a frontier community that lacks integration as a whole, or a community may be underorganized, without enough different organizations to meet the needs of its people. Thus, a community that has no church, or one in which there are no organizations for youth, or women or men, may be considered unorganized in the sense that it is underorganized. In contrast we have overorganized communities, where there seems to be too many organizations, or where there are so many to cause duplication of efforts, competition and conflict, which give rise to the need for better integration."[8] Professor Coleman talks of a "mass society" which takes the form of disorganized community in the urban areas and of a tribal or traditional rural society which is underorganized community. In his view in a vast urban community, the local community, fast becoming a specialized living place, has begun to take on a form similar to that of these voluntary associations. "It holds only a small part of the interests of most of its members, whose other interests have become fractionated into many parts, most of them outside the community. Only those few merchants and others whose livelihood is within the community, or who are part of its government, are centrally involved." The community thus tends towards a "mass society", with a small organized elite, and a large unorganized, undifferentiated mass. This is, not, of course, to say that its members are a "mass" from the point of view of the larger society. They are members of many groups, occupational, leisure-time, political, professional and other interest groups. But many of these are not local. Their members are, therefore, in effect a mass, not organized into interest groups

[7] Sanderson, D., and Polson, R. A., *Rural Community Organization* (1939), p. 75.

[8] *Ibid.*, p. 75.

and associations that play a role in community decisions. There are special consequences of such a structure, consequences which have much to do with conflict."[9]

However, he points out that such a mass society structure can come about through two exactly opposite societal forms : the members' having no important associations outside the family and close friends, so that no interest groups mediate between individual and government ; and the members' having all their associational ties in large associations that go beyond the bounds of the governmental units (in this case the community), and thus play no role in its decision-making. Though these associations can and do play a mediating role at the metropolitan, state, or national level, protecting and furthering their members' interests they cannot do so at the community level.

The first of these two forms of mass society is exemplified by traditional societies like those of Central America, where the large mass of the populace is only tied to family and friends. The second is exemplified by modern suburban communities. Following the above definition of Sanderson and Polson the metropolis community becomes disorganized, while the traditional one unorganized, where there is lack of community spirit. In the metropolis the elite govern the masses either through the city councils or becoming leaders in the large-scale organizations. At times the masses may revolt against the decision of the administrative elite. In the traditional society the masses are so confined to their family and clan interest that they ignore the community or national interests and are politically governed by other nations, who have organized governments.

Individual's Participation in Community Organization

The extent and the attitude of individual's participation in the life of the community at various levels determine the degree of organization or disorganization of the community. The individual participates in various groups such as family, church, business groups, in the community affairs where he resides and also in state and central organizations. The failure of the individual to participate in the life of the community except under the duress of personal ambition represents some fundamental changes in social attitudes and values of the community. Sharing in community interests and co-operative membership in local institutions become increasingly

[9] *Ibid.*, p. 601.

rare as each person seeks his own independence. This attitude is manifest at present both in the urban and rural communities. In the rural areas this attitude of the individual is a relic of the British rule as well as of so many other factors as disintegration of panchayats, narrow outlook of the cast groups, poverty and illiteracy of masses, zamindari system, etc. In the urban areas due to different social classes, castes and specialized interest groups the effective participation of individuals in community welfare is decreasing. Instead of taking interest in local activities for the welfare of community most men and women turn towards commercialized recreation and other such activities outside their local areas.

Community organization and disorganization are the direct functions of the activities of the citizens and their participation in community and civic affairs. Therefore, a community may be considered efficient or inefficient in accordance with the number of individuals actively interested and participating in its life and operation. As the percentage of persons who participate directly in communal life declines, disorganization often results. But it is also to be mentioned that no single individual fails completely to participate in community activities just as there is no one who participates in every enterprise. There are certain phases of community life in which every adult citizen plays its role. For example, an average person obeys the laws, pays the taxes, willingly or reluctantly. The measure of relative social solidarity is based rather on the degree of participation than on the gross number of participants. This participation is carried on partly through the intermediary institutions and partly through institutions serving directly the local community, e.g. a community welfare centre, a recreational centre, an educational institution, etc. and other programmes run by the corporation or local panchayat. The community exists as a group of institutions in a definite area. The individual participates in community life largely through membership of such institutions. He is a member of a religious sect, a recreational club, a study circle, a member of the school board, a welfare centre and a voter. If he fills these institutional roles with dignity and intelligence and keeping community interest above personal interest he is considered to be a good citizen.

Process of Community Disorganization

The process of community disorganization is a complex one

and develops out of many factors. The process of individual, family and community disorganization is an interrelated one. Community disorganization cannot logically be separated from the disorganization of the individual as well as family which compose the community. However, there are certain aspects of the disorganization process which are more closely related to the community than to the individuals and the families which make it up.

The process of community growth is a reciprocal and correlative performing a dual function of disorganization and reorganization. A certain amount of personal and social disorganization is inevitable and normal in the growth of the community, but when it exceeds its limit the result is widespread community disorganization. Again the community's working is complex and must be understood in proper perspective in any given situation. An individual takes part in various activities as a member of various groups, such as religious, economic, social ; as a member of the local community or mohalla or neighbourhood ; as a member of the city corporation ; a state or a region ; and a nation. Thus, his participation at various levels has to be balanced so as to promote group interest, community interest, regional interest or the national interest. Many a times they are all working in the same direction, that is, for the welfare of the community. But sometimes there is a clash between his own interest and the interest of the community or the nation. However, here we shall confine our study only to the community at the village or city level, and shall see how the interest of the community is promoted along with the welfare of the individual and the various groups. Professor Kaufman makes this point clear. He says sociologists have frequently designated the community as a social group. The precise nature of this group, however, has seldom if ever been made clear. Community, especially in the modern world, is seldom if ever expressed through only one association.[10] A great variety of groups may at one time or another be involved in community action. They range from the coffee-break clique through the civic club to the more institutionalized groups such as the board of eldermen. In addition to groups in which primary contacts are dominant, publics such as that of the local newspaper are important. Only a few organizations, such as perhaps a community improvement

[10] Kaufman, Harold F., *Toward an Interactional Conception of Community, Social Forces*, October, 1959, p. 12.

association, are engaged entirely in community activity. On the other hand, some never appear in the community field.[11]

Making explicit the criteria of community action which set off community from non-community activities is a crucial problem in interactional theory. Six types of characteristics, dimensions or criteria are suggested for differentiating community action from that not appropriate to the community field. The dimensions noted are (1) the degree of comprehensiveness of interests pursued and needs met, (2) the degree to which the action is identified with the locality, (3) relative number, status, and degree of involvement of local residents, (4) relative number and significance of local associations involved, (5) degree to which the action maintains or changes the local society, and (6) extent of organization of the action.

In this context if in an Indian village a gram panchayat constructs a panchayat ghar, where most of the people participate in the programme it will be a community programme as against a farmer's club or youth club in which only one group participates. Although the work done by a particular group adds to the welfare of the community, yet from the community consciousness point of view the community event is more important and has its own contribution in community development or welfare.

Community Disorganization and Social Change

The community is well organized if it is achieving the objectives laid down by the society and meeting the challenges of social change. We have already discussed the causes of social change and the objectives to be achieved in our society in Chapter I. The achievement of these two objectives depends upon the proper operation of the institutions and organizations within that community. These institutions may be in the sphere of economics, religion, education, health, politics, recreation, social welfare, etc. However, generally these institutions resist change for two main reasons : (1) because the human beings as such resist change, and (2) the vested interests whose position is threatened by such changes resist it.

Many institutions often tend to lose touch with life, whether the temple, the local government or the national government. On the other hand, institutions can survive and the community can progress if the institutions develop sufficient elasticity to conform

[11] *Ibid.*, p. 12.

to the changing times. Such changes require dynamic and foresighted leaders.

In the last two or three centuries the technological forces, new beliefs, and ideas in the field of religion, economics, politics, scientific inventions ; changes in communication and the concept of welfare state have changed the situation to such an extent that the institutions must adopt themselves to the new situation if the communities and the nation has to survive. However, the situation on the whole is that the institutions have not adopted to the new situations, and there is either inactivity in the organizations and apathy among leaders or there is conflict.

Community Conflicts and Inactivity

We have already mentioned above that there may be either conflict or inactivity in any situation. There may be three types of conflicts within the community. (1) Individual in conflict with community, (2) family conflict effecting children and ultimately the community, and (3) conflict between various groups in the society. We have already discussed in detail about the first two aspects. The individual is in conflict with community when for example a criminal, a juvenile delinquent, diseased, physically or mentally handicapped, drunkard, sexually disorganized affects the community in one way or the other. When the number of such persons is large they take the form of major social problems, which ultimately threaten the stability of the community as a whole. Similarly, there may be conflict in the family which may lead to divorce or separation and affects not only the husband and the wife, but their children as well. This may ultimately affect the community, if the affected children are to be supported by the community for their education, training, etc. The third is the group conflicts or community conflicts and here we are mainly concerned with this last aspect. This conflict between various groups may be in the sphere of economic, political, religious, social, rural-urban, regional, lingual, state basis, etc. There are always some conflicts in a dynamic society whether between the individual and the society, or in the family or among various groups, but so long as they do not cross a certain limit, there is no danger to community stability and only when they cross this limit that the stability of the community is threatened and community disorganization appears. The inactivity may be in existence when people do not want to change their ideas, belief, institutions to serve the new goals set by society and this is mostly the position in underdeveloped countries.

Some maintain that the basic conflict is economic and perhaps they are right to a great extent. Man's fundamental struggle is to make living and his endeavours often diminish the possibility of other man's economic enhancement. Thus, there is struggle between different classes, i.e. upper and lower. Strikes, violence and revolutions are some of the evidences in this type of conflict.

Then there are political conflicts in a democratic society, one party believing in a particular type of programme, while the other in another programme. Parliamentary system may be a check against undue privilege and authority, but it also possesses certain disorganizing qualities, and there is political corruption in such a system. Then there may be regional conflicts based on cultural difference such as language, etc. Similarly there are religious conflicts, ending in communal riots. Such instances are often found in many countries. Then there is conflict between rural and urban communities, where the interests of the two clash. There may be differences over the taxation issues or certain other amenities. Further, there are conflicts between various castes and clans. Similarly, there may be conflicts between various professional groups as to their status and privileges. Or, there may be conflicts within an association or organization such as a university, corporation or panchayat. In fact wherever social beings exist there is some type of conflict between one group or the other.

These conflicts in values and attitudes are important in the disorganization of community. But along with these are the basic underlying factors, which produce differences in values. These are the technological change, the mass migration from rural to urban areas, the decay of institutions and the failure of institutions to meet the new needs. Many of the factors in community disorganization cannot be measured directly. The breakdown of community consensus is one important indication in the community disorganization process. In collective aspects of community disorganization and underorganization we may discuss (1) problems of displaced persons, (2) conflict and inactivity in urban and rural communities, (3) caste conflicts, (4) class conflicts, (5) communal conflicts, (6) regional and lingual conflicts, and (7) conflicts in complex organizations such as universities and political parties, etc. However, before we discuss these conflicts, let us deal with some of the changes which have come into this country in the last two centuries.

India and Social Change

In India there have been vast changes in the last two hundred years and these may be discussed in two phases, viz. changes during the British period and changes after Independence.

Changes During the British Period

During the British period certain changes were introduced, which affected the life of the community in many ways. The introduction of zamindari system, new system of justice, bureaucratic administration, laissez-faire policy of the government, prejudicial taxation policy, changes in personal laws and rapid expansion of railways affected the life of the community in many ways. Our economic and industrial growth was hampered, agriculture remained in a primitive stage, gross inequalities were created by zamindari system, pressure of population on land increased because of slow industrialization, caste system was strengthened because of introduction of jantoo and Muslim law, communal feelings were increased by creation of communal parties, the growth of village panchayats was arrested by a new system of justice, lingual and cultural contiguity was ignored by creating provinces on administrative basis, no planning was done and there was no liberalization in political rights. Therefore, the industrial revolution in the West which affected the life of the people there in certain ways, affected differently in our country. Of course, there was some expansion in education, in the means of communication, health services, some change in fiscal policy after the end of the First World War, but on the whole, the country could not have the full effects of changes brought about by industrial revolution in the European countries.

Changes After Independence

After Independence vast changes have taken place in the country. The effects of these changes have been varied. Majority of these changes have been beneficial to the community, but some of them have been harmful too. New Constitution has been framed, which declares India to be a welfare State.

The Reserve Bank of India, the Imperial Bank of India and

Insurance Companies have been nationalized. The sphere of public sector has greatly increased. Zamindari system has been abolished. Ceilings on land are being fixed. Taxation policy has been entirely recasted. Estate duty and wealth tax are some of its outstanding features. The states have been reorganized on cultural or lingual basis. The Planning Commission has been set up to formulate the plans of development to raise the standard of living of the people. Our constitution guarantees free and compulsory education to all children up to 14 years of age. The scope of social services is gradually increasing. The Panchayati Raj has been established in the rural areas and the community development programme is in progress. But in spite of all these rapid changes there is some resistance to change because of certain vested interests or the conservatism of the people who are not changing their attitudes with the time. They are unable to adjust to the vast changes which are being brought out by technological or other factors. Similarly, certain problems are being brought into existence by these new changes which can be solved only gradually. In the light of these changes we may discuss the community conflicts in India on the lines indicated above.

(1) *Migration and Community Disorganization.* Social mobility is considered to be both a cause and an index to social disorganization. Improved transport and communication have made the community too mobile. In social mobility, which involves both physical and psychological change there is a breakdown of primary group control. Overcrowding and slums become another cause of community disorganization leading to delinquency, crime, prostitution, gambling, etc. Employment is an important factor these days, which leads to social mobility when thousands of persons have to migrate from rural to urban areas due to lack of employment opportunities at the former place or they are employed for a temporary period and move from place to place to seek employment. However, the sudden exodus of a large number of refugees from Pakistan after partition created a great problem for the government, as well as for those who became refugees. These displaced persons had to adjust themselves in new environments.

Whereas social mobility may be movement from place to place, migration is often referred to from one place to the other. Thus, migration may be from one country to another, or from village to the city. The former type of migration may include large number of persons migrated from West Pakistan as well as East Pakistan after the partition while the latter type of migration is the result of industrialization and is likely to increase with further industrialization and rationalization of agriculture. The persons who move from one country to the other or from village to the city often experience a cultural shock, which may result in social disorganization if migration is on a large scale. In case of migration if people move in large groups and carry their own culture, little disorganization results because individuals and families are not cut off from their familiar cultural surroundings and forced to adjust themselves to an alien environment. But often when they move in small groups or as individuals they do not bring their culture with them, nor find a familiar culture when they arrive, rather they are forced to give up much that is dear and familiar to adjust themselves to a totally different milieu. In case of migration from rural to urban areas, the abrupt change in social environment often results in social disorganization. Adolescents are particularly affected by cinema and other commercialized recreational activities leading to delinquency among them.

Migration of Displaced Persons. The mass migration of people from West Pakistan in 1947 just after Independence brought vast social disorganization in this country. Many of these families became homeless and set out wandering from one place to the other. These men, women and children lost traditional community relationships and broke family ties. These refugees were the persons who did not leave their homes voluntarily but were forced to do so because of threat of persecution by the Muslims there. These persons did not migrate for economic betterment, but to save their life and that of their families. They often had no choice about the time of departure from their home, nor any ultimate or approximate idea about the destination. Due to their sudden departure they could not take many things with them except their clothes and such knowledge and skills which they had acquired in their lifetime. They were displaced not only geographically but also socially and economically. There was disorganization of the family due to persecution, death and imprisonment of many of their family members. In some families there was separation of husband from wife and children from parents. In many cases some members of the family were lost. Many an individual did not know whether his wife, son, daughter or any such near relation was still alive. Often they felt a sense of sudden separation and many of them were mentally disorganized. The Governments, Central as well as States did their best to solve their problem and rehabilitate them by providing residential accommodation, preference in employment, vocational training, loans for business and settlement of their property claims. But in spite of all this, many families could not be rehabilitated because of the hugeness of the problem and death of certain earning family members, which brought economic dependence and disorganization in those families. Unfortunately this migration from East Pakistan still continues and their satisfactory rehabilitation is not possible due to heavy pressure on land and economic life in West Bengal.[12]

(2) *Conflict and Inactivity in Rural and Urban Communities.* In India, a concentrated effort has been made since 1947 to utilize the heritage of British political institutions in order to achieve comparable results by democratic means. This effort involves a policy of rapid industrialization and of community development which aims to advance the social and economic level of the bulk of the Indian population in the rural areas. But as Professor Bendix points out that in the past the insulation of villages from government authority was a by-product of caste dominance. This decisive dominance of a caste may mean oppression of a whole village.[13] "However decisive dominance of the leaders of one caste over the whole village is not the only, and perhaps the most general condition. The possible dimensions of dominance such as ritual status, education, numerical preponderance, economic power, and others may be distributed among several castes in a village. When this is true, factionalism becomes exacerbated often within a dominant caste as much as between castes. Together with his followers and dependents each leader represents an 'enclave' of solidarity which he seeks to protect and enhance vis-a-vis other leaders and their factions. Thus, the interests of factional groups and personal interests are more important than the interests of the village as a whole."[14] Even when there are factions in the village, they may resist intervention from outside.

Thus, due to factions in villages, or vested interests of dominant caste or lack of interest in development due to literacy of masses

[12] *Third Five-Year Plan* (1961), p. 726.

[13] Bendix, Reinhard, *Nation-Building and Citizenship—Studies of our Changing Order* (1964), p. 224.

[14] *Ibid.* p. 224

there are community conflicts or lack of community enterprise and the community development programme is not making much headway.

Both in the urban as well as rural areas the elite are separated from masses and actually there is absence of middle class. "Although the elite are separated from the masses in every complex society the gulf between them is increased when the educated few move far ahead—if only in the realm of ideas—while the masses of the people remain tied to traditional ways. It is probable that in Western Europe the social distance between the elites and the masses narrowed as both were affected by rapid industrialization and democratization, whereas the distance has increased in most of the countries that are late-comers to these processes of development."[15] It is because of lack of leadership among the middle classes that community development programmes in the rural and urban areas have not made much progress. Various welfare services in urban areas such as urban community welfare centres, economic programmes for women, consumer co-operative stores, services for physically, socially and mentally handicapped are envisaged to be developed under the five-year plans, but not much success has been achieved because of the apathy of educated intellectuals in these programmes. The problem of leadership and community development have been discussed in detail in Volume III, while the problem of casteism has been discussed in the next section.

(3) *Casteism and Community Disorganization.* It is very difficult to trace the origin of caste system. Various theories have been given regarding its origin and growth such as traditional Hindu theory, racial theory, occupational or functional theory, religious theory, mana theory, etc. but none of them explains the phenomenon in a scientific way.[16] It is generally believed that there were four varnas in the beginning, i.e. Brahman, Kshatriya, Vaishya and Sudra and in due course of time these were divided into a number of castes and sub-castes due to different occupations and professions, each distinguished from others in customs, which would not allow any inter-marriage or inter-dining between one caste and another. Thus, it was a sort of social stratification dividing society into various groups on the basis of occupation, customs, marriage

[15] Bendix, R., *op. cit.*, p. 233.

[16] For details see my book, *Changing Pattern of Indian Villages* (1964), Chapter on Rural Institutions.

restrictions and some type of superiority-inferiority vis-à-vis the other castes.

The caste has been defined as an endogamous and hereditary group or section of the society which occupies a relatively fixed place on a scale of superordination to subordination. Blunt defines "Caste as an endogamous group, or collection of endogamous groups, bearing a common name membership of which is hereditary ; imposing on its members certain restrictions in the matter of social intercourse ; either following a common traditional occupation or claiming a common origin ; and generally regarded as forming single homogenous community."[17]

This caste system may have served certain useful functions in the past and may be having certain advantages even now as we shall see here, but due to its rigidity and certain other harmful effects relegating certain castes to the lowest position it has become inconsistent with the present democratic structure and industrial age where the dignity of manual labour and equality has to be emphasized. These evil effects of caste system have been termed as casteism. Professor Sushil Chandra observes, "In the closeness and rigidity of the above four ranks is found the beginning of casteism. Devotion and loyalty to one's primary groups was a value of paramount importance. But with the change of time the virtue of old has assumed the form of deviation of the worst order of today. . . . In the modern democratic era such loyalties lead to undemocratic results and thus a virtue of the ancients becomes a deviation of today and tomorrow."[18] Sri Kalekar remarks, "This rigid social regimentation of life produces a peculiarly strong almost indissoluble loyalty to the members of the caste to each other, both for maintaining a standard and of looking after each other's self-interest. 'My castemen and my caste, right and wrong' seems to be the motto of this caste loyalty. Experience has shown that this caste-loyalty often proves stronger than loyalty to the whole body politics, to the nation and to humanity. Caste loyalty frequently drives a man to subordinate his sense of justice, fairplay and humanity to the interest of caste. This oversiding loyalty is known as casteism. Casteism, therefore, is an oversiding, blind and supreme group loyalty that ignores the healthy social standards of justice,

[17] Blunt, E. A. H., *The Caste System of Northern India* (1931), p. 5.
[18] Chandra, Sushil, *op. cit.*, p. 178.

fairplay, equity and universal brotherhood."[19] He further observes that this casteism is not only peculiar to the Hindu society, but it is prevalent in Muslims and Christians as well. However, before we discuss its harmful effects in detail let us mention some of its advantages.

According to Prof. J. H. Hulton some of the advantages of caste system are : (1) It provides a person with a fixed social status from which neither richness nor poverty can remove him unless of course he so violates the standards of behaviour laid down by caste that it expels him out temporarily or permanently. (2) The caste acts as his trade union, his friend or beneficent society and his social security agency. (3) It dictates to each member customs to be observed in the matter of diet and ceremonial uncleanliness, and rituals to be observed at the time of birth, initiation, marriage, death, etc. In short it hands down from generation to generation the pattern of skill, knowledge and behaviour which we speak as culture. (4) It enables the caste to act corporately and to control the behaviour of its component members. In this way it can raise its position in society. (5) In the religious sphere the caste system so operates that the caste can change or modify its social and religious observances in accordance with changing ethical standards or with the trend of public opinion. (6) It has created a plural society which has proved very stable. It has afforded a place to every group whether racial, social or occupational to become a part of the social whole. (7) The caste system provides for the various functions necessary to social life, functions ranging from education to scavanging and from government to domestic service of the most menial kind under the sanction of a religious dogma, the belief in karma.

In spite of all these advantages the caste system has many disadvantages too, which are rather more harmful particularly in the present age. (1) The caste system imposes some type of inflexibility in occupation. People want to follow their occupation, even if they are capable of giving it up. (2) People are not allowed to change their occupation because of caste restrictions, which is a great hindrance in the division of labour in the industrial age. (3) There have been clashes between the castes which have been responsible for foreign invasions. Thus, there is a lack of national

[19] *Report of the Seminar on Casteism and Removal of Untouchability* (1955), pp. 44-45.

life. (4) The observance of caste rules is considered to be more important than that of moral laws. Thus, certain castes justify their antisocial conduct by an appeal to the practices of their castes. For example, criminal castes justify their behaviour towards their fellowmen by following their caste practices. (5) The caste system has been effectively utilized by the Brahman priesthood to their own advantage and the inferior castes have been kept to the lowest status. Although sacred books lay down a rule of strict asceticism of public service for the Brahmans, the rule is not followed strictly by the generality of Brahman castes. (6) Certain callings are despised by upper caste Hindus, e.g. killing of cattle, which keeps outside the pale tanners, cobblers and those who deal in the products of dead bodies. Unfortunately in such cases the nature of taboos is such that the contagion of the polluted occupation contaminates all members of the caste, whatever their individual occupation may be. (7) The caste members vote for their candidates in elections irrespective of their qualifications. (8) Favouritism is done in the selection of candidates for public posts. (9) Educational and social welfare institutions are sometimes run on the basis of caste. (10) Due to prejudicial attitudes in discrimination and segregation there arise serious tension and many a time there is a conflict. The Seminar on Casteism and Removal of Untouchability organized by the Indian Conference of Social Work points out, "There is no sector of our life private or public, that it does not permeate. In fact its role has increased in several respects since the inception of British rule and certain processes set in motion in Independent India have also aided it. Adult franchise, which prevails today, means that a great number of votes are cast, in favour of an elector's caste. This is explicitly recognised during elections. And contrary to popular belief, our cities are the strongholds of casteism—we find these hostels, housing societies, charities, marriage halls and clubs run on caste lines."[20]

The fear of upper castes is both biological and socio-economic. If there is biological intermixture this may cause biological contamination and if they are able to take up higher professions or political participation their economic and social status may be lowered. Regarding the first the fear is baseless as there is no conclusive

[20] *Report of the Seminar on Casteism and Removal of Untouchability*, organized by the Indian Conference of Social Work, (1955), p. 143,

evidence that certain races are superior, but only that a number of castes are economically, socially and educationally advanced. Regarding the second in a democratic set up no caste can have the monopoly and everybody must get equal opportunity.

Remedies and Reforms. To remove the evils of casteism there can be two views, the extreme and the moderate. The extremists think that the caste system should be abolished all at once and heavy penalties should be imposed upon those who advocate caste system. The moderate view can be that the evils of caste system should be removed without destroying it. The unfortunate position of the exterior castes may be improved. The present position is the result of prejudices and taboos which have been operative for centuries and cannot be got rid of in a night. This is a process which can be accomplished in the course of time and with the help of education in the broadest sense. Modification in those beliefs which are already taking place will bring about in their turn a modification of the caste system. At the same time a great improvement should be brought out in the position of backward and scheduled castes without destroying the social order, which perform a number of useful functions.

The Central as well as State Governments have recently taken various measures to remove untouchability and ameliorate the conditions of lower castes. Untouchability has been abolished by our Constitution and its practice in any form made an offence. Among other measures may be included (1) economic, (2) social, (3) educational, (4) religious, (5) propaganda, etc. Among the economic measures suggested for their uplift are the land reforms, redistribution of land, their settlement on new lands and more employment opportunities through the revival of cottage industries and expansion of large scale industries. Social measures include intercaste marriages, camps, common dining, co-operative settlements with no segregation in housing, and group therapy in the form of Kirtans, Bhajans, Shramdan, Children's play, etc. In the educational sphere democratic pattern should inculcate feeling of equality and more education for the lower castes. In the sphere of religion the true religion be interpreted, i.e. all men are equal. Scriptures which advocate caste system in a strict sense may be banned, while teachings of those who propagate equality such as of Buddha, Nanak, Kabir, etc. should be encouraged. Propaganda through modern techniques, i.e. radio, newspapers, films, kathas, kirtans and cinemas should be carried out for the removal of untouchability and other prejudices.

Other measures should include abolition of surnames and titles, introduction of new common greetings such as Jai Hind instead of Jai Ram ji ki, Pai lagi, etc. and technological improvement in degraded occupations such as use of wheelbarrow and the development of sewage system. But in spite of all this, caste system cannot be rooted out at once. The Seminar rightly concludes that caste performs several functions as well and mere propaganda that caste is evil in all its manifestation will not go far in removing it till the time comes when there are other agencies to take over these functions. "We should try our utmost to hasten the economic development of the country and should work hard for the realization of welfare state, if we wish caste to disappear in the near future."[21]

(4) *Class Tension and Community Disorganization.* Besides caste tensions there are also class tensions which have mounted in the present capitalistic system, where there is a wide gap of income between different types of groups. The society is divided into different classes on the basis of income and there is often clash between the labourers and the employers. Although certain steps have been taken under the Five-Year Plans to remove these wide gaps, yet there is often conflict between the labourers and employers and there are many strikes.[22]

(5) *Communal Tensions and Community Disorganization.* Besides class and caste tensions there are religious tensions between different groups. There is a prejudice, which involves a dogmatic pattern of social attitudes. Prejudice is characterized by strong emotional overtone. Attitudes of prejudice are the products of a disorganized society or one that is likely to be disorganized. Prejudice is a social attitude and reflects a complex social milieu. The formation of prejudice is an extremely complicated phenomenon.

Religious tensions have been there in this country since the Mohammedan invaders came to India. But the degree of such tension has been high or low with the time. During the British rule it was deliberately created by the Britishers whose policy was "divide and rule". Electorate was formed on the basis of religion and a new

[21] *Ibid.*, p. 143.

[22] For details regarding the step taken to avoid industrial disputes see Chapter on *Labour Welfare*, Vol. II.

party called Muslim League was created. This led to great bloodshed during the year 1942 and just after Independence in 1947. Though the communal tension has lessened to some extent after Independence yet it has not completely died out, as the recent incidents in Madhya Pradesh and Uttar Pradesh show. Though true religion is based upon the spirit of brotherhood, transcending class, caste and race and gives a feeling that all human beings are partners in a common enterprise, yet often this social value is more honoured in the breach than the observance because certain prejudices enter into the minds of persons.

Prejudice is essentially a "prejudgement" of a particular situation before all the facts are in and is often in direct contradiction to the facts. Such prejudices often lead to discrimination. Both these elements, i.e. prejudices and discrimination are symptoms of social disorganization as well as the causes of social disorganization.

The chief reasons given for such prejudices are (1) cultural, (2) religious, (3) endogamous, and (4) personal factor. The cultural factor involves special dietary habits, special rhythms of work and holidays, and special family relationships. The religious factor involves different conception about God and the different ways of finding it. Endogamous factors involve marriage within the group and intermarriage is regarded with disfavour. Personal factors include some fear, frustration and insecurity among the group, manifesting in occasional aggressive and offensive behaviour.

The individual is not born with prejudice against any race, creed or religious group. He learns those prejudices from others in his immediate environment, who have in turn learned or absorbed them as part of their cultural heritage. In this sense, prejudices are part of the cultural pattern. The person who learns or absorbs the prejudices is not necessarily disorganized himself, but is merely responding as he has been taught. If he has prejudice, it is because of desires for social conformity, a wish to be like his fellows. A large number of persons fall into this category and express attitudes of prejudice merely because they have learned them in the course of their personality development.

But this explanation does not account for the origin of prejudice in the first instance or prejudices held by certain individuals who propagate for such prejudices in the masses. The origin and formation of prejudice are extremely complicated phenomenon and includes factors such as (1) biological differences, (2) economic competition, (3) frustration-aggression, (4) rural-urban conflicts, (5) social neurosis, and (6) value conflicts. The biological differences it is believed often make the individual in the dominant group prejudice against others who differ in physical traits from him. The theory of economic competition maintains that the individual is prejudiced against another group if he comes into economic competition with it. The theory of frustration-aggression maintains that frustration tends to produce aggression. The theory of rural-urban conflict, advocates that rural dwellers have often hostility for the urban persons. The theory of social neurosis maintains that the persons of a particular group brand persons of the other group as communists and international bankers, weak and strong, oversexed and impotent, or possess some other sets of completely antithetical characteristics. The value conflict theory is based upon the contradiction between discrimination and the democratic creed, i.e. profession different from practice.

It is often stated by sociologists, psychologists, anthropologists, psychiatrists and others that the deeply prejudiced individual is also in many ways a disorganized person who is usually unhappy and frustrated and has not found a satisfactory status in his own group and vents his satisfactions on other groups through prejudice. He often feels insecure—his sense of not belonging to his group, has a stereotyped thinking, is aggressive and has lack of insight. The prejudiced person is thus fundamentally weak, insecure and disorganized individual.

The prejudices in groups often remain latent and come out in critical times. When the social structure in general is relatively stable and the life of the group continues in tranquil and traditional channels, the masses of people can adjust to the frustrations and inadequacies of normal life, and only when stability is threatened, these frustrations become magnified into mass movements directed against minority groups.

These groups often have social discrimination having different clubs, hotels, resorts and the like or educational discrimination having different institutions. Prejudices are also created through religious education, e.g. Hindus are Kafirs or Muslims favour cow killing. Sometimes there is an organized movement of the religious group against the other. For example, the Muslim league made a strong propaganda against the Hindus before Independence. This propaganda was counteracted by Jan Sangh organization. The members of such organizations are often the persons who are affected by current changes.

There are often riots. But the causes of riots lie more in the frustration of those participating than in the fact community itself. "Riots are a form of mob behaviour and follow the mob pattern : (1) an event provokes the gathering of a crowd ; (2) there is milling ; (3) this leads to excited rumours and hysteria ; (4) anonymity develops ; (5) brutalized emotions arise ; (6) excited leadership takes over ; and (7) violence takes place. Then the mob becomes destructive and irresponsible."[23]

(6) *Lingual and Regional Conflicts.* Due to phenomenal development of regional languages in the nineteenth century there arose an emotional integration of different language groups and the development among them of a consciousness of being a distinct cultural unit (speaking the same language and following the same tradition and culture). Therefore, when progressive public opinion in India crystallized in favour of rationalism of administrative units, the objective was more or less sought in terms of linguistically homogenous units.

The Indian National Congress also supported this view. In 1920 in its annual session at Nagpur, the Congress accepted the linguistic redistribution of provinces as a clear political objective.[24]

However, the Congress which was pledged to reconstitute the provinces on linguistic and cultural basis changed its stand after Independence. The Prime Minister, Mr. Nehru, speaking before the Constituent Assembly in November, 1947 while conceding the linguistic principle remarked, "First things must come first and the first thing is the security and stability of India."[25] The Linguistic Provinces Commission appointed on the recommendation of the Drafting Committee of the Constituent Assembly also remarks, "In forming provinces the emphasis should be primarily on administrative convenience. The homogeneity of language should enter into consideration only as a matter of administrative convenience. Among many other factors which should be given due weight are history, geography, economy and culture."[26] It further pointed out that everything which helped the growth of nationalism had to

[23] Elliott, M. A., and Merrill, F. E., *op. cit.*, p. 658.

[24] *Report of the States Reorganization Commission* (1955), p. 53.

[25] Report, *op. cit.*, p. 4.

[26] *Report of Linguistic Provinces Commission* (1948) p. 131.

go forward and everything which impeded it had to be rejected or should stand over.

The Government of India's Resolution appointing the States Reorganization Commission stated, "The language and culture of an area have an undoubted importance as they represent a pattern of living which is common in that area. In considering a reorganization of States, however, there are other important factors which have also to be borne in mind. The first essential consideration is the preservation and strengthening of the unity and security of India. Financial, economic and administrative considerations are almost equally important, not only from the point of view of each State, but for the whole nation."[27]

The States Reorganization Commission also remarked, "While internal adjustments at state level are to be desired, it is imperative to ensure that these do not lead to maladjustments at the interstate or national level. From the point of view of national unity, reorganization has to aim at a two-fold objective : (*a*) firm discouragement of disruptive sentiments such as provincialism or linguistic fanaticism ; and (*b*) consistent with national solidarity, provision of full scope for the unhampered growth of the genius of each group of people."[28]

The advocates of linguistic principle advocate that the demand for linguistic states does not represent mere cultural revivalism. But it seeks to secure for different linguistic groups political and economic justice, because in multilingual states political leadership and administrative authority remains the monopoly of the dominant language groups, and linguistic minorities are denied an effective voice in the governance of their states. Besides there may be other advantages too, such as a real consciousness of identity of interests between the people and the Government and both work in co-ordination and understanding. Language is a rich and powerful vehicle of expression creating a sense of unity among the peoples speaking them and avoids the multiplicity of languages which lead to weakness and inefficiency in administration. But there are also weighty considerations which are urged against accepting language as the determining principle in the creation of states. This would encourage exclusivism ; blur the feeling of national unity by the emphasis it places on local culture, language and history, create

[27] *Report of the States Reorganization Commission* (1955), p. 25.
[28] *Ibid.*, p. 32.

feeling of superiority as compared to others, intolerance and aggressiveness. Considering both aspects of language problem the State Reorganization Commission came to the conclusion that, "it is neither possible nor desirable to reorganize states on the basis of the single test of either language or culture, but that a balanced approach to the whole problem is necessary in the interest of our national unity."[29] Such a balanced approach was to recognize linguistic homogeneity as an important factor conducive to administrative convenience and efficiency but not to consider it as an exclusive and binding principle overriding all other considerations, administrative, financial and political.

Similarly, the feeling of provincialism cuts at the unity of nation. If the different states pursue policies of their own without regard to the interests of the nation as a whole, the national security may be jeopardized. The States Reorganization Commission rightly remarks, "There has been a tendency during the last few years during which the new Constitution has been in force to lay more and more emphasis on the autonomy of the States. Indian nationalism, on the other hand, has still to develop into a positive concept. It must acquire a deeper content before it becomes ideologically adequate to withstand the gravitational pull of the traditional narrower loyalties."[30]

The sense of Indian unity is a plant of recent origin which is not only to be watered and nourished but protected against hailstorms and gales and against unfriendly climate. This in a measure was recognized by the framers of our Constitution and thus a number of provisions were included in it to safeguard the unity of India. They were : (1) the concurrent list of subjects in respect of which the Union Parliament has overriding legislative authority, (2) provision to legislate in matters of state list in case of grave emergency, (3) provisions enabling Parliament and President to assume legislative and executive functions in states when normal constitutional machinery breaks down, and (4) provisions empowering the Union Government to ensure compliance of laws made by Parliament. However, these special provisions are primarily remedial in character and under the Constitution the states have a large measure of autonomy. Under such circumstances the tendency of states to lay emphasis on their autonomy may jeopardize our national unity

[29] Report, *op. cit.*, p. 405.
[30] Report, *op. cit.*, p. 43.

and security. This tendency of regional and state loyalty must be curbed if Indian nationalism is to develop into a positive concept and if the broader sense of the unity of the country is to be maintained and the links between the centre and the states in order to secure a greater co-ordinated working of national policies and programmes are to be reinforced. However, unfortunately after Independence the tendencies toward lingualism, and regionalism have been on the increase ignoring the national interest. The Anti-Hindu agitation in the South and the Shiv Sena in Maharashtra are instances in point.

Conflicts and Groupism in Larger Organizations—Universities, Municipal Corporations and Legislative Assemblies

We have already mentioned about caste conflicts at the village level and of lingualism at the regional level. Unfortunately they have also taken roots in other important spheres such as Universities, Municipal Corporations, Panchayati Raj Institutions, public administration and political parties. We often find conflict or groupism in our local bodies in Panchayat Samities, Zilla Parishads, etc. Although some type of disagreement or groupism is natural in a democratic country but when they are formed on castes, language or communal basis they are very harmful. Then the real issues are ignored and many appointments or other matters are considered on the basis of caste or creed. This causes undue loss to the nation, when right persons are not put at the right place.

In the case of political parties there are some which are getting aid from outside countries and are thus anti-national in character. Some political parties are formed on communal or linguistic basis. Some are divided just on the basis of personal leadership. Some are too much nationalistic ignoring the social reforms and social service to the masses. Too many political parties are leading to unstable governments which are unable to make any substantial contributions.

CHAPTER XVII

CRITICAL APPRAISAL

We have discussed in the foregoing pages some of the social problems which the country is facing at present. Some of these problems are almost the same as are being faced by some of the industrially advanced countries of the world, e.g. the problems of mental disorder, suicide, delinquency and crime, alcoholism, prostitution, etc. though their extent may be different. However, some are such which are peculiar to this country, e.g. large-scale poverty and unemployment, population explosion, undernutrition, illiteracy, decay of religious institutions, casteism, etc.

We have discussed in each chapter the steps which are necessary to solve these problems. However, there are some more important suggestions which we would like to give in this concluding chapter to reconstruct our society in the light of objectives laid down in the Indian Constitution and these are mostly the objectives of all Democratic Welfare States.[1]

In Chapter I we have pointed out some of the factors leading to Social Disorganization. Among these factors we have mentioned the competition and conflict in the spheres of economic, political and cultural fields, maladjustment in the existing institutions, disbalance in the material and non-material culture, physical or geographical factors, biological factors, the ecological factors, degeneration of values, *laissez faire* policy, disintegration and confusion in roles, political subservience, etc. We have already made an attack on some of these factors after Independence to reorganize the society by the introduction of planning, control of physical factors, family planning, etc. However, some of these factors have still not been touched, e.g. the regeneration of values through reorganization of religious institutions, mass scale programme of adult education, etc. Our contention is that the balanced advance on all the fronts is essential to move in the direction of modernization (not Westernization).

[1] For objectives of a Democratic Welfare State see my book, *Welfare State and Democratic Planning.*

Chapter II deals with Individual Disorganization. We have divided disorganized persons into three broad categories, viz. (1) non-conformists, (2) rebels and revolutionists, and (3) maladjusted or disintegrated persons. In the last category are included the mentally ill or deranged and those who commit suicide. In this chapter we have specially dealt with their problems. The number of mentally ill is not known in this country due to lack of facilities for diagnosis. We need adequate institutions for such persons. Those in mental hospitals are also not given adequate care. We need adequately trained staff and more beds for such persons. The suicide statistics have been collected for the first time in 1964. The suicide rate is quite high in the country, but to know the correct position comparative analysis with respect to some other countries is desirable.

There is a great variation in suicide rates from state to state. The main cause of suicide was dreadful disease, while the next was the quarrel with parents or in-Laws. The first shows that there are not adequate facilities for dreadful diseases in our country. Steps are needed to create such facilities. The second shows that conflict among young couples and parents or in-Laws are very common in our country. Unless the parents change their attitude with changing environments it may not be possible to reduce the number of such cases.

Chapter III deals with Crime and its Causes. Besides the biological and environmental factors which lead to crime generally, three additional factors have been mentioned in reference to our country. These are (1) superstitions, (2) faction and feuds, and (3) exploitation of children by adults. To minimize the number of crimes due to superstitions we need reform in religion and education among masses. The factions and feuds are mainly the result of caste prejudices and narrow loyalties to their groups. To avoid such crimes we need to broaden the outlook of people through adult education and emphasis on constructive programmes to redirect their energies in useful channels. To avoid exploitation of children by adults we need change in the morals of ordinary citizens.

Chapter IV deals with Juvenile Delinquency in India. The statistics show that the juvenile delinquency is on the increase. Many suggestions have already been made in the chapter for the prevention and treatment of juvenile delinquents. Here we would like to point out two important steps which need further attention. As the U. N. O. report on Juvenile Delinquency points out, "perhaps the weakest link in the entire chain of early diagnosis, prevention, treatment and control of juvenile delinquency in this region is the preventive aspect. It has been seen that it is not so much the juvenile as his social environment which creates a predisposition towards delinquency. Hence most of the protective and preventive legislation is directed not towards the potential or pre-delinquency in the juvenile himself, but towards the prevention of cruelty to juveniles or of crime against juveniles by adults and towards the punishments of adults who victimize juveniles. There is hardly any diagnostic or prognostic services which might lead to early detection of the problem personality."[2] In other words, there are no child guidance clinics. Also in India there is very little to differentiate the juvenile jail, Borstals and Reformatory. "Custody-complex is the ruling feature more or less in all the three types of institutions. The importance of individualization, personal contacts and intimate staff-inmate relationship and fostering an inner response in the lad has not been realised. Some rudiments in education and vocational training are thought to be enough. After dusk the lads are locked up in dormitories and thrown on their own resources while in English Borstals there is 15 hours programme and where methodical training, physical and vocational are given."[3]

Chapter V deals with Adult Offenders. We have already mentioned the several steps which have been taken since 1920 for the treatment of adult offenders and improvement of amenities in the prisons. However, first not much has been done for the prevention of crime at the initial stages. The formation of vigilance committees in the villages and towns who could assist the police in this task is essential. Secondly, the jails are still a place of custody than of reformation. The attitude of jail staff is often repressive which need change. For this the training of such jail staff in the methods of social work and modern correctional work is necessary. The opening of jail training schools as has been done in Uttar Pradesh can be a step in the right direction. Thirdly, there is also need of more model prisons and open prisoners camps to facilitate the rehabilitation of prisoners after release. Fourthly, "in the overcrowded jails the largest number are serving short term sentences that have hardly

[2] United Nations Department of Social Affairs, *Comparative Survey of Juvenile Delinquency* (Part IV, Asia and the Far East), (1953), p. 101.

[3] Bhattacharya, B. K., *Juvenile Delinquency and Borstals* (1962), p. 55.

any penological value."[4] The system of probation needs wider use. However, this will require a network of probation services.

Chapter VI deals with Alcoholism and Drug Addiction. The programme introduced in many states since 1946 has not made much headway in the country. Except two or three states which have enforced complete prohibition, the rest have not taken adequate steps for its enforcement. The Study Team on Prohibition (1963) rightly observes, "Despite the fact that prohibition is enshrined in the Constitution as a Directive Principle, no serious or substantial steps of sufficient intensity or extent have been taken which could be proportionate to or in consonance with the magnitude of the problem. So far not even lip sympathy has been given to education on alcohol or alcoholism whereas, misleading propaganda is receiving wide publicity and people have started accepting half truths which are being broadcast by liquor interests. The idea has been spread that prohibition cannot succeed and is doomed to failure. The truth of the matter is that it has not been given a fair trial. The hostile forces are endeavouring to stifle it almost from the date of birth and those who believe in prohibition can hardly be said to have raised their little fingers in support of it."[5] Thus, the recommendations made by the study team for complete prohibition need much serious attention and enforcement than before.

In the case of other drugs like charas, ganja and bhang although most of the states have prohibited their sale, the illegal import from neighbouring countries is still not uncommon. More stern measures are needed in this direction.

Chapter VII deals with Gambling and Smoking. In order to check gambling as a commercial vice there is the Public Gambling Act, 1867, which is applicable to the states of Uttar Pradesh, Punjab and Delhi. Some other states such as Bengal, Bombay, Madras, Rajasthan, Orissa also have special gambling acts to check public gambling. However, in the rest of the states there is no special legislation to check gambling and persons engaged in gambling activities can only be punished under Section 290 of the Indian Penal Code, if it can be shown that their acts cause common injury, danger and annoyance to the public.

Even where the acts exist horse racing under certain conditions and gaming in private houses are still permitted. Not only that

[4] Kerawalla, P. C., *A Study in Indian Crime* (1959), p. 16.

[5] *Report of the Study Team on Prohibition* (1963), pp. 351-52.

there are many loopholes in these acts : (1) Mostly these Acts are applicable to urban areas. (2) In many cases it is difficult to prove that the gambling was being done for commercial purposes. Therefore, unless private gambling was prohibited it is difficult to check gambling completely. There should be comprehensive legislation on all-India basis to check gambling throughout the country. Besides changes in legislation and strict supervision by police it requires strong public opinion to check gambling in homes and at horse races.

We have seen that the use of tobacco products on the whole has increased after Independence. This is particularly so in the case of cigarettes and bidis and snuff. Cigarettes and bidis are more harmful than hookah, while snuff is much time consuming. No serious thought has been given to the bad effects of this evil either by the Congress Party or the Planners, although Mahatma Gandhi advocated for its eradicacy. There are juvenile smoking Acts under which sale of tobacco products is prohibited to children. But they are not enforced properly. To lessen the use of smoking habit in India the whole question requires examination by an expert committee. There should be restriction on such publicity which encourages smoking. The suggestions made by Dr. Oschner to stop smoking need wide publicity.

Chapter VIII deals with the problems of Prostitution. Since the enforcement of the Suppression of Immoral Traffic Act, from April 1958 some good work has, of course, been done in the suppression of immoral traffic. There are training programme for such women in the protective homes. However, there are many difficulties to suppress this evil completely. (1) It is very difficult to prove that a prostitute when living in a separate room is being exploited by the pimp, procurer or brothel-keeper. To get conviction the police must produce, positive evidence, which is a difficult task, as decent persons want to keep away themselves from such things. On the other hand, the evidence of police is not considered enough by the courts. Thus, the only remedy appears to be introduction in the Act of "Presumptive Proof" rather than direct and positive proof. (2) It is also argued that the closure of open brothels will increase the incidence of clandestine prostitution resulting in the establishment of camouflaged brothels all over the cities. But it should not be forgotten that open brothels are the centres of the underworld and many crimes are committed there. Therefore, to avoid the exploitation of victimized women on the one hand and to make their access difficult for men, it is necessary to destroy these brothels. (3) The ordinary police is overburdened by multifarious duties. Therefore, special staff need to be appointed to enforce this Act as has been done in Punjab.[6] It would be better if some special training is provided to such staff in the field of prostitution as has recently been done in Japan. There is also specialized women police to deal with prostitutes.[7] (4) It is true that evils like this cannot be eradicated completely by legislation alone. Therefore, prominent part has to be played by individuals as well as by the society in removing the causes which encourage and facilitate this traffic and also by reporting the suspected cases to the authorities. The other measures to check this crime have already been discussed. Some social workers argue that prostitution should be totally abolished. But how far it is possible is a debatable question, as the present Act only aims at the suppression of immoral traffic and not its total abolition.

Chapter IX deals with the problem of Beggary. It is a complex problem. Since 1956 about 60 beggar homes had been set up in various states for the old, diseased and disabled beggars. A scheme has also been introduced to check juvenile beggary and vagrancy. However, much more remains to be done. (1) There should be all-India Legislation to check beggary in all the states. (2) Those able-bodied adult beggars who *wilfully* and professionally beg should be punished like criminals as recommended by the Study Group 1965. (3) Efforts should be made to provide help to the poor at their homes through social security measures. However, the problem of beggary is related to large-scale poverty and unemployment and unless that is solved it might be difficult to eradicate it.

Chapter X relates to Poverty and Unemployment. We have seen in the foregoing pages that poverty and unemployment are rampant in our country. In spite of our three five-year plans, the number of unemployed has increased from 5 millions in 1956 to 12 millions in 1966, while the per capita income has not increased substantially. It was Rs. 275 in 1951 and rose to Rs. 325 in 1966 giving a small rise of 8 per cent. This is because of rapid growth in population and defective planning. However, the most important factor for this situation is our social climate, where due to joint family system,

[6] Aneaja, S. P., *Trafficking in Women*, Social Welfare, September, 1963, p. 19.

[7] Dr. Edward, Galway, *Seminar on Social Defence* (1964), p. 26.

caste system, religious beliefs and social values many young educated want employment in the offices and do not resort to business or start small industries requiring manual labour and involving some risk. Thus, they will have to break the tradition of their families if this problem is to be adequately solved. The United Nations Population Division rightly observes, "In all the under-developed countries there is a scarcity of workers who possess the skill and abilities required for efficient operation and maintenance of machinery and for technical, clerical and managerial occupations. It is not even easy to find suitable trainees for such jobs among a population composed mainly of peasant farmers and a few artisans using simple tools and little or no machinery. The formation of an efficient labour force depends not only on the abilities and aptitudes of the people but also on their willingness to learn and to do the kind of work in question. The change of occupations often means a complete readjustment of the workers' way of living, and perhaps moving from the homes of their forefathers to new and strange communities. It is not surprising that the material comforts that can be purchased with the wages of new employments are not always sufficient to attract a large number of workers or to hold them permanently."[8]

Chapter XI deals with Population and Health Problems. Although there has been considerable developments in the field of health and related services, there still remains much to be done. The number of primary health units and dispensaries in relation to the needs of the rural areas is quite inadequate. Even in dispensaries there was absence of qualified staff particularly the doctors. Progress in the control of communicable diseases was also hampered due to shortage of trained personnel and the supplies of equipments. There was also lack of safe drinking water supply in the rural areas. In many urban areas the problem of drainage has been accentuated on account of rapid growth of population.[9]

It may also be pointed out that during the three five-year plans there has been no concentrated effort to improve nutrition, change food habits or create great awareness of the problem.

The school health programme cannot make much success due to inadequacy of medical personnel in rural areas. Although the

[8] United Nations Population Division, *Population Growth and Standards of Living in Under-developed Countries*, Proceedings of the World Population Conference, Vol. V (1954), p. 1105.

[9] *Third Five-Year Plan* (1961), p. 652.

Prevention of Food Adulteration Act, 1954 has been amended to inflict more severe punishments on offenders yet much achievement is not possible unless moral standards improve as officials and non-officials both combine to do such acts.

The success of family planning programme has been limited so far. Although the Government has increased the staff and facilities, yet unless people themselves realize its urgency, it cannot make much progress. It has been seen that there is a positive correlation between the economic and education status of women to the family planning practices. This was also revealed in a recent survey of 500 working and non-working women from rural and urban areas of Uttar Pradesh. The survey concludes that family planning has received encouragement among the urban working class with higher income and education.[10] Thus, there is need of education among women and also rise in their income so that the programme may be a success.

Chapter XII deals with Educational and Religious Institutions. In the educational sphere we have dealt with three problems, i.e. (1) adult and social education, (2) students' indiscipline, and (3) education to students in moral and spiritual values. The problem of adult literacy has been recognized since long. Some efforts in this direction were made before Independence too. However, the success has not been much due to various reasons particularly the apathy of many adults who do not realize its importance. However, as adult literacy is the basis of all progress and modernization it cannot be left to its own fate. The pilot experiments being made in Gorakhpur and Lucknow districts in Uttar Pradesh and in certain other states can be a useful guide in this direction. In Gorakhpur the Adult Literacy Pilot Project Programme is being conducted under the Institute of Rural Growth and Planning, Gorakhpur, while in Lucknow the functional literacy programme is being run under the Education Department of Uttar Pradesh.[11]

The students' indiscipline is a complex problem arising from so many factors. However, the basic factor is that many young persons want to achieve success without putting in due labour. In the examination they want to achieve success by copying. In the field

[10] Dr. (Mrs.) Roy, P., "Family Planning Among Indian Women—A Field Study", in *Some Aspects of Women Welfare* (1967), (Ed.), Madan, G. R., p. 61.

[11] Dr. Mehrotra, S. N., "Farmers' Education and Functional Literacy", *National Herald*, February 18, 1968.

of leadership they want to achieve popularity not through success in academic career or social service but by antisocial activities. The elders in authority also have not the courage to check them even when they can do so because of their own moral weakness. Thus, the solution for this difficulty is the imparting of moral education to all.

The imparting of religious and moral values in the schools and colleges has been recommended by various committee and commissions. However, no practical steps have been taken in this direction. It would be better if the scheme is introduced on a pilot basis in certain schools and colleges and then later on extended to other institutions after assessing its drawbacks and difficulties. However, the basic problem is of giving religious education in religious institutions.

In order to impart right type of religious education two steps are needed. Firstly, the reinterpretation of religious literature in the light of scientific advance and modern democracy and secondly consolidation and reorganization of religious institutions. The interpretation of religious literature is an enormous task and needs the co-operation of many scholars and mendicants. The reorganization of religious institutions requires the co-operation of many educated persons who should take active interest in their own religious institutions so as to run them on proper lines. The ad hoc sermons by wandering mendicants are not going to have a lasting effect unless supported by regular sermons by educated priests and laity in their own religious institutions.

Chapter XIII deals with Leisure and Recreation. Although leisure and recreation generally go together yet it is not always so. Recreation must be healthy and useful for the individual as well as society. In the urban areas although we have many parks, playgrounds and various types of clubs for all groups of people, yet their number is inadequate in comparison to the needs. Very few people take part in organized activities like clubs which are useful for the participants as well as for the society as they take up some welfare activities too. Such activities are particularly lacking among women. The Rashtriya Swayam Sewak Sangh, a cultural organization has played a good role in providing healthy recreation as well as developing character of various age groups. However, this is not enough. We need many more civic clubs for various groups where people meet not only for recreation but also to do some constructive work.

I was much impressed by the civic clubs in America in which men and women participated regularly. They contemplate on current social problems and do some social service too. The international club, the rotary club, the lion club and clubs of this type need much encouragement in our country.

In the villages the community centres, the adult education centres, Bhajan Mandalis and such other cultural organizations need proper encouragement. This can be possible only when the post of Social Education Organizer is given due weight and much idle energy is utilized for constructive purposes.

Chapter XIV deals with Political Institutions and Corruption. We have seen that though democracy is the best form of government, yet it has many weaknesses. The change in social values and increasing functions of government have also led to increase in corruption. The politicians, officials and businessmen, all combine to indulge in corruption. Recently the government has taken many steps to check corruption. However, unless the moral values change, it is difficult to lessen it. The tone has to be set up by the political leaders, high officials, and businessmen whose practices are imbibed by the masses.

Chapter XV deals with Family Disorganization. No statistics are available about the desertation and divorce rate in India. However, it is presumed that due to economic dependence of women on their husbands and caste barriers at present the divorce rates are not as high as in the Western countries. But with increasing education among women, their employment, less control of caste and community, and more opportunities of meeting with the opposite sex, the increase in love marriages, conflicts and divorce rate is likely to go up. In such a situation the opening of marriage and family counselling agencies in urban areas with some assistance from Government is desirable.

Chapter XVI deals with Community and National Disorganization. Besides the problems of rehabilitation of displaced persons, communal tensions, caste and class conflicts, regional and lingual conflicts, the conflicts and groupism in institutions like municipal corporations and panchayati samitis, there is the problem of under-organization in rural and urban communities. The Congress party did some constructive work under the leadership of Mahatma Gandhi. Some social reforms were also undertaken under the social reform movement before 1933. But unfortunately after independence the leadership in Congress has not shown much interest in constructive programme. So far other parties have been too small to have any force in the country. But in the changing situation if other democratic political parties particularly the Jan Sangh which is the next to Congress could give some attention to development work along with national outlook, we might be able to move towards the goals laid down in the Constitution.

However, the role of all intellectuals irrespective of their political affiliations, caste and creed in the development of the country cannot be undermined. They must take active part in various institutions and organizations so that they may function properly and help in the development of the community whether at the village, town, district, regional or central level. The various programmes and activities which need to be properly developed have been discussed in these two volumes.

Part Six

POSTSCRIPT

CHAPTER XVIII

SOCIAL DEFENCE PROGRAMMES

THE SOCIAL defence programmes are concerned with those members of the society whose anti-social behaviour is harmful not only to the society but also to their own family members and sometimes even to their own well-being. Such persons include juvenile delinquents, adult offenders, alcoholics, drug addicts, gamblers, prostitutes, beggars, the mentally ill, etc. There are some writers who confine social defence programmes to the area of delinquency and crime. As Dr. Srivastava points out, the "Philosophy of social defence besides other things specifically strives to achieve significant results in preventing or forestalling criminality and treating and rehabilitating the institutional offenders."[1] Shri Ursekar observes, "The idea of social welfare has given rise in recent years to the concept of Social Defence. The idea of Social Defence was envisaged by the U.N.O. and it now includes all programmes which defend the society. The defence of society means the defence of the members of the society. The society needs a protective shield against social delinquents and anti-social elements. One of the means and measures to protect the society is by preventing crime and correcting the criminal, so that a criminal will no more go astray and harm the society but will be reformed and rehabilitated into a good citizen. In short, the soul of Social Defence is the philosophy of change of heart which can be brought about by humane treatment of the offender."[2] However, we have taken a broader view of the social defence programmes as done by the Government of India.

[1] Srivastava, S.P., "Role of Social Workers in Prevention of Crime and Treatment of Offenders" in *Social Defence,* January 1976, Vol. XI, No. 43, p. 4.

[2] Ursekar, H.S., "Role of the Judiciary in relation to Correctional Law and Procedure" in Social defence, April 1972, Vol. VII, No. 28, p. 21.

The Government of India has taken up some special programmes in the area of social defence since the beginning of the Second Five-Year Plan, reference to some of which has already been made in the foregoing chapters.[3] In this chapter we shall like to discuss some of the developments which have taken place since then and specially after 1966. A Government of India publication points out, "In order to curb various forms of personal and social misorganisations, government has taken up special programmes for maladjusted groups and individuals. These programmes known as Social Defence Programmes are organised mainly within the framework of specific legislations and allied measures. These measures include preventive, correctional and rehabilitative services in various areas of social defence such as welfare of prisoners, delinquency control, probation, beggary control and social and moral hygiene."[4] In order to implement the various social defence programmes envisaged under the Second Five-Year Plan, the Government of India set up the Central Bureau of Correctional Services in 1961. This was later reconstituted and renamed in 1975 as the National Institute of Social Defence. The same publication points out, "The Central Bureau of Correctional Services, established in 1961, was reconstituted and renamed on 1st January, 1975 as the National Institute of Social Defence. The Institute has been assigned technical functions with regard to the coordination, standardisation and development of social defence programme in various areas including those relating to the prevention of alcoholism, gambling, suicide and drug addiction."[5] In a way "the Institute is concerned with a wide range of preventive, corrective and rehabilitative services in various areas of social defence, including welfare of prisoners, prisons, reform and administration, juvenile vagrancy, delinquency and crime, probation, beggary, social and moral

[3] See Chapter V, p. 145.

[4] Research and Reference Division, Ministry of Information and Broadcasting, India—A Reference Annual. 1977 and 1978 (New Delhi: Publications Division, Ministry *of* Information and Broadcasting, Government of India, 1978), p. 116.

[5] *Ibid.*, p. II6. Also *see Indian Social Problems,* Vol. II, Social Work (1987) Chapter XXI.

hygiene, alcoholism, gambling, suicide and drug addiction".[6] With a view to achieving the envisaged tasks separate divisions for research, training and common facilities have been created in the Institute.

Individual Disorganization and the Mentally Ill

We have pointed out in Chapter II that personality disorganization occurs when a person abandons the campaign for achieving social approval and retreats into a subjective world. Such persons may have developed psychoneuroses (neuroses) which are relatively mild mental disorders. The symptoms in such cases are: excessive fatigue and bodily complaints, loss of memory or of sensory or motor functions (hysteria) and abnormal anxiety. Persons afflicted with such disorders may be much distressed and a source of nuisance to their associates; yet they are not so dangerous as those suffering from psychoses who have hallucinations and delusions. They are dangerous to themselves and to those around them and must be placed under treatment. Any crisis—a death in the family, an unexpected illness, an injury from an accident, loss of job, disappointment in friendship, etc.—may bring anxiety, while some people create crisis by their own emotional responses to situations. Such persons become fearful and suspicious of those with whom they are associated and thus become mentally disturbed. Any further crisis in their lives may upset the balance even more and lead to insanity and suicide.

We have already pointed out that services for the mentally ill in our country are much less than in certain advanced countries like the U.S.A. Dr. R.M. Verma points out that rapid social change due to technology, urbanization and industrialization has created certain situations in which an individual finds that his social functioning is threatened or that he cannot cope with the tensions and strains which threaten to engulf him. Such people tend to drift away from the mainstream of the society and come to be labelled as 'misfits' and other similar terms. The situation highlighted above could be tackled if the social planners and administrators seriously think of

[6] Ministry of Social Welfare, Government of India, National Institute of Social Defence—*A Perspective,* New Delhi, 1980, p. 3.

developing various large-scale facilities for serving the emotionally sick persons. Such facilities, of necessity, will include child guidance centres, observation-cum-recreational centres for the youth and adults, mental hospitals and mental care clinics and expansion of mental care facilities in each hospital. It will also require the creation of various institutions which are willing to pick up the 'misfit' or the 'drop-out' from the community, provide him a congenial atmosphere for the growth of his personality besides offering him education and training, if necessary.

There is no doubt that the magnitude of the problem is going to increase in the time to come. The need of the day, therefore, is to pay serious attention to this problem and not shy away from it under the plea that we do not have the wherewithal to meet the situation.[7]

Suicide

As regards suicide, the trend is towards an increase in its rate. Shri Sundaram observes that there has been an increase in the suicide rate. In 1969, it was 8.1 per one lakh; which rose to 8.8 in 1973. It is around 10 now. However, the incidence of suicide is not the same in all the States. It is very high in State like Gujarat, For instance, in 1971, 1,010 women ended their lives in Gujarat. It was 700 in 1970, and 650 in 1969.[8] He further adds that a significant percentage of suicides have their origin in social and domestic issues like maladjustment, quarrels between members of the family, ill-treatment by husband and parents-in-law, pregnancy through illicit relationship and disappointment in love. The Indian society is still in the grip of traditional taboos and the woman is often subjected to the traditional enslavement and oppression by the parents-in-law. The obnoxious dowry system has greatly reduced her status. In State like Gujarat, young women are constantly ill-treated and harassed by the elders, particularly mothers-in-laws. Even the husband is nonchalant to this. In Gujarat, the large incidence of suicide among women attracted public attention

[7] Verma, R.M., "Prevention of Suicides" in *Social Welfare,* June 1976, Vol. XXIII, No. 3, p. 12.

[8] Sundaram, Satya, "Anatomy of Suicides" in *Social Welfare,* June 1976, p. 1.

and led to the appointment of a Committee in 1965.[9] The report of the Committee which was based on police records and information obtained through individuals and welfare agencies also came to the above conclusions.[10]

Shri Sundaram further adds that unemployment, debts, dismissal from job due to inefficiency and poverty are some economic reasons leading to suicide. Sometimes suicides are due to purely psychological factors. A person may feel that his life has become so burdensome that it is not worth living. Sometimes, people suffering from prolonged illness resort to suicide. He concludes that there has been a fall in the incidence of suicide among women after the gradual breakup of joint families and the spread of education among them. "We should think of remedial measures for the growing number of suicides. We should ceaselessly make efforts to eradicate poverty, raise educational standards, offer adequate medical and psychiatric help to the poor who have been constantly subjected to mental strains. Since suicide is a social problem, the community should pay personal attention to the problems of the potential suicides. A large number of volunteers may be trained to look into the problems of those who are prone to suicide. Social education alone can solve this problem.

No purpose will be served by simply declaring suicide attempt a crime. The Indian Law Commission which submitted its report to Parliament on November 16, 1971 pleaded for a more humane attitude to the problem of suicides. If the people know the art of treating others, the problem of suicides can be solved, to a large extent".[11]

Crime and its Causes

We have stated in Chapters III and XVII, the changes which have taken place in the concept of crime and the causes which led to it, especially in India. Shri Venugopal Rao points out that there has been a vast change in the trends of crime in this country

[9] Ranade, S.N., "Social Work Research" in *A Survey of Research in Sociology and Social Anthropology,* Bombay, Popular Prakashan, 1974, Vol. II, p. 539.

[10] *Report of the Suicide Enquiry Committee,* Ahmedabad: Government Press, p. 966.

[11] *Ibid,* p. 2.

during the last twenty years or so. After describing twenty types of crimes committed in this country during the seventies, he concludes: "The twenty incidents which have been culled from newspapers and journals of 1978 and 1979 may be taken as typical manifestations of crime and violence in the seventies. They are not isolated instances involving abnormal individuals, but have to be viewed in the light of acts which are approved and rationalised by whole groups or subgroups of people. These fragmented sections make up our society and the totality of their acts and attitudes which back them determine the quality of life. This societal fragmentation occurs in distinct groups based on religion, community, caste and sub-caste, vocation or profession, ethnicity, language, traditional beliefs and cults, political affiliation and ideology. Admittedly no society can be homologous and culture conflict is inherent in every social structure. But in India, the typical incidents which have been narrated at length reflect the deepening crisis of class and culture conflicts superimposed on each other. Each emerging group develops a subculture of its own and accepts criminality in certain situations and under some conditions as an acceptable way of life. The degree of seriousness of their criminal acts may vary according to the artificial confines of law within which they are defined and adjudged. Punishment may not necessarily follow for a variety of reasons. Not surprisingly, crimes of large segments of society are not even known or exposed, a point which has to be constantly kept in mind since the dimensions of unreported crime establishes the inherent criminality of a larger number of people than those who are legally "labelled as criminal".[12] On the basis of motivation for committing a crime, he divides crime into four classes viz., traditional, organized, white collar and political and opines that crimes of the last three categories are increasing in number, though not reported officially, and when reported they are not punished. He observes, "Some categories of cheating and criminal breach of trust are generally reported and registered in urban areas, but

[12] Rao, Venugopal, S., *Crime in Our Society—A Political Perspective*. New Delhi: Vikas Publishing House, 1983, p. 13.

the whole range of such offences committed at higher socio-economic levels and in business circles are never brought into light."[13]

He also points out that no doubt the present correctional ideology which lays emphasis on reformation and rehabilitation of erring criminal for prevention of crime has its own value, yet some deterrent punishment and speedy justice are also desirable to keep a check on crime. He further adds that there is complete and unabashed neglect of the victims of crime in the present system of justice. There is an increasing concern for the treatment of the criminal and the virtual blackout of the unfortunate situation of the victim. The welfare state must protect its citizens against crime and compensation should be paid to the victims for their injury. The scheme of restitution for victims of crimes of violence needs to be introduced.

He concludes by saying that we must restructure our criminal law and procedure to meet the realities of today and the forbidding challenges of tomorrow.[14] Criminals are no longer the pervert but common citizens of upper strata. "He can be seen in the astute businessman who cheats a whole community, the blackmarketeer who cleverly plays upon the economic theories of demand and supply, the tax evader as well as the collector, the bureaucrat who savours the sense of power, the trade union leader, the caste elder, the landlord, the spiritualist, the politician in the web of incessant manipulations for power and the man with cause."[15] However, we do not totally agree with Shri Rao as mere changes in law cannot bring improvement in our society, and moral regeneration of the country as suggested in Chapters XIV and XIX under the head Corruption is desirable to solve this problem to some extent.

Juvenile Delinquency

"Crime and delinquency rates show that the problem of juvenile delinquency is on the increase not only in India but also all over the world. To explain this phenomenon, a number of factors have been cited. Processes like industrialisation,

[13] *Ibid.*, p. 36.
[14] *Ibid.*, p. 147.
[15] *Ibid.*, p. 46.

urbanisation and modernisation have created a crisis of values throwing the entire social structure off-balance... Young boys and girls in sizeable proportions take to social unacceptable forms of behaviour like vagrancy, alcohol and drug abuse, gambling, sexual promiscuity and the like. In a number of places, abstaining from classes and taking to rampage on slightest pretext have become almost a routine. What is more, they offer plausible rationalisation for their behaviour."[16]

As stated above, juvenile delinquency is on the increase, although the figures given below do not indicate the correct picture. There are many reasons for this: (1) The figures of delinquency are collected from courts or from police and do not include the misconduct of youthful offenders. (2) A large number of violations and violators are seldom detected. Even if they are detected, only a small proportion of them are reported to the police, a still smaller proportion go to the court. (3) The delinquent acts of the affluent and the highly placed are rarely reported.

TABLE 33[17]

TOTAL COGNIZABLE CRIME AND JUVENILE CRIME IN INDIA

Year	*Population in millions*	*Total cognizable crime under IPC*	*Juvenile crime under IPC*	*Percentage of juvenile crime to total crime*	*Volume of juvenile crime per lakh of population*
1968	511.1	862016	21385	2.5	4.2
1972	563.5	984773	31199	3.2	5.5
1976	613.3	1090887	36655	3.4	6.0
1981	6901	1385757	61019	4.4	8.8
1986	7661	1405835	55887	4.0	7.3
1989	8118	1529844	18457	1.2	2.3
1990	8270	1604449	15230	0.9	1.8

The above Table 33 indicates that the total number of crimes committed by juveniles slightly decreased in 1986 and much

[16] National Institute of Social Defence, Ministry of Social Welfare, Government of India, *Towards Delinquency Control,* New Delhi: 1979, p. 1.

[17] The figures for the years 1968 to 1976 have been taken from the publication "Towards Delinquency Control" (1979), op. cit, p. 11 while figures from 1981 to 1990 are from Crime in India 1990 (1991) brought by National Crime Record Bureau, Ministry of Home Affairs, Government of India, New Delhi: p. 136.

more in 1989 and 1990. So far as steep decline in the number of crimes committed in 1989 and after is concerned, it has to be stated that definition of juveniles changed under the new Juvenile Justice Act, 1986 as the National Crime Record Bureau points out that the new definition of juveniles compared to old one excludes male in the age group of 16 to 21 years and females in the age group of 18 to 21 years. "Crime cases attributed to juveniles are therefore reduced. It is for this reason that juvenile delinquency under IPC has substantially decreased in 1989."[18] As stated above, the share of juvenile delinquency in total crimes also decreased from 1.2 per cent in 1989 to 0.9 per cent in 1990. This may be a good sign. But as stated earlier, the reported juvenile crimes do not indicate the correct position as most of these crimes remain unreported and the problem of neglected and orphan children is also there.

The Eighth Plan points out that the decline in social obligations by extended family members towards children who become orphaned, the breakdown of families and the absence of support to single-parent women-headed households has increased the problem of child neglect and child abuse. Although there is no reliable data about the magnitude of the problem, its increasing visibility, specially in urban areas in the form of street children, beggary and vagrancy, is a pointer.[19]

As stated in Chapter IV, there cannot be a single solitary reason for the commission of crime but it is the result of many factors. These factors may be broadly divided into two, viz., (i) inside the home, and (ii) outside the home. The factors are parental discord, unhappy home background, wrong parental attitudes, comparison and jealousy between siblings, poverty, poor housing, etc. For want of basic needs inside the home, the child seeks opportunities outside and in the process meets with vulnerable situations with the result that he becomes a victim of the vice of juvenile delinquency.

The factors outside the home contributing to juvenile delinquency are bad company, gang influence, indifferent school authorities, inadequate recreational facilities, truancy, vagrancy, indecent film shows, prospect of easy earning, etc. One of these

[18] Crime in India 1990 (1991), op. cit., p. 132.
[19] Eighth Five-Year Plan (1992), p. 398.

factors or a combination of more than one factor paves the way for delinquency of child.[20]

Prevention and Control of Delinquency

The Asian and Pacific Regional Preparatory Meeting for the Sixth United Nations Congress on the prevention of crime and the treatment of offenders held at Manila in May, 1978 deliberated over the problem of juvenile delinquency and came out with a number of valuable suggestions. The Preparatory Meeting observed, "There is no substitute for strong family ties in relation to juvenile delinquency. It was emphasised that community-based actions were more successful than government interventions. Experiments have dispelled the notion that non-punitive or social welfare approach towards the juvenile offenders encourages disregard for law. In the view of the delegates, the endangered youngsters should be dealt with by their families, voluntary agencies and not by juvenile courts, but such neglected inmates should either be placed with foster homes or with community-based facilities.[21]

Each delinquent child offers a unique set of problems and should be studied in relation to his own local situations. The home, the school, the neighbourhood where he moves, the place of work and leisure time, all influence the individual and enter into the making of his personality. Therefore, a community programme of delinquency prevention should be based on creating a happy home situation, harmonious social adjustment, proper facilities of education, training and recreation, while developing a proper sense of values and respect for laws. The major constituents in this programme are the home, the neighbourhood, and the school. Thus the emphasis has to be on non-institutional services for the prevention of juvenile delinquency. As Shrimati J. Shah rightly points out, "Prevention of delinquency, vagrancy and beggary at the local neighbourhood level has a great potential, which has not been realised. Instead of allowing a child with behaviour problems and maladjustment at home, and at school to drift into delinquency, it is far more economical

[20] Central Bureau of Correctional Services, Department of Social Welfare, Government of India, *Juvenile Delinquency—A Challenge,* New Delhi: 1970, p. 2.

[21] *Towards Delinquency Control* (1979), *op. cit.,* p. 14.

to tap the resources of the community to prevent the future problems. The purpose of *non-institutional* services is to recognise pre-delinquent traits at an early stage; provide channels for aggressive behaviour into socially approved patterns and to equip them for better adjustment in society. Large industrial towns, with poor housing, and lack of recreational facilities, require at every neighbourhood level boys' clubs or youth centres which can provide (i) counselling and guidance to predelinquent children, (ii) organised recreational activities for them, (iii) training units for those who drop out from school, and (iv) contact-clubs for organising the community for preventing delinquency in collaboration with voluntary social work agencies on a neighbourhood basis."[22]

Protection and Treatment of Juvenile Delinquents

We have already pointed out in Chapter IV that to deal effectively with neglected and delinquent children, the Central Government passed the Children Act, 1960, which is often regarded as a milestone in this direction. The Act was to be applicable to Union Territories only, yet some other States including Assam, Rajasthan, Haryana, Madhya Pradesh, Jammu & Kashmir which did not have such Acts in the past, incorporated its main features into their Children Acts. The Children Act, 1960, was amended in 1978 to remove certain lacunae so as to make the legislation more effective in relation to the treatment of different categories of neglected and delinquent children. Under the present Act, the children were rigidly classified under two categories, i.e., either neglected or delinquent, which overlooked the fact that more often than not delinquency was the result of neglect. In the amendment, this classification was given up to make it more fluid. As a consequence, the cases could be transferred from the Juvenile Court to the Child Welfare Board which was not possible under the existing provision. Similarly, now it was not necessary to keep all the delinquents during the period of trial in Observation Homes and a child could be sent to another place of safety where he may get individual care and warmth.

[22] *Juvenile Delinquency—A Challenge*, 1970, *op. cit.*, p. 5.

Juvenile Justice Act, 1986

With a view to providing a uniform pattern of justice to juveniles throughout the country, the Juvenile Justice Act, 1986 was enacted by Parliament in December 1986 replacing Children's Acts in various States/Union Territories. The Act came into force from 2nd October, 1987 throughout the country except Jammu and Kashmir. It provides for care, protection, treatment, development and rehabilitation of neglected or delinquent juveniles and adjudication of certain matters relating to, and disposition of delinquents. It lays down a uniform legal framework so as to ensure that no child under any circumstances is lodged in jail or police lock-up. Juvenile welfare boards and juvenile courts have been established to provide for a specialised approach towards neglected and delinquent juveniles respectively. During the pendency of any enquiry regarding the juvenile, he shall, unless he is kept with his parents or guardians, be sent to an observation home or a place of safety. After the enquiry is complete (unless institutionalisation is considered necessary) neglected and delinquent juveniles shall be lodged in juvenile homes and special homes respectively. The Act represents a blueprint for fair, equitable and just treatment of juveniles with due emphasis on the rights of child.[23]

In order to effectively implement this Act by establishing and strengthening requisite infrastructure in States/Union Territories, Ministry of Welfare is implementing a centrally-sponsored scheme for prevention and control of juvenile maladjustment since 1986-87. Under this scheme, assistance is provided for setting up/upgradation of observation homes, juvenile homes, special homes and after-care facilities as well as training of functionaries. Expenditure is shared between Central and State governments equally.

The infrastructure for implementation of the Juvenile Justice Act, 1986 was to be set up in all the States to provide care, protection, development and rehabilitation to neglected and delinquent children. Existing facilities and standards of services in the institutions were to be improved. Diversified vocational

[23] India: A Reference Annual (1990), pp. 229-30.

training programmes were to be developed and linked with the existing vocational training institutions.[24]

There is a dearth of after-care organisations for the rehabilitation of juveniles who have no one to bank upon after their release from the correctional institutions. As Professor K.S. Shukla points out, "After-care schemes were started in the last decade of the last century, but they have not show signs of growth numerically or structurally. Although they have an unenviable role in the rehabilitative process and are important for a released juvenile, yet except in Maharashtra, Tamil Nadu, U.P., West Bengal and Delhi, they have not been able to assume systematised and concrete shape. Both official and non-official agencies may have to share the blame for inadequate attention to this scheme."[25] Thus special efforts will have to be made to make up this deficiency in States which lack these facilities. The number of institutions for neglected and delinquent children under the Juvenile Justice Act, 1986 in different States/UTs during the year 1998-99 may be seen from Table 34.

In the enforcement of juvenile legislation and prevention of delinquency, the role of the police is very important. As such some of the States have organized Juvenile Aid Bureaux or Juvenile Aid Police Units. These units have generally been set up in major cities with police officers specially trained in handling juvenile delinquents and with female officers and constables to deal with girls. However, most of the States have still to establish such units.

Although, as stated above, in the case of treatment of children non-institutional services have a prominent role and legislation provides a wide scope for such services, the community participation in the prevention and control of juvenile delinquency in India is negligible. Similarly, voluntary organisations also have not taken much interest in this work, with the exception of a few States like Gujarat, Maharashtra, and Tamil Nadu which have such institutions as Children's Aid Society; Society for the Care, Treatment and Training of Children in need of Special Care, etc. Much more effort will be

[24] Eighth Five-Year Plan (1992), p. 400.

[25] Shukla, K.S., Juvenile Delinquency in Encyclopedia of Social Work, Vol. II, Ministry of Welfare, Government of India, (1987) p. 141.

needed in this direction. As regards probation as non-institutional method of treatment of delinquents, this we have discussed under the head 'Treatment of Adult Offenders'.

An Integrated Programme for Juvenile Justice

During the year 1998-99, the scheme for Prevention and Control of Juvenile Social Maladjustment which the Ministry has been operating since 1986-87 was also revised with a view to strengthening the implementation of the Juvenile Justice Act, 1986 in the country and bringing about a qualitative improvement in the services provided under the scheme to both neglected as well as delinquent children. The salient features of the revised scheme which is called: "A Programme for Juvenile Justice" are as follows:

(i) Establishment of a National Advisory Board (NAB) on juvenile justice to advise the government on matters relating to the implementation of Juvenile Justice Act, 1986 in the country including the quality of infrastructure and the staff available under the Act. The Chairperson of the NAB is the Secretary, Ministry of Social Justice and Empowerment and it has representations from other Ministries of the Government of India, State Governments, Juvenile Welfare Boards, Juvenile Courts, Schools of Social Work, Law Schools and NGOs.

(ii) Creation of a Juvenile Justice Fund.

(iii) Establishment of a secretariat for the National Advisory Board.

(iv) Constitution of a Social Audit Pane (SAP) comprising 5-6 eminent persons to report upon juvenile justice facilities in the country.

(v) Institution of a chair on Juvenile Justice at the Child and the Law Centre of the National Law School of India University, Bangalore.

(vi) Appointment of observers to report upon implementation of the Act in different States/UTs.

(vii) Institution of awards for the best maintained Juvenile Justice Institutions in each State and at the National level.

(viii) Training, orientation and sensitization of judicial, administrative, Police and NGO personnel responsible for implementation of the Juvenile Justice Act, 1986.

(ix) Provision of 100% financial assistance to States/UTs/ voluntary organisations to facilitate creation of infrastructure prescribed under the Act in hitherto uncovered districts of the country.

(x) Financial assistance to bring about a qualitative improvement in the existing infrastructure.

(xi) Expansion of non-institutional services such as sponsorship, foster-care, probation, etc. as alternatives to institutional care.

(xii) Provision of scholarships to children being processed under the Act for excelling in academics or in extra-curricular activities.[26]

Juvenile Justice Act 2000 and After

In this Act, it is stated that "Whereas, the General Assembly of the United Nations has adopted the convention on the Rights of Child on the 20th November, 1989; and whereas, the convention on the Rights of the Child has prescribed a set of standards to be adhered to by all State parties in securing the best interests of the child and whereas the Convention on the Rights of Child emphasizes social reintegration of child victims, to the extent possible, without resorting to judicial proceedings, and whereas the government of India has ratified the Convention on the 11th December, 1992, and whereas, it is expedient to re-enact the existing law relating to Juveniles, this act has been enacted by Parliament in 2000. The Convention on the Right of the Child lays down four sets of rights for the child: The Right to Survival, The Right to Protection, the Right to Development and the Right to Participation.[27]

This Act was further amended in 2006. The new provision in this amendment is to provide for the effective implementation of the Act through constitution of Child Protection Units at States and district level.

As stated above, some action had already been taken on the basis of this Convention, but due to certain limitations in the earlier act, more action could be taken on the basis of this New Act of 2000 as amended in 2006.

[26] Annual Report (1998-99), Ministry of Social Justice and Empowerment, p. 68.

[27] The Juvenile Justice (Care and Protection of Children) Act, 2000, Ministry of Social Justice and Empowerment, Government of India, p. 9.

A separate Ministry for Women and Child Development came into existence from 30th January, 2006. All subjects relating to child welfare/protection like the Juvenile Justice (Care and Protection of Children) Act 2000, Central Adoption Resource Agency (CARA) and Adoption which were earlier under M/o Social Justice and Empowerment have since been transferred to the newly created Ministry of Women and Child Development.

The Juvenile Justice Act, 2000 recognizes the legal necessity of care and protection of children i.e. below 18 years. It has been enforced in the entire country from 1-4-2001. The Act lays down the setting up of Juvenile Justice Boards consisting of a Metropolitan Magistrate/Judicial magistrate and two social workers, one of which shall be female worker in every district. The State Governments were also required to set up Child Welfare Committees for discharging all functions regarding children in need of care and protection as laid down in the Act.

There is also an Integrated Child Protection Scheme for setting up of child protection units in each State and District with financial assistance from the Government of India to provide institutional as well as non institutional support for children in difficult circumstances. Thus both Juvenile in conflict with law and child in the need of care and protection are provided with adequate services.[28]

Treatment of Adolescent Offenders

As pointed out in Chapter XVII, the custody-complex was the feature in the Borstal institutions in most of the States, and the importance of individualisation, personal contacts and intimate staff inmates relationship and fostering an inner response in the lad was not realised. Moreover, the existing facilities for the treatment and training of adolescent offenders were inadequate. Statistics available from various States and Union Territories indicate that in the year 1980, there were about 15 thousand persons of the age 16 to 21 in prisons. The Conference of Chief Secretaries held in 1979 considered the inadequacy of Borstal institutions in the country, and recommended that each big State should have at least one Borstal school and small

[28] Annual Report 2006-2007, Ministry of Women and Child Development, Government of India, pp. 66-67. For more details also see Chapters IV and XXI on Child Welfare Services in Vol. II of this book Indian Social Problems.

States could set up a joint institution at a suitable place. There were juvenile jails in some of the States where young age of the offender was the only consideration and benefits of some other statutory provisions of the Borstal School Act were not available to the inmates of juvenile jails. As such there was an urgent need for establishment of Borstal schools in all the States.[29]

TABLE 34[30]

STATEWISE INSTITUTIONS FOR NEGLECTED AND DELINQUENT CHILDREN UNDER THE JUVENILE JUSTICE ACT, 1986

S. No.	*State/UTs*	*Observation Home*	*Juvenile Home*	*Special Home*	*After-Care Institutions*	*Total*
1.	Andhra Pradesh	9	5	2	1	17
2.	Arunachal Pradesh	1	1	-	-	2
3.	Assam	7	25	1	1	34
4.	Bihar	10	8	5	2	25
5.	Goa	2	2	2	-	6
6.	Gujarat	25	5	2	14	46
7.	Haryana	3	3	1	1	8
8.	Himachal Pradesh	-	1	1	-	2
9.	Karnataka	22	19	_	11	52
10.	Kerala	12	5	2	-	19
11.	Madhya Pradesh	22	2	3	1	28
12.	Maharashtra	45	101	3	3	152
13.	Manipur	1	2	1	-	4
14.	Meghalaya	I	-	-	-	1
15.	Mizoram	3	3	-	-	6
16.	Nagaland	-	1	1	-	2
17.	Orissa	12	2	-	-	14
18.	Punjab	7	2	1	2	12
19.	Rajasthan	11	4	1	-	16
20.	Sikkim	1	-	-	-	1
21.	Tamilnadu	14	17	3	3	37
22.	Tripura	1	1	-	-	2
23.	Uttar Pradesh	59	10	1	-	70
24.	West Bengal	7	19	4	6	36
25.	A &N Islands	-	-	-	-	-
26.	Chandigargh	1	1	1	-	3
27.	Dadra & Nigar Haveli	-	-	-	-	-
28.	Daman & Diu	-	-	-	-	-
29.	Delhi	3	11	-	-	14
30.	Laks had weep	-	-	-	-	-
31.	Pondicherry	1	1	I	1	4
	Total	280	251	36	46	613

[29] Bhatlacharayya, S.K., *Social Defence-Art Indian Perspective,* Delhi, Manas Publications, 1985, p. 47.

[30] Annual Report (1998-99), Ministry of Social Justice and Empowerment, p. 191.

Treatment of Adult Offenders

As recommended by various committees appointed by the Government in the past, the undertrials are now kept separate from the convicts. But all the persons under trial, irrespective of the nature of the offence they are charged with, are herded together. It would be better if they are kept separate on the basis of the nature of the crime committed. Further, according to the provisions of the Jail Manual, undertrials cannot be put to any kind of labour except when they elect to do so. Such persons whose body and brain remain idle are bound to create trouble for others. Therefore, some kind of work should be provided to all types of undertrials. Shri Misra points out that "Amongst the terms of reference of the All India Jail Manual Committee, 1957-59, was included the question of classification of prisoners on scientific lines for purposes of reformatory treatment and abolition of short-term sentences. Both these things are still lacking in our prison administration."[31]

To provide better facilities and treatment in jails, the All India Jail Manual Committee, 1957-59, recommended that certain additional officers including Chief Officer, Vocational Training Projects; Chief Officer, Education and Cultural Activities; Chief Officer, Agriculture; Chief Officer, Physical Education; and Chief Supervisor, Buildings, be appointed at the State headquarters of prison administration. But such officers have not been appointed so far. Shri Misra concluded by saying, "The scientific classification and treatment of the prisoners as well as the psychological effect of the environment in which they undergo punishment are important considerations. Looked at from that point of view, our jail buildings are grossly inadequate to the requirements. There can be no scientific classification if the prisoners are herded together in barracks. The locking up of short-term prisoners as well as of undertrials along with convicts also adversely affect all the inmates of a person. The scope for scientific treatment does not exist. . . What a prison should look like and how it should be built are major problems. We can only get sound advice from an architect when we are

[31] Misra, B.K., "A Glimpse into Jail Administration" in *The Journal of Correctional Work.* 1976, No. XXII, Lucknow, Jail Training School, Government of Uttar Pradesh, p, 56.

clear in our minds about our requirements and have the ability to pay for what we want. In the existing conditions, neither of these factors are present. Prison architecture has engaged the attention of very progressive countries against the background of jail reforms... Our prison buildings are mostly about hundred years old and some are older... These basic difficulties of buildings and paucity of funds preclude any large scale improvement and reforms in jail administration in the foreseeable future."[32]

It may further be stated that the Model Prison Manual prepared by the Committee provided broad guidelines for the State Governments to revise their respective jail manual. In pursuance of one of the recommendations, the Central Bureau of Correctional Services was established in 1961 under the Ministry of Home Affairs as a Central Organisation to bring about uniformity in the implementation of policies and programmes in the field of prisons and other correctional services in the country. This organisation has been striving to persuade the State Governments to revise their jail manuals, so that a broad uniformity could be achieved in respect of maintenance of prisons and treatment of prisoners. "Despite the relentless efforts by the Government of India, several States are yet to revise their jail manuals in accordance with the guidelines contained in the Model Prison Manuals."

In 1972, the Government of India appointed a Working Group on Prisons to examine measures for streamlining and improving the jail administration and living conditions of prison inmates. The Working Group studied various aspects of prison administration, viz., overcrowding in prisons, prison buildings, vocational training for prisoners, staff structure and training of prison personnel and made a fervent plea that the prison administration should be treated as a part of national development plan so that sufficient funds could be made available for the improvement of the existing facilities. In order to bring about a uniform pattern of administration, the Working Group also made a suggestion for the transfer of the subject from State List to Concurrent List. But these recommendations of the Group did not find favour with the State Governments or the Government of India. However, the Government of India

[32] *Ibid.*, p. 58.

in the years 1977-78 and 1978-79, made a provision of Rs. 2 crores and Rs. 4 crores respectively for financial assistance to the State Governments to enable them to initiate action for improvement in areas, such as improvement of buildings, modernisation of prison, industry and agriculture, provision of scientific and technological facilities in prisons, equipments for training programmes, etc.

There is overcrowding in the prisons and the buildings are dilapidated. All types of prisoners including undertrials, convicts, casuals, habituals, juvenile and young adult offenders, female offenders, mentally sick and physically handicapped are generally lodged in the same institution, leaving little scope for their specialised treatment and training. According to the All India Committee on Jail Reforms, 1980-83, there were 76 Central Prisons, 250 district prisons, 822 sub-jails, 27 open jails and 20 special jails in 1980. The total capacity of all these institutions was 79,544, 63,654, 26,057, 6,640 and 4,626 respectively. There were also 6 institutions for women offenders, 8 juvenile jails and 11 Borstal schools with an inmate capacity of 975, 1,827 and 2,102 respectively. Out of a total of 1,59,692 prisoners, 92,276 were undertrials.[33] Thus more than half of the total prison population were undertrials. While commenting on the problem of overcrowding, the Committee observed, "Overcrowded prisons tend to be unmanageable on correctional lines. In some of the States, prison barracks are so overcrowded that inmates have to sleep in shifts. Under such conditions custody of inmates becomes the primary, and probably the only, concern of the staff and even the care and welfare of inmates is neglected. The frequent influx of large number of agitators further worsens the situation and aggravates the problem of prison management."[34]

The Supreme Court of India in various judgments have brought out the shortcomings in the prison administration in the country and pointed out the inadequacy of prisons to function as centres of reformation. The Government of India, therefore, in July 1980 set up an All India Committee on Jail

[33] *Report of the All India Committee on Jail Reforms, 1980-83* (New Delhi: Ministry of Home Affairs, Government of India, 1983), Vol. I, p. 19.

[34] *Ibid.*, p. 21.

Reforms to study and analyse various prison problems. The Committee made a thorough study of the problems of overcrowding, prolonged detention of undertrial prisoners, lack of proper treatment programmes, etc. and have put forward a large number of valuable recommendations for the improvement of existing conditions in prisons in keeping with the modern objectives of reformation and rehabilitation of prisoners in society. "Based on the recommendations, certain areas were identified as essential to be taken on a priority basis and the financial requirement for implementing that was projected to the Eighth Finance Commission. The Commission has recommended certain outlays and it has been decided to release to various State Governments funds to the extent of Rs. 137.56 crores over the four-year period, i.e. 1985-89. These funds are proposed to be utilised for creating additional jail capacity for undertrials, young offenders, women prisoners, lunatic prisoners and for providing prison amenities, i.e., water supply, sanitary latrines, electrification."[35]

The Ministry of Welfare has recently formulated a scheme for welfare of prisoners for providing counselling and guidance to prisoners and setting up of rehabilitation homes for facilitating reintegration of offenders within the community. It is a Centrally-sponsored scheme where expenditure is equally borne by State Governments and Central Government. Objective of the scheme is to identify the cases of institutionalised offenders who need prolonged care, protection and assistance in the community, on their release.[36]

Probation

As stated in Chapter V, the Central Probation of Offenders Act was passed in 1958. Since then all the States except Nagaland, Jammu & Kashmir and Sikkim, have enforced this Act in their areas.[37] The scope of this Act is wider than the earlier Probation of Offenders Acts of the States. The States

[35] Publications Division, Ministry of Information and Broadcasting, Government of India, *India 1985—A Reference Annual*, New Delhi: 1986, pp. 529-30.

[36] India: A Reference Annual 1990, p. 23.

[37] Bhattacharayya, S.K., "Origin and Development of Probation" in *The Journal of Correctional Work*, 1976, *op. cit.*, p. 17.

Acts had restricted the use of probation to first offenders only, whereas the Central Act extends its use to all offenders except those who are found guilty of having committed an offence punishable with death or imprisonment for life. 'The State Probation of Offenders Act did not make any provision for pre-sentence enquiries of cases by Probation Officers. Under section 6 of the Central Act, this enquiry has been made compulsory. This section imposes restrictions on imprisonment of offenders below 21 years of age and makes pre-sentence enquiry in respect of such offenders obligatory. Besides, the Act should be applied more liberally than hitherto in all cases where it can be and particularly in the case of youthful offenders. The Probation Officers should be professionally qualified persons with necessary aptitude. It need be stated that the year 1971 was observed as a Probation Year with a view to focusing attention on the extramural treatment of offenders. The Central Bureau of Correctional Services on that occasion pointed out, "Annually, a total number of 13.5 lakhs of people approximately pass through the portals of the prisons for various reasons as undertrials or convicts. Of these about 20% are children and young persons below 21 years of age, i.e., as many as 2.7 lakhs of young persons pass through ordinary prisons. This does not include children who are tried by juvenile courts under Children Acts. . . . The task of preventing the admission of the entire group of 2.7 lakhs of young prisoners, passing through prisons, is stupendous... The Probation Year seeks to initiate a new trend of thinking as regards the real aim of punishment among the police, courts, judiciary, prison officers and Probation Officers. It does not need hard thinking to realise that a prison term does no good to children and young people."[38] Enlightened citizens and voluntary organisations can also contribute a lot in this direction by helping offenders in offering bail, by offering surety for bonds to the courts, by working as voluntary Probation Officers to help them in getting jobs and readjustment to normal life in the community. In countries like Japan, there are thousands of voluntary Probation Officers who help offenders in various ways without any monetary gain.[39]

[38] Central Bureau of Correctional Services, *Probation Year 1971*. New Delhi: 1971, p. 5.

[39] *Ibid.*, p. 9.

The probation of offenders rules of all States provide for the appointment of part-time probation officers and voluntary probation officers. The idea is to promote public participation in the field of probation and allied measures for the treatment of offenders under the community. "It is felt that there should be short training courses for all voluntary probation officers soon after their selection."[40]

Treatment through Community Services

It was pointed out in Chapter V that the idea gradually veered round the fact that prisons did not serve the purpose of training and rehabilitation of all categories of prisoners and the futility of short-term imprisonment was brought into focus and importance of rehabilitating prisoners back into the society through abolition of life sentence and institution of indeterminate sentence was considered more desirable. Thus, in course of time, various extramural methods of treatment were developed including probation, parole, premature release, pre-release guidance centres, community residential training centres, half way houses, community service, work-release, day-five system, etc.[41]

The Working Group on Prisons (1972) had made some valuable suggestions for introducing certain new modes of punishment such as externment, payment of compensation to victims, corrective labour and public censure. However, the corrective labour scheme is yet to be put into use, which can be helpful to the society. The criminal justice system in India envisages active participation of the public in the process of apprehension, trial, treatment, reformation and rehabilitation of offenders. In fact, the success of social defence schemes covering various aspects of the prevention of crime and treatment of offenders depends on the extent to which the cooperation of voluntary welfare agencies can be purposefully utilised in the community. The scheme of voluntary probation officers is much dependent on public cooperation. Some voluntary organisations like Children's Aid Society, Bombay; the Guild of Service, Madras; the Crime Prevention Societies in some States are doing some useful

[40] Bhattacharayya, S.K., *op. cit.*, 1985, p. 85.

[41] *Ibid.*, p. 100.

service. The idea of community service by offenders is comparatively of recent development in respect of the non-custodial treatment of offenders. It was realised that the people who committed minor offences would be better occupied doing a service to their fellow citizens than sitting alongside others in a crowded jail. The scheme of community service has become very popular in Britain and need to be developed in India.

Under the Criminal Justice Act, 1972, the courts in Britain were empowered to order offenders to perform unpaid work as a service to the community. It was alternative to short custodial sentence as a means of making people pay for their offences rather than merely spend a short time in an overcrowded prison. It is a court order ranging from 40 to 240 hours and performed during leisure mainly on a week basis. It may include various tasks, either work of practical nature or work with people engaged in community service. The work is administered by the probation service in cooperation with other organisations, usually voluntary agencies. The service has been developed extensively in view of the mountaing problem of prisons' population and at the same time to harness the energy of offenders for the benefit of society. Thus punishment is used as constructive work.

After-Care of Prisoners: As pointed out in Chapter V that Prisoners Aid Societies were formed in some States on the basis, of recommendations made by the Indian Jails Committee (1918-19). However good work was done by these societies only in three or four States. The Advisory Committee on After-Care Programme (1954) again emphasised on after-care programme to be taken up by voluntary organisations for orphan children, physically handicapped, the delinquent children, the widows and beggars. But there was not much progress reported in these programmes from the voluntary agencies as observed by the Study Team on Social Welfare (1959). However on the basis of recommendations made by the Advisory Committee (1954), district shelters were set up in some States where discharged prisoners could stay about three months and received help to readjust to society. "State homes for men and women were also set up where ex-prisoners could stay for longer periods and get training in various crafts."[42] The All India Jail Manual Committee (1957) and the All India Seminar on Correctional Services held in Delhi in 1969 again laid emphasis on the improvement of after-care services for the discharged prisoners. However due to the dearth of voluntary workers and organisations, not much has been done in this field, although on an average about 4,00,000 prisoners are released every year from jails in this country.

Alcoholism and Drug Addiction

It was pointed out in Chapter VI that the prohibition programme was not being followed uniformly in all the States. In some States, there was complete prohibition, in some others prohibition was partial, while the remaining States were mostly wet. The Planning Commission in the Second Five-Year Plan on the basis of recommendations made by the Prohibition Enquiry Committee gave certain guidelines to the States to be followed by them. In the States, which were still wet the following steps were to be taken: advertisements connected with drinking were to be banned; drinking in public premises such as hotels, restaurants, clubs, etc. was to be stopped; the number of liquor shops was to be progressively reduced; the number of dry days in each week was to be increased; supplies as well as proof strengths of liquor were to be reduced; consumption of inexpensive and soft drinks was to be encouraged. In the States where there was partial prohibition, they were to increase the dry areas and in States where there was complete prohibition it was to be implemented in a better way. However, the progress in this respect was slow as noted by the Planning Commission in the Third Plan. The Study Team on Prohibition (1964) again stressed that there should be complete prohibition by 1975-76 and for this suggested a four-phased programme. However, this recommendation was not given due consideration by the political party in power. "Recent studies in the field reveal that approximately 10 per cent of our population has taken to drinking and at least one person out of every hundred Indians is likely to indulge in heavy drinking and become an alcoholic. A problem which is affecting not only the economic condition of the country (about 5 per cent to 22 per cent of the total expenses

[42] Bhattacharayya, S.K., *op. cit.*, p. 116.

of drinking families is devoted to drinking), but the mental health of the nation too... The alcohol consumption, irrespective of the amount and degree, can result in a 'family disease' affecting physically, mentally and spiritually all the members of the family. One could go to the extent of saying that drinking of any one member in the family tends to distort the personalities of all in close proximity with him."[43] The All India Seminar on "Alcohol and its effect on Women and Homes" organised by the All India Prohibition Council in collaboration with the Central Social Welfare Board, the Kasturba Gandhi National Memorial Trust, and the All India Women's Conference in the context of International Women's Year, 1975, held in March 1975 at Sevagram, pointed out that it was a pity that alcoholism was becoming a widespread phenomenon.[44] Breweries and distilleries were coming up in different parts of India with an increasing number of drinkers including teenaged boy's and girls. It was time that the present policy of reliance on excise revenue was reviewed, as the social costs of alcoholism offset the quantum of revenues. There was the paradox of opening more liquor shops and at the same time subsidising prohibition campaigns in the States. The Seminar urged upon the State Governments to introduce total prohibition during the International Women's Year. However, no action was taken by the State Governments.

The credit for enforcing complete prohibition within a specified period of four years goes to the Janata Party with Shri Morarji Desai as Prime Minister, which came into power in 1977. "A meeting of the Central Prohibition Committee held on 30th July, 1977 in New Delhi resolved that total prohibition should be achieved throughout the country within next four years."[45] However, this policy of the Janata government was reversed by the Congress government which again came into power in 1980. "Responsibility for fulfilling the Constitutional obligation in regard to prohibition rests largely with State Governments. The Central Government has, however, been

[43] Nischai, K., "Family Counselling for Alcoholism" in *Social Welfare*, May 1975, Vol. XXII, No. 2, p. 8.

[44] Nair, G.R., "Alcoholism: Impact on the Family—A Seminar Report" in *Social Welfare*, May 1975, p. 11.

[45] *India—A Reference Annual*, 1977 and 1978, p. 118.

continuously making efforts to educate people about ill effects of drinking through mass media and also encouraging voluntary organisations through grants for educative publicity."[46]

Drug Addiction

As stated earlier in Chapters VI and XVII, the sale of drugs like *ganja* and *bhang* is now prohibited in most of the States, though illegal imports of these articles still continue to some extent. However, it is sad to note that the use of some new drugs like LSD, marijuana, methedrine (commonly known as 'speed'), STP (along with *ganja, bhang, etc.)* has become very common among the students. Shri Bandyopadhyay observes that cannabis (marijuana, hashish, *charas, ganja* or *bhang)* and LSD have now established their popularity and have considerably replaced the conventional drugs like opium, opiate and heroin. Cannabis, although mostly smoked in cigarettes or in pipes, is also chewed or drunk. LSD, popularly known as 'acid', is the abbreviation for lysergic acid diethylamide and is a very potent drug. It is 200 times more powerful than the narcotic cocaine. It can be taken in liquid or powder form. "Marijuana or hashish, considered to be milder as compared to LSD, lasts for one or two hours normally; LSD or 'speed' trips last for 8 to 12 hours; and STP, the mega-hallucinogen, takes 3 to 4 days before one can 'come down'."[47] Often use of one drug leads to the use of the other-a milder one being replaced by a comparatively stronger one. With amazing promptness, addicts learn the qualities of new and synthetic drugs and try to procure them by fair means or foul. With the least hesitation, an addict would indulge in theft or would forge prescriptions to obtain his favourite drug. Once a person becomes a 'convert' to the drug creed, he starts utterly neglecting personal hygiene and ceases to take care of his body, and as a result suffers from various skin diseases and his general health is ruined. He also generally develops an indifference to, or a disregard for, the accepted code of civilised behaviour. Eventually, he tries to escape the realities of life and

[46] India: A Reference Annual, *op. cit.*, p. 231.

[47] Bandyopadhyay, P.K., "Drugs—Their Effect on Human Mind" in *Social Welfare*, May 1973, Vol. XX, No. 2, p. 5.

drops out of school or college, office or factory, and ceases to be a useful and responsible citizen.

Apart from the fact that a person's basic character or his personality, disorder may lead to drug addiction, accidental stresses, like poverty, successive failures in life, frustration in love, parental neglect, loss of dear ones and the like may also be the contributing factors. Group or gang participation too often converts youngsters to the drug cult.

The reactions of various drugs, particularly marijuana and LSD, are very serious, leading to loss of confidence, epileptic seizures, prolonged psychosis, hallucination and suicide. Shri Bandyopadhyay concludes by saying that despite these dangerous consequences the family of drug addicts is growing in number every day all over the world. One reason for this may be the irresistible urge in adolescents and youngmen to know the unknown, to face the dangerous, and generally to widen the field of human experience. But a good number of the drug addicts, it is believed, are escapists who find the stress and strain of modem living too much a price for all that one gets out of normal life. They prefer to drop out of the mad rat-race. "Our social planners should, therefore, pause at the crucial juncture of human civilisation and make a fresh appraisal of our social values so that the tension of everyday life does not grow out of proportion to human capacity to adjust."[48]

It may be mentioned here that as the problem of drug abuse was gradually rearing its ugly head in India, a National Committee on Drug Addiction was appointed by the Government of India in 1976. The Committee evaluated the current prevalence of drug abuse in the total population on the basis of data available from a few studies conducted at the national level. In its opinion, these studies had several methodological flaws and as such the conclusions drawn from them could not be trustworthy. However, on the basis of the data available, the Committee came to the conclusion that "the drug problem exists in the population as a whole. The drugs most frequently misused are alcohol, tobacco, opium and cannabis, while the psychotropic drugs are just making their entry. The proportion of non-users is very large; but it is admitted that there is small hard core of addicts,

[48] *Ibid.*, p. 6.

many of whom become mentally ill and some of whom are treated in our psychiatric units and mental hospitals or by private practitioners."[49] The Committee observed that although the extent of the drug problem is limited at present, except for alcohol and tobacco, yet in the opinion of the Committee there were disturbing signs which showed that the situation in the country was likely to worsen and get out of hand if adequate measures were not adopted to curb the evil. They recommended that planned comprehensive and sustained measures should be taken without delay to prevent and control drug abuse in the total population in general and among the students in particular. Among the measures recommended were "the creation of a National Advisory Board of Drug Control; the enactment of a Single Law to deal with the problem in respect of all drugs except alcohol which is a State subject; the evolution of a national policy regarding alcohol in consultation with the States; removing inadequacies and plugging loopholes that have been noticed in the existing law, prescription of more stringent penalties for violation of legal provisions; registering service for drug addicts, strengthening the implementing machinery, and securing co-ordination between Central officials and the State Police".[50] According to this Committee, the common abused drugs in India were:

1. Cannabis and its products, Bhang, Ganja and Charas.
2. Hallucinogens (e.g. L.S.D.).
3. Tranquillisers.
4. Barbiturates.
5. Amphitamines.
6. Tobacco.
7. Other Narcotic drugs (opium, morphine, heroin).
8. Alcohol. (The problem of alcohol was not dealt by this Committee as already there were many reports on it).

The Central Advisory Board on Social Defence in its IX Meeting held in 1979, recommended that in the face of an increasing incidence of drug abuse among certain population groups especially the youth, the existing legislation on the

[49] *Drug Abuse in India: Report of the Committee appointed by the Government of India* (New Delhi: Ministry of Health and Family Welfare, 1977), p. 45.

[50] *Ibid.*, p. 1.

production, regulation and control of drugs should be reviewed and replaced by a single law to deal with the problem in all its dimensions. The Seventh Five-Year Plan points out, "Recent studies indicate that the consumption of narcotics, alcoholic drinks and addictive drugs which were deleterious to physical and mental health is on the increase, particularly among the younger-age groups. . . . This would have to be discouraged with sustained propaganda and community education through the mass media, particularly television and films."[51] However, to check this menace as pointed out by Dr. Bhattacharya, an inter-disciplinary approach by all concerned including the Department of health, education, social welfare, excise, police and voluntary organisations, parents and students organisations is essential. Different mass media like radio, television, audio-visual aids, newspapers may be used for disseminating the ill effects of drug addiction all over the country. To make this programme more effective, counselling and guidance centres with suitable referal services may be set up at campuses of universities, colleges and schools on the lines of family life institutes run by some voluntary welfare organisations.[52]

On the basis of recommendations made by the Central Advisory Board on Social Defence, the Narcotic Drug and Psychotropic Substances Act was enacted in 1985. Under this Act, stringent provisions have been made for the control and regulation of operations relating to the narcotic drugs and psychotropic substances and for other matters concerned with them. Under the Act, the cultivation or sale of coco plant, coco leaves, opium, poppy opium, consumption and use of psychotropic substances have been restricted and those violating the provisions may be imprisoned for a period ranging from 10 to 20 years for different offences committed under the Act.

The Narcotic Drug and Psychotropic Act, 1985 was further amended in 1988 which authorised confiscation and attachment of property acquired through trafficking. No sentence awarded under this Act can be commuted, suspended or remitted. Enhanced punishment for second conviction is death penalty.

[51] *Seventh Five-Year Plan* (1985), p. 311.

[52] Bhattacharayya, S.K., *op. cit.*, p. 158.

It also restricts the grant of bail to offender apprehended under the Act.

Another legislation enacted in 1988 was the Prevention of Illicit Traffic in Narcotic Drugs and Psychotropic Substances Act. It provides for detention for a period of 1-2 years for persons engaged in illicit cultivation, production, manufacture, possession, sale, transportation, warehousing and concealment of narcotics as well as financing of these activities. It need be mentioned here that in the same year, i.e., 1988, there was United Nations Convention Against Illicit Traffic in Narcatic Drugs and Psychotropic Substances.

It was realised that drug abuse is a psycho-socio-medico problem. To deal with it a community-based approach is required to enable the society to strengthen itself. Thus, Government adopted an integrated approach to tackle this problem which involves identification, referral services, treatment, mass awareness, education, rehabilitation aspects and training of functionaries, besides controlling supply of illicit trafficking. A number of ministries/departments are concerned with various aspects of this problem. The Welfare Ministry is looking into the educational and social welfare aspects of drug addiction. A concerted effort to deal with the problem in its entirety was made from 1985-86. Since then 26 de-addiction-cum-rehabilitation centres for treatment of drug addicts, 91 counselling centres and five after-care centres for their rehabilitation have been set up in voluntary sector.[53]

New Strategy for Drug Abuse Prevention

"In order to tackle the problem of drug abuse, a two pronged strategy has been adopted by the Govt. of India, i.e. (a) supply control and (b) demand reduction. While supply control aspect is taken care of by the Narcotic Control Bureau and the Police, the Ministry of Social Justice and Empowerment has been given the responsibilities of looking after the social welfare and educational aspects of drug addiction. In fulfilling this objective, the Ministry has formulated three pronged strategy with the following components:

[53] India: A Reference Annual, 1990, p. 231.

(i) Building awareness and educating people about ill-effects of drug abuse.

(ii) Dealing with the addicts through a well rounded up programme of motivation, counselling, treatment, follow-up and social reintegration of cured drug addicts.

(iii) To impart drug abuse prevention rehabilitation training to volunteers having in view to build up an educated cadre of drug abuse control operators."[54]

The Ministry has established a Centre for Drug Abuse Prevention under the aegis of the National Institute of Social Defence, New Delhi, to meet the growing demand of rehabilitation professional in the country. The Centre has started three months' Certificate Course on Deaddiction Counselling and Rehabilitation of Drug Abusers from November 16th, 1998.

Beginning with seven centres established in Delhi in 1985-86, the total number of centres has reached 414 as on 31st December, 1998 of which 218 are Drug Awareness Centres and 196 De-addiction-cum-rehabilitation Centres.

As a result of the impact of the implementation of the programme, the number of drug addicts registered in these centres was 2.49 lakhs in 1997-98 of which about 0.90 lakhs were detoxified. During the year 1998-99 (upto September, 1998) about 1.29 lakhs drug addicts were registered and 51,164 were detoxified in these centres.[55]

"It need also be stated that special focus has been given to the Drug Abuse Prevention Programme in North-East keeping in view the enormity of the problem. A three pronged strategy has been adopted for the North-East:

(a) Training and enhancing the capabilities of the NGOs in the area.

(b) Extending the outreach of drug abuse prevention scheme of the Ministry by opening of new centres; and

(c) Awareness and education programme for the North-East."[56]

[54] Annual Report (1998-99), Ministry of Social Justice and Empowerment, p. 71.

[55] *Ibid.*, p. 73

[56] Annual Report (1998-99), Ministry of Social Justice and Empowerment, p. 73.

"A committee has been constituted by the Ministry to visit the north eastern states for reviewing the working of the existing NGOs, explore the possibilities for opening of new centres and identify service provides for the purpose of training."[57]

Integration on HIV/AIDS Prevention Programmes with Substance Abuse Precaution

Realizing the commonality of concerns and the target groups for drug/Alcohol abuse and HIV/AIDs, the Ministry of Social Justice and Empowerment and National AIDs Control Organization (NACO), Ministry of Health and Family Welfare, the specialized field workers for the NGO run Drug De-Dedication centres, funded through the NACO undertake the following activities related to HIV/AIDs prevention i.e. (1) Conduct awareness programmes on the basics of HIV/AIDs, (2) Conduct small group meetings, (3) Provide information on basic health issues related to HIV/AIDs/STDs, Sex and sexuality. Presently 200 NGOs run de-addiction centres supported by the Ministry of Social Justice are taking this programme, with an additional specialized field workers 100 more NGOs are likely take up of this programme funded by NACO.[58]

Gambling and Smoking

It was pointed out in Chapters VII and XVII that there was the Public Gambling Act, 1867, which was applicable to the States of Uttar Pradesh, Punjab, Haryana and Delhi, Some States like West Bengal, Maharashtra, Tamil Nadu and Rajasthan had special Gambling Acts to check public gambling. In other States, gambling activities could be checked under section 290 of the Indian Penal Code. Horse racing under certain conditions was still permitted. There was no uniform legislation to check gambling throughout the country. We feel that such legislation should be enacted as early as possible to check gambling activities throughout the country. The system of lotteries introduced in many States during the last two decades is also very harmful as it creates false hopes in the minds of

[57] *Ibid.*, p. 73.

[58] Annual Report (2006-07), Ministry of Social Justice and Empowerment, Govt. of India, p. 48.

certain persons and leads to wastage of money and time. Encouragement of such activities by the State is not desirable from the point of view of social welfare.

The use of tobacco in the form of cigarettes and bidis is on the increase, particularly among the youth. The Ministry of Social Welfare, Government of India, sponsored a multi-disciplinary research project to assess the incidence of drug abuse among students. The study was conducted at the three metropolitan centres viz., Bombay, Delhi and Madras and three non-metropolitan centres, i.e., Jaipur, Hyderabad and Jabalpur and one residential university at Varanasi. "The prevalence rate of alcohol ranged from 15 per cent in Bombay and 9.0 per cent in Hyderabad. The prevalence rate of tobacco was highest (15.2 per cent) in Madras and lowest (6.3 per cent) in Hyderabad. The prevalence rate of pain killers was highest in Delhi (20.9 per cent) and lowest in Madras (1.2 per cent).[59] It showed that smoking was the most popular habit among the university students. This was also the conclusion arrived at by the Committee of 1976 as seen above. The problem as to how the spread of this evil practice among the growing generation can be checked needs to be examined by an expert committee as smoking leads to other evils like drinking, gambling, etc. In a poor country like ours, where people cannot afford even bare minimum necessities, the practice of smoking, apart from injuring the health of the smoker, comes in the way of building up a healthy, prosperous society, as the money spent on smoking could be utilised for better food, clothing, education of children, etc.

Prostitution

It was stated in Chapter VIII that the Suppression of Immoral Traffic in Women and Girls Act was passed in 1956. The Parliament hoped to prevent exploitation of women by unscrupulous persons and also to see that this evil is not practised in a manner causing annoyance to other members of the public, "While prostitution itself is the result of several factors, what is sought to be achieved by this Act is to protect the individuality and the dignity of a human being who is forced

[59] Bhattacharayya, S.K., *op. cit.*, p. 159.

by circumstances to take up this profession from the tentacles of exploiters. The profession by itself is a blot on humanity but the Act, while not hoping to eliminate prostitution, only contemplates to prevent trafficking in women and the unearned incomes to third parties who want to trade on the flesh of unfortunate women."[60]

TABLE 35

PERSONS INVOLVED UNDER THE IMPLEMENTATION OF S.I.T. ACT, 1956 (1968-72)[61]

		1968	*1970*	*1972*
1.	Number of cases started under S.I.T. Act	N.A.	5,324	7,718
2.	Number of persons involved (both men and women)	6,595	4,918	8,265
3.	Number of men involved	N.A.	856	778
4.	Number of cases registered under sections 363, 265, 365A, 366B, 367, 368, 370, 371, 372 and 373 of IPC	1,403	1,483	1,911
5.	Number of persons whose cases were disposed of during the year under S.I.T. Act (details given below; items 6 to 11)	5,891	4,925	7,650
6.	Number of persons discharged or acquitted	698	569	650
7.	Number of persons released under section 562 of Cr. P.C. on probation or admonition	453	485	417
8.	Number ordered to be detained in the Protective Homes	133	30	273
9.	Number sentenced to pay fine only	3,687	3,117	5,766
10.	Number sentenced to imprisonment with or without fine	824	645	408
11.	Dealt with in any other manner	96	79	136

Shri Rama Rao who collected statistics for three years, i.e., for 1971, 1972 and 1973, in the State of Andhra Pradesh, found that around 1,800 women were prosecuted under the Act every year out of whom about 1,500 were convicted. Apart from this, many more prosecutions were launched under section 294 of the Indian Penal Code to maintain order in public places. Judging from the number of convictions he came to the conclusion that there has not been any appreciable reduction in the number of prostitutes in various parts of the State. The

[60] Rama Rao, V.K., "Working of the Advisory Bodies and the Police for Prevention of Immoral Traffic in Andhra Pradesh" in *Social Defence,* April 1973, Vol. XIII, No. 32, p. 24.

[61] *Social Defence,* January 1976, Vol. XI, No. 43, pp. 54-56.

same conclusion can be drawn from the all-India statistics given in Table 35.

It need be mentioned here that in the year 1971, out of the 7,716 cases, started in the whole of the country under the S.I.T. Act, 1,859 were in Andhra Pradesh, 1,828 in Kamataka, 3,279 in Tamil Nadu, 399 in Maharashtra and the remaining 351 in all the other States.[62] It means that the Act was properly being enforced in some of the States while the remaining States did not take any action in this regard.

Shri Rama Rao further observes that there are not enough facilities for rescuing the women. The Act has both punitive and welfare aspects, but the latter aspect has generally been ignored. Even if the police want to send the women to protective homes, the State does not have a sufficient number of such homes. So he suggests that there should be a sufficient number of protective homes to prevent at least some women from going back to the profession. The homes should have enough facilities for vocational training so that the inmates after release could stand on their own feet.

He also observes that under section 13, sub-section 3, of the S.I.T. Act, the State Governments formed Advisory Committees in selected towns to review the implementation of the Act and other connected matters. But these Advisory Committees met very rarely and the attendance was also thin. The police officers who were supposed to call the meetings of these Advisory Committees were preoccupied with much more pressing and urgent matters, particularly of law and order, and the members of the Advisory Committee with a few exception did not take any active part in them. He suggests that the advisory bodies should be made statutory under the Act and these should be made responsible for the proper enforcement of the Act.

One of the main difficulties in the enforcement of the Act as stated in Chapter XVII is the difficulty in securing evidence against persons running a brothel. Thus section 3 of the Act needs to be amended. The law of presumption should be extended to this area as well. The punishments which are awarded to the offenders under section 3 are very lenient. There

[62] Central Bureau of Correctional Services, *Social Defence—A Statistical Handbook*, New Delhi, 1974, p. 226.

should be no leniency towards such offenders. The persons arrested under this section also get bail easily and continue to trade. It is felt that offences under this section should be made non-bailable. It may be mentioned here that the Department of Social Welfare, Government of India, had set up a Committee in 1967 which suggested certain amendments to the Act. It is heartening to note that the Act was amended in 1978 and some of the lacunae mentioned above have been removed: (1) A special Police officer has been redefined as an officer not below the rank of an Inspector of Police, in place of a Deputy Superintendent of Police; (2) During a raid by the Police, in place of a respectable woman of the same locality, a woman from another locality serve as a witness; (3) The use of probation has been restricted to certain cases only. With these changes some of the loopholes in the Act have been plugged and it will be possible to check the offenders in a more effective manner.[63]

The S.I.T. Act, 1956 was further amended in 1986 and it was renamed as the Immoral Traffic (Prevention) Act, 1986 (previously known as the Suppression of Immoral Traffic in Women and Girls Act, 1956). The Immoral Traffic (Prevention) Act, 1986 is applicable to both the sexes. The detention of a woman for purposes of prostitution is now punishable with a minimum of 7 years imprisonment: equally stringent punishment will be awarded to those procuring children for prostitution. The Act provides for the appointment of a special Police officer for investigating offences with inter-State ramifications.

Shrimati Jyotsna H. Shah is of the view that the abolitionist approach is not the solution under Indian conditions. "The institution cannot be abolished until society took up arms against this institution and until socio-economic conditions are such that there is absolutely no need for some women to choose the oldest profession. To deal with the problem of prostitution, legislation alone cannot control the vice. It is necessary to intensify literacy campaign all over the country so that the ignorant masses can realise the implication of this vice racket. It is necessary to enlist cooperation of the people in the community and voluntary organisations working in the field of

[63] *Social Defence*, January 1979, Volume XIV, No. 55.

moral and social hygiene."[64] The Association of Social Health in India (previously known as the Association of Moral and Social Hygiene in India) has a special role to play in this regard. As poverty is one of the main causes leading to prostitution among women, some minimum income to each family should be assured through social security programmes.

According to a study on problem of prostitution conducted by the Central Social Welfare Board (CS WB) in 1991, the estimated number of prostitutes in six metropolitan cities of Mumbai, Calcutta, Chennai, Delhi, Bangalore and Hyderabad ranged from 70,000 to 1,00,000. Of this, the number of child prostitutes has been estimated to 12 to 15%. The religious practices of offering young girls to temples in the name of Devadasi, Basavi, Yellamma and Jogin etc. are prevalent in certain parts of the country.

Child Prostitution

To contain the social evil of child prostitution, the Central Government has decided to make the Immoral Traffic (Prevention) Act, 1956 (as amended in 1986) more specific, through amendments, to the problem of child prostitution and also make the punishment more stringent. The Central Advisory Committee on Child Prostitution set up in 1994 at the instance of the Supreme Court is activated to review the situation from time to time and suggest effective steps in eradicating this social evil. A rehabilitation package for those weared out/withdrawn from the profession will also be put into action not only to keep the children away from prostitution but also to keep them tied up with alternative education-cum-income generation programmes."[65]

"The growing incidence of trafficking for prostitution is a matter of growing concern, especially as it is estimated that as much as 40% of the prostitutes are children. To deal with this problem the Ministry is implementing a pilot project for prevention and combating trafficking in source, destination and

[64] Report of the Seminar on Implementation of the Suppression of Immoral Traffic in Women and Girls Act, 1956, held in March 1973 in New Delhi, in *Social Defence*, April 1973, Vol. VIII, No. 32, p. 29.

[65] Ninth Five-Year Plan, 1997-2002 (1999), Vol. II, p. 347.

traditional areas. During the year 2006-2007, the Ministry initiated action to deal with the emerging problems such as repatriation of cross border victims, development of training modules and training and capacity building of various functionaries, streamlining interstate rescue and repatriation measures etc. The premier legislation, Immoral Traffic (Prevention) Act, 1956 is being amended in order to widen its scope, focus on the trafficker and prevent victimization of the victims.[66]

Schemes providing relief, Protection and Rehabilitation of women. Providing relief, protection and rehabilitation of women in distress is one of the focused area and this in achieved through Swadhar Shelter Homes, Short Stay Homes and Women Help lines. The women in the Swadhar and Short Stay Homes are provided shelter, food, clothing emotional support and counseling in order to rehabilitate them socially and economically.[67]

Beggary

In India the problem of beggary has assumed a stupendous proportion. According to the 1971 census there were 7.4 lakh beggars and vagrants in the country out of whom 4.7 lakhs were males and 2.7 lakhs females. Out of these 1 lakh were children below 14 years of age.[68]

The problem of begging by children has assumed an alarming proportion. The Government of India set up a Committee in 1968 to go into the problem of kidnapping of children for purpose of begging. The Committee suggested stringent measures against the exploiters of children and suggested that a minimum sentence of 3 years be provided under section 363A: (1) of the Indian Penal Code. It also suggested that the definition of begging under section 363(4)(a) be amended to make it more comprehensive in conformity with the anti-beggary legislation of some States.

[66] Annual Report 2006-07, Ministry of Women and Child Development, *op. cit.*, p. 6.

[67] *Ibid.*, p. 7.

[68] Bhattacharayya, S.K., "Prevention of Begging" in *Social Defence,* January 1975, Vol. X, No. 39, p. 12.

As stated earlier, there is no all-India legislation against begging as such. Section 109(b) of the Cr. P.C. prohibits vagrancy. Section 133 of the Cr. P.C. provides for public nuisance. It might be used against begging insofar as it is a public nuisance. There are municipal Acts which make importunate begging and exposure of diseased limbs for the purpose of begging as offences. Some States, as stated earlier, have enforced anti-beggary Acts in their respective areas. All these Acts provide for the prevention of begging through detention, training and employment of beggars and also for the custody, trial and punishment of beggars. Begging is a cognizable offence under these Acts and special Police squads operate in areas where the anti-beggary legislation is in force. The Police round up beggars and produce them before the court. In passing any order under the provisions of the Act, the court considers the report of the Probation Officer with regard to the age, character, circumstances and conditions in which he is living, his health, etc., and if he is found to be a beggar, he is sent to an institution for treatment, care and training for a period of not less than one year, but not more than three years.

As stated in Chapter IX, during the Second and Third Five-Year Plans, a Centrally-sponsored programme of controlling beggary in the country was take up. Some beggar homes were set up under the scheme. In 1971 there were 98 beggar homes in the country with about 12,500 inmates. Out of these 98 beggar homes, 11 were in Gujarat, 11 in Kerala, 30 in Maharashtra, 10 in Tamil Nadu, 9 in West Bengal and the remaining 18 in the rest of the 16 States including 8 in the Union Territory of Delhi.[69]

As a result of the follow up programme suggested by the Study Group (1965), 14 States and 2 Union Territories enforced special legislation for beggary prevention in specified area to the end of 1979.[70] "Despite the enforcement of Anti-Beggary legislations, the problem still continues to exist in its worst form as begging has become a profession for many, as they find it as an easy means of livelihood. The other problems related to

[69] Central Bureau of Correctional Services, *Social Defence—A Statistical Handbook.* New Delhi, 1974, p. 254.

[70] National Institute of Social Defence, *A Perspective,* 1980, *op. cit.*, p. 36.

begging include: ineffective enforcement of legislation, non-existence/inadequate number of Reception Homes/Beggars' Homes, and lack of standards in the services provided in the mandatory institutions owing to the existing variations in their respective legal provisions and administrative procedures. Presently, the approach for tackling this problem is based primarily on punitive devices with very little scope for any diversified programmes of treatment and rehabilitation, neither for the able-bodied nor for the disabled beggars.[71]

"In the Ninth Plan, for the prevention of the age-long problem of beggary, a three-way approach will be adopted. The first step being preventive in nature, special squads will be activated to round up the beggars from all the public places especially at religious/pilgrimage centres on a continuing basis, till no such people are visible in the public places. The second and the third are curative and rehabilitative in nature. While all those who become beggars due to poverty, will be dealt by keeping them gainfully employed through various employment-cum-income generation programmes/ social assistance programmes, those who opt wilfully and adopt begging as a profession, will be tackled through effective implementation of legislation and stringent measures of punishment."[72]

At present, 16 State Governments and 2 Union Territory Administrations have enacted Anti-Beggary Legislations. The Ministry of Welfare initiated a scheme for Beggary Prevention in 1992-93. Under this scheme, grant-in-aid was extended to NGOs for establishing Vocational Training Centres for the care, treatment and rehabilitation of beggars. Services in this field lacked uniformity.

However, the question arises whether such a comprehensive legislation alone can prevent the evil of begging. The answer should be in the negative. Unless the public are made conscious of the futility of indiscriminate charity and cooperate with the Government in the implementation of the Act, this problem will continue to defy all attempts as its solution. Giving alms to an individual does neither help him nor society as a whole; rather such benevolence aggravates the socio-economic

[71] Ninth Five-Year Plan, 1997-2002 (1999), Vol. II, p. 388.
[72] *Ibid.*, p. 394.

problems and encourages indolence in society. This idea should be disseminated through various kinds of mass media like radio, television newspapers, magazines, pamphlets, etc. An Anti-Beggary Week may also be observed once in a year and an extensive campaign undertaken to arouse people's interest in solving this problem.[73] In a country where the majority of the people live below poverty line some social security measures may also be necessary.

Voluntary Action in Social Defence Programmes

We have already pointed out in the foregoing pages that the role of voluntary social workers and agencies is crucial in the social defence programme. It has now been realised that the crime is committed by the individuals due to various factors which are mostly beyond his control. The criminal is the product of the community and as such it is for the community to deal with the problem of crime. As a result the community participation has been emphasised in the implementation of preventive and correctional programme in the country. These programmes are mainly organised within the framework of prison legislation, Juvenile Justice Act, Probation of Offenders Act, Immoral Traffic (Prevention) Act, Anti-beggary Act, etc. All the Acts in this field include provision for the utilisation of voluntary services of the people in the community. The first effort to enlist public cooperation in the implementation of correctional programmes was made through the Apprentices Act of 1850. Under this Act, Magistrates were authorised to commit such children as apprentices to employers and provided for controlling the relations between them.[74] Similarly under the Reformatory School Act, 1897, the Superintendent of a reformatory with the sanction of visitors could entrust any youth offender above the age of 14 years to any trustworthy and respectable person who was willing to take charge of him on the condition that the employer shall keep such youthful offender employed in trade, occupation or calling. The Children Acts provide for the utilisation of voluntary welfare services in the institutional and non-institutional programmes. There is

[73] Bhattacharayya, S.K., *op. cit.*, p. 12.

[74] See Chapter IV, p. 99.

provision for the release of inmates of Children Act institutions on licence under the care and guardianship of voluntary social workers and social welfare agencies. In the case of institutions run by the government, managing committees and boards of visitors are appointed with the specified number of persons from the locality. There is also provision for the after-care services both for child and adult offenders by voluntary agencies. The prison manuals of different States and Union Territories contain provision for boards of visitors consisting of non-official members which can offer suggestions for the improvement of treatment and training methods in prisons. Similarly in the field of probation, the probation rules provide for the appointment of voluntary probation officers and placement of probationers under the care and supervision of voluntary welfare organisations. Similarly the Borstal School Acts of various States provide for the formation of visiting committees with non-officials as some members and placing the inmates in the custody of non-officials after their retention in the institution for a particular period. Voluntary organisations and workers also assist the government in the suppression of immoral traffic in various ways. Even in the maintenance of law and order, the formation of defence committee and utilisation of the services of home guards is envisaged. Thus the role of voluntary organisations and voluntary social workers is crucial in the implementation of social defence programmes. However, the recent studies show that public at large was ignorant about the utility of correctional programmes and as such there was no effective public cooperation forthcoming in the implementation of these programmes.[75]

We have pointed out in the foregoing pages that social defence programmes such as prevention of delinquency and crime, treatment of juvenile delinquents and adult offenders, check on alcoholism, gambling, prostitution, beggary, etc. are not being followed uniformly in all the States. Some States like Maharashtra, Gujarat, Tamil Nadu, Andhra Pradesh and Karnataka are much ahead of others. So far the implementation of some of these programmes is concerned, the difficulty is that the implementation

[75] Srivastava, S.P., *Public Participation in Social Defence*, New Delhi: D.K. Publishers and Distributors, 1981.

of these programmes is entirely within the purview of the States. Even in fields where a comprehensive legislation has been passed by the Central Government, for example, the Juvenile Justice Act, 1986, the Probation of Offenders Act, 1958, and the Immoral Traffic (Prevention) Act, 1986, these Acts are not being enforced properly by most of the States. Thus unless all the State Governments are serious about these programmes and create proper machinery for the implementation of various schemes not much progress seems possible. In some fields where there is no Central legislation, e.g., for beggary, gambling, etc., we need such legislation on an all-India basis. Then, again, for the success of these programmes the cooperation of voluntary social welfare organisations and community leaders is essential. However in most of the States (exception being Maharashtra, Gujarat, Tamil Nadu) such type of organisations and leadership is scarce. We need a coordinating body of voluntary organisations at an all-India level to guide the social welfare movement in the country. We hope that if the suggestions made above are accepted and implemented, we may, to some extent, achieve the objectives of a Welfare State as enshrined in the Indian Constitution.[76]

[76] For functions of a Welfare State, see Chapter XX.

CHAPTER XIX

PROBLEMS OF MAJOR INSTITUTIONS AND COMMUNITIES

THE MAJOR groups and institutions which function in a society are in the fields of economics, politics, religion, family and recreation. In a modern society, the two other important institutions involved are in the fields of health and education. Then there are the problems of communities from the village, city and regional level to the State and national level. There are also problems of social classes and castes. The bureaucratic structure of complex organisations, whether in the economic, political, or other fields, has its own problems in a modern society. It may not be possible to deal with all these problems in this chapter. Some of these have already been discussed in Parts IV and V of this book. Some of these have been discussed in later volumes under the title—India's Social Transformation, Volume II (1996) and India of Tomorrow (1998). Here we would confine our observations to some major problems concerned with (1) poverty and unemployment, (2) population and health, (3) educational and religious institutions, (4) leisure and recreation, (5) corruption, (6) family disharmony, (7) community conflicts and national integration, etc., in which some thinking has been done by the Government, the Planning Commission or some other agencies in recent years.

1. *Poverty and Unemployment*

Poverty, with reference to a country, may be defined as a social phenomenon in which a section of society is unable to fulfil even its basic necessities of life. Where a substantial segment of society is deprived of the minimum level of living and continues at a bare subsistence level, the society is said to be plagued with mass poverty. Attempts have been made to measure the extent of poverty in India and depending on the norms used, the 40-60 per cent of the population fall below the minimum acceptable standard. According to a recent estimate using minimum norms of 2,250 calories consumption, the percentage of population below the poverty line in 1977-78 was projected as 48 per cent in rural areas and 41 in urban areas.[1] Though these estimates may be debatable, yet it cannot be doubted that we have a long way to go to ensure a tolerable standard of living for the large numbers of the poor and destitute. The removal of poverty and unemployment has been one of the major objectives of the Five-Year Plans after Independence. However, not much could be done in this direction till the beginning of the Fourth Five-Year Plan when some special programmes like Drought Prone Areas Programme (DPAP), Command Area Development (CAD) Programme, Small Farmers and Agricultural Labour Development Agency (SFDA), crash scheme for rural employment etc. were taken up.[2] Later on, this was one of the major objectives laid down in the Fifth and subsequent Five-Year plans. The Planning Commission in the Fifth Plan observes, "Removal of poverty and attainment of self-reliance are the two major objectives that the country had set out to accomplish in the Fifth Plan."[3] The Sixth Five-Year Plan again points out that the basic task of economic planning in India is to bring about a structural transformation of the economy so as to achieve a high and sustained rate of growth, a progressive improvement in the standard of living of the masses leading to the eradication of poverty and unemployment and provide the material base for a self-reliant socialist economy. During the thirty years of planned development, which we have now completed, impressive progress has been made in agriculture, industry, science and technology, health and education, and in the development of infrastructure for a wide range of services. However the progress achieved has fallen short of objectives, needs and expectations.[4]

[1] *Draft Five-Year Plan, 1978-83* (1978), p. 3.
[2] For details see Madan, G.R., *India's Developing Villages* (1990), pp. 299-311.
[3] *Fifth Five-Year Plan* (1974), p. 16.
[4] *Sixth Five-Year Plan* (1981), p. 17.

As far as problem of unemployment is concerned it was estimated that there were 12.02 million unemployed persons in March 1980, while net addition to labour in 1980-85 was to be 34.24 million. To solve the problem of poverty and unemployment a new strategy of "Manpower Planning and Employment Generation" at the District level was to be adopted. The District Manpower Planning and Employment Generation Council was to be formed, which was to be assisted by the District Employment Exchange, District Industries Centre, District Agricultural Officers, Lead Bank and those connected with the organisation of services in preparing a portfolio of opportunities for salaried, self and wage employment during the Plan period. However there is no reference to this strategy in the Seventh Five-Year Plan.

The Eighth Plan points out that expansion of employment opportunities has been an important objective of development planning in India. There has been a significant growth in employment over the years. However, a relatively higher growth of population and labour force has led to an increase in the volume of unemployment from one Plan period to another. The Eighth Plan aims at bringing employment into a sharper focus in a medium-term perspective with the goal of reducing unemployment to negligible level within the next ten years.[5] The Plan also points out that the incidence of poverty (or underemployment) is much higher than that of unemployment. An overwhelming majority of the poor are thus not apparently unemployed but underemployed.

It was estimated that total employment in the beginning of 1992-93 was 302 million, while the labour force was estimated to be 319 million and thus the backlog of open unemployment was 17 million on April 1, 1992. The labour force was projected to increase by about 35 million during 1992-97. Thus the total number of persons requiring employment during 1992-97 was to be 52 million. The main programmes towards expansion of employment opportunities during the Eighth Plan are: (i) a faster and geographically diversified growth of agriculture, so that the hitherto lagging regions have a larger share in agricultural growth; and diversification of agriculture into high

[5] Eighth Five-Year Plan (1992), Vol. I, p. 16.

value, more labour intensive crops like vegetable and fruits, particularly in the agriculturally better developed regions; (ii) development of infrastructure and marketing arrangements for agro-based and allied activities like dairy, poultry, fishery and sericulture to accelerate growth to these sectors; (iii) an expanded programme of development and utilisation of wasteland for crop-cultivation and forestry; (iv) growth of non-agricultural manufacturing activities in rural areas, including rural towns; (v) decentralised manufacturing sector particularly in the production of consumption goods and manufactured exports; (vi) strengthening of basic health and education facilities in the rural areas; and (vii) greater flexibility in special employment programmes and their integration with sectoral development with a view to ensuring their contribution to growth and sustainable employment.[6]

Removal of Poverty and Underemployment in Rural Areas

For removing underemployment there were different schemes for rural and urban areas. The Eighth Plan points out that rural poverty is inextricably linked with low rural productivity and unemployment including underemployment. Employment at miserably low levels of productivity and incomes is already a problem of far greater magnitude than unemployment as such. "It is estimated that in 1987-88, the rate of unemployment was only 3 per cent and inclusive of the underemployed, it was around 5 per cent. As per the currently used methodology in the Planning Commission, poverty for the same year was estimated to be 30 per cent. This demonstrates that even though a large proportion of the rural population was 'working' it was difficult for them to eke out a living even at subsistence levels from it... In terms of absolute numbers of poor, the decline has been much less. While this can be attributed to the demographic factor, the fact remains that after 40 years of planned development about 200 million are stilll poor in rural India. In 1987-88, the rural poverty line in terms of per capita monthly expenditure was Rs. 131.80. The average incidence of rural poverty conceals wide inter-State differences which suggests that greater attention needs to be paid to the regions which

[6] *Ibid.*, p. 127.

have a greater concentration of the rural poor. In recent years, several issues have been raised about the methodology of poverty estimation, both by professionals and State governments. An Expert Group appointed by the Planning Commission is looking into these issues relating to the definition and measurement of poverty."[7]

Stress has been laid on three main programmes for the removal of poverty in the Eighth Plan as in the last three or four Five-Year Plans. These are: (1) special employment programmes; (2) area development programmes; and (3) land reforms. The role of the Panchayati Raj institutions and voluntary organisations in the implementation of these has also been stressed.

Some of the special programmes which were being implemented during the Seventh Plan were: (1) Integrated Rural Development Programme (IRDP); (2) Training of Rural Youth for Self-Employment (TRYSEM); (3) Development of Women and Children in Rural Areas (DWCRA); (4) Wage Employment Programmes of the Central Government (including the National Rural Employment Programme and Rural Landless Employment Guarantee Programme (RLEGP) which were merged into a single rural wage employment programme in 1989 called the Jawahar Rozgar Yojana); and (5) Selected State level employment programmes which included Maharashtra Employment Guarantee Scheme (EGS) (introduced in 1971) and Special Employment Programme of Gujarat (introduced in 1991). Among the area development programmes is included the Drought Prone Area Programme (DPAP) introduced in 1972-73. So far as the Land Reform is concerned, the land reform policy consisted of four elements: (a) abolition of intermediaries; (b) tenancy reforms with security to actual cultivators; (c) redistribution of surplus ceiling land; and (d) updating of land records.

All the above referred programmes were to be pursued during the Eighth Plan. However, certain deficiencies noted in these programmes were to be removed. As the Plan points out, "Experience indicates that while poverty alleviation programmes have been successful in providing a certain quantum of

[7] Eighth Five-Year Plan (1992), Vol. II, p. 27.

employment to people and have led to the creation of some durable assets in the villages, there is a perception that the achievements have not been commensurate with the resources spent on them. Under the IRDP, the very fact that about half the number of beneficiaries have overdues raises doubts about their ability to come out of the debt syndrome."[8] For making improvement in this programme the emphasis should be on need-based self-employment with an element of subsidy rather than a subsidy supplemented by bank credit. Similarly in case of Jawahar Rozgar Yojana the programme should be concentrated in some backward districts to provide at least 90-100 days of employment per person instead of providing 15 days of employment per person to raise them above the poverty line. As it is pointed out, "The programmes themselves need not be changed but the manner of implementing them would need some modification."

Poverty Alleviation in Rural India—Ninth Plan Strategy

(i) Direct poverty alleviation programmes will continue on an expanded scale in the Ninth Plan. But these programmes will be oriented towards strengthening the productive potential of the economy and providing more opportunities for involving the poor in the economic process.

(ii) The Integrated Rural Development Programme (IRDP) would continue to be the major self-employment programme targeted to families living below poverty line in the rural areas of the country. In the Ninth Plan, it would be implemented through an integrated approach under which the existing schemes of Training of Rural Youth for Self Employment (TRYSEM) and Supply of Improved Toolkits to Rural Artisans (SITRA), Development of Women and Children in Rural Areas (DWCRA) and Ganga Kalyan Yojna (GKY) would be subsumed into the main programme.

(iii) To facilitate higher levels of investment under the programme, there would be a strategic shift under IRDP from an individual beneficiary approach to a group and/or cluster approach. As part of the group approach, the focus

[8] *Ibid.*, p. 36.

of IRDP, would be on the formation of Self-Help Groups (SHGs) which would be the catalyst for organising the poor. The cluster approach would focus on the identification of a few specified viable activities based on the local resource endowment and occupational skills of the people of that area.

(iv) Land reforms will continue to be an important policy instrument for alleviating rural poverty. Access to land is still a major source of livelihood and its possession enhances the status of people in rural society. All efforts would be made to detect and redistribute the ceiling surplus land and to enforce the ceiling laws stringently. The poor should be given access to wastelands and common property resources. The land rights of women must be ensured.

(v) "In the Ninth Plan, the poverty alleviation programmes would be more effectively integrated with area development programmes and the various sectoral programmes within the umbrella of Panchayati Raj Institutions (PRIs). The PRIs will function as effective institutions of local self-government. These would prepare the plans for economic development and social justice through the District Planning Committees and implement them.

(vi) In the Ninth Plan, alternative strategies would be formulated for developing a suitable marketing infrastructure under Integrated Rural Development Programme (IRDP). These would include (a) provision of transport arrangements for carrying IRDP products to rural/urban markets, (b) introduction of insurance cover to mobile sellers, (c) provision of better storage facilities, (d) setting up and revamping of District Supply and Marketing Societies, (e) sale of IRDP products through Khadi & Village Industries Commission (KVIC) outlets, State Emporia etc. besides networking with DRDA showrooms/markets, (f) setting up of quality control centres and consultancy centres which the beneficiaries could approach for advice for improving the quality and standard of their products, (g) involvement of private sector in marketing by adoption of better packaging techniques, design, input, quality control, brand name etc. and (h) launching of a suitable advertisement campaign for IRDP products including organisation of exhibitions, melas.[9]

The Sampoorna Grameen Rozgar Yojana

The Sampoorna Grameen Rozgar Yojana (SGRY) was launched on 25the September 2001 by merging the on-going schemes of Jawahar Gram Samridhi Yojana (JGSY) and Employment Assurance Scheme (EAS).

The objectives of the programme are to provide additional wage employment in the rural areas as also food security, alongside the creation of durable community, social and economic infrastructure in the rural areas. The programme is self-targetting in nature with special emphasis to period Wage Employment to women, scheduled castes, scheduled tribes and parents of children withdrawn from hazardous occupations.[10]

The scheme is exclusively implemented by the Panchayati Raj Institutions at the District level, Block level and village level. 50% of the funds and food-grains were earmarked for the village panchayats and are distributed among them through DRDAs/District Panchayats. 20% of the resources are reserved for district levels panchayats. 30% for intermediate level panchayats. 22.5% of the annual allocation inclusive of food-grains allocated both at the level of district and intermediate level shall be earmarked for individual/group beneficiary Schemes of SC/ST families living below the poverty line (BPL) Efforts would be made to provide 30% of the employment opportunities for women. The SGRY is Centrally Sponsored Scheme. The wages under the scheme are to be paid partly in foodgrains and partly in cash.

Swarnjayanti Gram Swarozgar Yojana (SGSY)

"The Swarnjayanti Gram Swarozgar Yojana is a major on-going programme for the self-employment of rural poor. The programme was started from 1-4-1999 after restructuring the erstwhile Integrated Rural Development Programme and its atted programmes namely Training of Rural Youth for Self

[9] Ninth Five-Year Plan, 1997-2002 (1999), Vol. II, p. 26-32.

[10] Annual Report 2006-07, Ministry of Rural Development, Govt. of India, p. 10.

Employment (TRYSEM), Development of Women and Children in Rural Areas (DWCRA), Supply of Toolkits in Rural Areas (SITRA) and Ganga Kalyan Yojana, besides Million Wells Scheme (MWS).

The basic objective of the SGSY is to bring the assisted poor families (Swarozgaris) above the Poverty Line by providing them income-generating assets through a mix of bank credit and governmental subsidy. The programme aims at establishing a large number of micro enterprises in rural areas based upon the ability of poor and potential of each area."[11] The emphasis is on the formation of Self Help Groups. The NGOs have to play an active role in the formation and capacity building of SHGs. Focus is to be on vulnerable groups i.e. SC/ST, women and disabled and others below Poverty Line families. The SHG may consist of 10-20 persons belonging to families below the poverty line. A person should not be a member of more than one group. 50% of SH Groups should be exclusively for women. Each block may select about 10 key activities but focus should be on 4-5 key activities.

Training

Training and capacity building of Swarozgaris is an important component of SGSY. Under SGSY 10% of the financial allocation is earmarked for training and skill development of swarozgaris.

Rural Development and Self Employment Training Institutes (RUDSET) are being set up in different states. They will provide training to rural youths mostly from BPL households.[12]

The object is to train youths to develop the aptitude for working in rural areas in rural development projects etc. will assist trained youths in self-employment and as far as a possible in obtaining credit facilities from banks and other financial institutions.

Persons with Disabilities (Equal Opportunities, Protection of Right and Full Participation). The Guidelines of Swarnjayanti

[11] Annual Report 2006-2007, Ministry of Rural Development, Govt. of India, p. 38.

[12] *Ibid.*, p. 46.

Gram Swarozgar Yojana (CGSY) stipulates that disabled persons will account for at least 3% of the total swarogzaris.

National Rural Employment Guarantee Act 2005 (NREGA)

This programme has been launched for securing the livelihood of the people in the rural areas by guaranteeing 100 days of employment in a financial year to every household whose adult members volunteer to do unskilled manual work. The NREGA provides a social safety net for the vulnerable groups and an opportunity to combine growth with equity. For the first time in Indian history, employment has been conferred the status of a legal right through an Act of the Parliament. Channelisation of resources under these programmes in identified priority areas can go a long way towards enhancing and conserving our natural resources and creating durable, economic assets capable of triggering opportunities for economic activity. The assets created result in sustained employment for the area for future growth, employment and self-sufficiency.[13]

Programmes for Urban Areas

To remove poverty and unemployment in the urban areas there are two main programmes, viz., (1) Nehru Rozgar Yojana; and (2) Scheme for Educated Unemployed of Employment Generation in Urban Localities.

Nehru Rozgar Yojana (NRY). This was launched in October, 1989 to help the persons living below the poverty line (households with an annual household income of Rs. 11,850 at 1991-92 prices). Under the NRY, there were three schemes; (i) The Scheme of Urban-Micro Enterprises (SUME); (ii) The Scheme of Urban Wage Employment (SUWE); and (iii) The Scheme of Housing and Shelter Upgradation (SHASU).

The SUME is designed to encourage unemployed and under-employed youth to take up self-employment ventures in all urban settlements. The scheme envisages that 30% of beneficiaries should be women. The scheme has loan-cum-subsidy component and the training and infrastructure component.

The SUWE is designed to provide employment to the urban poor through the creation of socially and economically useful

[13] *Ibid.*, P. V and VI.

assets in the low income neighbourhood in towns with a population below one lakh. Works like community centres, common worksheds, common selling places for the poor, construction of drains, etc. were to be taken in the scheme.

The SHASU aims at providing employment for persons involved in housing and building activities. The scheme has two components viz., training and subsidy-cum-loan assistance. The training programme is meant for skill upgradation of masons, carpenters, plumbers, sanitary workers, electricians and others engaged in construction trades, as well as infrastructure support for common facilities to beneficiaries and machinery equipment to training institutions. The scheme is operative in urban settlements having a population between 1 and 20 lakhs with relaxation in the population criteria for hilly States.[14]

Swarna Jayanti Shahari Rozgar Yojana (SJSRY)

During the Golden Jubilee Year of Independence, a new programme known as Swarna Jayanti Shahari Rozgar Yojana (SJSRY) was introduced in 1997 and has been launched as a replacement for Nehru Rozgar Yojana (NRY), Urban Basic Services for the Poor (UBSP) and Prime Minister's Integrated Urban Poverty Eradication Programme (PMIUPEP) on 1.12.97. The SJSRY seeks to provide gainful employment to the urban unemployed or underemployed poor through encouraging the setting up of self-employment ventures and provision of wage employment.

The Swarna Jayanti Shahari Rozgar Yojana will be funded on 75:25 basis between the Centre and the States.

Salient Features

The SJSRY rests on a foundation of community empowerment. This programme relies on establishing and promoting community organisations and structure to provide supporting and facilitating mechanism for local development. Towards this end, community organisations like Neighbourhood Groups (NGs), Neighbourhood Committees (NCs) and Community Development Societies (CDSs) be set up in the target areas

[14] Ninth Five Year Plan (1997-2002).

based on the UBSP pattern. The CDS shall be the focal point for purposes of identification of beneficiaries, preparation of application, monitoring of recovery etc.

The CDS being a federation of different community based organisations shall be the nodal agency for this programme. The scheme consists of two special schemes namely:

(a) The Urban Self-Employment Programme (USEP)

(b) The Urban Wage-Employment Programme (UWEP)".[15]

A. The Urban Self-Employment Programme (USEP)

This programme has three distinct parts:

(i) Assistance to individual urban poor beneficiaries for setting up gainful self-employment ventures,

(ii) Assistance to groups of urban poor women for setting up gainful self-employment ventures. This sub-scheme is called Scheme for Development of Women and Children in the Urban Areas (DWCUA).

(iii) Training of beneficiaries, potential beneficiaries and other persons associated with the urban employment programme for upgradation and acquisition of vocational and enterpreneurial skills.

Coverage: (i) The programme will be applicable to all the towns in India, (ii) The programme will be implemented on a whole town basis with special emphasis on urban poor clusters.[16]

Development of Women and Children in Urban Areas

DWCUA aims at helping groups of urban poor women in taking up self-employment ventures. The group should consist of at least 10 women. The ceiling of subsidy under the scheme is Rs. 1.25 lakh or 50% of the cost of project whichever is less. Where the group sets itself up as Thrift and Credit Society in addition to its self-employment ventures, it will be eligible for an additional grant of Rs. 25,000 as Revolving Fund at the rate of Rs. 1,000 maximum per member. The fund is meant for purposes like purchase of raw materials and marketing, infrastructure support, one time expense on child care activity,

[15] Annual Report (1998-99), Ministry of Urban Affairs and Employment, p. 14.

[16] *Ibid.*, p. 14.

expenses upto Rs. 500 on travel cost of group members to bank, payment of insurance premium for self/spouse/child by maintaining savings for different periods by a member and any other expense allowed by the state in Group's interest.[17]

B. The Urban Wage-Employment Programme (UWEP)

This programme shall seek to provide wage employment to beneficiaries living below the poverty line within the jurisdiction of urban local bodies by utilising their labour for construction of socially and economically useful public assets.

This programme shall apply to urban local bodies the population of which was less than five lakhs as per the 1991 census.

The material labour ratio for works under this programme shall be maintained at 60:40. Community Development Societies (CDSs) shall survey and draw up a list of available basic minimum services in their areas. Missing basic services shall be listed thereafter.

The CDSs shall prioritise the above services into two lists "A" and "B". This prioritisation shall be final. List A will be the order of priority for the missing minimum services whereas List B shall be the order of priority for other required infrastructure. These lists along with the remarks of the CDS with respect to where such services should be located etc. shall be forwarded to the Town Poverty Eradication Cell at the beginning of the year.[18]

The Planning Commission's (modified Expert Group) estimates of urban poverty show a decline in the percentage of urban poor from 38% (1987-88) to 32.36% (1993-94). As per the modified Expert Group, the number of urban poor is 763.37 lakhs in 1993-94.

Programme for Employment during Tenth Plan and after

The Constitution (74th) Amendment Act, 1992 has given a more pocussed thrust to decentralization and the creation of a

[17] *Ibid.*, p. 15.

[18] *Ibid.*, p. 15

For *'Empowerment of Women'* and *'Employment for the Persons with Disabilities* see chapters *'Women Welfare'* and *'Social Assistance and the Handicapped'* respectively in Madan, G.R., *'Indian Social Problems'*. Vol. II.

democratic governance structure with local responsibilities being assumed and managed at the local level.

It is significant that apart from the traditional municipal functions, Article 243W of the Act allocates to ULBs the function of 'preparation of plans for economic development and social justice' and the Twelfth Schedule contains 'urban poverty alleviation' as a municipal responsibility. These take municipal bodies from being mere providers of civic amenities to a much wider area of action encompassing economic and social planning.[19]

It is further stated in the Plan that the city administrations should create urban poverty alleviation (UPA) cells at the municipal level. The UPA cells should draw up City Poverty Alleviation Plans in which the community organization of the poor created under the Swarn Jayanti Shahri Rozgar Yojana (SJSRY) should be involved. Besides other activities for the socio-economic upliftment of the slum populations should also be taken up making maximum use of SJSRY and similar schemes.[20]

Programmes for the Educated Unemployed

It was estimated that unemployment among the educated manpower, namely, matriculates and graduates and above, was 3.7 million in March 1985. 10.6 million educated who were seeking employment were to be added during 1985-90. It was envisaged that new jobs would be created for 9.4 million during Seventh Plan period. While the job opportunities for the matric pass and engineering diploma holders were to emanate both from the organised and unorganised sectors of economy, those for the higher categories were to be generated primarily in industry, banking, transport, communication and public services.

Characteristics of unemployed persons help in determining the nature of employment opportunities that need to be created to utilise the labour force that is seeking work. In regard to educational characteristics of the unemployed persons, there has been a substantial change since the years of early eighties.

[19] Tenth Five Year Plan, Volume II, 2002-2007, p. 611.

[20] *Ibid.*, p. 630.

Both the enumeration approach of the census in identifying the unemployed persons and the sampling approach of the National Sample Surveys on Employment and Unemployment reveal a substantial increase of literate among the unemployed persons."[21] (Table 36)

TABLE 36

EDUCATION PROFILE OF THE UNEMPLOYED IN INDIA[22]

	LEVEL OF EDUCATION					
Year	*Illiterate*	*Primary*	*Middle*	*Secondary and above*	*Literate*	*All unemployed*
CENSUS OF POPULATION (ALL AGE GROUPS) 1, 3, 4						
1981	29.62	14.57	16.84	38.97	70.38	100.00
1991	19.56	12.17	20.89	47.38	80.44	100.00
SAMPLE SURVEYS ON EMPLOYMENT AND UNEMPLOYMENT (15 YRS. AND ABOVE) 1, 2						
1983	6.10	19.32	27.58	47.00	93.90	100.00
1993-94	5.24	11.01	20.20	63.55	94.76	100.00

Notes:

(1) The concepts used for identifying the unemployed in the population census are not exactly the same as those used in the National Sample Surveys on employment and unemployment.

(2) Sample survey estimates are according to usual activity taking into consideration the subsidiary economic status of persons categorised as "not working".

(3) Education level secondary and above includes also those literates assigned education status as education level not classifiable in 1981 and 1991 census.

(4) Information on 1991 census is based on advanced tabulation of 100% data for States with population below 10 million and 10% sample data for States with population 10 million and above.

Scheme for Educated Unemployed of Employment Generation in Urban Localities (SEEGUL). It seeks to provide self-employment opportunities for the educated unemployed in towns with population above one lakh. The scheme aims at providing training to beneficiaries for the enhancement of their technical skills. The scheme is targetted at all the unemployed persons who are matriculates, ITI diploma holders or have attended a Government sponsored technical training course of

[21] Ninth Five-Year Plan, 1997-2002 (1999), Vol. I, p. 204.

[22] Ninth Five-Year Plan, 1997-2002 (1999), Vol. I, p. 205.

at least six months duration and whose family income does not exceed a specified level.[23]

Programme for Female Employment

It has been observed that female unemployment rates are higher than male unemployment rates on the weekly and daily status basis as smaller proportion of women want employment on whole-time basis. The nation is committed to a steady improvement in the status of women and to achieve this objective it is necessary to secure for them a fair share of employment opportunities. For that purpose the Planning Commission recommended that: (1) there should be more education and training opportunities for women; (2) in occupations preferred by women, such as office work, work in textiles, chemical and electronic industries, etc., preference should be given to qualified women; and (3) women should be given equal opportunity under the employment guarantee scheme in the rural areas.[24]

There has been special emphasis in the Sixth Plan and after to provide increasing opportunities to women in wage employment as mentioned in the next Chapter.

Our field investigations of the 'Food for Work Programme' carried out in a Community Development Block in Lucknow District reveal the following weakness of the programme[25]: (1) There was no proper planning of the road construction programme. (2) In some cases where land of the dominant castes of the village was involved, the path was changed and the land and houses of poor persons were encroached upon. (3) The payment to the workers was not made regularly with the result that the mates (supervisors) misused their position, advanced loans to the labourers and later on got foodgrains from the Block authorities and sold the foodgrains for more money. (4) The distribution of grains was not made on the spot, causing great inconvenience to the workers. (5) There was no employment of women as envisaged by the Planning Commission. All these deficiencies need be removed to make this programme more successful.

[23] Eighth Five-Year Plan (1992), Vol. II, p. 357.

[24] Draft Five-Year Plan, 1978-83 (1978), pp. 85 and 90.

[25] The programme in the Chinhat Block which was visited on 14-1-80.

2. *Population and Health Problems*

According to Thompson and Lewis, the three main questions of population study are: (1) How many people live in a given population group, what changes are taking place in the size of the group, and how are these changes in size effected? (2) What kind of people live in the population group, and how do they differ from the people in another group? This study of the characteristics of population is usually discussed under the general heading of the 'composition of the population'. (3) How are people distributed in the area under study, and what changes are taking place in their distribution? These three major elements of study can be remembered easily in terms of the three words emphasised above: size, composition and distribution. The population student is interested in a population's size, composition, and distribution; and in changes in these aspects through time, and the causes of these changes. Ultimately he is interested in these changes because they are related to human welfare.[26] Although to study population problems of our country all these three aspects need our attention, yet the first one is the most important and demands our immediate attention, because the main problem which the country is facing at present is concerned with the size, i.e., more increase in population than required.

The population which was 437 million in 1961 rose to 548 in 1971, 685 in 1981 and to 844 million in 1991, almost double the figure of 1961. India is the first country in the world to have a government-level programme of family welfare and planning. "In 1966, the programme was consolidated, expanded and extended, and a new Family Planning Department was created in the Ministry of Health. However the programme received a setback during the years 1977-79. The effective couple protection rate which touched a figure of 23.7 per cent in 1976-77, slipped down to 22.5 per cent in 1979-80, the beginning of the Sixth Five-Year Plan.[27]

A Working Group on Population Policy was set up by the Planning Commission in 1979. This group recommended the adoption of the long-term demographic goal of reducing the Net

[26] Thompson, W.S. and Lewis, D.T., *Population Problems* (1965), p. 5.

[27] Seventh Five-Year Plan (1985), p. 279.

Reproduction Rate (NRR) to 1 by the year 1996 for the country as a whole and by 2001 in all the States. The implications of this long-term demographic goals were spelt out as follows:

(1) The average size of the family would be reduced from 4.2 children to 2.3 children.

(2) The birth rate per 1000 population would be reduced from the level of 33 in 1978 to 21.

(3) The death rate per 1000 population would be reduced from about 14 in 1978 to 9 and the infant mortality would be reduced from 129 to 60 or less.

(4) As against about 22 per cent of the eligible couples protected with family planning, 60 per cent would be protected by the year 2000 A.D.

If these goals are achieved, the population of India would be around 950 million by the turn of the century and stabilise at 1200 million by the year 2050 A.D.

"The Sixth Plan emphasised that the family planning and welfare programme must rise above all controversies and should be accorded high priority. It was reiterated that the programme would not be the sole responsibility of any one department of the Government but the responsibility of the Government as a whole. The role of extension education, motivation and involvement of official and voluntary agencies was stressed.[28]

Against a target of 24 million sterilisations by the end of Sixth Plan, about 17 million sterilisation were carried out. Against the target of 7.9 million IUD about 7 million IUD insertions were done, and against a 11 million target of CC users in 1984-85, only 9.31 million were enrolled during the year. Thus the achievements fell short of the target particularly in the case of sterilisation. The effective couple protection was raised from 22 to 32 per cent but it was still below the Sixth Plan target to 36.6 per cent. The performance was much below the average in the States of Uttar Pradesh, Bihar and Rajasthan which account for a sizeable population of the country.

The performance of family planning was also not satisfactory during the Seventh Plan period. The Eighth Plan points out that while the Seventh Plan targets of achieving CPR of 42% was achieved, this was not matched by a commensurate decline

[28] *Ibid.*, p. 280.

in the birth rate, possibly because of improper selection of the cases. The performance in terms of various methods of couple protection was not uniform. While the targets for Intra Uterine Device (IUD) were fully achieved and those for oral contraceptives and conventional contraceptives were exceeded, the targets for sterilisation operations fell short by about a quarter.[29] Thus the slow progress of family planning programme is a matter of great concern for the planners. As the Eighth Plan points out, "High growth rate of the population continues to be one of the major problems facing the country. Although 1991 census recorded a marginal decline in the annual growth rate of population from 2.22% in 1971-81 to 2.11% in 1981-91. This would mean an addition of 18 million people to the country's population annually.

To give a major thrust in this priority area, which constitutes the pivotal point for the success of all developmental efforts, a National Population Policy needs to be enunciated and adopted by the Parliament. Given the political commitment at all levels, it must generate a cascading effect to become a people's movement. Social determinates such as female literacy, age of marriage, employment opportunities for women, and their status in the society are as important as achieving a reduction in infant mortality, improving health and nutrition of pre-school child and providing a comprehensive package of maternal health care services. Such an inter-sectoral interaction, supported by political commitment and a popular mass movement, will constitue the approach to strategic interventions during the Plan period."[30]

The targeted reduction in the birth rate will be the basis of designing, implementing and monitoring the programme against the current method of couple protection rate. Identification and registration of eligible couples, enforcement of civil registration scheme, registration of mothers and children for child survival and safe motherhood activities are areas requiring official monitoring.

"The role of voluntary organisations in a mass movement such as population control is critical for generation of

[29] Eighth Five-Year Plan, 1992-97 (1992), p. 232.

[30] *Ibid.*, pp. 331 and 334-35.

momentum and accelerating the pace of progress. There is a need to incorporate family planning as a major objective of all voluntary organisations concerned with health and/or education-related activities... The establishment of an apex organisation to develop networking between all such voluntary organisations committed to the promotion of national efforts in this important area of human endeavour will be considered."[31]

Special efforts will be made to involve the community in the family planning programme. Panchayats, youth clubs, village committees, Nehru Yuvak Kendras, women's organisations, etc., can play an important role in community motivation, organisation of camps and contraceptive distribution. Grassroot level functionaries, e.g., village dais, Village Health Guides (VHGs), Auxiliary Nurse Midwives (ANMs), Anganwadi workers, village extension workers, primary school teachers, gram panchayat staff, etc. will play a supportive role in population control movement. The possibilities of introducing certain disincentives to the non-adopters of family planning was also to be explored and introduced with due regard to the freedom and fundamental rights of the people.

The Medical Termination of Pregnancy Act (1971) is a legislative measure for improving maternal health through the stipulation of conditions under which pregnancies may be terminated. It was envisaged that MTP services would be provided at all primary health centres. Medical Termination of Pregnancy (MTP) was to play an important role in the entire scheme of family planning in the Eighth Plan.

Health Services

India is signatory to the Alma Ata Declaration (1978) whereby it is committed to achieving "Health for All by 2000 A.D.". The programme initiated and executed over the last three decades have strengthened the health care system, particularly in the field of communicable disease. Measures have been initiated to correct the regional imbalances prevalent within the system and to augment health-care services in the rural areas through the Minimum Needs Programme (MNP). Life expectancy at birth has gone up from 32 years in 1947 to 58

[31] *Ibid.*, p. 337.

years in 1990 while the infant mortality rate has come down from 129 per thousand live births in 1970 to 80 in 1990. The health infrastructure has been strengthened considerably. The country had about 83,000 sub-centres, 11,000 primary and subsidiary health centres and 650 community health centres in 1985. This infrastructure is supported by curative and specialist care facilities at the higher institutions.

Rural Health Programme. The new National Health Policy was adopted by the Parliament in 1982. Under this policy, Health Care Programmes were restructured and reoriented towards this policy. Priority has been given to extension and expansion of the rural health infrastructure through a network of community health centres, primary health centres and sub-centres. High priority was given to the development of primary health care located as close to the people as possible. Under the minimum needs programme, population norms have been revised to one sub-centre for 5,000 population, one primary health centre for 30,000 and one community health centre with four basic specialities for a population coverage of 1 lakh. The number of sub-centres, primary health centres and community health centres was to be raised to 1,37,000, 23,000, and 2,202 respectively by the year 1990.

Thus the three-tier system of sub-centres, Primary Health Centres (PHC) and Community Health Centres (CHC) was to be further strengthened during the Seventh Plan period, by converting the existing Maternity and Child Health (MCH) centres and rural dispensaries into PHCs and sub-district hospitals into CHCs and by setting up new functional units wherever necessary.[32] The training of uni-purpose health workers into multi-purpose functionaries had not progressed satisfactorily during the Sixth Plan period. Lack of rationalisation of pay scales of the multi-purpose functionaries by the States was a serious impediment to the successful progress of the scheme. Thus the Multi-Purpose Workers (MPW) scheme was to be extended and emphasis on training for ensuring attitudinal changes and developing the required skills among them was to be laid in the Seventh Plan. Effective deployment of trained personnel and the resolution of administrative problems, e.g.,

[32] Seventh Five-Year Plan (1985), p. 273.

connected with rationalisation of pay scale, was also important. It need be stated here that the scheme of multi-purpose workers remained controversial for a long time with the result that the health and family welfare programme suffered. 'The various committees appointed from 1963 to 1973 in connection with health programmes by the Government of India (e.g., Chadah Committee, Mukerji Committee 1965, Mukerji Committee 1966, Jungalwalla Committee 1967 and Kartar Singh Committee 1973) made different recommendations regarding the role of health workers posted in the community development blocks in the rural areas."[33] This controversy was finally set atrest by the Srivastava Committee (1975) which recommended for multi-purpose health workers at the centre/sub-centre level and local Community Health Workers (CHW) at the village level.

Measures for encouraging community participation in the programme were to be encouraged. Village Health Committees need to be activised. The block and district level panchayats were to be fully involved in the planning, organising and running of health services.

Urban Health Services

In the urban areas, there were multiple agencies providing health services but poor coordination among them results in duplication and inefficiency of services. Thus there was urgent need for a coordinated, organised, integrated urban development programme, which would include proper health services as an essential and integrated part.

The Eighth Plan points out, "More than one quarter of the population in the country now lives in urban areas. In metropolitan and large cities, about 40-50% of the urban dwellers are estimated to be living in slum areas where the health status of the people is as bad as, if not worse than in rural areas. But infrastructure for primary health care in urban areas hardly exists. Serious attempts will be made to develop urban health services as per the recommendations of Krishnan Committee. Organic linkage will be forged with the urban development schemes including Urban Basic Services for a comprehensive

[33] Madan, G.R., *India's Developing Villages*, 1990, p. 424.

development of health and welfare services. Local hospitals will be made responsible to run these centres and treat them as their extension counters for providing health services to the community. Voluntary organisations and local bodies would be encouraged to develop partnership and ultimately taking full responsibility for carrying out these programmes. Health system research to develop a mode of urban primary health care services will be undertaken."[34] It may be mentioned here that the Krishnan Committee (1982) recommended that a scheme should be so devised as might provide the basic health services (preventive, promoted and curative) and family welfare services at a place with a walking distance of about 15 minutes from the slum area.[35] The proposed Health Post should cover an area whose population had at least 40% living in slum or slum-like areas with predominantly weaker sections. The Population to be covered by a post/centre was to vary between 5000 to 50,000 depending upon the area and the staff appointed.

Communicable diseases account for more than two-thirds of the total morbidity and mortality in the country. Programmes for their control and eradication were to be further strengthened.

Mental health care activities are vital for obviating the ill-effects of major socio-economic changes, A beginning in this direction was made in the Seventh Plan by according priority to strengthening the existing psychiatry departments, promotion of community psychiatry by provision of drugs and services through the primary health care system and organisation of training programmes.

During the Eighth Plan, mental health services were to be given priority. A psychiatric centre in each of the districts/divisions was to be established. Also every medical college was to be encouraged to start a separate department of psychiatry, so that the required manpower, both medical and para-medical, could be trained.[36]

[34] Eighth Five-Year Plan, (1992), p. 323.

[35] *Report of the Working Group on Reorganisation of Family Welfare and Primary Health Care Services in Urban Areas (Ministry of Health and Family Welfare, 1982)*, p. 5.

[36] Eighth Five-Year Plan (1992), p. 329.

Progress so far made in the promotion of health education is far from satisfactory. Efforts were to be made for the active use of different types of media to create awareness among the people and motivate them to utilise health services and to adopt healthful practices.

Some Programmes in the Field of Population Control and Health

(a) India Population Projects

To overcome the constraints faced by the family welfare programme such as: (i) weak infrastructure (ii) poor skills of health functionaries and (iii) inadequate and poor quality of services mainly in low income and backward states due to resource constraints, India Population Projects (IPPs) have been taken up since 1973 through the assistance of World Bank and other donor agencies in selected states and backward districts. Upto this day, seven India Population Projects have been successfully completed and presently two IPPs (IPP VIII and IFF IX) are in operation.

(b) Integrated Population and Development (IPD) Project

It is proposed to take up an Integrated Population and Development Project with the assistance of UNFPA in four districts and five urban areas in Maharashtra State namely, Dhule, Gadchiroli, Thane and Chandrapur and urban slums of Kalyan, Bhwandi, Thane, Ulhasnagar and Pune at a total cost of Rs. 33.67 crores and Alwar, Bhilwara, Udaipur, Chittorgarh, Sawai Madhopur and Bharatpur at a total cost of Rs. 42.82 crores. The project is for a period of four years i.e. from 1998 to 2001.[37]

(c) Reproductive and Child Health Programme (RCH)

During the Ninth Plan, the RCH programme has integrated all the related programmes of the Eighth Plan. The concept of RCH is to provide to the beneficiaries need based, client-centered, demand-driven, high quality and integrated RCH services. The RCH programme incorporates components covered under the Child Survival and Safe Motherhood Programme and includes two additional components, one relating to Sexually

[37] Annual Report (1998-99), Ministry of Health and Family Welfare, p. 99.

Transmitted Diseases (STD) and the other relating to Reproductive Tract Infection (RTI)."[38]

(d) Community Needs Assessment Approach (CNAA)

This family welfare programme was being implemented under the Target Free Approach (TFA) since 1st April, 1996 all over India and under the system of decentralised participatory planning. TFA has been renamed as Community Needs Assessment Approach (CNAA) from 1997. Under this approach, planning of family welfare services will be formulated in consultation with the community at the grassroot level. This approach is expected to bring about improvement in quality of services and client satisfaction."[39]

AIDS—A Major Health Hazard

AIDS is the abbreviated form used to describe the Acquired Immuno Deficiency Syndrome whereas HIV (Human Immunodeficiency Virus) is the virus which can lead to AIDS. AIDS is in fact a syndrome of more than thirty distinct life threatening conditions that can follow HIV infection. Since AIDS is a medical as well as social problem many steps have been taken to prevent it. Some of the major steps are:

(i) Realising the gravity of epidemiological situation of HIV infection prevailing in the country, the Government of India launched a National AIDS Control Programme in 1987. A comprehensive five year strategic plan was launched during the Eighth Plan period with the assistance from World Bank to the tune of US $ 1.5 million in the form of technical assistance from World Health Organisation.

(ii) A National AIDS Helpline has been set up with a toll free number 1097 for telephonic counselling which maintains the confidentiality and privacy of the caller.

(iii) A School AIDS Education Programme has been started to provide lifestyle education and information on HIV/AIDS to the students and youth.

(iv) For control of sexually transmitted diseases which have a

[38] *Ibid.*, p. 8.
[39] *Ibid.*, p. 13.

direct correlation with HIV/AIDS, 504 STD clinics in district hospitals have been taken up for modernization.[40]

Nutrition Programme

The first two Five-Year Plans recognised the need for combating the ill-effects of malnutrition. Some programmes were initiated during the Third and Fourth Five-Year Plans. However, it was only in the Fifth Plan that the nutrition programmes were intensified. "Two important Supplementary Feeding Programmes of the Fifth Plan were the Special Nutrition Programme for pre-school children in the age-group of 0-6 years, pregnant and nursing mothers in urban slums, tribal, drought prone rural and hill areas, and Mid-day Meals Programme for school children in the age-group of 6-11 years belonging to weaker sections of the society... As a part of the revised Minimum Needs Programme, it is proposed to cover about one million additional beneficiaries under the Special Nutrition Programme and four million beneficiaries under the Mid-day Meals Programme."[41] However, the supply of free or subsidised food under the Supplementary Feeding Programmes was not an adequate answer to the problem. The nutritional status of the population could only be ensured by increasing food production, imparting proper nutrition education and improving the economic status of the people so that the families can afford to buy and consume a balanced diet. For this purpose, creation of more employment opportunities in the rural areas is the only remedy. The difficulties in achieving this objective have already been discussed.

3. *Educational and Moral Problems*

We have already pointed out in Chapter XII that some of the defects and the deficiencies removed in the field of education in the country up to the time when the Education Commission (1962-64) was appointed.[42] The Education Commission made

[40] Annual Report (1998-99), Ministry of Health and Family Welfare, p. 165-167.

[41] Draft Sixth Five-Year Plan (1978), p. 252. For further details see *Indian Social, Problems,* Volume II, 1987, Chapter XXI.

[42] These points have been discussed in detail in our book *India of Tomorrow,* 1985, " Chapter VI. Also see *India's Developing Villages,* 1990, Chapter XVIII.

many useful recommendations on the basis of which New Education Policy was announced by the Government of India in 1968, in which emphasis was laid on elementary and adult education, to delink the degree from the job, to lay more emphasis on evening and correspondence courses and increase the vocational element in secondary education. The system often plus two, to be followed by three years' degree course was also gradually to be introduced all over the country to have a uniform standard of education. Science and mathematics were introduced as compulsory subjects at the secondary level. The implementation of this policy was also reflected in the Fifth and Sixth Five-Year Plans. The Seventh Five-Year Plan points out, "The Sixth Plan provided, inter-alia, for mass education through programmes of elementary education (formal and non-formal streams) and adult education. The Plan also envisaged increased bias towards the practical in secondary education, vocationalisation of higher secondary education and restructuring of undergraduate courses with a vocational bias.

Forging beneficial linkages between education, employment and development was another objective in the field of higher education ... Some of the notable measures taken for the promotion of elementary education were: 'earn while you learn' scheme, mid-day meals for children, innovative curriculum renewal schemes and special emphasis on appointment of women teachers."[43]

However in the Seventh Five-Year Plan, some changes in the educational policy were suggested. The Plan points out, "Although the Indian education scene since independence has been characterised by massive quantitative expansion at all levels, it is still to undergo the kind of transformation envisaged in the National Policy. It is faced with a staggering backlog; the level of illiteracy is as high as 63 per cent; to achieve universal elementary education, as enjoined by the Constitution. There will be need to enrol fifty million more children; vocationalisation of secondary education has yet to make headway; there is very significant pressure on the higher educational system and a decline in the standards of quality. There is an urgent need for a new design of education."[44]

[43] *Seventh Five-Year Plan* (1985), p. 253.

[44] *Ibid.*, p. 252.

In order to remove these deficiencies, the Planning Commission reiterated that the Resolution on the National Policy on Education adopted in 1968 declared that the radical reconstruction of eduction as envisaged involved: (i) a transformation of the system to relate it more closely to the life of the people; (ii) a continuous effort to expand educational opportunity; (iii) a sustained and intensive effort to raise the quality of education at all levels; (iv) an emphasis on the development of science and technology; and (v) cultivation of moral and social values. According to the Resolution, the educational system must produce young men and women of character and ability committed to national service and development.[45]

The Seventh Plan provided for reorientation of the educational system so as to prepare the country to meet the challenges of the next century.[46] The main thrust areas in the Seventh Plan were to be: (i) achievement of universal elementary education; (ii) eradication of illiteracy in the age-group 15-35 years; (iii) vocationalisation and skill-training programmes at different levels of education; (iv) upgradation of standards and modernisation at all stages of education with effective links with the world of work and with special emphasis on science and environment and on value orientation; (v) provision of facilities for education of high quality and excellence in every district of the country where talented students will be provided free education, and (vi) removal of obsolescence and modernisation of technical education. The major strategies for achieving these objectives were to include effective decentralised planning and organisational reforms, promotion of non-formal and open learning systems, adoption of low cost alternatives and optimum use of resources, forging of beneficial linkages with industry and development agencies and mobilisation of community resources and societal involvement.

As a result, a New Educational Policy was declared by the Government of India in May, 1986. In this policy, it is envisaged that we should have concrete results. "All teachers should teach

[45] *Ibid.*, p. 252.
[46] *Ibid.*, p. 255.

and all students should study"[47] and the semester system to be introduced from the secondary stage. The main features of this policy were earlier indicated in the Seventh Plan.

The Eighth Plan points out, "Although the country has not so far achieved the goals of universalisation of elementary education and eradication of adult illiteracy, the 1991 census results reveal a literacy rate of over 52%, with a higher rate of growth for female literacy. This is highly encouraging and the country can hope to achieve the broader goals of 'Education For All' (EFA) by 2000 A.D., which has incidentally received international recognition at the world conference of EFA held at Jomtien in March 1990. The commitment of the Government to the National Policy on Education (NPE), implemented from 1986-87 onwards and reviewed in 1990, has been reaffirmed with revised formulation in respect of a few paras, placed before the Parliament on 7.5.1992. On the eve of Eighth Plan, therefore, the country is poised to make a real break-through in achieving its long-cherished educational goals as well as in supporting the drive of higher rate of economic growth."[48]

(i) Elementary Education

The new thrust in elementary education emphasised the aspects of: (i) universal enrolment and universal retention; and (ii) substantial improvement in the quality of education. As part of implementation of NPE, the new scheme of "Operation Blackboard" (OB) was launched. Besides, the scheme of Non-Formal Education (NFE) was revised and a number of schemes for teacher education were also taken up. By March 1992, the scheme of OB covered about 80 per cent of the blocks and 49 experimental, innovative NFE projects were sanctioned. There were 27,342 NFE centres run by 419 voluntary agencies and there were 2.72 lakh State-run NFE centres.

(ii) Imparting of Moral Education

All the Commissions or Committees appointed in the field of education have laid emphasis on the development of fundamental

[47] Ministry of Human Resource Development, Government of India, Department of Education, *National Policy on Education.* 1986, New Delhi, 1986, p. 20.

[48] Eighth Five-Year Plan (1992), p. 283.

social, moral and spiritual values in the educational institutions as stated in Chapter XII. Even in the Educational Policy (1986), emphasis has been laid on value orientation to produce young men and women of character and ability and committed to national service and development. However, in our view, mere educational institutions cannot perform this job. It is the conduct of teachers and other elite groups in society which affects the younger generation and the role of religious and other institutions like family, government, labour groups, politicians and mass media are important. However, as stated earlier, the role of religious institutions is the most important.

(iii) Adult Education Programme

After the report of the Education Commission (1964-66), certain programmes in the field of education were taken up. But it was with the coming of Janata Government in power, in 1977, that a massive programme of adult education was taken up. The Draft Five-Year Plan 1978-83, points out, "The existing programmes of adult education, viz., (1) the farmers' functional literacy project for rural areas, (2) the Shramik Vidyapeeths and polyvalent adult education centres for urban areas, (3) adult education departments in universities, (4) the Nehru Yuvak Kendras, (5) the National Service Scheme, and (6) assistance to voluntary organisations for adult education will be continued, improved and expanded where necessary. But the main feature of the Plan is the proposal to mobilise all these efforts and organise a very large, intensive and nation-wide programme of adult education, with special emphasis on the age-group 15-35. Whereas in the past the total number of adults made literate every year was about 5 lakhs, it is now proposed that programmes of adult education and literacy in the Plan will cover about 650 lakhs in total; 15 lakhs in the first year, 45 lakhs in the second, 90 lakhs in the third, 180 lakhs in the fourth and 320 lakhs in the fifth and final year."[49] Besides literacy, the 'main elements of the programme will include an appropriate 'mix', suited to the needs and interests of the individual of such themes as general education including

[49] Draft Five-Year Plan, 1973-83 (1978), p. 221.

citizenship training, health education and family planning, upgrading of vocational skills, deeper understanding of science and technology in day-to-day life and physical education and cultural activities.

A National Board of Adult Education was established at the Centre to guide the programme. Suitable agencies were also set up with similar objectives at the State, district, block and local community levels.

This programme was also accepted by the Congress Government when it came to power in 1980 and was a part of the Sixth and the Seventh Five-Year Plans. The Seventh Five-Year Plan points out, "Eradication of adult illiteracy and the development of a programme of continuing adult education is a major thrust area in the Seventh Plan. This task of covering all the illiterates in the age-group 15-35 years by 1990 is a formidable one. As motivation of the learner is crucial for success and as the number to be covered is about 90 million, the strategy to achieve the goal can only be through a mass movement involving social institutions, voluntary organisations, students, teachers, employers and the community ... Community participation in all literacy programme will be an essential feature from village level upwards to give proper direction and orientation and lend effective support to this national programme."[50]

Training in functional skills relevant to their economic activities was another aspect of adult education, which was to receive due attention. Similarly non-formal education for the achievement of universalisation of elementary education for those who were not able or willing to attend full-time schools was given great importance in the Seventh Plan.

Eighth Plan points out, "The NPE and the Programme Of Action (POA) envisaged that the Adult Education Programme (AEP) would cover 4 crore illiterates by 1990 and another 6 crores by 1995. With the launching of the National Literacy Mission (NLM) in 1988, the targets were reformulated and strategies recast. Accordingly, 3 crore illiterates were expected to be covered by 1990 and 5 crores by 1995. While Rural Functional Literacy Programme (RFLP), the post-literacy

[50] Seventh Five-Year Plan (1985), pp. 257-58.

teaching-learning processes were modified, new strategies like area-specific and time-bound approach to achieve 100 per cent Total Literacy (TL), massive participation of Non-Governmental Organisations (NGOs) and students and effective utilisation of traditional and folk theatre forms in literacy work were evolved. By 1991-92, the post-literacy programme was institutionalised in the form of 32,000 Jan Shikshan Nilayams (JSN). Apart from the introduction of Improved Pace and Content of Learning (IPCL) method, which reduced the duration of learning from 500 to 200 hours, technology demonstration programmes were initiated in 42 selected districts. The scheme of Shramik Vidyapeeths (SVs) was reviewed, suggesting a need for expansion. A National Institute of Adult Education was set up in January 1991 to augment the technical and academic resource support to adult education and to undertake quality research and evaluation studies."[51]

Area-specific and time-bound mass campaigns for TL first launched in Kottayam town and Ernakulam district in Kerala in 1989 with the active participation of students and voluntary agencies were extended to other districts. By March 1992, twenty-five districts had achieved total literacy (in the sense of 85 per cent literacy) and TL campaigns were at different stages of progress in 80 districts of different States covering over 3 crore illiterates with the help of about 30 lakh volunteers.

"Universalisation of elementary education, eradication of illiteracy in the age-group of 15-35 and strengthening of Vocational Education (VE) so as to relate it to the emerging needs in the urban and rural settings are the major thrust areas of the Eighth Plan in the Education Sector ... The changed approach, improved methodology of teaching, increased participation of NGOs and student volunteers have infused a new vitality into the literacy programme and have given it a fresh momentum. The aim would be to impart a similar vitality and momentum to the universal primary education programme with a definite edge in its favour... Within the overall school-age population, the focus would be on girls, who account for two-thirds of target, and among adults the focus would be on women's literacy which has a beneficial impact on children's

[51] Eighth Five-Year Plan (1992), p. 284.

literacy as well as other national objectives like population control and family welfare."[52]

"Keeping in view the way the National Literacy Mission has moved the following new strategies have evolved:

1. Preparation of time-bound action plans for Total Literacy Campaign (TLC) coverage of uncovered districts in the states of Bihar, Punjab, Jammu and Kashmir and north eastern states.
2. Non-cash incentives for motivating volunteers so as not to defeat their spirits.
3. Instituting linkages between literacy campaigns and Panchayati Raj Institutions.
4. Linking literacy schemes and other development programmes.
5. Regular and systematic monitoring by holding state level monthly meetings.
6. Compilation and dissemination of accurate field-level data.
7. Concurrent and final evaluations of campaigns by independent social research agencies with proven track record.
8. Decentralisation and delegation of authority for implementation of literacy programmes to State Governments by establishing State Literacy Mission Authorities (SLMAs).
9. Strengthening State Directorates of Adult Education to act as nodal agencies of monitoring and evaluation.
10. Augmenting State Resource Centres (SRCs) for providing improved techno-pedagogic and training support to literacy programmes."[53]

"In the field of education, literacy campaigns have already covered 447 districts, of which 215 are in Total Literacy Campaigns and 173 are in Post Literacy Campaigns and 59 are in Continuing Education Phase. In addition, 38 districts have been covered under Rural Functional Literacy Projects. Hence, the total coverage comes to 485 districts. Efforts would be made to bring the remaining 40 odd districts under the coverage of Literacy."[54]

[52] *Ibid.*, p. 285.

[53] Annual Report (1998-99), Department of Education, p. 83.

[54] *Ninth Five-Year Plan, 1997-2002 (1999), Vol. II, p. 121.*

(iv) Indiscipline among Students

We have already discussed the causes leading to indiscipline among the students and also made certain suggestions for improving the situation. However, there has not been much change in the situation except during the internal emergency (1975 to 1977). Canalising students' energy into such constructive activities as National Cadet Corps, National Service Scheme, and also sports, games and other cultural activities may produce good results.[55] However, in our opinion much responsibility for this indiscipline rests with the teachers who do not give adequate attention to their welfare. The lack of parents' interest in their wards may also be responsible for this phenomenon. Another important cause is the lack of moral education among youngsters through religious institutions. As Shrimati Ranjan Amin points out, "Formerly, religion and religious institutions gave children a philosophy of life and a code of behaviour. It taught them to honour and respect parents, to be faithful in marriage, to be humble and forgiving, to be content with what was given to them and so on... Today, parents are afraid to talk of anything as old-fashioned as religion. It embarrasses adults to uphold positive principles because these days everything is relative... Not only are children denied education in the frames of reference once provided by religion, but what they see around them in a mass of contradictions. On the one hand, marriage is called a 'sacrament' and on the other permissiveness is present; honesty is said to be good yet one goes all out to give the lie to what one is—financially, educationally, socially; kindness is upheld as an admirable quality, but one is kind to those who can return it. As a result of this chaos, the child comes to the adolescent stage insecure in his behaviour and in the meaning of life. As parents and teachers, our responsibility in guiding moral development begins from the child's earliest years and it begins with ourselves. We must be sure of our own values and constantly endeavour to live by them."[56]

[55] SeeMadan.G.R., *Indian Social Problems,* Vol. II, 1987, Chapter on Youth Welfare Services.

[56] Amin, Ranjan, "Parents, Teachers and Guidance of Adolescents" in *The Indian Family in the Change and Challenge of the Seventies* (Selected Papers of a Seminar organised by the Family Life Centre of the Indian Social Institute, New Delhi), New Delhi, Sterling Publishers, 1972, p. 134.

Education Policy during 10th Five Year Plan and after

The National Policy on Education (NPE) 1986 as updated in 1992, envisages improvement and expansion of education in all sectors, elimination of disparities in access and laying greater access on improvement in the quality and relevance of education at all levels, including technical and professional education. It also emphasizes that education must play a positive and interventionist role in correcting social and regional imbalances, empowering women and a securing a rightful place for the disadvantaged, linguistic groups and minorities.

With the vigorous implementation of the Sarva Siksha Abhiyan (SSA) and cooked Mid Day Meal (MDM Scheme) the number of out of school children has come down to less than 5% of the total population in the age groups of 6 to 14 years i.e. from 4.4 crores in 2001-02 to 70 lakhs in 2006.

In the field of adult education and literacy, out of 600 district in the country 597 have since been covered under various programmes—101 under total literacy campaigns, 171 under post literacy programme and 325 under continuing education programme. About 120.39 million persons have been covered under literacy programes as on 31-3-2006. About 60% of the beneficiaries are women while 22% and 12% belong to scheduled castes and scheduled tribes respectively.[57]

Programme of Higher Education in Eleventh Five Year Plan

The Eleventh Plan must also focus on the pressing need to expand capacity in our institutions of higher education and technical and professional education (Engineering, Medicine, Law etc.). The Gross Enrolment Ratio (GER) for higher education (percentage of the 18-23 age group enrolled in higher education institutions) currently is around 11% whereas it is 25% for many other developing countries. China has increased its GER in higher education from 10% in 1998 to 21% in 2005. We must aim at increasing the GER to 15% by the end of the Plan and reach 21% by the end of the Twelfth Plan. This is necessary not only to meet the needs of a growing economy, but also to meet

[57] *Annual Report 2006-2007, Department of School Education and Literacy, Department of Higher Education, Ministry of Human Resource Development, Govt. of India. P. 2*

the aspirations of younger people who see education as an essential requirement for advancement. Along with expansion, it is also necessary to aim at improvement in quality. While the best of our institutions of higher education compare well internationally a large number suffer from serious quality problems. A general improvement in the quality of existing universities is necessary, including upgrading of facilities and improved methods of teaching.

There will be establishment of 30 new Central universities, one in each of the 16 States which do not have a Central university at present, and 14 other Central universities in different parts of the country. Similarly that will be establishment of eight IITs, seen IIMs and five Indian Institute of Science Education and Research during the Eleventh Plan.[58]

Religious Institutions and Democratic Society

Religion plays a very important role in controlling the behaviour of an individual in a democratic society. Although the tenets of Hinduism are of positive nature and can help in moulding the character of people in the right direction, yet at present, their impact is not wholesome due to their defective teaching to the masses. The recommendations made by the Hindu Religious Endowment Commission (1962) in this regard need serious consideration by some religious bodies like the Vishwa Hindu Parishad. The Commission recommended that each State should set up one or more religious institutions for systematic instructions to temple priests in Sanskrit, Hindu scriptures and rituals. However, to achieve the goals of a Welfare State, the emphasis should be on purity of life, self-sacrifice and social service as stated in the Brihad-Aranyaka Upanishad. The Upanishad laid emphasis on three cardinal virtues for a human being to attain moksha. These were: (i) self-control, (ii) generosity, and (iii) compassion. While the first virtue was stressed more for the Brahmins, the second was for the king and the third for all the three varnas bound up with apathetic mystical ecstasy.[59] For children, the stories given in the

[58] *Eleventh Five Year Plan 2007-2012 Volume-I, Inclusive Growth, Planning Commission Government of India (2008) pp. 17-18*

[59] See Madan, G.R., *Western Sociologist on Indian Society,* London, 1979, p. 146, and Ram, *G.M., Bible of Hinduism,* 1985, p. 111.

Panchatantra and Hitopadesa should be freely translated in all languages and taught in the schools and homes.

4. *Leisure and Recreation*

It was pointed out in Chapter XIII that with the introduction of modern technology, the leisure time for the common man has increased tremendously, and it was presumed that the common man will use this leisure wisely, devoting much time to self-improvement and social betterment rather than spending it in idleness, mischief and even criminal activities. That some have used leisure properly is evidenced by the progress of community recreation, cultural activities and welfare programmes, yet many have misused it leading to group conflicts and litigation in villages and filling the cinemas and drinking shops in the urban areas. The expansion of adult education programme, the reading groups and libraries, expansion of social welfare activities, more attendance in religious gatherings, increase in healthy cultural and physical activities are some of the programmes which need more attention. Unfortunately adequate attention has not been paid to healthy recreational programmes with the result that there has not been much improvement in the social health of the nation. Our own survey in two villages of Uttar Pradesh reveals that there are not many regular and well organised recreational activities there. Men and women generally gossip within their own caste groups. In these villages, there was no regular social, educational, physical, cultural or religious programme in which people of all caste groups could participate. In one village, there was open conflict between Harijans and a dominant caste faction of the village which ultimately led to litigation. In the other village, there was conflict between two factions of the same dominating caste, with the result that no community work such as construction of a school building or an approach road was possible.[60]

As regards urban areas, our field experience shows that though we were running one recreational centre through a voluntary welfare organisation, and government assistance was also available, local leaders did not take much interest in

[60] See Madan, G.R., *Village Development in India* (1983), Chapter VIII.

running the centre properly. It is unfortunate that no healthy tradition is being built for some type of recreational activities.

TABLE 37

NUMBER OF CINEMAS IN INDIA[61]

Cinemas	*1965-66*	*1971-72*	*1973-74*	*1975-76*
Permanent	3,808	4,590	5,304	5,650
Touring	1,639	2,711	2,932	3,367
Total	5,447	7,3M	8,236	9,017

The increase in the number of cinemas in recent years as shown in Table 37 is also not a healthy sign.

No doubt Central and State Governments have assisted in establishing certain academies in the fields of art, music, drama, etc. after Independence.[62] Yet more attention is needed in the playground activities in an organised manner.

Dr. Shipstone points out that the most important single change that has affected family life in India is the breaking up of the joint family system and the emergence of the unitary family. In this new family pattern, often both the parents work and go their own way; children go their own way. Often working parents have little time to spend together as a family; and the youth, pulsating with new energy and full of new experiences and questions, begins to get estranged from his part-time parents. The youth is now deprived of an opportunity to imbibe the culture and traditional values which he formerly did through the grand-parents, mothers and aunts in the joint family situation. His leisure is now spent in spurious pursuits or in company with his peers. He needs guidance for leisure time. "The two or three most common recreational activities of the young people today are movies, talking and aimless wandering in shopping and restaurant areas. Our youth have the most leisure and they are the most wasteful of time.[63] She suggests that educational institutions should provide them wholesome

[61] *India-Reference Annual,* 1977 and 1978, 1978, p. 149.

[62] See Madan, G.R., *India's Social Transformation,* Vol. I, 1979, Chapter VI.

[63] Dr. Shipstone, Eva, "Educating the Indian Adolescent" in *The Indian family in the Change and Challenge of the Seventies,* 1972, *op. cit.*, p. 113.

recreational activities like N.C.C., girl guides, scouting, social service camps, games, etc.

5. *Political Institutions and Corruption*

There are various forms of Government which have been in vogue from time to time in different countries. Their working has been discussed in some detail in another volume.[64] The working of democratic institutions from the village level to the Central level, i.e., Village Panchayats, Panchayat Samitis, Zila Parishads, State Assemblies and Parliament has been discussed in detail in the same series.[65] With the extensive area of operation of the elected leaders, where the people are not able to supervise the conduct of their elected leaders, expansion in the functions of the Government, store of wealth in the form of paper money, limitless increase in the number of material goods which a person can purchase for his material comforts such as radio, television, scooter, car, spacious and expensive houses, less fear of God, lack of organised public opinion against corruption are some of the factors responsible for increase in corruption in public life. The two Government Committees or Commissions appointed to look into this aspect of corruption were the Committee on Prevention of Corruption (1962) and the Administrative Reforms Commission (1966).[66] We have already dealt with the recommendations made by the Committee on Prevention of Corruption. On the recommendations of this Committee, the Central Vigilance Commission at the Centre and vigilance departments in the States were set up to check corruption among public servants. However, no steps were taken to check corruption in Public Undertakings or corruption among legislators or ministers. Similarly, on the recommendations of the Administrative Reforms Commission, Lokpals and Lokayuktas have been appointed in various States to look into the conduct of legislators, ministers and officers working in Government Undertakings. During the Janata Government regime, some special Commissions were also appointed in 1977

[64] For details see Madan.G.R., *India's Social Transformation*, Vol. II, 1984, Chapter IV.

[65] See Madan,G.R., *India of Tomorrow: Problems of Social Reconstruction* (1985). Chapter VIII.

[66] For details see Madan, G.R., *India of Tomorrow* (1985), Chapter VII.

to look into the conduct of the Prime Minister and other ministers and officers. These included the Shah Commission, the Gupta Commission, etc. However, we do not see any improvement in the situation and corruption is on the increase. The assumption of the Committee on Prevention of Corruption (1962) that after the introduction of certain administrative measures and vigilance establishments corruption will be reduced, seems to have proved wrong. Perhaps the Committee never looked into the changes which the reformed religion in Western countries brought into their conduct of life. In a democratic society, where there are so many loopholes in the law and where there is corruption in all spheres and at all levels, it becomes difficult to curtail it in the existing set-up. A change in the life of the people can come only through good religious instructions and example of simple living set by the leaders. Unless that is done no amount of legislation can help in checking corruption. The responsibility of maintaining integrity lies with top administrators, political leaders, businessmen, intellectuals and religious leaders. Unless they lead a simple life and are honest in their dealings not much can be expected from the lower ranks.

It may be mentioned here that the Prevention of Corruption Act, 1947 was replaced by a new Act known as Prevention of Corruption Act, 1988. Its scope is wider and it covers officials working in universities, local bodies, cooperatives, social and cultural institutions, etc.[67]

As a result of the implementation of the Prevention of Corruption Act, 1988, many corruption cases, scandals and scams came to limelight since the very beginning of this decade (1990-2000).

Early 90s witnessed scandals after scandals in which many Congress Ministers, MPs and bureaucrats were involved. Some of these included Security Scam by Harshad Mehta and payment to many political leaders by Jain Brothers amounting to Rs. 65 crores in Hawala Case to gain undue favour. Similarly there was Sugar Scam, Fodder Scam, Urea Scam, etc.[68] Even a former

[67] Ministry of Law and Justice, Government of India, Acts of Parliament, 1988 (1989), pp. 463-475.

[68] Madan, G.R., *India of Tomorrow*, p. 337.

Prime Minister of India, Mr. P.V. Narasimha Rao, had two corruption cases against him—one of St. Kitts and other of Jharkhand Mukti Morcha (JMM).

Corruption has its roots in the field of administration too. The year 1999 witnessed many such instances in which top IAS, IPS and IFS officers were booked for corruption by the Central Vigilance Commission. The Vigilance Department filed cases against a former Indian Forest Services official, Chandra Gupta and several others during the month of July in 1999. According to the department sources, these officers including some of the employees belonging to the U.P. Forest Corporation have been charged with embezzlement and causing financial loss to the department.

In March 1999, various such incidents happened in which many top government officials were caught in vigilance net. In U.P., a vigilance enquiry was started against five IPS officers. The State Govt. also sought centre's approval to prosecute one IAS officer out of the four against whom vigilance enquiry had been completed. The four officers included one secretary, a departmental commissioner and a special secretary in the Bureau of Public Enterprises.

In Mandi Parishad Scam, services of the Mandi Parishad employees recruited after April 1996, were declared to be terminated soon. It was alleged that all the appointments made after April 1, 1996 were illegal and several PCS officers, who were holding the deputy director posts in various divisions were in the enquiry net.

In another incident of the 42 cases which were referred to the Vigilance Cell of the Food and Civil Supplies Department (U.P. Government) for probe in 1998, 14 gazetted and 14 non-gazetted officers were found guilty and actions were recommended against them.

More recently in 2000, a 30,000 crore match fixing scam has been unearthed in which along with many others, the captain of South African cricket team, Mr. Hansie Cronje is also one of the accused.

In India, the first evidence of match- fixing was gathered by the officials of the Directorate of Revenue Income (DRI), Mumbai on 6-7 Nov. 1996 when they were tapping the telephonic conversation between an Indian residing in Mumbai and Anees

Ibrahim—brother of Dubai based mafia, Dawood Ibrahim, in connection with a smuggling case. This conversation was related to the fixing of a match in which it was decided that India will win in the Titan series which was scheduled to be played in Wankhede Stadium, Mumbai. In that series, India won by 35. runs. DRI handed over the cassette of this conversation to CBI in May 2000.[69] Manoj Prabhakar, an ex-cricket player also gave a video cassette to CBI which shows the conversation about match-fixing between many top cricketers and officials. Based on these evidences, some Indian cricketers who are suspected of being involved in match-fixing by CBI are: Mohd. Azharuddin, Ajay Jadeja, Kapil Dev, Nayan Mongia, etc.

6. *Family Disorganization*

We discussed in Chapter XV that some of the causes leading to family disorganization and the measures needed to avoid family tensions. Some major causes were the differences in attitude and temper of spouses, conflict with in-laws, low family income, old authoritative attitudes of husbands towards their educated and employed wives and ill-health in the family. In the joint family set-up in India, "where the role of women is still overwhelmingly a subsidiary one and where there are too many commands to obey and a large number of conventions to follow, it is natural that a new bride may end up with hysteria when she is expected to cope with the uphill task of emotional integration with her in-laws. Hysteria is quite frequent in a new bride who happens to be in a joint family where the capacity of an individual is much restricted in terms of total adaptation."[70]

Mental illness is a product of the 'sick family', that is, of parental pathology or pathological patterns of interpersonal relationship in the family, "The education of the family members together with the restructuring of existing family patterns may

[69] India Today (Hindi Edition, 31 May 2000), p. 38.

[70] Nathawat, S.S., "Family Patterns and Mental Illness" in *The Indian Family in the Change and Challenge of the Seventies* (Selected Papers of a Seminar organised by the Family Life Centre of the Indian Social Institute, New Delhi), New Delhi, Sterling Publishers, 1972, p. 43.

both bring about a decline in mental illness and help in its treatment."[71]

Dr. Kapur who carried out a socio-psychological study of the change in the attitudes of educated earning women points out that the attitudes of the educated woman have undergone a considerable change regarding her role and status in society, whereas the attitudes of the husband and of the in-laws towards her role and relationship in the family have remained comparatively unchanged. In her study, she found "that if the employed wife demands the assistance of her husband and in-laws in the performance of household duties, feeling that by virtue of being a working wife she could legitimately claim to have such assistance, she is accused of being vain, impertinent, inefficient and not a good wife and daughter-in-law."[72] Marital maladjustment resulted when working women, who had to carry out household chores along with their jobs and who needed and expected help from their husbands or in-laws, did not receive that assistance in carrying out these responsibilities. It was found that 84 per cent of the employed wives who had certain expectations from their husbands but could not get them were found to be maladjusted in their married life. Another source of tension was the fact that the working wife was not given the right to spend her earned money as she liked. Thus some of the traditions and norms with regard to women's role and status need to be changed to reduce tensions in the family.

Shrimati Modak points out that there is also need for imparting sex education to our growing children and adolescents so that they may lead good family life later on. Infantile masturbation tends to become harmful when parents express their disapproval in such a way as to suggest that there is something unclear about the genitals. It is certainly undesirable that the child should indulge in excessive masturbation but it is equally undesirable to load him with feelings of shame and guilt by scolding or punishing him for masturbating. An important point is that masturbation, like thumb sucking, is a way of deriving contentment and a child indulging excessively

[71] *Ibid.*, p. 45.

[72] Kapur, Promilla, "The Changing Role and Status of Women" in *The Indian Family in the Change and Challenge of the Seventies* (1972), *op. cit.*, pp. 53-55.

in it is probably deprived of a satisfactory emotional life and proper love and affection from parents. So the important thing is to attempt to eradicate the cause and not the symptom.

At puberty and adolescence, when many physical and emotional changes take place, they become anxious and worried and even feel guilty and ashamed about the feelings of attraction that they are beginning to have for the opposite sex. However, these feelings are as perfectly normal and natural as it is to feel angry or hungry. And just as one exercises control in the latter emotions which becomes part of our nature through constant practice, so it should be with our sex desires. In this way, the sexual urge of adolescence may be used as a means of building up character through self-discipline. It is equally important for them to have a healthy outlet for these developing emotions through association with each other in work and play.

Today children enjoy a much greater freedom to mix and are exposed to much more sexual stimulation than formerly because of movies, cheap literature and other media of communication. Yet it is important for them to know that greater freedom brings with it greater obligations and responsibilities. They should know that free mingling does not mean physical intimacy as it is likely to create serious problems. The adolescents should also be given guidance as to the meaning of love, factors which are important in the choice of a marriage partner, the nature of the marriage relationships, etc. Teaching should not only aim at providing sex instructions but should also impart what is morally desirable from a personal and social point of view. Well planned sex education given at home, and in schools and colleges can help in developing wholesome attitudes toward sex and may also constitute the foundation for marriage preparation. "Many marriages that show signs of breaking up can be saved if young people are helped to acquire right attitudes to sex."[73]

7. *Community Conflicts and National Integration*

We discussed in Chapter XIV that there are various groups and organisations within a community and then there are

[73] Modak, Usha, "Sex Education" in *The Indian Family in the Change and Challenges" of the Seventies* (1972), *op. cit.*. p. 170.

communities within a community. There are economic, political, religious, recreational and class or caste groups within a community. Then there are villages, towns, cities, regions and States within a nation. In every community, there are some tensions and disruptions, some institutions that are not functioning properly and some signs of incomplete consensus. Community vitality is measured by the degree of harmony with which any action affecting the community as a whole is carried out. When the local citizens cease to be concerned about their community welfare, the proper functioning of the community is threatened. There will be more social integration if the various groups in the community work in a harmonious manner to develop individual and group responsibilities, and at the same time work for the welfare of the community. Again there are disorganised, under-organised and unorganised communities and the social workers and the local leaders have to see how they can be made well organized communities. But this is not an easy task. It will require the proper understanding of the community structure and a large number of dedicated workers to build up the community.

We have already discussed earlier, the community conflicts under several heads, viz.: (1) migration and community disorganisation; (2) conflict and inactivity in rural and urban communities; (3) casteism and community disorganisation; (4) class tensions and community disorganisation; (5) communal tensions and community disorganization; (6) lingual and regional conflicts; and (7) conflicts and groupism in large organisations, i.e., universities, municipal corporations, and political parties, and have given our suggestions for improving the situation. There is one aspect, i.e., national integration, which has been much debated upon in recent years and need further discussion.

Problems of National Integration

Prior to Independence, the one major goal before the political leaders and the people was the attainment of political independence on the basis of nationalism forgetting the narrow interests on caste, lingual and communal basis. But once independence was achieved, the conflicts started on caste, lingual or communal basis, again disrupting the national integrity. Also there was increase in the number of conflicts between employers and employees, students and authorities, disrupting the community life. These incidents have since agitated the mind of political leaders and intellectuals. Shri Jawaharlal Nehru, the first Prime Minister of India, once remarked, "We should not become parochial, narrow-minded, provincial, communal and caste-minded, because we have a great mission to perform. Let us, the citizens of the Republic of India, stand up straight with straight backs, and look up at the skies, keeping our feet firmly planted on the ground, and bring about this synthesis, this integration of the Indian people. Political integration has already taken place to some extent, but what I am after is something much deeper than that-an emotional integration of the Indian people so that we might be welded into one and made into one strong national unit, maintaining at the same time all our wonderful diversity."[74] We may define national integration as a psycho-social process that involves, beyond parochial loyalties, a common participation of all groups towards the accomplishment of nationally accepted goals.[75] However, it may be mentioned that national integration is an abstract concept because the gap between the desired and the real level would always exist. As a reality, it may have four components or more:

(1) *Political Integration:* This implies political stability, territorial integrity, ideological commitment and national identity.
(2) *Economic Integration:* This refers to an equal share in the national produce.
(3) *Socio-Cultural Integration:* This is meant to harmonise religious, caste, regional and linguistic groups for the ultimate prosperity of the whole nation. This would also imply a socially constructive relationship between the more and less educated people, the rural and the urban, as well as the ruler and the ruled.

[74] Nehru, Jawaharlal, speech at Bangalore, October 1995. Also see *Report of the Committee on Emotional Integration,* New Delhi, Government of India, Ministry of Education, 1962, p. 3.

[75] *Brij Mohan, India's Social Problems, Analysing Basic Issues,* Allahabad, Indian International Publications, 1972, p. 108.

(4) *Psychological Integration:* This implies the development of a 'national psyche'.

The State Education Ministers' Conference held in November, 1960 in New Delhi, felt distressed at the frequency with which disruptive tendencies were making themselves felt in the country and stressed the importance of the role of education in counteracting such divisive trends and in fostering unity.[76] It recommended that a committee be set up by the Union Ministry of Education to study the problems and suggest positive educational measures for promoting integration. As a result, a committee was appointed by the Government of India in May 1961 to examine the role of education in promoting emotional integration in national life with Dr. Sampumanand as Chairman. This subject of national integration was also discussed at the Conference of Governors as well as the Conference of State Chief Ministers held in New Delhi. At the Chief Ministers' Conference, it was resolved that attention should be paid to all aspects of integration including cultural, educational, linguistic and administrative.[77] The All India Congress Committee appointed a National Integration Committee under the chairmanship of Shrimati Indira Gandhi in 1961, to study the problem in depth. The Committee recommended reorientation of education, equipping students with knowledge of freedom movement, encouraging activities and studies helpful toward better understanding between States and communities and creation of responsibility among citizens. They suggested definite guidance for textbook committee, publication of books on regional heroes, and creation of communal harmony through mass education.[78] They also emphasised on social and economic equality and equal opportunity in industry, trade and commerce for backward people along with provision of technical and professional training for them.

The Planning Commission in the Third Plan observed that the success of economic planning in India will largely depend

[76] *Report of the Committee on Emotional Integration* (1962), p. XIII.

[77] Siddiqui, A.H., *National Integration in India-A Sociological Approach,* Aligarh, Three Men Publications, 1971, p. 33.

[78] Siddiqui, A.M., *op. cit.*, p. 31.

upon our capacity to hold together as a nation in the midst of diversity of language, region, caste and religion. Unity in a democracy must be based on the consciousness of a common cultural heritage and commonly accepted future goals and on a constant effort to realise them. The essentials of its culture and broadmindedness and mutual tolerance, balance between the material and the spiritual, and the cooperative way of life in which various individuals in a group are bound together by commonly accepted rights and obligations. India's future goals are embodied in the Constitution and her development plans are among the principal means for realising them.[79] They further observed that educational institutions have a vital role to play in bringing about national integration and social cohesion among the young generation. The question of achieving emotional integration and promoting national consciousness through educational institutions is being studied by a special committee and educational policies and programmes will be reviewed in the light of its recommendations.

Committee on Emotional Integration (1961)

The Committee observed that emotional integration of the Indian people is a challenge that cannot be ignored by any person in any part of the country and tolerance, charity and compassion must be practised by all the citizen in their true spirit. The Committee emphasised that it was necessary to evolve an effective national policy in education, the implementation of which would bring the States and Union Territories closer together. The idea of national unity and the unity of mankind should be introduced from the outset in the curriculum with regard to children's age and understanding. The teaching of geography should be made compulsory. A special subject dealing with national integration should be made compulsory at the college level. In the adult schools and industrial training institutes, certain programmes should be included to help students have a basic knowledge of their country and to realise the need for wholehearted cooperation in its developmental activities. Although it is not possible to provide religious

[79] Planning Commission, Government of India, *Third Five-Year Plan*. New Delhi, 1961, p. 602.

education as a part of the curriculum for schools in a secular State, students should be helped to appreciate the spiritual values which the various religions present to the people through talks given by competent persons.[80]

Colloquium on National Integration (1966)

The most important deliberation on the issue was the Colloquium on Ethical and Spiritual Values as the Basis of National Integration held in Bombay in 1966-67, in which about 300 people from different section of the society including religious heads, governors, ex-governors, union ministers, university vice-chancellors, ex-judges, members of Parliament, philosophers, authors, artists, educationists, retired I.C.S. men, journalists, sociologists, economists, scientists and lawyers took part. The problem for the Colloquium as set out in the invitation was as follows: "We seem to have lost the purposive all-India outlook, the spirit of oneness and the sense of mission which characterised our activities during our struggle for freedom and in the first few years of Independence. Centrifugal forces and group-sentiments have been sedulously at work in our country in recent years, impairing our unity and submerging our robust nationalism. We are trying to build up so-called regional cultures. Even as secessionist outlook is discernible in certain regions. We have totally ignored the aspect of reconstruction of man by simultaneously fostering ethical and spiritual values which alone go to build up character: character alone can provide the solid foundation for stable reconstruction-economic, social and political. The youth of the land are being denied the inspiration and guidance provided in our great sacred texts and by the pioneers of Indian renaissance."[81] "It was to this danger that this Colloquium was to draw attention and suggest certain remedies. Although there were more than 15 sections of the Colloquium which dealt with different aspects of Indian society, we are here mainly concerned with the sections closely connected with national integration.

[80] *Committee Report* (1962), *op. cit.*, pp. 139-60.

[81] *All India Colloquium on Ethical and Spiritual Values as the Basis of National Integration,* Dec. 30, 1966 to Jan. 2, 1977, Bombay, Bharatiya Vidya Bhavan, 1967, p. 2.

(i) Linguistic States and National Integration. In the section on 'National Integration' the main discussion revolved round the desirability or otherwise of linguistic States. The majority view was that linguistic States have come into being as a result of historical circumstances, there was no real advantage to undo what has already happened. Linguistic reorganisation was not merely a whim or a fancy but was the result of a long process which went back many years. Instead of trying to undo the process of linguistic reorganisation, the stress should be laid upon mitigating the ill-effects of that by broadening the national feelings.[82] It is particularly important that there should be no conflict between devotion to one's mother tongue and the broader loyalty to the nation, because if India continues to exist, then all the regions-whether Maharashtra or Gujarat or Bengal-will continue to flourish, and if India is weakened, then every one of these regions will be weakened. It was suggested that in the educational system, in particular, stress must be laid upon inculcating national values. In this the role of English as an important link language, apart from Hindi, was stressed. It was also felt that somewhere in our educational system Sanskrit, which has already been a great unifying factor from the Vedic times, should be taught. The desirability of having a common script, either Devanagari script or Roman script, was also suggested.

(ii) Emphasis on Ethical and Spiritual Values. In the section on 'Ethical and Spiritual Values' it was recognised that "there has been a decline in these values in the life of communities and individuals and it was felt that unless we arrested this decline, our life as a nation with a great historical past will be jeopardised. So, it is necessary to devise measures to strengthen the hold of ethical and spiritual values on the life of the people... It was recognised that ethical and spiritual values cut across all the divisions of religion, community, caste, etc., because every society has to bind itself together through values which are ethical as well as spiritual."[83] In the section on 'Religion and Secularism', it was observed that while religious instruction has disappeared from educational institutions, it has not been

[82] *Ibid.*, p. 664.
[83] *Ibid.*, p. 666.

substituted by the imparting of ethical and spiritual values. Therefore it was felt that ethical and spiritual values ought to be conveyed to the younger generation and in a general way to the public at large. It was agreed that "while religious neutrality by the Government may be continued, the education of students, and indeed of the people as a whole, in ethical and spiritual values, must be the responsibility of the State. The people's welfare, even secularism of the hedonistic type, cannot succeed without ethical and spiritual values. Possibly spiritual values may be interpreted differently; but honesty, truthfulness, helpfulness to each other, friendliness, cooperation, mutual aid-are all ethical values."[84]

(iii) Emphasis on Moral Instruction in Educational Institutions. In the section on 'Education and Youth' it was recommended that the suggestions of the Sri Prakasa Committee should be implemented. The content of instruction in spiritual and moral values should not include any denominational or religious instruction as such, but instruction of the type as envisaged in the report of the Sri Prakasa Committee consisting of prayers of universal character at lower levels, and lives of great saints and philosophers, extracts and passages from their writings, discussions on the individual philosophies and comparative religion, etc., at higher levels-as modulated in a proper manner so as to inculcate in the minds of the students, the fundamental principles of right life and conduct and true citizenship which would make them useful and social human beings. A miserable situation prevails in various educational institutions throughout the country. Joint councils of teachers and students should eliminate politicians from the field of education and prevent the minds of the students from being polluted by political and other extraneous influences of a deleterious character.[85]

(iv) Sincere Leadership at the Top. In the concluding session, it was stressed that national integration was necessary in order that the nation that had come into being should not only continue to function but should fulfil the mission for which a free and national democratic republic was created. It was also stressed

[84] *Ibid.*, p. 667.

[85] *Ibid.* , p. 675.

that the political and spiritual values were far away from men and women who had to struggle to get two meals a day. As Sri Ramkrishna often said, "Religion is not for empty bellies." But at the same time, even to improve our economy, even to improve our society, we need ethical values. We cannot cooperate with one another unless we have ethical motivation, and we cannot advance the country without cooperation. It was also stressed that national integration was not to mean rigid uniformity, but an overriding sense of national unity and of oneness which transcended all lesser barriers and lesser loyalties. Those in power should adhere to ethical values. In this case, we must learn from the British people, the value that they set on honesty and integrity in their high positions.

(v) Organization of Youth Forums and Camps. In the final meeting of the Steering Committee of the Colloquium where reports of various sections were discussed, it was decided to continue the work which the Colloquium had started. Thus a Continuing Committee of the Colloquium to carry out its aims and objectives and to give shape and form to the main question of national integration was formed. The Continuing Committee which met in New Delhi in March 1967, resolved to organise youth forums in universities and colleges in collaboration with the Integration Sub-Committee of the Gandhi Centenary Celebrations Committee and also to organise camps of teachers, students and educational authorities to discuss the basic problems and steps to be taken to translate the resolutions in personal and social life. The basic purpose of the youth forums was to create in the minds of the youth an awareness of ethical and spiritual values with a view to canalizing their energies into constructive nation-building activities. Dr. K.M. Munshi, Chairman of the Committee, addressing the Press Conference on this occasion, stated, "India is at present passing through a critical phase in its political and cultural development. The ethos of Indian society is today characterised by an all-pervading sense of moral confusion and a steadily enlarging vacuum in the sphere of ethical values, social goals and political objectives. As things are, neither the parents, nor the teachers, nor the religious heads and institutions enjoy moral influence which they used to have in the past. The restoration of such moral influence is

essential for a stable and creative society."[86] It was decided to have a permanent Executive Committee of the Colloquium in Bombay located in the Bharatiya Vidya Bhavan to continue the programme. However, it is doubtful if any success could be achieved by the Colloquium in the prevailing atmosphere.

National Integration Council

A Conference of all major political parties and eminent personalities was held in Delhi to discuss the question of integration. The leaders of the main political parties, chief ministers, union ministers, vice-chancellors, scientists, industrialists and eminent persons from other walks of life attended the Conference. The Conference drew attention of all thinking people to the pressing need of unity and integration. It formulated a Code of Conduct for all political parties in view of the forthcoming general election. It prohibited aggravation of existing differences, creation of mutual hatred or tension between communities.

It recognized the importance of regional balance in economic development at a positive factor of integration, stressed priority and rapid development of economically backward regions in any State. It also considered the question of education from primary to university levels, medium of instruction, medium of inter-State communication and methods for inculcating love for the country and the sense of unity and oneness. It decided to set up a 37-member National Integration Council with Prime Minister as Chairman.[87]

The Council after its formation took note of disrupting force during elections and expressed concern over agitations carried out in certain parts of the country for regional separation and over the persistence of communalism. It also considered issues relating to the medium of instruction in educational institutions, a code for the press to develop a feeling of unity, etc. At its meeting in October 1968, the Standing Committee of the Council recommended the setting up of a number of committees composed

[86] *Ibid.*, p. 716.

[87] Siddiqui, A.M., *National Integration in India-A Sociological Approach*, 1971, *op. cit.*, pp. 34-35.

of members drawn from various fields of national life to act as spearheads for a mass movement in the cause of national integration. The main objects of these committees were:

(a) to consider with a sense of urgency, and in some detail the contributions which specialised groups can make towards the promotion of national integration and, in particular, the prevention of communal and regional tensions; and

(b) to create an awareness at different levels and sectors of national life of the programme and recommendations of the Council and of the paramount need for solidarity and fraternity.[88]

National Integration Samitis in Universities and Colleges

Following this recommendation in the educational sphere, a Committee of educationists and leaders of youth and student organisations was set up in 1969 by the Ministry of Education to study syllabi and textbooks with a view to emphasising values that would promote unity and mutual tolerance and to recommend measures for eliminating from the minds of students and teachers all narrow and communal feelings. This Committee, besides making other suggestions, also recommended that to promote the sense of national oneness on the university campuses, National Integration Samitis should be organised in all universities and also, to the extent possible, in affiliated colleges.

Some National Integration Samitis had already been set up by the Gandhi Centenary Committee in certain universities in 1969. After the work of the Gandhi Centenary Committee was over, these Samitis were to continue and, where they did not exist, new Samitis were to be set up. A National Cell was created in the Ministry of Education to coordinate activities of all National Integration Samitis. A Counterpart cell was also opened in the University Grants Commission. One staff member in each university was to work as liaison officer for all matters pertaining to the National Integration Samiti functioning in that university. It was suggested that the Samitis could form

[88] Ministry of Education and Youth Services, Government of India, *National Integration Programmes of Union Ministry of Education*, New Delhi, 1971, p. 1.

themselves into mohalla/ward-wise sub-committee for taking up a minimum action programme for:[89]

(a) promoting recreational facilities and running sports clubs in the mohallas;
(b) running adult literacy centres;
(c) making continuous studies in depth regarding difficulties and disadvantages of all type of minorities including the weaker sections of the community living in that area and making recommendations to the vice-chancellor/principal, for taking up the matter with the appropriate authorities; and
(d) cooperating with the civic authorities in fighting false rumours and in restoring friendly feelings among all sections of the community.

These Samitis and Sub-Committees might have worked well in the beginning, but gradually their enthusiasm languished. We do not think such a programme can succeed unless there is a well thought out integrated scheme for all the youth in the universities and colleges.

All India Scholars' Conference on National Integration

The First All India Scholars' Conference on National Integration held in Bombay in 1969 came to the conclusion that the problem of national integration has ramifications in the field of literature, art, education, culture and economic planning. "There are several factors present in the situation which inhibit the development of an integrated society. They are, firstly, the social stratification based on the caste system; secondly, the socio-economic stratification based on the feudal past; thirdly, the economic classes with wide disparities of income; fourthly, wide disparities of economic development between different regions; and finally, the alienation of the educated elite from the masses. These several factors and similar others have prevented and continue to prevent large sections of the society from participating in the national life. This is recognised and public policy is pledged to eliminate all such inhibiting stratification and fragmentation of the society. We urge that active steps be taken to pursue this policy with greater zeal

[89] *Ibid.*, p. 8

and expedition than in the past.[90] Among other factors which prevented integration the three important elements which they mentioned were language, religion and pockets of tribal culture.

However, whatever be the differences of language, religion and culture, all must recognise that lack of common courtesy and civil manners is no part of the cultural heritage of any community in this country. It is a genuine respect for another man's faith and feelings, and a sincere appreciation of the variety that exists in human needs that constitute the key to the vexed problem of emotional integration in a multi-cultural society. There was also the problem of relation between two States and problems of relations between the States and the Union. There should be laid down some general principles and criteria on the basis of which such problems could be solved.

It is clear from the above that problem of emotional and national integration is not so simple and needs attack on many fronts. National integration has different aspects and many dimensions including political, economic, social, cultural and religious. There exists in the country, many religious and bilingual groups, regional disparities, conflicting ideologies, etc. leading to tension and violence. There has been a tendency after Independence among certain leaders to incite communal, lingual or regional sentiments of the people as stated earlier. However this increased particularly during the eighties as some foreign countries, smugglers and peddlars became more involved than previously. Thus there has been an increase in communal riots and smuggling activities, racial riots in Assam and other eastern States and terrorism in Punjab. The assassination of Prime Minister Indira Gandhi in October 1984, attack on the Prime Minister Rajiv Gandhi in Delhi on October 2, 1986 and killing of innocent persons in Assam, Punjab and Tamil Nadu is part of this phenomena.

In 1976, a Working Group of the NIC recommended a seven-point action plan aimed at promoting communal and regional harmony. After Shrimati Indira Gandhi again assumed power

[90] Indian Institute of Asian Studies, *Integration in India* (Papers and Proceedings of the First All India Scholars' Conference on National Integration), (Ed.) M.R. Sinha, Bombay, 1971, p. IX.

at the centre in January 1980, the NIC was revived. The NIC which met in November 1980 set up a Standing Committee to keep a constant watch on the activities of communal and other derisive forces. It drew up an eight-point action plan to curb communalism.[91]

The Constitution was amended in 1963 to permit State Governors to impose restrictions on activities aimed at the disintegration of the country. The Indian Penal Code was amended to make disturbances of communal harmony a criminal offence. The National Security Act was passed in 1980 to apprehend those who incite people for disturbances. However there has not been much change in the situation. The problem is particularly dangerous in the border States.

The question of maintaining peace in the border areas, checking smuggling activities, infiltration of foreigners, insurgencies, communal disturbances caused in collusion with foreign powers and other anti-national activities are some of the problems of border areas. It is often stated that the smuggling activities in the border areas of Punjab, Jammu and Kashmir, Rajastban, Maharashtra, etc. are carried out by some smugglers who have links with political bosses. The detention of Haji Mastan, Karim Lala and 16 others during the Bhiwandi and Bombay riots in May 1984 under the Maintenance of National Security Act for their alleged involvement in communal riots and then their sudden release by the Maharashtra Government was an instance in the point.[92] Sri Saksena observes that the disturbances in the border States are connected with the smuggling activities which have been on increase for the last few years.[93]

The Central Security Agencies like Border Security Force, the Central Reserve Police Force, the intelligence wing, etc., have a crucial role to play in this respect. However, it is the people and their leaders whose cooperation cannot be minimised

[91] Agnihotri, V.K. and Others, *IAS Advanced General Studies* (New Delhi, Allied Publishers, 1985), p. 447.

[92] For details see Madan, G.R., *India of Tomorrow-Problems of Social Reconstruction,* 1985, p. 322.

[93] Saksena, N.S., *Smuggling Network in India,* in Proceedings of the XIX Internal Security Seminar, Mount Abu, October 1984.

in this task. The people should follow the true religious teachings and the leaders should be honest and impartial in their dealings, only then some peace and national integration can be maintained. Shri J.F. Ribeiro, Police Chief in Punjab observes, "Paramilitary forces could be withdrawn only if those making the demand came out in the open against terrorists, which they were not doing. The task of curbing terrorism could be done only by the police and not the army, this has been borne out by the experience of the British army in Ireland where too, the battle was being fought by the police. Terrorism could not be wiped out because it is the heart and mind of those perpetuating it in the cause of misplaced sentiments or philosophy. Terrorism can be controlled to a manageable extent as has been done in Ireland.[94]

Shri Masud explaining the official conception of National Integration states, "Integration has come to be used officially for bringing about, with the consent of all concerned, a social and religious climate in the country wherein it may be possible for all citizens, irrespective of religious differences or social status, to live a life of peace and tranquillity devoted entirely to a common purpose of building up a strong, prosperous and forward-looking society which can contribute its own share to the peace of the world."[95]

According to Professor Khan, the policy of national integration should take into consideration the following facts, i.e. (i) there are diversities in the country in the form of region, language, culture, religion, tribes, castes and classes; (ii) there are possibilities of differences and even clashes at both levels—(a) horizontal, i.e., ethnic, religious, linguistic and tribal; and (b) vertical, i.e., classes, castes and sectarian groups; (iii) the integration process towards nation-building works in three phases simultaneously, viz., ideologically, socially and institutionally. Ideologically there has to be created a national ideology, a minimum value consensus, duly adopted in Constitution (which is already there) and constantly adopted in practice by the leaders, to be gradually accepted by the

[94] *Times of India*, Lucknow, dated 12.1.87.

[95] Masud, M.N., *Official Conception of National Integration in Secular Democracy*, February 1970. Also see Khan, Ziauddin, *op. cit.*, p. 5.

society. Socially the primordial sentiments (created through social existence in family, communities, social practices and regional living) to be converted into civil sentiments (created by interaction with other groups linked together under the political system with a claim for superseding loyalty in matters political, politico-economic and politico-social). Institutionally, by setting up of national institutions (such as Community Development Programme, Panchayati Raj, Economic Planning, 20-Point Programme for the amelioration of poor and backward communities)[96]. However, he points out in the end that this process of ideological, social and politico-institutional working is beset with various difficulties such as religious, regional administrative capacity, leadership in political and voluntary organisations.

[96] Khan, Ziauddin, *National Integration in India-Issues and Dimensions,* New Delhi, Associated Publishing House, 1983, p. 9.

CHAPTER XX

SOCIAL WELFARE AND FIVE-YEAR PLANS

THE TERM 'welfare' is a dynamic one and its meaning has changed with the passage of time.[1] In the beginning, the welfare measures were only in palliative terms, i.e., helping the poor, orphans, widows, physically handicapped, etc., but the term assumed a wider connotation later on and included the provision of health, educational and housing services, legislation for the protection of the working class, social security measures, etc. However, even this represented only one aspect of 'welfare' as any measure taken for the benefit of the weaker sections of the society vis-a-vis the stronger one could be included under the term 'welfare'. For example, the tax imposed and collected from the rich and used for the welfare of the poor may be called an aspect of economic welfare. The utilitarian concept "greatest good of the greatest number" could be considered as a 'welfare' measure in this broader context. Professor Titmus divides all collective interventions to meet certain needs of the individual and/or to serve the wider interests of society into three major categories of welfare: Social Welfare (or Social Service), Fiscal Welfare, and Occupational Welfare.[2]

Without elaborating the term in its various aspects, viz., economic welfare, social welfare, moral welfare, educational welfare, political welfare, etc. we shall confine ourselves to the 'social welfare' aspect as used in the field of social work of social service.

[1] Madan, G.R., *Welfare Slate and Problems of Democratic Planning,* 1972, p. 27 or see its second revised edition, *India's Social Transformation,* Vol. II, *Problems of Welfare and Planning.* 1984, p. 25.

[2] *Ibid.,* p. 29. Also see Titmus, R.M., "The Social Division of Welfare" in *Essays on the Welfare State* (1958), p. 42.

Social Welfare and other Related Concepts

The terms 'social welfare', 'social work', and 'social service' are often used interchangeably. The distinction can be made only while going into minute details. The Department of Social Welfare United Nations, points out: "The field of social welfare has not settled into fixed or uniform patterns and is therefore resistant to clear-cut definition. This fact is reflected in widespread confusion as to what constitutes qualified personnel and appropriate training. In no country have the frontiers of social welfare or social service or social work been established beyond cavil."[3] To this confusion two reasons are attributed: (1) social welfare or social service or social work is, in each country, a dynamic activity that has grown out of, and is constantly influenced by, evolving social, economic, political and cultural trends and for this very reason could acquire fixed meaning only at the price of failing to meet new situations; and (2) the term 'social welfare' is used not only to describe certain specific activities, but is often used synonymously with the term 'social policy' to describe what, in some countries, is regarded as a central responsibility of the State, i.e., the provision and maintenance of an acceptable standard of social and economic well-being for the entire population, which cut across the fields of health, education, labour, etc.

However, there are certain writers who have tried to draw the distinction between these various terms. Prof. Friedlander says: "Social welfare is the organised system of social services and institutions, designed to aid individuals and groups to attain satisfying standards of life and health. It aims at personal and social relationship which permit individuals the development of their full capacities and the promotion of their well-being in harmony with the needs of the community. Whereas social work is a professional service, based upon scientific knowledge and skill in human relations, which assists individuals, alone or in groups, to obtain social and personal satisfaction and independence. It is usually performed by a social agency or a related organisation.

[3] United Nations, Department of Social Welfare, *Training for Social Work-An International Survey* (1950), p. 6.

The term 'social welfare' has a broader implication than professional social work."[4] He further adds that the term 'social services' is often used in a very broad sense. Mr. Harry M. Cassidy defines social services as "those organised activities that are primarily and directly concerned with the conservation, the protection and the improvement of human resources"[5] and includes as social services: social assistance, social insurance, child welfare, corrections, mental hygiene, public health, education, recreation, labour protection, and housing. Shrimati Durgabai Deshmukh points out: "The concept of social welfare is distinct from that of general social services like education and health, etc. Social welfare is specialised work for the benefit of the weaker and more vulnerable sections of the population and would include social services for the benefit of women, children, the physically handicapped, the mentally retarded and those specially handicapped in many ways."[6]

She further adds, "Social welfare was the result and social work was the process employed to secure it. Social workers were the people working through social work for social welfare... If the process was understood, the attendant skills were appreciated, the information on subjects of direct concern and on allied fields together with the necessary relevant background material was carefully compiled and presented and the social policy-makers, social pianners, social administrators, professional and lay social workers were properly equipped, the quality of social welfare services would improve and expansion of social welfare programmes and services would be less difficult, more economic and efficient."[7]

Scope of Social Welfare in India

Taking the view as expressed above by Shrimati Durgabai Deshmukh, as also that taken by the Planning Commission in the Five-Year Plans, we may include in social welfare services those services which are designed for the welfare of the weaker

[4] Friedlander, W.A., *introduction to Social Welfare* (1959), p. 4.

[5] Cassidy, Harry M., *Social Security and Reconstruction in Canada* (1942), p. 13. Also see Friedlander's book, *op., cit.*, p. 4.

[6] Planning Commission, Government of India, *Social Welfare in India* (1955), Preface.

[7] *Encyclopedia of Social Work in India* (1968), Vol. I, Preface, p. viii.

groups such as children, youth, women, the family, the under-privileged groups, etc.

The Planning Commission in the First Five-Year Plan points out that "The object of social welfare is the attainment of social health, which implies the realisation of such objectives as adequate living standards, the assurance of social justice, opportunities for cultural development through individual and group self-expression and readjustment of human relations leading to social harmony. A comprehensive concept of living standards will include the satisfaction of basic needs like food, clothing and shelter as well as normal satisfaction of family life, enjoyment of physical and mental health, opportunities for the expression of skills and recreational abilities, and active and pleasurable social participation. These objectives can be achieved mainly by revitalising the nation's economic and social structure.

The aim of social service in the past was essentially curative, and efforts were directed towards relief for the handicapped and the uplift of the underprivileged sections of society. It is now essential to maintain vigilance over weaknesses and strains in the social structure and to provide against them by organising social services. The aim of all social work now has to be the gradual rehabilitation of all weak, handicapped and anti-social elements in society.

Some of the important social problems like poverty, ignorance, overpopulation and rural backwardness are of a general nature and, in varying degrees, they are influenced by factor like squalor and bad housing, malnutrition and physical and mental ill-health, neglected childhood, family disorganisation and a low standard of living. For a long time, society has remained apathetic to these conditions; but with the awakening of political consciousness and the enthusiasm of organisations and workers to improve social conditions, there is a possibility of developing programmes which could gradually remedy the present situation. The economic programmes of the Five-Year Plan will mitigate these problems to some extent, but the gains of economic development have to be maintained and consolidated by well-conceived and organized social welfare programmes spread over the entire country. In this chapter, it is proposed to consider some of the more important problems of social welfare which need the special attention of both State and private welfare agencies.[8]

The principal social welfare problems dealt with in this category are problems relating to women, children, youth, the family, underprivileged groups and social vice. The main problems dealt under social vices are prostitution, crime and delinquency, alcoholism and drug addiction, gambling, and beggary. In the underprivileged groups are included the scheduled castes, scheduled tribes, other backward classes, and the socially and physically handicapped. Family welfare includes the problems of divorce, desertion, treatment of maladjusted members of the family, etc. The urban community welfare centres are dealt with under social welfare while rural community development programme is treated separately. The problems of social security are dealt with under labour welfare, while social services, viz., education, health and housing are treated separately.

Social Welfare Services and Welfare State

The scope of social welfare services has increased with the changing concept of social welfare or social work on the one hand and the emergence of the concept of 'welfare state' on the other. The social work activities which were in the form of palliative activities in the beginning (e.g. assistance to the poor or the handicapped in cash or kind) later took the form of rehabilitative and protective activities.[9] Social work as a profession came to be recognised only in the present century and especially after the Second World War. As regards the concept of 'welfare state', which is now accepted in almost all the democratic countries of the world, its objectives and scope became clear only in the present century and particularly so after the Second World War. As Mr. Purcell observes, "The 'welfare state' which has become for many in the twentieth century a synonym for social justice has not been a sudden or violent growth. On the other hand, it has been a gradual

[8] Planning Commission, Government of India, *first Five-Year Plan* (1952), Chapter on Social Welfare, p. 613.

[9] For details see Madan, G.R., *Indian Social Problems*, Vol. II. *Social Work*, 1987, Chapter I.

evolution, a development rather than upheaval."[10] It is the sum of efforts over many years to remedy the practical social difficulties and evils of a modern system of economic organisation which grew with but little regard for the majority of those who became involved in it, and which, indeed, insisted that development must be left to take their course.[11]

As regards its functions, Professor Myrdal points out, "In the last half-century, the State, in all the rich countries in the Western world, has become a democratic 'welfare state' with fairly explicit commitments to the broader goals of economic development, full employment, equality of opportunity for the young, social security, and protected minimum standards as regards not only income, but nutrition, housing, health and education, for people of all regions and social groups." In nutshell, the functions of a democratic welfare state are: "(1) provision of social services, (2) social security measures, (3) economic development and full employment, (4) nationalisation of certain industries, (5) protection of civil liberties, (6) other social controls, and (7) people's participation."[12]

Thus, besides the attainment of certain other objectives, the provision of social services is one of the important functions of a 'welfare state'. The scope of social services in a welfare state as seen by Professor Robson is as follows:

"One of their primary aims has been the provision of protective services. The better protection of children, for example, is the purpose of a mass of legislation which safeguards or rescues children from neglect, cruelty, exploitation in labour market and other evils. There is legislation to protect adult workers from conditions injurious to their health and welfare in factories, mines and shops. And there are many other protective services.

A second group of social services aims at the rehabilitation of injured, derelict or diseased persons. A welfare state must provide for the training of persons suffering from blindness, deafness, end other handicaps so that they may lead useful lives in occupations for which they are suited.

[10] Purcelt, M.P.O., *The Modern Welfare State* (1953), p. 1.

[11] Bruce Maurice, *The Coming of a Welfare State* (1961), p. 17.

[12] Madan, G.R., *Welfare State and Problems of Democratic Planning (1972)*, p. 28.

A third group of services consists of those which are essentially a form of social investment in the young. The system of publicly administered or publicly financed education is an investment of this kind, the purpose of which is to produce well-educated, alert, intelligent citizens whose creative powers have been developed and enhanced.

A fourth group of services comprises those which aim at the prevention and cure of sickness. This was the original aim of the public health movement and it remains of fundamental importance. A fifth group of social services is directed towards fostering the arts and the provision of recreation amenities. The earlier activities of the state in this sphere were concerned with the creation and maintenance of art galleries museums and public libraries and the care of public monuments. To these must now be added public service broadcasting and television, the support and encouragement of drama, opera, ballet, music, sculpture, films, festivals and exhibitions.

Lastly, there are the services which offer moral guidance to those in need of it. These include the moral welfare services for delinquents and unmarried mothers; the probation services for those who have been sentenced by the criminal courts; and the youth service which provides clubs and recreation centres for young persons. This is the vast structure of collective activity administered by the public authorities or by voluntary bodies aided with public money."[13]

Besides social services, provision of social security measures is also another important function of a welfare state as mentioned by Professor Robson. Without going into details about the functions of a welfare state let us discuss the relation between welfare state and planning.[14]

Welfare State and Planning

As the functions of a welfare state increase, there arises the need to coordinate the various activities of the State in a rational manner to have the maximum utilisation of limited resources. The objectives of welfare state and planning are almost the same

[13] Robson, W.A., *The Welfare State* (1957), pp. 11-13.

[14] For details about the functions of a Welfare State see Madan, G.R., *op. cit.*, pp. 27-40.

in a democratic society. In the words of Professor Myrdal, "Planning means conscious attempts by the government of a country-usually with the participation of other collective bodies-to coordinate public policies more rationally in order to reach more fully and rapidly the desirable ends of future development which are determined by the political process as it evolves."[15]

Economic versus Social Planning

The word 'planning' is used in many situations. We may have planning of an individual's daily routine, planning of a family budget or a business organisation. However, here we use the word in the sense of planning of a country's socio-economic life with certain definite goals in view.

Again the word planning has many adjectives, i.e., economic planning, social planning, democratic planning, fascist planning, communist planning, etc., having different objectives in view.[16] The word planning is generally used in the sense of economic planning as the allocation of resources both of State as well as private agencies has to be made in terms of money. In this sense, then planning is concerned with the proper production and distribution of wealth. According to Professor Harris, "Planning is general allocation of resources to goals determined by authority instead of allocation of resources in response to price and income investment."[17] In other words, planning is the anti-thesis of laissez-faire. As stated earlier, the term 'planning' is used in the economic sense but even in this sense it has social implications and thus economic planning also includes social planning. However, in a narrower sense the term 'social planning' is restricted to planning of various social welfare services. Shri Tarlok Singh observes, "The objectives of planning are both economic and social and are interrelated. In its economic aspect, planning seeks a higher rate of growth, greater balance between industry and agriculture, better harnessing of natural and human resources of employment opportunities at a reasonable level of income for the entire labour force. In comparison with

[15] Myrdal, G., *Beyond the Welfare Slate,* London, Gerald Duckworth & Co. (1960), p. 15.

[16] For different types of Planning see Madan., G.R., *op. tit.,* pp. 41-62.

[17] Harris, *S.E., Economic Planning (19W),* p. 26.

social planning, the aims and methods of economic planning are more narrowly defined and more capable of measurement. On the other hand, social planning has broader goals, notably creation of conditions of equal opportunity for different sections of the population and a fuller-life for every citizen, and these can become precise only over a period of effort and struggle. On a broader view, social planning may be said to comprise four main areas of efforts: (a) development of basic social services such as education, health and housing; (b) social welfare, including provision of minimum amenities and rural and urban welfare; (c) welfare of the weaker and more vulnerable sections of the community; and (d) social security."[18] According to Professor Reckless, "Social planning is concerned with the improvement of condition of masses through better housing, greater economic security, better health, more leisure time, more education, and pushing the existing facilities and programmes for handling social problems into higher and better operational gear."[19]

In fact, there is no contradiction between economic and social planning, and both are part of national planning, whether it takes the form of democratic or non-democratic planning.

Social Planning and Social Policy

Social planning (or national planning) is closely related with social policy of any country. According to Wilhelm Keilhau, "Social planning is that planning which is directed to a particular social policy."[20] Whereas social policy is described as measures taken by the State in order to promote the welfare of those classes within the society which economically are called lower classes. Previously this social policy was mostly in the hands of private persons. This social policy in its origin was motivated by the knowledge of human wants engendered by four sets of economic conditions such as: (1) those who, through infancy, illness, mental incapacity, etc. needed support; (2) to prevent the effects of natural catastrophes or misfortunes, e.g., war or earthquakes; (3) existence of foreseeable dangers which required

[18] Singh, Tarlok, "The Process of Social Planning" in *Yojana*, July 1964, p. 2.

[19] Reckless, W.C., *Criminal Behaviour* (1940), p. 421.

[20] Keilhau, Wihelm, *Principles of Private and Public Planning* (1919), p. 229.

insurance policy; and (4) condition of labour market which does not give work and measures for unemployment insurance and to have full employment. Two more were added later on such as: (a) house building, and (b) food distribution.

According to Freeman and Sherwood, the term 'social policy' is used in many senses: as a philosophical concept, as a product, as a process, and as a framework for action. They add, "Social policy is the principle whereby the members of large organisations and political entitlies collectively seek enduring solutions to the problems that affect them-almost the opposite of rugged individualism... Viewed as a product, social policy consists of the conclusions reached by persons concerned with the betterment of community conditions and social life, and with the amelioration of deviance and social disorganisation... As a process, social policy is the fundamental process by which enduring organisations maintain an element of stability and at the same time seek to improve conditions of their members— As a framework of action, social policy is both product and process. It assumes the availability of a well-delineated policy which is to be implemented within the context of potential changes in the values, structures and conditions of the group affected. Thus social policies are continually modified in the face of changing conditions and values."[21]

So far as India is concerned, Shri Tarlok Singh points out that at present the tasks which social policy should accomplish may be looked at in terms of programmes and measures directed towards the following objectives:

(a) expansion of social services and their qualitative improvement, for instance in education, health, family planning, nutrition and housing;
(b) welfare and development of the weaker and more vulnerable sections of the population, especially of non-integrated groups such as scheduled castes and the tribal people;
(c) development of supplementary welfare services (such as provision of facilities for pre-school children, and for children out of school, mid-day meals in schools, promoting

[21] Freeman, Howard E. and Sherwood, Clarence C., *Social Research and Social Policy* (1971), pp. 2-3.

health education, etc.) at the level of the local area and the local community;

(d) social reform;

(e) provision of social security; and

(f) social change, including reduction in disparities of income and wealth, prevention of concentration of economic power and steps to equalise opportunities within the community.[22]

Planning of Social Welfare Services

When we are planning the economy of the country as a whole, there has to be detailed planning in every sector of the economy, besides the overall planning. In India's Five-Year Plans, there are various sectors to be planned including agriculture and community development, irrigation and power, industry and mining, transport and communication, social services, etc. Thus social services is one of the sectors in which planning is to be done and social welfare forms a part of it. In social services are included: (i) education, (ii) health, (iii) housing, (iv) welfare of backward classes, (v) social welfare, (vi) labour welfare, and (vii) others. Here the term 'social welfare' has been used in a narrower sense and includes services for the handicapped, maladjusted and unadjusted groups, though we have used the term in the following pages in a broader sense.

As there is need of planning for the total economy of the country to achieve certain objectives and to utilise the scarce resources in such a way that there is balanced development in all spheres, there should be no wastage or duplication of services and priorities are to be fixed in accordance with the objectives. The same principle will apply in the sphere of social welfare. In order to plan for social welfare services: (1) assessment of resources is to be done; (2) priorities are to be fixed to achieve certain objectives; (3) targets are to be laid down to achieve certain results within a given time; (4) there has to be coordination among the activities to avoid wastage and overlapping; (5) there has to be planning at all levels, i.e., at the Central level, State level, regional level, district level and block and village levels; (6) planning has to be done with the

[22] Singh, Tarlok, "Social Policy" in *Encyclopaedia of Social Work in India*, Vol. II (1968), p. 286.

consent of the people; and (7) there has to be planning in this sphere in consonance with overall planning.

It is particularly to be seen that planning for social welfare implies the simultaneous and to some extent basic planning for economic well-being. The two go together and support each other and social thinkers and planners have clearly to realise how much social welfare is dependent on the economic self-sufficiency of the family. Also that a large number of individual and social ills, though certainly not all, arise from unemployment, underemployment, economic want and relatively low standard of physical living.

Instead of 'social welfare planning' some writers have used the terms 'community organistions', 'social inter-group work process', 'social welfare organisation', or 'social engineering'. According to Friedlander, the three main objectives of community welfare organisation are: (i) to determine the social needs, (ii) to arrange for careful and conscientious planning to meet the needs of the population, and (iii) to mobilise the forces of the community in the best way to achieve this goal.[23]

Social Welfare and Five-Year Plans

As stated earlier, the Planning Commission have tried in the Five-Year Plans to distinguish between social services and social welfare services. The term 'social services' is meant to connote established services in the fields of education, health and housing meant for the entire community. 'Social welfare services', on the other hand, are those services which are specialised services, meant to enable handicapped and maladjusted individuals and groups to reach their full potential. A school for the blind, a home for the destitutes, a certified institution for the delinquents, after-care of discharged prisoners, or rehabilitation of women rescued from moral danger are some of the examples of social welfare services. Welfare services for children, youth and women are also included in this category.

The responsibility for the provision of education and health services largely rests with the Government. However, the main

[23] Friedtander, W.A., *op.cit.*. p. 589. Also see Madan, G.R., *Indian Social Problems*, Vol. II, chapter on Urban Community Welfare.

responsibility in the field of social welfare services before Independence had been mainly of private welfare agencies. After Independence, Government has taken positive responsibility in this field also. The Government has now begun to assist private social welfare agencies by providing them adequate financial assistance so that they may work effectively and has started where necessary its own agencies in those fields where there was deficiency. In order to fulfil these functions, the Central Social Welfare Board was created in August 1953 by a Government of India Resolution in the Ministry of Education. Its main function is to administer the programme of grant-in-aid to existing voluntary welfare organisations and to sponsor and assist the development of new welfare services through non-official organisations. The Central Social Welfare Board has set up State Social Welfare Advisory Boards at the State level to implement its programme in the various States. Besides, it has organised a number of other programmes, including economic programmes under urban family welfare projects, welfare extension projects, after-care programmes, etc. In the year 1984-85, the Board assisted about 12,000 voluntary organisations all over the country in the field of children, women and handicapped.

Amount Spent and the Activities Developed

The Planning Commission in the Third Plan points out that the development of the human resources of the country through the provision of facilities for education, health and social welfare is one of the major objectives of planned development. In the First as well as the Second Five-Year Plans, considerable importance was attached to social services and altogether Rs. 1,289 crores were spent for their development during the decade, but unfortunately the needs to be met were much larger.[24] The programmes under the head 'social services' included education, health and family planning, water supply and sanitation, housing and urban development, welfare of backward classes, social welfare, labour welfare, training of craftsmen and rehabilitation of displaced persons from Pakistan. The expenditures incurred on social services and

[24] Government of India, Planning Commission, *Third Five-Year Plan* (1961), p. 44.

social welfare programmes during the successive Five-Year Plans may be seen from the following table.

TABLE 38

PUBLIC SECTOR EXPENDITURE ON SOCIAL SERVICES IN FIVE-YEAR PLANS

(Rs. in crores)

	First Plan	*Second Plan*	*Third Plan*	*Fourth Plan*	*Fifth Plan*	*Sixth Plan*	*Seventh Plan*	*Eighth Plan*	*Ninth Plan*
1. Total outlay	1960	4600	7500	15902	37250	97500	180000	434100	859200
2. Expenditure on Social Services	459	830	1300	2579	5790	14035	29350	79012	183273
3. Percentage	23%	18%	17%	16%	15%	14.4%	16.3%	18.2%	21.3%
4. Social Welfare Programmes only	1.6	15	28	41.4	83	272	1012	3855	4556.75

During the First and Second Five-Year Plans, the social welfare programmes, which were implemented by voluntary organisations with the assistance of the Central and State Governments, included among others, welfare extension projects undertaken by the Central and State Social Welfare Board, programmes relating to social defence, social and moral hygiene and after-care services, and other welfare programmes.

Besides grants to voluntary organisations through the Central Social Welfare Board and State Social Welfare Departments an important step taken during the First Plan was the setting up of welfare extension projects in rural areas, each serving some 25 villages, and providing maternity and child health services, craft classes, social education for women and care of children through balwadis. During the Second Plan, an outlay of about Rs. 15 crores was incurred on social welfare. Among the main development programmes were welfare extension projects and the assistance given to voluntary organisations by the Central Social Welfare Board (about Rs. 10 crores), for social defence, social and moral hygiene and after-care services, and welfare schemes of State Government (about Rs. 5 crores). Under the programme for social defence, social and moral hygiene and after-care services, 327 institutions were established and 128 probation officers were appointed.[25]

In the Third Plan, the social welfare programmes involved an outlay of Rs. 28 crores-Rs. 16 crores at the Centre and Rs. 12 crores in the States. The programmes of the Central Social Welfare Board, including assistance to voluntary organisations and welfare extension projects envisaged a total outlay of Rs. 12 crores, In addition, schemes for child welfare and pre-primary education with a provision of Rs. 3 crores were included under 'Education'. Other schemes to be implemented under' Social Welfare' related to urban community welfare projects, training, research and surveys, social defence and after-care and the setting up of a Central Bureau of Correctional Administration. The Central Social Welfare Board's principal programmes during the Third Plan period were grants to about 6,000 voluntary organisations, assistance to mahila mandals which were running about 1,700 centres, welfare extension projects, socio-economic programmes for women, condensed courses of training for adult women, urban welfare projects, night shelters, holiday homes for children, the technical guidance to aided institutions.[26]

The Fourth Plan pointed out, "A review of the development of welfare services during the last eight years shows certain weakness. In the previous Plans, inadequate attention was paid to the needs of destitute children. Absence of counselling or advisory services, lack of statistical data, deficiencies in management and supervision at the field level, and absence of proper coordination between the Central Social Welfare Board and State Department of Social Welfare have been the other limitations."[27] A major programme that was to continue during the Fourth Plan period in the Central sector was that of the family and child welfare projects in rural areas. To remove nutritional deficiency in pre-school children an outlay of Rs. 6 crores was made for the feeding of such children. The scheme of pre-vocational training which was evaluated by a study team

[25] *Third Five-Year Plan* (1961), p. 718.

[26] *Ibid.*, pp. 718-19.

[27] *Fourth Five-Year Plan* (1970), p. 409.

was to be reoriented. Diversification of training, starting of part-time courses and starting of new centres for girls were some of the steps to be taken. Among children those who were destitutes were to receive higher priority. Although the Children Acts in most of the States and Union Territories covered both neglected and delinquent children, neglected children did not receive much attention. This defect was to be remedied by providing assistance through the Central Social Welfare Board to voluntary organisaitons working for the welfare of destitute children and for experimenting with non-institutional services like foster-care and adoption.[28] The programme for social defence which included prevention and treatment of juvenile delinquency, probation, suppression of immoral traffic in women and girls, social and moral hygiene and eradiction of beggary was to be expanded. Voluntary organisations were to be assisted in creating public opinion in favour of prohibition.

Fifth Five-Year Plan

A major thrust in the field of social welfare during the Fifth Plan period was the expansion of preventive and developmental programmes of social welfare. There was to be integration between the social and economic aspects of planning for the weaker sections particularly for children and women. Welfare services were promoted taking the family as a unit of development and integrated with programmes of employment, economic development and distributive justice. Simultaneously, efforts were to be made to provide basic health services such as maternity care, family planning, immunisation, functional literacy, child care, nutrition, and other social services to families in general, and particularly those of the weaker sections. These efforts were further supplemented by the Minimum Needs Programme to cater primarily to the needs of families of vulnerable groups. Welfare programmes for women and children in need of care and protection as also assistance to the aged and the handicapped were to be further expanded and strengthened with the ultimate object of developing a comprehensive social security programme.[29]

[28] *Ibid,*, p. 411.

[29] *Draft Fifth Five-Year Plan* (1974), Vol. II, p. 278.

The Fifth Plan points out, "For the care, education, training and rehabilitation of delinquent and neglected children, it is necessary to extend the application of the Children Act on a wider scale. Preventive services such as setting up contact clubs, play centres, juvenile guidance units, workshops, parental counselling, etc., particularly in slum areas of metropolitan cities and big towns, will be encouraged. Expansion of probation system, improvement of services for social and moral hygiene, development of parole services, appointment of welfare officers in prisons, expansion of after-care services and enforcement of minimum standards in correctional and non-correctional institutions are some of the priority areas to which attention will be paid during the Fifth Plan period."[30]

The Five-Year Plan 1978-83, points out that in the Fifth Plan child welfare was accorded the highest priority, a major programme being the "Integrated Child Development Services" (ICDS). During the Plan period, schemes for the welfare and development of children and women would have to be accorded higher priority with increased bias towards preventive and developmental services. Various other schemes like distribution of cooperative credit for weaker sections, health programmes, functional literacy and nutrition schemes would have to be dovetailed so as to promote family welfare and improve economic capacity."[31] Social defence programmes for the reformation and rehabilitation of social deviants will be expanded and strengthened. The National Institute of Social Defence will continue to offer guidance and advice to the States and Union Territories. Sustained educational programmes through mass media to mould public opinion in favour of prohibition would be undertaken. Voluntary agencies and local bodies like Panchayati Raj institutions will be associated in the implementation of the programme.[32] The scheme of ICDS, on the basis of experience gained so far, will be modified to offer services in an integrated manner.

Sixth Five-Year Plan to Eight Five-Year Plan

It need be mentioned here that in the Fifth Five-Year Plan (1974-79), 'Social Welfare and Welfare of Backward Classes'

[30] *Ibid.*, p. 279.

[31] *Draft Five-Year Plan*, 1978-83 (1978), p. 250.

[32] *Ibid.*, p. 257.

was dealt in one chapter, while 'Nutrition' was part of the chapter on 'Health and Family Planning'. However in the Sixth Plan, there are three separate chapters one each on: (1) Welfare of Backward Classes, (2) Woman Welfare, and (3) Social Welfare. In the Seventh Plan, 'Nutrition' became a part of the chapter on 'Social Welfare' and it was renamed as 'Social Welfare and Nutrition'. In the Sixth Plan, there was special emphasis on development of tribals and scheduled castes. Similarly after a Report of the Committee on the Status of Women, there was emphasis on women welfare and there is a separate chapter on Women Welfare.

In the Seventh Plan, 'Nutrition' becomes part of social welfare as ICDS programme which is administered by the Social Welfare Department has nutrition an important component. The two other chapters are renamed as 'Socio-Economic Programmes for Women' and Socio-Economic Programmes for Scheduled Castes and Scheduled Tribes'. In the Eighth Plan, there are two chapters: one on 'Social Welfare' and the other on 'Welfare and Development of Scheduled Castes and Scheduled Tribes'. Thus the emphasis has changed from welfare to development.

In the Sixth Five-Year Plan, the programmes already in progress in the field of social welfare were to continue, but due to limited finances emphasis was to be on areas which were most backward and prone to the handicapped or social disorder. "In these areas, the families belonging to weaker sections, i.e., scheduled castes and scheduled tribes were to be identified. Among the families, the most vulnerable members, namely, the children of the age-group 0-6, pregnant and nursing mothers, the physically handicapped, the aged and the infirm were to be helped."[33] The Seventh Plan points out, During the Sixth Plan, several Central programmes had a number of achievements to their credit. These included the sanctioning of additional 896 ICDS projects bringing the total number of projects to 1019; institutional and non-institutional services to 32,000 children in need of care and protection; 4785 condensed and vocational training courses benefiting 1,11,000 women; 3589 socio-economic units covering 47,011 women and disabled persons; continuation of the national institutes for the handicapped, and

[33] *Sixth Five-Year Plan* (1981), p. 432.

assistance to 58 voluntary organisations for assisting about 25,000 disabled persons to acquire aids and appliances, besides providing various training and research programmes. In addition, 7,000 creche units covering 1,75,000 children and 344 working women's hostels with a total capacity of 22,150 inmates were functioning by the end of 1984-85.

Social welfare programmes received further momentum in the State sector as well. Taking advantage of the Central ICDS model, more State Governments initiated similar projects. By March 1985, 117 projects had been sanctioned. The other programmes under implementation were creches, balwadis, training-cum-production centres for women, institutional and non-institutional services for socially and physically handicapped, etc. Children's Acts were enacted in all the States except Nagaland. However, their enforcement is yet to be extended to about one-third of the districts in the country, and services under this legislation were not uniformly available in the covered districts."[34] Various services under Children's Act like the establishment of Children's Courts, Children's Boards, remand homes, certified schools, appointment of probation officers, etc. were to be suitably expanded.[35]

As regards Prohibition, the policy of total prohibition introduced by the Janata Government was reversed and only excessive consumption through heavy taxation and educational campaign for temperence through voluntary organisations were considered enough.

In the Sixth Plan, as stated above, besides emphasis on social welfare in general, there was greater emphasis on the welfare of backward classes and women. The Sixth Plan points out that three decades of development have not had the desired impact on these socially, economically and educationally handicapped groups and therefore Sixth Five-Year Plan lays special emphasis on measures to solve their problems. "The major objective of the Sixth Plan (1980-85) is to wage an all-out war on poverty and mobilise all our latent energies for the creation of a more dynamic and more equitable society. This will be achieved only if the scheduled castes/scheduled tribes who constitute the bulk

[34] *Seventh Five-Year Plan,* 1985-90 (1985), p. 307.

[35] *Sixth Five-Year Plan* (1981), p. 435.

of the poorer sections of the population receive their due share from the Plan programmes. In view of this, special Component Plans will be formulated as part of various programmes as to enable scheduled castes families to cross the poverty line within a short time."[36] For the tribals, the scheme of the Tribal Sub-Plans was introduced during the Fifth Plan in areas where there was concentration of scheduled tribes and funds were earmarked for their development. During the Sixth Plan, pockets with 50 per cent or more tribals in a population of 10,000 in contiguous areas were included in the Sub-Plan Areas from 1979-80.

The strategy of special Component Plans was adopted particularly for States/Union Territories having large scheduled castes population. Thus comprehensive development plans were formulated for these groups keeping in view the special problems and needs of each of these communities. These programme were to be integrated with other general programmes in the context of overall development strategy of the Plan.

As regards development of women, it was pointed out that in spite of general and some special programmes taken up under the different Five-Year Plans, women have lagged behind men in almost all sectors. The infant mortality was more among female babies as compared to males, the literacy rate was low, girls were married at a younger age and the percentage of women employed was low. The major thrust in the Sixth Plan in the field of welfare of women was to be their economic upliftment through greater opportunities for salaried, self and wage employment to increase their economic independence to improve their status in society.

In the Seventh Plan, the programmes initiated in the earlier Plans were to continue and emphasis was to be on increasing the income of the family. The Plan points out, "The welfare of children, women and the disabled is linked with the development of the family, the basic unit. Family welfare can best be promoted by providing to its members greater opportunities for employment to augment their income substantially, for the most part, these opportunities would be in rural development, agriculture, animal husbandry and other

[36] *Sixth Five-Year Plan* (1981), p. 418.

such sectors."[37] Child welfare would be given the highest priority. Preventive and developmental services of a domiciliary nature would be accorded priority over institutional care. In programmes for women, greater stress would be laid in the generation of both skilled and unskilled employment and promotion of opportunities for higher level skills through proper education and vocational training. Physically handicapped would be encouraged to pursue education and vocational training through scholarships and promotional aids in order to draw them closer to the normal stream of life.

So far as the scheduled castes and scheduled tribes are concerned in the Sixth Plan for the first time a target of assisting economically 50 per cent of the SC/ST families to cross over the poverty line was fixed. The aim of the Seventh Plan was to continue the thrust towards the socio-economic development of the SCs/STs. The emphasis on the Component Plans was to continue.

In the Eighth Plan, there is a chapter on 'Social Welfare' which deals with development of women, child development, nutrition and other welfare programmes. There is another chapter with the title 'Welfare and Development of Scheduled Castes and Scheduled Tribes'. It is clear from above that the emphasis has shifted from welfare to development programmes.

So far as development of women is concerned, the Eighth Plan points out that a National Perspective Plan for Women (1988-2000) has been drawn up (as recommended by the U.N. Commission on the Status of Women) which provides directions for allround development of women. The National Commission on Self-Employed Women and Women in Informal Sector submitted a comprehensive report titled *Shramshakti* analysing the problems affecting large number of women in the informal sector and the steps needed to give them a better deal. A significant step taken in the Seventh Plan towards improving women's status was the identification of a number of beneficiary-oriented programmes under various sectors of development.

In the Seventh Plan, the number of women beneficiaries under the IRDP was 34.33 lakhs and it increased from 9.9 per

[37] *Seventh Five-Year Plan* (1985), p. 308.

cent in 1985-86 to 25.6% in 1989-90. Under TRYSEM, 4.59 lakh women were trained for self-employment. Under both the programmes, the minimum percentage of women beneficiaries has now been raised to 40. Under Jawahar Rozgar Yojana, 30 per cent employment opportunities are reserved for women. Development of Women and Children in Rural Areas (DWCRA), launched in 1982-83, to increase rural women's access to employment, skills, training, credit and other support services, covered 187 districts in 1990-91. In 1986-87, a scheme to provide support to training and employment of women (STEP) was launched.

The strategy in the Eighth Plan will be to ensure that the benefits of development from different sectors do not by-pass women and special programmes are implemented to complement the general development programmes... The flow of benefits to women in education, health and employment need to be monitored. Voluntary agencies will be supported in their advocacy and social activism programmes for gender equality and prevention of atrocities on women.

A major thrust in the strategy for women's development will be on the formation and strengthening of grassroot level women's groups, which will articulate local women's needs and play an important role in decentralised planning and implementation of programmes. Services for women under various programmes of employment, education, health care, family welfare, drinking water and nutrition would be made available at the grassroot level in the form of a package through convergence and integration.[38]

So far as child development is concerned, the Eighth Plan points out that the Seventh Plan continued the strategy of promoting early childhood survival and development through programmes in different sectors, important among these being ICDS, universal immunisation, maternal and child care services, nutrition, pre-school education, protected drinking water, environmental sanitation and hygiene and family planning.

Since human development was to be the main focus of the Eighth Plan, policies and programmes relating to child survival

[38] Eighth Five-Year Plan (1992), pp. 391-392.

and development were to receive high priority. The national programme of ICDS was to continue to be the basic strategy for child survival and early childhood development with special focus on areas predominantly inhabited by the tribal people, scheduled castes, drought-prone regions and urban slums. The universal programme of immunisation was to be expanded and strengthened to increase the effective levels of coverage. The enforcement of Child Labour Prohibition and Regulation Act, 1986 was to be strengthened. More industries were to be identified in which child labour was to be prohibited.[39]

Nutrition. The Eighth Plan points out that the nutritional status of a nation has close relationship with other indicators like the extent of economic growth, food adequacy had its effective distribution, level of poverty, status of women, rate of population growth and access to health, education, hygiene and other social services. A multi-sectoral approach is, therefore, required to tackle the problem of malnutrition and other associated disorders.

The various programmes implemented in the successive Five-Year Plans, particularly in the Seventh Plan including the programmes of poverty alleviation, population control, increased production of cereals, pulses, etc. and expansion of social services particularly health, water supply and housing had an impact on the nutritional status of the population. Special programmes were implemented in different sectors for improving nutritional status through a combination of direct measures covering nutrition, education and extension; development and promotion of nutritious foods; fortification and enrichment of foods, supplementary feeding; and prophylaxis programmes.

"A major objective in the Eighth Plan will be to bring about an overall improvement in the nutritional status of the population Absence of an effective machinery for coordination of policies and programmes implemented by different departments which have a bearing on nutrition has been a great handicap. It will be desirable to set up a body, preferably a high-powered Nutrition Council, at the national level, to facilitate development of an integrated food and nutrition policy and its monitoring,..

[39] *Ibid.*, pp. 399-400.

At the State level, too a high power coordinative body will be necessary."[40]

Other Welfare Programmes

Among other welfare programmes, the programmes discussed in the Eighth Plan relate to the problems of physically and socially handicapped, problems of drug abuse, and problems relating to beggary and immoral traffic in women and girls.

The Plan points out that the Seventh Plan and Annual Plans (1990-92) saw a significant expansion of programmes and services for the welfare of the handicapped in different sectors. The eradication of smallpox, the extensive coverage of infants under the immunisation and prophylaxis programme against Vitamin 'A' deficiency, iodine deficiency and anaemia were expected to reduce significantly the incidence of handicap in early childhood. The extensive network of primary health care and the hospital-based curative services also played their role in identification of handicaps, treatment and cure.

For the education of the handicapped, almost all the States implemented programmes to provide stipends and other incentives to the handicapped at the elementary school stage. The Central Government continued the scheme to award scholarships to physically handicapped students to pursue general, technical and professional courses from Class IX onwards on the basis of a means-cum-merit test.

For the care of the elderly, the most important welfare measure was the scheme of the old-age pension of those without any means or support. By the end of the Seventh Plan, all the States and Union Territories had old-age pension schemes, the extent of coverage depending upon the resources of the State. Several States implemented special programmes for poor widowed women. While the older among them, without any means of support, received maintenance allowances, for the others, education, training and employment programmes were organised, including residential care for those without shelter. Short-stay home facilities were organised for women in distress. Assistance for marriage of widows was also provided. The main thrust of the policy for the Eighth Plan was to be to make as

[40] *Ibid.*, pp. 403 and 405.

many handicapped persons as possible active, self-dependent and productive members of the nation through opportunities for education, vocational training and economic rehabilitation. The coverage of elderly persons without any means of support was to be expanded through the schemes of old age pensions of the State Governments.[41]

So far as programmes in the field of social defence during the Eighth Plan are concerned these have already been dealt in Chapter XVIII and therefore have not been discussed in this chapter. The programmes for the welfare of scheduled castes and scheduled tribes have been discussed in Volume II.[42]

Ninth Five-Year Plan (1997-2002)

The name of Ministry of Welfare was renamed as Ministry of Social Justice and Empowerment in May, 1998. As the name implies, it incorporates two components—empowerment and social justice. The word 'empowerment' encompasses social as well as economic empowerment. As regards social justice, affirmative action and legislative measures being the most powerful instruments to ensure social justice to the socially disadvantaged groups, the Government commits to bring forth into action a 'National Charter for Social Justice' based on the principle of social harmony. An amount of Rs. 4556.75 crore has been allocated in the Ninth Five-Year Plan (1997-2002) for the Social Welfare sector.

While a total outlay of Rs. 5399.50 crore has been earmarked for both Central and Centrally sponsored schemes including Special Central Assistance (SCA) to Special Component Plan (SCP) for SCs, an amount of Rs. 9568.68 crore (Provisional) has been allocated for State Sector schemes for empowering the socially disadvantaged groups viz. SCs, STs, OBCs and Minorities in the Ninth Five-Year Plan (1997-2002).

The Ninth Plan commits to empower the SCs, STs, OBCs and Minorities as the agents of socio-economic change and development. While formulating/implementing programmes for these groups, the Ninth Plan will strive to ensure 'People-Centered Development' and 'People's Participation' with effective

[41] *Ibid.*, p. 411.
[42] See *Indian Social Problems*. Volume II (1993), Chapter XXI.

involvement of Panchayati Raj Institutions, in pursuance of the recent Constitutional (73rd and 74th) Amendments. In the context of adopting the special strategy of Women's Component Plan' in the Ninth Plan, action will be taken by the nodal Ministry of Social Justice and Empowerment to earmark funds/ benefits under all its programmes exclusively for women belonging to these socially disadvantaged groups."[43]

During VIII Plan, Rs. 118.67 lakhs SC families were assisted against a target of Rs. 127.6 lakhs. During IX Plan, Rs. 124 lakhs SC families have been targetted to be assisted.

The Persons with Disabilities Act, 1995

As regards empowerment of the Persons with Disabilities is concerned (1) every effort was to be made towards effective enforcement of the *Persons with Disabilities Act, 1995,* (2) a special strategy of family/Community Based Rehabilitation (CBR) was to be adopted by pooling the resources of both financial and manpower of all the concerned, (3) special efforts were to be made to prevent disabilities through supplementary nutritional feeding for both children and expectant/nursing mothers, early detection and timely intervention and (4) setting up of a National Trust to ensure total care and custodianship of those with Mental Retardation and Cerebral Palsy.[44]

To tackle the ever-increasing problem of street children, Ninth Plan includes:

(a) More emphasis on preventive measures through various developmental services for children like Integrated Child Development Services, compulsory primary education, supplementary feeding programmes, health and referral services etc. and (b) Priority for non-institutional services through restoring the street children to their families and foster families.

So far as policy commitments for the well-being of older persons is concerned, there was to be emphasis on:

(i) Direct Policy Prescriptions to extend support for financial security, health care, shelter, welfare and other needs of older

[43] *Ninth Five-Year Plan,* 1997-2002 (1999), Vol. II, pp., 366-367.

[44] *Ninth Five-Year Plan,* 1997-2002 (1999), Vol. II, pp., 389.

persons, and (ii) to provide protection against the dangers of life and property, abuse and exploitation of older persons.[45]

"In the field of Women and Child Development, the Integrated Child Development Services (ICDS) continues to be the major intervention for the overall development of children. It caters to the pre-school children below 6 yrs. and expectant and nursing mothers with a package of services viz. immunization, health check-ups, referral services, supplementary nutrition, pre-school education and health and nutrition education. The Eighth Plan contemplated universalisation of ICDS by the end of 1995-96, by expanding the services to all over the country. Out of the 5614 ICDS projects sanctioned till 1996, 4200 became operationalised during the Eighth Plan. The process of universalisation will continue during the Ninth Plan till all the 5614 ICDS projects become operationalised. With the operationalisation of 4200 ICDS projects, the total number of beneficiaries has risen from 16.6 million in 1991-92 to 23.3 million in 1997-98 which included 19.8 million children and 3.5 million expectant and nursing mothers. Of the 19 million child beneficiaries, about 11.0 million received the services of pre-school education.[46]

The Department of Social Welfare

At the Centre, there was the Department of Social Welfare created in 1964, which was a part of the Ministry of Education and Social Welfare, looked after child welfare, women welfare, family welfare, welfare of physically and mentally handicapped, social defence, rehabilitation of displaced persons, welfare of the scheduled castes and backward classes, etc. Some of these functions were previously dealt with in the Ministries of Education, Health and Home Affairs.

With the formation of the new Government after the general elections in December 1984, the Ministry of Social Welfare was renamed as Ministry of Social and Women's Welfare. With the reorganisation of several Ministries in September 1986, the erstwhile Ministry of Social and Women's Welfare was reorganised

[45] *Ibid.*, p. 395.
[46] *Ibid.*, p. 349. For more details see *Indian Social Problems*, Vol. II (1994).

into the Ministry of Welfare and the Department of Women and Child Development.

The Ministry of Welfare was to look after the welfare of scheduled castes, scheduled tribes, minorities and other backward classes, welfare of the disabled, social defence programmes, wakf matters, etc. The activities of the Ministry were carried out through three divisions and two cells. These were Scheduled Castes and Backward Classes Division, Tribal Development Division, and Social Welfare Division; Backward Classes Cell and Minorities Cell.

The Department of Women's Welfare was now part of the Ministry of Human Resource Development which was under the charge of a Cabinet Minister. There was a Minister of State for Women's Welfare, Youth and Sports. The newly formed Department had two Bureaus: (i) Nutrition and Child Development; and (ii) Women's Welfare and Development. The Central Social Welfare Board and the National Institute of Public Cooperation and Child Development were attached to this Department.

Changes made in Ninth Five Year Plan (1997-2002) and after

There has been change in the concept of 'Social Welfare' to 'Human Development' since the beginning of Ninth Five Year Plan. This is in consonance with the concept of Human Development given by the United Nations Organization in 1948 and later on in various conferences held by it from time to time.[47] Recognising the shortfall in the achievement, of the basic minimum standards of life for all sections of the people, a bold initiative was taken by the Chief Ministers' Conference held in July, 1996 to ensure access to all of certain basic Minimum services (BMS) in a time bound manner. The seven basic services indentified for priority attention were:

1. Universalisation of Primary education;
2. 100 per cent coverage of primary health service facilities in rural and urban areas;
3. 100 per cent coverage of provision of safe drinking water in rural and urban areas;

[47] See Madan G.R., Sociology of Development (2003) P. 406. Also see Madan, G.R., Indian Social Problems Vol. 2 (2002) Chapter XIX pp. 433-448.

4. Extension of Mid-day Meal Programme in primary schools, to all rural blocks and urban slums and disadvantaged sections;
5. Provision of Public Housing Assistance to shelter less poor families;
6. Provision of connectively to all un-connected villages and habitations; and
7. Streamlining of the Public Distribution System with focus upon the poor.[48]

Main Emphasis in Tenth Five Year Plan (2002-2007)

In the Tenth Five Year Plan, it is stated that the Approach Paper also recognized that economic growth can not be the only objective of National Planning, and development objectives should be specified in the broader sense of enhancement of human well-being. It is important to emphsise that these human development-related targets of the Plan, which are extremely important and are being introduced for the first time in Indian planning, are intimately linked to the growth objective, and attainment of one may not be possible without the attainment of the others. For example, high rates of growth are essential if we want to provide a sufficient expansion of sustainable gainful employment opportunities to our expanding labour force and to ensure a sufficient increase in incomes of the poor and the disadvantaged. It is equally true that high growth rates may not be sustainable if they are not accompanied by a dispersion of purchasing power which can provide the demand needed to support the increase in output. Similarly, improvements in social and environmental indicators are essential for the sustainability of the growth process, while the later provides the resources for undertaking the necessary investments for the former.[49]

Furthermore, there are cross linkages that exist within the set of the social and environmental indicators, which need to be given due recognition. For instance, environmental degradation can have serious consequences on the health status of the

[48] Ninth Five Year Plan (1999) Vol. II p. 92.

[49] Planning Commission, Government of India, Tenth Five Year Plan 2002-207, Vol. II, Sectoral Policies and Development Programmes, p. 3.

population, which environmental protection and rejuvenation will be difficult without the awareness that is brought about through education.

The essence of planning is to weave all these seemingly disparate strands into a cohesive and well knit strategy so that the various cross-linkages operate in a synergistic manner in order to attain the ultimate objective of all development initiatives —namely human development. Conceptually, the aggregative objectives and targets that are set for the nation can be thought as being comprised of two sets of sub-targets across sectors and across regions which are consistent with the aggregates. Thus, there are at least three broad dimensions in which a Plan needs to be presented—the national aggregates, the sectoral requirements and the state-wise distributions. Furthermore, the conduct of policies and design of programmes for attaining the targets must also reflect this tri-dimensinality.

For the reasons enumerated above, the Tenth Five Year Plan is being presented in Three Volumes.

The first volume covers the broad perspectives and strategy of development, the macroeconomic and economy wide issues relating to growth, investment and employment, and certain general observations on institutional design, governance and implementation methodologies. The state level issues are taken up in Vol III. Volume II, therefore gives the details of the secotral policies and programmes that are necessary to attain the Plan objectives.

The presentation in this volume II is structured around three broad themes (a) Growth, Poverty and Employment, (b) Social Development and Quality of Life; and (c) Sustainability of Growth and Development.

(a) Growth, Poverty and Employment

There are three main dimensions to this strategy.

(i) Agricultural development to be viewed as a core element of the Plan, since growth in this sector is likely to lead to the widest spread of benefits, especially to the rural poor. (ii) Ensuring rapid growth of those sectors which are most likely to create gainful employment opportunities. These include sectors such as agriculture in its extended sense, construction, tourism, transport, SS1 retailing. IT and a range of other new services (iii) continuing need to supplement the impact of growth with special programmes aimed at special targets groups which may not benefit, sufficiently from the normal growth process. Such programmes have long been part of our development strategy and will be continued in the Tenth Plan.

(b) Social Development and Quality of Life

Most of the monitorable targets of the Tenth Plan relate to significant improvements in social indicators, particularly in the areas of education, health and family welfare. These are not only important in themselves, but they also have an important bearing on the achievement of the growth and employment targets. These sectors are highly employment intensive and are also perceived to be particularly suitable for providing employment to women.

There has been less than adequate decentralization of the functions of Government, to the detriment of the delivery of a number of key services. The spirit of the 73rd and 74th Constitutional Amendments has not been observed in many of the states. It is believed that little improvement will be possible until such decentralisation becomes effective, both in terms of functions and resources. But decentralization cannot stop at the level of Panchayati Raj Institutions (PRIs) and urban local bodies (ULBs). The potential of civic society organizations, such as health and education committees to name only a few, to improve delivery of services is vast, and advantage must be taken of these possibilities through appropriate devolution of functions and authority.

Performance in the field of education is one of the most disappointing aspects of India's development strategy. Out of the approximately 200 million children in the age group of 6-14 yrs, only 120 million are in schools and net attendance in the primary level is only 66% of the enrolement.

Mere establishment of schools and hiring of teachers will not lead to an improvement in education if teachers remain absent as happens in many parts of the country, especially in rural areas. It is therefore essential that control over the schools and teachers should be transferred to local bodies which have a direct interest in teacher performance. Efforts should also be made for social mobalisation of local communities for adult literacy campaigns and for promotion of primary education.

While planning for the social development of the country, as a whole, cognizance needs to be taken of the fact that there are segments of our population which may not be able to take full advantage of the facilities or may have special needs. Women and children and disadvantaged sections have requirements which have to be addressed specifically.

(a) Intra-household disadvantages faced by women and children need to be recognized and redressed. It is proposed to operationalise the Women's Empowerment Policy and National commission for Children to ensure protection of their rights.

(b) For the socially disadvantaged groups, including tribals, who have their own special needs, it is proposed to institute a National Charter for Social Justice, eradicate manual scavenging and National Policy and Plan of Action for Empowering Tribals.

(c) It is proposed to have, a Special Component Plan for the disabled and a national programme for demand reduction for substance abusers. Appropriate legislation will have to be passed for the protection of the aged.

(c) Sustainability of Growth and Development.

Agricultural development is not only central to the attainment of the growth objective, it is also critical for the sustainability of the development process. Emphasis has to be laid on the sustainable development of our national resources, particularly land and water. The Tenth Plan aims at a revival of major and medium irrigation capacity and on water management. Greater attention will also be paid to rain water harvesting and increasing the irrigation potential through scientific watershed development and minor irrigation.

People's participation in land and water management is also necessary. There is a Lok Nayak Jai Prakash Narayan Land and Wasteshed Mission for holistic development of degraded and wastelands with emphasis on integration of conservation and production systems.

Forests are natural assets and provided a variety of benefits to the economy. Recorded forest area is about 23 per cent of the geographical area but 41 percent of these are degraded. These need to the improved to meet the forest produce need of the people, industry and other sectors.[50]

Details about the development of these activities which are mentioned here are discussed in detail in the chapters concerned with these sectors.

Eleventh Plan (2007-2012)

In this Eleventh Plan, it is pointed out that India has entered the Eleventh Plan period with an impressible record of economic growth. After a lackluster performance in the Ninth Plan period (1997-1998 to 2001-2002), when Gross Domestic Product (GDP) grew at only 5.5% per annum, the economy accelerated in the Tenth Plan period (2002-2003 to 2006-2007) to record an average growth of 7.7%, the highest in any plan period so far.[51]

The positive factors notwithstanding, a major weakness in the economy is that the growth is not perceived as being sufficiently inclusive for many groups, especially scheduled castes (SCs), Scheduled Tribes (STs) and minorities.

Indicators of human development such as literacy and education and maternal and infant mortality show steady improvement but they also suggest the progress is slow and we continue to lag behind several other Asian countries.

Vision of the Eleventh Plan

The central vision of Eleventh Plan is to build on our strengths to trigger a development process which ensures broad-based improvement in the quality of life of the people especially the SC/STs, other backward classes (OBCs), minorities and women. The National Development Council (NDC) in approving the Approach Plan, endorsed a target of 9% GDP growth for the country as a whole.

This broad vision of the Eleventh Plan includes several inter-related components, rapid growth that reduces poverty and creates employment opportunities, access to essential services in health and education especially for the poor, equality of opportunity, empowerment through education and skill development, employment opportunities underpinned by the National Rural

[50] *Ibid.*, pp. 3-16.

[51] Eleventh Five Year Plan 2007-2012, Volume I, Inclusive Growth, Planning Commission, Government of India, p. 1.

Employment Guarantee, environmental sustainability, recognition of women's agency and good governance.[52]

A key feature of the inclusive growth strategy in the Eleventh Plan is that growth of GDP should not be treated as an end in itself, but only as a means to an end. This is best done by adopting monitorable targets which should reflect multi-dimensional economic and social objectives of inclusive growth.

The 27 national targets at the national level fall in six major categories. The six major categories are:

(i) Income and Poverty (ii) Education (iii) Health (iv) Women and Children (v) Infrastructure (vi) Environment.

The 27 National Targets

Twenty-seven targets at the national level fall in six major categories. The six categories are: (i) Income and Poverty; (ii) Education; (iii) Health; (iv) Women and Children; (v) Infrastructure; and (vi) Environment. The targets in each of these categories are given below.

(i) Income and Poverty

- Average GDP growth rate of 9% per year in the Eleventh Plan period.
- Agricultural GDP growth rate at 4% per year on the average.
- Generation of 58 million new work opportunities.
- Reduction of unemployment among the educated to less than 5%.
- 20% rise in the real wage rate of unskilled workers.
- Reduction in the head-count ratio of consumption poverty by 10 percentage points.

(ii) Education

- Reduction in the dropout rates of childrern at the elementary level from 52.2% in 2003-04 to 20% by 2011-12.
- Developing minimum standards of educational attainment in elementary schools, to ensure quality education.

[52] *Ibid.*, p. 2

- Increasing the literacy rate for persons of age 7 years or more to 85% by 2011-12.
- Reducing the gender gap in literacy to 10 percentage points by 2011-12.
- Increasing the percentage of each cohort going to higher education from the present 10% to 15% by 2011-12.

(iii) Health

- Infant mortality rate (IMR) to be reduced to 28 and maternal mortality ratio (MMR) to 1 per 1000 live births by the end of the Eleventh Plan.
- Total Fertility Rate to be reduced to 2.1 by the end of the Eleventh Plan.
- Clean drinking water to be available for all by 2009, ensuring that there are no slip-backs by the end of the Eleventh Plan.
- Malnutrition among children of age group 0-3 to be reduced to half its present level by the end of the Eleventh Plan.
- Anaemia among women and girls to be reduced to half its present level by the end of the Eleventh Plan.

(iv) Women and Children

- Sex ratio for age group 0-6 to be raised to 935 by 2011-12 and to 950 by 2016-17.
- Ensuring that at least 33% of the direct and indirect beneficiaries of all government schemes are women and girl children.
- Ensuring that all children enjoy a safe childhood, without any compulsion to work.

(v) Infrastructure

- To ensure electricity connection to all villages and BPL households by 2009 and reliable power by the end of the Plan.
- To ensure all-weather road connection to all habitations with population 1000 and above (50,0 and above in hilly and tribal areas) by 2009, and all significant habitations by 2015.
- To connect every village by telephone and provide broadband connectivity to all villages by 2012.

- To provide homestead sites to all by 2012 and step up the pace of house construction for rural poor to cover all the poor by 2016-17.

(vi) Environment

- To increase forest and tree cover by 5 percentage points. To attain WHO standards of air quality in all major cities by 2011-12.
- To treat all urban waste water by 2011-12 to clean river waters.
- To increase energy efficiency by 20% by 2016-17.

The 13 State-Specific Targets

The Eleventh Plan has been formulated in a manner whereby 13 of the 27 monitorable national targets have been disaggregated into appropriate targets for individual States. These are:

(i) GDP growth rate
(ii) Agricultural growth rate
(iii) New work opportunities
(iv) Poverty ratio
(v) Drop out rate in elementary schools
(vi) Literacy rate
(vii) Gender gap in literacy rate
(viii) Infant Mortality Rate (IMR)
(ix) Maternal Mortality Ratio (MMR)
(x) Total Fertility Rate (TFR)
(xi) Child malnutrition
(xii) Anaemia among women and girls
(xiii) Sex-ratio.[53]

State Social Welfare Department

We have already mentioned above the main functions of the Ministry of Welfare and the Department of Women and Child Development at the Centre. It may be stated here that only a part of the functions of these two agencies consist in direct implementation of the programmes, their main role being to

[53] *Ibid.*, pp. 23-24

provide the supportive financial assistance through grants. Largely, programmes are implemented by either the State Government or voluntary organistions or local self-government institutions like panchayati raj institutions and municipal boards. For the programmes directly administered by the Central Social Welfare Department or for routing financial assistance given by it, the Department functions through four main institutions, viz., the Central Social Welfare Board, the Central Bureau of Correctional Services (now called National Institute of Social Defence), the Social Welfare and Rehabilitation Directorate, and the Commissioner for Scheduled Castes and Scheduled Tribes.

At the State level the administrative machinery for social welfare programmes differs from State to State in respect of its structure and programme coverage. In several States, different social welfare programmes are being handled in different departments, e.g., Juvenile Delinquency in Education Department or Home Department or Social Welfare Department and Social Defence in Home Department or Social Welfare Department. Like the Central Government, the State Governments also give grants to voluntary organisations in their respective States but, by and large, their activities in the field of social welfare are concentrated on social defence schemes.

To have uniformity at the State level, there should be a unified Social Welfare Department in each State dealing with social welfare subjects as also the welfare of backward classes. However, the executive machinery for social welfare and for the welfare of backward classes may be kept separate as the schemes for the welfare of backward classes cover the entire sector of development and are of a different nature from that of the social welfare schemes, which have predominantly a welfare content. The subjects to be dealt with by this unified department should be the same as those of the Social Welfare Department at the Centre. The departments should be manned by tried as well as trained social workers.

At the District level, there should be a District Social Welfare Officer to-look after the development of welfare services. As the position exists at present, full use should be made, where possible of the panchayati raj institutions and municipal organisations for implementation of welfare programmes. There should be separate cells/divisions within these organisations with clearly identifiable personnel for undertaking social welfare activities.[54]

In Uttar Pradesh, there is a Directorate of Harijan and Social Welfare under the charge of a Director. He is assisted at the headquarters by two Deputy Directors, many Assistant Directors and Special Officers. Under the Deputy Director, Harijan Welfare, there are four Assistant Directors dealing with (1) education, (2) development schemes (help in setting up of cottage industries, housing work, etc.), (3) grants to individuals and voluntary organisations working for the welfare of Harijans, and (4) tribal welfare. Under the Deputy Director, Social Welfare, there are three Assistant Directors, looking after various social welfare schemes. One Assistant Director deals with schemes relating to Social and Moral Hygiene, the Immoral Traffic (Prevention) Act, the Juvenile Justice Act and institutions for handicapped persons. One Assistant Director is in change of schemes connected with child welfare such as children's homes and after-care, beggary, grants to voluntary organisations, etc. The third Assistant Director looks after industrial and vocational education (such as tailoring and embroidery schools for women, etc.). One Special Officer looks after the nutrition programme for children in the urban areas. There are two Probation Officers (one male and other female) who look after probation and reformation work being done in the State. The Lady Probation Officer is attached to Nari Bandi Niketan (women's prison) which is a part of the Model Jail of Lucknow. She looks after rehabilitation, after-care and follow-up of women prisoners. All the districts in the State are covered under the Probation Scheme.

At the District level, there is a Harijan and Social Welfare Officer in each district to look after Harijan and other Social Welfare works. They recommend grants to voluntary welfare organisations on the basis of their work. The various institutions run by the Government in the fields of social welfare and social defence such as protective homes, rescue homes, after-care homes, beggar homes, schools for the blind, etc. are directly

[54] *Report of the Working Group on Administrative Machinery for Welfare Programmes* (Cyclostyled Report, Government of India, Planning Commission, 1968), p. 19.

supervised by the Assistant Directors at the State headquarters. In the districts where the Probation Act and Juvenile Justice Act are enforced, there are Probation and Reformation Officers to look after probation and reformation work such as attending cases in juvenile courts, looking after remand homes and approved schools, probation work, etc.

The scope of social welfare is very wide and as the State Governments have confined themselves mainly to the social defence programme, most of the work is done by the voluntary welfare organisations. Many of these organisations which have secular character receive grants both from the State Social Welfare Department and the State Social Welfare Advisory Board. The latter is directly connected with the Central Social Welfare Board.

Voluntary Social Welfare Agencies

In all societies, and at all times, people have been giving something, either in cash or in kind, and services for the welfare of the needy, the destitute, the handicapped and the victims of natural calamities. Indian history is replete with striking examples of voluntary work. Social work in the past was, however, mainly identified with the practice of charity which was enjoined by religion. This did not encourage an organised programme of prevention and treatment of problems of the handicapped like the sick, the destitutes, the dependant and the delinquent. In the new concept of 'social work', the programme of rehabilitation and prevention for the handicapped on systematic lines was most desirable, particularly in a welfare state.

About the present position of voluntary social work in the country, the Working Group on Administrative Machinery for Welfare Programmes (1968) in its report observes that the sphere of social welfare is still very largely the domain of voluntary workers and voluntary organisations. They constitute the king-pin of the machinery for the implementation of welfare programmes. No complete or reliable data are available about the total number of voluntary organisations in the country but about 5,000 are known to be receiving grants from the Central Social Welfare Board and a much large number is probably functioning with their own resources derived from religious and charitable organisations, private donations and gifts, etc. In their aims and ideals, quality of personnel and standard of services, voluntary organisations are known to show wide variations, from some old well-established organisations with a distinguished record of dedicated services at the one end to a few new organisations which have sprung up to take advantage of Government grants available for specific welfare activities at the other.[55] The level at which these organisations function and the range of their activities also vary; some are all-India organisations concerned with a wide range of activities; others are at the district or sub-district level. There is similarly a wide range of variations in regard to the resources at the disposal of these organisations. Except for those voluntary organisations which are receiving grants-in-aid and are required to comply with certain conditions of grants or those which are licensed under law for running orphanages and women's homes, etc., there seems to be no means at present of obtaining a continuous flow of information about the activities of voluntary organisations, keeping a tab on their work and influencing their activities.[56]

Generally there is a multiplicity of organisations working in the same area and an identical and similar fields with the result that there is considerable duplication and consequent waste of resources. Besides, the quality of service rendered by these agencies is rather poor. Some of the reasons are lack of finances, employment of untrained personnel, lack of proper equipment and building, lack of coordination among agencies and inadequate recognition of good voluntary workers. What is needed is proper planning and coordination among the various agencies under the auspices of some National Council of Social Welfare Agencies. The Council should have its branches at the State and District levels, and should work in coordination with the representatives of State Social Welfare Departments, State Social Welfare Advisory Boards, local welfare agencies and prominent social workers of the areas. Thus, planning in the social welfare field can be possible only when such a machinery is established.

[55] *Report of the Working Group on Administrative Machinery for Welfare Programmes, op. cit.*, p. 12.

[56] *Ibid.*, p. 13

We have described in this chapter, the main functions of a Welfare State, the programmes of Social Welfare taken up under the Five-Year Plans and the agencies involved in running these programmes. In Volume Two are discussed in detail the various social welfare programmes going on in the country in different fields such as child welfare, women welfare, youth welfare, family welfare, welfare of the backward classes, etc.

INDEX

Abottwood Committee (1937), 299
Acts
Apprentices Act (1850), 99, 472
Bengal Rural Poor and Unemployment Relief Act (1939), 242
Bengal Suppression of Immoral Traffic Act (1933), 212
Bengal Vagrancy Act (1943), 241
Bombay Beggars Act (1945), 234
Bombay Devadasi Protection Act (1939), 212
Bombay Prevention of Gambling Act (1887), 189
Bombay Prevention of Prostitution Act (1923), 212
Bombay Probation of Offenders Act (1938), 137
Borstal Schools Acts for Adolescents, 105,473
Cantonment Act (1934), 212
Central Children Act (1960), 112, 113, 441, 451, 472
Central Probation of Offenders Act (1958), 453
Child Labour Prohibition and Regulation (1986), 556
Children Acts in other States, 104
Criminal Justice Act (1972), 454
Employees' Provident Fund Act (1952), 271
Employees' State Insurance Act (1948), 257, 268, 271
Gambling Act (1867), 188,463
Immoral Traffic (Prevention) Act 1986, 467,460,472
Indian Factories Act, 268
Juvenile Justice Act 1986, 439, 442-443, 467, 472
Juvenile Smoking Act, 104
Madras Children Act (1920), 101
Madras Devadasi (Prevention of Dedication) Act (1947), 212
Madras Gambling Act, 189
Madras Probation of Offenders Act (1937), 137
Medical Termination of Pregnancy Act (1971), 494
Municipal Acts, 468
Narcotic Drugs and Psychotropic Substances 1985, 460
National Security (1980), 531
Prevention of corruption 1947, 354
Prevention of corruption 1988, 513
Provontion of illicit Traffic in Narcotic Drugs and Psychotropic Substances 1988, 460
Prevention of Food Adulteration Act (1954), 425
Prisons Act of (1894), 130
Probation of Offenders Act, 105, 451
Punjab Prisoners Probational Release for Good Conduct Act (1926), 140
Race Course Licensing Act, 189
Reformatory Schools Act, 100, 102, 106, 472
Regulating Act (1773), 126
Suppression of Immoral Traffic Acts to Protect Young Girls, 105, 467
Suppression of Immoral Traffic in Women and Girls Act (1956), 217, 463-67

United Provinces First
Offenders Act (1938), 137
Uttar Pradesh Municipalities Act
(1916), 242
U.P. Naik Girls Protection Act
(1929), 242
Addams, Janes 330
Adler and Alexander, 69
Adolescent Offenders, 448
Treatment of, 448
Adult Literacy, 302
Adult Offenders, 115, 448
Correctional Programmes in
India, 125
Future Programmes for, 146
Forms of Punishment, 121
From Punishment to
Reformation, 119
Individualization of Treatment,
124
Justification of Punishment, 120
Treatment of, 119, 447-448
Trends of Punishment, 123, 437
After-care of Prisoners, 454
Agarwal, S.K., 296
Agarwal, S.N., 295, 296
Agnihotri, V.K. 531
Agricultural Labour Enquiry (1954),
267
AIDS-A Major Health Hazard, 495
Alcoholic, 431
Alcoholism, 153, 179, 432, 454-462
and Drug Addiction, 153-179
All India
Bharat Sadhu Samaj, 316
Committee on Jail Reforms
(1980-83), 449-450
Jail Manual Committee (1957-
59), 448, 455
National Integration Council, 521
Prohibition Council, 456
Scholars' Conference on National
Integration, 523
Women's Conference, 475
Alma Ata Declaration (1978), 490
Amin, Ranjan, 508
Aneajtt, S.P., 422
Applied Sociology, 5
Scope of, 6
and Social Work, 7
Aristotelian Golden Mean, 37
Aschaffenburg, 118
Ashrama System, 312
Association of Moral and Social
Hygiene, 227, 228, 238, 468
Atwood, B.S. and Swideler, F.H., 75
Auxiliary Homes, 108

Bahadur, S., 233
Bandyopadhyay, P.K., 443-44
Barnes, H.E., 84
Barnes, H.E. and Teeters, N.K.,
56, 135, 140, 142
Basu, Smt. Sita, 113
Beccaria, C.B., 121, 122
Beggars, 431
Beggars, Types of, 233
Able-Bodied Adult Beggars, 233
Hereditary Beggars, 233
Infirm or Old, 234
Mentally Deficient, 234
Physically Disabled, 234
Religious Mendicants, 234
Sick or Diseased Beggars, 234
Beggary, 226, 469-71
Anti-Beggary Bill, 469
Causes of, 228
Biological, 231
Economic, 229
Religious, 232
Social, 230
Control, 432
Definition, 228
Extent of Begging in India, 238
Future Programme, 244
Measures Taken in Ancient
India, 238

Present Methods of
Rehabilitation, 240
Techniques of, 234
Deforming of Body, 237
Employed by Religious
Mendicants, 236
Ordinary, 234
Use of Coercive Methods, 237
Use of Tricks, 237
Bendix Reinhard, 404, 405
Benjamin Rush, 194
Bentham Jeremy, 122
Bernier, 161
Bergler Edmund, 181, 183,
184,185, 191
Beveridge, 260
Bharat Sewak Samaj, 316
Bhattacharayya, B.K., 419,
Bhattacharayya, S.K., 447-448,
451-452, 454, 463, 468, 470
Bhushan, Vidya, 126
Birth Rate and Death Rate, 284
Blumer, H. and Hauser, P.M., 78,
334, 335
Blum, E.A.H., 406
Board
Advisory on Social Defence, 459
Central Social Welfare (see
under Central)
Child Welfare Board (see
under Child)
Drug Control, 459
State Social Welfare Advisory,
518
Bogen, Emil, 158
Bonger, W.A., 79, 154, 156, 203
Borstal Institutions, 109, 419, 446
Brahmans, 192
Breckinridge, P. and Abbot, E., 71
British People
Honesty, 520
Integrity, 520
Brooks, R.C., 340
Bruce, Maurice, 539
Buckle, 60
Burgers, E.W., 35
Burgers, E.W. and Cattrell, L.S., 376
Burgers, E.W. and Locke, H.J.,
356, 359
Burns, C.D., 322
Burl Cyril, 66, 71, 73, 77, 78, 87, 336
Caltin, George E.C. 154, 156
Carpenter, Miles, 328
Carstens, C.C., 94
Cassidy, Harry M., 536
Casual to Habitual Drinker, 156
Central Advisory Board of Education,
307
Central Bureau of
Correctional Services, 432,449,
470
Central Health Bureau (1956), 289
Central Organization for Drug
Addiction, 178
Central Social Welfare Board, 4, 216,
451, 518-20, 531, 534
Certified Schools, 108
Charas, 177
Chandrashekhar, 284
Chandra, Sushil, 87, 145, 206, 244
Children Acts, 104, 451
Children Aid Society, 453
Chinoy, Ely, 9, 391
Cinema
and Disorganization, 330
and the Role of the Movies, 330
Effects of, 333
Inculcation of Anti-Social
Attitudes, 333
Its Relationship to Delinquent
Behaviour, 334
Its Relationship to Sex
Delinquency, 335
Movies and Adolescents, 332
Coleman, James S., 392, 393, 394

Commercial Recreation
and Disorganization, 324
Causes of, 328
Meaning of, 328
Commissions,
Administrative Reforms
Commission (1966) 513
Calcutta University
Commission (1917), 227
Central Vigilance Commission
513
Education Commission (1966),
30, 296, 307, 308, 309, 500
Gupta Commission, 514
Hindu Religious Endowment
Commission, 315, 510
Indian Education Commission
(1882), 299
Indian Law Commission, 435
Linguistic Provinces
Commission (1948), 413
Secondary Education
Commission (1953), 299
Shah Commission 519
State Reorganisation
Commission (1955), 413, 414
University Grants Commission,
528 *Also see* under Reports
Committees
Advisory on Social and Moral
Hygiene (1954), 200, 206,
207, 213, 216, 218, 227
Advisory on Social Questions,
League of Nations, 203, 219,
224, 232
Advisory on the Traffic in
Women and Children
(1922), 224
Chadah, 491
Gandhi Centenary, 520
Indian Excise (1905), 162
Joint Committee on Methods
of Preventing Delinquency
New York (1925), 93
Jungalwalla (1967), 496
Kartar Singh (1973), 496
Krishnan (1982), 492
Mukerji (1965), 496
On Drug Addiction (1976), 455, 457
On Emotional Integration, 514
On Prevention of Corruption
(1964), 339, 345
Prohibition Enquiry Committee
(1954-55), 165,
Sri Prakash Committee, 525
Srivastava Committee, 496
Traffic in Women and Child Welfare
Committee (1937), 224
Also see under Reports
Community Conflicts, 399, 490-91
and Inactivity, 399
and National Integration, 490
Groupism in Larger
Organizations, 436
In Rural and Urban
Communities, 404
Lingual and Regional Conflicts,
413
Community Disorganization
and Social Disorganization, 391
and Social Change, 398
Casteism and, 405
Class Tension and, 410
Migration and, 402
Nature of, 392
Organized Crime and, 367
Process of, 396
Vice and, 209
Comprehensive Social Security
Measures, 270
Conference of Chief Secretaries
(1979), 446
Cooley, Charles, H., 23, 33
Correctional
Brief History of Prison
Administration, 125
Ideology, 437
Programme in India, 125

Corruption, 338
Among Politicians, 343
Businessmen and, 345
Causes of, 341
Change in Values, 343
Close Connection between Big Business and Politics, 342
Expanding Activities of the Government, 342
Expansion of Money Economy, 343
Lack of Adequate Machinery to deal with Corruption, 343
Large Areas of Political Bodies, 341
Spoil System of Democratic Government, 342
Defined, 339
Extent of Corruption in India, 348
Forms of, 343
Businessmen and, 345
Graft and the Police, 345
Individuals and, 346
Officials and, 344
Politicians and, 343
In Ancient Period, 239
Measures for Controlling, 350
Administration Measures to Avoid Delays, 353
Change in Social Values, 353
Civic Sense Among General Public, 353
Honesty Among Public, 351
Legislative Measures, 354
Proper Machinery for Enforcement of Laws, 354
Restriction on Government Functions, 354
Crime, 55, 436, 472
Causes Leading to Delinquency and, 58, 435
Causes of, 117
Classes of, 436
Conception of, 55, 437
Extent of crime in India. 115
Factors of, 20
Areal and Regional Differences in, 61
Class, Sex, Age, Race, etc., 62
Physical Factors, 60
Sociological Factors, 60
Specific Factors, 62
Biological, 63
Economic Condition, 78
Environmental Factors, 70
Mental and Psychological, 68
Religious and Other Factors, 81
Motivation of, 436
Prevention of, 118
Prevention of Crime and U.N.O., 145
Trends of, 436
Criminals
Classification of, 115
White-Collar, 340
Criminality
Causes of White-Collar Criminality, 84
Criminal Procedure Code, 126, 330
Cyclic Unemployment, 260

Das, S.K., 182
Dastur, Z.N., 306
Davis Jerome, 6
Davis, J. and Barnes, H.E., 6
Davis, Kingsley, 281
Delinquency
Juvenile, 86, 472 (Also see under Juvenile)
Department of
Education, 551
Home, 570
Social Welfare, 554 (Also see under Social)
Women and Child Development, 555
Desai, Morarji, 456

Deshmukh, Durgabai, 536
Development of Women and Children in Rural Areas, 555
Disintegration of Personality, 44
Disorganization
Community, 391 (Also see under Community)
Family, 356 (Also see under Family) Individual, 33 (Also see under Individual)
Personal, 380 (Also see under Personal)
Social, 16 (Also see under Social)
Divorce, 380
and Economic Position, 382
and Injured Ego, 381
and Sex Adjustment, 381
and Social Relationship, 382
Avoidance of Family Tension and, 385
Children of Divorced Persons, 383
Consequences of Desertion and, 380
Desirability and Undesirability of, 384
Personal Disorganization of Divorced Persons, 380
Drinkers, 157
Casual Habitual Drinker, 157
Drinking, 451
and Community Disorganization, 160
and Family Disorganization, 160
and Individual Disorganization, 160
Causes of, 154
Bad Housing and Lack of Recreational Facilities, 155
Fashion, 155
for Business Reasons, 155
for Companionship and Fun, 155
God's Curse of Gift, 155
Ignorance, 155
Inherent Nervous Defects, 155
Misery Drinking, 154
Occupational facior, 155
Social Inadequacy, 156
Sudden Success in Business, 155
Urbanization, 155
History of Drinking in India, 161
Progress After Independence, 164
Drug Addiction, 176, 431, 456-462
and Charas, Ganja and Bhang, 177
and Cocaine, 178
and Opium, 176
New Strategy for Drug Abuse Prevention, 461
Dugdale, R.L., 65
Dunham, 69
Durfee, Charles, 154 Dutta,G.C., 86
Dull Gupta, Bela, 28, 320, 357

East, Dr., 68
Education,
Adult, 304, 499
Health, 289
On Social, Moral and Spiritual Values, 307
Policy (1968), 501
Policy (1986), 502
Social and Adult, 301
Educational
and Moral Problems, 500
and Religious Institutions, 298
Institutions, 299
Elliott, M.A. and Merrill, F.E., 9, 11, 13, 17, 19, 37, 41, 45, 49, 91, 114, 157, 200, 204, 209, 210, 220, 261, 262, 328, 340, 351, 361, 363, 385, 386, 391, 393, 413
Ellen Key, 370
Ellwood, C.A. 359
Elmer, M.C., 77

Ely Chinoy, 9, 391
Employees' State Insurance Act, 268, 270
Employment, and Third Five-Year Plan, 269
  for the Older Worker, 270

Fahien, 161
Fairchild, H.P., 319
Family and Society, 357
Family Disorganization, 356, 510-512
  Causes of, 371
    Personal Factors, 372
    Clashing Temperament, 374
    Personal Behaviour Pattern, 374
    Philosophy of Life, 374
    Psychopathic Personalities, 375
    Romantic Fallacy, 372
    Social and Cultural Factors, 372
    Differences in Cultural Background, 376
    Disparity in Age, 376
    Economy Tensions, 375
    III Health, 377
    Interference of In laws, 377
    Occupation Tensions, 376
    Parent-Child Relationship, 377
  Concept of, 362
  Effects of Family Tension, 379
Family Organization, 360
  Characteristics of Family Organization
    Unity of Objective, 361
    Unity of Personal Ambitions, 361
    Unity of Interest, 361
  Future of, 388
  The Nature of, 360
Fairs, R.E.L., 11, 27, 28, 30
Fit Persons Institutions, 108
Food for Work Programme, 485
Ford, James, 6
Foster Homes, 108
Freeman, Howard, E., 543,
Freud, 48, 351
Friedlander, W.A., 87, 96, 100, 110, 111, 530, 545
Frictional and Technological Unemployment, 259

Galway, Edward, 422
Gambler, 431
  Occasional and Habitual, 184
  Treatment of, 191
Gambling, 180, 432, 463 472
  Activities, 183
  and Demoralization, 186
  and Family Disorganization, 187
  and Personal Disorganization, 186
  and Smoking, 192, 463
  and Social Disorganization, 187
  and Speculation, 180
  Causes of, 185
  Control of, 188
  Disadvantages of, 185
Gaming, Wagering and Betting, 182
Gandhi, Indira, 530
  Kasturba, 456
Gandhi, Mahatma, 163, 190, 191, 196, 198, 295, 421, 426
  Gandhi, Rajiv, 530
Ganja and Bhang, 177
Geoffrey, May, 200
Giddings, F.H., 18
Gillin, J.L., 55, 60
Gillin, J.L. and Giltin, J.P., 6, 17, 251
Gita, 313
Gobindaswamy, M.V., 47
Goddard, H.H., 68
Golda Van Bushirk, 303
Goring, 65, 68
Goring and Boas, 64
Greenson, R.R., 185, 191
Green, Scott A., 9

Groves, E.R. and Moore, H.E., 6, 7
Gundlach and Mohr, 65

Hardly, Charles, O., 181
Harris, S.E., 541
Hauser, Philip, M., 334, 335
Hawlrey, 260
Health, 286, 491-497
  Causes of Low Health, 287
  Health Education, 289
  Medical Care and Public Health, 287
  Mental Health, 292
  Other Health Problems, 291
  School Health, 291
  Social, 531
Healy, William, 59, 69, 73, 75, 76, 78, 83, 93
Healy, William and Bronner, A.F., 73, 74
Hertzler, J.O., 310
Hinduism and Social Progress, 312
  Hitopadesha, 505
Hobson, 260
Homes
  Auxiliary, 108
  Foster, 108
  Remand, 107
  Howard, John, 122
Hutton, J.H., 407
Huntington, 60

India's Social transformation, 473
Indian
  Education Commission (1882), 299
  Excise Committee (1905), 162
  Factories Act 268, 270
  Law Commission, 435
  National Congress, 163
  Penal Code, 126, 210, 213, 464, 525
Indiscipline among Students, 305, 503, 504
Individual and Society, 35
  Life Organization, 36
Individual Disorganization, 433-434
  Causes of, 39
  Stages in, 40
Industrial Revolution, 280
Industrial Workshop of the World, 255
International Convention for the Suppression of Immoral Traffic, 230
International Women's Year, 455
Involuntary Unemployment or Under employment, 260

Jagannadham, V., 98
Jain, R.K., 327, 331, 336
Jan Shikshan Nilayam, 506
Janata Parly, 456
Jayakar, R.B.K., 210, 222
JenetPiere, 154, 156, 157
Jevons, 260
Joint Committee of the Indian Council of Medical and Agricultural Research, 290
Johnston, Lennox, 195
Jukes, 65
Juvenile
  Aid Bureaux, 443
  Aid Police Units, 443
  Delinquents, 431
  Jails, 447
  Justice, 446
Juvenile Delinquency, 86, 437-440
  Causes of, 90
  Defined, 87
  Extent in India, 88
  Methods of Rehabilitation, 99
    New Policy After Independence, 111
  Programmes Before Independence, 99
  preventive Measures, 96
    Assistance to Under-privileged Children, 97

A Team Work of Private and Public Agencies devoted to Preventive work, 96
Education of the Family, 97
Establishment of Child Guidance Clinics, 97
Establishment of Wholesome Re-creation Agencies, 97
Propaganda, 27
Training of Members and Staff of all Organizations, 97
Juvenile Vagrancy, 93
Methods of Controlling, 95

Kabir, Humayun, 302
Kabir, Shanti, 205, 215, 222
Kalekar, 406
Kapur, Promila, 517
Karl Marx, 11
Karma Theory, 259, 312
Kasturba Gandhi Memorial Trust, 456
Kaufman, Harold F., 397, 398
Kautilya, 210, 239, 240, 241
Keilhau, Wilhelm,542
Kerawalla, P.C., 77, 420
Key, Ellen, 370
Khan, Nasir Ali, 378
Khan, Ziauddin, 527
Khanna, Raj Nath, 91, 92, 93
Kimball, Young, 58
Kingsley, Davis, 201
Kinberg, Olof, 63, 65
Kinsey, A.C., 363
Kishore, B.R.,87
Koskowski, W., 192, 193
Kretschmer, 65, 67
Kulkarni, D.V., 101
Kumarappa, M., 228

Laissez faire, 4, 21, 26, 27, 29
Lala, Karim, 525
Landis, J.T., 367
Landis, Paul, H., 386
Lange, Johannes, 66
Laski, H.J., 338
League of Nations, Advisory Committee on Social Questions, 232, 239
Legislation on Prostitution, 210
Leisure
and Recreation, 318, 319, 505-507
Income and Leisure, 332
Misuse of Leisure Time and Disorganisation, 336
Lemert, Edwin M., 10
Lennox Johnston, 195
Lenz, Adolph, 67, 69, 70
Lescohier, Don D., 263
Lewis, D.T., 472
Lindsay, A.D., 338
Lingual and Regional Conflicts, 413, 519
Lombroso Cesare, 60, 64, 76, 83
Luhach, Frank C., 304
Lundberg, G.A., 320, 322

Macaulay, Lord, 127
Maciver, R.M. and Page, C.H., 9, 365, 357, 365, 370
Madan, G.R., 474, 496, 508, 510, 531, 533
Major Institutions, Problems of, 473
Maladjustment in Institutions, 249
Malthus, 280
Manila, 440
Mannheim, Karl, 19, 26, 27
Manu, 188, 226, 227, 240
Marx and Engels, 79
Marx, Karl, 11
Mastan, Haji, 525
Masud, M.N., 532
Mead, George H., 35, 36
Measurement of Poverty, 252
Medical Care and Public Health, 287
Mehrotra, S.N., 424

Menninger, Karl A., 48
Mentally Deranged, 45
Mental Illness, 433-434
  Causes of, 46
  In India, 47
  Services for, 47
Merchant, K.T., 284
Merton, R.K., 28, 29
Merton, R.K. and Nisbet Robert, A., 8, 392
Michael, J. and Adler, M J., 56
Miller, Justine, 56, 57
Minimum Needs Programme, 495
  Minimum Wages Act, 268
Ministry' of
  Education, 555
  Health, 555
  Home Affairs, 555
  Rehabilitation, 555
  Social and Women Welfare, 555
  Social Welfare, 555
  Welfare, 555
Misra, B.K., 447
Mitra, K., 153, 154
Modak, Usha, 511-518
Model Prison Manual, 449
Mohan, Brij, 378, 520
Moharnmadan Laws, 188
Mohr and Gundlach, 65
Montague-Chelmsford Reforms, 129
Montesquieu, 122
Madras Gaming Act (1930), 189
Moore, 260
Moorthy, M.V., 238
Morrison, Douglas, 80
Mowrer, E.R., 15, 17, 18, 23, 32, 33, 34, 41
Muhar, P.S., 340
Mukherjee, R.K., 26, 229, 230, 231, 255, 293, 299
Mukherjee, S.N., 299
Mukerji, 491
Multipurpose Workers, 477
Munn, N.L., 45
Munshi, K.M., 526
Myrdal G., 541

Nadel, S.F., 9,10
Nair, G.R.,455
Nanda, Gulzari Lai, 316
Naoroji, Dadabhoy, 253
Narain, Raj, 303
Nathawat, S.S., 516
National
  Board of Adult Education, 505
  Cadet Corps, 508
  Commission on Self-employed Women and Women in Informal Sector, 549
  Council of Social, Welfare, Agencies, 560
  Crime Record Bureau, 439
  Income of India, 253
  Institute of Adult Education, 506
  Institute of Social Defence, 432
  Integration, 513-527
  Literacy Mission, 507
  Rural Employment Programme, 477
  Sample Survey, 267
  Service Scheme, 499
National Income Committee, 254
Nehru, Jawaharlal, 514
Neumeyer, M.H. and Neumeyer, E.S., 318
Niles, Carpenter, 328
Nimkoff, M.E., 358
Nischal, K., 455
Nurullah, S. and Naik, J.P., 299
Nutrition, 290

Observation Home, 441
Occasional and Habitual Gambler, 184
Oshsner, Alton, 193, 194, 195, 199
Ogburn, W.F., 21
Ojha, P.O. and Bhatt, N.V., 274
Opium, 186
Osier, 194

Page, C.H., 9 (Also see under
Maciver, R.M.)
Park, R.E. and Burgess, E.W., 19, 20
Parishad, Vishwa Hindu, 504
Parole, 139
Parsons, E.C., 370
Pearl, Raymond, 159
Personal Disorganization, 40, 433
of Divorced Persons, 380
Stages in, 40
Pigou, A.C., 257, 258
Planning
and Welfare State, 540
Economic, 541
of Social Welfare Services, 544
Social, 541
Plant, James S., 39
Population, 280
and Health Problems, 280, 491, 494
Birth Rate and Death Rate, 284
Control of Population, 292
Family Planning, 294
Growth of India's Population, 280
Increase in Production, 293
Migration of Population, 293
Optimum Theory, 281
Theories of Population, 280
Poverty, 251
Absolute and Relative, 251
and Disorganization, 257
and Unemployment, 257
Causes of, 254
Biological Factors, 256
Personal and Economic Factors, 255
Political and Economic Factors, 255
Social Factors, 256
Technological and Environmental Factors, 254
Measurement of, 252
Prabhu, P.N., 356, 358
Prison
Types of, 125, 450
Working of, 130
Prisoners,
Treatment through Community Services, 453-454
Welfare Schemes for, 450-451
Prisoners' Open Camp, 134
Prisons Act of 1894, 130
Probation, 110, 135, 433, 451-452
of Offenders Rules, 452
Working of Probabtion Acts, 137
Working of Probation in India, 136
Programme
Command Area, 474
Drought Prone Area, 474
Family Planning, 294, 491
Food For Work, 490
Minimum Needs, 494
Nutrition, 500
Small Farmers, 474
Social Defence, 431
Prohibition, 165
Central Organizations, 178
Difficulties Encountered, 167
Economic Benefits, 166
Methods of Enforcement of, 170
Education and Propaganda, 171
Financial Aspect, 171
Preventive Measures, 171
Prohibition Boards, 170
Prohibition Enquiry Committee (1954-55), 165
Study Team on Prohibition (1964), 173, 174, 455
Procurers, 218
Prostitution, 200, 464-467, 473
and Family Disorganization, 208
and Personal Disorganization, 207
and Welfare Organizations, 223

Causes of, 201
for Females, 202
Desire for new Experience, 204
Devadasi System, 205
Economic Factors, 203
Ignorance, 204
Inordinate Sex Desire, 204
Mental Deficiency of Certain Temperamental Traits, 204
Restrictions on Widow Remarriage, 205
Social Values Against Unchastity, 203
Unhappy Marital Relations, 204
Vested Interests, 204
for Males, 201
Future Programme, 219
Legislation on, 210
Venereal Diseases and, 220
Punekar, S.D. and Rao, Kamla, 202, 205, 206
Purcel, M.P., 539

Queen, S.A. and Mann, D.M., 40
Quetelet, L.A J., 80

Race-Course Licensing Act, 189
Radhakrishnan, S., 312
Raizaday, B.N., 188
Raju, V.B., 183
Rameshwari Nehru, 224 ,
Ramakrishna, 526
Ramakrishna Mission, 316
Rama Rao, V.K., 464
Ranade, S.N., 435
Ranganayaki, 220
Rao, S. Venugopala, 81, 82, 118, 435-36
Rebels and Revolutionists, 42
Reckless, W.C., 56, 58, 59, 65, 68, 69, 83, 144, 148, 180, 183, 207, 542
Recreation
and Disorganization, 329
Causes of, 329
Commercial, 327
Forms of Recreation, 323
In Modern Society, 320
Meaning of, 328
Leisure and, 319
Leisure and Recreation Defined, 319
Recreational Activities Among Adults, 323
Reformatory Schools, 109
Reformatory Schools Act (1897), 100
Regional Women Institutes, 216
Regulating Act (1773), 126
Rehabilitation of Physically Handicapped, 269
Religious Institutions, 298, 309
Reinterpretation of Religious Literature, 313
Reorganization of, 314
Remand Homes, 107, 216
Robson W.A. 540
Report of
Advisory Committee on Aftercare Programmes (1954), 145
Advisory Committee on Social and Moral Hygiene (1954), 200, 206, 207, 213, 216
Agricultural Labour Enquiry Committee (1954), 267
All-India Jail Manual Committee (1957-59), 145, 448
Crime Commission of New York State; From Truancy to Crime (1928), 92
Education Commission (1964-66), 298, 306, 307, 308
Indian Excise Committee (1905-06), 162, 308
Indian Jails Committee (1919), 129
Joint Committee on Methods of Preventing Delinquency, New York (1925), 93

Linguistic Provinces
Commission (1948), 413
Prohibition Enquiry
Committee (1954), 163
State re-Organization Commission (1955), 413, 414, 415
Study Team on Prohibition
(1964), 174, 455
Study Team on Social Welfare
and Welfare of Backward
Classes (1959), 144
Suicide Enquiry Committee
(1966), 435
Working Group on
Administrative Machinery
for Welfare Pro-grammes
(1968), 571
see also under Commission,
Committee
Report on
Delinquent Children and
Juvenile Offenders in India
(1950), 89, 112
Research Group of the Political
and Economic Planning
Organization, London, 293
Ribeiro, 532
Robson, W.A., 540
Ross, 357
Roy, P., 424
Russel, Bertrand, 19, 20, 21
Russel, Dora, 370

Saksena, N.S., 504
Sami, S.M.A, and Iyer, K.J., 189
Sampurnananda, 521
Samyukta Sadachari Samiti, 316
Sanderson, D. and Palson, R.A.,
394, 395
Scheme
Training Rural Youth for Self-employment, 479
Scholapp and Smith, 67
Seasonal and Causal
Unemployment, 258
Secondary Education Commission
(1953), 290
Sellen Thorsten, 58
Semple, 60
Sen Gupta, N.N., 235
Sen, N. and Das, S.K., 182
Senath, M.J., 114, 148, 149
Sethi, (Miss) Nirmal and Agarwal
S.K., 296
Shah, Jyotsna H., 466
Shanti Kabir, 205, 215, 222
Shaw, C. and McKay, H.D., 62, 71,
74
Shaw, C.R., 22
Sheth, Hansa, 82
Shipstone, Eva, 507
Shivananda Divine Life Society, 316
Shukla, K.S., 443
Siddiqui, A.H., 521, 527
Singh, Tarlok, 542, 544
Singh, V.N., 326
Sinha, M.R., 530
Sletto, Raymond F., 72
Smith, D.E., 316
Smith, W.C., 309, 310
Smokers, 194
Classification of, 194
Smoking, 192
Advantages and Disadvantages
of, 192
Bad Effects of, 193
Biological Effects, 193
Economic and Social Effects, 193
Causes of, 195
Control of, 198
Removal of Nicotine, 198
Restriction of Excessive Use,
198
Extent of Smoking in India, 196
Social Change
and Social Disorganization, 17

Social Organization and, 11
Causes of, 12
Community Disorganization and, 398
in Industrial and Pre-industrialized Societies, 12
India and, 401
Social Control
and Social Disorganization, 14
Social Defence,
Central AdvisoryBoard on, 460
Programmes, 431-472
Social Disorganization
and Social Organization, 17
Causes of, 18
Biological Factors, 22
Cultural Factors, 21
Degeneration of Values, 23
Disintegration and Confusion of, 227
Ecological, 22
Individual Disorganization Leading to, 23
Lack of Proper Planning Leading to, 26
Physical Factors, 22
Political Subservicence, 28
Psychological Factors, 20
Social Problems Leading to, 23
Concept of, 16
in India, 29
Social Organization
and Modern Society, 14
and Social Change, 11
Defined, 9
its Equilibrium and Disequilibrium, 16
Social Planning, 542-544
and Social Policy, 542
Social Problems, 3-31
a Field of Applied Sociology, 5
and Individual Disorganization, 8
and Social Disorganization, 7
Natural of Social Problems in India, 5
Study of Indian, 3
Social Welfare
Agencies, 572
and Five Year Plans, 545-574
and other Related Concepts, 535-536
Department, 426-27
Scope of, 536-538
Services, 538
State Departments of, 569-572
Society
Children's Aid, 443
Sorokin, P.A., 19, 23, 24, 25
Special Component Plan, 547
Spencer, 60
Spengler, 24
Speculation, 180
Srinivas, M.R., 314
Srivastava, M.P., 58
Srivastava, S.P., 431, 472
Srivastava, S.S., 94
Starling, E.H., 154
Statistical Department of the U.N., 254
Slocking, Collis, 180, 185
Study Group on Educated Unemployed (1955), 275
Suicide, 47, 434-35
Causes of, 49
in India, 49
Theories of, 48
Sullivan, Edward D., 350, 353
Sundaram, Satya, 434
Suppression of Immoral Traffic in Women and Girls Act (1956), 217
Supreme Court of India, 450
Sutherland, E.H., 62, 84, 85, 346
Swarna Jayanti Shahari Rozgar Yojana, 481

Taft, D.R., 23

Tata Institute of Social Sciences, 4
Tavemier, 161
Teeters, N.K. and Reinemann, J.O., 97
Thomas, Parran, 220
Thomas, W.I., 69, 208, 299, 373
Thomas, W.I. and Znaniecki, F., 36, 38, 393
Thompson, W.S., 491
Thurston Henry W.,336
Titmus, R.M., 534
Todd, Arthur J., 328
Treatment of Adult Offender, 119
  Also see under Adult Offenders
Treatment of Gamblers, 191
Tripathi, B.D., 314, 316
Truancy, 91
Turf Club, 191

Uncarcd Children Institutions, 109
Unemployment, 257, 473
  and Community Disorganization, 265
  and Low Healthh, 264
  and Family Disorganization, 264
  and Poverty, 473
  Among Educated, 275, 483
  Female, 485
  Extent of Unemployment in India, 265
  Removal of, 476
  Rural Unemployment, 267, 476
  Urban Unemployment, 266, 270
  Types of, 258
  Cylic, 260
  Frictional and Technological, 259
  Involuntary, 260
  Seasonal or Casual, 258
  Shortage of Capital Equipment, 260
  Temporary, 259
  Voluntary, 259
UN Commission on the Status of women, 549
UNESCO, 304
United Nations
  Department of Social Welfare, 535
  Convention against Illicit Traffic, 460
Upanishad, 510
Ursekar, H.S., 431

Vagrancy, 93,438
Varma, Paripurnanand, 52
Varma, 312
Vasco Da Gama, 161
Venereal Diseases, 220
  and Prostitution, 220
  Extent of Venereal Diseases in India, 22
  Social Control of, 222
    Establishment of Venereal Diseases Clinics, 233
  Segregation of Diseased Patients, 223
  Social Rejection of the Profession, 222
  Spread of Information, 223
Verma, R.M., 434
Vorvaeck, Louis, 64
Vice and Community Disorganization, 209
Virginia Woolf, 369
Voluntary
  Action in Social Defence, 472
  Organizations, 443, 453, 540
  Probation Officers, 472
  Social Welfare Agencies, 559
  Social Work, 529, 532
Von Mayer, George, 81

Wadia, P.A. and Merchant, K.T., 253, 282, 284
Walsh, Cecial, 57, 74
Weber, Max, 311
Weinberg, S. Kirson, 3, 8

Welfare
    Fiscal, 534
    Occupational, 534
    Social, *see* Social Welfare
Welfare State, 4, 354, 417, 437, 538
White-Collar Criminality, 84
    Causes of, 84
William H. Sheldon, 87
William, Lillie, 312
Winslow, E.A., 81
W.I.T. Club, 190
Witty, Paul A. and Golda, Von
    Buskirk, 303
Working Group
    on Population Policy (1979), 487
    on Prisons (1972), 449-453
World Health Organization Expert
    Committee, 153
Workmen Compensation, 269, 270
Writh, Louis, 16

Youth
    Camps, 526
    Forums, 526

Zamindari System, 256
Znaniecki, F. and Thomas, W.I., 36,
    38, 39 (Also *see* under Thomas)